COGNITIVE PSYCHOLOGY

Connecting Mind, Research, and Everyday Experience | 5E

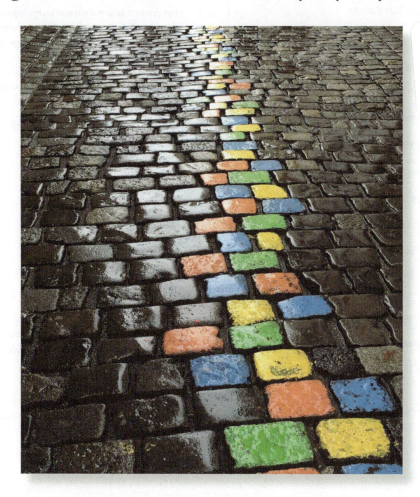

E. Bruce Goldstein

University of Pittsburgh
University of Arizona

✷ Cengage

Australia • Brazil • Canada • Mexico • Singapore • United Kingdom • United States

Cognitive Psychology: Connecting Mind, Research, and Everyday Experience,
Fifth Edition
E. Bruce Goldstein

Product Director: Marta Lee-Perriard

Product Team Manager: Star Burruto

Product Manager: Erin Schnair

Content Developer: Linda Man

Product Assistant: Leah Jenson

Digital Content Specialist: Allison Marion

Marketing Manager: Heather Thompson

Content Project Manager: Ruth Sakata Corley

Production and Composition: MPS Limited

Intellectual Property Analyst: Deanna Ettinger

Intellectual Property Project Manager:
Carly Belcher

Illustrator: Jan Troutt

Art Director: Vernon Boes

Text and Cover Designer: Cheryl Carrington

Cover Image: E. Bruce Goldstein

For product information and technology assistance, contact us at
**Cengage Customer & Sales Support, 1-800-354-9706
or support.cengage.com.**

For permission to use material from this text or product,
submit all requests online at **www.copyright.com.**

Library of Congress Control Number: 2017951368

Student Edition:
ISBN: 978-1-337-40827-1
Loose-leaf Edition:
ISBN: 978-1-337-61628-7

Cengage
200 Pier 4 Boulevard
Boston, MA 02210
USA

Cengage is a leading provider of customized learning solutions with employees residing in nearly 40 different countries and sales in more than 125 countries around the world. Find your local representative at: **www.cengage.com.**

To learn more about Cengage platforms and services, register or access your online learning solution, or purchase materials for your course, visit **www.cengage.com.**

Printed at CLDPC, USA, 01-23

To Barbara

E. BRUCE GOLDSTEIN is Associate Professor Emeritus of Psychology at the University of Pittsburgh and Adjunct Professor of Psychology at the University of Arizona. He received the Chancellor's Distinguished Teaching Award from the University of Pittsburgh for his classroom teaching and textbook writing. After receiving his bachelor's degree in chemical engineering from Tufts University, he had a revelation that he wanted to go to graduate school in psychology, rather than engineering, and so received his PhD in psychology, specializing in visual physiology, from Brown University. He continued his research in vision as a post-doctoral fellow in the Biology Department at Harvard University and then joined the faculty at the University of Pittsburgh. He continued his research at Pitt, publishing papers on retinal and cortical physiology, visual attention, and the perception of pictures, before focusing exclusively on teaching (Sensation & Perception, Cognitive Psychology, Psychology of Art, Introductory Psychology) and writing textbooks. He is the author of *Sensation and Perception,* 10th edition (Cengage, 2017), and edited the *Blackwell Handbook of Perception* (Blackwell, 2001) and the two-volume *Sage Encyclopedia of Perception* (Sage, 2010). In 2016, he won "The Flame Challenge" competition, sponsored by the Alan Alda Center for Communicating Science, for his essay, written for 11-year-olds, on *What Is Sound?*

Brief Contents

Contents

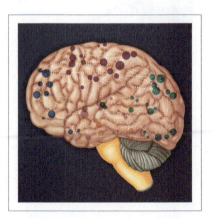

CHAPTER 3
Perception   59

The Nature of Perception   60

Why Is It So Difficult to Design a Perceiving Machine?   65

Information for Human Perception   67

CHAPTER 11

Language   321

CHAPTER 12

Problem Solving & Creativity   355

CogLab Experiments

Numbers in parentheses refer to the experiment number in CogLab.

The first experiments in each chapter are "Primary Experiments" that are directly or closely related to discussion in the text.

Asterisks (*) indicate "Related Experiments." These experiments are relevant to the topic of the chapter, but are not directly related to the discussion in the text.

Chapter 1

Simple Detection (2) A simple reaction time task that measures how fast you react to the appearance of a dot.

Chapter 2

Brain Asymmetry (15)* How speed of processing for shapes and words may be different in the left and right hemispheres.

Chapter 3

Signal Detection (1)* Collect data that demonstrate the principle behind the theory of signal detection, which explains the processes behind detecting hard-to-detect stimuli.

Apparent Motion (3) Determining how fast two dots have to be flashed, one after another, to achieve an illusion of movement.

Garner Interference: Integral Dimensions (4)* Making light-dark judgments for a square. A one-dimensional task.

Garner Interference: Separable Dimensions (5)* Making light-dark judgments for squares of different sizes. An additional dimension is added.

Müller-Lyer Illusion (6)* Measure the size of a visual illusion.

Blind Spot (14)* Map the blind spot in your visual field that is caused by the fact that there are no receptors where the optic nerve leaves the eye.

Metacontrast Masking (16)* How presentation of a masking stimulus can impair perception of another stimulus.

Categorical Perception: Discrimination (39)* Demonstration of categorical perception based on the ability to discriminate between sounds.

Categorical Perception: Identification (40)* Demonstration of categorical perception based on the identification of different sound categories.

Statistical Learning (47) How learning can occur in response to exposure to sequences of forms.

Chapter 4

Visual Search (7) Feature search experiment. Searching for a green circle among blue lines, with different numbers of blue lines.

Attentional Blink (8)* Testing your ability to detect stimuli that are presented in rapid succession.

Change Detection (9) A task involving detecting changes in alternating scenes.

Inhibition of Return (10) Inhibition of return (10) How presentation of a target away from fixation can cause a slowing of responding.

Simon Effect (11)* How speed and accuracy of responding are affected by the location of the response to a stimulus.

Spatial Cueing (12) How cueing attention affects reaction time to the cued area. Evidence for the spotlight model of attention.

Stroop Effect (13) How reaction time to naming font colors is affected by the presence of conflicting information from words.

Von Restorff Effect (32)* How the distinctiveness of a stimulus can influence memory.

Chapter 5

Modality Effect (17)* How memory for the last one or two items in a list depends on whether the list is heard or read.

Partial Report (18) The partial report condition of Sperling's iconic memory experiment.

Brown-Peterson Task (20) How memory for trigrams fades.

Position Error (21)* Memory errors when trying to remember the order of a series of letters.

Sternberg Search (22)* A method to determine how information is retrieved from short-term memory.

Irrelevant Speech Effect (22) How recall for items on a list is affected by the presence of irrelevant speech.

Memory Span (24) Measuring memory span for numbers, letters, and words.

Operation Span (25) Measuring the operation-word span, a measure of working memory.

Phonological Similarity Effect (26) How recall for items on a list is affected by how similar the items sound.

Word Length Effect (27) Measurement of the word length effect.

Von Restorff Effect (32)* How the distinctiveness of a stimulus can influence memory.

Neighborhood Size Effect (42)* How recall in a short-term memory task is affected by the size of a word's "neighborhood" (how many words can be created by changing a letter or phoneme).

Chapter 6

Suffix Effect (19)* How adding an irrelevant item to the end of a list affects recall for the final items on a list in a serial position experiment.

Serial Position (31) How memory for a list depends on an item's position on the list.

Remember/Know (36) Distinguishing between remembered items in which there is memory for learning the item and items that just seem familiar.

Implicit Learning (45) How we can learn something without being aware of the learning.

Chapter 7

Encoding Specificity (28) How memory is affected by conditions at both encoding and retrieval, and the relation between them.

Levels of Processing (29) How memory is influenced by depth of processing.

Von Restorff Effect (32)* How the distinctiveness of a stimulus can influence memory.

Production Effect (30)* How memory depends on whether words are read out loud or silently.

Chapter 8

False Memory (33) How memory for words on a list sometimes occurs for words that were not presented.

Forgot it All Along Effect (34) How it is possible to remember something and also have the experience of having previously forgotten it

Memory Judgment (35) A test of how accurate people are at predicting their memory performance.

Chapter 9

Lexical Decision (41) Demonstration of the lexical decision task, which has been used to provide evidence for the concept of spreading activation.

Absolute Identification (44)* Remembering levels that have been associated with a stimulus.

Prototypes (46) A method for studying the effect of concepts on responding.

Chapter 10

Link Word (37) A demonstration of how imagery can be used to help learn foreign vocabulary.

Mental Rotation (38) How a stimulus can be rotated in the mind to determine whether its shape matches another stimulus.

Chapter 11

Categorical Perception: Identification (40)* Demonstration of categorical perception based on the identification of different sound categories.

Categorical Perception: Discrimination (39)* Demonstration of categorical perception based on the ability to discriminate between sounds.

Lexical Decision (41) Demonstration of the lexical decision task.

Neighborhood Size Effect (42)* How recall in a short-term memory task is affected by the size of a word's "neighborhood" (how many words can be created by changing a letter or phoneme).

Word Superiority (43) How speed of identifying a letter compares when the letter is isolated or in a word.

Chapter 12

None

Chapter 13

Monty Hall (49)* A simulation of the Monty Hall three-door problem, which involves an understanding of probability.

Decision Making (48) An experiment that demonstrates how decisions can be affected by the context within which the decision is made.

Risky Decisions (50) How decision making is influenced by framing effects.

Typical Reasoning (51) How the representativeness heuristic can lead to errors of judgment.

Wason Selection Task (52) Two versions of the Wason four-card problem.

Demonstrations

Methods

Preface to Instructors

▶ The Evolution of a Cognitive Psychology Textbook

This edition is the culmination of a process that began in 2002, when I decided to write the first edition of this book. From a survey of more than 500 instructors and my conversations with colleagues, it became apparent that many teachers were looking for a text that not only covers the field of cognitive psychology but is also accessible to students. From my teaching of cognitive psychology, it also became apparent that many students perceive cognitive psychology as being too abstract and theoretical, and not connected to everyday experience. With this information in hand, I set out to write a book that would tell the story of cognitive psychology in a concrete way that would help students appreciate the connections between empirical research, the principles of cognitive psychology, and everyday experience.

I did a number of things to achieve this result. I started by including numerous **real-life examples** in each chapter, and **neuropsychological case studies** where appropriate. To provide students with firsthand experience with the phenomena of cognitive psychology, I included more than 40 **Demonstrations**—easy-to-do mini-experiments that were contained within the narrative of the text—as well as 20 additional suggestions of things to try, throughout the chapters. The Demonstrations in this edition are listed on page xxi.

One thing I avoided was simply presenting the results of experiments. Instead, whenever possible, I **described how experiments were designed**, and what participants were doing, so students would understand how results were obtained. In addition, most of these descriptions were supported by illustrations such as pictures of stimuli, diagrams of the experimental design, or graphs of the results.

Students also received access to more than 45 online **CogLab experiments** that they could run themselves and could then compare their data to the class average and to the results of the original experiments from the literature. The first edition (2005) therefore combined many elements designed to achieve the goal of covering the basic principles of cognitive psychology in a way that students would find interesting and easy to understand. My goal was for students to come away feeling excited about the field of cognitive psychology.

The acceptance of the first edition was gratifying, but one thing I've learned from years of teaching and textbook writing is that there are always explanations that can be clarified, new pedagogical techniques to try, and new research and ideas to describe. With this in mind as I began preparing the second edition (2008), I elicited feedback from students in my classes and received more than 1,500 written responses indicating areas in the first edition that could be improved. In addition, I also received feedback from instructors who had used the first edition. This feedback was the starting point for the second edition, and I repeated this process of eliciting student and instructor feedback for the third and fourth editions, as well. Thus, in addition to updating the science, I revised many sections that students and instructors had flagged as needing clarification.

▶ Retained Features

All of the features described above were well received by students and instructors, and so they are continued in this new fifth edition. Additional pedagogical features that have been retained from previous editions include **Test Yourself** sections, which help students review the material, and end-of-chapter **Think About It** questions, which ask students to consider questions that go beyond the material.

Methods sections, which were introduced in the second edition, highlight the ingenious methods cognitive psychologists have devised to study the mind. Over two dozen Methods sections, which are integrated into the text, describe methods such as brain imaging, the lexical decision task, and think-aloud protocols. This not only highlights the importance of the method but makes it easier to return to its description when it is referred to later in the text. See page xxiv for a list of Methods.

The end-of-chapter **Something to Consider** sections describe cutting-edge research, important principles, or applied research. A few examples of topics covered in this section are *Technology Determines What Questions We Can Ask* (Chapter 2); *Autobiographical Memories Determined by Odors and Music* (Chapter 8); and *The Dual Systems Approach to Thinking* (Chapter 13). **Chapter Summaries** provide succinct outlines of the chapters, without serving as a substitute for reading the chapters.

What Is New in the Fifth Edition

As with previous editions of this book, this edition features updates to material throughout, and in a few cases chapters have been rewritten or reorganized to improve clarity and pedagogy. One indication of the updating of this edition is the inclusion of 96 new boldfaced terms in the text, which also appear in the Glossary. Following is a list that highlights a few of the new or updated topics in this edition. *Italicized* items are new section headings.

CHAPTER 1 Introduction to Cognitive Psychology
- ➤ What is consciousness? fMRI study of a comatose person.
- ➤ *Paradigms and Paradigm Shifts*
- ➤ *The Evolution of Cognitive Psychology*

CHAPTER 2 Cognitive Neuroscience
- ➤ *Structural Connectivity*
- ➤ *Functional Connectivity*
- ➤ *Method: Resting State Functional Connectivity*
- ➤ *The Default Mode Network*
- ➤ *The Dynamics of Cognition*
- ➤ *Technology Determines What Questions We Can Ask*

CHAPTER 3 Perception
- ➤ *Knowledge, Inference, and Prediction.*

CHAPTER 4 Attention
- ➤ *Method: Experience Sampling*
- ➤ *Distraction Caused by Mind Wandering*
- ➤ Prediction controlling eye movements
- ➤ *Attentional Networks*
- ➤ Effective connectivity

CHAPTER 5 Short-Term and Working Memory
- ➤ *Why Is More Working Memory Better?*

CHAPTER 6 Long-Term Memory: Structure

➤ *Interactions Between Episodic and Semantic Memory*

➤ *Loss of Semantic Memory Can Affect Episodic Memories*

➤ *Back to the Future* (Episodic memory and imagining the future, updated)

➤ *Procedural Memory and Attention*

➤ *A Connection Between Procedural Memory and Semantic Memory*

CHAPTER 7 Long-Term Memory: Encoding and Retrieval

➤ The involvement of hippocampus in remote memory—fMRI evidence.

➤ *Alternative Explanations in Cognitive Psychology*

CHAPTER 8 Everyday Memory and Memory Errors

➤ *Music and Odor-Elicited Autobiographical Memories*

CHAPTER 10 Visual Imagery

➤ *Individual Differences in Imagery*

➤ Contrasting object imagery and spatial imagery

CHAPTER 11 Language

➤ Major revision: 25 references deleted; 30 new references added; 11 figures replaced by 8 new figures; 17 new key terms

➤ Updated: Garden path sentences; multiple meanings of words; common ground in conversation.

➤ *Language and Music*

CHAPTER 12 Problem Solving and Creativity

➤ *Brain "Preparation" for Insight and Analytical Problem Solutions*

➤ *Opening the Mind to Think "Outside the Box"*

➤ *Networks Associated With Creativity*

➤ *Wired to Create: Things Creative People Do Differently*

➤ *Method: Transcranial Direct Current Stimulation*

CHAPTER 13 Judgment, Decisions, and Reasoning

➤ Poor decision making in the NBA draft.

➤ Evaluating false evidence, linking to idea of fake news

➤ Illusory truth, backfire effect

➤ Neuroeconomics, updated

▶ Ancillaries to Support Your Teaching

Instructor Ancillaries

Online Instructor's Manual: The manual includes key terms, a detailed chapter outline, lesson plans, discussion topics, student activities, video links, and an expanded test bank.

Online PowerPoints: Helping you make your lectures more engaging while effectively reaching your visually oriented students, these handy Microsoft PowerPoint® slides outline the chapters of the main text in a classroom-ready presentation. The PowerPoint slides are updated to reflect the content and organization of the new edition of the text.

Cengage Learning Testing, powered by Cognero®: Cengage Learning Testing, Powered by Cognero®, is a flexible online system that allows you to author, edit, and manage test bank content. You can create multiple test versions in an instant and deliver tests from your LMS in your classroom.

CogLab

CogLab Online is a series of virtual lab demonstrations designed to help students understand cognition through interactive participation in cognitive experiments. Students with instructors that adopt CogLab also receive access to more than 50 online CogLab experiments that they can run themselves, then compare their data to the class average and to the results of the original experiments from the literature. To view a demo, visit coglab.cengage.com.

MindTap

MindTap® Psychology: *MindTap® for Cognitive Psychology,* 5th edition, is the digital learning solution that helps instructors engage and transform today's students into critical thinkers. Through paths of dynamic assignments and applications that you can personalize, real-time course analytics, and an accessible reader, MindTap helps you turn cookie cutter into cutting edge, apathy into engagement, and memorizers into higher-level thinkers. As an instructor using MindTap, you have at your fingertips the right content and unique set of tools curated specifically for your course, all in an interface designed to improve workflow and save time when planning lessons and course structure. The control to build and personalize your course is all yours, focusing on the most relevant material while also lowering costs for your students. Stay connected and informed in your course through real-time student tracking that provides the opportunity to adjust the course as needed based on analytics of interactivity in the course.

Animated and experiential demonstrations are available in the MindTap. The purpose of these activities is to extend the students' experience beyond simply reading a description of an experiment, a principle, or a phenomenon, by giving them the opportunity to experience these things more fully and actively. This is achieved in a number of ways. Students may observe something unfolding on the screen or respond in some way, such as participating in a mini-experiment.

Preface to Students

As you begin reading this book, you probably have some ideas about how the mind works from things you have read, from other media, and from your own experiences. In this book, you will learn what we actually do and do not know about the mind, as determined from the results of controlled scientific research. Thus, if you thought that there is a system called "short-term memory" that can hold information for short periods of time, then you are right; when you read the chapters on memory, you will learn more about this system and how it interacts with other parts of your memory system. If you thought that some people can accurately remember things that happened to them as very young infants, you will see that there is a good chance that these reports are inaccurate. In fact, you may be surprised to learn that even more recent memories that seem extremely clear and vivid may not be entirely accurate due to basic characteristics of the way the memory system works.

But what you will learn from this book goes much deeper than simply adding more accurate information to what you already know about the mind. You will learn that there is much more going on in your mind than you are conscious of. You are aware of experiences such as seeing something, remembering a past event, or thinking about how to solve a problem—but behind each of these experiences are a myriad of complex and largely invisible processes. Reading this book will help you appreciate some of the "behind the scenes" activity in your mind that is responsible for everyday experiences such as perceiving, remembering, and thinking.

Another thing you will become aware of as you read this book is that there are many practical connections between the results of cognitive psychology research and everyday life. You will see examples of these connections throughout the book. For now, I want to focus on one especially important connection—what research in cognitive psychology can contribute to improving your studying. This discussion appears on pages 199–202 of Chapter 7, but you might want to look at this material now, rather than waiting until later in the course. I invite you to also consider the following two principles, which are designed to help you get more out of this book.

Principle 1: It is important to know what you know.

Professors often hear students lament, "I came to the lecture, read the chapters a number of times, and still didn't do well on the exam." Sometimes this statement is followed by "... and when I walked out of the exam, I thought I had done pretty well." If this is something that you have experienced, the problem may be that you didn't have a good awareness of what you knew about the material and what you didn't know. If you think you know the material but actually don't, you might stop studying or might continue studying in an ineffective way, with the net result being a poor understanding of the material and an inability to remember it accurately, come exam time. Thus, it is important to test yourself on the material you have read by writing or saying the answers to the Test Yourself questions in the chapter.

Principle 2: Don't mistake ease and familiarity for knowing.

One of the main reasons that students may think they know the material, even when they don't, is that they mistake familiarity for understanding. Here is how it works: You read the chapter once, perhaps highlighting as you go. Then later, you read the chapter again, perhaps focusing on the highlighted material. As you read it over, the material is familiar because you remember it from before, and this familiarity might lead you to think, "Okay, I know that." The problem is that this feeling of familiarity is not necessarily equivalent to knowing the material and may be of no help when you have to come up with an answer on the exam. In fact, familiarity can often lead to errors on multiple-choice exams because you might pick a choice that looks familiar, only to find out later that although it was something you had read, it wasn't really the best answer to the question.

This brings us back again to the idea of testing yourself. One finding of cognitive psychology research is that the very act of *trying* to answer a question increases the chances that you will be able to answer it when you try again later. Another related finding is that testing yourself on the material is a more effective way of learning it than simply rereading the material. The reason testing yourself works is that *generating* material is a more effective way of getting information into memory than simply *reviewing* it. Thus, you may find it effective to test yourself before rereading the chapter or going over your highlighted text.

Whichever study tactic you find works best for you, keep in mind that an effective strategy is to rest (take a break or study something else) before studying more and then retesting yourself. Research has shown that memory is better when studying is spaced out over time, rather than being done all at once. Repeating this process a number of times— testing yourself, checking back to see whether you were right, waiting, testing yourself again, and so on—is a more effective way of learning the material than simply looking at it and getting that warm, fuzzy feeling of familiarity, which may not translate into actually knowing the material when you are faced with questions about it on the exam.

I hope you will find this book to be clear and interesting and that you will sometimes be fascinated or perhaps even surprised by some of the things you read. I also hope that your introduction to cognitive psychology extends beyond just "learning the material." Cognitive psychology is endlessly interesting because it is about one of the most fascinating of all topics—the human mind. Thus, once your course is over, I hope you will take away an appreciation for what cognitive psychologists have discovered about the mind and what still remains to be learned. I also hope that you will become a more critical consumer of information about the mind that you may encounter on the Internet or in movies, magazines, or other media.

Acknowledgments

The starting point for a textbook like this one is an author who has an idea for a book, but other people soon become part of the process. Writing is guided by feedback from editors and reviewers on writing and content. When the manuscript is completed, the production process begins, and a new group of people take over to turn the manuscript into a book. This means that this book has been a group effort and that I had lots of help, both during the process of writing and after submitting the final manuscript. I would therefore like to thank the following people for their extraordinary efforts in support of this book.

➤ **ERIN SCHNAIR**, product manager. Thank you, Erin, for supporting the production of this book in both print and digital formats, and for providing the resources I needed to create the best book possible.

➤ **SHANNON LEMAY-FINN**, developmental editor. Writing a book is a solitary pursuit, but I was fortunate enough to have Shannon comment on everything I wrote. Thank you, Shannon, for focusing your uncanny critical radar on my writing, and for letting me know when my writing didn't make sense, or parse well, or had left out an essential part of the story. Thank you also, for appreciating my writing and for being interested in cognitive psychology. Working with you is one of the things that makes writing these books worthwhile.

➤ **LINDA MAN**, senior content developer. Thanks, Linda, for being on top of this book from the early planning stages all the way through to the end. You handled everything from reviewing photos to managing MindTap activities, plus the countless other details involved in getting the manuscript ready for production, and creating the final book. Thank you for taking care of everything with such efficiency and grace, and for being such a joy to work with.

➤ **LYNN LUSTBERG**, senior project manager, MPS Limited. Producing a book is a complex process that involves close attention to detail, while meeting deadlines. Thank you, Lynn, for shepherding my book through the production process, and especially for dealing with all of my corrections and suggestions as the process of production progressed.

➤ **VERNON BOES**, art director. Thanks, yet again, Vernon, for coordinating the design and art program. It's been fun working with you, all these years.

➤ **CHERYL CARRINGTON**. Thank you, Cheryl, for your beautiful text and cover designs.

I also thank the following people whose work was essential to this project: **Ruth Sakata Corley**, senior content project manager; **Chris Sabooni**, copy editor; **Jan Trout**, ilustrations; and **Carly Belcher**, intellectual property manager.

In addition to the help I received from the above people on the editorial and production side, I received a great deal of help from teachers and researchers who gave me feedback on what I wrote and made suggestions regarding new work in the field. I thank the following people for their help.

▶ Specialist Reviewers

A number of experts were commissioned to read one of the chapters from the fourth edition and provide suggestions on updating the content for the fifth edition. What made many of these reviews especially helpful were suggestions that combined the reviewers' expertise with their experience of presenting the material in their classes.

CHAPTER 4   **Attention**
Michael Hout
New Mexico State University

CHAPTER 5   **Short-Term and Working Memory**
Brad Wyble   Daryl Fougnie
Penn State University   *New York University*

CHAPTER 6   **Long-Term Memory: Structure**
Megan Papesh
Louisiana State University

CHAPTER 7   **Long-Term Memory: Encoding and Retrieval**
Andrew Yonelinas   Barbara Knowlton
University of California, Davis   *University of California, Los Angeles*

CHAPTER 8   **Everyday Memory and Memory Errors**
Jason Chan   Jennifer Talarico
Iowa State University   *Lafayette College*

CHAPTER 9   **Conceptual Knowledge**
Brad Mahon   Jamie Reily
University of Rochester   *Temple University*

CHAPTER 10   **Visual Imagery**
Frank Tong
Vanderbilt University

CHAPTER 11   **Language**
Bob Slevc   Adrian Staub
University of Maryland   *University of Massachusetts*

Tessa Warren
University of Pittsburgh

CHAPTER 12   **Problem Solving**
Evangelia Chrysikou
University of Kansas

CHAPTER 13   **Judgment, Decisions, and Reasoning**
Sandra Schneider
University of South Florida

In addition, the following reviewers read parts of chapters to check for accuracy in their areas of expertise, or took the time to answer questions that I posed.

Jessica Andrews-Hanna
University of Arizona

Ying-Hui Chou
University of Arizona

Marc Coutanche
University of Pittsburgh

Jack Gallant
University of California Berkeley

Måns Holgersson
Kristianstad University, Sweden

Almut Hupbach
Lehigh University

Alexender Huth
University of California, Berkeley

Marcia Johnson
Yale University

Matthew Johnson
University of Nebraska, Lincoln

Lo Tamborini
Kristianstad University, Sweden

Timothy Verstynen
Carnegie-Mellon University

I also thank the following people, who donated photographs and research records for illustrations that are new to this edition.

Ying-Hui Chou
University of Arizona

Jack Gallant
University of California, Berkeley

Alex Huth
University of California, Berkeley

These floating umbrellas, besides being pretty, symbolize many of the cognitive processes we will be describing in this book: Perception (Seeing colors and shapes); Attention (Where your eyes move when observing this scene); Memory (Seeing umbrellas might stimulate memories); Knowledge (You know what umbrellas are used for, and that they usually don't float); and Problem Solving (Floating umbrellas! What's that all about?). What unfolds, as you read this book, is a fascinating story about how the mind works to create these cognitions and more. This chapter begins by describing the history of cognitive psychology.

Introduction to Cognitive Psychology

1

It's been 16 years since the accident. Sam, lying in the long-term care facility, has been in a coma ever since. Observing Sam, who shows no signs of awareness or ability to communicate, it seems reasonable to conclude that "there's nobody in there." But is that true? Does the fact that Sam hasn't moved or responded to stimulation mean he doesn't have a mind? Is there any probability that his eyes, which appear to be vacantly staring into space, could be perceiving, and that these perceptions might be accompanied by thoughts?

These are the questions Lorina Naci and coworkers (2014, 2015) were asking when they placed Sam in a brain scanner that measured increases and decreases in electrical activity throughout his brain, and then showed him an 8-minute excerpt from an Alfred Hitchcock television program called "Bang. You're Dead." At the beginning, a 5-year-old boy is playing with his toy gun. But then he discovers a real gun and some bullets in his uncle's suitcase. The boy loads one bullet into the gun, spins the chamber that contains the single bullet, and shoves the weapon into his toy-gun holster.

As the boy roams the neighborhood, pointing the gun at a number of different people, the tension mounts. He points the gun at someone! He pulls the trigger! The gun doesn't fire because the single bullet isn't in the firing chamber. But thoughts such as "Will the gun go off?" and "Will someone be killed?" are racing through the viewers' minds, knowing that the boy's "play" could, at any moment, turn tragic. (There was a reason Hitchcock was called "the master of suspense.") In the last scene, back at the boy's house, the boy's father, realizing that he is pointing a real gun, lunges toward the boy. The gun fires! A mirror shatters. Luckily, no one is hurt. The boy's father grabs the gun, and the audience breathes a sigh of relief.

When this film was shown to healthy participants in the scanner, their brain activity increased and decreased at the same time for all of the participants, with changes in brain activity being linked to what was happening in the movie. Activity was highest at suspenseful moments in the film, such as when the child was loading the gun or pointing it at someone. So the viewer's brains weren't just responding to the images on the screen; their brain activity was being driven both by the images *and* by the movie's plot. And— here's the important point—to understand the plot, it is necessary to understand things that weren't specifically presented in the movie, like "guns are dangerous when loaded," "guns can kill people," and "a 5-year-old boy may not be aware that he could accidentally kill someone."

So, how did Sam's brain respond to the movie? Amazingly, his response was the same as the healthy participants' responses: brain activity increased during periods of tension and decreased when danger wasn't imminent. This indicates that Sam was not only seeing the images and hearing the soundtrack, but that he was reacting to the movie's plot! His brain activity therefore indicated that Sam was consciously aware; that "someone was in there."

This story about Sam, who appears to have a mental life despite appearances to the contrary, has an important message as we embark on the adventure of understanding the mind. Perhaps the most important message is that the mind is hidden from view. Sam is an extreme case because he can't move or talk, but you will see that the "normal" mind also holds many secrets. Just as we can't know exactly what Sam is experiencing, we don't know exactly what other people are experiencing, even though they are able to tell us about their thoughts and observations.

And although you may be aware of your own thoughts and observations, you are unaware of most of what's happening in your mind. This means that as you understand what you are reading right now, there are hidden processes operating within your mind, beneath your awareness, that make this understanding possible.

As you read this book, you will see how research has revealed many of these secret aspects of the mind's operation. This is no trivial thing, because your mind not only makes it possible for you to read this text and understand the plots of movies, but it is responsible for who you are and what you do. It creates your thoughts, perceptions, desires, emotions, memories, language, and physical actions. It guides your decision making and problem solving. It has been compared to a computer, although your brain outperforms your smartphone, laptop, or even a powerful supercomputer on many tasks. And, of course, your mind does something else that computers can't even dream of (if only they could dream!): it creates your consciousness of what's out there, what's going on with your body, and, simply, what it's like to be you!

In this book, we will be describing what the mind is, what it does, and how it does it. The first step in doing this is to look at some of the things the mind does. As we do this, we will see that the mind is multifaceted, involving multiple functions and mechanisms. We begin this chapter by looking at the multifaceted nature of the mind and then describing some of the history behind the field of cognitive psychology.

▶ Cognitive Psychology: Studying the Mind

You may have noticed that we have been using the term *mind* without precisely defining it. As we will see, **mind**, like other concepts in psychology such as intelligence or emotion, can be thought of in a number of different ways.

What Is the Mind?

One way to approach the question "What is the mind?" is to consider how "mind" is used in everyday conversation. Here are a few examples:

1. "He was able to call to mind what he was doing on the day of the accident." (The mind as involved in memory)
2. "If you put your mind to it, I'm sure you can solve that math problem." (The mind as problem-solver)
3. "I haven't made up my mind yet" or "I'm of two minds about this." (The mind as used to make decisions or consider possibilities)
4. "He is of sound mind and body" or "When he talks about his encounter with aliens, it sounds like he is out of his mind." (A healthy mind being associated with normal functioning, a nonfunctioning mind with abnormal functioning)
5. "A mind is a terrible thing to waste." (The mind as valuable, something that should be used)
6. "He has a brilliant mind." (Used to describe people who are particularly intelligent or creative)

These statements tell us some important things about what the mind is. Statements 1, 2, and 3, which highlight the mind's role in memory, problem solving, and making decisions, are related to the following definition of the mind: *The mind creates and controls mental functions such as perception, attention, memory, emotions, language, deciding, thinking, and reasoning.* This definition reflects the mind's central role in determining our various mental abilities, which are reflected in the chapter titles in this book.

Another definition, which focuses on how the mind operates, is this: *The mind is a system that creates representations of the world so that we can act within it to achieve our goals.* This definition reflects the mind's importance for functioning and survival, and also provides the beginnings of a description of how the mind achieves these ends. The idea of creating representations is something we will return to throughout this book.

These two definitions of the mind are not incompatible. The first one indicates different types of **cognition**—the mental processes, such as perception, attention, and memory, which is what the mind creates. The second definition indicates something about how the mind operates (it creates representations) and its function (it enables us to act and to achieve goals). It is no coincidence that all of the cognitions in the first definition play important roles in acting to achieve goals.

Statements 4, 5, and 6 emphasize the mind's importance for normal functioning, and the amazing abilities of the mind. The mind is something to be used, and the products of some people's minds are considered extraordinary. But one of the messages of this book is that the idea that the mind is amazing is not reserved for "extraordinary" minds, because even the most "routine" things—recognizing a person, having a conversation, or deciding what courses to take next semester—become amazing in themselves when we consider the properties of the mind that enable us to achieve these familiar activities.

Cognitive psychology is the study of mental processes, which includes determining the characteristics and properties of the mind and how it operates. Our goals in the rest of this chapter are to describe how the field of cognitive psychology evolved from its early beginnings to where it is today, and to begin describing how cognitive psychologists approach the scientific study of the mind.

Studying the Mind: Early Work in Cognitive Psychology

In the 1800s, ideas about the mind were dominated by the belief that it is not possible to study the mind. One reason given for this belief was that it is not possible for the mind to study itself, but there were other reasons as well, including the idea that the properties of the mind simply cannot be measured. Nonetheless, some researchers defied the common wisdom and decided to study the mind anyway. One of these people was the Dutch physiologist Franciscus Donders, who in 1868, 11 years before the founding of the first laboratory of scientific psychology, did one of the first experiments that today would be called a cognitive psychology experiment. (It is important to note that the term *cognitive psychology* was not coined until 1967, but the early experiments we are going to describe qualify as cognitive psychology experiments.)

Donders's Pioneering Experiment: How Long Does It Take to Make a Decision?

Donders was interested in determining how long it takes for a person to make a decision. He determined this by measuring **reaction time**—how long it takes to respond to presentation of a stimulus. He used two measures of reaction time. He measured **simple reaction time** by asking his participants to push a button as rapidly as possible when they saw a light go on (**Figure 1.1a**). He measured **choice reaction time** by using two lights and asking his participants to push the left button when they saw the left light go on and the right button when they saw the right light go on (**Figure 1.1b**).

The steps that occur in the simple reaction time task are shown in **Figure 1.2a**. Presenting the stimulus (the light flashes) causes a mental response (perceiving the light), which leads to a behavioral response (pushing the button). The reaction time (dashed line) is the time between the presentation of the stimulus and the behavioral response.

(a) Press J when light goes on. (b) Press J for left light, K for right.

➤ **Figure 1.1** A modern version of Donders's (1868) reaction time experiment: (a) the simple reaction time task and (b) the choice reaction time task. In the simple reaction time task, the participant pushes the J key when the light goes on. In the choice reaction time task, the participant pushes the J key if the left light goes on and the K key if the right light goes on. The purpose of Donders's experiment was to determine how much time it took to decide which key to press in the choice reaction time task.

But remember that Donders was interested in determining how long it took for a person to make a decision. The choice reaction time task added decisions by requiring participants to first decide whether the left or right light was illuminated and then which button to push. The diagram for this task, in **Figure 1.2b**, changes the mental response to "Perceive left light" and "Decide which button to push." Donders reasoned that the difference in reaction time between the simple and choice conditions would indicate how long it took to make the decision that led to pushing the correct button. Because the choice reaction time took one-tenth of a second longer than simple reaction time, Donders concluded that the decision-making process took one-tenth of a second.

Donders's experiment is important, both because it was one of the first cognitive psychology experiments and because it illustrates something extremely significant about studying the mind: Mental responses (perceiving the light and deciding which button to push, in this example) cannot be measured directly, but must be inferred from behavior. We can see why this is so by noting the dashed lines in Figure 1.2. These lines indicate that when Donders measured reaction time, he was measuring the relationship between presentation of the stimulus and the participant's response. He did not measure mental responses directly, but inferred how long they took from the reaction times. The fact that mental responses cannot be measured directly, but must be inferred from observing behavior, is a principle that holds not only for Donders's experiment but for all research in cognitive psychology.

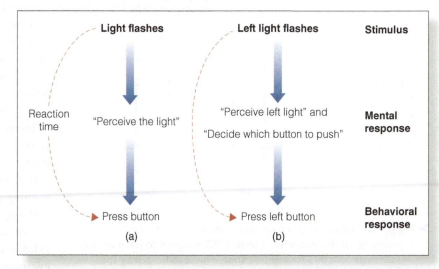

➤ **Figure 1.2** Sequence of events between presentation of the stimulus and the behavioral response in Donders's experiments: (a) simple reaction time task and (b) choice reaction time task. The dashed line indicates that Donders measured reaction time—the time between presentation of the light and the participant's response.

Wundt's Psychology Laboratory: Structuralism and Analytic Introspection In 1879, 11 years after Donders's reaction time experiment, Wilhelm Wundt founded the first laboratory of scientific psychology at the University of Leipzig in Germany. Wundt's approach, which dominated psychology in the late 1800s and early 1900s, was called **structuralism**. According to structuralism, our overall experience is determined by combining basic elements of experience the structuralists called *sensations*. Thus, just as chemistry developed a periodic table of the elements, which combine to create molecules, Wundt wanted to create a "periodic table of the mind," which would include all of the basic sensations involved in creating experience.

Wundt thought he could achieve this scientific description of the components of experience by using **analytic introspection**, a technique in which trained participants described their experiences and thought processes in response to stimuli. Analytic introspection required extensive training because the participants' goal was to describe their experience in terms of elementary mental elements. For example, in one experiment, Wundt asked participants to describe their experience of hearing a five-note chord played on the piano. One of the questions Wundt hoped to answer was whether his participants were able to hear each of the individual notes that made up the chord. As we will see when we consider perception in Chapter 3, structuralism was not a fruitful approach and so was abandoned in the early 1900s. Nonetheless, Wundt made a substantial contribution to psychology by his commitment to studying behavior and the mind under controlled conditions. In addition, he trained many PhDs who established psychology departments at other universities, including many in the United States.

Ebbinghaus's Memory Experiment: What Is the Time Course of Forgetting?
Meanwhile, 120 miles from Leipzig, at the University of Berlin, German psychologist Hermann Ebbinghaus (1885/1913) was using another approach to measuring the properties of the mind. Ebbinghaus was interested in determining the nature of memory and forgetting—specifically, how rapidly information that is learned is lost over time. Rather than using Wundt's method of analytic introspection, Ebbinghaus used a quantitative method for measuring memory. Using himself as the participant, he repeated lists of 13 nonsense syllables such as DAX, QEH, LUH, and ZIF to himself one at a time at a constant rate. He used nonsense syllables so that his memory would not be influenced by the meaning of a particular word.

Ebbinghaus determined how long it took to learn a list for the first time. He then waited for a specific amount of time (the delay) and then determined how long it took to relearn the list. Because forgetting had occurred during the delay, Ebbinghaus made errors when he first tried to remember the list. But because he had retained something from his original learning, he relearned the list more rapidly than when he had learned it for the first time.

Ebbinghaus used a measure called **savings**, calculated as follows, to determine how much was forgotten after a particular delay: Savings = (Original time to learn the list) − (Time to relearn the list after the delay). Thus, if it took 1,000 seconds to learn the list the first time and 400 seconds to relearn the list after the delay, the savings would be 1,000 − 400 = 600 seconds. **Figure 1.3**, which represents original learning and relearning after three different delays, shows that longer delays result in smaller savings.

According to Ebbinghaus, this reduction in savings provided a measure of forgetting, with smaller savings meaning more forgetting. Thus, the plot of percent savings versus time in **Figure 1.4**, called a **savings curve**, shows that memory drops rapidly for the first 2 days after the initial learning and then levels off. This curve was important because it demonstrated that memory could be quantified and

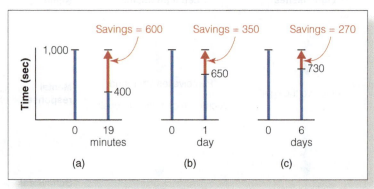

▶ **Figure 1.3** Calculating the savings score in Ebbinghaus's experiment. In this example, it took 1,000 seconds to learn the list of nonsense syllables for the first time. This is indicated by the lines at 0. The time needed to relearn the list at delays of (a) 19 minutes, (b) 1 day, and (c) 6 days are indicated by the line to the right of the 0 line. The red arrows indicate the savings score for each delay. Notice that savings decrease for longer delays. This decrease in savings provides a measure of forgetting.

that functions like the savings curve could be used to describe a property of the mind—in this case, the ability to retain information. Notice that although Ebbinghaus's savings method was very different from Donders's reaction time method, both measured behavior to determine a property of the mind.

William James's *Principles of Psychology*   William James, one of the early American psychologists (although not a student of Wundt's), taught Harvard's first psychology course and made significant observations about the mind in his textbook, *Principles of Psychology* (1890). James's observations were based not on the results of experiments but on observations about the operation of his own mind. One of the best known of James's observations is the following, on the nature of attention:

> Millions of items . . . are present to my senses which never properly enter my experience. Why? Because they have no interest for me. My experience is what I agree to attend to. . . . Everyone knows what attention is. It is the taking possession by the mind, in clear and vivid form, of one out of what seem several simultaneously possible objects or trains of thought. . . . It implies withdrawal from some things in order to deal effectively with others.

The observation that paying attention to one thing involves withdrawing from other things still rings true today and has been the topic of many modern studies of attention. As impressive as the accuracy of James's observations, so too was the range of cognitive topics he considered, which included thinking, consciousness, attention, memory, perception, imagination, and reasoning.

The founding of the first laboratory of psychology by Wundt, the quantitative experiments of Donders and Ebbinghaus, and the perceptive observations of James provided what seemed to be a promising start to the study of the mind (**Table 1.1**). However, research on the mind was soon to be curtailed, largely because of events early in the 20th century that shifted the focus of psychology away from the study of the mind and mental processes. One of the major forces that caused psychology to reject the study of mental processes was a negative reaction to Wundt's technique of analytic introspection.

➤ **Figure 1.4** Ebbinghaus's savings curve. Ebbinghaus considered the percent savings to be a measure of the amount remembered, so he plotted this versus the time between initial learning and testing. The decrease in savings (remembering) with increasing delays indicates that forgetting occurs rapidly over the first 2 days and then occurs more slowly after that.

(Source: Based on data from Ebbinghaus, 1885/1913.)

TABLE 1.1

Early Pioneers in Cognitive Psychology

Person	Procedure	Results and Conclusions	Contribution
Donders (1868)	Simple reaction time versus choice reaction time	Choice reaction time takes 1/10 seconds longer; therefore, it takes 1/10 second to make a decision	First cognitive psychology experiment
Wundt (1879)	Analytic introspection	No reliable results	Established the first laboratory of scientific psychology
Ebbinghaus (1885)	Savings method to measure forgetting	Forgetting occurs rapidly in the first 1 to 2 days after original learning	Quantitative measurement of mental processes
James (1890)	No experiments; reported observations of his own experience	Descriptions of a wide range of experiences	First psychology textbook; some of his observations are still valid today

▶ Abandoning the Study of the Mind

Many early departments of psychology conducted research in the tradition of Wundt's laboratory, using analytic introspection to analyze mental processes. This emphasis on studying the mind was to change, however, because of the efforts of John Watson, who received his PhD in psychology in 1904 from the University of Chicago.

Watson Founds Behaviorism

The story of how John Watson founded an approach to psychology called **behaviorism** is well known to introductory psychology students. We will briefly review it here because of its importance to the history of cognitive psychology.

As a graduate student at the University of Chicago, Watson became dissatisfied with the method of analytic introspection. His problems with this method were (1) it produced extremely variable results from person to person, and (2) these results were difficult to verify because they were interpreted in terms of invisible inner mental processes. In response to what he perceived to be deficiencies in analytic introspection, Watson proposed a new approach called behaviorism. One of Watson's papers, "Psychology As the Behaviorist Views It," set forth the goals of this approach to psychology in this famous quote:

> Psychology as the Behaviorist sees it is a purely objective, experimental branch of natural science. Its theoretical goal is the prediction and control of behavior. Introspection forms no essential part of its methods, nor is the scientific value of its data dependent upon the readiness with which they lend themselves to interpretation in terms of consciousness. . . . What we need to do is start work upon psychology making behavior, not consciousness, the objective point of our attack. (Watson, 1913, pp. 158, 176; emphasis added)

This passage makes two key points: (1) Watson rejects introspection as a method, and (2) observable behavior, not consciousness (which would involve unobservable processes such as thinking, emotions, and reasoning), is the main topic of study. In other words, Watson wanted to restrict psychology to behavioral data, such as Donders's reaction times, and rejected the idea of going beyond those data to draw conclusions about unobservable mental events. Watson eliminated the mind as a topic for investigation by proclaiming that "psychology . . . need no longer delude itself into thinking that it is making mental states the object of observation" (p. 163). Watson's goal was to replace the mind as a topic of study in psychology with the study of directly observable behavior. As behaviorism became the dominant force in American psychology, psychologists' attention shifted from asking "What does behavior tell us about the mind?" to "What is the relation between stimuli in the environment and behavior?"

Watson's most famous experiment was the "Little Albert" experiment, in which Watson and Rosalie Rayner (1920) subjected Albert, a 9-month-old-boy, to a loud noise every time a rat (which Albert had originally liked) came close to the child. After a few pairings of the noise with the rat, Albert reacted to the rat by crawling away as rapidly as possible.

Watson's ideas are associated with **classical conditioning**—how pairing one stimulus (such as the loud noise presented to Albert) with another, previously neutral stimulus (such as the rat) causes changes in the response to the neutral stimulus. Watson's inspiration for his experiment was Ivan Pavlov's research, begun in the 1890s, that demonstrated classical conditioning in dogs. In these experiments (**Figure 1.5**), Pavlov's pairing of food (which made the dog salivate) with a bell (the initially neutral stimulus) caused the dog to salivate to the sound of the bell (Pavlov, 1927).

Watson used classical conditioning to argue that behavior can be analyzed without any reference to the mind. For Watson, what was going on inside Albert's head (or inside

Pavlov's dog's head!), either physiologically or mentally, was irrelevant. He cared only about how pairing one stimulus with another affected behavior.

Skinner's Operant Conditioning

In the midst of behaviorism's dominance of American psychology, B. F. Skinner, who received his PhD from Harvard in 1931, provided another tool for studying the relationship between stimulus and response, which ensured that this approach would dominate psychology for decades to come. Skinner introduced **operant conditioning**, which focused on how behavior is strengthened by the presentation of positive reinforcers, such as food or social approval (or withdrawal of negative reinforcers, such as a shock or social rejection). For example, Skinner showed that reinforcing a rat with food for pressing a bar maintained or increased the rat's rate of bar pressing. Like Watson, Skinner was not interested in what was happening in the mind, but focused solely on determining how behavior was controlled by stimuli (Skinner, 1938).

➤ **Figure 1.5** In Pavlov's famous experiment, he paired ringing a bell with presentation of food. Initially, presentation of the food caused the dog to salivate, but after a number of pairings of bell and food, the bell alone caused salivation. This principle of learning by pairing, which came to be called *classical conditioning*, was the basis of Watson's "Little Albert" experiment.

The idea that behavior can be understood by studying stimulus–response relationships influenced an entire generation of psychologists and dominated psychology in the United States from the 1940s through the 1960s. Psychologists applied the techniques of classical and operant conditioning to classroom teaching, treating psychological disorders, and testing the effects of drugs on animals. **Figure 1.6** is a time line showing the initial studies of the mind and the rise of behaviorism. But even as behaviorism was dominating psychology, events were occurring that were to lead to the rebirth of the study of the mind.

Setting the Stage for the Reemergence of the Mind in Psychology

Although behaviorism dominated American psychology for many decades, some researchers were not toeing the strict behaviorist line. One of these researchers was Edward Chace Tolman. Tolman, who from 1918 to 1954 was at the University of California at Berkeley, called himself a behaviorist because his focus was on measuring behavior. But in reality, he was one of the early cognitive psychologists, because he used behavior to infer mental processes.

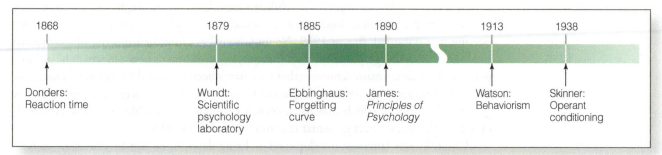

| 1868 | 1879 | 1885 | 1890 | 1913 | 1938 |

Donders: Reaction time | Wundt: Scientific psychology laboratory | Ebbinghaus: Forgetting curve | James: *Principles of Psychology* | Watson: Behaviorism | Skinner: Operant conditioning

➤ **Figure 1.6** Time line showing early experiments studying the mind in the 1800s and the rise of behaviorism in the 1900s.

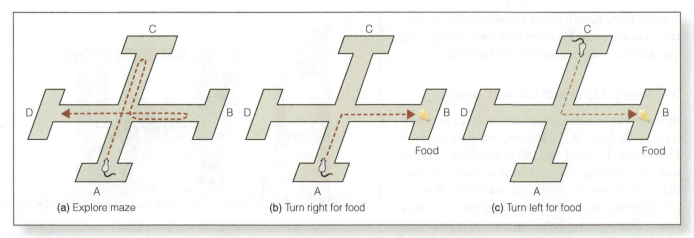

(a) Explore maze   (b) Turn right for food   (c) Turn left for food

> **Figure 1.7** Maze used by Tolman. (a) The rat initially explores the maze. (b) The rat learns to turn right to obtain food at B when it starts at A. (c) When placed at C, the rat turns left to reach the food at B. In this experiment, precautions are taken to prevent the rat from knowing where the food is based on cues such as smell.

In one of his experiments, Tolman (1938) placed a rat in a maze like the one in **Figure 1.7**. Initially, the rat explored the maze, running up and down each of the alleys (**Figure 1.7a**). After this initial period of exploration, the rat was placed at point A and food was placed at point B, and the rat quickly learned to turn right at the intersection to obtain the food. This is exactly what the behaviorists would predict, because turning right was rewarded with food (**Figure 1.7b**). However, when Tolman (after taking precautions to be sure the rat couldn't determine the location of the food based on smell) placed the rat at point C, something interesting happened. The rat turned left at the intersection to reach the food at point B (**Figure 1.7c**). Tolman's explanation of this result was that when the rat initially experienced the maze it was developing a **cognitive map**—a conception within the rat's mind of the maze's layout (Tolman, 1948). Thus, even though the rat had previously been rewarded for turning right, its mental map indicated that when starting from the new location it needed to turn left to reach the food. Tolman's use of the word *cognitive*, and the idea that something other than stimulus–response connections might be occurring in the rat's mind, placed Tolman outside of mainstream behaviorism.

Other researchers were aware of Tolman's work, but for most American psychologists in the 1940s, the use of the term *cognitive* was difficult to accept because it violated the behaviorists' idea that internal processes, such as thinking or maps in the head, were not acceptable topics to study. It wasn't until about a decade after Tolman introduced the idea of cognitive maps that developments occurred that led to a resurgence of the mind in psychology. Ironically, one of these developments was the publication, in 1957, of a book by B. F. Skinner titled *Verbal Behavior*.

In his book, Skinner argued that children learn language through operant conditioning. According to this idea, children imitate speech that they hear, and repeat correct speech because it is rewarded. But in 1959, Noam Chomsky, a linguist from the Massachusetts Institute of Technology, published a scathing review of Skinner's book, in which he pointed out that children say many sentences that have never been rewarded by parents ("I hate you, Mommy," for example), and that during the normal course of language development, they go through a stage in which they use incorrect grammar, such as "the boy hitted the ball," even though this incorrect grammar may never have been reinforced.

Chomsky saw language development as being determined not by imitation or reinforcement, but by an inborn biological program that holds across cultures. Chomsky's idea that language is a product of the way the mind is constructed, rather than a result of reinforcement, led psychologists to reconsider the idea that language and other complex behaviors, such as problem solving and reasoning, can be explained by operant conditioning. Instead, they began to realize that to understand complex cognitive behaviors, it is necessary not only to measure observable behavior but also to consider what this behavior tells us about how the mind works.

▶ The Rebirth of the Study of the Mind

The decade of the 1950s is generally recognized as the beginning of the **cognitive revolution**—a shift in psychology from the behaviorist's focus on stimulus–response relationships to an approach whose main thrust was to understand the operation of the mind. Even before Chomsky's critique of Skinner's book, other events were happening that signaled a shift away from focusing only on behavior and toward studying how the mind operates. But before we describe the events that began the cognitive revolution, let's consider the following question: What is a revolution—and specifically a scientific revolution? One answer to this question can be found in philosopher Thomas Kuhn's (1962) book *The Structure of Scientific Revolutions*.

Paradigms and Paradigm Shifts

Kuhn defined a **scientific revolution** as a shift from one paradigm to another, where a **paradigm** is a system of ideas that dominate science at a particular time (Dyson, 2012). A scientific revolution, therefore, involves a **paradigm shift**.

An example of a paradigm shift in science is the shift that occurred in physics in the beginning of the 20th century, with the introduction of the theory of relativity and quantum theory. Before the 20th century, classical physics, founded by Isaac Newton (1642–1727), had made great progress in describing things like how objects are affected by forces (Newton's laws of motion) and the nature of electrical fields (Maxwell's laws, which described electromagnetism). The principles of classical physics did not, however, adequately describe subatomic phenomena and the relation between time and motion. For example, classical physics conceived of the flow of time as an absolute constant, which was the same for everyone. But in 1905, Albert Einstein, a young clerk in the Bern, Switzerland, patent office, published his theory of relativity, which proposed that the measurement of space and time are affected by an observer's motion, so clocks run slower when approaching the speed of light. He also proposed that there is an equivalence of mass and energy, as expressed in his famous equation $E = mc2$ (energy equals mass times the speed of light squared). Einstein's relativity theory, along with the newly introduced quantum theory, which explained the behavior of subatomic particles, marked the beginning of modern physics.

Just as the paradigm shift from classical physics to modern physics provided a new way of looking at the physical world, the paradigm shift from behaviorism to the cognitive approach provided a new way to look at behavior. During the reign of behaviorism, behavior was considered an end in itself. Psychology was dominated by experiments studying how behavior is affected by rewards and punishments. Some valuable discoveries resulted from this research, including psychological therapies called "behavioral therapies," which are still in use today. But the behaviorist paradigm did not allow any consideration of the mind's role in creating behavior, so in the 1950s the new cognitive paradigm began to emerge. We can't mark the beginning of this new paradigm by the publication of a single paper, like Einstein's (1905) proposal of relativity theory, but rather we can note a series of events, which added together culminated in a new way of studying psychology. One of these events was the introduction of a new technology that suggested a new way of describing the operation of the mind. That new technology was the digital computer.

Introduction of the Digital Computer

The first digital computers, developed in the late 1940s, were huge machines that took up entire buildings, but in 1954 IBM introduced a computer that was available to the general public. These computers were still extremely large compared to the laptops of today, but they found their way into university research laboratories, where they were used both to analyze data and, most important for our purposes, to suggest a new way of thinking about the mind.

Flow Diagrams for Computers   One of the characteristics of computers that captured the attention of psychologists in the 1950s was that they processed information in stages, as illustrated in **Figure 1.8a**. In this diagram, information is first received by an "input processor." It is then stored in a "memory unit" before it is processed by an "arithmetic unit," which then creates the computer's output. Using this stage approach as their inspiration, some psychologists proposed the **information-processing approach** to studying the mind—an approach that traces sequences of mental operations involved in cognition. According to the information-processing approach, the operation of the mind can be described as occurring in a number of stages. Applying this stage approach to the mind led psychologists to ask new questions and to frame their answers to these questions in new ways. One of the first experiments influenced by this new way of thinking about the mind involved studying how well people are able to focus their attention on some information when other information is being presented at the same time.

Flow Diagrams for the Mind   Beginning in the 1950s, a number of researchers became interested in describing how well the mind can deal with incoming information. One question they were interested in answering followed from William James's idea that when we decide to attend to one thing, we must withdraw from other things. Taking this idea as a starting point, British psychologist Colin Cherry (1953) presented participants with two auditory messages, one to the left ear and one to the right ear, and told them to focus their attention on one of the messages (the attended message) and to ignore the other one (the unattended message). For example, the participant might be told to attend to the left-ear message that began "As Susan drove down the road in her new car . . ." while simultaneously receiving, but not attending to, the right-ear message "Cognitive psychology, which is the study of mental processes . . ."

The result of this experiment, which we will describe in detail when we discuss attention in Chapter 4, was that when people focused on the attended message, they could hear the sounds of the unattended message but were unaware of the contents of that message. This result led another British psychologist, Donald Broadbent (1958), to propose the first flow diagram of the mind (**Figure 1.8b**). This diagram represents what Broadbent believed happens in a person's mind when directing attention to one stimulus in the environment. Applied to Cherry's attention experiment, "input" would be the sounds of both the attended and unattended messages; the "filter" lets through the attended message and filters out the unattended message; and the "detector" records the information that gets through the filter.

Applied to your experience when talking to a friend at a noisy party, the filter lets in your friend's conversation and filters out all the other conversations and noise. Thus, although you might be aware that there are other people talking, you are not aware of detailed information such as what the other people are talking about.

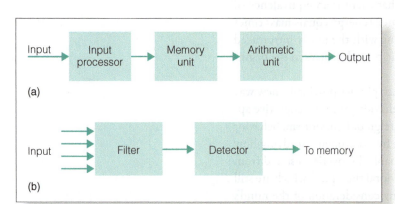

(a)

(b)

➤ **Figure 1.8** (a) Flow diagram for an early computer. (b) Flow diagram for Broadbent's filter model of attention. This diagram shows many messages entering a "filter," which selects the message to which the person is attending for further processing by a detector and then transfer to short-term memory. We will describe this diagram more fully in Chapter 4.

Broadbent's flow diagram provided a way to analyze the operation of the mind in terms of a sequence of processing stages and proposed a model that could be tested by further experiments. You will see many more flow diagrams like this throughout this book because they have become one of the standard ways of depicting the operation of the mind. But the British psychologists Cherry and Broadbent weren't the only researchers finding new ways of studying the mind. At about the same time in the United States, researchers organized two conferences that, taking their cue from computers, conceived of the mind as a processor of information.

Conferences on Artificial Intelligence and Information Theory

In the early 1950s, John McCarthy, a young professor of mathematics at Dartmouth College, had an idea. Would it be possible, McCarthy wondered, to program computers to mimic the operation of the human mind? Rather than simply asking the question, McCarthy decided to organize a conference at Dartmouth in the summer of 1956 to provide a forum for researchers to discuss ways that computers could be programmed to carry out intelligent behavior. The title of the conference, *Summer Research Project on Artificial Intelligence*, was the first use of the term **artificial intelligence**. McCarthy defined the artificial intelligence approach as "making a machine behave in ways that would be called intelligent if a human were so behaving" (McCarthy et al., 1955).

Researchers from a number of different disciplines—psychologists, mathematicians, computer scientists, linguists, and experts in information theory—attended the conference, which spanned 10 weeks. A number of people attended most of the conference, others dropped in and out, but perhaps the two most important participants—Herb Simon and Alan Newell from the Carnegie Institute of Technology—were hardly there at all (Boden, 2006). The reason they weren't there is that they were busy back in Pittsburgh trying to create the artificial intelligence machine that McCarthy had envisioned. Simon and Newell's goal was to create a computer program that could create proofs for problems in logic—something that up until then had only been achieved by humans.

Newell and Simon succeeded in creating the program, which they called the *logic theorist*, in time to demonstrate it at the conference. What they demonstrated was revolutionary because the logic theorist program was able to create proofs of mathematical theorems that involve principles of logic. This program, although primitive compared to modern artificial intelligence programs, was a real "thinking machine" because it did more than simply process numbers—it used humanlike reasoning processes to solve problems.

Shortly after the Dartmouth conference, in September of the same year, another pivotal conference was held, the *Massachusetts Institute of Technology Symposium on Information Theory*. This conference provided another opportunity for Newell and Simon to demonstrate their logic theorist program, and the attendees also heard George Miller, a Harvard psychologist, present a version of a paper "The Magical Number Seven Plus or Minus Two," which had just been published (Miller, 1956). In that paper, Miller presented the idea that there are limits to a human's ability to process information—that the capacity of the human mind is limited to about seven items (for example, the length of a telephone number).

As we will see when we discuss this idea in Chapter 5, there are ways to increase our ability to take in and remember information (for example, we have little trouble adding an area code to the seven digits of many telephone numbers). Nonetheless, Miller's basic principle that there are limits to the amount of information we can take in and remember was an important idea, which, you might notice, was similar to the point being made by Broadbent's filter model at about the same time.

The Cognitive "Revolution" Took a While

The events we have described—Cherry's experiment, Broadbent's filter model, and the two conferences in 1956—represented the beginning of a shift in psychology from behaviorism to the study of the mind. Although we have called this shift the *cognitive revolution*, it is

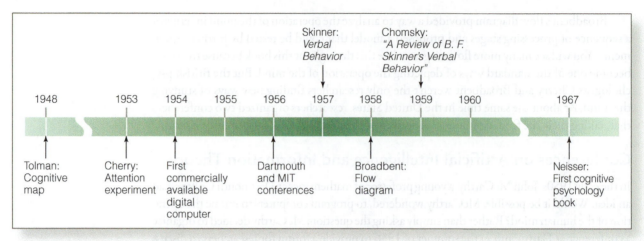

> **Figure 1.9** Time line showing events associated with the decline of the influence of behaviorism (above the line) and events that led to the development of the information-processing approach to cognitive psychology (below the line).

worth noting that the shift from Skinner's behaviorism to the cognitive approach, which was indeed revolutionary, occurred over a period of time. The scientists attending the conferences in 1956 had no idea that these conferences would, years later, be seen as historic events in the birth of a new way of thinking about the mind or that scientific historians would someday call 1956 "the birthday of cognitive science" (Bechtel et al., 1998; Miller, 2003; Neisser, 1988). In fact, even years after these meetings, a textbook on the history of psychology made no mention of the cognitive approach (Misiak & Sexton, 1966), and it wasn't until 1967 that Ulrich Neisser published a textbook with the title *Cognitive Psychology* (Neisser, 1967). **Figure 1.9** shows a time line of some of the events that led to the establishment of the field of cognitive psychology.

Neisser's textbook, which coined the term *cognitive psychology* and emphasized the information-processing approach to studying the mind, is, in a sense, the grandfather of the book you are now reading. As often happens, each successive generation creates new ways of approaching problems, and cognitive psychology has been no exception. Since the 1956 conferences and the 1967 textbook, many experiments have been carried out, new theories proposed, and new techniques developed; as a result, cognitive psychology, and the information-processing approach to studying the mind, has become one of the dominant approaches in psychology.

▶ The Evolution of Cognitive Psychology

We have been describing the events in the 1950s and 1960s as the cognitive revolution. But it is important to realize that although the revolution made it acceptable to study the mind, the field of cognitive psychology continued to evolve in the decades that followed. One way to appreciate how cognitive psychology has evolved from the 1950s and 1960s until today is to look at the contents of Neisser's (1967) book.

What Neisser Wrote

We can appreciate where cognitive psychology was in the 1960s by looking at the first cognitive psychology textbook, Ulrich Neisser's (1967) *Cognitive Psychology*. The purpose of this book, as Neisser states in Chapter 1, is "to provide a useful and current assessment of the existing state of the art" (p. 9). Given this purpose, it is instructive to consider the book's Table of Contents.

Most of the book is devoted to vision and hearing. There are descriptions of how information is taken in by vision and held in memory for short periods of time, and how people search for visual information and use visual information to see simple patterns. Most of the discussion is about the intake of information and holding information in the mind for brief periods of time, such as how long people can remember sounds like strings of numbers. But it isn't until page 279 of the 305-page book that Neisser considers "higher mental processes" such as thinking, problem solving, and long-term remembering. The reason Neisser gives for this scant treatment is that in 1967, we just didn't know much about higher mental processes.

Another gap in coverage is the almost complete absence of physiology. Neisser says that "I do not doubt that human behavior and consciousness depends entirely on the activity of the brain and related processes" (p. 5), but then he goes on to argue that he is interested in how the mind operates, but not in the physiological mechanisms behind this operation.

These two gaps in Neisser's book highlight what are central topics in present-day cognitive psychology. One of these topics is the study of higher mental processes, and the other is the study of the physiology of mental processes.

Studying Higher Mental Processes

A big step toward the study of higher mental processes was Richard Atkinson and Richard Shiffrin's (1968) model of memory, which was introduced a year after the publication of Neisser's book. This model, shown in **Figure 1.10**, pictures the flow of information in the memory system as progressing through three stages. *Sensory memory* holds incoming information for a fraction of a second and then passes most of this information to *short-term memory*, which has limited capacity and holds information for seconds (like an address you are trying to remember until you can write it down). The curved arrow represents the process of rehearsal, which occurs when we repeat something, like a phone number, to keep from forgetting it. The blue arrow indicates that some information in short-term memory can be transferred to *long-term memory*, a high-capacity system that can hold information for long periods of time (like your memory of what you did last weekend, or the capitals of states). The green arrow indicates that some of the information in long-term memory can be returned to short-term memory. The green arrow, which represents what happens when we remember something that was stored in long-term memory, is based on the idea that remembering something involves bringing it back into short-term memory.

By distinguishing between different components of the memory process, this model opened the way for studying each part separately. And once researchers discovered more details about what was going on inside each of the model's boxes, they were able to subdivide these boxes into smaller units, which then could be studied in more depth. For example, Endel Tulving (1972, 1985), one of the most prominent early memory researchers, proposed that long-term memory is subdivided into three components (**Figure 1.11**). *Episodic memory* is memory for events in your life (like what you did last weekend). *Semantic memory* is memory for facts (such as the capitals of the states). *Procedural memory* is memory for physical actions (such as how to ride a bike or play the piano). Subdividing the long-term memory box into types of long-term memory added detail to the model that provided the basis for research into how each of these components operates. As you will see in every chapter of this book, the study of higher mental processes has extended to areas beyond memory. As you read this book, you will see how researchers

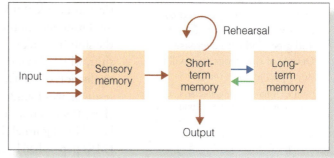

➤ **Figure 1.10** Atkinson and Shiffrin's (1968) model of memory. See text for details.

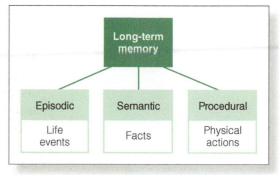

➤ **Figure 1.11** Endel Tulving (1972) divided long-term memory into three components.

have often subdivided cognitive processes into smaller units in order to create a more detailed picture of how these processes operate.

Studying the Physiology of Cognition

While researchers were working to understand memory and other cognitive functions by doing behavioral experiments, something else was happening. Physiological research, which we will see in Chapter 2 had been making advances since the 1800s, was providing important insights into the "behind the scenes" activity in the nervous system that creates the mind.

Two physiological techniques dominated early physiological research on the mind. **Neuropsychology**, the study of the behavior of people with brain damage, had been providing insights into the functioning of different parts of the brain since the 1800s. **Electrophysiology**, measuring electrical responses of the nervous system, made it possible to listen to the activity of single neurons. Most electrophysiology research was done on animals. As we will see in Chapter 2, both neuropsychology and electrophysiology have provided important insights into the physiological basis of the mind.

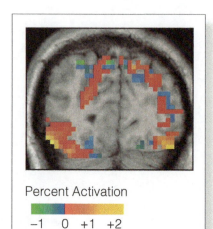

Percent Activation

−1   0   +1   +2

▶ **Figure 1.12** Record of brain activation determined using fMRI. Colors indicate locations of increases and decreases in brain activity. Red and yellow indicate increases in activity caused by perceiving pictures of faces. Blue and green indicate decreases. Details of this procedure will be described in Chapter 2.

(Source: Ishai, A., Ungerleider, L. G., Martin, A., & Haxby, J. V. (2000). The Representation of Objects in the Human Occipital and Temporal Cortex. *Journal of Cognitive Neuroscience, 12*, 36-51.)

But perhaps the most significant physiological advance wasn't to come until a decade after Neisser's book, when the technique of **brain imaging** was introduced. A procedure called *positron emission tomography* (PET), which was introduced in 1976, made it possible to see which areas of the human brain are activated during cognitive activity (Hoffman et al., 1976; Ter-Pogossian et al., 1975). A disadvantage of this technique was that it was expensive and involved injecting radioactive tracers into a person's bloodstream. PET was therefore replaced by *functional magnetic resonance imaging* (fMRI), which didn't involve radioactive tracers and which was capable of higher resolution (Ogawa et al., 1990). **Figure 1.12** shows the results of an fMRI experiment.

The introduction of fMRI brings us back to the idea of revolutions. Thomas Kuhn's idea of paradigm shifts was based on the idea that a scientific revolution involves a shift in the way people think about a subject. This was clearly the case in the shift from the behavioral paradigm to the cognitive paradigm. But there's another kind of shift in addition to the shift in thinking: a shift in how people *do* science (Dyson, 2012; Galison, 1997). This shift, which depends on new developments in technology, is what happened with the introduction of the fMRI. *Neuroimage*, a journal devoted solely to reporting neuroimaging research, was founded in 1992 (Toga, 1992), followed by *Human Brain Mapping* in 1993 (Fox, 1993). From its starting point in the early 1990s, the number of fMRI papers published in all journals has steadily increased. In fact, it has been estimated that about 40,000 fMRI papers had been published as of 2015 (Eklund et al., 2016).

There are limitations to fMRI research, so other scanning techniques have also been developed. But there is no question that the trend started by the introduction of fMRI in 1990 caused its own revolution within cognitive psychology, which, as we will see in Chapter 2, has led to a vast increase in our knowledge of how the brain functions.

New Perspectives on Behavior

So how has cognitive psychology evolved since Neisser's 1967 "progress report"? As we have already mentioned, current cognitive psychology involves more-sophisticated flow diagrams of the mind, a consideration of higher mental processes, and also a large amount of physiological research.

Beyond developing more research on higher-level processes and physiology that we knew little about in 1967, researchers began taking research out of the laboratory. Most early research was done in laboratories, with participants sitting in one place looking at flashed stimuli, as in Donders's reaction time experiment. But it became clear that to fully understand the mind, we have to also study what happens when a person is moving through

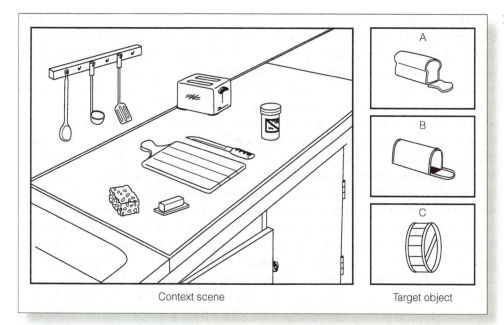

▶ Figure 1.13 Stimuli used in Palmer's (1975) experiment. The scene at the left is presented first, and then one of the objects on the right is briefly flashed. Participants in this experiment were more accurate in identifying the bread. This indicates that their knowledge of what is usually found in kitchens influenced their performance.

the environment and acting on it. Modern cognitive psychology therefore features an increasing amount of research on cognition in "real-world" situations.

Researchers also realized that humans are not "blank slates" that just accept and store information, so they began doing experiments that demonstrated the importance of knowledge for cognition. For example, consider the picture in **Figure 1.13**, which was used by Stephen Palmer (1975) to illustrate how our knowledge about the environment can influence our perception. Palmer first presented a context scene such as the kitchen scene on the left and then briefly flashed one of the target pictures on the right. When Palmer asked observers to identify the object in the target picture, they correctly identified an object like the loaf of bread (which is appropriate to the kitchen scene) 80 percent of the time, but correctly identified the mailbox or the drum (two objects that don't fit into the scene) only 40 percent of the time. Apparently, Palmer's observers were using their knowledge of objects that are likely to be found in kitchens to help them perceive the briefly flashed loaf of bread. Of course, knowledge isn't just an interesting effect to be demonstrated in a perception experiment; it is central to most of our cognitive processing. You will see evidence for the importance of such knowledge in cognition because it appears in every chapter!

As you read this book, you will encounter a wide range of perspective and approaches. You will see how physiological research adds another dimension to our understanding of the mind; how cognitive psychology is studied in the laboratory and in real-world environments; and how the knowledge a person brings to a situation plays a central role in cognition.

▶ SOMETHING TO CONSIDER

Learning from This Book

Congratulations! You now know how some researchers began doing cognitive psychology experiments in the 19th century, how the study of the mind was suppressed in the middle of the 20th century, how the study of the mind made a glorious comeback in the 1950s, and how present-day psychologists approach the study of the mind. One of the purposes of this chapter—to orient you to the field of cognitive psychology—has been accomplished.

Another purpose of this chapter is to help you get the most out of this book. After all, cognitive psychology is the study of the mind, and there are things that have been discovered about memory that can help you improve your study techniques so you can get as much as possible from this book and from the course you are taking. One way to appreciate how cognitive psychology can be applied to studying is to look at pages 199–202 in Chapter 7. It would make sense to skim this material now, rather than waiting. There will be some terms that you may not be familiar with, but these aren't crucial for what you want to accomplish, which is picking up some hints that will make your studying more efficient and effective. Two terms worth knowing, as you read these pages, are *encoding*—which is what is happening as you are learning the material—and *retrieval*—what is happening when you are remembering the material. The trick is to encode the material during your studying in a way that will make it easier to retrieve it later. (Also see page xxii in the preface.)

Something else that might help you learn from this book is to be aware of how it is constructed. As you read the book, you will see that often a basic idea or theory is presented and then it is supported by examples or experiments. This way of presenting information breaks the discussion of a particular topic into a series of "mini-stories." Each story begins with an idea or phenomenon and is followed by demonstrations of the phenomenon and usually evidence to support it. Often there is also a connection between one story and the next. The reason topics are presented as mini-stories is that it is easier to remember a number of facts if they are presented as part of a story than if they are presented as separate, unrelated facts. So, as you read this book, keep in mind that your main job is to understand the stories, each of which is a basic premise followed by supporting evidence. Thinking about the material in this way will make it more meaningful and therefore easier to remember.

One more thing: Just as specific topics can be described as a number of small stories that are linked together, the field of cognitive psychology as a whole consists of many themes that are related to each other, even if they appear in different chapters. Perception, attention, memory, and other cognitive processes all involve the same nervous system and therefore share many of the same properties. The principles shared by many cognitive processes are part of the larger story of cognition that will unfold as you progress through this book

TEST YOURSELF 1.1

1. What was the point of the opening story about Sam?
2. What are two ways of defining the mind?
3. Why could we say that Donders and Ebbinghaus were cognitive psychologists, even though in the 19th century there was no field called cognitive psychology? Describe Donders's experiment and the rationale behind it, and Ebbinghaus's memory experiments. What do Donders's and Ebbinghaus's experiments have in common?
4. Who founded the first laboratory of scientific psychology? Describe the method of analytic introspection that was used in this laboratory.
5. What method did William James use to study the mind?
6. Describe the rise of behaviorism, especially the influence of Watson and Skinner. How did behaviorism affect research on the mind?
7. How did Edward Tolman deviate from strict behaviorism?
8. What did Noam Chomsky say about Skinner's book *Verbal Behavior*, and what effect did that have on behaviorism?

9. What is a scientific revolution, according to Thomas Kuhn? How is the cognitive revolution similar to the revolution that occurred in physics at the beginning of the 20th century?

10. Describe the events that led to the "cognitive revolution." Be sure you understand the role of digital computers and the information-processing approach in moving psychology toward the study of the mind.

11. What was the state of cognitive psychology in 1967, according to Neisser's (1967) book?

12. What are neuropsychology, electrophysiology, and brain imaging?

13. What new perspectives on behavior emerged as cognitive psychology developed?

14. What are two suggestions for improving your ability to learn from this book?

CHAPTER SUMMARY

1. Cognitive psychology is the branch of psychology concerned with the scientific study of the mind.

2. The mind creates and controls mental capacities such as perception, attention, and memory, and creates representations of the world that enable us to function.

3. The work of Donders (simple versus choice reaction time) and Ebbinghaus (the forgetting curve for nonsense syllables) are examples of early experimental research on the mind.

4. Because the operation of the mind cannot be observed directly, its operation must be inferred from what we can measure, such as behavior or physiological responding. This is one of the basic principles of cognitive psychology.

5. The first laboratory of scientific psychology, founded by Wundt in 1879, was concerned largely with studying the mind. Structuralism was the dominant theoretical approach of this laboratory, and analytic introspection was one of the major methods used to collect data.

6. William James, in the United States, used observations of his own mind as the basis of his textbook, *Principles of Psychology*.

7. In the first decades of the 20th century, John Watson founded behaviorism, partly in reaction to structuralism and the method of analytic introspection. His procedures were based on classical conditioning. Behaviorism's central tenet was that psychology was properly studied by measuring observable behavior, and that invisible mental processes were not valid topics for the study of psychology.

8. Beginning in the 1930s and 1940s, B. F. Skinner's work on operant conditioning ensured that behaviorism would be the dominant force in psychology through the 1950s.

9. Edward Tolman called himself a behaviorist but studied cognitive processes that were out of the mainstream of behaviorism.

10. The cognitive revolution involved a paradigm shift in how scientists thought about psychology, and specifically the mind.

11. In the 1950s, a number of events occurred that led to what has been called the cognitive revolution: a decline in the influence of behaviorism and a reemergence of the study of the mind. These events included the following: (a) Chomsky's critique of Skinner's book *Verbal Behavior*; (b) the introduction of the digital computer and the idea that the mind processes information in stages, like a computer; (c) Cherry's attention experiments and Broadbent's introduction of flow diagrams to depict the processes involved in attention; and (d) interdisciplinary conferences at Dartmouth and the Massachusetts Institute of Technology.

12. Even after the shift in psychology that made studying the mind acceptable, our understanding of the mind was limited, as indicated by the contents of Neisser's (1967) book. Notable developments in cognitive psychology in the decades following Neisser's book were (1) development of more-sophisticated models; (2) research focusing on the physiological basis of cognition; (3) concern with cognition in the real world, and (4) the role of knowledge in cognition.

13. Two things that may help in learning the material in this book are to read the study hints in Chapter 7, which are based on some of the things we know about memory research, and to realize that the book is constructed like a story, with basic ideas or principles followed by supporting evidence.

THINK ABOUT IT

1. What do you think the "hot topics" of cognitive psychology are, based on what you have seen or heard in the media? Hint: Look for stories such as the following: "Scientists Race to Find Memory Loss Cure"; "Defendant Says He Can't Remember What Happened."

2. The idea that we have something called "the mind" that is responsible for our thoughts and behavior is reflected in the many ways that the word *mind* can be used. A few examples of the use of *mind* in everyday language were cited at the beginning of the chapter. See how many more examples you can think of that illustrate different uses of the word *mind*, and decide how relevant each is to what you will be studying in cognitive psychology (as indicated by the Table of Contents of this book).

3. The idea that the operation of the mind can be described as occurring in a number of stages was the central principle of the information-processing approach, which was one of the outcomes of the cognitive revolution that began in the 1950s. How can Donders's reaction time experiment from the 1800s be conceptualized in terms of the information-processing approach?

4. Donders compared the results of his simple and choice reaction time experiments to infer how long it took, when given a choice, to make the decision as to which button to push. But what about other kinds of decisions? Design an experiment to determine the time it takes to make a more complex decision. Then relate this experiment to the diagram in Figure 1.2.

KEY TERMS

Analytic introspection, 8

Artificial intelligence, 15

Behaviorism, 10

Brain imaging, 18

Choice reaction time, 6

Classical conditioning, 10

Cognition, 6

Cognitive map, 12

Cognitive psychology, 6

Cognitive revolution, 13

Electrophysiology, 18

Information-processing approach, 14

Mind, 5

Neuropsychology, 18

Operant conditioning, 11

Paradigm, 13

Paradigm shift, 13

Reaction time, 6

Savings, 8

Savings curve, 8

Scientific revolution, 13

Simple reaction time, 6

Structuralism, 8

COGLAB EXPERIMENTS   Numbers in parentheses refer to the experiment number in CogLab.

Simple Detection (2)

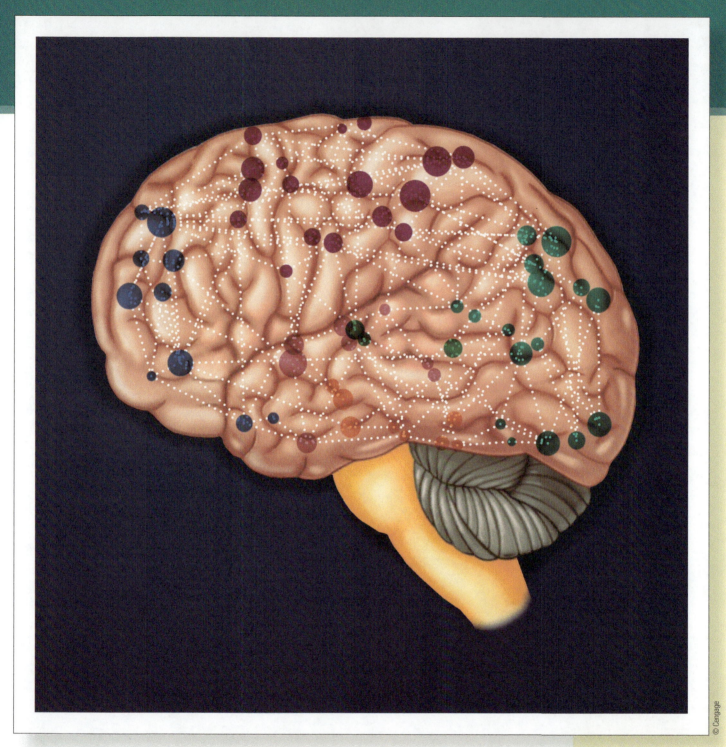

To fully understand cognition, we need to understand the brain. As we will see in this chapter, the brain has been studied at levels ranging from single neurons to complex networks that interconnect areas throughout the brain. This picture represents, in simplified form, the complexity of the interconnections between different places in the brain. These interconnections are determined both by physical connections created by neurons, and by the specific functions that the brain is carrying out at a particular time. The brain, therefore, is not only extremely complex, but its functioning is changeable and dynamic, in keeping with the dynamic nature of the cognitions it creates.

Cognitive Neuroscience

2

▶ What is cognitive neuroscience, and why is it necessary? (26)

▶ How is information transmitted from one place to another in the nervous system? (29)

▶ How are things in the environment, such as faces and places, represented in the brain? (42)

▶ What are neural networks, and what is their role in cognition? (45)

As we discussed in Chapter 1, research on the mind has been on a roller-coaster ride that began with a promising start in the 1800s with the early research of Donders and Ebbinghaus, only to be derailed by Watson's behaviorism in the early 1900s and Skinner's operant conditioning in the 1930s. Finally, in the 1950s and 1960s, clearer minds decided that it was important to return to the study of the mind and began doing experiments based on the information-processing model that was inspired by digital computers.

But just as this cognitive revolution was beginning, something else was happening that would have a huge impact on our understanding of the mind. In the 1950s, a number of research papers began appearing that involved recording nerve impulses from single neurons. As we will see, research studying the relationship between neural responding and cognition began long before the 1950s, but technological advances led to a large increase in physiological research beginning just about the same time the cognitive revolution was happening.

In this chapter, we take up the story of **cognitive neuroscience**—the study of the physiological basis of cognition. We begin by discussing the idea of "levels of analysis," which is our rationale behind studying the physiology of the mind, and we then go back in time to the 19th and early 20th century to look at the early research that set the stage for amazing discoveries that were to be made beginning in the 1950s.

▶ Levels of Analysis

Levels of analysis refers to the idea that a topic can be studied in a number of different ways, with each approach contributing its own dimension to our understanding. To understand what this means, let's consider a topic outside the realm of cognitive psychology: understanding the automobile.

Our starting point for this problem might be to take a car out for a test drive. We could determine its acceleration, its braking, how well it corners, and its gas mileage. When we have measured these things, which come under the heading of "performance," we will know a lot about the particular car we are testing. But to learn more, we can consider another level of analysis: what is going on under the hood. This would involve looking at the mechanisms responsible for the car's performance: the motor and the braking and steering systems. For example, we can describe the car as being powered by a four-cylinder 250 HP internal combustion engine and having independent suspension and disc brakes.

But we can look even deeper into the operation of the car by considering another level of analysis designed to help us understand how the car's engine works. One approach would be to look at what happens inside a cylinder. When we do this, we see that when vaporized gas enters the cylinder and is ignited by the spark plug, an explosion occurs that pushes the cylinder down and sends power to the crankshaft and then to the wheels. Clearly, considering the automobile from the different levels of driving the car, describing the motor, and observing what happens inside a cylinder provides more information about cars than simply measuring the car's performance.

Applying this idea of levels of analysis to cognition, we can consider measuring behavior to be analogous to measuring the car's performance, and measuring the physiological processes behind the behavior as analogous to what we learned by looking under the hood. And just as we can study what is happening under a car's hood at different levels, we can study the physiology of cognition at levels ranging from the whole brain, to structures within the brain, to chemicals that create electrical signals within these structures.

Consider, for example, a situation in which Gil is talking with Mary in the park (**Figure 2.1a**), and then a few days later he passes the park and remembers what she was wearing and what they talked about (**Figure 2.1b**). This is a simple behavioral description of having an experience and later having a memory of that experience.

But what is going on at the physiological level? During the initial experience, in which Gil perceives Mary as he is talking with her, chemical processes occur in Gil's eyes and ears, which create electrical signals in neurons (which we will describe shortly); individual brain structures are activated, then multiple brain structures are activated, all leading to Gil's perception of Mary and what is happening as they talk (Figure 2.1a).

Meanwhile, other things are happening, both during Gil's conversation with Mary and after it is over. The electrical signals generated as Gil is talking with Mary trigger chemical and electrical processes that result in the storage of Gil's experiences in his brain. Then, when Gil passes the park a few days later, another sequence of physiological events is triggered that retrieves the information that was stored earlier, which enables him to remember his conversation with Mary (Figure 2.2b).

We have gone a long way to make a point, but it is an important one. To fully understand any phenomenon, whether it is how a car operates or how people remember past experiences, it needs to be studied at different levels of analysis. In this book, we will be describing research in cognition at both the behavioral and physiological levels. We begin our description of physiology by considering one of the basic building blocks of the nervous system: the neuron.

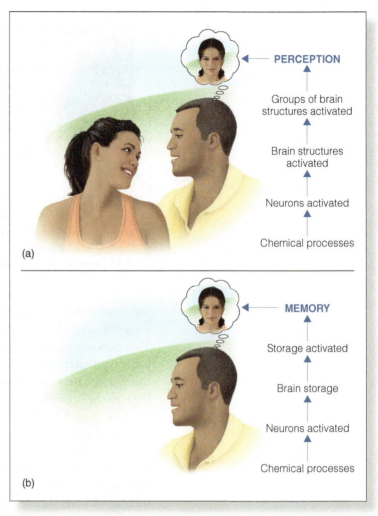

➤ **Figure 2.1** Physiological levels of analysis. (a) Gil perceives Mary and their surroundings as he talks with her. The physiological processes involved in Gil's perception can be described at levels ranging from chemical reactions to single neurons, to structures in the brain, to groups of structures in the brain. (b) Later, Gil remembers his meeting with Mary. The physiological processes involved in remembering can also be described at different levels of analysis.

▶ Neurons: Basic Principles

How is it possible that the 3.5-pound structure called the brain could be the seat of the mind? The brain appears to be static tissue. Unlike the heart, it has no moving parts. Unlike the lungs, it doesn't expand or contract. And when observed with the naked eye, the brain looks almost solid. As it turns out, to understand the relation between the brain and the mind—and specifically to understand the physiological basis for everything we perceive, remember, and think—it is necessary to look within the brain and observe the small units called **neurons** that create and transmit information about what we experience and know.

Early Conceptions of Neurons

For many years, the nature of the brain's tissue was a mystery. Looking at the interior of the brain with the unaided eye gives no indication that it is made up of billions of smaller units. But in the 19th century, anatomists applied special stains to brain tissue, which increased

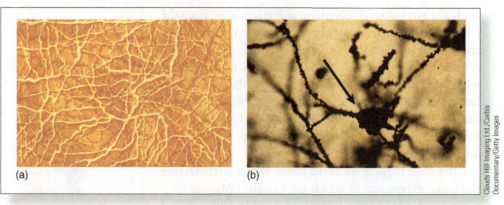

➤ **Figure 2.2** (a) Nerve net theory proposed that signals could be transmitted throughout the net in all directions. (b) A portion of the brain that has been treated with Golgi stain shows the shapes of a few neurons. The arrow points to a neuron's cell body. The thin lines are dendrites or axons (see **Figure 2.3**).

the contrast between different types of tissue within the brain. When they viewed this stained tissue under a microscope, they saw a network they called a **nerve net** (**Figure 2.2a**). This network was believed to be continuous, like a highway system in which one street connects directly to another, but without stop signs or traffic lights. When visualized in this way, the nerve net provided a complex pathway for conducting signals uninterrupted through the network.

One reason for describing the microstructure of the brain as a continuously interconnected network was that the staining techniques and microscopes used during that period could not resolve small details, and without these details the nerve net appeared to be continuous. However, in the 1870s, the Italian anatomist Camillo Golgi (1843–1926) developed a staining technique in which a thin slice of brain tissue was immersed in a solution of silver nitrate. This technique created pictures like the one in **Figure 2.2b**, in which fewer than 1 percent of the cells were stained, so they stood out from the rest of the tissue. (If all of the cells had been stained, it would be difficult to distinguish one cell from another because the cells are so tightly packed.) Also, the cells that were stained were stained completely, so it was possible to see their structure.

Meanwhile, the Spanish physiologist Ramon y Cajal (1852–1934) was using two techniques to investigate the nature of the nerve net. First, he used the Golgi stain, which stained only some of the cells in a slice of brain tissue. Second, he decided to study tissue from the brains of newborn animals, because the density of cells in the newborn brain is small compared with the density in the adult brain. This property of the newborn brain, combined with the fact that the Golgi stain affects less than 1 percent of the neurons, made it possible for Cajal to clearly see that the nerve net was not continuous but was instead made up of individual units connected together (Kandel, 2006). Cajal's discovery that individual units called neurons were the basic building blocks of the brain was the centerpiece of **neuron doctrine**—the idea that individual cells transmit signals in the nervous system, and that these cells are not continuous with other cells as proposed by nerve net theory.

Figure 2.3a shows the basic parts of a neuron. The **cell body** is the metabolic center of the neuron; it contains mechanisms to keep the cell alive. The function of **dendrites** that branch out from the cell body is to receive signals from other neurons. **Axons** (also called **nerve fibers**) are usually long processes that transmit signals to other neurons. **Figure 2.3b** shows a neuron with a receptor that receives stimuli from the environment—pressure, in this example. Thus, the neuron has a receiving end and a transmitting end, and its role, as visualized by Cajal, was to transmit signals.

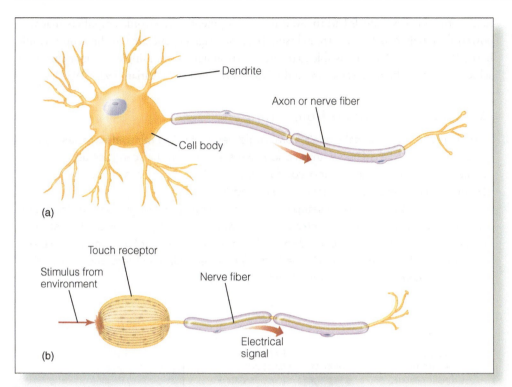

(a)

(b)

> **Figure 2.3** (a) Basic components of a neuron in the cortex. (b) A neuron with a specialized receptor in place of the cell body. This receptor responds to pressure on the skin.

Cajal also came to some other conclusions about neurons: (1) There is a small gap between the end of a neuron's axon and the dendrites or cell body of another neuron. This gap is called a **synapse** (**Figure 2.4**). (2) Neurons are not connected indiscriminately to other neurons but form connections only to specific neurons. This forms groups of interconnected neurons, which together form **neural circuits**. (3) In addition to neurons in the brain, there are also neurons that are specialized to pick up information from the environment, such as the neurons in the eye, ear, and skin. These neurons, called **receptors** (**Figure 2.3b**), are similar to brain neurons in that they have an axon, but they have specialized receptors that pick up information from the environment.

Cajal's idea of individual neurons that communicate with other neurons to form neural circuits was an enormous leap forward in the understanding of how the nervous system operates. The concepts introduced by Cajal—individual neurons, synapses, and neural circuits—are basic principles that today are used to explain how the brain creates cognitions. These discoveries earned Cajal the Nobel Prize in 1906, and today he is recognized as "the person who made this cellular study of mental life possible" (Kandel, 2006, p. 61).

The Signals That Travel in Neurons

Cajal succeeded in describing the structure of individual neurons and how they are related to other neurons, and he knew that these neurons transmitted signals. However, determining the

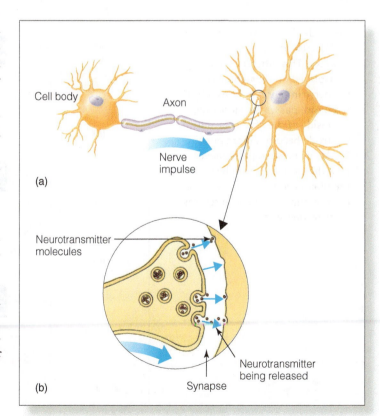

(a)

(b)

> **Figure 2.4** (a) Neuron synapsing on the cell body of another neuron. (b) Close-up of the synapse showing the space between the end of one neuron and the cell body of the next neuron, and neurotransmitter being released.

exact nature of these signals had to await the development of electronic amplifiers that were powerful enough to make the extremely small electrical signals generated by the neuron visible. In the 1920s, Edgar Adrian was able to record electrical signals from single sensory neurons, an achievement for which he was awarded the Nobel Prize in 1932 (Adrian, 1928, 1932).

METHOD Recording from a Neuron

Adrian recorded electrical signals from single neurons using **microelectrodes**—small shafts of hollow glass filled with a conductive salt solution that can pick up electrical signals at the electrode tip and conduct these signals back to a recording device. Modern physiologists use metal microelectrodes.

Figure 2.5 shows a typical setup used for recording from a single neuron. There are two electrodes: a **recording electrode**, shown with its recording tip inside the neuron,[1] and a **reference electrode**, located some distance away so it is not affected by the electrical signals. The difference in charge between the recording and reference electrodes is fed into a computer and displayed on the computer's screen.

➤ **Figure 2.5** Recording an action potential as it travels down an axon. (a) When the nerve is at rest, there is a difference in charge, called the resting *potential*, of −70 millivolts (mV) between the inside and outside of the axon. The difference in charge between the recording and reference electrodes is fed into a computer and displayed on a computer monitor. This difference in charge is displayed on the right. (b) As the nerve impulse, indicated by the red band, passes the electrode, the inside of the fiber near the electrode becomes more positive. (c) As the nerve impulse moves past the electrode, the charge in the fiber becomes more negative. (d) Eventually the neuron returns to its resting state.

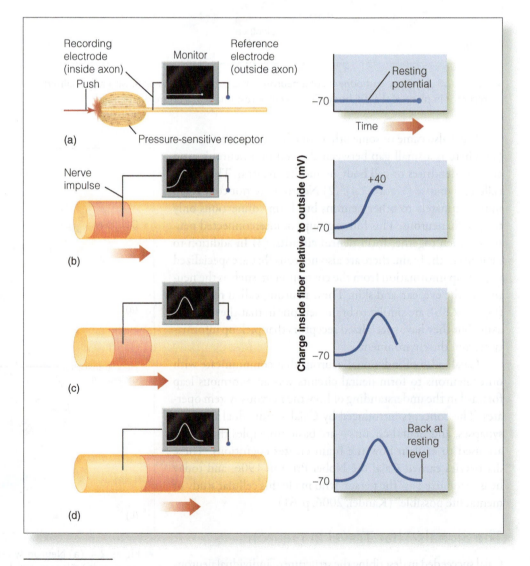

When the axon, or nerve fiber, is at rest, the meter records a difference in potential between the tips of the two electrodes of −70 millivolts (a millivolt is 1/1000 of a volt), as shown on the right in **Figure 2.5a**. This value, which stays the same as long as there are no signals in the neuron, is called the **resting potential**. In other words, the inside of the neuron has a charge that is 70 mV more negative than the outside, and this difference continues as long as the neuron is at rest.

Figure 2.5b shows what happens when the neuron's receptor is stimulated so that a **nerve impulse** is transmitted down the axon. As the impulse passes the recording electrode, the charge inside the axon rises to +40 millivolts, compared to the outside. As the impulse continues past the electrode, the charge inside the fiber reverses course and starts becoming negative again (**Figure 2.5c**), until it returns to the resting potential (**Figure 2.5d**). This impulse, which is called the **action potential**, lasts about 1 millisecond (1/1000 of a second).

Figure 2.6a shows action potentials on a compressed time scale. Each vertical line represents an action potential, and the series of lines indicates that a number of action potentials are traveling past the electrode. **Figure 2.6b** shows one of the action potentials on an expanded time scale, as in Figure 2.5. There are other electrical signals in the nervous system, but we will focus here on the action potential because it is the mechanism by which information is transmitted throughout the nervous system.

In addition to recording action potentials from single neurons, Adrian made other discoveries as well. He found that each action potential travels all the way down the axon without changing its height or shape. This property makes action potentials ideal for sending signals over a distance, because it means that once an action potential is started at one end of an axon, the signal will still be the same size when it reaches the other end.

At about the same time Adrian was recording from single neurons, other researchers were showing that when the signals reach the synapse at the end of the axon, a chemical called a **neurotransmitter** is released. This neurotransmitter makes it possible for the signal to be transmitted across the gap that separates the end of the axon from the dendrite or cell body of another neuron (see Figure 2.4b).

Although all of these discoveries about the nature of neurons and the signals that travel in them were extremely important (and garnered a number of Nobel Prizes for their discoverers), our main interest is not in how axons transmit signals, but in how these signals contribute to the operation of the mind. So far, our description of how signals are transmitted is analogous to describing how the Internet transmits electrical signals, without describing how the signals are transformed into words and pictures that people can understand. Adrian was acutely aware that it was important to go beyond simply describing nerve signals, so he did a series of experiments to relate nerve signals to stimuli in the environment and therefore to people's experience.

Adrian studied the relation between nerve firing and sensory experience by measuring how the firing of a neuron from a receptor in the skin changed as he applied more pressure to the skin. What he found was that the shape and height of the action potential remained the same as he increased the pressure, but the *rate* of nerve firing—that is, the number of action potentials that traveled down the axon per second—increased (**Figure 2.7**). From this result, Adrian drew a connection between nerve firing and experience. He describes this connection in his book *The Basis of Sensation* (1928) by stating that if nerve impulses "are crowded closely together the sensation is intense, if they are separated by long intervals the sensation is correspondingly feeble" (p. 7).

What Adrian is saying is that electrical signals are *representing* the intensity of the stimulus, so pressure that generates "crowded" electrical signals feels stronger than pressure that

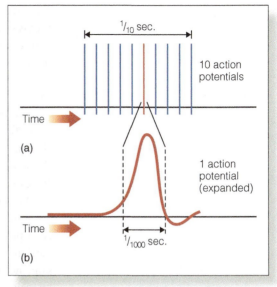

➤ **Figure 2.6** (a) A series of action potentials displayed on a time scale that makes each action potential appear as a thin line. (b) Changing the time scale reveals the shape of one of the action potentials.

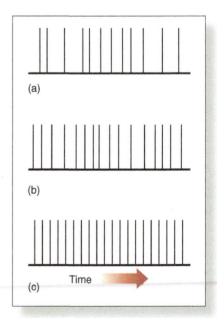

➤ **Figure 2.7** Action potentials recorded from an axon in response to three levels of pressure stimulation on the skin: (a) light, (b) medium, and (c) strong. Increasing stimulus intensity causes an increase in the rate of nerve firing.

generates signals separated by long intervals. Later experiments demonstrated similar results for vision. Presenting high-intensity light generates a high rate of nerve firing and the light appears bright; presenting lower intensity light generates a lower rate of nerve firing and the light appears dimmer. Thus, the rate of neural firing is related to the intensity of stimulation, which, in turn, is related to the magnitude of an experience, such as feeling pressure on the skin or experiencing the brightness of a light.

Going beyond Adrian's idea that the magnitude of experience is related to the rate of nerve firing, we can ask, how is the *quality* of experience represented in neural firing? For the senses, quality *across the senses* refers to the different experience associated with each of the senses—perceiving light for vision, sound for hearing, smells for olfaction, and so on. We can also ask about quality *within a particular sense*, such as for vision: color, movement, an object's shape, or the identity of a person's face.

One way to answer the question of how action potentials determine different qualities is to propose that the action potentials for each quality might look different. However, Adrian ruled out that possibility by determining that all action potentials have basically the same height and shape. If all nerve impulses are basically the same whether they are caused by seeing a red fire engine or remembering what you did last week, how can these impulses stand for different qualities? The short answer to this question is that different qualities of stimuli, and also different aspects of experience, activate different neurons and areas in the brain. We begin the long answer to this question in the next section by taking up the idea of representation, which we introduced in Chapter 1.

▶ Representation by Neural Firing

In Chapter 1, we defined the mind as *a system that creates representations of the world so that we can act within it to achieve our goals* (page 6). The key word in this definition is *representations*, because what it means is that everything we experience is the result of something that *stands for* that experience. Putting this in neural terms, the **principle of neural representation** states that everything a person experiences is based on representations in the person's nervous system. Adrian's pioneering research on how nerve impulses represent the intensity of a stimulus, in which he related high nerve firing to feeling greater pressure, marks the beginning of research on neural representation. We now move ahead to the 1960s to describe early research that involved recording from single neurons in the brain.

The Story of Neural Representation and Cognition: A Preview

In the 1960s, researchers began focusing on recording from single neurons in the primary visual receiving area, the place where signals from the eye first reach the cortex (**Figure 2.8a**). The question being asked in these experiments was "what makes this neuron fire?" Vision dominated early research because stimuli could be easily controlled by creating patterns of light and dark on a screen and because a lot was already known about vision.

But as research progressed, researchers began recording from neurons in areas outside the primary visual area and discovered two key facts: (1) Many neurons at higher levels of the visual system fire to complex stimuli like geometrical patterns and faces; and (2) a specific stimulus causes neural firing that is distributed across many areas of the cortex (**Figure 2.8b**). Vision, it turns out, isn't created only in the primary visual receiving area, but in many different areas. Later research, extending beyond vision, found similar results for other cognitions. For example, it was discovered that memory is not determined by a single "memory area," because there are a number of areas involved in creating memories and remembering them later. In short, it became obvious that large areas of the brain are involved in creating cognition.

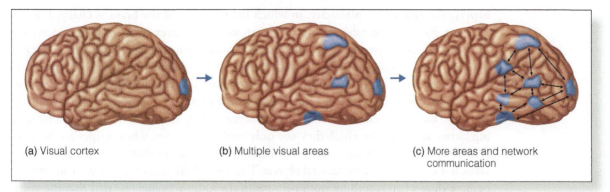

(a) Visual cortex   (b) Multiple visual areas   (c) More areas and network communication

➤ **Figure 2.8** (a) Early work on neural representation and cognition focused on recording from single neurons in the visual cortex, where signals first arrive at the cortex. (b) Researchers then began to explore other places in the brain and found that visual stimulation causes activity that is distributed across many areas of the cortex. (c) Recent work has focused on looking at how these distributed areas are connected by neural networks and how activity flows in these networks. Note that, with the exception of the visual area in (a), the locations of the areas in this figure do not represent the locations of actual areas. They are for illustrative purposes only.

As it became clear that understanding neural representation involves casting a wide net across the brain, many researchers began considering the way different areas are connected to one another. The idea of neural signals transmitted between many destinations in an interconnected brain has led to today's conception of the brain as containing a vast highway system that can be described in terms of "neural networks" (**Figure 2.8c**). We will now fill in the details, beginning with the discovery of neural feature detectors.

Feature Detectors

One possible answer to the question "how can nerve impulses stand for different qualities?" is that perhaps there are neurons that fire only to specific qualities of stimuli. Early research found some evidence for this (Hartline, 1940; Kuffler, 1953), but the idea of neurons that respond to specific qualities was brought to the forefront by a series of papers by David Hubel and Thorsten Wiesel, which would win them the Nobel Prize in 1981.

In the 1960s, Hubel and Wiesel started a series of experiments in which they presented visual stimuli to cats, as shown in **Figure 2.9a**, and determined which stimuli caused specific neurons to fire. They found that each neuron in the visual area of the cortex responded to a specific type of stimulation presented to a small area of the retina. **Figure 2.9b** shows some of the stimuli that caused neurons in and near the visual cortex to fire (Hubel, 1982; Hubel & Wiesel, 1959, 1961, 1965). They called these neurons **feature detectors** because they responded to specific stimulus features such as orientation, movement, and length.

The idea that feature detectors are linked to perception was supported by many different experiments. One of these experiments involved a phenomenon called

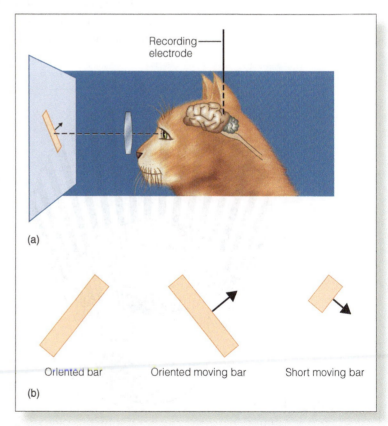

(a)

(b)

Oriented bar   Oriented moving bar   Short moving bar

➤ **Figure 2.9** (a) An experiment in which electrical signals are recorded from the visual system of an anesthetized cat that is viewing stimuli presented on the screen. The lens in front of the cat's eye ensures that the images on the screen are focused on the cat's retina. The recording electrode is not shown. (b) A few of the types of stimuli that cause neurons in the cat's visual cortex to fire.

experience-dependent plasticity, in which the structure of the brain is changed by experience. For example, when a kitten is born, its visual cortex contains feature detectors that respond to oriented bars (see Figure 2.9). Normally, the kitten's visual cortex contains neurons that respond to all orientations, ranging from horizontal to slanted to vertical, and when the kitten grows up into a cat, the cat has neurons that can respond to all orientations.

But what would happen if kittens were reared in an environment consisting only of verticals? Colin Blakemore and Graham Cooper (1970) answered this question by rearing kittens in a space in which they saw only vertical black and white stripes on the walls (**Figure 2.10a**). After being reared in this vertical environment, kittens batted at a moving vertical stick but ignored horizontal objects. The basis of this lack of response to horizontals became clear when recording from neurons in the kittens' brains revealed that the visual cortex had been reshaped so it contained neurons that responded mainly to verticals and had no neurons that responded to horizontals (**Figure 2.10b**). Similarly, kittens reared in an environment consisting only of horizontals ended up with a visual cortex that contained neurons that responded mainly to horizontals (**Figure 2.10c**). Thus, the kittens' brains had been shaped to respond best to the environment to which they had been exposed.

Blakemore and Cooper's experiment is important because it is an early demonstration of experience-dependent plasticity. Their result also has an important message about neural representation: When a kitten's cortex contained mainly vertically sensitive neurons, the kitten *perceived* only verticals, and a similar result occurred for horizontals. This result supports the idea that perception is determined by neurons that fire to specific qualities of a stimulus (orientation, in this case).

This knowledge that neurons in the visual system fire to specific types of stimuli led to the idea that each of the thousands of neurons that fire when we look at a tree fire to different features of the tree. Some neurons fire to the vertically oriented trunk, others to

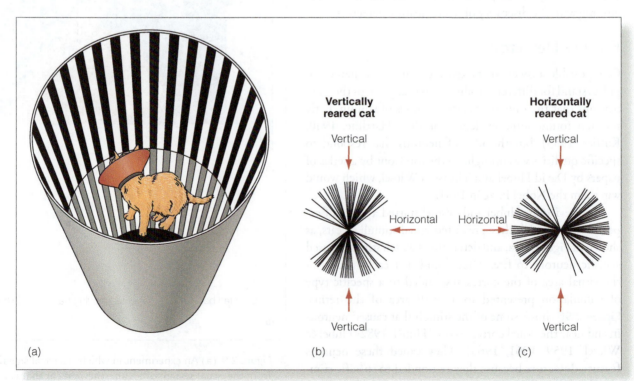

(a)

(b)

(c)

➤ **Figure 2.10** (a) Striped tube used in Blakemore and Cooper's (1970) selective rearing experiments. (b) Distribution of orientations that caused maximum firing for 72 cells from a cat reared in an environment of vertical stripes and (c) for 52 cells from a cat reared in an environment of horizontal stripes.

the variously oriented branches, and some to more complex combinations of a number of features. The idea that the tree is represented by the combined response of many feature detectors is similar to building objects by combining building blocks like Legos. But it is important to realize that the visual cortex is an early stage of visual processing, and that vision depends on signals that are sent from the visual cortex to other areas of the brain.

Figure 2.11 indicates the location of the **visual cortex** in the human brain, as well as additional areas that are involved in vision, and some other areas we will be discussing later. The vision areas are part of a vast network of areas that make up about 30 percent of the cortex (Felleman & Van Essen, 1991). Some of these visual areas receive signals directly from the visual cortex. Others are part of a sequence of interconnected neurons, some of which are far down the line from the visual cortex. Following Hubel and Wiesel's pioneering research, other researchers who began exploring these "higher" levels of the visual pathway discovered neurons that respond to stimuli more complex than oriented lines.

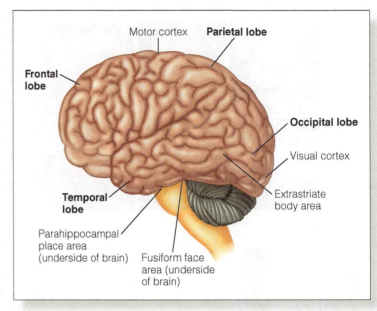

➤ **Figure 2.11** Some of the structures of the human brain that we will be referring to in this chapter. Pointers indicate the locations of these areas, each of which extends over an area of the cortex.

Neurons That Respond to Complex Stimuli

How are complex stimuli represented by the firing of neurons in the brain? One answer to this question began to emerge in the laboratory of Charles Gross. Gross's experiments, in which he recorded from single neurons in the monkey's **temporal lobe** (Figure 2.11), required a great deal of endurance by the researchers, because the experiments typically lasted 3 or 4 days. In these experiments, the results of which were reported in now classic papers in 1969 and 1972 (Gross et al., 1969, 1972), Gross's research team presented a variety of different stimuli to anesthetized monkeys. On a projection screen like the one shown in Figure 2.9a, they presented lines, squares, and circles. Some stimuli were light and some dark.

The discovery that neurons in the temporal lobe respond to complex stimuli came a few days into one of their experiments, when they had found a neuron that refused to respond to any of the standard stimuli, like oriented lines or circles or squares. Nothing worked, until one of the experimenters pointed at something in the room, casting a shadow of his hand on the screen. When this hand shadow caused a burst of firing, the experimenters knew they were on to something and began testing the neuron with a variety of stimuli, including cutouts of a monkey's hand. After a great deal of testing, they determined that this neuron responded best to a handlike shape with fingers pointing up (far-right stimuli in **Figure 2.12**) (Rocha-Miranda, 2011; also see Gross, 2002). After expanding the types of stimuli presented, they also found some neurons that responded best to faces. Later researchers extended these results and provided many examples of neurons that respond to faces but don't respond to other types of stimuli (Perrett et al., 1982; Rolls, 1981) (**Figure 2.13**).

Let's stop for a moment and consider the results we have presented so far. We saw that neurons in the visual cortex respond to simple stimuli like oriented bars, neurons in the temporal lobe

➤ **Figure 2.12** Some of the shapes used by Gross et al. (1972) to study the responses of neurons in the temporal lobe of the monkey's cortex. The shapes are arranged in order of their ability to cause the neuron to fire, from none (1) to little (2 and 3) to maximum (6).

(Source: Based on Gross et al., 1972.)

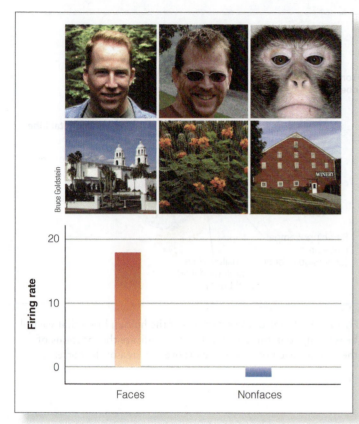

➤ **Figure 2.13** Firing rate, in nerve impulses per second, of a neuron in the monkey's temporal lobe that responds to face stimuli but not to nonface stimuli.

(Source: Based on E. T. Rolls & M. J. Tovee, 1995.)

respond to complex geometrical stimuli, and neurons in another area of the temporal lobe respond to faces. What is happening is that neurons in the visual cortex that respond to relatively simple stimuli send their axons to higher levels of the visual system, where signals from many neurons combine and interact; neurons at this higher level, which respond to more complex stimuli such as geometrical objects, then send signals to even higher areas, combining and interacting further and creating neurons that respond to even more complex stimuli such as faces. This progression from lower to higher areas of the brain is called **hierarchical processing**.

Does hierarchical processing solve the problem of neural representation? Could it be that higher areas of the visual system contain neurons that are specialized to respond only to a specific object, so that object would be represented by the firing of that one type of specialized neuron? As we will see, this is probably not the case, because neural representation most likely involves a number of neurons working together.

Sensory Coding

The problem of neural representation for the senses has been called the **problem of sensory coding**, where the **sensory code** refers to how neurons represent various characteristics of the environment. The idea that an object could be represented by the firing of a specialized neuron that responds only to that object is called **specificity coding**. This is illustrated in **Figure 2.14a**, which shows how a number of neurons respond to three different faces. Only neuron 4 responds to Bill's face, only neuron 9 responds to Mary's face, and only neuron 6 responds to Raphael's face. Also note that the neuron specialized to respond only to Bill, which we can call a "Bill neuron," does not respond to Mary or Raphael. In addition, other faces or types of objects would not affect this neuron. It fires only to Bill's face.

Although the idea of specificity coding is straightforward, it is unlikely to be correct. Even though there are neurons that respond to faces, these neurons usually respond to a number of different faces (not just Bill's). There are just too many different faces and other objects (and colors, tastes, smells, and sounds) in the world to have a separate neuron dedicated to each object. An alternative to the idea of specificity coding is that a number of neurons are involved in representing an object.

Population coding is the representation of a particular object by the pattern of firing of a large number of neurons (**Figure 2.14b**). According to this idea, Bill's, Mary's and Raphael's faces are each represented by a different pattern. An advantage of population coding is that a large number of stimuli can be represented, because large groups of neurons can create a huge number of different patterns. There is good evidence for population coding in the senses and for other cognitive functions as well. But for some functions, a large number of neurons aren't necessary.

Sparse coding occurs when a particular object is represented by a pattern of firing of only a small group of neurons, with the majority of neurons remaining silent. As shown in **Figure 2.14c**, sparse coding would represent Bill's face by the pattern of firing of a few neurons (neurons 2, 3, 4, and 7). Mary's face would be signaled by the pattern of firing of a few different neurons (neurons 4, 6, and 7), but possibly with some overlap with the neurons representing Bill, and Raphael's face would have yet another pattern (neurons 1, 2, and 4).

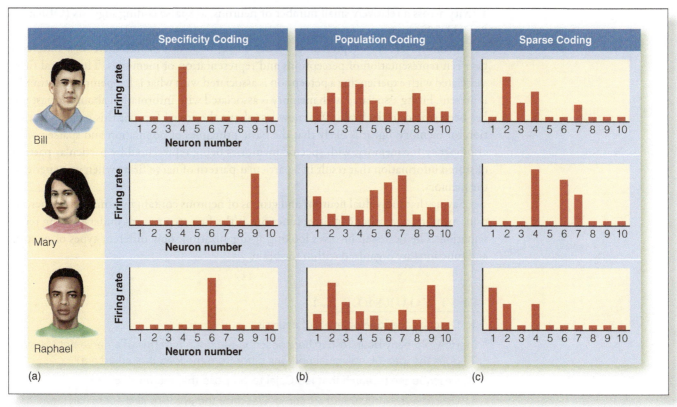

➤ Figure 2.14 Three types of coding: (a) Specificity coding. The response of 10 different neurons to each face on the left is shown. Each face causes a different neuron to fire. (b) Population coding. The face's identity is indicated by the pattern of firing of a large number of neurons. (c) Sparse coding. The face's identity is indicated by the pattern of firing of a small group of neurons.

Notice that a particular neuron can respond to more than one stimulus. For example, neuron 4 responds to all three faces, although most strongly to Mary's.

Recently, neurons were discovered when recording from the temporal lobe of patients undergoing brain surgery for epilepsy. (Stimulating and recording from neurons is a common procedure before and during brain surgery, because it makes it possible to determine the exact layout of a particular person's brain.) These neurons responded to very specific stimuli. Figure 2.15 shows the records for a neuron that responded to pictures of the actor Steve Carell and not to other people's faces (Quiroga et al., 2007). However, the researchers who discovered this neuron (as well as other neurons that responded to other people) point out that they had only 30 minutes to record from these neurons, and that if more time were available, it is likely that they would have found other faces that would cause this neuron to fire. Given the likelihood that even these special neurons are likely to fire to more than one stimulus, Quiroga and coworkers (2008) suggested that their neurons are probably an example of sparse coding.

There is also other evidence that the code for representing objects in the visual system, tones in the auditory system, and odors in the olfactory system may involve the pattern of

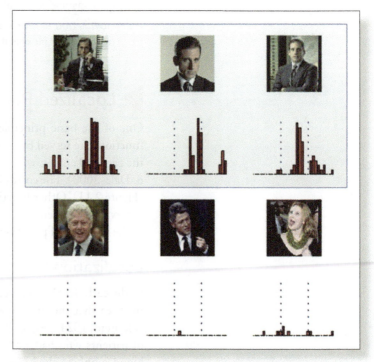

➤ Figure 2.15 Records from a neuron in the temporal lobe that responded to different views of Steve Carell (top records) but did not respond to pictures of other well-known people (bottom records).
(Source: Quiroga et al., 2008)

activity across a relatively small number of neurons, as sparse coding suggests (Olshausen & Field, 2004).

Memories are also represented by the firing of neurons, but there is a difference between representation of perceptions and representation of memories. The neural firing associated with experiencing a perception is associated with what is happening as a stimulus is present. Firing associated with memory is associated with information about the past that has been stored in the brain. We know less about the actual form of this stored information for memory, but it is likely that the basic principles of population and sparse coding also operate for memory, with specific memories being represented by particular patterns of stored information that result in a particular pattern of nerve firing when we experience the memory.

Saying that individual neurons and groups of neurons contain information for perception, memory, and other cognitive functions is the first step toward understanding representation. The next step involves looking at organization: how different types of neurons and functions are organized within the brain.

TEST YOURSELF 2.1

1. Describe the idea of levels of analysis.

2. How did early brain researchers describe the brain in terms of a nerve net? How does the idea of individual neurons differ from the idea of a nerve net?

3. Describe the research that led Cajal to propose the neuron doctrine.

4. Describe the structure of a neuron. Describe the synapse and neural circuits.

5. How are action potentials recorded from a neuron? What do these signals look like, and what is the relation between action potentials and stimulus intensity?

6. How has the question of how different perceptions can be represented by neurons been answered? Consider both research involving recording from single neurons and ideas about sensory coding.

7. How is neural representation for memory different from neural representation for perception? How is it similar?

 ## Localized Representation

One of the basic principles of brain organization is **localization of function**—specific functions are served by specific areas of the brain. Many cognitive functions are served by the **cerebral cortex**, which is a layer of tissue about 3 mm thick that covers the brain (Fischl & Dale, 2000). The cortex is the wrinkled covering you see when you look at an intact brain (Figure 2.11). Other functions are served by **subcortical areas** that are located below the cortex. Early evidence for localization of function came from **neuropsychology**—the study of the behavior of people with brain damage.

Localization Determined by Neuropsychology

In the early 1800s, an accepted principle of brain function was **cortical equipotentiality**, the idea that the brain operated as an indivisible whole as opposed to specialized areas (Flourens, 1824; Pearce, 2009). But in 1861, Paul Broca published work based on his study of patients who had suffered brain damage due to strokes that caused disruption of the blood supply to the brain. These strokes caused damage to an area in the frontal lobe that came to be called **Broca's area** (**Figure 2.16**).

One of Broca's patients was famously called *Tan*, because the word *tan* was the only word he could say. Other patients with frontal lobe damage could say more, but their speech was slow and labored and often had jumbled sentence structure. Here is an example of the speech of a modern patient, who is attempting to describe when he had his stroke, which occurred when he was in a hot tub:

> Alright. . . . Uh ... stroke and un. . . . I . . . huh tawanna guy. . . . H . . . h . . . hot tub and. . . . And the. . . . Two days when uh. . . . Hos . . . uh. . . . Huh hospital and uh . . . amet . . . am . . . ambulance. (Dick et al., 2001, p. 760)

Patients with this problem—slow, labored, ungrammatical speech caused by damage to Broca's area—are diagnosed as having **Broca's aphasia**. The fact that damage to a specific area of the brain caused a specific deficit of behavior was striking evidence against the idea of equipotentiality and for the idea of localization of function.

Eighteen years after Broca reported on his frontal lobe patients, Carl Wernicke (1879) described a number of patients who had damage to an area in their temporal lobe that came to be called **Wernicke's area**. Wernicke's patients produced speech that was fluent and grammatically correct but tended to be incoherent. Here is a modern example of the speech of a patient with **Wernicke's aphasia**:

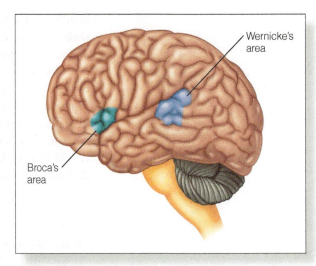

> ➤ **Figure 2.16** Broca's area, in the frontal lobe, and Wernicke's area, in the temporal lobe, were identified in early research as being specialized for language production and comprehension, respectively.

> It just suddenly had a feffort and all the feffort had gone with it. It even stepped my horn. They took them from earth you know. They make my favorite nine to severed and now I'm a been habed by the uh stam of fortment of my annulment which is now forever. (Dick et al., 2001, p. 761)

Patients such as this not only produce meaningless speech but are unable to understand other people's speech. Their primary problem is their inability to match words with their meanings, with the defining characteristic of Wernicke's aphasia being the absence of normal grammar (Traxler, 2012).

Broca's and Wernicke's observations showed that different aspects of language—production of language and comprehension of language—were served by different areas in the brain. As we will see later in this chapter, modern research has shown that the strict separation of language functions in different areas was an oversimplification. Nonetheless, Broca's and Wernicke's 19th-century observations set the stage for later research that confirmed the idea of localization of function.

Further evidence for localization of function came from studies of the effect of brain injury in wartime. Studies of Japanese soldiers in the Russo-Japanese war of 1904–1905 and Allied soldiers in World War I showed that damage to the **occipital lobe** of the brain, where the visual cortex is located (Figure 2.11), resulted in blindness, and that there was a connection between the area of the occipital lobe that was damaged and the place in visual space where the person was blind (Glickstein & Whitteridge, 1987; Holmes & Lister, 1916; Lanska, 2009). For example, damage to the left part of the occipital lobe caused an area of blindness in the upper-right part of visual space.

As noted earlier, other areas of the brain have also been associated with specific functions. The auditory cortex, which receives signals from the ears, is in the upper *temporal lobe* and is responsible for hearing. The somatosensory cortex, which receives signals from the skin, is in the **parietal lobe** and is responsible for perceptions of touch, pressure, and pain. The **frontal lobe** receives signals from all of the senses and is responsible for coordination of the senses, as well as higher cognitive functions like thinking and problem solving.

Another effect of brain damage on visual functioning, reported in patients who have damage to the temporal lobe on the lower-right side of the brain, is **prosopagnosia**—an inability to recognize faces. In one type of prosopagnosia, people can tell that a face is a face, but they can't recognize whose face it is, even for people they know well such as friends and family members. In some cases, in one type of prosopagnosia, people look into a mirror and, seeing their own image, wonder who the stranger is looking back at them (Burton et al., 1991; Hecaen & Angelergues, 1962; Parkin, 1996).

One of the goals of the neuropsychology research we have been describing is to determine whether a particular area of the brain is specialized to serve a particular cognitive function. Although it might be tempting to conclude, based on a single case of prosopagnosia, that the damaged brain area in the lower temporal lobe is responsible for recognizing faces, modern researchers realized that to reach more definite conclusions about the function of a particular area, it is necessary to test a number of different patients with damage to different brain areas in order to demonstrate a *double dissociation*.

METHOD   Demonstrating a Double Dissociation

A **double dissociation** occurs if damage to one area of the brain causes function A to be absent while function B is present, and damage to another area causes function B to be absent while function A is present. To demonstrate a double dissociation, it is necessary to find two people with brain damage that satisfy the above conditions.

Double dissociations have been demonstrated for face recognition and object recognition, by finding patients with brain damage who can't recognize faces (Function A) but who can recognize objects (Function B), and other patients, with brain damage in a different area, who can't recognize objects (Function B) but who can recognize faces (Function A) (McNeal & Warrington, 1993; Moscovitch et al., 1997). The importance of demonstrating a double dissociation is that it enables us to conclude that functions A and B are served by different mechanisms, which operate independently of one another.

The results of the neuropsychology studies described above indicate that face recognition is served by one area in the temporal lobe and that this function is separate from mechanisms associated with recognizing other types of objects, which is served by another area of the temporal lobe. Neuropsychological research has also identified areas that are important for perceiving motion and for different functions of memory, thinking, and language, as we will see later in this book.

Localization Determined by Recording from Neurons

Another tool for demonstrating localization of function is recording from single neurons. Numerous studies, mostly on animals, used single-neuron recording to demonstrate localization of function. For example, Doris Tsao and coworkers (2006) found that 97 percent of neurons within a small area in the lower part of a monkey's temporal lobe responded to pictures of faces but not to pictures of other types of objects. This "face area," as it turns out, is located near the area in humans that is associated with prosopagnosia. The idea that our perception of faces is associated with a specific area of the brain is also supported by research using the technique of **brain imaging** (see Chapter 1, page 18), which makes it possible to determine which areas of the brains of humans are activated by different cognitions.

Localization Demonstrated by Brain Imaging

We noted in Chapter 1 that technological advances that cause a shift in the way science is done can be called a revolution. On that basis, it could be argued that the introduction of the brain-scanning techniques positron emission tomography (PET) in 1976 and functional magnetic resonance imaging (fMRI) in 1990 marked the beginning of the "imaging revolution."

As you will see throughout this book, brain scanning, and especially fMRI, has played an important role in understanding the physiological basis of cognition. Here we consider what fMRI research tells us about localization of function in the brain. We begin by describing the basic principle behind fMRI.

METHOD   Brain Imaging

Functional magnetic resonance imaging (fMRI) takes advantage of the fact that neural activity causes the brain to bring in more oxygen, which binds to hemoglobin molecules in the blood. This added oxygen increases the magnetic properties of the hemoglobin, so when a magnetic field is presented to the brain, these more highly oxygenated hemoglobin molecules respond more strongly to the magnetic field and cause an increase in the fMRI signal.

The setup for an fMRI experiment is shown in **Figure 2.17a**, with the person's head in the scanner. As a person engages in a cognitive task such as perceiving an image, the activity of the brain is determined. Activity is recorded in **voxels**, which are small, cube-shaped areas of the brain about 2 or 3 mm on a side. Voxels are not brain structures but are simply small units of analysis created by the fMRI scanner. One way to think about voxels is that they are like the small, square pixels that make up digital photographs or the images on your computer screen, but because the brain is three-dimensional, voxels are small cubes rather than small squares. **Figure 2.17b** shows the result of an fMRI scan. Increases or decreases in brain activity associated with cognitive activity are indicated by colors, with specific colors indicating the amount of activation.

It bears emphasizing that these colored areas do not appear as the brain is being scanned. They are determined by a procedure that involves taking into account how the brain is responding when the person is not engaged in a task and the change in activity triggered by the task. Complex statistical procedures are used to determine the **task-related fMRI**—the change in brain activity that can be linked specifically to the task. The results of these calculations for each voxel are then displayed as colorful activation patterns, like the one in Figure 2.17b.

Many of the brain-imaging experiments that have provided evidence for localization of function have involved determining which brain areas were activated when people observed pictures of different objects.

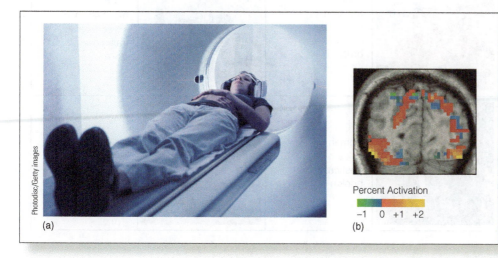

(a)   (b)

➤ **Figure 2.17** (a) Person in a brain scanner. (b) fMRI record. Colors indicate locations of increases and decreases in brain activity. Red and yellow indicate increases in brain activity; blue and green indicate decreases.

(Source: Part b from Ishai et al., 2000)

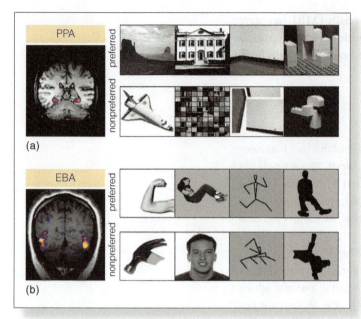

(a)

(b)

> ➤ **Figure 2.18** (a) The parahippocampal place area (PPA) is activated by places (top row) but not by other stimuli (bottom row). (b) The extrastriate body area (EBA) is activated by bodies (top) but not by other stimuli (bottom).
>
> (Source: Chalupa & Werner, 2003)

Looking at Pictures We've already seen how neuropsychology research and single neuron recording identified areas that are involved in perceiving faces. A face area has also been identified by having people in a brain scanner look at pictures of faces. This area, which is called the **fusiform face area (FFA)** because it is in the fusiform gyrus on the underside of the temporal lobe (Kanwisher et al., 1997), is the same part of the brain that is damaged in cases of prosopagnosia (Figure 2.11).

Further evidence for localization of function comes from fMRI experiments that have shown that perceiving pictures representing indoor and outdoor scenes like those shown in **Figure 2.18a** activates the **parahippocampal place area (PPA)** (Aguirre et al., 1998; Epstein et al., 1999). Apparently, what is important for this area is information about spatial layout, because increased activation occurs when viewing pictures both of empty rooms and of rooms that are completely furnished (Kanwisher, 2003). Another specialized area, the **extrastriate body area (EBA)**, is activated by pictures of bodies and parts of bodies (but not by faces), as shown in **Figure 2.18b** (Downing et al., 2001).

Looking at Movies Our usual experience, in everyday life, involves seeing scenes that contain many different objects, some of which are moving. Therefore, Alex Huth and coworkers (2012) conducted an fMRI experiment using stimuli similar to what we see in the environment, by having participants view film clips. Huth's participants viewed 2 hours of film clips while in a brain scanner. To analyze how the voxels in these participants' brains responded to different objects and actions in the films, Huth created a list of 1,705 different objects and action categories and determined which categories were present in each film scene.

Figure 2.19 shows four scenes and the categories (labels) associated with them. By determining how each voxel responded to each scene and then analyzing his results using a complex statistical procedure, Huth was able to determine what kinds of stimuli each voxel

> ➤ **Figure 2.19** Four frames from the movies viewed by participants in Huth et al.'s (2012) experiment. The words on the right indicate categories that appear in the frames (n = noun, v = verb).
>
> (Huth et al., 2012)

Movie Clip	Labels	Movie Clip	Labels
	butte.n desert.n sky.n cloud.n brush.n		city.n expressway.n skyscraper.n traffic.n sky.n
	woman.n talk.v gesticulate.v book.n		bison.n walk.v grass.n stream.n

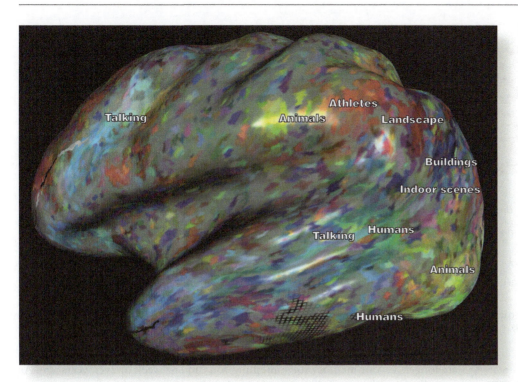

➤ **Figure 2.20** The results of Huth et al.'s (2012) experiment, showing locations on the brain where the indicated categories are most likely to activate the brain.

(Source: Courtesy of Alex Huth)

responded to. For example, one voxel responded well when streets, buildings, roads, interiors, and vehicles were present.

Figure 2.20 shows the types of stimuli that cause voxels across the surface of the brain to respond. Objects and actions similar to each other are located near each other in the brain. The reason there are two areas for humans and two for animals is that each area represents different features related to humans or animals. For example, the area labeled "Humans" at the bottom of the brain (which is actually on the underside of the brain) corresponds to the fusiform face area (Figure 2.11), which responds to all aspects of faces. The area labeled "Humans" higher on the brain responds specifically to facial expressions. The areas labeled "Talking" correspond to Broca's and Wernicke's areas.

The results in Figure 2.20 present an interesting paradox. On one hand, the results confirm the earlier research that identified specific areas of the brain responsible for the perception of specific types of stimuli like faces, places, and bodies. On the other hand, these new results reveal a map that stretches over a large area of the cortex. As we will now see, even though there is a great deal of evidence for localization of function, we need to consider the brain as a whole in order to understand the physiological basis of cognition.

▶ Distributed Representation

Let's consider Huth's map of categories in the brain in Figure 2.20, which shows that there are two locations for "Humans." The explanation—that different areas respond to different features of humans—illustrates a central principle of cognition: most of our experience is **multidimensional**. That is, even simple experiences involve combinations of different qualities. Consider, for example, looking at a person's face.

Looking at a Face

Looking at a face triggers responses to many different aspects of the face. So in addition to identifying an object as a face ("that's a face"), we also respond to the following additional aspects of faces: (1) emotional aspects ("she is smiling, so she is probably happy," "looking at his face makes me happy"); (2) where someone is looking ("she's looking at me");

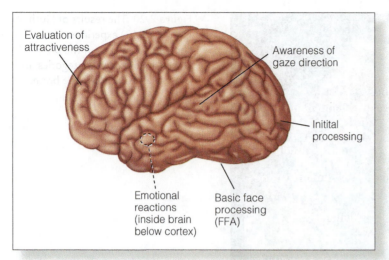

Evaluation of attractiveness

Awareness of gaze direction

Inititial processing

Emotional reactions (inside brain below cortex)

Basic face processing (FFA)

➤ **Figure 2.21** Areas of the brain that are activated by different aspects of faces.

(Sources: Adapted from Ishai, 2008; based on data from Calder et al., 2007; Gobbini & Haxby, 2007; Grill-Spector et al., 2004; Haxby et al., 2000; Ishai et al., 2004.)

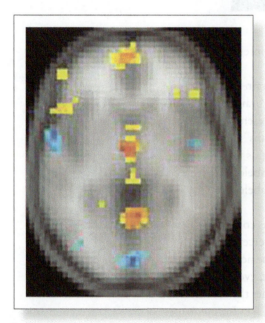

➤ **Figure 2.22** Brain showing areas activated by episodic and semantic memories. Yellow = episodic. Blue = semantic.

(Source: From Levine et al., 2004)

(3) how parts of the face move ("I can understand him better by watching his lips move"); (4) how attractive a face is ("he has a handsome face"); and (5) whether the face is familiar ("I remember her from somewhere"). This multidimensional response to faces is reflected in distributed neural responses throughout the cortex (**Figure 2.21**).

The fact that looking at a face activates many areas of the brain is called **distributed representation**. Cognitions, be they perceptions from looking at something, or processes such as remembering or thinking, activate numerous, sometimes widely separated, areas of the brain. Let's examine two additional examples of distributed neural representation.

Remembering

Memories are complicated. Some memories, called short-term memories, last fleetingly, for only about 10 to 15 seconds unless repeated over and over, as you might do to remember a phone number you forgot to store in your cell phone. Other memories are longer, as your memory for something you did last week or even years ago. As we will see in Chapter 5, there is evidence that short-term and long-term memories are served by different areas of the brain (Curtis & D'Esposito, 2003; Harrison & Tong, 2009).

But memories also differ in another way. *Episodic memories* are memories for events in a person's life, like remembering what you did yesterday. *Semantic memories* are memories for facts, like knowing that the capital of California is Sacramento. **Figure 2.22** shows the results of a brain-scanning experiment, which indicates that thinking about episodic and semantic memories activates different areas of the brain (Levine et al., 2004).

We will see in Chapters 5 through 7 that some areas of the brain play important roles in forming new memories and retrieving old ones, but there is also evidence that remembering activates areas throughout the brain. Memories can be visual (picturing someplace you often visit), auditory (remembering a favorite song), or olfactory (smell triggering memories for a familiar place). Memories often have emotional components, both good and bad (thinking about someone you miss). Most memories are combinations of many of these components, each of which activates different areas of the brain. Memories, therefore, create a symphony of neural activity throughout the brain.

Producing and Understanding Language

When we told the story about Broca and Wernicke, we focused on how their descriptions of two areas of the brain—one for producing speech, the other for comprehending speech—provided the impetus for the idea of localized functions. But in telling that story, we left something out: In addition to proposing an area for speech comprehension, Wernicke also suggested that language goes beyond isolated regions to include connections between them, and to other areas as well (Ross, 2010).

As it turns out, Wernicke's proposal of connectivity stayed in the background after it was proposed, in favor of the idea of localized brain function, and it wasn't until the 20th century that his ideas about connectivity became well known and other researchers showed that explaining the physiology of language involved more than just two separate, localized language areas (Geshwind, 1964; Ross, 2010).

Modern researchers have shown that damage to areas outside of Broca's and Wernicke's areas can cause problems in producing and understanding language (Ross, 2010). There is also evidence that nonlanguage functions are associated with parts of Broca's area (Federencko et al., 2012) and that processing of sentence grammar occurs throughout the language system (Blank et al., 2016). Results such as this led to a much more complex picture of how language is processed.

Figure 2.23 shows a modern diagram of language pathways. In this diagram, the language system is organized into two sets of pathways: one (in blue), which is involved with processing sounds, production of speech, and saying words, and the other (in red), which is involved in understanding words. Both sets of pathways are also involved in understanding sentences (Gierhan, 2013). This diagram represents the results of "research in progress," because much remains to be learned about how language is represented in the brain. However, there is no question that the representation of language is distributed throughout many areas.

One thing that the examples of perceiving faces, remembering, and language have in common is that they involve experiences that activate many separated brain areas, and there is evidence that many of these areas are linked either by direct neural connections or by being part of a number of interconnected structures. This brings us to an important new way of understanding the physiology of cognition that involves *neural networks*.

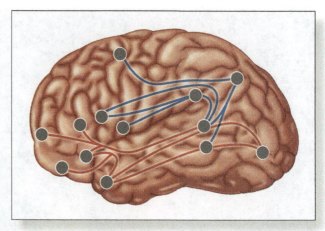

➤ **Figure 2.23** Pathways that have been reported to be involved in language processing. This diagram is based on the results of a large number of studies. Specific functions have been associated with each of the pathways, but the overall picture can be summarized by noting that the pathways shown in blue are involved in processing sounds, producing speech, and saying words, and the pathways shown in red are involved in understanding words, with both sets of pathways being involved in understanding sentences.

(Source: Gierhan, 2013)

▶ Neural Networks

Neural networks are interconnected areas of the brain that can communicate with each other (Bassett & Sporns, 2017). The idea of neural networks is a logical extension of the idea of distributed processing, because it makes sense that if many areas are involved in a particular type of cognition, that they might be connected.

As we tell the story of how researchers are discovering the properties of neural networks, we will be introducing four principles:

1. There are complex structural pathways called *networks* that form the brain's information highway.

2. Within these structural pathways there are functional pathways that serve different functions.

3. These networks operate dynamically, mirroring the dynamic nature of cognition.

4. There is a resting state of brain activity, so parts of the brain are active all the time, even when there is no cognitive activity.

We begin by considering how neural networks have been described structurally.

Structural Connectivity

Structural connectivity is the brain's "wiring diagram" created by nerve axons that connect different brain areas. Early researchers determined these connections using classical neuroanatomical techniques in which slices of brain tissue were stained to highlight axons, which enabled them to see the neural pathways with a microscope. But recently, new techniques have been developed that make more extensive mapping of the brain's connections possible.

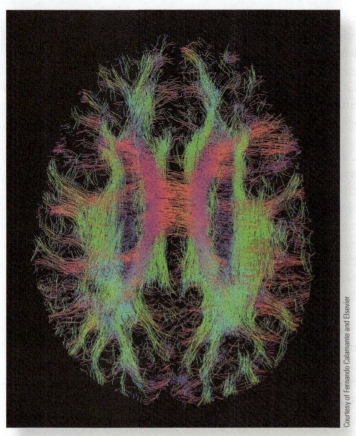

➤ **Figure 2.24** The connectome. Nerve tracts in the human brain determined by track-weighted imaging.
(Source: Calamante et al., 2013)

One of these techniques, called **track-weighted imaging (TWI)**, is based on detection of how water diffuses along the length of nerve fibers. **Figure 2.24** shows nerve tracts determined by this technique (Calamante, 2013). New techniques like this are constantly being developed to determine more precisely how areas of the brain communicate (Bressler & Menon, 2010; Sporns, 2015).

Pictures of the brain's pathways obtained by these new techniques led to the coining of the term **connectome** to indicate the "structural description of the network of elements and connections forming the human brain" (Sporns et al., 2005), or more simply, the "wiring diagram" of neurons in the brain (Baronchelli et al., 2013).

Determining the brain's wiring diagram is an important step in understanding how different areas of the brain communicate, because communication depends on structural connections. Interestingly, maps of structural connectivity of the brain have recently been likened to "fingerprints" that are different for every person, so it could be argued that the brain's wiring makes us who we are (Finn et al., 2015; Seung, 2012; Yeh et al., 2016). But to fully understand how the brain's structural network makes us who we are, or how it helps create cognition, it is necessary to determine how groups of neurons within the connectome form *functional* connections that are related to specific types of cognition.

Functional Connectivity

Picture the road network of a large city. On one set of roads, cars are streaming toward the shopping mall just outside the city, while other roads are funneling cars toward the city's business and financial district. One group of people is using roads to reach places to shop. Another group is using roads to get to work or to conduct business. Just as different parts of the city's road network are involved in achieving different goals, so different parts of the brain's neural network are involved in carrying out different cognitive or motor tasks.

How is it possible to determine what parts of a neural network are involved in different functions? One way this question has been answered is by measuring **functional connectivity**, with functional connectivity being determined by the extent to which neural activity in two brain areas are correlated (Harmelech & Malach, 2013; Pessoa, 2014). If the responses of two brain areas are correlated with each other, this means that they are functionally connected.

One method of determining whether the responding of two areas is correlated is based on **resting-state fMRI**—the fMRI response measured while a person is at rest (that is, not performing a cognitive task). The procedure for measuring **resting-state functional connectivity** was introduced by Bharat Biswal and coworkers (1995).

METHOD   Resting-State Functional Connectivity

Resting-state functional connectivity is measured as follows:

1. Use task-related fMRI to determine a brain location associated with carrying out a specific task. For example, movement of the finger causes an fMRI response at the location marked *Motor (L)* in **Figure 2.25a**. This location is called the **seed location**.

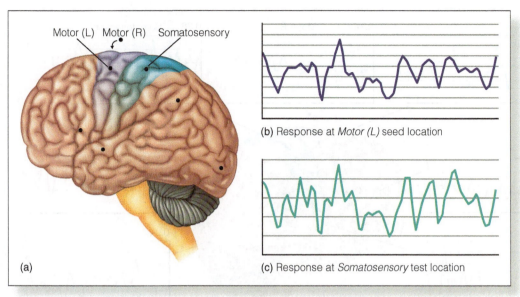

(b) Response at *Motor (L)* seed location

(c) Response at *Somatosensory* test location

(a)

➤ **Figure 2.25** (a) Left hemisphere of the brain, showing the seed location *Motor (L)* in the left motor cortex, and a number of test locations, each indicated by a dot. Test location *Motor (R)* is in the right motor cortex on the other side of the brain from *Motor (L)*. Test location *Somatosensory* is in the somatosensory cortex, which is involved in perceiving touch. (b) Resting level fMRI response of the *Motor (L)* seed location. (c) Resting level fMRI response of the *Somatosensory* test location. The responses in (b) and (c) are 4 seconds long.

(Source: Responses courtesy of Ying-Hui Chou)

2. Measure the *resting-state fMRI* at the seed location. The resting-state fMRI of the seed location, shown in **Figure 2.25b**, is called a **time-series response** because it indicates how the response changes over time.

3. Measure the resting-state fMRI at another location, which is called the **test location**. The response of the test location *Somatosensory*, which is located in an area of the brain responsible for sensing touch, is shown in **Figure 2.25c**.

4. Calculate the correlation between the seed- and test-location responses. The correlation is calculated using a complex mathematical procedure that compares the seed and test responses at a large number of places along the horizontal time axis. **Figure 2.26a** shows the response at the *Somatosensory* test location superimposed on the seed response. The correspondence between these responses results in a high correlation, which indicates high functional connectivity. **Figure 2.26b** shows the seed response and the response at another test location. The poor match between these two responses results in a low correlation, which indicates poor or no functional connectivity.

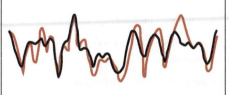

Seed response (black) and test response at *Somatosensory* test location (red)
Correlation = 0.86

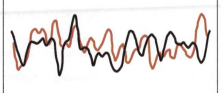

Seed response (black) and test response at another test location (red)
Correlation = 0.04

➤ **Figure 2.26** Superimposed seed response (black) and test location response (red). (a) Response of the *Somatosensory* test location, which is highly correlated with the seed response (correlation = 0.86). (b) Response of another test location, which is poorly correlated with the seed response (correlation = 0.04).

(Source: Responses courtesy of Yin-Hui Chou)

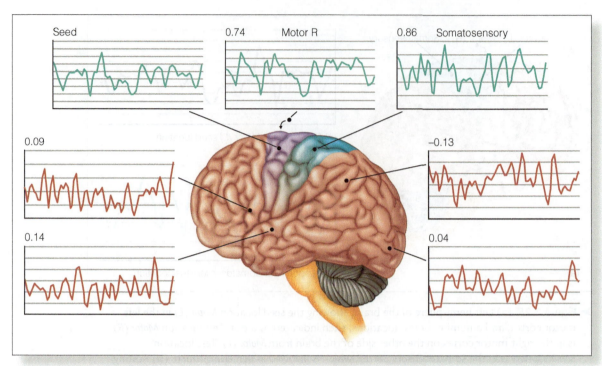

> ➤ **Figure 2.27** Resting-state fMRI responses for the *Motor (L)* seed, test locations *Motor (R)*, *Somatosensory*, and five test locations in other parts of the brain. The numbers indicate correlations between the seed response and each test-location response. Responses *Motor (R)* and *Somatosensory* have been singled out because they have high correlations, which indicates high functional connectivity with the seed. The other locations have low correlations so are not functionally connected to the seed location.
>
> (Responses courtesy of Ying-Hui Chou.)

Figure 2.27 shows time-series for the seed location and a number of test locations, and the correlations between the seed and test locations. The test locations, *Somatosensory* and *Motor (R),* are highly correlated with the seed response and so have high functional connectivity with the seed location. This is evidence that these structures are part of a functional network. All of the other locations have low correlations so are not part of the network.

Resting-state functional fMRI connectivity has become one of the main methods for determining functional connectivity. **Figure 2.28** shows networks determined for a number of different functions using this procedure. **Table 2.1** summarizes the functions of these networks.

TABLE 2.1

Six Common Functional Networks Determined by Resting-State fMRI

Network	Function
Visual	Vision; visual perception
Somato-motor	Movement and touch
Dorsal Attention	Attention to visual stimuli and spatial locations
Executive Control	Higher-level cognitive tasks involved in working memory (see Chapter 5) and directing attention during tasks
Salience	Attending to survival-relevant events in the environment
Default mode	Mind wandering, and cognitive activity related to personal life-story, social functions, and monitoring internal emotional states

Sources: From Barch, 2013; Bressler & Menon, 2010; Raichle, 2011; Zabelina & Andrews-Hanna, 2016. Note that there are other networks as well, including networks involved in hearing, memory, and language.

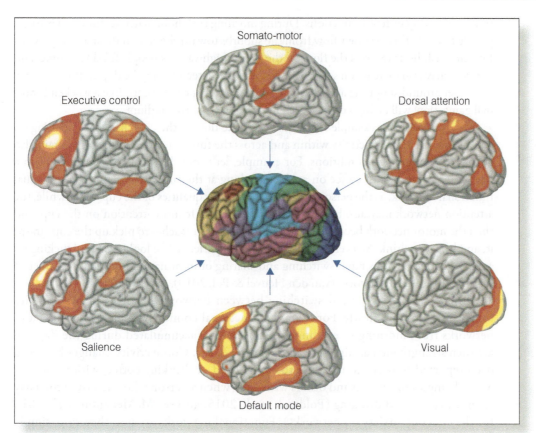

➤ **Figure 2.28** Six major brain networks determined by the resting-state fMRI procedure. Note that all of these networks increase activity during a task and decrease activity when at rest, *except* the default mode network, which decreases activity during a task, and increases activity when there is no task. See Table 2.1 for brief descriptions of these networks.
(Source: From Zabelina & Andrews-Hanna, 2016)

There are also other ways to determine functional connectivity. For example, functional connectivity can be determined by measuring the task-related fMRI at the seed and test locations and determining the correlations between the two responses, as we did for resting-state fMRI. It is important to note that saying two areas are *functionally connected* does not necessarily mean that they directly *communicate* by neural pathways. For example, the response from two areas can be highly correlated because they are both receiving inputs from another area. Functional connectivity and structural connectivity are not, therefore, the same thing, but they are related, so regions with high structural connectivity often show a high level of functional connectivity (Poldrack et al., 2015; van den Heuvel & Pol, 2010).

The pictures in Figure 2.28 show that the overall structural map of the brain is divided into smaller functional maps, so different cognitions activate different groups of neurons. But to really understand what is happening during cognition, we need to go beyond just identifying areas that serve different functions. We need to consider the *dynamics* of cognition.

The Dynamics of Cognition

To understand what we mean by the dynamics of cognition, let's return to our analogy between the structural map of the brain and a big-city street system. Imagine climbing into a helicopter and flying above the city so you can observe the patterns of traffic flow at various times of day. As you hover above the city, you notice how this flow changes when the street system is serving different functions. During morning rush hour, when its function is to get people to work, there is heavy flow from the suburbs toward the city on the major highways. Evening rush hour reverses the flow on the major highways, as people head for home, and the flow may also increase on suburban streets a little later. During the day, traffic flow may be higher around shopping areas; and before and after special events, like a weekend football game, flow will be high on roads leading to and from the stadium.

The point of this example is that just as traffic flow in the city changes depending on conditions, the flow of activity within and across the functional networks in the brain also changes, depending on conditions. For example, let's consider what is happening when a person looks at a cup of coffee on a table. Looking at the cup causes activity in the visual functional network, as the person perceives the various qualities of the cup. Meanwhile, the attention network may also be activated, as the person focuses attention on the cup, and then the motor network becomes activated as the person reaches to pick up the cup, grasps it, and lifts it to drink. So even a simple everyday experience like looking at and picking up a cup of coffee involves rapid switching and sharing of information between a number of different functional networks (van den Heuvel & Pol, 2010).

In addition to this rapid switching between networks, changes in connectivity can also occur more slowly. For example, functional connectivity changes in memory networks from morning to evening as memories are accumulated during the day and are then strengthened at night (Shannon et al., 2013). Connectivity changes have also been reported to occur in response to eating food or drinking coffee, with some networks being strengthened and others weakened when a person who had fasted for a day resumed eating and drinking (Poldrack et al., 2015; also see McMenamin et al., 2014 for the effect of anxiety on networks). Functional networks are not, therefore, simply static diagrams but involve constantly changing activity within and across networks (Mattar et al., 2015).

Many of the ideas about networks and connectivity that we have been describing are based on recent research that logically follows from the idea of distributed representation. After all, if functions are represented by structures in many different areas of the brain, it makes sense that they would be able to communicate with each other. But in the process of discovering ideas about how networks work, one finding, made in just the last two decades, was extremely unexpected. A network was discovered that responded not when people were engaged in tasks—but when they weren't! This network is called the *default mode network*.

The Default Mode Network

The **default mode network (DMN)**, which is shown at the bottom of Figure 2.28, is a network of structures that respond when a person is not involved in specific tasks. The story behind the discovery of this network begins with a paper by Gordon Shulman and coworkers (1997), who noted a few earlier fMRI studies in which presentation of a task caused a *decrease* in activity in some areas of the brain, and stopping the task caused an increase in activity in the same areas. This was different than the usual result, in which presentation of a task is associated with an increase in activity and stopping the task is associated with a decrease in activity.

Following up on this observation, Marcus Raichle and coworkers (2001), in a paper titled "A Default Mode of Brain Function," proposed that the areas that decrease activity during tasks represent a "default mode" of brain function—that is, a mode of brain function that occurs when it is at rest.

To make things even more interesting, research using the resting-state functional connectivity method indicated that areas in the frontal and parietal lobes that decrease activity during tasks (**Figure 2.29a**) have correlated resting state activity (**Figure 2.29b**)

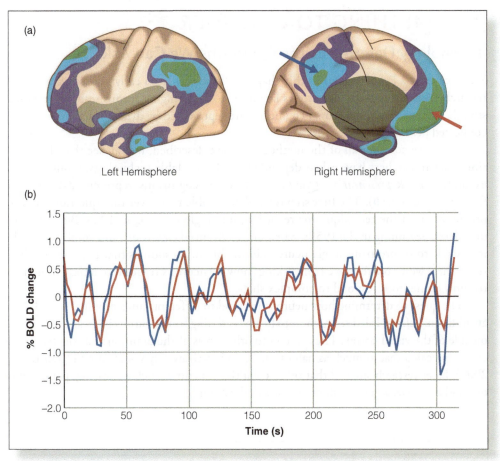

➤ **Figure 2.29** (a) Brain areas that decrease their activity during task performance.
(b) Resting-state activity at two points in the right hemisphere, indicated by the arrows
above. The fact that the resting state activity is correlated indicates that these areas are
functionally connected. All of these areas, taken together, are called the *default mode network*.
(Source: From Raichle, 2015)

(Greicius et al., 2003). These areas are, therefore, part of a functional network, which is
identified as the default mode network (DMN) in Figure 2.28.

There has been a great deal of speculation and research about the purpose of the
DMN. One interesting observation is that when the DMN is active, people's minds tend to
wander (Killingsworth & Gilbert, 2010; Smallwood & Schooler, 2015). This is probably
something you have experienced. One minute you are driving along the highway, paying
close attention to your driving, but then, without even realizing it, you find your mind
wandering to thoughts about what you are going to do later or how to deal with some ongoing concern. What happened? Your brain switched from task-related networks involved
in driving to your default mode network. As you might expect, mind wandering during
driving, as well as during other tasks, isn't necessarily a good thing for performance. This
idea is confirmed by a large body of research that shows that mind wandering decreases performance on tasks that require focused attention (Lerner, 2015; Moneyham & Schooler,
2013; Smallwood, 2011).

But the DMN must have a purpose other than creating mind wandering that distracts
you from your work! After all, it is one of the brain's largest networks and accounts for a
large portion of the brain's activity when it is at rest. In some of the chapters that follow,
we will consider evidence that shows that the DMN is involved in processes ranging from
attention to memory to creativity.

▶ SOMETHING TO CONSIDER

Technology Determines the Questions We Can Ask

We've covered a lot of ground in this chapter, all the way from early neuropsychological research on how brain damage affects language, to how single neurons respond to visual stimuli, to how multidimensional cognitions are represented by dynamic activity in interconnected neural networks.

When we consider all of the methods we have described, we can see that the questions that researchers have asked depended on the available technology. Consider, for example, *The Representation Question*: "How are cognitions represented by neural firing?" (**Figure 2.30**). The first step toward being able to answer that question was the introduction of the technique for recording for single neurons in 1928. But it wasn't until later, beginning in the 1950s, when more-advanced electrodes and amplifiers made it possible to record from single neurons in the brain. As soon as that became possible, researchers were able to move from asking "how do neurons respond to a flash of light?" to "how do neurons respond to complex shapes?"

The quest to determine how neurons respond to different kinds of visual stimuli had an additional effect. It led researchers to begin recording from neurons in areas of the brain outside of the visual cortex. These forays to other areas of the brain, such as the temporal cortex, revealed that as much as half of the brain is activated by visual stimuli (Van Essen, 2004). Later research showed that other cognitive functions, such as hearing, pain, memory, and language, activate numerous areas of the brain.

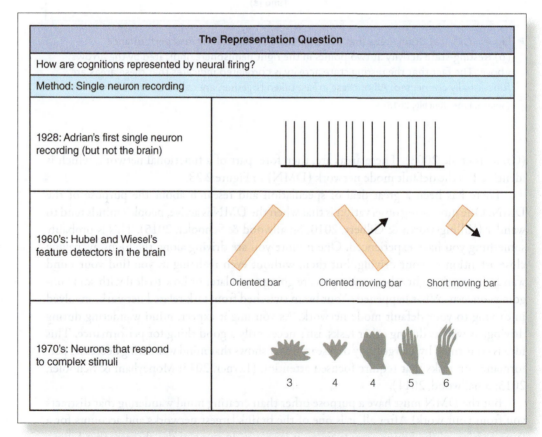

The Representation Question	
How are cognitions represented by neural firing?	
Method: Single neuron recording	
1928: Adrian's first single neuron recording (but not the brain)	
1960's: Hubel and Wiesel's feature detectors in the brain	Oriented bar Oriented moving bar Short moving bar
1970's: Neurons that respond to complex stimuli	3 4 4 5 6

▶ **Figure 2.30** Technology involved in research studying how cognitions are represented by neural firing. Advances in technology made it possible to record from the brain and study how neurons respond to more complex stimuli.

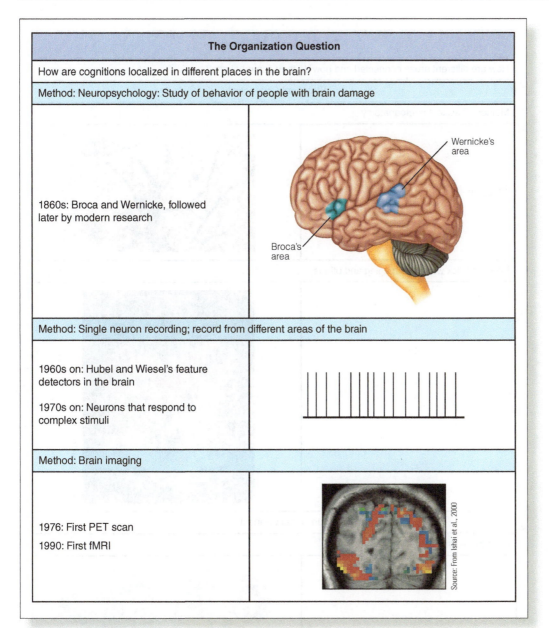

> Figure 2.31 Technology involved in research studying how cognitions are localized in different areas of the brain. Three different methods have been used: Neuropsychology (1860 on); Single neuron recording (1960s on); and Brain imaging (beginning in 1976 with PET, picking up steam in 1990, with the introduction of fMRI).

The discovery that stimuli can activate a large area of the brain brings us to *The Organization Question*: "How are cognitions localized in different areas of the brain?" (**Figure 2.31**). This question was first studied in humans in the 1800s by Broca and Wernicke's research on brain-damaged patients and then in animals in the 1960s and 70s using single neuron recording. Although a tremendous amount was learned about brain organization using these techniques, research on human brain organization took off when brain-scanning technology was introduced—first PET scans in 1976 and then fMRI in 1990, which made it possible to map patterns of brain activity in humans.

But just determining which brain areas were activated wasn't enough for researchers. They wanted to go beyond determining static maps to study dynamic communication, and so they posed *The Communication Question*: "How are different areas of the brain connected and how do they communicate?" (**Figure 2.32**). The idea that neurons form circuits

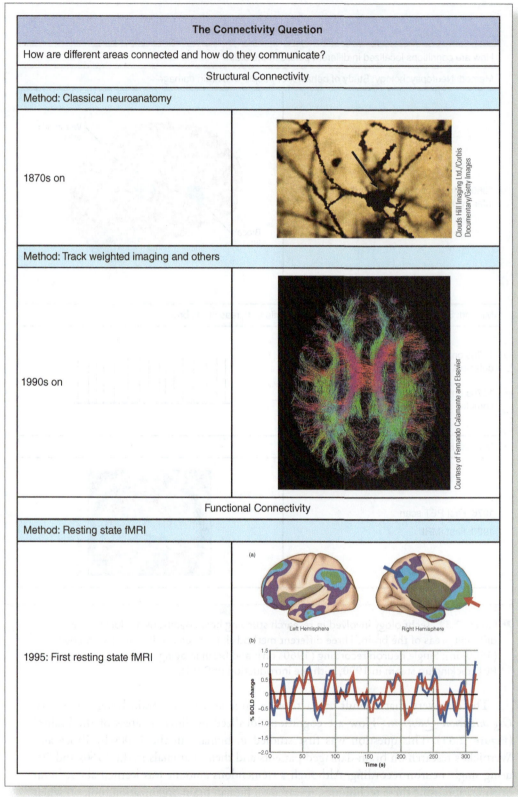

The Connectivity Question
How are different areas connected and how do they communicate?
Structural Connectivity
Method: Classical neuroanatomy
1870s on
Method: Track weighted imaging and others
1990s on
Functional Connectivity
Method: Resting state fMRI
1995: First resting state fMRI

➤ **Figure 2.32** Technology involved in research studying how different areas of the brain are connected and how they communicate. Structural connectivity was studied in the 1800s using neuroanatomical techniques and beginning in the 1990s using brain imaging. The study of functional connectivity took off with the introduction of the resting-state fMRI method in 1995.

dates back to early anatomy experiments from the 1800s, which, like the single neuron re- cordings, were carried out on animals. But the introduction of brain imaging and other technologies made it possible to begin determining structural connectivity (the "roadmap" of the brain) and functional connectivity (the "traffic pattern" of the brain).

The events we have been describing show that technology has determined not only what can be learned about the functioning of the brain but also the types of behaviors that can be studied. Early research involved simple behaviors—the ability to perceive a flash of light, an oriented line, or a geometrical shape. Even later, when researchers began presenting more complex objects like faces, they were usually presented as briefly flashed pictures. But present-day research involves more naturalistic stimuli, such as events depicted in films. And perhaps more important, although early research focused largely on visual stimuli, current research has expanded to include cognitive behaviors ranging from remembering the past and imagining the future to understanding sen- tences and making decisions.

But before we get too carried away by the wonders of technology, let's not lose sight of the fact that although it may be nice to know how neurons work, where brain struc- tures are located, or how neurons communicate in networks, psychologists are not really interested in studying physiology for its own sake. They are interested in determining the relationship between physiological mechanisms and experiences, thoughts, and actions.

The approach in this book is, therefore, based on the idea that the best way to explain cognition is by conducting both behavioral and physiological experiments. As you read this book, you will encounter many examples of situations in which the results of behavioral and physiological experiments have been used together to provide a richer understanding of the mind than would be provided by either alone.

TEST YOURSELF 2.2

1. What is localization of function? Describe how localization has been demonstrated by neuropsychology and recording from neurons. Be sure you understand the principle of double dissociations.

2. Describe the basic principles behind functional magnetic resonance imaging.

3. Describe brain-imaging evidence for localization of function. Describe experiments that involved looking at still pictures and that involved looking at movies. What does each type of experiment tell us about localization of function?

4. What is distributed representation? How is distributed representation related to the multidimensional nature of experience? How is distributed processing illustrated by how the brain responds to looking at faces, remembering and language?

5. What is a neural network?

6. What is structural connectivity? How is it measured?

7. What is functional connectivity? How is it measured and what are some networks that have been determined using this technique?

8. What does it mean to say that the operation of brain networks is dynamic?

9. What is the default mode network? How is it different than other networks?

10. Describe the connection between advances in technology and research on the physiology of cognition.

CHAPTER SUMMARY

1. Cognitive neuroscience is the study of the physiological basis of cognition. Taking a levels-of-analysis approach to the study of the mind involves research at both behavioral and physiological levels.

2. Ramon y Cajal's research resulted in the abandonment of the neural net theory in favor of the neuron doctrine, which states that individual cells called *neurons* transmit signals in the nervous system.

3. Signals can be recorded from neurons using microelectrodes. Edgar Adrian, who recorded the first signals from single neurons, determined that action potentials remain the same size as they travel down an axon and that increasing stimulus intensity increases the rate of nerve firing.

4. The principle of neural representation states that everything that a person experiences is based not on direct contact with stimuli, but on representations in the person's nervous system.

5. Representation by neurons can be explained by considering feature detectors, neurons that respond to complex stimuli, and how neurons are involved in specificity coding, population coding, and sparse coding.

6. The idea of localization of function in perception is supported by the existence of a separate primary receiving area for each sense, by the effects of brain damage on perception (for example, prosopagnosia), by recording from single neurons, and from the results of brain-imaging experiments.

7. Brain imaging measures brain activation by measuring blood flow in the brain. Functional magnetic resonance imaging (fMRI) is widely used to determine brain activation during cognitive functioning. Brain-imaging experiments have measured the response to still pictures to identify areas in the human brain that respond best to faces, places, and bodies, and the response to movies to create a brain map indicating the kinds of stimuli that activate different areas of the brain.

8. The idea of distributed processing is that specific functions are processed by many different areas in the brain. One reason for the activation of many areas is the multidimensional nature of experience. This principle is illustrated by the multidimensional nature of seeing a face, remembering, and producing and understanding language.

9. Neural networks are groups of neurons or structures that are connected structurally and also that are functionally related.

10. Structural connectivity defines the neural highway system of the brain. It has been measured using track weighted imaging.

11. Functional connectivity occurs when different areas have temporally correlated responses. Measuring resting-level fMRI has emerged as one of the ways to measure functional connectivity, but functional connectivity can also be measured by task-related fMRI.

12. A number of different functional networks, such as visual, auditory, salience, executive function, and motor networks, have been determined using resting-level fMRI.

13. A full description of networks needs to include the dynamic aspects of network activity.

14. The default mode network is different than other networks because its activity decreases when a person is engaged in a task, but then increases when the brain is at rest. The function of the DMN is still being researched, but it has been suggested that it may play important roles in a number of cognitive processes, which we will discuss later in the book.

15. Progress in understanding the physiology of cognition has depended on advances in technology. This is demonstrated by considering the connection between technology and answering three basic questions: The Representation Question, The Organization Question, and The Communication Question.

THINK ABOUT IT

1. Some cognitive psychologists have called the brain the mind's computer. What are computers good at that the brain is not? How do you think the brain and computers compare in terms of complexity? What advantage does the brain have over a computer?

2. People generally feel that they are experiencing their environment directly, especially when it comes to sensory experiences such as seeing, hearing, or feeling the texture of a surface. However, our knowledge of how the nervous system operates indicates that this is not the case. Why would a physiologist say that all of our experiences are indirect?

3. When brain activity is being measured in an fMRI scanner, the person's head is surrounded by an array of magnets and

must be kept perfectly still. In addition, the operation of the machine is very noisy. How do these characteristics of brain scanners limit the types of behaviors that can be studied using brain scanning?

4. It has been argued that we will never be able to fully understand how the brain operates because doing this involves using the brain to study itself. What do you think of this argument?

KEY TERMS

Action potential, 31

Axons, 28

Brain imaging, 40

Broca's aphasia, 39

Broca's area, 38

Cell body, 28

Cerebral cortex, 38

Cognitive neuroscience, 26

Connectome, 46

Cortical equipotentiality, 38

Default mode network (DMN), 50

Dendrites, 28

Distributed representation, 44

Double dissociation, 40

Experience-dependent plasticity, 34

Extrastriate body area (EBA), 42

Feature detectors, 33

Frontal lobe, 39

Functional connectivity, 46

Functional magnetic resonance imaging (fMRI), 41

Fusiform face area (FFA), 42

Hierarchical processing, 36

Levels of analysis, 26

Localization of function, 38

Microelectrodes, 30

Multidimensional, 43

Nerve fibers, 28

Nerve impulse, 31

Nerve net, 28

Neural circuits, 29

Neural networks, 45

Neuron doctrine, 28

Neurons, 27

Neuropsychology, 38

Neurotransmitter, 31

Occipital lobe, 39

Parahippocampal place area (PPA), 42

Parietal lobe, 39

Population coding, 36

Principle of neural representation, 32

Prosopagnosia, 39

Receptors, 29

Recording electrode, 30

Reference electrode, 30

Resting-state fMRI, 46

Resting-state functional connectivity, 46

Resting potential, 31

Seed location, 46

Sensory code, 36

Sparse coding, 36

Specificity coding, 36

Structural connectivity, 45

Synapse, 29

Task-related fMRI, 41

Temporal lobe, 35

Test location, 47

Time-series response, 47

Track-weighted imaging (TWI), 46

Visual cortex, 35

Voxels, 41

Wernicke's aphasia, 39

Wernicke's area, 39

COGLAB EXPERIMENTS   Numbers in parentheses refer to the experiment number in CogLab.

Brain Asymmetry (*15*)

You may have had little trouble perceiving this as a staircase, without being aware of the complex processes that led to your perception. Among the perceptual feats you accomplished were telling the difference between the railing and the shadow on the wall, realizing that the vertical bars of the railing are half in shadow and half in sunlight (they aren't two different colors), and that the red "object" on the left is most likely part of a doorway. It may have taken you a little longer to decide that the shadow on the wall was cast not by the railing you can see, but by another railing on the floor above. One of the themes of this chapter is that although perception is usually easy, it is created by complex processes that often operate without your awareness.

Perception

3

▶ Why can two people experience different perceptions in response to the same stimulus? (68)

▶ How does perception depend on a person's knowledge about characteristics of the environment? (74)

▶ How does the brain become tuned to respond best to things that are likely to appear in the environment? (79)

▶ What is the connection between perception and action? (80)

Crystal begins her run along the beach just as the sun is rising over the ocean. She loves this time of day, because it is cool and the mist rising from the sand creates a mystical effect. She looks down the beach and notices something about 100 yards away that wasn't there yesterday. "What an interesting piece of driftwood," she thinks, although it is difficult to see because of the mist and dim lighting (**Figure 3.1a**). As she approaches the object, she begins to doubt her initial perception, and just as she is wondering whether it might not be driftwood, she realizes that it is, in fact, the old beach umbrella that was lying under the lifeguard stand yesterday (**Figure 3.1b**). "Driftwood transformed into an umbrella, right before my eyes," she thinks.

Continuing down the beach, she passes some coiled rope that appears to be abandoned (**Figure 3.1c**). She stops to check it out. Grabbing one end, she flips the rope and sees that, as she suspected, it is one continuous strand. But she needs to keep running, because she is supposed to meet a friend at Beach Java, a coffee shop far down the beach. Later, sitting in the coffeehouse, she tells her friend about the piece of magic driftwood that was transformed into an umbrella.

▶ The Nature of Perception

We define **perception** as experiences resulting from stimulation of the senses. To appreciate how these experiences are created, let's return to Crystal on the beach.

Some Basic Characteristics of Perception

Crystal's experiences illustrate a number of things about perception. Her experience of seeing what she thought was driftwood turn into an umbrella illustrates how perceptions

(a) (b) (c)

Bruce Goldstein

➤ **Figure 3.1** (a) Initially Crystal thinks she sees a large piece of driftwood far down the beach. (b) Eventually she realizes she is looking at an umbrella. (c) On her way down the beach, she passes some coiled rope.

can change based on added information (Crystal's view became better as she got closer to the umbrella) and how perception can involve a process similar to reasoning or problem solving (Crystal figured out what the object was based partially on remembering having seen the umbrella the day before). (Another example of an initially erroneous perception followed by a correction is the famous pop culture line, "It's a bird. It's a plane. It's Superman!") Crystal's guess that the coiled rope was continuous illustrates how perception can be based on a perceptual rule (*when objects overlap, the one underneath usually continues behind the one on top*), which may be based on the person's past experiences.

Crystal's experience also demonstrates how arriving at a perception can involve a *process*. It took some time for Crystal to realize that what she thought was driftwood was actually an umbrella, so it is possible to describe her perception as involving a "reasoning" process. In most cases, perception occurs so rapidly and effortlessly that it appears to be automatic. But, as we will see in this chapter, perception is far from automatic. It involves complex, and usually invisible, processes that resemble reasoning, although they occur much more rapidly than Crystal's realization that the driftwood was actually an umbrella.

Finally, Crystal's experience also illustrates how perception occurs in conjunction with action. Crystal is running and perceiving at the same time; later, at the coffee shop, she easily reaches for her cup of coffee, a process that involves coordination of seeing the coffee cup, determining its location, physically reaching for it, and grasping its handle. This aspect of Crystal's experiences is what happens in everyday perception. We are usually moving, and even when we are just sitting in one place watching TV, a movie, or a sporting event, our eyes are constantly in motion as we shift our attention from one thing to another to perceive what is happening. We also grasp and pick up things many times a day, whether it is a cup of coffee, a phone, or this book. Perception, therefore, is more than just "seeing" or "hearing." It is central to our ability to organize the actions that occur as we interact with the environment.

It is important to recognize that while perception creates a picture of our environment and helps us take action within it, it also plays a central role in cognition in general. When we consider that perception is essential for creating memories, acquiring knowledge, solving problems, communicating with other people, recognizing someone you met last week, and answering questions on a cognitive psychology exam, it becomes clear that perception is the gateway to all the other cognitions we will be describing in this book.

The goal of this chapter is to explain the mechanisms responsible for perception. To begin, we move from Crystal's experience on the beach and in the coffee shop to what happens when perceiving a city scene: Pittsburgh as seen from the upper deck of PNC Park, home of the Pittsburgh Pirates.

A Human Perceives Objects and a Scene

Sitting in the upper deck of PNC Park, Roger looks out over the city (**Figure 3.2**). He sees a group of about 10 buildings on the left and can easily tell one building from another. Looking straight ahead, he sees a small building in front of a larger one, and has no trouble telling that they are two separate buildings. Looking down toward the river, he notices a horizontal yellow band above the right field bleachers. It is obvious to him that this is not part of the ballpark but is located across the river.

All of Roger's perceptions come naturally to him and require little effort. But when we look closely at the scene, it becomes apparent that the scene poses many "puzzles." The following demonstration points out a few of them.

Bruce Goldstein

➤ **Figure 3.2** It is easy to tell that there are a number of different buildings on the left and that straight ahead there is a low rectangular building in front of a taller building. It is also possible to tell that the horizontal yellow band above the bleachers is across the river. These perceptions are easy for humans but would be quite difficult for a computer vision system. The letters on the left indicate areas referred to in the Demonstration.

DEMONSTRATION   Perceptual Puzzles in a Scene

The following questions refer to the areas labeled in Figure 3.2. Your task is to answer each question and indicate the reasoning behind each answer:

What is the dark area at A?

Are the surfaces at B and C facing in the same or different directions?

Are areas B and C on the same building or on different buildings?

Does the building at D extend behind the one at A?

Although it may have been easy to answer the questions, it was probably somewhat more challenging to indicate what your "reasoning" was. For example, how did you know the dark area at A is a shadow? It could be a dark-colored building that is in front of a light-colored building. On what basis might you have decided that building D extends behind building A? It could, after all, simply end right where A begins. We could ask similar questions about everything in this scene because, as we will see, a particular pattern of shapes can be created by a wide variety of objects.

One of the messages of this demonstration is that to determine what is "out there," it is necessary to go beyond the pattern of light and dark that a scene creates on the retina—the structure that lines the back of the eye and contains the receptors for seeing. One way to appreciate the importance of this "going beyond" process is to consider how difficult it has been to program even the most powerful computers to accomplish perceptual tasks that humans achieve with ease.

A Computer-Vision System Perceives Objects and a Scene

A computer that can perceive has been a dream that dates back to early science fiction and movies. Because movies can make up things, it was easy to show the droids R2-D2 and C3PO having a conversation on the desert planet Tatooine in the original *Star Wars* (1977). Although C3PO did most of the talking (R2D2 mainly beeped), both could apparently navigate through their environment with ease, and recognize objects along the way.

But designing a computer vision system that can actually perceive the environment and recognize objects and scenes is more complicated than making a *Star Wars* movie. In the 1950s, when digital computers became available to researchers, it was thought that it would take perhaps a decade to design a machine-vision system that would rival human vision. But the early systems were primitive and took minutes of calculations to identify simple isolated objects that a young child could name in seconds. Perceiving objects and scenes was, the researchers realized, still the stuff of science fiction.

It wasn't until 1987 that the *International Journal of Computer Vision*, the first journal devoted solely to computer vision, was founded. Papers from the first issues considered topics such as how to interpret line drawings of curved objects (Malik, 1987) and how to determine the three-dimensional layout of a scene based on a film of movement through the scene (Bolles et al., 1987). These papers and others in the journal had to resort to complex mathematical formulas to solve perceptual problems that are easy for humans.

Flash-forward to March 13, 2004. Thirteen robotic vehicles are lined up in the Mojave Desert in California for the Defense Advanced Projects Agency's (DARPA) Grand Challenge. The task was to drive 150 miles from the starting point to Las Vegas, using only GPS coordinates to define the course and computer vision to avoid obstacles. The best performance was achieved by a vehicle entered by Carnegie-Mellon University, which traversed only 7.3 miles before getting stuck.

Progress continued through the next decade, however, with thousands of researchers and multi-million-dollar investments, until now, when driverless cars are no longer a novelty. As I write this, a fleet of driverless Uber vehicles are finding their way around the winding streets of Pittsburgh, San Francisco, and other cities (**Figure 3.3**).

One message of the preceding story is that although present accomplishments of computer-vision systems are impressive, it turned out to be extremely difficult to create the systems that made driverless cars possible. But as impressive as driverless cars are, computer-vision systems still make mistakes in naming objects. For example, **Figure 3.4** shows three objects that a computer identified as a tennis ball.

➤ **Figure 3.3** Driverless car on the streets of San Francisco.

➤ **Figure 3.4** Even computer-vision programs that are able to recognize objects fairly accurately make mistakes, such as confusing objects that share features. In this example, the lens cover and the top of the teapot are erroneously classified as a "tennis ball." (Source: Based on K. Simonyan et al., 2012)

In another area of computer-vision research, programs have been created that can describe pictures of real scenes. For example, a computer accurately identified a scene similar to the one in **Figure 3.5** as "a large plane sitting on a runway." But mistakes still occur, as when a picture similar to the one in **Figure 3.6** was identified as "a young boy holding a baseball bat" (Fei-Fei, 2015). The computer's problem is that it doesn't have the huge storehouse of information about the world that humans begin accumulating as soon as they are born. If a computer has never seen a toothbrush, it identifies it as something with a similar shape. And, although the computer's response to the airplane picture is accurate, it is beyond the computer's capabilities to recognize that this is a picture of airplanes on display, perhaps at an air show, and that the people are not passengers but are visiting the air show. So on one hand, we have come a very long way from the first attempts in the 1950s to design computer-vision systems, but to date, humans still out-perceive computers. In the next section, we consider some of the reasons perception is so difficult for computers to master.

➤ **Figure 3.5** Picture similar to one that a computer vision program identified as "a large plane sitting on a runway."

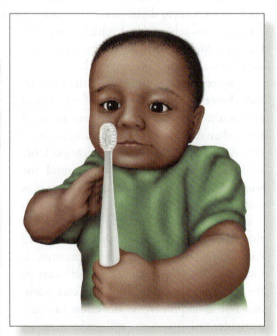

➤ **Figure 3.6** Picture similar to one that a computer vision program identified as "a young boy holding a baseball bat."

▶ Why Is It So Difficult to Design a Perceiving Machine?

We will now describe a few of the difficulties involved in designing a "perceiving machine." Remember that although the problems we describe pose difficulties for computers, humans solve them easily.

The Stimulus on the Receptors Is Ambiguous

When you look at the page of this book, the image cast by the borders of the page on your retina is ambiguous. It may seem strange to say that, because (1) the rectangular shape of the page is obvious, and (2) once we know the page's shape and its distance from the eye, determining its image on the retina is a simple geometry problem, which, as shown in **Figure 3.7**, can be solved by extending "rays" from the corners of the page (in red) into the eye.

But the perceptual system is not concerned with determining an object's image on the retina. It *starts* with the image on the retina, and its job is to determine what object "out there" created the image. The task of determining the object responsible for a particular image on the retina is called the **inverse projection problem**, because it involves starting with the retinal image and extending rays out from the eye. When we do this, as shown by extending the lines in Figure 3.7 out from the eye, we see that the retinal image created by the rectangular page could have also been created by a number of other objects, including a tilted trapezoid, a much larger rectangle, and an infinite number of other objects, located at different distances. When we consider that a particular image on the retina can be created by many different objects in the environment, it is easy to see why we say that the image on the retina is ambiguous. Nonetheless, humans typically solve the inverse projection problem easily, even though it still poses serious challenges to computer-vision systems.

Objects Can Be Hidden or Blurred

Sometimes objects are hidden or blurred. Look for the pencil and eyeglasses in **Figure 3.8** before reading further. Although it might take a little searching, people can find the pencil in the foreground and the glasses frame sticking out from behind the computer next to the picture, even though only a small portion of these objects is visible. People also easily perceive the book, scissors, and paper as whole objects, even though they are partially hidden by other objects.

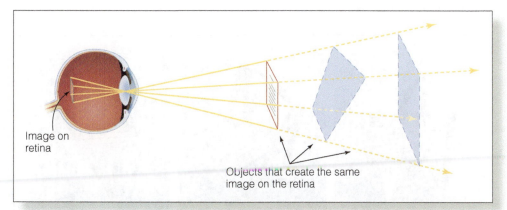

Image on retina

Objects that create the same image on the retina

▶ **Figure 3.7** The projection of the book (red object) onto the retina can be determined by extending rays (solid lines) from the book into the eye. The principle behind the inverse projection problem is illustrated by extending rays out from the eye past the book (dashed lines). When we do this, we can see that the image created by the book can be created by an infinite number of objects, among them the tilted trapezoid and large rectangle shown here. This is why we say that the image on the retina is ambiguous.

Bruce Goldstein

➤ **Figure 3.8** A portion of the mess on the author's desk. Can you locate the hidden pencil (easy) and the author's glasses (hard)?

This problem of hidden objects occurs any time one object obscures part of another object. This occurs frequently in the environment, but people easily understand that the part of an object that is covered continues to exist, and they are able to use their knowledge of the environment to determine what is likely to be present.

People are also able to recognize objects that are not in sharp focus, such as the faces in **Figure 3.9**. See how many of these people you can identify, and then consult the answers on page 91. Despite the degraded nature of these images, people can often identify most of them, whereas computers perform poorly on this task (Sinha, 2002).

Objects Look Different from Different Viewpoints

Another problem facing any perceiving machine is that objects are often viewed from different angles, so their images are continually changing, as in **Figure 3.10**. People's ability to recognize an object even when it is seen from different viewpoints is called **viewpoint invariance**. Computer-vision systems can achieve viewpoint invariance only by a laborious process that involves complex calculations designed to determine which points on an object match in different views (Vedaldi, Ling, & Soatto, 2010).

s_bukley/Shutterstock.com; Featureflash/Shutterstock.com; dpa picture alliance archive/Alamy Stock Photo; Peter Muhly/Alamy Stock Photo; s_bukley/Shutterstock.com; Joe Seer/Shutterstock.com; DFree/Shutterstock.com

➤ **Figure 3.9** Who are these people? See page 91 for the answers.
(Source: Based on Sinha, 2002)

(a)   (b)   (c)

Bruce Goldstein

➤ **Figure 3.10** Your ability to recognize each of these views as being of the same chair is an example of viewpoint invariance.

Scenes Contain High-Level Information

Moving from objects to scenes adds another level of complexity. Not only are there often many objects in a scene, but they may be providing information about the scene that requires some reasoning to figure out. Consider, for example, the airplane picture in Figure 3.5. What is the basis for deciding the planes are probably on display at an air show? One answer is knowing that the plane on the right is an older-looking military plane that is most likely no longer in service. We also know that the people aren't passengers waiting to board, because they are walking on the grass and aren't carrying any luggage. Cues like this, although obvious to a person, would need to be programmed into a computer.

The difficulties facing any perceiving machine illustrate that the process of perception is more complex than it seems. Our task, therefore, in describing perception is to explain this process, focusing on how our human perceiving machine operates. We begin by considering two types of information used by the human perceptual system: (1) environmental energy stimulating the receptors and (2) knowledge and expectations that the observer brings to the situation.

▶ Information for Human Perception

Perception is built on a foundation of information from the environment. Looking at something creates an image on the retina. This image generates electrical signals that are transmitted through the retina, and then to the visual receiving area of the brain. This sequence of events from eye to brain is called **bottom-up processing**, because it starts at the "bottom" or beginning of the system, when environmental energy stimulates the receptors.

But perception involves information in addition to the foundation provided by activation of the receptors and bottom-up processing. Perception also involves factors such as a person's knowledge of the environment, and the expectations people bring to the perceptual situation. For example, remember the experiment described in Chapter 1, which showed that people identify a rapidly flashed object in a kitchen scene more accurately when that object fits the scene (Figure 1.13)? This knowledge we have of the environment is the basis of **top-down processing**—processing that originates in the brain, at the "top" of the perceptual system. It is this knowledge that enables people to rapidly identify objects and scenes, and also to go beyond mere identification of objects to determining the story behind a scene. We will now consider two additional examples of top-down processing: perceiving objects and hearing words in a sentence.

Perceiving Objects

An example of top-down processing, illustrated in **Figure 3.11**, is called "the multiple personalities of a blob," because even though all of the blobs are identical, they are perceived as different objects depending on their orientation and the context within which they are seen (Oliva & Torralba, 2007). The blob appears to be an object on a table in (b), a shoe on a person bending down in (c), and a car and a person crossing the street in (d). We perceive the blob as different objects because of our knowledge of the kinds of objects that are likely to be found in different types of scenes. The human advantage over computers is therefore due, in part, to the additional top-down knowledge available to humans.

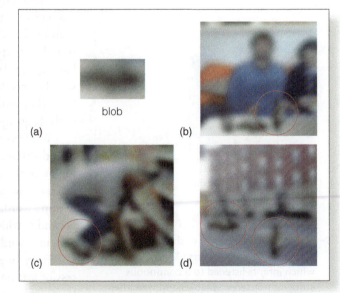

blob

(a)   (b)

(c)   (d)

▶ **Figure 3.11** "Multiple personalities of a blob." What we expect to see in different contexts influences our interpretation of the identity of the "blob" inside the circles. (Source: Adapted from A. Oliva & A. Torralba, 2007)

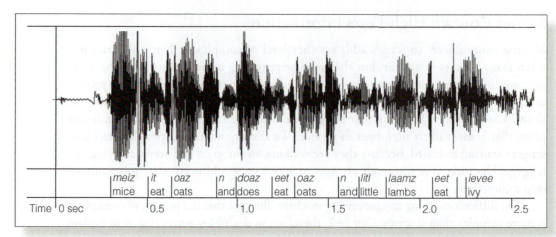

➤ **Figure 3.12** Sound energy for the sentence "Mice eat oats and does eat oats and little lambs eat ivy." The italicized words just below the sound record indicate how this sentence was pronounced by the speaker. The vertical lines next to the words indicate where each word begins. Note that it is difficult or impossible to tell from the sound record where one word ends and the next one begins.

(Source: Speech signal courtesy of Peter Howell)

Hearing Words in a Sentence

An example of how top-down processing influences speech perception occurs for me as I sit in a restaurant listening to people speaking Spanish at the next table. Unfortunately, I don't understand what they are saying because I don't understand Spanish. To me, the dialogue sounds like an unbroken string of sound, except for occasional pauses and when a familiar word like *gracias* pops out. My perception reflects the fact that the physical sound signal for speech is generally continuous, and when there are breaks in the sound, they do not necessarily occur between words. You can see this in **Figure 3.12** by comparing the place where each word in the sentence begins with the pattern of the sound signal.

The ability to tell when one word in a conversation ends and the next one begins is a phenomenon called **speech segmentation**. The fact that a listener familiar only with English and another listener familiar with Spanish can receive identical sound stimuli but experience different perceptions means that each listener's experience with language (or lack of it!) is influencing his or her perception. The continuous sound signal enters the ears and triggers signals that are sent toward the speech areas of the brain (bottom-up processing); if a listener understands the language, their knowledge of the language creates the perception of individual words (top-down processing).

While segmentation is aided by knowing the meanings of words, listeners also use other information to achieve segmentation. As we learn a language, we are learning more than the meaning of the words. Without even realizing it we are learning **transitional probabilities**—the likelihood that one sound will follow another within a word. For example, consider the words *pretty baby*. In English it is likely that *pre* and *ty* will be in the same word (**pre-tty**) but less likely that *ty* and *ba* will be in the same word (pre*tty ba*by).

Every language has transitional probabilities for different sounds, and the process of learning about transitional probabilities and about other characteristics of language is called **statistical learning**. Research has shown that infants as young as 8 months of age are capable of statistical learning.

Jennifer Saffran and coworkers (1996) carried out an early experiment that demonstrated statistical learning in young infants. **Figure 3.13a** shows the design of

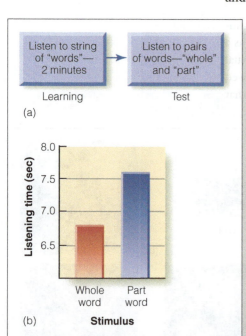

➤ **Figure 3.13** (a) Design of the experiment by Saffran and coworkers (1996), in which infants listened to a continuous string of nonsense syllables and were then tested to see which sounds they perceived as belonging together. (b) The results, indicating that infants listened longer to the "part-word" stimuli.

this experiment. During the learning phase of the experiment, the infants heard four non-sense "words" such as *bidaku, padoti, golabu,* and *tupiro,* which were combined in random order to create 2 minutes of continuous sound. An example of part of a string created by combining these words is *bidaku**padoti**golabu**tupiro**padotibidaku*.... In this string, every other word is printed in boldface in order to help you pick out the words. However, when the infants heard these strings, all the words were pronounced with the same intonation, and there were no breaks between the words to indicate where one word ended and the next one began.

The transitional probabilities between two syllables that appeared *within* a word were always 1.0. For example, for the word *bidaku,* when /*bi*/ was presented, /*da*/ always followed it. Similarly, when /*da*/ was presented, /*ku*/ always followed it. In other words, these three sounds always occurred together and in the same order, to form the word *bidaku.*

The transitional probabilities between the *end* of one word and the *beginning* of another were only 0.33. For example, there was a 33 percent chance that the last sound, /*ku*/ from *bidaku,* would be followed by the first sound, /*pa*/, from *padoti,* a 33 percent chance that it would be followed by /tu/ from *tupiro,* and a 33 percent chance it would be followed by /*go*/ from *golabu.*

If Saffran's infants were sensitive to transitional probabilities, they would perceive stimuli like *bidaku* or *padoti* as words, because the three syllables in these words are linked by transitional probabilities of 1.0. In contrast, stimuli like **tibida** (the end of *padoti* plus the beginning of **bidaku**) would not be perceived as words, because the transitional probabilities were much smaller.

To determine whether the infants did, in fact, perceive stimuli like *bidaku* and *padoti* as words, the infants were tested by being presented with pairs of three-syllable stimuli. Some of the stimuli were "words" that had been presented before, such as *padoti.* These were the "whole-word" stimuli. The other stimuli were created from the end of one word and the beginning of another, such as *tibida.* These were the "part-word" stimuli.

The prediction was that the infants would choose to listen to the part-word stimuli longer than to the whole-word stimuli. This prediction was based on previous research that showed that infants tend to lose interest in stimuli that are repeated, and so become familiar, but pay more attention to novel stimuli that they haven't experienced before. Thus, if the infants perceived the whole-word stimuli as words that had been repeated over and over during the 2-minute learning session, they would pay less attention to these familiar stimuli than to the more novel part-word stimuli that they did not perceive as being words.

Saffran measured how long the infants listened to each sound by presenting a blinking light near the speaker where the sound was coming from. When the light attracted the infant's attention, the sound began, and it continued until the infant looked away. Thus, the infants controlled how long they heard each sound by how long they looked at the light. **Figure 3.13b** shows that the infants did, as predicted, listen longer to the part-word stimuli. From results such as these, we can conclude that the ability to use transitional probabilities to segment sounds into words begins at an early age.

The examples of how context affects our perception of the blob and how knowledge of the statistics of speech affects our ability to create words from a continuous speech stream illustrate that top-down processing based on knowledge we bring to a situation plays an important role in perception.

We have seen that perception depends on two types of information: bottom-up (information stimulating the receptors) and top-down (information based on knowledge). Exactly how the perceptual system uses this information has been conceived of in different ways by different people. We will now describe four prominent approaches to perceiving objects, which will take us on a journey that begins in the 1800s and ends with modern conceptions of object perception.

▶ Conceptions of Object Perception

An early idea about how people use information was proposed by 19th-century physicist and physiologist Hermann von Helmholtz (1866/1911).

Helmholtz's Theory of Unconscious Inference

Hermann von Helmholtz (1821–1894) was a physicist who made important contributions to fields as diverse as thermodynamics, nerve physiology, visual perception, and aesthetics. He also invented the ophthalmoscope, versions of which are still used today to enable physicians to examine the blood vessels inside the eye.

One of Helmholtz's contributions to perception was based on his realization that the image on the retina is ambiguous. We have seen that ambiguity means that a particular pattern of stimulation on the retina can be caused by a large number of objects in the environment (see Figure 3.7). For example, what does the pattern of stimulation in **Figure 3.14a** represent? For most people, this pattern on the retina results in the perception of a blue rectangle in front of a red rectangle, as shown in **Figure 3.14b**. But as **Figure 3.14c** indicates, this display could also have been caused by a six-sided red shape positioned behind or right next to the blue rectangle.

Helmholtz's question was, How does the perceptual system "decide" that this pattern on the retina was created by overlapping rectangles? His answer was the **likelihood principle**, which states that we perceive the object that is *most likely* to have caused the pattern of stimuli we have received. This judgment of what is most likely occurs, according to Helmholtz, by a process called **unconscious inference**, in which our perceptions are the result of unconscious assumptions, or inferences, that we make about the environment. Thus, we *infer* that it is likely that Figure 3.14a is a rectangle covering another rectangle because of experiences we have had with similar situations in the past.

Helmholtz's description of the process of perception resembles the process involved in solving a problem. For perception, the problem is to determine which object has caused a

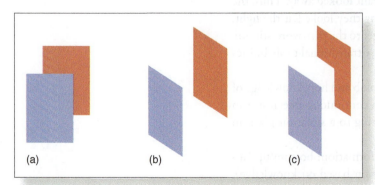

➤ **Figure 3.14** The display in (a) is usually interpreted as being (b) a blue rectangle in front of a red rectangle. It could, however, be (c) a blue rectangle and an appropriately positioned six-sided red figure.

particular pattern of stimulation, and this problem is solved by a process in which the perceptual system applies the observer's knowledge of the environment in order to infer what the object might be.

An important feature of Helmholtz's proposal is that this process of perceiving what is most likely to have caused the pattern on the retina happens rapidly and unconsciously. These unconscious assumptions, which are based on the likelihood principle, result in perceptions that seem "instantaneous," even though they are the outcome of a rapid process. Thus, although you might have been able to solve the perceptual puzzles in the scene in Figure 3.2 without much effort, this ability, according to Helmholtz, is the outcome of processes of which we are unaware. (See Rock, 1983, for a more recent version of this idea.)

The Gestalt Principles of Organization

We will now consider an approach to perception proposed by a group called the **Gestalt psychologists** about 30 years after Helmholtz proposed his theory of unconscious inference. The goal of the Gestalt approach was the same as Helmholtz's—to explain how we perceive objects—but they approached the problem in a different way.

The Gestalt approach to perception originated, in part, as a reaction to Wilhelm Wundt's structuralism (see page 7). Remember from Chapter 1 that Wundt proposed that our overall experience could be understood by combining basic elements of experience called *sensations*. According to this idea, our perception of the face in **Figure 3.15** is created by adding up many sensations, represented as dots in this figure.

The Gestalt psychologists rejected the idea that perceptions were formed by "adding up" sensations. One of the origins of the Gestalt idea that perceptions could not be explained by adding up small sensations has been attributed to the experience of psychologist Max Wertheimer, who while on vacation in 1911 took a train ride through Germany (Boring, 1942). When he got off the train to stretch his legs at Frankfurt, he bought a stroboscope from a toy vendor on the train platform. The stroboscope, a mechanical device that created an illusion of movement by rapidly alternating two slightly different pictures, caused Wertheimer to wonder how the structuralist idea that experience is created from sensations could explain the illusion of movement he observed.

Figure 3.16 diagrams the principle behind the illusion of movement created by the stroboscope, which is called **apparent movement** because, although movement is perceived, nothing is actually moving. There are three components to stimuli that create apparent movement: (1) One light flashes on and off (**Figure 3.16a**); (2) there is a period of darkness, lasting a fraction of a second (**Figure 3.16b**); and (3) the second light flashes on and off (**Figure 3.16c**). Physically, therefore, there are two lights flashing on and off separated by a period of darkness. But we don't see the darkness because our perceptual system adds something during the period of darkness—the perception of a light moving through the space between the flashing lights (**Figure 3.16d**). Modern examples of apparent movement are electronic signs that display moving advertisements or news headlines, and movies. The perception of movement in these displays is so compelling that it is difficult to imagine that they are made up of stationary lights flashing on and off (for the news headlines) or still images flashed one after the other (for the movies).

Wertheimer drew two conclusions from the phenomenon of apparent movement. His first conclusion was that apparent movement cannot be explained by sensations, because there is nothing in the dark space between the flashing lights. His second conclusion became one of the basic principles of Gestalt psychology: *The whole is different than the sum of its parts.* This conclusion follows from the fact that the perceptual system creates the perception of movement from stationary images. This idea that the whole is different than the sum of its parts led the Gestalt psychologists to propose a number of **principles of perceptual organization** to explain the way elements are grouped together to create larger

➤ **Figure 3.15** According to structuralism, a number of sensations (represented by the dots) add up to create our perception of the face.

(a) One light flashes

(b) Darkness

(c) The second light flashes

(d) Flash—dark—flash

➤ **Figure 3.16** The conditions for creating apparent movement. (a) One light flashes, followed by (b) a short period of darkness, followed by (c) another light flashing at a different position. The resulting perception, symbolized in (d), is a light moving from left to right. Movement is seen between the two lights even though there is only darkness in the space between them.

➤ **Figure 3.17** Some black and white shapes that become perceptually organized into a Dalmatian. (See page 91 for an outline of the Dalmatian.)

objects. For example, in **Figure 3.17**, some of the black areas become grouped to form a Dalmatian and others are seen as shadows in the background. We will describe a few of the Gestalt principles, beginning with one that brings us back to Crystal's run along the beach.

Good Continuation The **principle of good continuation** states the following: *Points that, when connected, result in straight or smoothly curving lines are seen as belonging together, and the lines tend to be seen in such a way as to follow the smoothest path. Also, objects that are overlapped by other objects are perceived as continuing behind the overlapping object.* Thus, when Crystal saw the coiled rope in Figure 3.1c, she wasn't surprised that when she grabbed one end of the rope and flipped it, it turned out to be one continuous strand (**Figure 3.18**). The reason this didn't surprise her is that even though there were many places where one part of the rope overlapped another part, she didn't perceive the rope as consisting of a number of separate pieces; rather, she perceived the rope as continuous. (Also consider your shoelaces!)

Pragnanz Pragnanz, roughly translated from the German, means "good figure." The **law of pragnanz**, also called the **principle of good figure** or the **principle of simplicity**, states: *Every stimulus pattern is seen in such a way that the resulting structure is as simple as possible.*

➤ **Figure 3.18** (a) Rope on the beach. (b) Good continuation helps us perceive the rope as a single strand.

The familiar Olympic symbol in **Figure 3.19a** is an example of the law of simplicity at work. We see this display as five circles and not as a larger number of more complicated shapes such as the ones shown in the "exploded" view of the Olympic symbol in **Figure 3.19b**. (The law of good continuation also contributes to perceiving the five circles. Can you see why this is so?)

Similarity   Most people perceive **Figure 3.20a** as either horizontal rows of circles, vertical columns of circles, or both. But when we change the color of some of the columns, as in **Figure 3.20b**, most people perceive vertical columns of circles. This perception illustrates the **principle of similarity**: *Similar things appear to be grouped together.* A striking example of grouping by similarity of color is shown in **Figure 3.21**. Grouping can also occur because of similarity of size, shape, or orientation.

There are many other principles of organization, proposed by the original Gestalt psychologists (Helson, 1933) as well as by modern psychologists (Palmer, 1992; Palmer & Rock, 1994), but the main message, for our discussion, is that the Gestalt psychologists realized that perception is based on more than just the pattern of light and dark on the retina. In their conception, perception is determined by specific organizing principles.

But where do these organizing principles come from? Max Wertheimer (1912) describes these principles as "intrinsic laws," which implies that they are built into the system. This idea that the principles are "built in" is consistent with the Gestalt psychologists' idea that although a person's experience can *influence* perception, the role of experience is minor compared to the perceptual principles (also see Koffka, 1935). This idea that experience plays only a minor role in perception differs from Helmholtz's likelihood principle, which proposes that our knowledge of the environment enables us to determine what is most likely to have created the pattern on the retina and also differs from modern approaches to object perception, which propose that our experience with the environment is a central component of the process of perception.

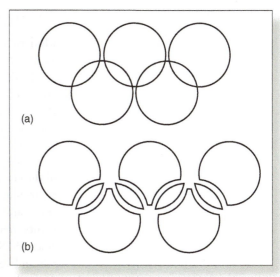

(a)

(b)

➤ **Figure 3.19** The Olympic symbol is perceived as five circles (a), not as the nine shapes in (b).

➤ **Figure 3.21** This photograph, Waves, by Wilma Hurskainen, was taken at the exact moment that the front of the white water aligned with the white area on the woman's clothing. Similarity of color causes grouping; differently colored areas of the dress are perceptually grouped with the same colors in the scene. Also notice how the front edge of the water creates grouping by good continuation across the woman's dress.

(Source: Courtesy of Wilma Hurskainen)

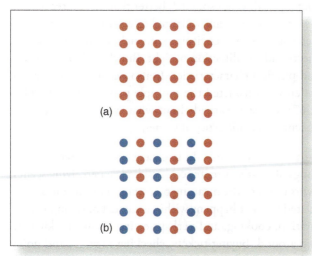

(a)

(b)

➤ **Figure 3.20** (a) This pattern of dots is perceived as horizontal rows, vertical columns, or both. (b) This pattern of dots is perceived as vertical columns.

Taking Regularities of the Environment into Account

Modern perceptual psychologists take experience into account by noting that certain characteristics of the environment occur frequently. For example, blue is associated with open sky, landscapes are often green and smooth, and verticals and horizontals are often associated with buildings. These frequently occurring characteristics are called **regularities in the environment**. There are two types of regularities: *physical regularities* and *semantic regularities*.

Physical Regularities   **Physical regularities** are regularly occurring physical properties of the environment. For example, there are more vertical and horizontal orientations in the environment than oblique (angled) orientations. This occurs in human-made environments (for example, buildings contain lots of horizontals and verticals) and also in natural environments (trees and plants are more likely to be vertical or horizontal than slanted) (Coppola et al., 1998) (**Figure 3.22**). It is therefore no coincidence that people can perceive horizontals and verticals more easily than other orientations, an effect called the **oblique effect** (Appelle, 1972; Campbell et al., 1966; Orban et al., 1984). Another example of a physical regularity is that when one object partially covers another one, the contour of the partially covered object "comes out the other side," as occurs for the rope in Figure 3.18.

Another physical regularity is illustrated by **Figure 3.23a**, which shows indentations created by people walking in the sand. But turning this picture upside down, as in **Figure 3.23b**, transforms the indentations into rounded mounds. Our perception in these two situations has been explained by the **light-from-above assumption**: We usually assume that light is coming from above, because light in our environment, including the sun and most artificial light, usually comes from above (Kleffner & Ramachandran, 1992). **Figure 3.23c** shows how light coming from above and from the left illuminates an indentation, leaving a shadow on the left. **Figure 3.23d** shows how the same light illuminates a bump, leaving a shadow on the right. Our perception of illuminated shapes is influenced by how they are shaded, combined with the brain's assumption that light is coming from above.

One of the reasons humans are able to perceive and recognize objects and scenes so much better than computer-guided robots is that our system is adapted to respond to the physical characteristics of our environment, such as the orientations of objects and the direction of light. But this adaptation goes beyond physical characteristics. It also occurs because, as we saw when we considered the multiple personalities of a blob (page 67), we have learned about what types of objects typically occur in specific types of scenes.

Semantic Regularities   In language, *semantics* refers to the meanings of words or sentences. Applied to perceiving scenes, *semantics* refers to the meaning of a scene. This meaning is often related to what happens within a scene. For example, food preparation, cooking, and perhaps eating occur in a kitchen; waiting around, buying tickets, checking luggage, and going through security checkpoints happen in airports. **Semantic regularities** are the characteristics associated with the functions carried out in different types of scenes.

Bruce Goldstein

➤ **Figure 3.22** In these two scenes from nature, horizontal and vertical orientations are more common than oblique orientations. These scenes are special examples, picked because of the large proportion of verticals. However, randomly selected photos of natural scenes also contain more horizontal and vertical orientations than oblique orientations. This also occurs for human-made buildings and objects.

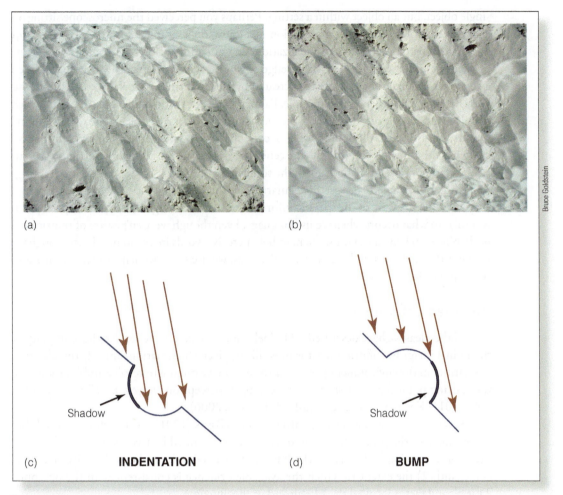

➤ **Figure 3.23** (a) Indentations made by people walking in the sand. (b) Turning the picture upside down turns indentations into rounded mounds. (c) How light from above and to the left illuminates an indentation, causing a shadow on the left. (d) The same light illuminating a bump causes a shadow on the right.

One way to demonstrate that people are aware of semantic regularities is simply to ask them to imagine a particular type of scene or object, as in the following demonstration.

DEMONSTRATION Visualizing Scenes and Objects

Your task in this demonstration is simple. Close your eyes and then visualize or simply think about the following scenes and objects:

1. An office
2. The clothing section of a department store
3. A microscope
4. A lion

Most people who have grown up in modern society have little trouble visualizing an office or the clothing section of a department store. What is important about this ability, for our purposes, is that part of this visualization involves details within these scenes. Most people see an office as having a desk with a computer on it, bookshelves, and a chair. The department store scene contains racks of clothes, a changing room, and perhaps a cash register. What did you see when you visualized the microscope or the lion? Many people report seeing not just a single object, but an object within a setting. Perhaps you perceived the microscope sitting on a lab bench or in a laboratory and the lion in a forest, on a savannah, or in a zoo. The point of this demonstration is that our visualizations contain information based on our knowledge of different kinds of scenes. This knowledge of what a given scene typically contains is called a **scene schema,** and the expectations created by scene schemas contribute to our ability to perceive objects and scenes. For example, Palmer's (1975) experiment (Figure 1.13), in which people identified the bread, which fit the kitchen scene, faster than the mailbox, which didn't fit the scene, is an example of the operation of people's scene schemas for "kitchen." In connection with this, how do you think your scene schemas for "airport" might contribute to your interpretation of what is happening in the scene in Figure 3.5?

Although people make use of regularities in the environment to help them perceive, they are often unaware of the specific information they are using. This aspect of perception is similar to what occurs when we use language. Even though we aren't aware of transitional probabilities in language, we use them to help perceive words in a sentence. Even though we may not think about regularities in visual scenes, we use them to help perceive scenes and the objects within scenes.

Bayesian Inference

Two of the ideas we have described—(1) Helmholtz's idea that we resolve the ambiguity of the retinal image by inferring what is most likely, given the situation, and (2) the idea that regularities in the environment provide information we can use to resolve ambiguities—are the starting point for our last approach to object perception: *Bayesian inference* (Geisler, 2008, 2011; Kersten et al., 2004; Yuille & Kersten, 2006).

Bayesian inference was named after Thomas Bayes (1701–1761), who proposed that our estimate of the probability of an outcome is determined by two factors: (1) the **prior probability,** or simply the **prior,** which is our initial belief about the probability of an outcome, and (2) the extent to which the available evidence is consistent with the outcome. This second factor is called the **likelihood** of the outcome.

To illustrate Bayesian inference, let's first consider **Figure 3.24a**, which shows Mary's *priors* for three types of health problems. Mary believes that having a cold or heartburn is likely to occur, but having lung disease is unlikely. With these priors in her head (along with lots of other beliefs about health-related matters), Mary notices that her friend Charles has a bad cough. She guesses that three possible causes could be a cold, heartburn, or lung disease. Looking further into possible causes, she does some research and finds that coughing is often associated with having either a cold or lung disease, but isn't associated with heartburn (**Figure 3.24b**). This additional information, which is the *likelihood*, is combined with Mary's *prior* to produce the conclusion that Charles probably has a cold (**Figure 3.24c**)

➤ **Figure 3.24** These graphs present hypothetical probabilities to illustrate the principle behind Bayesian inference. (a) Mary's beliefs about the relative frequency of having a cold, lung disease, and heartburn. These beliefs are her *priors*. (b) Further data indicate that colds and lung disease are associated with coughing, but heartburn is not. These data contribute to the *likelihood*. (c) Taking the priors and likelihood together results in the conclusion that Charles's cough is probably due to a cold.

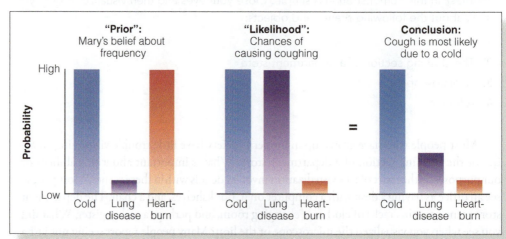

(Tenenbaum et al., 2011). In practice, Bayesian inference involves a mathematical procedure in which the prior is multiplied by the likelihood to determine the probability of the outcome. Thus, people start with a prior and then use additional evidence to update the prior and reach a conclusion (Körding & Wolpert, 2006).

Applying this idea to object perception, let's return to the inverse projection problem from Figure 3.7. Remember that the inverse projection problem occurs because a huge number of possible objects could be associated with a particular image on the retina. So, the problem is how to determine what is "out there" that is causing a particular retinal image. Luckily, we don't have to rely only on the retinal image, because we come to most perceptual situations with prior probabilities based on our past experiences.

One of the *priors* you have in your head is that books are rectangular. Thus, when you look at a book on your desk, your initial belief is that it is likely that the book is rectangular. The *likelihood* that the book is rectangular is provided by additional evidence such as the book's retinal image, combined with your perception of the book's distance and the angle at which you are viewing the book. If this additional evidence is consistent with your prior that the book is rectangular, the likelihood is high and the perception "rectangular" is strengthened. Additional testing by changing your viewing angle and distance can further strengthen the conclusion that the shape is a rectangle. Note that you aren't necessarily conscious of this testing process—it occurs automatically and rapidly. The important point about this process is that while the retinal image is still the starting point for perceiving the shape of the book, adding the person's prior beliefs reduces the possible shapes that could be causing that image.

What Bayesian inference does is to restate Helmholtz's idea—that we perceive what is most likely to have created the stimulation we have received—in terms of probabilities. It isn't always easy to specify these probabilities, particularly when considering complex perceptions. However, because Bayesian inference provides a specific procedure for determining what might be out there, researchers have used it to develop computer-vision systems that can apply knowledge about the environment to more accurately translate the pattern of stimulation on their sensors into conclusions about the environment. (Also see Goldreich & Tong, 2013, for an example of how Bayesian inference has been applied to tactile perception.)

Comparing the Four Approaches

Now that we have described four conceptions of object perception (Helmholtz's unconscious inference, the Gestalt laws of organization, regularities in the environment, and Bayesian inference), here's a question: Which one is different from the other three? After you've figured out your answer, look at the bottom of the page.

The approaches of Helmholtz, regularities, and Bayes all have in common the idea that we use data about the environment, gathered through our past experiences in perceiving, to determine what is out there. Top-down processing is therefore an important part of these approaches.

The Gestalt psychologists, in contrast, emphasized the idea that the principles of organization are built in. They acknowledged that perception is affected by experience but argued that built-in principles can override experience, thereby assigning bottom-up processing a central role in perception. The Gestalt psychologist Max Wertheimer (1912) provided the following example to illustrate how built-in principles could override experience: Most people recognize **Figure 3.25a** as *W* and *M* based on their past experience with these letters. However, when the letters are arranged as in **Figure 3.25b**, most people see two uprights plus a

Answer: The Gestalt approach.

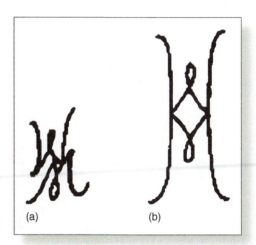

➤ **Figure 3.25** (a) W on top of M. (b) When combined, a new pattern emerges, overriding the meaningful letters.

(Source: From M. Wertheimer, 1912)

▶ **Figure 3.26** A usual occurrence in the environment: Objects (the men's legs) are partially hidden by another object (the grey boards). In this example, the men's legs continue in a straight line and are the same color above and below the boards, so it is highly likely that they continue behind the boards.

pattern between them. The uprights, which are created by the principle of good continuation, are the dominant perception and override the effects of past experience we have had with *W*s and *M*s.

Although the Gestalt psychologists deemphasized experience, using arguments like the preceding one, modern psychologists have pointed out that the laws of organization could, in fact, have been created by experience. For example, it is possible that the principle of good continuation has been determined by experience with the environment. Consider the scene in **Figure 3.26**. From years of experience in seeing objects that are partially covered by other objects, we know that when two visible parts of an object (like the men's legs) have the same color (principle of similarity) and are "lined up" (principle of good continuation), they belong to the same object and extend behind whatever is blocking it. Thus, one way to look at the Gestalt principles is that they describe the operating characteristics of the human perceptual system, *which happen to be determined at least partially by experience.* In the next section, we will consider physiological evidence that experiencing certain stimuli over and over can actually shape the way neurons respond.

TEST YOURSELF 3.2

1. Describe Helmholtz's theory of unconscious inference. What is the likelihood principle?
2. Describe the Gestalt approach to perception, focusing on the principles of organization. How do these principles originate, according to the Gestalt psychologists?
3. What are regularities of the environment, and how do they influence perception? Distinguish between physical regularities and semantic regularities. What is a scene schema?
4. Describe Bayesian inference in terms of how it would explain the "coughing" example and the inverse projection problem.
5. How does the Gestalt approach differ from the other three? How do modern psychologists explain the relation between experience and the principles of organization?

Neurons and Knowledge About the Environment

We will now follow up on the idea that experience can shape the way neurons respond. Our starting point is the finding that there are more neurons in the animal and human visual cortex that respond to horizontal and vertical orientations than to oblique (slanted) orientations.

Neurons That Respond to Horizontals and Verticals

When we described physical regularities in the environment, we mentioned that horizontals and verticals are common features of the environment (Figure 3.22), and behavioral experiments have shown that people are more sensitive to these orientations than to other orientations that are not as common (the *oblique effect*; see page 74). It is not a coincidence, therefore, that when researchers have recorded the activity of single neurons in the visual cortex of monkeys and ferrets, they have found more neurons that respond best to horizontals and verticals than neurons that respond best to oblique orientations (Coppola et al., 1998; DeValois et al., 1982). Evidence from brain-scanning experiments suggests that this occurs in humans as well (Furmanski & Engel, 2000).

Why are there more neurons that respond to horizontals and verticals? One possible answer is based on the **theory of natural selection**, which states that characteristics that enhance an animal's ability to survive, and therefore reproduce, will be passed on to future generations. Through the process of evolution, organisms whose visual systems contained neurons that fired to important things in the environment (such as verticals and horizontals, which occur frequently in the forest, for example) would be more likely to survive and pass on an enhanced ability to sense verticals and horizontals than would an organism with a visual system that did not contain these specialized neurons. Through this evolutionary process, the visual system may have been shaped to contain neurons that respond to things that are found frequently in the environment.

Although there is no question that perceptual functioning has been shaped by evolution, there is also a great deal of evidence that *learning* can shape the response properties of neurons through the process of *experience-dependent plasticity* that we introduced in Chapter 2 (page 34).

Experience-Dependent Plasticity

In Chapter 2, we described Blakemore and Cooper's (1970) experiment in which they showed that rearing cats in horizontal or vertical environments can cause neurons in the cat's cortex to fire preferentially to horizontal or vertical stimuli. This shaping of neural responding by experience, which is called *experience-dependent plasticity*, provides evidence that experience can shape the nervous system.

Experience-dependent plasticity has also been demonstrated in humans using the brain imaging technique of fMRI (see Method: Brain Imaging, page 41). The starting point for this research is the finding that there is an area in the temporal lobe called the fusiform face area (FFA) that contains many neurons that respond best to faces (see Chapter 2, page 42). Isabel Gauthier and coworkers (1999) showed that experience-dependent plasticity may play a role in determining these neurons' response to faces by measuring the level of activity in the FFA in response to faces and also to objects called Greebles (**Figure 3.27a**). Greebles are families of computer-generated "beings" that all have the same basic configuration but differ in the shapes of their parts (just like faces). The left pair of bars in **Figure 3.27b** show that for "Greeble novices" (people who have had little experience in perceiving Greebles), the faces cause more FFA activity than the Greebles.

Gauthier then gave her subjects extensive training over a 4-day period in "Greeble recognition." These training sessions, which required that each Greeble be labeled with a specific name, turned the participants into "Greeble experts." The right bars in Figure 3.27b show that after the training, the FFA responded almost as well to Greebles as to faces. Apparently, the FFA contains neurons that respond not just to faces but to other complex objects as well. The particular objects to which the neurons respond best are established by experience with the objects. In fact, Gauthier has also shown that neurons in the FFA

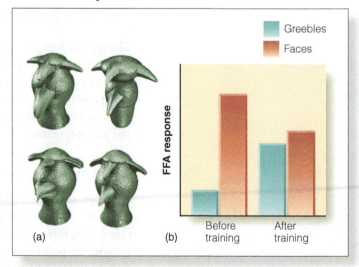

➤ **Figure 3.27** (a) Greeble stimuli used by Gauthier. Participants were trained to name each different Greeble. (b) Magnitude of FFA responses to faces and Greebles before and after Greeble training.

(Source: Based on I. Gauthier et al., 1999)

of people who are experts in recognizing cars and birds respond well not only to human faces but to cars (for the car experts) and to birds (for the bird experts) (Gauthier et al., 2000). Just as rearing kittens in a vertical environment increased the number of neurons that responded to verticals, training humans to recognize Greebles, cars, or birds causes the FFA to respond more strongly to these objects. These results support the idea that neurons in the FFA respond strongly to faces because we have a lifetime of experience perceiving faces.

These demonstrations of experience-dependent plasticity in kittens and humans show that the brain's functioning can be "tuned" to operate best within a specific environment. Thus, continued exposure to things that occur regularly in the environment can cause neurons to become adapted to respond best to these regularities. Looked at in this way, it is not unreasonable to say that neurons can reflect knowledge about properties of the environment.

We have come a long way from thinking about perception as something that happens automatically in response to activation of sensory receptors. We've seen that perception is the outcome of an interaction between bottom-up information, which flows from receptors to brain, and top-down information, which usually involves knowledge about the environment or expectations related to the situation.

At this point in our description of perception, how would you answer the question: "What is the purpose of perception?" One possible answer is that the purpose of perception is to create our awareness of what is happening in the environment, as when we see objects in scenes or we perceive words in a conversation. But it becomes obvious that this answer doesn't go far enough, when we ask, *why* it is important that we are able to experience objects in scenes and words in conversations?

The answer to that question is that an important purpose of perception is to enable us to interact with the environment. The key word here is *interact*, because interaction implies taking action. We are taking action when we pick something up, when we walk across campus, when we have an interaction with someone we are talking with. Interactions such as these are essential for accomplishing what we want to accomplish, and often are essential for our very survival. We end this chapter by considering the connection between perception and action, first by considering behavior and then physiology.

▶ Perception and Action: Behavior

The approach to perception we have described so far could be called the "sitting in a chair" approach to studying perception, because most of the situations we have described could occur as a person sits in a chair viewing various stimuli. In fact, that is probably what you are doing as you read this book—reading words, looking at pictures, doing "demonstrations," all while sitting still. We will now consider how movement helps us perceive, and how action and perception interact.

Movement Facilitates Perception

Although movement adds a complexity to perception that isn't there when we are sitting in one place, movement also helps us perceive objects in the environment more accurately. One reason this occurs is that moving reveals aspects of objects that are not apparent from a single viewpoint. For example, consider the "horse" in **Figure 3.28**. From one viewpoint, this object looks like a metal sculpture of a fairly normal horse (**Figure 3.28a**). However, walking around the horse reveals that it isn't as normal as it first appeared (**Figures 3.28b** and **3.28c**). Thus, seeing an object from different viewpoints provides added information that results in more accurate perception, especially for objects that are out of the ordinary, such as the distorted horse.

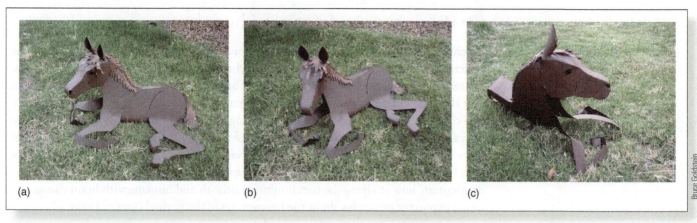

(a)   (b)   (c)

Bruce Goldstein

➤ **Figure 3.28** Three views of a "horse." Moving around an object can reveal its true shape.

The Interaction of Perception and Action

Our concern with movement extends beyond noting that it helps us perceive objects by revealing additional information about them. Movement is also important because of the coordination that is continually occurring between perceiving stimuli and taking action toward these stimuli. Consider, for example, what happens when Crystal, resting in the coffee shop after her run, reaches out to pick up her cup of coffee (**Figure 3.29**). She first identifies the coffee cup among the flowers and other objects on the table (**Figure 3.29a**). Once the coffee cup is perceived, she reaches for it, taking into account its location on the table (**Figure 3.29b**). As she reaches, avoiding the flowers, she positions her fingers to grasp the cup, taking into account her perception of the cup's handle (**Figure 3.29c**); then she lifts the cup with just the right amount of force, taking into account her estimate of how heavy it is based on her perception of its fullness. This simple action requires continually perceiving the position of the cup, and of her hand and fingers relative to the cup, while calibrating her actions in order to accurately grasp the cup and then pick it up without spilling any coffee (Goodale, 2010). All this just to pick up a cup of coffee! What's amazing about this sequence is that it happens almost automatically, without much effort at all. But as with everything else about perception, this ease and apparent simplicity are achieved with the aid of complex underlying mechanisms. We will now describe the physiology behind these mechanisms.

(a) Perceive cup   (b) Reach for cup   (c) Grasp cup

➤ **Figure 3.29** Picking up a cup of coffee: (a) perceiving and recognizing the cup; (b) reaching for it; (c) grasping and picking it up. This action involves coordination between perceiving and action that is carried out by two separate streams in the brain, as described in the text.

Perception and Action: Physiology

Psychologists have long recognized the close connection between perceiving objects and interacting with them, but the details of this link between perception and action have become clearer as a result of physiological research that began in the 1980s. This research has shown that there are two processing streams in the brain—one involved with perceiving objects, and the other involved with locating and taking action toward these objects. This physiological research involves two methods: *brain ablation*—the study of the effect of removing parts of the brain in animals, and *neuropsychology*—the study of the behavior of people with brain damage, which we described in Chapter 2 (see page 38). Both of these methods demonstrate how studying the functioning of animals and humans with brain damage can reveal important principles about the functioning of the normal (intact) brain.

What and Where Streams

In a classic experiment, Leslie Ungerleider and Mortimer Mishkin (1982) studied how removing part of a monkey's brain affected its ability to identify an object and to determine the object's location. This experiment used a technique called **brain ablation**—removing part of the brain.

METHOD   Brain Ablation

The goal of a brain ablation experiment is to determine the function of a particular area of the brain. This is accomplished by first determining an animal's capacity by testing it behaviorally. Most ablation experiments studying perception have used monkeys because of the similarity of the monkey's visual system to that of humans and because monkeys can be trained to demonstrate perceptual capacities such as acuity, color vision, depth perception, and object perception.

Once the animal's perception has been measured, a particular area of the brain is ablated (removed or destroyed), either by surgery or by injecting a chemical in the area to be removed. Ideally, one particular area is removed and the rest of the brain remains intact. After ablation, the monkey is tested to determine which perceptual capacities remain and which have been affected by the ablation. Ablation is also called *lesioning*.

Ungerleider and Mishkin presented monkeys with two tasks: (1) an object discrimination problem and (2) a landmark discrimination problem. In the **object discrimination problem**, a monkey was shown one object, such as a rectangular solid, and was then presented with a two-choice task like the one shown in **Figure 3.30a**, which included the "target" object (the rectangular solid) and another stimulus, such as the triangular solid. If the monkey pushed aside the target object, it received the food reward that was hidden in a well under the object. The **landmark discrimination problem** is shown in **Figure 3.30b**. Here, the tall cylinder is the landmark, which indicates the food well that contains food. The monkey received food if it removed the food well cover closer to the tall cylinder.

In the ablation part of the experiment, part of the temporal lobe was removed in some monkeys. Behavioral testing showed that the object discrimination problem became very difficult for the monkeys when their temporal lobes were removed. This result indicates that the neural pathway that reaches the temporal lobes is responsible for determining an object's identity. Ungerleider and Mishkin therefore called the pathway leading from the striate cortex to the temporal lobe the **what pathway** (**Figure 3.31**).

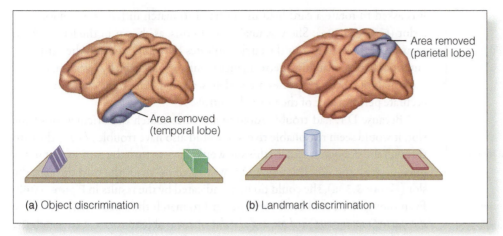

➤ **Figure 3.30** The two types of discrimination tasks used by Ungerleider and Mishkin. (a) Object discrimination: Pick the correct shape. Lesioning the temporal lobe (purple-shaded area) makes this task difficult. (b) Landmark discrimination: Pick the food well closer to the cylinder. Lesioning the parietal lobe makes this task difficult.

(Source: Adapted from M. Mishkin et al., 1983)

Other monkeys, which had their parietal lobes removed, had difficulty solving the landmark discrimination problem. This result indicates that the pathway that leads to the parietal lobe is responsible for determining an object's location. Ungerleider and Mishkin therefore called the pathway leading from the striate cortex to the parietal lobe the **where pathway** (Figure 3.31).

The *what* and *where* pathways are also called the **ventral pathway** (what) and the **dorsal pathway** (where), because the lower part of the brain, where the temporal lobe is located, is the ventral part of the brain, and the upper part of the brain, where the parietal lobe is located, is the dorsal part of the brain. The term *dorsal* refers to the back or the upper surface of an organism; thus, the dorsal fin of a shark or dolphin is the fin on the back that sticks out of the water. **Figure 3.32** shows that for upright, walking animals such as humans, the dorsal part of the brain is the top of the brain. (Picture a person with a dorsal fin sticking out of the top of his or her head!) *Ventral* is the opposite of dorsal, hence it refers to the lower part of the brain.

Applying this idea of *what* and *where* pathways to our example of a person picking up a cup of coffee, the *what* pathway would be involved in the initial perception of the cup and the *where* pathway in determining its location—important information if we are going to carry out the action of reaching for the cup. In the next section, we consider another physiological approach to studying perception and action by describing how studying the behavior of a person with brain damage provides further insights into what is happening in the brain as a person reaches for an object.

➤ **Figure 3.31** The monkey cortex, showing the what, or perception, pathway from the occipital lobe to the temporal lobe and the where, or action, pathway from the occipital lobe to the parietal lobe.

(Source: Adapted from M. Mishkin et al., 1983)

Perception and Action Streams

David Milner and Melvyn Goodale (1995) used the neuropsychological approach (studying the behavior of people with brain damage) to reveal two streams, one involving the temporal lobe and the other involving the parietal lobe. The researchers studied D.F., a 34-year-old woman who suffered damage to her temporal lobe from carbon monoxide poisoning caused by a gas leak in her home. One result of the brain damage was revealed when D.F.

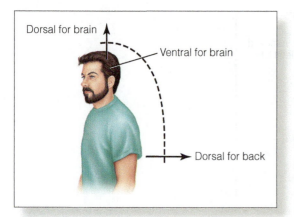

➤ **Figure 3.32** *Dorsal* refers to the back surface of an organism. In upright standing animals such as humans, dorsal refers to the back of the body *and* to the top of the head, as indicated by the arrows and the curved dashed line. Ventral is the opposite of dorsal.

was asked to rotate a card held in her hand to match different orientations of a slot (**Figure 3.33a**). She was unable to do this, as shown in the left circle in **Figure 3.33b**. Each line in the circle indicates how D.F. adjusted the card's orientation. Perfect matching performance would be indicated by a vertical line for each trial, but D.F.'s responses are widely scattered. The right circle shows the accurate performance of the normal controls.

Because D.F. had trouble rotating a card to match the orientation of the slot, it would seem reasonable that she would also have trouble *placing* the card through the slot because to do this she would have to turn the card so that it was lined up with the slot. But when D.F. was asked to "mail" the card through the slot (**Figure 3.34a**), she could do it, as indicated by the results in **Figure 3.34b**. Even though D.F. could not turn the card to match the slot's orientation, *once she started moving the card toward the slot*, she was able to rotate it to match the orientation of the slot. Thus, D.F. performed poorly in the static orientation matching task but did well as soon as *action* was involved (Murphy, Racicot, & Goodale, 1996). Milner and Goodale interpreted D.F.'s behavior as showing that there is one mechanism for judging orientation and another for coordinating vision and action.

Based on these results, Milner and Goodale suggested that the pathway from the visual cortex to the temporal lobe (which was damaged in D.F.'s brain) be called the **perception pathway** and the pathway from the visual cortex to the parietal lobe (which was intact in D.F.'s brain) be called the **action pathway** (also called the *how pathway* because it is associated with how the person takes action). The perception pathway corresponds to the *what* pathway we described in conjunction with the monkey experiments, and the action pathway

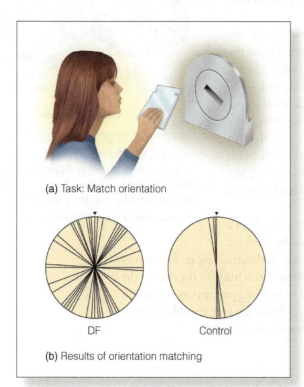

(a) Task: Match orientation

DF   Control

(b) Results of orientation matching

➤ **Figure 3.33** (a) D.F.'s orientation task. A number of different orientations were presented. D.F.'s task was to rotate the card to match each orientation. (b) Results for the orientation task. Correct matches are indicated by vertical lines.

(Source: Based on A. D. Milner & M. A. Goodale, 1995)

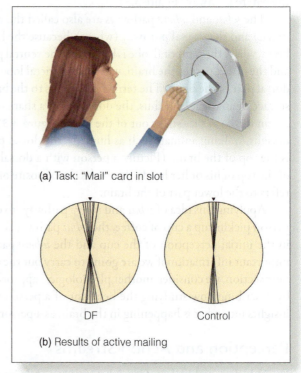

(a) Task: "Mail" card in slot

DF   Control

(b) Results of active mailing

➤ **Figure 3.34** (a) D.F.'s "mailing" task. A number of different orientations were presented. D.F.'s task was to "mail" the card through the slot. (b) Results for the mailing task. Correct orientations are indicated by vertical lines.

(Based on A. D. Milner & M. A. Goodale, 1995)

corresponds to the *where* pathway. Thus, some researchers refer to *what* and *where* pathways and some to *perception* and *action* pathways. Whatever the terminology, the research shows that perception and action are processed in two separate pathways in the brain.

With our knowledge that perception and action involve two separate mechanisms, we can add physiological notations to our description of picking up the coffee cup (Figure 3.29) as follows: The first step is to identify the coffee cup among the vase of flowers and the glass of orange juice on the table (*perception* or *what pathway*). Once the coffee cup is perceived, we reach for the cup (*action* or *where pathway*), taking into account its location on the table. As we reach, avoiding the flowers and orange juice, we position our fingers to grasp the cup (*action pathway*), taking into account our perception of the cup's handle (*perception pathway*), and we lift the cup with just the right amount of force (*action pathway*), taking into account our estimate of how heavy it is based on our perception of the fullness of the cup (*perception pathway*).

Thus, even a simple action like picking up a coffee cup involves a number of areas of the brain, which coordinate their activity to create perceptions and behaviors. A similar coordination between different areas of the brain also occurs for the sense of hearing, so hearing someone call your name and then turning to see who it is activates two separate pathways in the auditory system—one that enables you to hear and identify the sound (the auditory *what* pathway) and another that helps you locate where the sound is coming from (the auditory *where* pathway) (Lomber & Malhotra, 2008).

The discovery of different pathways for perceiving, determining location, and taking action illustrates how studying the physiology of perception has helped broaden our conception far beyond the old "sitting in the chair" approach. Another physiological discovery that has extended our conception of visual perception beyond simply "seeing" is the discovery of mirror neurons.

Mirror Neurons

In 1992, G. di Pelligrino and coworkers were investigating how neurons in the monkey's premotor cortex (**Figure 3.35a**) fired as the monkey performed an action like picking up a piece of food. **Figure 3.35b** shows how a neuron responded when the monkey picked up food from a tray—a result the experimenters had expected. But as sometimes happens in science, they observed something they didn't expect. When one of the experimenters picked up a piece of food while the monkey was watching, the same neuron fired (**Figure 3.35c**). What was so unexpected was that the neurons that fired to observing the experimenter pick up the food were the same ones that had fired earlier when the monkey had picked up the food.

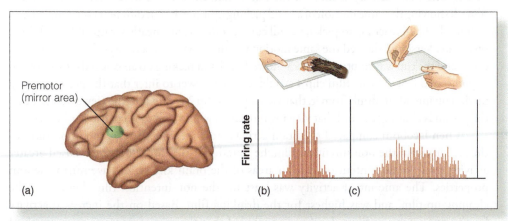

(a)   (b)   (c)

➤ **Figure 3.35** (a) Location of the monkey's premotor cortex. (b) Responses of a mirror neuron when the monkey grasps food on a tray and (c) when the monkey watches the experimenter grasp the food.

(Source: Rizzolatti et al., 2000)

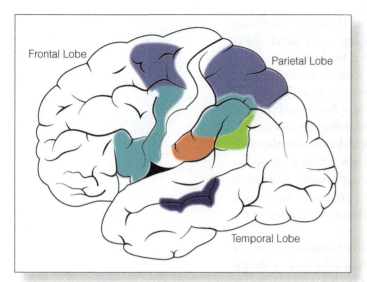

➤ **Figure 3.36** Cortical areas in the human brain associated with the mirror neuron system. Colors indicate the type of actions processed in each region. Turquoise: movement directed toward objects; purple: reaching movements; orange: tool use; green: movements not directed toward objects; blue: upper limb movements.

(Source: Adapted from Cattaneo & Rizzolatti, 2009)

This initial observation, followed by many additional experiments, led to the discovery of **mirror neurons**—neurons that respond both when a monkey observes someone else grasping an object such as food on a tray and when the monkey itself grasps the food (Gallese et al., 1996; Rizzolatti et al., 2006; Rizzolatti & Sinigaglia, 2016). They are called mirror neurons because the neuron's response to watching the experimenter grasp an object is similar to the response that would occur if the monkey were performing the same action. Although you might think that the monkey may have been responding to the anticipation of receiving food, the type of object made little difference. The neurons responded just as well when the monkey observed the experimenter pick up an object that was not food.

At this point, you might be wondering whether mirror neurons are present in the human brain. Some research with humans does suggest that our brains contain mirror neurons. For example, researchers who were using electrodes to record the brain activity in people with epilepsy in order to determine which part of their brains was generating their seizures have recorded activity from neurons with the same mirror properties as those identified in monkeys (Mukamel et al., 2010). Additional work done using fMRI in neurologically normal people has further suggested that these neurons are distributed throughout the brain in a network that has been called the **mirror neuron system** (**Figure 3.36**) (Caspers et al., 2010; Cattaneo & Rizzolatti, 2009; Molenbergs et al., 2012).

What is the purpose of these mirror neurons? One suggestion is that they are involved in determining the *goal* or *intention* behind an action. To understand what this means, let's return to Crystal reaching for her coffee cup. She could be reaching for the cup for a number of reasons. Maybe she intends to drink some coffee, although if we notice that the cup is empty, we might instead decide that she is going to take the cup back to the counter of the coffee shop to get a refill, or if we know that she never drinks more than one cup, we might decide that she is going to place the cup in the used cup bin. Thus, a number of different intentions can be associated with perception of the same action.

What is the evidence that the response of mirror neurons can be influenced by different intentions? Mario Iacoboni and coworkers (2005) did an experiment in which they measured participants' brain activity as they watched short film clips. There were three versions of the film, all showing the same motion of a hand picking up a cup, but in different contexts. Version 1 showed a hand reaching to pick up a full cup of coffee from a neatly set up table, with food on a plate. Version 2 showed the same motion but the cup was on a messy table, the food was eaten, and the cup was empty. Version 3 showed the hand picking up an isolated cup. Iacoboni hypothesized that viewing film clip 1 would lead the viewer to infer that the person picking up the cup intends to drink from it, that viewing film clip 2 would lead the viewer to infer that the person is cleaning up, and that viewing film clip 3 would lead to no particular inference.

When Iacoboni compared the brain activity from viewing the two intention films to the activity from the non-intention film, he found that the intention films caused greater activity than the non-intention film in areas of the brain known to have mirror neuron properties. The amount of activity was least for the non-intention film, higher for the cleaning-up film, and was highest for the drinking film. Based on the increased activity for the two intention films, Iacoboni concluded that the mirror neuron area is involved with understanding the intentions behind the actions shown in the films. He reasoned that if the mirror neurons were just signaling the action of picking up the cup, then a similar response would occur regardless of whether a context surrounding the cup was present.

Mirror neurons, according to Iacoboni, code the "why" of actions and respond differently to different intentions (also see Fogassi et al., 2005 for a similar experiment on a monkey).

If mirror neurons do, in fact, signal intentions, how do they do it? One possibility is that the response of these neurons is determined by the sequence of motor activities that could be *expected* to happen in a particular context (Fogassi et al., 2005; Gallese, 2007). For example, when a person picks up a cup with the intention of drinking, the next expected actions would be to bring the cup to the mouth and then to drink some coffee. However, if the intention is to clean up, the expected action might be to carry the cup over to the sink. According to this idea, mirror neurons that respond to different intentions are responding to the action that is happening *plus* the sequence of actions that is most likely to follow, given the context.

When considered in this way, the operation of mirror neurons shares something with perception in general. Remember Helmholtz's likelihood principle—we perceive the object that is *most likely* to have caused the pattern of stimuli we have received. In the case of mirror neurons, the neuron's firing may be based on the sequence of actions that are *most likely* to occur in a particular context. In both cases the outcome—either a perception or firing of a mirror neuron—depends on knowledge that we bring to a particular situation.

The exact functions of mirror neurons in humans are still being debated, with some researchers assigning mirror neurons a central place in determining intentions (Caggiano et al., 2011; Gazzola et al., 2007; Kilner, 2011; Rizzolatti & Sinigaglia, 2016) and others questioning this idea (Cook et al., 2014; Hickock, 2009). But whatever the exact role of mirror neurons in humans, there is no question that there is some mechanism that extends the role of perception beyond providing information that enables us to take action, to yet another role—inferring why other people are doing what they are doing.

▶ SOMETHING TO CONSIDER: KNOWLEDGE, INFERENCE, AND PREDICTION

"Brains, it has recently been argued, are essentially prediction machines" Clark (2013)

Two terms that have appeared throughout this chapter are *knowledge* and *inference*. Knowledge was the foundation of Helmholtz's theory of unconscious inference, and the basis of the likelihood principle. Inference depends on knowledge. For example, we saw how inference based on knowledge helps resolve the ambiguity of the retinal image and how knowledge of transitional probabilities helps us infer where one word in a conversation ends and the other begins. Knowledge and the inferences that follow are the basis of top-down processing (p. 67).

Another way to think about knowledge and inference is in terms of *prediction*. After all, when we say that a particular retinal image is caused by a book (Figure 3.7), we are making a prediction of what is probably out there. When we say that a briefly presented shape on a kitchen counter is probably a loaf of bread (Figure 1.13), we are making a prediction based on what is likely to be sitting on a kitchen counter. We are making predictions about what is out there constantly, which is the basis of the assertion that "brains . . . . are essentially prediction machines" at the beginning of this section (Clark, 2013).

A hint that prediction extends beyond simply seeing is provided by the **size-weight illusion**: When a person is presented with two similar objects, such as two cubes, that are the same weight but different sizes, the larger one seems lighter when they are lifted together. One explanation for this is that we predict that larger objects will be heavier than smaller objects, because objects of the same type typically get heavier as they get larger (Buckingham et al., 2016; Plaisier & Smeets, 2015). We are therefore surprised when the larger one is lighter than predicted. Just as perception is guided by predictions, so are the actions associated with perceptions.

As it turns out, prediction is a central principle that operates throughout cognition. Here is a preview of a few of the predictions we will encounter in the chapters that follow:

➤ Chapter 4 (Attention)—Prediction guides where we direct our eyes as we scan a scene.

➤ Chapter 7 (Memory)—Our ability to predict what might happen in the future is based on our ability to remember events from the past.

➤ Chapter 11 (Language)—Not only does prediction help us perceive individual words in the speech stream, as we saw in this chapter, but it also helps us understand the meanings of sentences, follow conversations, and understand stories.

➤ Chapter 13 (Thinking)—People sometimes use "rules of thumb" called heuristics to make predictions that help them make decisions or determine solutions to problems.

Although the idea of prediction is nothing new, having been proposed by Helmholtz in the 19th century, it has become an important topic across a number of different areas of cognition.

TEST YOURSELF 3.3

1. What is the oblique effect? Describe how this effect could be caused by evolution and by experience.

2. Describe the interaction between perceiving and taking action, giving a specific example from everyday perception.

3. Describe the Ungerleider and Mishkin experiment. How did they use the procedure of brain ablation to demonstrate *what* and *where* streams in the cortex?

4. Describe how Milner and Goodale's testing of D.F. demonstrated pathways for matching orientation and for combining vision and action. Describe the perception pathway and the action pathway. How do these pathways correspond to Ungerleider and Mishkin's *what* and *where* streams?

5. Describe how the perception and action pathways both play a role in an action such as picking up a cup of coffee.

6. What are mirror neurons? What have some researchers proposed about how mirror neurons might link perception and action?

7. What is the connection among knowledge, inference, and prediction?

CHAPTER SUMMARY

1. The example of Crystal running on the beach and having coffee later illustrates how perception can change based on new information, how perception can be based on principles that are related to past experiences, how perception is a process, and how perception and action are connected.

2. We can easily describe the relation between parts of a city scene, but it is often challenging to indicate the reasoning that led to the description. This illustrates the need to go beyond the pattern of light and dark in a scene to describe the process of perception.

3. Attempts to program computers to recognize objects have shown how difficult it is to program computers to perceive at a level comparable to humans. A few of the difficulties facing computers are (1) the stimulus on the receptors is ambiguous, as demonstrated by the inverse projection problem; (2) objects in a scene can be hidden or blurred; (3) objects look different from different viewpoints; and (4) scenes contain high-level information.

4. Perception starts with bottom-up processing, which involves stimulation of the receptors, creating electrical signals that

reach the visual receiving area of the brain. Perception also involves top-down processing, which is associated with knowledge stored in the brain.

5. Examples of top-down processing are the multiple personalities of a blob and how knowledge of a language makes it possible to perceive individual words. Saffran's experiment has shown that 8-month-old infants are sensitive to transitional probabilities in language.

6. The idea that perception depends on knowledge was proposed by Helmholtz's theory of unconscious inference.

7. The Gestalt approach to perception proposed a number of laws of perceptual organization, which were based on how stimuli usually occur in the environment.

8. Regularities of the environment are characteristics of the environment that occur frequently. We take both physical regularities and semantic regularities into account when perceiving.

9. Bayesian inference is a mathematical procedure for determining what is likely to be "out there"; it takes into account a person's prior beliefs about a perceptual outcome and the likelihood of that outcome based on additional evidence.

10. Of the four approaches to object perception—unconscious inference, Gestalt, regularities, and Bayesian—the Gestalt approach relies more on bottom-up processing than the others. Modern psychologists have suggested a connection between the Gestalt principles and past experience.

11. One of the basic operating principles of the brain is that it contains some neurons that respond best to things that occur regularly in the environment.

12. Experience-dependent plasticity is one of the mechanisms responsible for creating neurons that are tuned to respond to specific things in the environment. The experiments in which people's brain activity was measured as they learned about Greebles supports this idea. This was also illustrated in the experiment described in Chapter 2 in which kittens were reared in vertical or horizontal environments.

13. Perceiving and taking action are linked. Movement of an observer relative to an object provides information about the object. Also, there is a constant coordination between perceiving an object (such as a cup) and taking action toward the object (such as picking up the cup).

14. Research involving brain ablation in monkeys and neuropsychological studies of the behavior of people with brain damage have revealed two processing pathways in the cortex—a pathway from the occipital lobe to the temporal lobe responsible for perceiving objects, and a pathway from the occipital lobe to the parietal lobe responsible for controlling actions toward objects. These pathways work together to coordinate perception and action.

15. Mirror neurons are neurons that fire both when a monkey or person takes an action, like picking up a piece of food, and when they observe the same action being carried out by someone else. It has been proposed that one function of mirror neurons is to provide information about the goals or intentions behind other people's actions.

16. Prediction, which is closely related to knowledge and inference, is a mechanism that is involved in perception, attention, understanding language, making predictions about future events, and thinking.

THINK ABOUT IT

1. Describe a situation in which you initially thought you saw or heard something but then realized that your initial perception was in error. (Two examples: misperceiving an object under low-visibility conditions; mishearing song lyrics.) What were the roles of bottom-up and top-down processing in this situation of first having an incorrect perception and then realizing what was actually there?

2. Look at the picture in **Figure 3.37**. Is this a huge giant's hand getting ready to pick up a horse, a normal-size hand picking up a tiny plastic horse, or something else? Explain, based on some of the things we take into account in addition to the image that this scene creates on the retina, why it is unlikely that this picture shows either a giant hand or a tiny horse. How does your answer relate to top-down processing?

3. In the section on experience-dependent plasticity, it was stated that neurons can reflect knowledge about properties of the environment. Would it be valid to suggest that the response of these neurons represents top-down processing? Why or why not?

4. Try observing the world as though there were no such thing as top-down processing. For example, without the aid of

Kristin Durr

➤ **Figure 3.37** Is a giant hand about to pick up the horse?

top-down processing, seeing a restaurant's restroom sign that says "Employees must wash hands" could be taken to mean that we should wait for an employee to wash our hands! If you try this exercise, be warned that it is extremely difficult because top-down processing is so pervasive in our environment that we usually take it for granted.

KEY TERMS

Action pathway, 84

Apparent movement, 71

Bayesian inference, 76

Bottom-up processing, 67

Brain ablation, 82

Direct pathway model, 00

Dorsal pathway, 83

Gestalt psychologists, 71

Inverse projection problem, 65

Law of pragnanz, 72

Landmark discrimination problem, 82

Light-from-above assumption, 74

Likelihood, 76

Likelihood principle, 70

Mirror neuron, 85

Mirror neuron system, 86

Object discrimination problem, 82

Oblique effect, 74

Perception, 60

Perception pathway, 84

Physical regularities, 74

Placebo, 00

Placebo effect, 00

Principle of good continuation, 72

Principle of good figure, 72

Principle of similarity, 73

Principle of simplicity, 72

Principles of perceptual organization, 71

Prior, 76

Prior probability, 76

Regularities in the environment, 74

Scene schema, 76

Semantic regularities, 74

Size-weight illusion, 87

Speech segmentation, 68

Statistical learning, 68

Theory of natural selection, 79

Top-down processing, 67

Transitional probabilities, 68

Unconscious inference, 70

Ventral pathway, 83

Viewpoint invariance, 66

What pathway, 82

Where pathway, 83

COGLAB EXPERIMENTS   Numbers in parentheses refer to the experiment number in CogLab.

Signal Detection (*1*)

Apparent Motion (*3*)

Garner Interference: Integral
   Dimensions (*4*)

Garner Interference: Separable
   Dimensions (*5*)

Müller-Lyer Illusion (*6*)

Blind Spot (*14*)

Metacontrast Masking (*16*)

Categorical Perception:
   Discrimination (*39*)

Categorical Perception:
   Identification (*40*)

Statistical Learning (*49*)

Answers for **Figure 3.9**

Faces from left to right: Will Smith, Taylor Swift, Barack Obama, Hillary Clinton, Jackie Chan, Ben Affleck, Oprah Winfrey

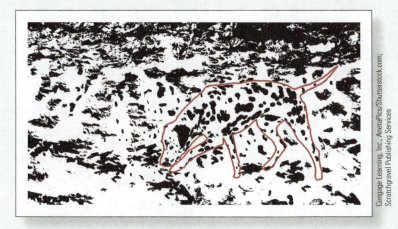

Cengage Learning, Inc., AnetaPics/Shutterstock.com; Scratchgravel Publishing Services

➤ **Figure 3.38** The Dalmatian in Figure 3.17.

It's a rainy day in Barcelona, and the photographer, looking down from a window high above, freezes the umbrellas of three people crossing the street. When you looked at this picture, the umbrellas or the white lines of the crosswalk probably grabbed your attention first. But if you had been observing this scene as it was happening, movement would also have influenced your attention. You might have focused on how the umbrellas were moving relative to one another, or you might have tracked the movement of one of the umbrellas, because of its color, or direction or speed of movement. And what's that yellow thing on the sidewalk? Curiosity might lead you to look more closely at that object. Every time you open your eyes and look out at a scene, attention is one of the major processes determining what you experience, and what you take away from that experience.

Attention

4

▶ Is it possible to focus attention on just one thing, even when there are many other things going on at the same time? (95)

▶ Under what conditions can we pay attention to more than one thing at a time? (110)

▶ What does attention research tell us about the effect of talking on cell phones while driving a car? (112)

▶ Is it true that we are not paying attention to a large fraction of the things happening in our environment? (115)

Roger, sitting in the library, is attempting to do his math homework when some people at the next table start talking. He is annoyed because people aren't supposed to talk in the library, but he is so focused on the math problems that it doesn't distract him (**Figure 4.1a**). However, a little later, when he decides to take a break from his math homework and play an easy game on his cell phone, he does find their conversation distracting (**Figure 4.1b**). "Interesting," he thinks. "Their talking didn't bother me when I was doing the math problems."

Deciding to stop resisting his listening to the conversation, Roger begins to consciously eavesdrop while continuing to play his cell phone game (**Figure 4.1c**). But just as he is beginning to figure out what the couple is talking about, his attention is captured by a loud noise and commotion from across the room, where it appears a book cart has overturned, scattering books on the floor. As he notices that one person seems upset and others are gathering up the books, he looks from one person to another and decides he doesn't know any of them (**Figure 4.1d**).

➤ **Figure 4.1** Roger's adventures with attention. (a) Selective attention: doing math problems while not being distracted by people talking. (b) Distraction: playing a game but being distracted by the people talking. (c) Divided attention: playing the game while listening in on the conversation. (d) Attentional capture and scanning: a noise attracts his attention, and he scans the scene to figure out what is happening.

Roger's experiences illustrate different aspects of **attention**—the ability to focus on specific stimuli or locations. His attempt to focus on his math homework while ignoring the people talking is an example of **selective attention**—attending to one thing while ignoring others. The way the conversation in the library interfered with his cell phone game is an example of **distraction**—one stimulus interfering with the processing of another stimulus. When Roger decides to listen in on the conversation while simultaneously playing the game, he is displaying **divided attention**—paying attention to more than one thing at a time. Later, his eavesdropping is interrupted by the noise of the overturned book cart, an example of **attentional capture**—a rapid shifting of attention usually caused by a stimulus such as a loud noise, bright light, or sudden movement. Finally, Roger's attempt to identify the people across the room, looking from one person's face to another, is an example of **visual scanning**—movements of the eyes from one location or object to another.

With all of these different aspects of attention in mind, let's return to William James's (1890) definition of attention, which we introduced in Chapter 1:

> Millions of items … are present to my senses which never properly enter my experience. Why? Because they have no interest for me. My experience is what I agree to attend to…. Everyone knows what attention is. It is the taking possession by the mind, in clear and vivid form, of one out of what seem several simultaneously possible objects or trains of thought…. It implies withdrawal from some things in order to deal effectively with others.

Although this definition is considered a classic, and certainly does capture a central characteristic of attention—withdrawal from some things in order to deal effectively with others—we can now see that it doesn't capture the diversity of phenomena that are associated with attention. Attention, as it turns out, is not one thing. There are many different aspects of attention, which have been studied using different approaches.

This chapter, therefore, consists of a number of sections, each of which is about a different aspect of attention. We begin with a little history, because early research on attention helped establish the information processing approach to cognition, which became the central focus of the new field of cognitive psychology.

▶ Attention as Information Processing

Modern research on attention began in the 1950s with the introduction of Broadbent's filter model of attention.

Broadbent's Filter Model of Attention

Broadbent's **filter model of attention**, which we introduced in Chapter 1 (page 14), was designed to explain the results of an experiment done by Colin Cherry (1953). Cherry studied attention using a technique called **dichotic listening**, where *dichotic* refers to presenting different stimuli to the left and right ears. The participant's task in this experiment is to focus on the message in one ear, called the attended ear, and to repeat what he or she is hearing out loud. This procedure of repeating the words as they are heard is called **shadowing** (Figure 4.2).

Cherry found that although his participants could easily shadow a spoken message presented to the attended ear, and they could report whether the unattended message was spoken by a male or female, they couldn't report what was being said in the unattended ear. Other dichotic listening experiments confirmed that people are not aware of most of the information being presented to the unattended ear. For example, Neville Moray (1959) showed that participants were unaware of a word that had

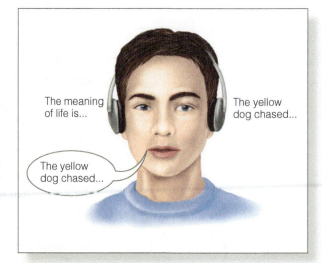

The meaning of life is...

The yellow dog chased...

The yellow dog chased...

▶ **Figure 4.2** In the shadowing procedure, which involves dichotic listening, a person repeats out loud the words that they have just heard. This ensures that participants are focusing their attention on the attended message.

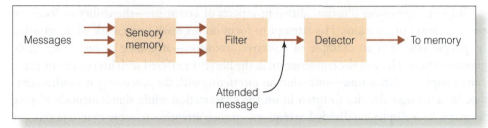

> Figure 4.3 Flow diagram of Broadbent's filter model of attention.

been repeated 35 times in the unattended ear. The ability to focus on one stimulus while filtering out other stimuli has been called the **cocktail party effect**, because at noisy parties people are able to focus on what one person is saying even if there are many conversations happening at the same time.

Based on results such as these, Donald Broadbent (1958) created a model of attention designed to explain how it is possible to focus on one message and why information isn't taken in from the other message. This model, which introduced the flow diagram to cognitive psychology (see page 14), proposed that information passes through the following stages (**Figure 4.3**):

> ➤ *Sensory memory* holds all of the incoming information for a fraction of a second and then transfers all of it to the filter. (We will discuss sensory memory in Chapter 5.)

> ➤ The **filter** identifies the message that is being attended to based on its physical characteristics—things like the speaker's tone of voice, pitch, speed of talking, and accent—and lets only this attended message pass through to the detector in the next stage. All of the other messages are filtered out.

> ➤ The **detector** processes the information from the attended message to determine higher-level characteristics of the message, such as its meaning. Because only the important, attended information has been let through the filter, the detector processes all of the information that enters it.

> ➤ The output of the detector is sent to *short-term memory*, which holds information for 10–15 seconds and also transfers information into *long-term memory*, which can hold information indefinitely. We will describe short- and long-term memory in Chapters 5–8.

Broadbent's model is called an **early selection model** because the filter eliminates the unattended information right at the beginning of the flow of information.

Modifying Broadbent's Model: More Early Selection Models

The beauty of Broadbent's filter model of attention was that it provided testable predictions about selective attention, which stimulated further research. One prediction is that since all of the unattended messages are filtered out, we should not be conscious of information in the unattended messages. To test this idea, Neville Moray (1959) did a dichotic listening experiment in which his participants were instructed to shadow the message presented to one ear and to ignore the message presented to the other ear. But when Moray presented the listener's name to the unattended ear, about a third of the participants detected it (also see Wood & Cowan, 1995).

Moray's participants had recognized their names even though, according to Broadbent's theory, the filter is supposed to let through only one message, based on its physical characteristics. Clearly, the person's name had not been filtered out, and, most important, it had been analyzed enough to determine its meaning. You may have had an experience similar to Moray's laboratory demonstration if, as you were talking to someone in a noisy room, you suddenly heard someone else say your name.

Following Moray's lead, other experimenters showed that information presented to the unattended ear is processed enough to provide the listener with some awareness of its meaning. For example, J. A. Gray and A. I. Wedderburn (1960), while undergraduates at the University of Oxford, did the following experiment, sometimes called the "Dear Aunt Jane" experiment. As in Cherry's dichotic listening experiment, the participants were told to shadow the message presented to one ear. As you can see in **Figure 4.4**, the attended (shadowed) ear received the message "Dear 7 Jane," and the unattended ear received the message "9 Aunt 6." However, rather than reporting the "Dear 7 Jane" message that was presented to the attended ear, participants reported hearing "Dear Aunt Jane."

Switching to the unattended channel to say "Aunt" means that the participant's attention had jumped from one ear to the other and then back again. This occurred because they were taking the meaning of the words into account. (An example of top-down processing! See page 67.)

Because of results such as these, Anne Treisman (1964) proposed a modification of Broadbent's model. Treisman proposed that selection occurs in two stages, and she replaced Broadbent's filter with an attenuator (**Figure 4.5**). The **attenuator** analyzes the incoming message in terms of (1) its physical characteristics—whether it is high-pitched or low-pitched, fast or slow; (2) its language—how the message groups into syllables or words; and (3) its meaning—how sequences of words create meaningful phrases. Note that the attenuator represents a process and is not identified with a specific brain structure.

Treisman's idea that the information in the channel is selected is similar to what Broadbent proposed, but in Treisman's **attenuation model of attention**, language and meaning can also be used to separate the messages. However, Treisman proposed that the analysis of the message proceeds only as far as is necessary to identify the attended message. For example, if there are two messages, one in a male voice and one in a female voice, then analysis at the physical level (which Broadbent emphasized) is adequate to separate the low-pitched male voice from the higher-pitched female voice. If, however, the voices are similar, then it might be necessary to use meaning to separate the two messages.

According to Treisman's model, once the attended and unattended messages have been identified, both messages pass through the attenuator, but the attended message emerges at full strength and the unattended messages are attenuated—they are still present but are weaker than the attended message. Because at least some of the unattended message gets through the attenuator, Treisman's model has been called a "leaky filter" model.

The final output of the system is determined in the second stage, when the message is analyzed by the dictionary unit. The **dictionary unit** contains words, stored in memory, each of which has a threshold for being activated (**Figure 4.6**). A threshold is the smallest signal strength that can barely be detected. Thus, a word with a low threshold might be detected even when it is presented softly or is obscured by other words.

According to Treisman, words that are common or especially important, such as the listener's name, have low thresholds, so even a weak signal in the unattended channel can activate that word, and

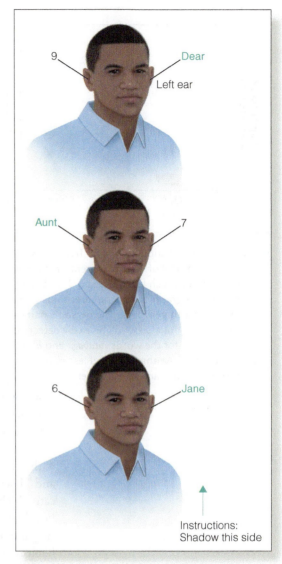

➤ **Figure 4.4** In Gray and Wedderburn's (1960) "Dear Aunt Jane" experiment, participants were told to shadow the message presented to the left ear. But they reported hearing the message "Dear Aunt Jane," which starts in the left ear, jumps to the right ear, and then goes back to the left ear.

Unless otherwise noted all items © Cengage

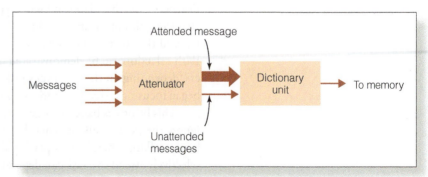

➤ **Figure 4.5** Flow diagram for Treisman's attenuation model of selective attention.

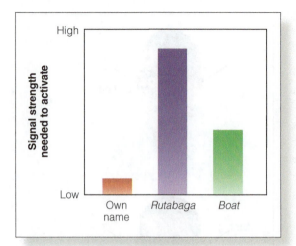

> **Figure 4.6** The dictionary unit of Treisman's attenuation model of selective attention contains words, each of which has a threshold for being detected. This graph shows the thresholds that might exist for three words. The person's name has a low threshold, so it will be easily detected. The thresholds for the words *rutabaga* and *boat* are higher, because they are used less or are less important to this particular listener.

we hear our name from across the room. Uncommon words or words that are unimportant to the listener have higher thresholds, so it takes the strong signal of the attended message to activate these words. Thus, according to Treisman, the attended message gets through, plus some parts of the weaker, unattended messages.

The research we have been describing so far was extremely important, not only because it defined some of the basic phenomena of attention but also because it demonstrated how an aspect of cognition could be conceptualized as a problem of information processing, in which information from the environment passes through various stages of processing. Like Broadbent's model, Treisman's is called an early selection model because it proposes a filter that operates at an early stage in the flow of information. Other models propose that selection can occur later.

A Late Selection Model

Other theories were proposed to take into account the results of experiments showing that messages can be selected at a later stage of processing, based primarily on their meaning. For example, in an experiment by Donald MacKay (1973), a participant listened to an ambiguous sentence, such as "They were throwing stones at the bank," that could be interpreted in more than one way. (In this example, "bank" can refer to a riverbank or to a financial institution.) These ambiguous sentences were presented to the attended ear while biasing words were presented to the other, unattended ear. For example, as the participant was shadowing "They were throwing stones at the bank," either the word "river" or the word "money" was presented to the unattended ear.

After hearing a number of ambiguous sentences, the participants were presented with pairs of sentences, such as "They threw stones toward the side of the river yesterday" and "They threw stones at the savings and loan association yesterday," and asked to indicate which of these two sentences was closest in meaning to one of the sentences they had heard previously. MacKay found that the meaning of the biasing word affected the participants' choice. For example, if the biasing word was "money," participants were more likely to pick the second sentence. This occurred even though participants reported that they were unaware of the biasing words that had been presented to the unattended ear.

MacKay proposed that because the meaning of the word *river* or *money* was affecting the participants' judgments, the word must have been processed to the level of meaning even though it was unattended. Results such as this led MacKay and other theorists to develop **late selection models of attention**, which proposed that most of the incoming information is processed to the level of meaning before the message to be further processed is selected (Deutsch & Deutsch, 1963; Norman, 1968).

The attention research we have been describing has focused on when selective attention occurs (early or late) and what types of information are used for the selection (physical characteristics or meaning). But as research in selective attention progressed, researchers realized that there is no one answer to what has been called the "early–late" controversy. Early selection can be demonstrated under some conditions and later selection under others, depending on the observer's task and the type of stimuli presented. Thus, researchers began focusing instead on understanding the many different factors that control attention.

This brings us back to Roger's experience in the library. Remember that he was able to ignore the people talking when he was doing his math homework but became distracted by the talking when he was playing the easy cell phone game. The idea that the ability to selectively attend to a task can depend both on the distracting stimulus and on the nature of the task has been studied by Nilli Lavie (2010), who introduced the concepts of *processing capacity* and *perceptual load*.

▶ Processing Capacity and Perceptual Load

How do people ignore distracting stimuli when they are trying to focus their attention on a task? Lavie answers this question by considering two factors: (1) **processing capacity**, which refers to the amount of information people can handle and sets a limit on their ability to process incoming information; and (2) **perceptual load**, which is related to the difficulty of a task. Some tasks, especially easy, well-practiced ones, have low perceptual loads; these **low-load tasks** use up only a small amount of the person's processing capacity. Tasks that are difficult and perhaps not as well practiced are **high-load tasks** and use more of a person's processing capacity.

Sophie Forster and Lavie (2008) studied the role of processing capacity and perceptual load in determining distraction by presenting displays like the one in **Figure 4.7a**. The participants' task was to respond as quickly as possible when they identified a target, either X or N. Participants pressed one key if they saw the X and another key if they saw the N. This task is easy for displays like the one on the left in Figure 4.7a, in which the target is surrounded by just one type of letter, like the small o's. However, the task becomes harder when the target is surrounded by different letters, as in the display on the right. This difference is reflected in the reaction times, with the hard task resulting in longer reaction times than the easy task. However, when a task-irrelevant stimulus—like the unrelated cartoon character shown in **Figure 4.7b**—is flashed below the display, responding slows for the easy task more than for the hard task.

Lavie explains results such as the ones in Figure 4.7b in terms of her **load theory of attention**, diagrammed in **Figure 4.8**, in which the circle represents the person's processing capacity and the shading represents the portion that is used up by a task. **Figure 4.8a** shows that with the low-load task, there is still processing capacity left. This means that resources are available to process the task-irrelevant stimulus (like the cartoon character), and even

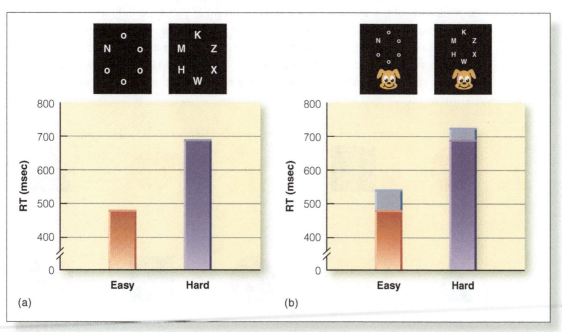

(a)   (b)

▶ **Figure 4.7** The task in Forster and Lavie's (2008) experiment was to indicate the identity of a target (X or N) as quickly as possible in displays like the ones shown here. (a) The reaction time for the easy condition like the display on the left, in which the target is accompanied by small o's, is faster than the reaction time for the hard condition, in which the target is accompanied by other letters. (b) Flashing a distracting cartoon character near the display increases the reaction time for the easy task more than it does for the hard task. The increase for each task is indicated by the gray extensions of the bars.

(Source: Adapted from S. Forster & N. Lavie, Failures to ignore entirely irrelevant distractors: The role of load, *Journal of Experimental Psychology: Applied*, 14 , 73–83, 2008.)

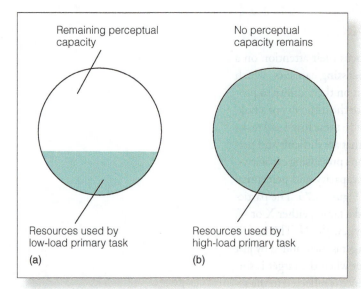

Remaining perceptual capacity

No perceptual capacity remains

Resources used by low-load primary task

Resources used by high-load primary task

(a)

(b)

➤ **Figure 4.8** The load theory of attention: (a) Low-load tasks that use few cognitive resources may leave resources available for processing unattended task-irrelevant stimuli, whereas (b) high-load tasks that use all of a person's cognitive resources don't leave any resources to process unattended task-irrelevant stimuli.

though the person was told not to pay attention to the task-irrelevant stimulus, it gets processed and slows down responding.

Figure 4.8b shows a situation in which all of a person's processing capacity is being used for a high-load task, such as the hard task in the experiment. When this occurs, no resources remain to process other stimuli, so irrelevant stimuli can't be processed and they have little effect on performance of the task. Thus, if you are carrying out a hard, high-load task, no processing capacity remains, and you are less likely to be distracted (as Roger found when he was focusing on the hard math problems). However, if you are carrying out an easy, low-load task, the processing capacity that remains is available to process task-irrelevant stimuli (as Roger found out when he was distracted from his easy cell phone game).

The ability to ignore task-irrelevant stimuli is a function not only of the load of the task you are trying to do but also of how powerful the task-irrelevant stimulus is. For example, while Roger was able to ignore the conversation in the library while he was focused on the difficult math problems, a loud siren, indicating fire, would probably attract his attention. An example of a situation in which task-irrelevant stimuli are difficult to ignore is provided by the *Stroop effect*, described in the following demonstration.

DEMONSTRATION The Stroop Effect

Look at **Figure 4.9**. Your task is to name, as quickly as possible, the color of ink used to print each of the shapes. For example, starting in the upper-left corner and going across, you would say, "red, blue, ..." and so on. Time yourself (or a friend you have enlisted to do this task), and determine how many seconds it takes to report the colors of all the shapes. Then repeat the same task for **Figure 4.10**, remembering that your task is to specify the color of the ink, not the color name that is spelled out.

➤ **Figure 4.9** Name the color of the ink used to print these shapes.

YELLOW	RED	BLUE	PURPLE	GREEN
ORANGE	YELLOW	GREEN	BLUE	RED
GREEN	PURPLE	ORANGE	RED	BLUE

➤ **Figure 4.10** Name the color of the ink used to print these words.

If you found it harder to name the colors of the words than the colors of the shapes, then you were experiencing the **Stroop effect**, which was first described by J. R. Stroop in 1935. This effect occurs because the names of the words cause a competing response and therefore slow responding to the target—the color of the ink. In the Stroop effect, the task-irrelevant stimuli are extremely powerful, because reading words is highly practiced and has become so automatic that it is difficult not to read them (Stroop, 1935).

The approaches to attention we have described so far—early information processing models and Lavie's load approach—are concerned with the ability to focus attention on a particular image or task. But in everyday experience you often shift your attention from place to place, either by moving your eyes or by shifting attention "in your mind" without moving your eyes. We discuss such shifts in attention next.

TEST YOURSELF 4.1

1. Give examples of situations that illustrate the following: selective attention, distraction, divided attention, attentional capture, and scanning.

2. How was the dichotic listening procedure used to determine how well people can focus on the attended message and how much information can be taken in from the unattended message? What is the cocktail party effect, and what does it demonstrate?

3. Describe Broadbent's model of selective attention. Why is it called an early selection model?

4. What were the results of experiments by Moray (words in the unattended ear) and Gray and Wedderburn ("Dear Aunt Jane")? Why are the results of these experiments difficult to explain based on Broadbent's filter model of attention?

5. Describe Treisman's attenuation model. First indicate why she proposed the theory, then how she modified Broadbent's model to explain some results that Broadbent's model couldn't explain.

6. Describe MacKay's "bank" experiment. Why does his result provide evidence for late selection?

7. Describe the Forster and Lavie experiment on how processing capacity and perceptual load determine distraction. What is the load theory of attention?

8. What is the Stroop effect? What does it illustrate about task-irrelevant stimuli?

Directing Attention by Scanning a Scene

Attention, according William James, involves "withdrawing from some things in order to effectively deal with others." Think about what this means when applied to everyday situations. There are lots of "things" out there that are potential objects of our attention, but we attend to some things and ignore others. How do we accomplish this, and how does directing our attention affect our experience? We begin by considering how we can direct our attention by moving our eyes to look at one place after another.

Scanning a Scene With Eye Movements

See how many people you can identify in **Figure 4.11** in a minute. Go!

As you did this task, you probably noticed that you had to scan the scene, checking each face in turn, in order to identify it. Scanning is necessary because good detail vision occurs only for things you are looking at directly.

Another way to experience the fact that we have to look directly at things we want to see in detail is to look at the word at the end of this line and, without moving your eyes, see how many words you can read to the left. If you do this without cheating (resist the urge to look to the left!), you will find that although you can read the word you are looking at, you can read only a few of the words that are farther off to the side.

Both of these tasks illustrate the difference between central vision and peripheral vision. *Central vision* is the area you are looking at. *Peripheral vision* is everything off to the side. Because of the way the retina is constructed, objects in central vision fall on a small area called the *fovea*, which has much better detail vision than the peripheral retina, on

➤ **Figure 4.11** How many people can you identify in this photo in 1 minute?

which the rest of the scene falls. Thus, as you scanned the scene in Figure 4.11, you were aiming your fovea at one face after another. Each time you briefly paused on one face, you were making a **fixation**. When you moved your eye to observe another face, you were making a **saccadic eye movement**—a rapid, jerky movement from one fixation to the next.

It isn't surprising that you were moving your eyes from one place to another, because you were trying to identify as many people as possible. But it may surprise you to know that even when you are freely viewing an object or scene without searching for anything in particular, you move your eyes about three times per second. This rapid scanning is shown in **Figure 4.12**, which is a pattern of fixations (dots) separated by saccadic eye movements (lines) that occurred as a participant viewed the picture of the fountain. Shifting attention from one place to another by moving the eyes is called **overt attention** because we can see attentional shifts by observing where the eyes are looking.

➤ **Figure 4.12** Scan path of a person freely viewing a picture. Fixations are indicated by the yellow dots and eye movements by the red lines. Notice that this person looked preferentially at areas of the picture such as the statues but ignored areas such as the water, rocks, and buildings.

We will now consider two factors that determine how people shift their attention by moving their eyes: bottom-up, based primarily on physical characteristics of the stimulus; and top-down, based on cognitive factors such as the observer's knowledge about scenes and past experiences with specific stimuli.

Scanning Based on Stimulus Salience

Attention can be influenced by **stimulus salience**—the physical properties of the stimulus, such as color, contrast, or movement. Capturing attention by stimulus salience is a bottom-up process because it depends solely on the pattern of light and dark, color and contrast in a stimulus (Ptak, 2012). For example, the task of finding the people with blonde hair in Figure 4.11 would involve bottom-up processing because it involves responding to the physical property of color, without considering the meaning of the image (Parkhurst et al., 2002). Determining how salience influences the way we scan a scene typically involves analyzing characteristics such as color, orientation, and intensity at each location in the scene and then combining these values to create a **saliency map** of the scene (Itti & Koch, 2000; Parkhurst et al., 2002; Torralba et al., 2006). For example, the person in red in **Figure 4.13** would get high marks for salience, both for the brightness of the color and because it contrasts with the expanse of white, which has lower salience because it is homogeneous.

Experiments in which people's eyes were tracked as they observed pictures have found that the first few fixations are more likely on high-salience areas. But after the first few fixations, scanning begins to be influenced by top-down, or cognitive, processes

➤ **Figure 4.13** The red shirt is visually salient because it is bright and contrasts with its surroundings.

that depend on things such as the observers' goals and expectations determined by their past experiences in observing the environment (Parkhurst et al., 2002).

Scanning Based on Cognitive Factors

One way to show that where we look isn't determined only by stimulus salience is by checking the eye movements of the participant looking at the scene in Figure 4.12. Notice that the person never looks at the bright blue water even though it is salient due to its brightness, color, and position near the front of the scene. The person also ignored the rocks and columns and several other prominent architectural features. Instead, the person focused on aspects of the fountain that might be more interesting, such as the statues. It is important to note, however, that just because this person looked at the statues doesn't mean everyone would. Just as there are large variations between people, there are variations in how people scan scenes (Castelhano & Henderson, 2008; Noton & Stark, 1971). Thus, another person, who might be interested in the architecture of the buildings, might look less at the statues and more at the building's windows and columns.

This example illustrates top-down processing, because scanning is influenced by preferences a person brings to the situation. Top-down processing also comes into play when scanning is influenced by **scene schemas**—an observer's knowledge about what is contained in typical scenes (see regularities of the environment, page 74). Thus, when Melissa Võ and John Henderson (2009) showed pictures like the ones in **Figure 4.14**, observers looked longer at the printer in **Figure 4.14b** than the pot in **Figure 4.14a** because a printer is less likely to be found in a kitchen. People look longer at things that seem out of place in a scene because their attention is affected by their knowledge of what is usually found in the scene.

Another example of how cognitive factors based on knowledge of the environment influences scanning is an experiment by Hiroyuki Shinoda and coworkers (2001) in which they measured observers' fixations and tested their ability to detect traffic signs as they drove through a computer-generated environment in a driving simulator. They found that the observers were more likely to detect stop signs positioned at intersections than those positioned in the middle of a block, and that 45 percent of the observers' fixations occurred close to intersections. In this example, the observers are using learning about regularities in the environment (stop signs are usually at corners) to determine when and where to look for stop signs.

Scanning Based on Task Demands

The examples in the last section demonstrate that knowledge of various characteristics of the environment can influence how people direct their attention. However, the last example, in which participants drove through a computer-generated environment, was different from the rest. The difference is that instead of looking at pictures of stationary scenes, participants were interacting with the environment. This kind of situation, in which people are shifting their attention from one place to another as they are doing things, occurs when people are moving through the environment, as in the driving example, and when people are carrying out specific tasks.

Because many tasks require attention to different places as the task unfolds, it isn't surprising that the timing of when people look at specific places is determined by the sequence of actions involved in the task. Consider, for example, the pattern of eye movements in **Figure 4.15**, which were measured as a person was making a peanut butter sandwich. The process of making

(a)

(b)

▶ **Figure 4.14** Stimuli used by Võ and Henderson (2009). Observers spent more time looking at the printer in (b) than at the pot in (a), shown inside the yellow rectangles (which were not visible to the observers).

(Source: M.L.-H.Vo, & J. M. Henderson, Does gravity matter? Effects of semantic and syntactic inconsistencies on the allocation of attention during scene perception, *Journal of Vision*, 9, 3:24, 1–15, Figure 1)

the sandwich begins with the movement of a slice of bread from the bag (A) to the plate (B). Notice that this operation is accompanied by an eye movement from the bag to the plate. The observer then looks at the peanut butter jar just before it is lifted and looks at the top just before it is removed (C). Attention then shifts to the knife, which is picked up and used to scoop the peanut butter and spread it on the bread (Land & Hayhoe, 2001).

The key finding of these measurements, and also of another experiment in which eye movements were measured as a person prepared tea (Land et al., 1999), is that the person's eye movements were determined primarily by the task. The person fixated on few objects or areas that were irrelevant to the task, and eye movements and fixations were closely linked to the action the person was about to take. Furthermore, the eye movement usually preceded a motor action by a fraction of a second, as when the person first fixated on the peanut butter jar and then reached over to pick it up. This is an example of the "just in time" strategy— eye movements occur just before we need the information they will provide (Hayhoe & Ballard, 2005; Tatler et al., 2011).

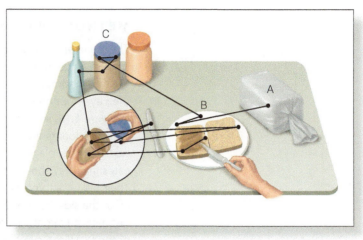

▶ **Figure 4.15** Sequence of fixations of a person making a peanut butter sandwich. The first fixation is on the loaf of bread.

(Source: Adapted from M. F. Land, N. Mennie, & J. Rusted, The roles of vision and eye movements in the control of activities of daily living, *Perception*, 28, 11, 1311–1328. Copyright © 1999 by Pion Ltd, London. Reproduced by permission. www.pion.co.uk and www.envplan.com.)

The examples we have described in connection with scanning based on cognitive factors and task demands have something in common: They all provide evidence that scanning is influenced by people's *predictions* (Henderson, 2017). Scanning anticipates what a person is going to do next as they make a peanut butter and jelly sandwich; scanning anticipates that stop signs are most likely to be located at intersections; and pausing scanning to look longer at an unexpected object occurs when a person's expectations are violated, as when a printer unexpectedly appears in a kitchen.

▶ Outcomes of Attention

What do we gain by attending? Based on the last section, which described *overt attention* that is associated with eye movements, we might answer that question by stating that shifting attention by moving our eyes enables us to see places of interest more clearly. This is extremely important, because it places the things we're interested in front-and-center where they are easy to see.

But some researchers have approached attention not by measuring factors that influence eye movements, but by considering what happens when we shift our attention without making eye movements. Shifting attention while keeping the eyes still is called **covert attention**, because the attentional shift can't be seen by observing the person. This type of attending involves shifting attention "with the mind" as you might do when you are paying attention to something off to the side while still looking straight ahead. (This has also been described as "looking out of the corner of your eye.")

One reason some researchers have studied covert attention is that it is a way of studying what is happening in the mind without the interference of eye movements. We will now consider research on covert attention, which shows how shifting attention "in the mind" can affect how quickly we can respond to locations and to objects, and how we perceive objects.

Attention Improves Our Ability to Respond to a Location

In a classic series of studies, Michael Posner and coworkers (1978) asked whether paying attention to a location improves a person's ability to respond to stimuli presented there. To answer this question, Posner used a procedure called **precueing**.

The general principle behind a precueing experiment is to determine whether presenting a cue indicating where a test stimulus will appear enhances the processing of the target stimulus. The participants in Posner and coworkers' (1978) experiment kept their eyes stationary throughout the experiment, always looking at the + in the display in **Figure 4.16**, so Posner was measuring covert attention.

Participants first saw an arrow cue (as shown in the left panel) indicating on which side of the display they should focus their attention. In **Figure 4.16a**, the arrow cue indicates that they should focus their attention to the right (while looking steadily at the +). Their task was to press a key as rapidly as possible when a target square was presented off to the side (as shown in the right panel). The trial shown in **Figure 4.16a** is a valid trial because the target square appears on the side indicated by the cue arrow. On 80 percent of the trials, the cue arrow directed participants' attention to the side where the target square appeared. However, on 20 percent of the trials, the arrow directed the participant's attention away from where the target was to appear (**Figure 4.16b**). These were the invalid trials. On both the valid and invalid trials, the participant's task was the same—to press the key as quickly as possible when the target square appeared.

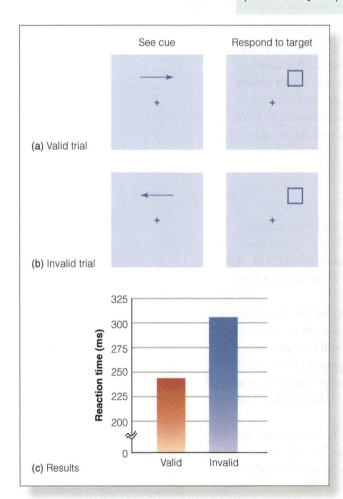

(a) Valid trial

(b) Invalid trial

(c) Results

▶ **Figure 4.16** Procedure for (a) valid trials and (b) invalid trials in Posner et al.'s (1978) precueing experiment; (c) the results of the experiment. The average reaction time was 245 ms for valid trials but 305 ms for invalid trials.

(Source: M. I. Posner, M. J. Nissen, & W. C. Ogden, Modes of perceiving and processing information. Copyright © 1978 by Taylor & Francis Group LLC–Books.)

The results of this experiment, shown in **Figure 4.16c**, indicate that participants reacted to the square more rapidly when their attention was focused on the location where the signal was to appear. Posner interpreted this result as showing that information processing is more effective at the place where attention is directed. This result and others like it gave rise to the idea that attention is like a spotlight or zoom lens that improves processing when directed toward a particular location (Marino & Scholl, 2005).

Attention Improves Our Ability to Respond to Objects

In addition to covertly attending to locations, as in Posner's experiment, we can also covertly attend to specific objects. We will now consider some experiments that show that (1) attention can enhance our response to objects and (2) when attention is directed to one place on an object, the enhancing effect of that attention spreads to other places on the object.

Consider, for example, the experiment diagrammed in **Figure 4.17** (Egly et al., 1994). As participants kept their eyes on the +, one end of the rectangle was briefly highlighted (**Figure 4.17a**). This was the cue signal that indicated where a target, a dark square (**Figure 4.17b**), would probably appear. In this example, the cue indicates that the target is likely to appear in position A, at the upper part of the right rectangle, and the target is, in fact, presented at A. (The letters used to illustrate positions in our description did not appear in the actual experiment.)

The participants' task was to press a button when the target was presented anywhere on the display. The numbers indicate the reaction times, in milliseconds, for three target locations when the cue signal had been presented at A. Not surprisingly, participants responded most rapidly when the target was presented at A, where the cue had been presented. However, the most interesting result is that participants responded more rapidly when the target was presented at B (reaction time = 358 ms) than when the target was presented at C (reaction time = 374 ms). Why does this occur? It can't be because B is closer to A than C, because B and C are exactly the same distance from A. Rather, B's advantage occurs because it is located within the object that was receiving the participant's attention. Attending at A, where the cue was presented, causes the maximum effect at A, but the effect of this attention spreads throughout the object so some enhancement occurs at B as well. The faster responding that occurs when enhancement spreads within an object is called the **same-object advantage** (Marino & Scholl, 2005; also see Driver & Baylis, 1989, 1998; Katzner et al., 2009; Lavie & Driver, 1996; and Malcolm & Shomstein, 2015 for more demonstrations of how attention spreads throughout objects).

Attention Affects Perception

Returning to the quote by James at the beginning of the chapter, let's focus on his description of attention to objects as "taking possession by the mind *in clear and vivid form.*" The phrase *in clear and vivid form* suggests that attending to an object makes it more clear and vivid—that is, attention affects perception. More than 100 years after James's suggestion, many experiments have shown that attended objects are perceived to be bigger and faster, and to be more richly colored and have better contrast than non attended objects (Anton-Erxleben et al., 2009; Carrasco et al., 2004; Fuller & Carrasco, 2006; Turatto et al., 2007). Attention therefore not only causes us to respond faster to locations and objects but affects how we perceive the object (Carrasco, 2011).

Attention Affects Physiological Responding

Attention has a number of different effects on the brain. One effect is to increase activity in areas of the brain that represent the attended location.

Attention to Locations Increases Activity in Specific Areas of the Brain

What happens in the brain when people shift their attention to different locations while keeping their eyes stationary? Ritobrato Datta and Edgar DeYoe (2009) answered this question by measuring brain activity using fMRI as participants kept their eyes fixed on the center of the display in **Figure 4.18** and shifted their attention to different locations in the display.

The colors in the circles in **Figure 4.18b** indicate the area of brain that was activated when the participant directed his or her attention to different locations indicated by the letters on the stimulus in Figure 4.18a. Notice that the yellow "hot spot," which is the place of greatest activation, moves out from the center and also becomes larger as attention

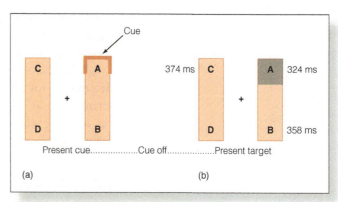

> **Figure 4.17** In Egly and coworkers' (1994) experiment, (a) a cue signal appears at one place on the display, then the cue is turned off and (b) a target is flashed at one of four possible locations, A, B, C, or D. The participants' task was to press a button when the target was presented anywhere on the display. Numbers are reaction times in ms for positions A, B, and C when the cue signal appeared at position A.

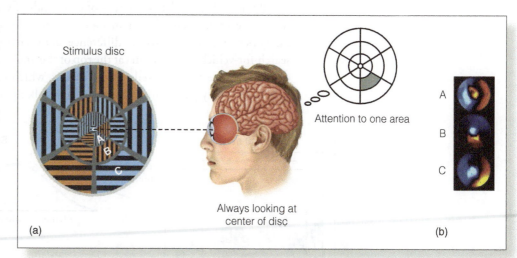

> **Figure 4.18** (a) Participants in Datta and DeYoe's (2009) experiment directed their attention to different areas of this circular display while keeping their eyes fixed on the center of the display. (b) Activation of the brain that occurred when participants attended to the areas indicated by the letters on the stimulus disc. The center of each circle is the place on the brain that corresponds to the center of the stimulus. The yellow "hot spot" is the area of the brain that is maximally activated by attention.

(Source: From R. Datta & E. A. DeYoe, I know where you are secretly attending! The topography of human visual attention revealed with fMRI, *Vision Research*, 49, 1037–1044, 2009.)

is directed farther from the center. By collecting brain activation data for all of the locations on the stimulus, Datta and DeYoe created "attention maps" that show how directing attention to a specific area of space activates a specific area of the brain.

What makes this experiment even more interesting is that after attention maps were determined for a particular participant, that participant was told to direct his or her attention to a "secret" place, unknown to the experimenters. Based on the location of the resulting yellow "hot spot" in the brain, the experimenters were able to predict, with 100 percent accuracy, the "secret" place where the participant was attending.

Attention Changes the Representation of Objects Across the Cortex   Datta and DeYoe's "hot spot" experiment is an elegant demonstration of how attention directed to a specific location results in enhanced activity at one place in the cortex. But what about a situation in which people might be directing their attention to numerous different locations as they search for something in a naturalistic environment? Tolga Cukur and coworkers (2013) considered this question by determining how attention affects the way different types of objects are represented across the brain as a whole.

The starting point for Cukur's experiment was Alex Huth's (2012) brain map that we described in Chapter 2 (see Figure 2.20). Huth's map illustrates how different categories of objects and actions are represented by activity that is distributed across a large area of the brain. Huth determined this map by having participants view movies in a scanner, and using fMRI to determine brain activity when different things were happening on the screen (see Figure 2.19).

Cukur did the same thing as Huth (they were working in the same laboratory and were involved in both papers), but instead of having his observers passively view the movies, he gave them a task that involved searching for either "humans" or "vehicles." A third group passively viewed the films, as in Huth's experiment. **Figure 4.19** shows what happened by plotting how a single voxel in the brain (see page 41 to review *voxel*) responded to different types of stimuli under two different search conditions. Notice in (a) that when the observer is searching for "humans" in the movie, the voxel responds well to "person," slightly to "animal," and hardly at all to "building" and "vehicle." However, in (b), when the observer is searching for "vehicle," the voxel's tuning shifts so it now responds well to "vehicle," slightly to "building," but not to "person" or "animal."

By analyzing the data from tens of thousands of voxels across the brain, Cukur created the whole brain maps shown in **Figure 4.20**. The colors indicate tuning to different categories. The most obvious difference between the search-for-people brain and the search-for-vehicles brain occurs at the top of the brain in this view. Notice that in the person condition there are more yellows and greens, which represent people or things related to people like body parts, animals, groups, and talking. However, in the vehicles condition,

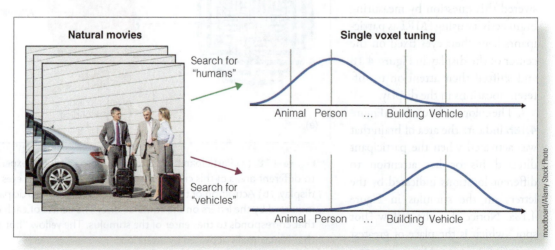

➤ **Figure 4.19** How tuning of a single voxel is affected by attention to (a) humans and (b) vehicles.

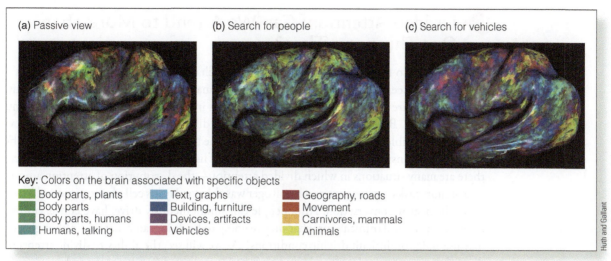

(a) Passive view   (b) Search for people   (c) Search for vehicles

Key: Colors on the brain associated with specific objects

Body parts, plants	Text, graphs	Geography, roads
Body parts	Building, furniture	Movement
Body parts, humans	Devices, artifacts	Carnivores, mammals
Humans, talking	Vehicles	Animals

Huth and Gallant

➤ **Figure 4.20** The map of categories on the brain changes for viewing a film. Colors indicate activation caused by different categories of stimuli. (a) Passive view indicates activation when not searching for anything. (b) Search for people causes activation indicated by yellow and green, which stand for people and things related to people. (c) Search for vehicles causes activation indicated by reds, which stand for vehicles and things related to vehicles.

colors shift to reds, which represent vehicles or things related to vehicles such as movement, road, and devices.

An important feature of these brain maps is that looking for a particular category shifts responding to the category and to additional things related to that category, so looking for people also affects responding to groups and clothing. Cukur calls this effect **attentional warping**—the map of categories on the brain changes so more space is allotted to categories that are being searched for, and this effect occurs even when the attended category isn't present in the movie. For example, when a person is on the lookout for vehicles, the brain becomes "warped" or "tuned" so that large areas respond best to vehicles and things related to vehicles. Then, when a vehicle, a road, or movement appears in a scene, a large response occurs. Other things, which the person is not looking for at the moment, would cause smaller responses.

TEST YOURSELF 4.2

1. What is the difference between central vision and peripheral vision? How is this difference related to overt attention, fixations, and eye movements?

2. What is stimulus salience? How is it related to attention?

3. Describe some examples of how attention is determined by cognitive factors. What is the role of scene schemas?

4. Describe the peanut butter experiment. What does the result tell us about the relation between task demands and attention?

5. What is covert attention? Describe the precueing procedure used by Posner. What does the result of Posner's experiment indicate about the effect of attention on information processing?

6. Describe the Egly precueing experiment. What is the same-object advantage, and how was it demonstrated by Egly's experiment?

7. What are three behaviorally measured outcomes of attention?

8. Describe how Data and DeYoe showed that attention to a location affects activity in the brain.

9. Describe Cukur's experiment, which showed how attention changes the representation of objects across the cortex.

▶ Divided Attention: Can We Attend to More Than One Thing at a Time?

Our emphasis so far has been on attention as a mechanism for focusing on one thing at a time. We have seen that sometimes we take in information from a task-irrelevant stimulus, even when we are trying ignore irrelevant stimuli, as in Forster and Lavie's experiment and the Stroop task. But what if you want to purposely distribute your attention among a few tasks? Is it possible to pay attention to more than one thing at a time? Although you might be tempted to answer "no," based on the difficulty of listening to two conversations at once, there are many situations in which divided attention—the distribution of attention among two or more tasks—can occur, as when Roger was able to play his cell phone game and listen in on the nearby conversation. Also, people can simultaneously drive, have conversations, listen to music, and think about what they're going to be doing later that day (although this may not hold for difficult driving conditions). As we will see, the ability to divide attention depends on a number of factors, including practice and the difficulty of the task.

Divided Attention Can Be Achieved With Practice: Automatic Processing

Experiments by Walter Schneider and Richard Shiffrin (1977) involved divided attention because they required the participant to carry out two tasks simultaneously: (1) holding information about target stimuli in memory and (2) paying attention to a series of "distractor" stimuli to determine whether one of the target stimuli is present among these distractor stimuli. **Figure 4.21** illustrates the procedure. The participant was shown a memory set like the one in **Figure 4.21a**, consisting of one to four characters called target stimuli. The memory set was followed by rapid presentation of 20 "test frames," each of which contained distractors (**Figure 4.21b**). On half of the trials, one of the frames contained a target stimulus from the memory set. A new memory set was presented on each trial, so the targets changed from trial to trial, followed by new test frames. In this example, there is one target stimulus in the memory set, there are four stimuli in each frame, and the target stimulus 3 appears in one of the frames.

At the beginning of the experiment, the participants' performance was only 55 percent correct; it took 900 trials for performance to reach 90 percent (**Figure 4.22**). Participants reported that for the first 600 trials, they had to keep repeating the target items in each memory set in order to remember them. (Although targets were always numbers and distractors letters, remember that the actual targets and distractors changed from trial to trial.) However, participants reported that after about 600 trials, the task had become automatic: The frames appeared and participants responded without consciously thinking about it. They would do this even when as many as four targets had been presented.

What this means, according to Schneider and Shiffrin, is that practice made it possible for participants to divide their attention to deal with all of the target and test items simultaneously. Furthermore, the many trials of practice resulted in **automatic processing**, a type of processing that occurs (1) without intention (it happens automatically without the person intending to do it) and (2) at a cost of only some of a person's cognitive resources.

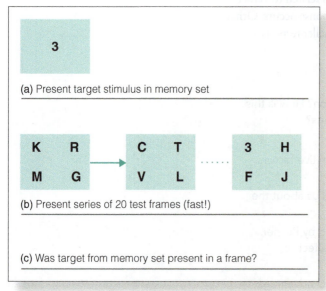

(a) Present target stimulus in memory set

(b) Present series of 20 test frames (fast!)

(c) Was target from memory set present in a frame?

▶ **Figure 4.21** Sample stimuli for Schneider and Shiffrin's (1977) experiment. In this experiment, there is one target stimulus in the memory set (the 3) and four stimuli in each frame. The target appears in the last frame in this example.

(Source: R. M. Shiffrin & W. Schneider, Controlled and automatic human information processing: Perceptual learning, automatic attending, and a general theory, *Psychological review*, 84, 127–190, 1977.)

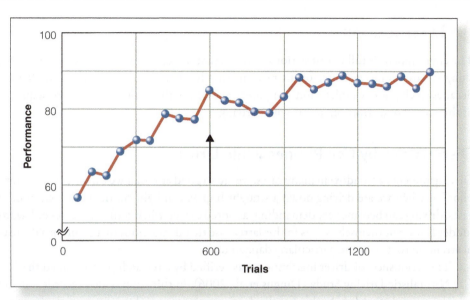

➤ **Figure 4.22** Improvement in performance with practice in Schneider and Schiffrin's (1977) experiment. The arrow indicates the point at which participants reported that the task had become automatic. This is the result of experiments in which there were four target stimuli in the memory set and two stimuli in each test frame

(Source: R. M. Shiffrin & W. Schneider, Controlled and automatic human information processing: Perceptual learning, automatic attending, and a general theory, *Psychological review*, 84, 127–190, 1977.)

Real-life experiences are filled with examples of automatic processing because there are many things that we have been practicing for years. For example, have you ever wondered, after leaving home, whether you had locked the door and then returned to find that you had? Locking the door has, for many people, become such an automatic response that they do it without paying attention. Another example of automatic processing (which is sometimes scary) occurs when you have driven somewhere and can't remember the trip once you get to your destination. In many cases, this involves being "lost in thought" about something else, yet driving has become so automatic that it seems to take care of itself (at least until a traffic "situation" occurs, such as road construction or another car cutting in front of you). Finally, you may carry out many motor skills, such as touch-typing or texting, automatically, without attention. Try paying attention to what your fingers are doing while typing and notice what happens to your performance. Concert pianists have reported that if they start paying attention to their fingers while they are playing, their performance falls apart.

Divided Attention Becomes More Difficult When Tasks Are Harder

What Schneider and Shiffrin's experiment shows is that divided attention is possible for some well-practiced tasks. However, in other experiments, they found that if task difficulty is increased—by using letters for both targets and distractors and by changing targets and distractors on each trial so a target on one trial can be a distractor on another—then automatic processing is not possible even with practice (also see Schneider & Chein, 2003).

An example of divided attention becoming difficult when the task is made too hard is provided by driving. You may find it easy to drive and talk at the same time if traffic is light on a familiar road. But if traffic increases, you see a flashing "Construction Ahead" sign, and the road suddenly becomes rutted, you might have to stop a conversation or turn off the radio, so you can devote all of your cognitive resources to driving. Because of the importance of driving in our society and the recent phenomenon of people talking on cell phones and texting while driving, researchers have begun to investigate the consequences of attempting to divide attention between driving and other distracting activities.

▶ Distractions

The environment is full of distractions—things that direct our attention away from something we are doing. A source of distractions that has become widespread in the last few decades is cell phones, tablets, and computers, and one of the most dangerous consequences of this source of distraction occurs while driving.

Distractions by Cell Phones while Driving

Driving presents a paradox: in many cases, we are so good at it that we can operate on "autopilot," as when we are driving down a straight highway in light traffic. However, in other cases, driving can become very demanding, as noted earlier, when traffic increases or hazards suddenly present themselves. It is in this latter case that distractions that result in a decrease in attention to driving are particularly dangerous.

The seriousness of driver inattention was verified by a research project called the 100-Car Naturalistic Driving Study (Dingus et al., 2006). In this study, video recorders in 100 vehicles created records of both what the drivers were doing and the view out the front and rear windows. These recordings documented 82 crashes and 771 near crashes in more than 2 million miles of driving. In 80 percent of the crashes and 67 percent of the near crashes, the driver was inattentive in some way 3 seconds beforehand. One man kept glancing down and to the right, apparently sorting through papers in a stop-and-go driving situation, until he slammed into an SUV. A woman eating a hamburger dropped her head below the dashboard just before she hit the car in front of her. One of the most distracting activities was pushing buttons on a cell phone or similar device. More than 22 percent of near crashes involved that kind of distraction, and it is likely that this number may be higher now because of increases in cell phone use since that study.

In a laboratory experiment on the effects of cell phones, David Strayer and William Johnston (2001) gave participants a simulated driving task that required them to apply the brakes as quickly as possible in response to a red light. Doing this task while talking on a cell phone caused participants to miss twice as many of the red lights as when they weren't talking on the phone (**Figure 4.23a**) and also increased the time it took them to apply the brakes (**Figure 4.23b**). Perhaps the most important finding of this experiment is that the same decrease in performance occurred regardless of whether participants used a hands-free or a handheld device.

Taking into account results such as these, plus many other experiments on the effects of cell phones on driving, Strayer and coworkers (2013) concluded that talking on the phone uses mental resources that would otherwise be used for driving the car (also see Haigney & Westerman, 2001; Lamble et al., 1999; Spence & Read, 2003; Violanti, 1998). This conclusion that the problem posed by cell phone use during driving is related to the use of mental resources is an important one. The problem isn't driving with one hand. It is driving with fewer mental resources available to focus on driving.

But even though research clearly shows that driving while talking on a cell phone is dangerous, many people believe it doesn't apply to them. For example, in response to a class assignment, one of my students wrote, "I do not believe my driving is affected by talking on the phone.... My generation learned to drive when cell phones were

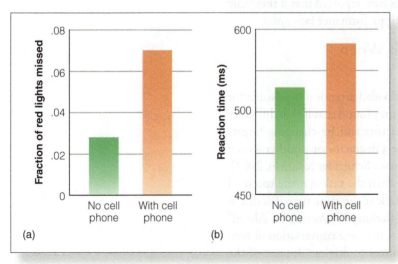

▶ **Figure 4.23** Result of Strayer and Johnston's (2001) cell phone experiment. When participants were talking on a cell phone, they (a) missed more red lights and (b) took longer to apply the brakes.

already out. I had one before driving, so while learning to drive, I also simultaneously learned to talk on the phone and drive." Thinking such as this may be why 27 percent of adults report that they sometimes text while driving, even in the face of overwhelming evidence that it is dangerous (Seiler, 2015; Wiederhold, 2016). For example, a study by the Virginia Tech Transportation Institute found that truck drivers who send text messages while driving were 23 times more likely to cause a crash or near crash than truckers who were not texting (Olson et al., 2009). Because of results such as these, which indicate that texting is even more dangerous than talking on a cell phone, most states now have laws against text-messaging while driving.

The main message here is that anything that distracts attention can degrade driving performance. And cell phones aren't the only attention-grabbing device found in cars. New car models feature small screens that can display the same apps that are on your phone. Some voice-activated apps enable drivers to make movie or dinner reservations, send and receive texts or emails, and post on Facebook. Ford calls their system an "infotainment system." But a recent study from the AAA Foundation for Traffic Safety, *Measuring Cognitive Distraction in the Automobile*, indicates that perhaps too much information and entertainment isn't a good thing. The study found that voice-activated activities were more distracting, and therefore potentially more dangerous, than either hands-on or hands-free cell phones. The study concludes that "just because a new technology does not take the eyes off the road does not make it safe to be used while the vehicle is in motion" (Strayer et al., 2013).

Distractions by the Internet

There is no question that distracted driving caused by cell phone use impacts the ability to drive safely. But cell phones, and the Internet in general, can also have negative effects on many other aspects of behavior.

Many research studies have documented high usage of cell phones and the Internet. For example, 92 percent of college students report that they have texted, browsed the web, sent pictures, or visited social networks during class time (Tindall & Bohlander, 2012). By checking college students' phone bills (with their permission!), Judith Gold and coworkers (2015) determined that they send an average of 58 text messages a day, and Rosen and coworkers (2013) showed that during a 15-minute study session, students averaged less than 6 minutes on-task before interrupting studying to stretch, watch TV, access websites, or use technology such as texting or Facebook.

Another method of determining ongoing daily behaviors such as texting is *experience sampling*.

METHOD   Experience Sampling

Experience sampling was developed to answer the question, "what percentage of the time during the day are people engaged in a specific behavior?" One way this question has been answered is to use a cell phone app that sends people text messages at random times during the day, asking them questions. For example, to determine the frequency of Internet usage, the question might be "Were you on the Internet?" Additional questions could also be inserted, such as "What type of online activity were you engaged in?" with choices such as "social networking," "email," and "browsing." When Moreno and coworkers (2012) sent students text-message probes at random times six times a day, they found that 28 percent of the probes arrived when the student was on the phone or Internet.

How often do you consult your cell phone? If you check your phone constantly, one explanation of your behavior involves **operant conditioning**, a type of learning named by behaviorist B.F. Skinner (1938) (see p. 11), in which behavior is controlled by rewards (called reinforcements) that follow behaviors. A basic principle of operant conditioning is that the best way to ensure that a behavior will continue is to reinforce it intermittently. So when you check your phone for a message and it's not there, well, there's always a chance it will be there the next time. And when it eventually appears, you've been intermittently reinforced, which strengthens future phone-clicking behavior. Some people's dependence on their phone is captured in the following sticker, marketed by Ephemera, Inc: "After a long weekend without your phone, you learn what's really important in life. Your phone." (See Bosker, 2016, for more on how cell phones are programmed to keep you clicking.)

Constant switching from one activity to another has been described as "continuous partial attention" (Rose, 2010), and here is where the problem lies, because as we saw for driving, distraction from a task impairs performance. It isn't surprising, therefore, that people who text more tend to have lower grades (Barks et al., 2011; Kuznekoff et al., 2015; Kuznekoff & Titsworth, 2013; Lister-Landman et al., 2015), and in extreme cases, some people are "addicted" to the Internet, where addiction is defined as occurring when Internet use negatively affects a number of areas of a person's life (for example, social, academic, emotional, and family) (Shek et al., 2016).

What's the solution? According to Steven Pinker (2010), given that the computer and Internet are here to stay, "the solution is not to bemoan technology, but to develop strategies of self-control, as we do with every other temptation in life." This sounds like good advice, but sometimes powerful temptations are difficult to resist. One example, for some people, is chocolate. Another is checking their cell phone. But even if you are able to resist chocolate and your cell phone, there is another distraction that is difficult to resist: the distraction that occurs when your mind wanders.

Distraction Caused by Mind Wandering

Let's return to Roger, who, at the beginning of the chapter, was sitting in the library wondering how to solve some math problems. Even though he is able to ignore the people talking next to him, he suddenly realizes that his mind has drifted away from doing his math problems to thinking about what he's going to do later, and then there's the problem of what to get his girlfriend for her birthday, and then . . . But wait a minute! What happened to the math problem? Roger's mind has been waylaid by **mind wandering**—thoughts coming from within—which have also been called *daydreaming* (Singer, 1975; Smallwood & Schooler, 2015) (**Figure 4.24**).

One of the properties of mind wandering is that it is extremely prevalent. Matthew Killingsworth and Daniel Gilbert (2010) used the experience sampling technique to contact people at random intervals during the day and ask them "What are you doing right now?" Mind wandering occurred 47 percent of the time and occurred when people were involved in a wide range of activities (**Table 4.1**). So mind wandering is extremely prevalent and, as shown in other studies, is distracting enough to disrupt an ongoing task (Mooneyham & Schooler, 2013). An example of disruption by mind wandering is what happens while reading, when you suddenly realize that you have no idea what you've just read because you were thinking about something else. This phenomenon, called *mindless reading* or *zoned-out reading*, is one example of how mind wandering decreases performance (Smallwood, 2011).

> ➤ **Figure 4.24** According to Killingsworth and Gilberts (2010), people are mind wandering about half the time when they are awake. Here, Roger is supposed to be focusing on doing math problems but seems to be drifting off onto other topics.
>
> (Source: Killingsworth and Gilberts, 2010)

TABLE 4.1

Activities During Which Mind Wandering Occurs, in Order of Frequency.

Most frequent activities are listed first, starting at the top left.		
Working	Eating	Playing
Talking/conversing	Reading	Exercising
Using a computer	Shopping, running errands	Walking
Commuting, traveling	Reading	Listening to music
Watching television	Doing housework	Making love
Relaxing	Grooming/self-care	Listening to the radio
Resting/sleeping	Taking care of children	Praying, meditating

Source: From Killingsworth & Gilbert, 2010.

Another property of mind wandering is that it is usually associated with activity in the default mode network (DMN). Remember, from Chapter 2 (page 50), that the DMN becomes activated when a person is not involved in a task. This may seem to contradict the preceding examples, when mind wandering is occurring during tasks like doing math problems or reading. But remember that once a person's mind begins to wander, he or she is no longer focusing their attention on a task. Mind wandering is a big problem if you need to stay focused. However, as we will see later in the book, when we consider memory, problem solving, and creativity, mind wandering also has benefits, such as helping us plan for the future and enhancing creativity.

▶ What Happens When We Don't Attend?

One thing that should be clear from our discussion so far is that attention is a precious, but limited, resource. We can attend to some things but not to everything. Dividing attention is possible but difficult, and there are forces out there in the world trying to distract us from paying attention to what we're supposed to be attending to. (Feel free to take a break here to check your cell phone for messages, but don't be distracted for too long, because there's still more to our story.)

There are many ways of showing that limits exist to our ability to attend, and we can demonstrate this by looking at what happens when we aren't attending to the right place at the right time. If we are paying attention to some things in a scene, we inevitably miss other things. This is dramatically illustrated by a tragic accident that occurred at a swimming pool in Iowa, described as follows by Lyndsey Lanagan-Leitzel and coworkers (2015):

> On 14 July 2010, approximately 175 teenage boys enjoyed a day of swimming at a local pool in Pella, Iowa, as part of a Fellowship of Christian Athletes camp held at Central College. When it was time to board busses to return to their rooms, two boys were discovered missing. A 15-minute search culminated in a tragic discovery—the bodies of two of the boys (ages 14 and 15 years) were discovered motionless on the bottom of the pool. Attempts to revive them failed (Belz, 2010).

What was particularly surprising about these drownings is that although at least 10 lifeguards and 20 camp counselors were observing the swimmers, nobody was aware of their drowning. According to Lanagan-Leitzel, although fatal drownings in lifeguarded pools are rare, there are reasons involving the limits of our ability to attend that might explain why this happened.

Consider the lifeguard's task. They are essentially carrying out a visual scanning task in which their job is to detect a rare event (someone drowning) amidst many similarly appearing distractors (boys splashing in a pool). Apparently, it isn't uncommon for people to drown without excessive splashing, and they often don't yell out for help because they are focusing their energy and attention on trying to breathe. There are other reasons it is sometimes difficult to spot someone who is drowning in a crowded pool, but the message,

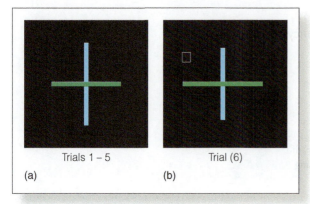

Trials 1 – 5   Trial (6)

(a)   (b)

➤ **Figure 4.25** Inattentional blindness experiment. (a) The cross display is presented for five trials. On each trial, one arm of the cross is slightly longer than the other. The participant's task is to indicate which arm (horizontal or vertical) is longer. (b) On the sixth trial, the participants carry out the same task, but a small square or other geometric object is included in the display. After the sixth trial, participants are asked whether they saw anything different than before.

(Source: Adapted from N. Lavie, Attention, distraction, and cognitive control under load, Current Directions in Psychological Science, 19, 143–148, 2010.)

for us, is that it is possible to be very attentive and still miss things. One example, called *inattentional blindness*, illustrates how we can miss things even if they are clearly visible.

Inattentional Blindness

Inattentional blindness occurs when people are unaware of clearly visible stimuli if they aren't directing their attention to them (Mack & Rock, 1998). For example, Cartwright-Finch and Nilli Lavie (2007) had participants view the cross stimulus shown in **Figure 4.25**. The cross was presented for five trials, and the observer's task was to indicate which arm of the briefly flashed cross was longer, the horizontal or the vertical. This is a difficult task because the arms were just slightly different in length, the cross was flashed rapidly, and the arm that was longer changed from trial to trial. On the sixth trial, a small outline of a square was added to the display (**Figure 4.25b**). Immediately after the sixth trial, participants were asked whether they noticed if anything had appeared on the screen that they had not seen before. Out of 20 participants, only 2 reported that they had seen the square. In other words, most of the participants were "blind" to the small square, even though it was located right next to the cross.

This demonstration of inattentional blindness used a rapidly flashed geometric test stimulus. But Daniel Simons and Christopher Chabris (1999) showed that attention can affect perception within a dynamic scene by having observers view a short film that showed two "teams" of three players each. One team, dressed in white, was passing a basketball around, and the other was "guarding" that team by following them around and putting their arms up as in a basketball game (**Figure 4.26**). Observers were told to count the number of passes, a task that focused their attention on the team wearing white. After about 45 seconds, one of two events occurred: Either a woman carrying an umbrella or a person in a gorilla suit walked through the "game," an event that took 5 seconds.

After seeing the video, observers were asked whether they saw anything unusual happen or whether they saw anything other than the six players. Nearly half of the observers—46 percent—failed to report that they saw the woman or the gorilla. This experiment demonstrates that when observers are attending to one sequence of events, they can fail to notice another event, even when it is right in front of them (also see Goldstein & Fink, 1981; Neisser & Becklen, 1975).

➤ **Figure 4.26** Frame from the film shown by Simons and Chabris in which a person in a gorilla suit walks through the basketball game.

(Source: D. J. Simons & C. F. Chabris, Gorillas in our midst:Sustained inattentional blindness for dynamic events, *Perception*, 28, 1059–1074, 1999. Pion Limited, London. Figure provided by Daniel Simons.)

Inattentional Deafness

The idea that inattention can cause us to miss visual stimuli has been extended to hearing. Dana Raveh and Nilli Lavie (2015) had participants carry out a visual search task, where **visual search** involves scanning a scene to find a specific object. They presented either an easy visual search task, like the one in **Figure 4.27a**, or a hard task like the one in **Figure 4.27b**. Participants were also asked to indicate whether they heard a tone that was presented during the visual display on about a fifth of the trials. The results, shown in **Figure 4.27c**, indicate that it was more difficult to detect the tone when engaged in the hard visual search task. This situation, in which focusing on a difficult visual task results in impaired hearing, is an example of **inattentional deafness**.

This result is significant both because it shows that inattentional effects can occur across vision and hearing and also because it shows how Lavie's *load theory of attention* (see page 99) can be applied to explaining the effects of inattention. Raveh and Lavie showed that being involved in a high-load task increases the chances of missing other stimuli. Looking back at the examples of inattentional blindness in vision, we can see that the tasks involved—detecting a slight difference in line length (see Figure 4.25) or counting basketball passes (Figure 4.26)—do involve highly focused attention, so it isn't surprising that participants missed the small square or the gorilla.

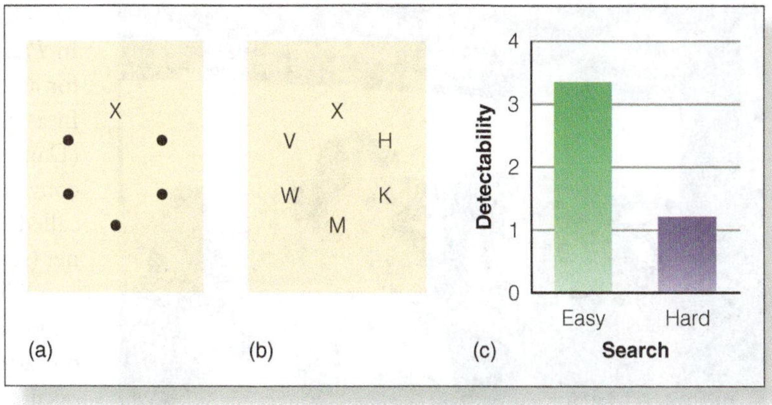

Change Detection

Researchers have also demonstrated how a lack of attention can affect perception using a procedure called **change detection**, in which one picture is presented followed by another picture, and the task is to determine what the difference is between them. To appreciate how this works, try the following demonstration before reading further.

> **Figure 4.27** Raveh and Lavie's (2015) inattentional deafness experiment. (a) Stimuli for easy search task. Find the X. (b) Stimuli for hard search task. (c) Result, showing detectability for a tone presented during the easy and hard search tasks. The high detectability during the easy search task means the tone was easier to detect.
> (Source: Based on Raveh and Lavie, 2015)

DEMONSTRATION   Change Detection

When you are finished reading these instructions, look at the picture in **Figure 4.28** for just a moment; then turn the page and see whether you can determine what is different in **Figure 4.29**. Do this now.

Were you able to see what was different in the second picture? People often have trouble detecting the change even though it is obvious when you know where to look. (Try again, paying attention to the sign near the lower-left portion of the picture.) Ronald Rensink and coworkers (1997) did a similar experiment in which they presented one picture, followed by a blank field, followed by the same picture but with an item missing, followed by a blank field. This sequence was repeated until observers were able to determine what was different about the two pictures. Rensink found that the sequence had to be repeated a number of times before the difference was detected. This difficulty in detecting changes in scenes is called **change blindness** (Rensink, 2002).

The frequency with which change blindness occurs can be startling. For example, in one study (Grimes, 1996), 100 percent of observers failed to detect a one-fourth increase in the size of a building, 92 percent failed to detect a one-third reduction in a flock of birds, 58 percent failed to detect a change in a model's swimsuit from bright pink to bright green, 50 percent failed to notice that two cowboys had exchanged their heads, and 25 percent failed to notice a 180-degree rotation of Cinderella's Castle at Disneyland!

If you find this hard to believe, you can reflect upon your own ability to detect changes while watching movies. Change blindness occurs regularly in popular films, in which some aspect of the scene, which should remain the same, changes from one shot to the next. In the *Wizard of Oz* (1939), Dorothy's (Judy Garland's)

> **Figure 4.28** Stimulus for the change detection demonstration.

Bruce Goldstein

➤ **Figure 4.29** Stimulus for the change detection demonstration.

hair changes length many times from short to long and back again. In *Pretty Woman* (1990), Vivian (Julia Roberts) began to reach for a croissant for breakfast that suddenly turned into a pancake. In a scene in *Harry Potter and the Sorcerer's Stone* (2001), Harry (Daniel Radcliff) suddenly changes where he is sitting during a conversation in the Great Hall. These changes in films, which are called **continuity errors**, have been well documented on the Internet (search for "continuity errors in movies").

Why does change blindness occur? The answer is that when we look at a scene in a still picture or at the ongoing action in a film, our attention is often not directed at the place where the change occurs.

What About Everyday Experience?

All of the experiments we have described—the inattentional blindness experiments, in which a distracting task kept people from noticing a test stimulus; the inattentional deafness experiment, in which focusing on a visual task results in impaired hearing; and the change blindness experiments, in which small but easily visible changes in pictures are not perceived—demonstrate that attending plays an important role in perceiving. This has implications for perception in our everyday experience, because there are a large number of stimuli present in the environment, and we are able to pay attention to only a small fraction of these stimuli at any moment. This means that we are constantly missing things in the environment.

Before you decide that our perceptual system is hopelessly flawed by its inability to detect large portions of our environment, consider the fact that we (and other animals) have somehow survived, so clearly our perceptual system is doing its job well enough to take care of most of the perceptual requirements posed by everyday life. In fact, it has been argued that the fact that our perceptual system focuses on only a small portion of the environment is one of its most adaptive features, because by focusing on what is important, our perceptual system is making optimal use of our limited processing resources.

Also even as we are focusing on what is important at the moment, our perceptual system has a warning system that responds to motion or intense stimuli, which causes us to rapidly shift our attention to things that might signal danger, such as a charging animal, a pedestrian on a collision course with us, a bright flash of light, or a loud noise. Once our attention has shifted, we can then evaluate what is happening at our new center of attention and decide whether we need to take action.

It is also important to realize that we don't need to be aware of all the details of what is happening around us. As you walk down a crowded sidewalk, you need to know where the other people are so you can avoid colliding, but you don't need to know that a particular person is wearing glasses or that another is wearing a blue shirt. You also don't need to be continually checking the details of what is happening around you because, from your past experience, you have scene schemas for city streets, country roads, or the layout of your campus that enable you to "fill in" what is around you without paying close attention (see Chapter 3, page 74).

What all of this means is that our perceptual systems are generally well adapted to take in the information we need to survive, even though we can only take in a small proportion of the information out there. But before you decide that the combination of focused attention, warning signals on the side, and filling in by schemas enables you to achieve feats of divided attention like driving and texting, remember that driving, texting, and cell phones are recent additions to the environment that weren't present when the human perceptual system evolved. Thus, as adaptive as our perceptual system might be, our modern world often puts us in situations that we are not designed to deal with and that, as we saw earlier, can lead to a dented fender, or worse.

▶ Attention and Experiencing a Coherent World

We have seen that attention is an important determinant of what we perceive. Attention brings things to our awareness and can enhance our ability to perceive and to respond. We now consider yet another function of attention, one that is not obvious from our everyday experience. This function of attention is to help create **binding**—the process by which features such as color, form, motion, and location are combined to create our perception of a coherent object.

We can appreciate why binding is necessary by considering an everyday event: You are sitting on a bench in the park, appreciating the colors of the Fall leaves, when all of a sudden a red ball rolls across your field of view, followed closely by a small child chasing the ball. When the ball rolls by, a number of different types of cells fire in your brain. Cells sensitive to the ball's round shape fire in your temporal cortex, cells sensitive to movement fire in an area specialized for motion, and cells sensitive to depth and color fire in other areas. But even though the ball's shape, movement, depth, and color cause firing in different areas of your cortex, you don't perceive the ball as separated shape, movement, depth, and color perceptions. You experience an integrated perception of a ball, with all of the ball's features being bound together to create the coherent perception of a "rolling red ball." The question of how an object's individual features become bound together, which is called the **binding problem**, has been addressed by Anne Treisman's (1986, 1988, 1999) feature integration theory.

Feature Integration Theory

According to **feature integration theory** (**FIT**), the first step in object processing is the **preattentive stage** (the first box in the flow diagram in **Figure 4.30**). As its name implies, the preattentive stage occurs *before* we focus attention on an object. Because attention is not involved, researchers argue that this stage is automatic, unconscious, and effortless. In this stage, the features of objects are analyzed independently in separate areas of the brain and are not yet associated with a specific object. For example, during the preattentive stage, the visual system of a person observing a rolling red ball would process the qualities of redness (color), roundness (form), and rightward movement (motion) separately. In the next stage of processing, called the **focused attention stage**, attention is focused on an object and the independent features are combined, causing the observer to become consciously aware of the rolling red ball.

In this two-stage process, you can think of visual features as components of a "visual alphabet." At the very beginning of the process, information about each of these components exist independently of one another, just as the letter tiles in a game of Scrabble exist as individual units when the tiles are scattered at the beginning of the game. However, just as the individual Scrabble tiles are combined to form words, the individual features combine to form perceptions of whole objects.

The idea that an object is automatically broken into features may seem counterintuitive because we always see whole objects, not objects that have been divided into individual features. The reason we aren't aware of this process of feature analysis is that it

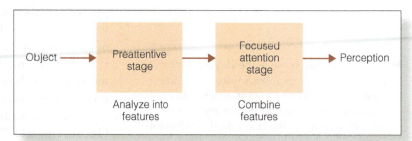

▶ **Figure 4.30** Steps in Treisman's feature integration theory. Objects are analyzed into their features in the preattentive stage, and the features are later combined with the aid of attention.

occurs early in the perceptual process, before we have become conscious of the object. Thus, when you see this book, you are conscious of its rectangular shape, but you are not aware that before you saw this rectangular shape, your perceptual system analyzed the book in terms of individual features such as lines with different orientations.

Evidence for Feature Integration Theory

To provide some perceptual evidence that objects are, in fact, analyzed into features, Anne Treisman and Hilary Schmidt (1982) did an experiment that involved a perceptual effect called *illusory conjunctions* in which one object can take on properties of another object.

Illusory Conjunctions Treisman and Schmidt presented displays like the one in **Figure 4.31**, in which four objects are flanked by two black numbers. They flashed this display onto a screen for one-fifth of a second, followed by a random-dot masking field designed to eliminate any residual perception that might remain after the stimuli were turned off. Participants were told to report the black numbers first and then to report what they saw at each of the four locations where the shapes had been. Thus, participants had to divide their a ttention across two tasks: identifying the numbers and identifying the shapes. By dividing participants' attention, Tresiman and Schmidt reduced their ability to focus attention on the shapes.

So what did participants report seeing? Interestingly, on about one-fifth of the trials, participants reported seeing shapes that were made up of a combination of features from two different stimuli. For example, after being presented with the display in Figure 4.31, in which the small triangle is red and the small circle is green, they might report seeing a small red circle and a small green triangle. These combinations of features from different stimuli are called **illusory conjunctions**. Illusory conjunctions can occur even if the stimuli differ greatly in shape and size. For example, a small blue circle and a large green square might be seen as a large blue square and a small green circle.

Although illusory conjunctions are usually demonstrated in laboratory experiments, they can occur in other situations as well. In a class demonstration to illustrate that observers sometimes make errors in eyewitness testimony, I had a male wearing a green shirt burst into the class, grab a yellow purse that was sitting on a desk (the owner of the purse was in on the demonstration), and run out of the room. This happened so rapidly that it surprised the students in the class, whose task was to describe what had happened as eyewitnesses to a "crime." Interestingly enough, one of the students reported that a male wearing a yellow shirt grabbed a green purse from the desk! Interchanging the colors of these objects is an example of illusory conjunctions (Treisman, 2005).

According to Treisman, illusory conjunctions occur because in the preattentive stage, each feature exists independently of the others. That is, features such as "redness," "curvature," or "tilted line" are, at this early stage of processing, not associated with a specific object. They are, in Treisman's (1986) words, "free floating," as shown in **Figure 4.32**, and can therefore be incorrectly combined if there is more than one object, especially in laboratory situations when briefly flashed stimuli are followed by a masking field.

When I describe this process in class, some students aren't convinced. One student said, "I think that when people look at an object, they don't break it into parts. They just see what they see." To convince such students (and the many others who, at the beginning of the course, are not comfortable with the idea that perception sometimes involves rapid processes we

➤ **Figure 4.31** Stimuli for illusory conjunction experiment. See text for details.

(Source: A. Treisman & H. Schmidt, Illusory conjunctions in the perception of objects, *Cognitive Psychology*, 14, 107–141, 1982.)

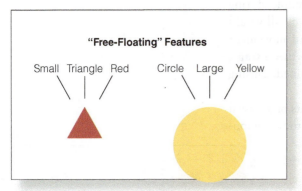

➤ **Figure 4.32** Illustration of the idea that in the preattentive stage an object's features are "free floating." Because they are not attached to a particular object, they can potentially become associated with any object in a display. When this happens, an illusory conjunction is created.

(Source: A. Treisman & H. Schmidt, Illusory conjunctions in the perception of objects, *Cognitive Psychology*, 14, 107–141, 1982.)

aren't aware of), I describe the case of R.M., a patient who had parietal lobe damage that resulted in a condition called **Balint's syndrome**. A crucial characteristic of Balint's syndrome is an inability to focus attention on individual objects.

According to feature integration theory, lack of focused attention would make it difficult for R.M. to combine features correctly, and this is exactly what happened. When R.M. was presented with two different letters of different colors, such as a red T and a blue O, he reported illusory conjunctions such as "blue T" on 23 percent of the trials, even when he was able to view the letters for as long as 10 seconds (Friedman-Hill et al., 1995; Robertson et al., 1997). The case of R.M. illustrates how a breakdown in the brain can reveal processes that are not obvious when the brain is functioning normally.

The feature analysis approach involves mostly bottom-up processing because knowledge is usually not involved. In some situations, however, top-down processing can come into play. For example, when Treisman and Schmidt (1982) did an illusory conjunction experiment using stimuli such as the ones in **Figure 4.33** and asked participants to identify the objects, the usual illusory conjunctions occurred; the orange triangle, for example, would sometimes be perceived to be black. However, when she told participants that they were being shown a carrot, a lake, and a tire, illusory conjunctions were less likely to occur, and participants were more likely to perceive the triangular "carrot" as being orange. In this situation, the participants' knowledge of the usual colors of objects influenced their ability to correctly combine the features of each object. In our everyday experience, in which we often perceive familiar objects, top-down processing combines with feature analysis to help us perceive things accurately.

➤ **Figure 4.33** Stimuli used to show that top-down processing can reduce illusory conjunctions.
(Source: A. Treisman & H. Schmidt, Illusory conjunctions in the perception of objects, *Cognitive Psychology*, 14, 107–141, 1982.)

Visual Search   Another approach to studying the role of attention in binding has used a type of visual search task called a **conjunction search.**

DEMONSTRATION   Searching for Conjunctions

We can understand what a conjunction search is by first describing another type of search called a feature search. Before reading further, find the horizontal line in **Figure 4.34a**. This is a feature search because you could find the target by looking for a single feature—"horizontal." Now find the green horizontal line in **Figure 4.34b**. This is a conjunction search because you had to search for a combination (or conjunction) of two or more features in the same stimulus—"horizontal" and "green." In Figure 4.34b, you couldn't focus just on green because there are vertical green lines, and you couldn't focus just on horizontal because there are horizontal red lines. You had to look for the conjunction of horizontal *and* green.

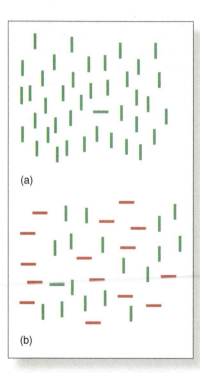

(a)

(b)

➤ **Figure 4.34** Find the horizontal line in (a) and then the green horizontal line in (b). Which task took longer?

Conjunction searches are useful for studying binding because finding the target in a conjunction search involves scanning a display in order to focus attention at a specific location. To test the idea that attention to a location is required for a conjunction search, a number of researchers have tested R.M., the Balint's patient, and have found that he cannot find the target when a conjunction search is required (Robertson et al., 1997). This is what we would expect because of R.M's difficulty in focusing attention. R.M. can, however, find targets when only a feature search is required, as in Figure 4.34a, because attention-at-a-location is not required for this kind of search. Visual scanning experiments, both on R.M. and normal observers, provides evidence that supports the idea that attention is an essential component of the mechanism that creates our perception of objects from a number of different features (Wolfe, 2012).

▶ SOMETHING TO CONSIDER

Attentional Networks

We've seen how attention can affect responding in the brain by enhancing activity at a location (page 107) or by expanding the area dedicated to a specific type of objects (page 108).

But we need to take a step further to fully understand the connection between attention and the brain. We need to look at how the brain is set up to make attention work. To do that, we consider the neural networks that transmit signals across many areas of the brain, which we introduced in Chapter 2 (see page 45).

Neuroimaging research has revealed that there are neural networks for attention associated with different functions. Consider, for example, how attention is directed by scanning a scene (page 103). We saw that attention is determined by stimulus salience—physical properties of stimuli—and by higher-level top-down functions such as scene schemas, as when an unusual object appears in a scene, or task demands, as in the example of making a peanut butter and jelly sandwich. Imaging experiments in which participants carried out tasks involving salience or involving top-down processes have revealed two different networks: the **ventral attention network**, which controls attention based on salience, and the **dorsal attention network**, which controls attention based on top-down processes (**Figure 4.35**).

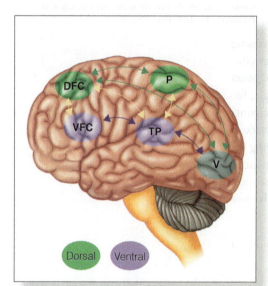

▶ **Figure 4.35** Main structures in the two attention networks. V = visual cortex. Dorsal attention network: P = parietal cortex; DFC = dorsal frontal cortex; Ventral attention network: TP = junction of temporal and parietal lobes; VFC = ventral frontal cortex.

(Source: Based on Vossel et al., 2014, Figure 1)

Identifying different networks for different functions was a big step toward understanding how the brain controls attention. But researchers have gone beyond just identifying networks to looking at the dynamics of how information flows in these networks. Remember the helicopter ride we took in Chapter 2 to observe the flow of traffic in a network of city streets, which represented a neural network (page 49). We noted that traffic flow changed depending on changing conditions. For example, traffic flow toward the stadium increased on the weekend of the big football game. Similarly, flow in attention systems changes depending on whether attention is being controlled by stimulus salience or by top-down factors, with more flow in the ventral network for control by salience and more in the dorsal network when flow is controlled by top-down factors.

But to fully understand the dynamic nature of attention, we need to go one step further. Different tasks don't just shift activity from one pathway to another. They also change the **effective connectivity** between different areas in a network. Effective connectivity refers to how easily activity can travel along a particular pathway.

We can illustrate effective connectivity by returning to our road network example, in which we noted that the flow of traffic is directed more toward the stadium on the day of the football game. Sometimes, when situations like this occur, the people in charge of regulating traffic in the city open up more lanes moving toward the stadium before the game, and then open more lanes moving away from the stadium after the game. In other words, the basic road system remains the same, but the flow becomes easier in certain directions, depending on conditions.

This is exactly what happens for attention when the effective connectivity between different structures in a network changes depending on conditions. How does this effective connectivity change? One mechanism that has been suggested, **synchronization**, is illustrated by the results of an experiment by Conrado Bosman and coworkers (2012) in which they recorded a response called the *local field potential (LFP)* from a monkey's cortex. LFPs, which are recorded by small disc electrodes placed on the surface of the brain, record signals from thousands of neurons near the electrode. LFP responses were recorded from an electrode at A on the brain, where signals from the visual stimulus arrive. Signals are also recorded from an electrode at B on the brain, which is connected to A and so receives signals from A (**Figure 4.36a**).

Bosman found that the visual stimulus caused an LFP response at A in the cortex and also at B, because A sends signals to B. He also found that when the monkey wasn't paying attention to the visual stimulus, the responses recorded from A and B were unsynchronized (**Figure 4.36b**). However, when the monkey focused attention on the visual stimulus, the signals from A and B become synchronized (**Figure 4.36c**). It has been hypothesized that synchronization such as this results in more effective communication between the two areas (see Bosman et al., 2012; Buschman & Kastner, 2015).

In addition to the ventral and dorsal attention networks, another network, called the **executive attention network**, has been proposed. This network is extremely complex and may involve two separate networks (Petersen & Posner, 2012). Rather than list all the structures involved, let's focus on what the executive attention network does.

The executive attention network is responsible for executive functions. **Executive functions** include a range of processes that involve controlling attention and dealing with conflicting responses. One example is the Stroop test (see page 100), in which the task involves focusing on the color of the ink and ignoring the color spelled out by the words. But executive attention extends into real life as well, any time there is conflict between different possible courses of action.

Dealing with conflict in everyday life has been called a number of things, including **cognitive control**, **inhibitory control**, and **willpower**. You can probably think of situations in which you were faced with a temptation that was difficult to resist. If so, your executive attention system was involved in dealing with this situation. As stated in the title of the song "Should I Stay or Should I Go," by the British punk rock group The Clash, decisions and temptation are a part of life. In the next chapter, we will see that there are connections between attention, cognitive control, and a type of memory called working memory.

•••

The story we have told in the last two chapters has been about interacting with things in the environment. We perceive objects visually, hear sounds, experience smells or someone touching us, and in some cases we pay attention to some of these things more than others. Both perception and attention support our ability to know about our environment and to act within it. But to take us beyond having immediate experiences, we need to be able to store some of what is happening to us so we can remember it later. This function is achieved by the process of memory, which not only helps us survive but also determines our identity as a person. This is so important that we will spend the next four chapters discussing the process of memory. As you will see, many of the things we have introduced in our discussion of perception and attention—the principle of representation, the importance of knowledge gained from experience, the way we use inference and prediction, and our active interaction with both ideas and things—are central to our understanding of memory.

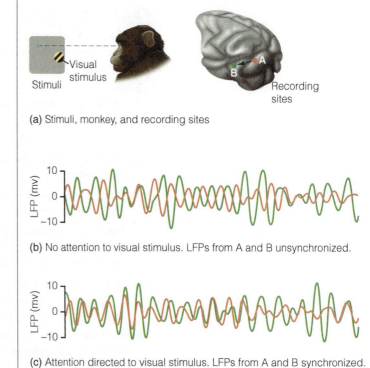

(a) Stimuli, monkey, and recording sites

(b) No attention to visual stimulus. LFPs from A and B unsynchronized.

(c) Attention directed to visual stimulus. LFPs from A and B synchronized.

▶ **Figure 4.36** Bosman et al. (2012) demonstration of synchronization caused by attention. (a) The monkey is looking at the blue dot on the screen. Local field potentials are being recorded from locations A and B on the cortex, which are connected. (b) When the monkey is not paying attention to the visual stimulus, the LFP responses from A and B are unsynchronized. (c) When the monkey focuses its attention on the visual stimulus, the LFP responses of A and B become synchronized.

(Source: Figure courtesy of Pascal Fries and Conrado Bosman)

TEST YOURSELF 4.3

1. Describe Schneider and Shiffrin's experiment that demonstrated automatic processing. What are some real-life examples of automatic processing? When is automatic processing not possible?

2. What conclusions can be reached from the results of experiments testing the ability to drive while talking on a cell phone?

3. What is the evidence that cell phones can affect performance in situations in addition to driving?

4. How can a principle of operant conditioning explain why some people check their cell phones so often?

5. What is mind wandering, and how does it affect the ability to focus attention on tasks? What brain network is associated with mind wandering?

6. Describe the following evidence that attention is sometimes necessary for perception: the inattentional blindness experiment; the "basketball-passing" experiment; the change detection experiments.

7. What is inattentional deafness, and what does the inattentional deafness experiment described in the text tell us about the relation between load theory and the effects of inattention?

8. Why can we say that we don't need to be aware of all of the details of what is happening around us?

9. What is binding, and why is it necessary? What is the binding problem?

10. Describe Treisman's feature integration theory. What does the theory seek to explain about perceiving objects? What are the stages of the theory, and at what point does attention become involved?

11. What are illusory conjunctions, and what do they demonstrate about feature analysis? How have illusory conjunction experiments supported the role of attention in feature analysis? How do experiments with Balint's syndrome patients support feature integration theory?

12. What is a feature search? A conjunction search? Which type of search did the Balint's patient find difficult? What does that tell us about the role of attention in feature integration?

13. Describe how attention is controlled by different types of attentional networks. Be sure you understand the functions of the dorsal attention network, the ventral attention network, and the executive attention network, and the principles of effective connectivity and synchronization.

CHAPTER SUMMARY

1. Selective attention, the ability to focus on one message while ignoring all others, has been demonstrated using the dichotic listening procedure.

2. A number of models have been proposed to explain the process of selective attention. Broadbent's filter model proposes that the attended message is separated from the incoming signal early in the analysis of the signal. Treisman's model proposes later separation and adds a dictionary unit to explain how the unattended message can sometimes get through. Late selection models propose that selection doesn't occur until messages are processed enough to determine their meaning.

3. Lavie proposes that our ability to ignore distracting stimuli can be explained by considering processing capacity and perceptual load. Her load theory of attention states that distraction is less likely for high-load tasks because no capacity remains to process potential distracting stimuli.

4. The Stroop effect demonstrates how a powerful task-irrelevant stimulus, such as meaningful words that result in a response that competes with the observer's task, can capture attention.

5. Overt attention is shifting attention by making eye movements. Overt attention is determined by bottom-up processes such as stimulus salience and by top-down processes such as scene schemas and task demands, which influence how eye movements are directed to parts of a scene.

6. Covert attention is shifting attention without making eye movements. Visual attention can be directed to different places in a scene even without eye movements. The effect of covert attention has been demonstrated by precueing experiments, which have shown that covert attention to a location enhances processing at that location.

7. Eagly's experiment demonstrates that responding is faster for cued locations on an object and that this effect spreads throughout an object—an effect called the same-object advantage.

8. Experiments have shown that attended objects are perceived to be bigger, faster, more richly colored, and higher in contrast than non attended objects.

9. Covert attention to a location causes an increase in activity at the place on the brain that corresponds to that location.

10. Attention to specific categories of objects, like people or cars, increases the area of the brain devoted to the attended category. This is called attentional warping.

11. Divided attention is possible for easy tasks or for highly practiced difficult tasks. Automatic processing is possible in these situations but is not possible for very difficult tasks.

12. Driver inattention is one of the major causes of automobile accidents. There is a large amount of evidence that using cell phones while driving is associated with increases in traffic accidents and decreases in performance of driving-related tasks. Hands-free and voice-activated devices are just as distracting as handheld devices.

13. The use of cell phones and the Internet in general has increased greatly recently. One explanation for frequent checking of cell phones involves principles of operant conditioning.

14. The distraction caused by cell phones and the Internet has been linked to lower grades, and in extreme cases to negative effects in many areas of a person's life.

15. Mind wandering is very prevalent and has been associated with disruption of ongoing tasks that require focused attention. Mind wandering is associated with activity of the default mode network.

16. Inattentional blindness experiments provide evidence that without attention we may fail to perceive things that are clearly visible in the field of view.

17. Inattentional deafness can occur when attention to a high-load visual search task impairs the ability to detect sounds.

18. Change blindness is the inability to detect changes in a scene. It is another example of how inattention can affect perception.

19. Although inattentional blindness and deafness and change blindness indicate that we don't notice everything that is happening, our perceptual system is well adapted for survival. We can be warned about possible danger by movement, and the perceptual system makes optimal use of limited processing resources by focusing on what is being attended.

20. Binding is the process by which object features are combined to create perception of a coherent object. Feature integration theory explains how binding occurs by proposing two stages of processing: preattentive processing and focused attention. The basic idea is that objects are analyzed into their features and that attention is necessary to combine these features to create perception of an object. Illusory conjunction, visual search, and neuropsychology experiments support feature integration theory.

21. A number of neural networks are involved in controlling attention. The ventral attention network controls attention based on salience. The dorsal attention network controls attention based on top-down processes. The executive attention network controls attention that involves dealing with conflicting responses. The mechanism of synchronization helps achieve effective connectivity between different areas in a network.

THINK ABOUT IT

1. Pick two items from the following list, and decide how difficult it would be to do both at the same time. Some things are difficult to do simultaneously because of physical limitations. For example, it is extremely dangerous to type on your computer and drive at the same time. Others things are difficult to do simultaneously because of cognitive limitations. For each pair of activities that you pick, decide why it would be easy or difficult to do them simultaneously. Be sure to take the idea of cognitive load into account.

Driving a car	Talking on a cell phone
Reading a book for pleasure	Flying a kite
Doing math problems	Walking in the woods
Talking to a friend	Listening to a story
Thinking about tomorrow	Writing a paper for class
Rock climbing	Dancing

2. Find someone who is willing to participate in a brief "observation exercise." Cover a picture (preferably one that contains a number of objects or details) with a piece of paper, and tell the person that you are going to uncover the picture and that their task is to report everything that they see. Then uncover the picture very briefly (less than a second), and have the person write down, or tell you, what they saw. Then repeat this procedure, increasing the exposure of the picture to a few seconds, so the person can direct his or her attention to different parts of the picture. Perhaps try this a third time, allowing even more time to observe the picture. From the person's responses, what can you conclude about the role of attention in determining what people are aware of in their environment?

3. Art composition books often state that it is possible to arrange elements in a painting in a way that controls both what a person looks at in a picture and the order in which a person looks at things. What would the results of research on visual attention have to say about this idea?

4. How does the attention involved in carrying out actions in the environment differ from the attention involved in scanning a picture for details, as in the "observation exercise" in problem 2?

5. As you sit in a stadium watching a football game, a lot is going on in the game, in the stands, and on the sidelines. Which things that you might look at would involve attention to objects, and which would involve attention to locations?

6. As the quarterback steps back to pass, the offensive line blocks the defense, so the quarterback has plenty of time to check out what is happening downfield and to throw to an open receiver. Later in the game, two 300-pound linemen get through to the quarterback. While he scrambles for safety, he fails to see the open receiver downfield and instead throws a pass toward another receiver that is almost intercepted. How can these two situations be related to the way selective attention is affected by task load?

7. Given the mounting evidence that talking on cell phones (even hands-free) while driving increases the chances of having an accident, it could be argued that laws should be passed making all cell phone use illegal while driving. (The majority of states currently have laws against texting while driving.) What would be your reaction if this occurred? Why?

KEY TERMS

Same-object advantage, 107
Scene schemas, 104
Selective attention, 95
Shadowing, 95
Stimulus salience, 103
Stroop effect, 101
Synchronizations, 122
Ventral attention network, 122
Visual scanning, 95
Visual search, 116
Willpower, 123

COGLAB EXPERIMENTS

Numbers in parentheses refer to the experiment number in CogLab.

Visual Search (*7*)
Attentional Blink (*8*)
Change Detection (*9*)
Inhibition of Return (*10*)
Simon Effect (*11*)
Spatial Cueing (*12*)
Stroop Effect (*13*)
Von Restorff Effect (*32*)

What does football have to do with memory? Just about everything we do depends on memory, and football is no exception. Memory involves holding information in the mind for short periods of time (short-term or working memory), and also holding information for long periods (long-term memory). A crucial task for a football player is using long-term memory to remember all of the plays in the playbook. Then, when the play is called in the huddle, they have to retrieve that play from all of the plays stored in their long-term memory. This play, and the snap count, which indicates when the ball will be snapped, is stored in short-term memory and, as the play unfolds, each player carries out their role—blocking, executing a pass route, taking a handoff—each of which, plus the specific skills involved, are part of the "football smarts" that are so well practiced, they happen with no thought to the memory processes that made them possible.

Short-Term and Working Memory

5

CHAPTER SUMMARY

THINK ABOUT IT

KEY TERMS

COGLAB EXPERIMENTS

SOME QUESTIONS
WE WILL CONSIDER

▶ Why can we remember a
telephone number long enough
to place a call, but then we
forget it almost immediately?
(138)

▶ How is memory involved in
processes such as doing a math
problem? (143)

▶ Do we use the same memory
system to remember things we
have seen and things we have
heard? (145)

So much has been written about memory—the advantages of having a good memory, the pitfalls of forgetting, or in the worst case, losing one's ability to remember—that it may hardly seem necessary to read a cognitive psychology textbook to understand what memory is. But as you will see over the next four chapters, "memory" is not just one thing. Memory, like attention, comes in many forms. One of the purposes of this chapter and the next is to introduce the different types of memory, describing the properties of each type and the mechanisms responsible for them. Let's begin with two definitions of memory:

➤ **Memory** is the process involved in retaining, retrieving, and using information about stimuli, images, events, ideas, and skills after the original information is no longer present.

➤ Memory is active any time some past experience has an effect on the way you think or behave now or in the future (Joordens, 2011).

From these definitions, it is clear that memory has to do with the past affecting the present, and possibly the future. But while these definitions are correct, we need to consider the various ways in which the past can affect the present to really understand what memory is. When we do this, we will see that there are many different kinds of memory. With apologies to the English poet Elizabeth Barrett Browning, whose famous poem to her husband begins "How do I love thee, let me count the ways," let's consider a woman we'll call Christine as she describes incidents from her life that illustrate a related question: "How do I *remember* thee, let me count the ways" (see **Figure 5.1**).

My first memory of you was brief and dramatic. It was the Fourth of July, and everyone was looking up at the sky to see the fireworks. But what I saw was your face—illuminated

➤ **Figure 5.1** Five types of memory described by Christine. See text for details.

for just a moment by a flash, and then there was darkness. But even in the darkness I held your image in my mind for a moment.

When something is presented briefly, such as a face illuminated by a flash, your perception continues for a fraction of a second in the dark. This brief persistence of the image, which is one of the things that makes it possible to perceive movies, is called *sensory memory*.

Luckily, I had the presence of mind to "accidentally" meet you later so we could exchange phone numbers. Unfortunately, I didn't have my cell phone with me or anything to write with, so I had to keep repeating your number over and over until I could write it down.

Information that stays in our memory for brief periods, about 10 to 15 seconds if we don't repeat it over and over as Christine did, is *short-term memory* or *working memory*.

And the rest is history, because I have countless memories of all the things we have done. I especially remember that crisp fall day when we went bike riding to that place in the woods where we had a picnic.

Long-term memory is responsible for storing information for long periods of time—which can extend from minutes to a lifetime. Long-term memories of *experiences* from the past, like the picnic, are *episodic memories*. The ability to ride a bicycle, or do any of the other things that involve muscle coordination, is a type of long-term memory called *procedural memory*.

I must admit, however, that as much as I remember many of the things we have done, I have a hard time remembering the address of the first apartment we lived in, although, luckily for me, I do remember your birthday.

Another type of long-term memory is *semantic memory*—memories of facts such as an address or a birthday or the names of different objects ("that's a bicycle").

We will describe sensory memory and short-term memory in this chapter, we will compare short-term and long-term memory at the beginning of Chapter 6, and then spend the rest of Chapter 6 plus Chapters 7 and 8 on long-term memory. We will see that although people often mistakenly use the term "short-term memory" to refer to memory for events that happened minutes, hours, or even days ago, it is actually much briefer. In Chapter 6 we will note that this misconception about the length of short-term memory is reflected in how memory loss is described in movies. People also often underestimate the importance of short-term memory. When I ask my students to create a "top 10" list of what they use memory for, most of the items come under the heading of long-term memory. The four top items on their list are the following:

Material for exams

Their daily schedule

Names

Directions to places

Your list may be different, but items from short-term memory rarely make the list, especially since the Internet and cell phones make it less necessary to repeat phone numbers over and over to keep them alive in memory. So what is the purpose of sensory and short-term memory?

Sensory memory is important when we go to the movies (more on that soon), but the main reason for discussing sensory memory is to demonstrate an ingenious procedure for measuring how much information we can take in immediately, and how much of that information remains half a second later.

The purpose of short-term memory will become clearer as we describe its characteristics, but stop for a moment and answer this question: What are you aware of right now? Some material you are reading about memory? Your surroundings? Noise in the background? Whatever your answer, you are describing what is in short-term memory. Everything you know or think about at each moment in time is in short-term memory. Thirty seconds from now your "old" short-term memories may have faded, but new ones will have taken over. Your "to do" list in long-term memory may be important, but as you are doing each of the things on your list, you are constantly using your short-term memory. As you will see in this chapter, short-term memory may be short in duration, but it looms large in importance.

We begin our description of sensory and short-term memory by describing an early and influential model of memory called the *modal model*, which places sensory and short-term memory at the beginning of the process of memory.

▶ The Modal Model of Memory

Remember Donald Broadbent's (1958) filter model of attention, which introduced the flow chart that helped usher in the information processing approach to cognition (Chapter 1, page 14; Chapter 4, page 95). Ten years after Broadbent introduced his flow diagram for attention, Richard Atkinson and Richard Shiffrin (1968) introduced the flow diagram for memory shown in **Figure 5.2**, which is called the **modal model of memory**. This model proposed three types of memory:

1. *Sensory memory* is an initial stage that holds all incoming information for seconds or fractions of a second.

2. Short-term memory (STM) holds five to seven items for about 15 to 20 seconds. We will describe the characteristics of short-term memory in this chapter.

3. Long-term memory (LTM) can hold a large amount of information for years or even decades. We will describe long-term memory in Chapters 6, 7, and 8.

➤ **Figure 5.2** Flow diagram for Atkinson and Shiffrin's (1968) modal model of memory. This model, which is described in the text, is called the modal model because it contains features of many of the memory models that were being proposed in the 1960s.

The types of memory listed above, each of which is indicated by a box in the model, are called the **structural features** of the model. As we will see, the short-term memory and long-term memory boxes in this diagram were expanded by later researchers, who modified the model to distinguish between the different types of short- and long-term memories. But for now, we take this simpler modal model as our starting point because it illustrates important principles about how different types of memory operate and interact.

Atkinson and Shiffrin also proposed **control processes**, which are dynamic processes associated with the structural features that can be controlled by the person and may differ from one task to another. An example of a control process that operates on short-term memory is **rehearsal**—repeating a stimulus over and over, as you might repeat a telephone number in order to hold it in your mind after looking it up on the Internet. Rehearsal is symbolized by the blue arrow in Figure 5.2. Other examples of control processes are (1) strategies you might use to help make a stimulus more memorable, such as relating the digits in a phone number to a familiar date in history, and (2) strategies of attention that help you focus on information that is particularly important or interesting.

To illustrate how the structural features and control processes operate, let's consider what happens as Rachel looks up the number for Mineo's Pizza on the Internet (**Figure 5.3**). When she first looks at the screen, all of the information that enters her eyes is registered in sensory memory (**Figure 5.3a**). Rachel uses the control process of selective attention to focus on the number for Mineo's, so the number enters her short-term memory (**Figure 5.3b**), and she uses the control process of rehearsal to keep it there (**Figure 5.3c**).

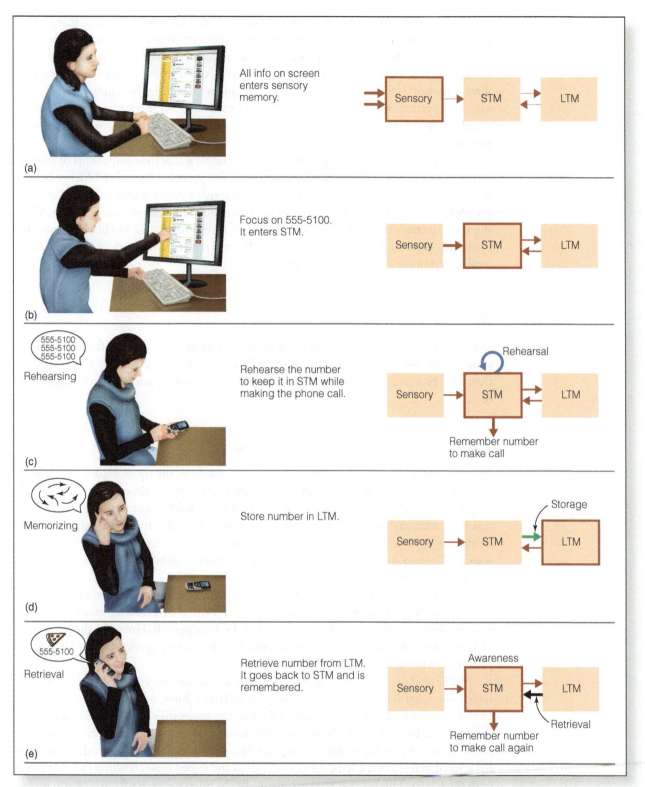

> ➤ **Figure 5.3** What happens in different parts of Rachel's memory as she is (a, b) looking up the phone number, (c) calling the pizza shop, and (d) memorizing the number. A few days later, (e) she retrieves the number from long-term memory to order pizza again. The parts of the modal model that are outlined in red indicate which processes are activated for each action that Rachel takes.

Rachel knows she will want to use the number again later, so she decides that in addition to storing the number in her cell phone, she is going to memorize the number so it will also be stored in her mind. The process she uses to memorize the number, which involves control processes that we will discuss in Chapter 6, transfers the number into long-term memory, where it is stored (**Figure 5.3d**). The process of storing the number in long-term memory is called *encoding*. A few days later, when Rachel's urge for pizza returns, she remembers the number. This process of remembering information that is stored in long-term memory is called *retrieval* (**Figure 5.3e**).

One thing that becomes apparent from our example is that the components of memory do not act in isolation. Thus, the phone number is first stored in Rachel's STM, but because information is easily lost from STM (as when you forget a phone number), Rachel transfers the phone number into LTM (green arrow), where it is held until she needs it later. When she then remembers the phone number later, it is returned to STM (black arrow), and Rachel becomes aware of the phone number. We will now consider each component of the model, beginning with sensory memory.

Sensory Memory

Sensory memory is the retention, for brief periods of time, of the effects of sensory stimulation. We can demonstrate this brief retention for the effects of visual stimulation with two familiar examples: the trail left by a moving sparkler and the experience of seeing a film.

The Sparkler's Trail and the Projector's Shutter

It is dark out on the Fourth of July, and you put a match to the tip of a sparkler. As sparks begin radiating from the tip, you sweep the sparkler through the air, creating a trail of light (**Figure 5.4a**). Although it appears that this trail is created by light left by the sparkler as you wave it through the air, there is, in fact, no light along this trail. The lighted trail is a creation of your mind, which retains a perception of the sparkler's light for a fraction of a second (**Figure 5.4b**). This retention of the perception of light in your mind is called the *persistence of vision*.

Persistence of vision is the continued perception of a visual stimulus even after it is no longer present. This persistence lasts for only a fraction of a second, so it isn't obvious in everyday experience when objects are present for long periods. However, the persistence of vision effect is noticeable for brief stimuli, like the moving sparkler or rapidly flashed pictures in a movie theater.

While you are watching a movie, you may see actions moving smoothly across the screen, but what is actually projected is quite different. First, a single film frame is positioned in front of the projector lens, and when the projector's shutter opens and closes, the image on the film frame flashes onto the screen. When the shutter is closed, the film moves on to the next frame, and during that time the screen is dark. When the next frame has arrived in front of the lens, the shutter opens and closes again, flashing the next image onto the screen. This process is repeated rapidly, 24 times per second, with 24 still images flashed on the screen every second and each image followed by a brief period of darkness (see **Table 5.1**). (Note that some filmmakers are now beginning to experiment with higher frame rates, as in Peter Jackson's *The Hobbit: An Unexpected Journey* (2012), shot at 48 frames per second, and Ang Lee's *Billy Lynn's Long Halftime Walk* (2016), shot at 120 frames per second.) A person viewing the film doesn't see the dark intervals between the images because the persistence of vision fills in the darkness by retaining the image of the previous frame.

➤ **Figure 5.4** (a) A sparkler can cause a trail of light when it is moved rapidly. (b) This trail occurs because the perception of the light is briefly held in the mind.

Perceptual trail

Gordon Langsbury/Alamy Stock Photo

TABLE 5.1

Persistence of Vision in Film*

What Happens?	What Is on the Screen?	What Do You Perceive?
Film frame 1 is projected.	Picture 1	Picture 1
Shutter closes and film moves to the next frame.	Darkness	Picture 1 (persistence of vision)
Shutter opens and film frame 2 is projected.	Picture 2	Picture 2

*The sequence indicated here is for movies projected using traditional film. Newer digital movie technologies are based on information stored on discs.

Sperling's Experiment: Measuring the Capacity and Duration of the Sensory Store

The persistence of vision effect that adds a trail to our perception of moving sparklers and fills in the dark spaces between frames in a film has been known since the early days of psychology (Boring, 1942). But George Sperling (1960) wondered how much *information* people can take in from briefly presented stimuli. He determined this in a famous experiment in which he flashed an array of letters, like the one in **Figure 5.5a**, on the screen for 50 milliseconds (50/1000 second) and asked his participants to report as many of the letters as possible. This part of the experiment used the **whole report method**; that is, participants were asked to report as many letters as possible from the entire 12-letter display. Given this task, they were able to report an average of 4.5 out of the 12 letters.

At this point, Sperling could have concluded that because the exposure was brief, participants saw only an average of 4.5 of the 12 letters. However, some of the participants in Sperling's experiment reported that they had seen all the letters, but that their perception had faded rapidly as they were reporting the letters, so by the time they had reported 4 or 5 letters, they could no longer see or remember the other letters.

Sperling reasoned that if participants couldn't report the 12-letter display because of fading, perhaps they would do better if they were told to just report the letters in a single 4-letter row. Sperling devised the **partial report method** to test this idea. Participants saw the 12-letter display for 50 ms, as before, but immediately after it was flashed, they heard a tone that told them which row of the matrix to report. A high-pitched tone indicated the top row; a medium-pitch indicated the middle row; and a low-pitch indicated the bottom row (**Figure 5.5b**).

Because the tones were presented immediately *after* the letters were turned off, the participant's attention was directed not to the actual letters, which were no longer present, but to whatever trace remained in the participant's mind after the letters were turned off. When the participants focused their attention on one of the rows, they correctly reported an average of about 3.3 of the 4 letters (82 percent) in that row. Because this occurred no matter which row they were reporting, Sperling concluded that immediately after the 12-letter display was presented, participants saw an average of 82 percent of all of the letters but were not able to report all of these letters because they rapidly faded as the initial letters were being reported.

Sperling then did an additional experiment to determine the time course of this fading. For this experiment, Sperling devised a **delayed partial report method** in which the letters were flashed on and off and then the cue tone was presented after a short delay (**Figure 5.5c**). The result of the delayed partial report experiments was that when the cue

➤ **Figure 5.5** Procedure for three of Sperling's (1960) experiments. (a) Whole report method: Person saw all 12 letters at once for 50 ms and reported as many as he or she could remember. (b) Partial report: Person saw all 12 letters, as before, but immediately after they were turned off, a tone indicated which row the person was to report. (c) Delayed partial report: Same as (b), but with a short delay between extinguishing the letters and presentation of the tone.

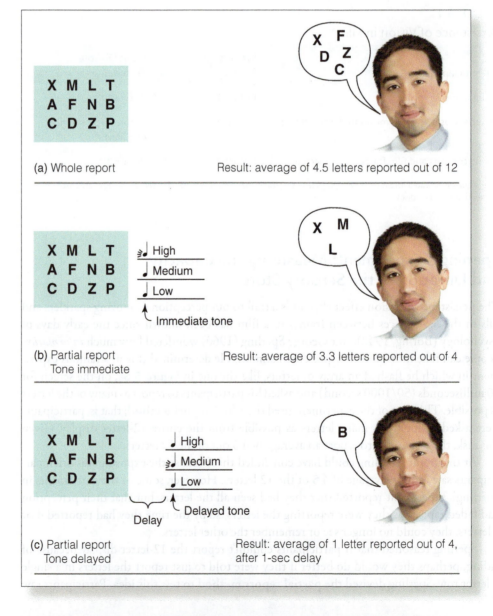

(a) Whole report — Result: average of 4.5 letters reported out of 12

(b) Partial report — Tone immediate — Result: average of 3.3 letters reported out of 4

(c) Partial report — Tone delayed — Result: average of 1 letter reported out of 4, after 1-sec delay

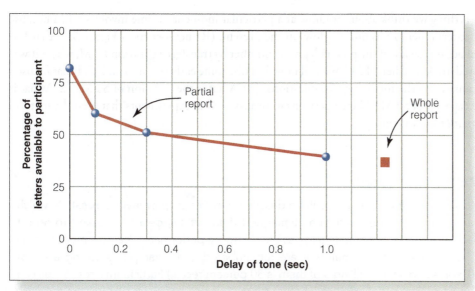

> **Figure 5.6** Results of Sperling's (1960) partial report experiments. The decrease in performance is due to the rapid decay of iconic memory (sensory memory in the modal model).

tones were delayed for 1 second after the flash, participants were able to report only slightly more than 1 letter in a row. **Figure 5.6** plots this result, showing the percentage of letters available to the participants from the entire display as a function of time following presentation of the display. This graph indicates that immediately after a stimulus is presented, all or most of the stimulus is available for perception. This is sensory memory. Then, over the next second, sensory memory fades.

Sperling concluded from these results that a short-lived sensory memory registers all or most of the information that hits our visual receptors, but that this information **decays** within less than a second. This brief sensory memory for visual stimuli, called **iconic memory** or the **visual icon** (icon means "image"), corresponds to the sensory memory stage of Atkinson and Shiffrin's modal model. Other research using auditory stimuli has shown that sounds also persist in the mind. This persistence of sound, called **echoic memory**, lasts for a few seconds after presentation of the original stimulus (Darwin et al., 1972). An example of echoic memory is when you hear someone say something, but you don't understand at first and say "What?" But even before the person can repeat what was said, you "hear" it in your mind. If that has happened to you, you've experienced echoic memory. In the next section, we consider the second stage of the modal model, short-term memory, which also holds information briefly, but for much longer than sensory memory.

Short-Term Memory: Storage

We saw in the preceding section that although sensory memory fades rapidly, Sperling's participants could report some of the letters. These letters are the part of the stimuli that has moved on to short-term memory in the flow diagram in Figure 5.2. **Short-term memory (STM)** is the system involved in storing small amounts of information for a brief period of time (Baddeley et al., 2009). Thus, whatever you are thinking about right now, or remember from what you have just read, is in your short-term memory. As we will see below, most of this information is eventually lost, and only some of it reaches the more permanent store of long-term memory (LTM).

Because of the brief duration of STM, it is easy to downplay its importance compared to LTM, but, as we will see, STM is responsible for a great deal of our mental life.

Everything we think about or know at a particular moment in time involves STM because short-term memory is our window on the present. (Remember from Figure 5.3e that Rachel became aware of the pizzeria's phone number by transferring it from LTM, where it was stored, back into her STM.) We will now describe some early research on STM that focused on answering the following two questions: (1) What is the duration of STM? (2) What is the capacity of STM? These questions were answered in experiments that used the method of *recall* to test memory.

METHOD   Recall

Most of the experiments we will be describing in this chapter involve **recall**, in which participants are presented with stimuli and then, after a delay, are asked to report back as many of the stimuli as possible. Memory performance can be measured as a percentage of the stimuli that are remembered. (For example, studying a list of 10 words and later recalling 3 of them is 30 percent recall.) Participants' responses can also be analyzed to determine whether there is a pattern to the way items are recalled. (For example, if participants are given a list consisting of types of fruits and models of cars, their recall can be analyzed to determine whether they grouped cars together and fruits together as they were recalling them.) Recall is also involved when a person is asked to recollect life events, such as graduating from high school, or to recall facts they have learned, such as the capital of Nebraska.

What Is the Duration of Short-Term Memory?

One of the major misconceptions about short-term memory is that it lasts for a relatively long time. It is not uncommon for people to refer to events they remember from a few days or weeks ago as being remembered from short-term memory. However, short-term memory, as conceived by cognitive psychologists, lasts 15 to 20 seconds or less. This was demonstrated by John Brown (1958) in England and Lloyd Peterson and Margaret Peterson (1959) in the United States, who used the method of recall to determine the duration of STM. Peterson and Peterson presented participants with three letters, such as FZL or BHM, followed by a number, such as 403. Participants were instructed to begin counting backwards by threes from that number. This was done to keep participants from rehearsing the letters. After intervals ranging from 3 to 18 seconds, participants were asked to recall the three letters. Participants correctly recalled about 80 percent of the three letter groups when they had counted for only 3 seconds, but recalled only about 12 percent of the groups after counting for 18 seconds. Results such as this have led to the conclusion that the effective duration of STM (when rehearsal is prevented, as occurred when counting backwards) is about 15 to 20 seconds or less (Zhang & Luck, 2009).

How Many *Items* Can Be Held in Short-Term Memory?

Not only is information lost rapidly from STM, but there is a limit to how much information can be held there. As we will see, estimates for how many items can be held in STM range from four to nine.

Digit Span   One measure of the capacity of STM is provided by the **digit span**—the number of digits a person can remember. You can determine your digit span by doing the following demonstration.

DEMONSTRATION   Digit Span

Using an index card or piece of paper, cover all of the numbers below. Move the card down to uncover the first string of numbers. Read the first set of numbers once, cover it up, and then write the numbers down in the correct order. Then move the card to the next string, and repeat this procedure until you begin making errors. The longest string you are able to reproduce without error is your digit span.

2 1 4 9

3 9 6 7 8

6 4 9 7 8 4

7 3 8 2 0 1 5

8 4 2 6 4 1 3 2

4 8 2 3 9 2 8 0 7

5 8 5 2 9 8 4 6 3 7

If you succeeded in remembering the longest string of digits, you have a digit span of 10 or perhaps more.

According to measurements of digit span, the average capacity of STM is about five to nine items—about the length of a phone number. This idea that the limit of STM is somewhere between five and nine was suggested by George Miller (1956), who summarized the evidence for this limit in his paper "The Magical Number Seven, Plus or Minus Two," described in Chapter 1 (page 15).

Change Detection   More recent measures of STM capacity have set the limit at about four items (Cowan, 2001). This conclusion is based on the results of experiments like one by Steven Luck and Edward Vogel (1997), which measured the capacity of STM by using a procedure called **change detection**.

METHOD   Change Detection

Following the "Change Detection" demonstration on page 117, we described experiments in which two pictures of a scene were flashed one after the other and the participants' task was to determine what had changed between the first and second pictures. The conclusion from these experiments was that people often miss changes in a scene.

Change detection has also been used with simpler stimuli to determine how much information a person can retain from a briefly flashed stimulus. An example of change detection is shown in **Figure 5.7**, which shows stimuli like the ones used in Luck and Vogel's experiment. The display on the left was flashed for 100 ms, followed by 900 ms of darkness and then the new display on the right. The participant's task was to indicate whether the second display was the same as or different from the first. (Notice that the color of one of the squares is changed in the second display.) This task is easy if the number of items is within the capacity of STM (**Figure 5.7a**) but becomes harder when the number of items becomes greater than the capacity of STM (**Figure 5.7b**).

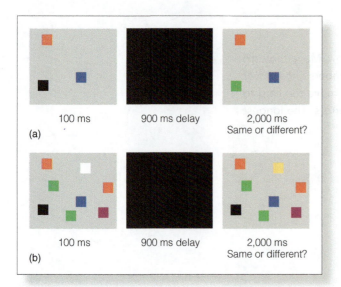

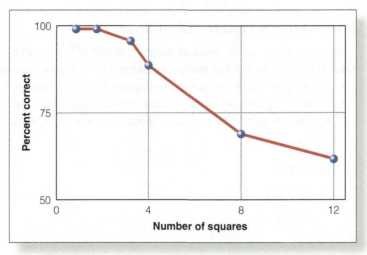

> **Figure 5.8** Result of Luck and Vogel's (1997) experiment, showing that performance began to decrease once there were four squares in the display.

(Source: Adapted from E. K. Vogel, A. W. McCollough, & M. G. Machizawa, Neural measures reveal individual differences in controlling access to working memory, *Nature*, 438, 500–503, 2005.)

> **Figure 5.7** (a) Stimuli used by Luck and Vogel (1997). The participant sees the first display and then indicates whether the second display is the same or different. In this example, the color of one square is changed in the second display. (b) Luck and Vogel stimuli showing a larger number of items.

(Source: Adapted from E. K. Vogel, A. W. McCollough, & M. G. Machizawa, Neural measures reveal individual differences in controlling access to working memory, *Nature*, 438, 500–503, 2005.)

The result of Luck and Vogel's experiment, shown in **Figure 5.8,** indicates that performance was almost perfect when there were one to three squares in the arrays, but that performance began decreasing when there were four or more squares. Luck and Vogel concluded from this result that participants were able to retain about four items in their short-term memory. Other experiments, using verbal materials, have come to the same conclusion (Cowan, 2001).

These estimates of either four or five times to nine items set rather low limits on the capacity of STM. If our ability to hold items in memory is so limited, how is it possible to hold many more items in memory in some situations, as when words are arranged in a sentence? The answer to this question was proposed by George Miller, who introduced the idea of *chunking* in his "Seven, Plus or Minus Two" paper.

Chunking Miller (1956) introduced the concept of **chunking** to describe the fact that small units (like words) can be combined into larger meaningful units, like phrases, or even larger units, like sentences, paragraphs, or stories. Consider, for example, trying to remember the following words: *monkey, child, wildly, zoo, jumped, city, ringtail, young.* How many units are there in this list? There are eight words, but if we group them differently, they can form the following four pairs: *ringtail monkey, jumped wildly, young child, city zoo.* We can take this one step further by arranging these groups of words into one sentence: The *ringtail monkey jumped wildly* for the *young child* at the *city zoo.*

A **chunk** has been defined as a collection of elements that are strongly associated with one another but are weakly associated with elements in other chunks (Cowan, 2001; Gobet et al., 2001). In our example, the word *ringtail* is strongly associated with the word *monkey* but is not as strongly associated with the other words, such as *child* or *city.*

Thus, chunking in terms of meaning increases our ability to hold information in STM. We can recall a sequence of 5 to 8 unrelated words, but arranging the words to form a meaningful sentence so that the words become more strongly associated with one another increases the memory span to 20 words or more (Butterworth et al., 1990). Chunking of a series of letters is illustrated by the following demonstration.

Although the second list has the same letters as the first group, it was easier to remember if you realized that this sequence consists of the names of four familiar organizations. You can therefore create four chunks, each of which is meaningful, and therefore easy to remember.

K. Anders Ericsson and coworkers (1980) demonstrated an effect of chunking by showing how a college student with average memory ability was able to achieve amazing feats of memory. Their participant, S.F., was asked to repeat strings of random digits that were read to him. Although S.F. had a typical memory span of 7 digits, after extensive training (230 one-hour sessions), he was able to repeat sequences of up to 79 digits without error. How did he do it? S.F. used chunking to recode the digits into larger units that formed meaningful sequences. S.F. was a runner, so some of the sequences were running times. For example, 3,492 became "3 minutes and 49 point 2 seconds, near world-record mile time." He also used other ways to create meaning, so 893 became "89 point 3, very old man." This example illustrates an interaction between STM and LTM, because S.F created some of his chunks based on his knowledge of running times that were stored in LTM.

Chunking enables the limited-capacity STM system to deal with the large amount of information involved in many of the tasks we perform every day, such as chunking letters into words as you read this, remembering the first three numbers of familiar telephone exchanges as a unit, and transforming long conversations into smaller units of meaning.

How Much *Information* Can Be Held in Short-Term Memory?

The idea that the capacity of short-term memory can be specified as a number of items, as described in the previous section, has generated a great deal of research. But some researchers have suggested that rather than describing memory capacity in terms of "number of items," it should be described in terms of "amount of information." When referring to visual objects, information has been defined as visual features or details of the object that are stored in memory (Alvarez & Cavanagh, 2004).

We can understand the reasoning behind the idea that information is important by considering storing pictures on a computer flash drive. The number of pictures that can be stored depends on the size of the drive *and* on the size of the pictures. Fewer large pictures, which have files that contain more detail, can be stored because they take up more space in memory.

With this idea in mind, George Alvarez and Patrick Cavanagh (2004) did an experiment using Luck and Vogel's change detection procedure. But in addition to colored squares, they also used more complex objects like the ones in **Figure 5.9a.** For example, for the shaded cubes, which were the most complex stimuli, a participant would see a display containing a number of different cubes, followed by a blank interval, followed by a display

➤ **Figure 5.9** (a) Some of the stimuli used in Alvarez and Cavanagh's (2004) change detection experiment. The stimuli range from low information (colored squares) to high information (cubes). In the actual experiments, there were six different objects in each set. (b) Results showing the average number of objects that could be remembered for each type of stimulus.

(Source: Adapted from G. A. Alvarez & P. Cavanagh, The capacity of visual short-term memory is set both by visual information load and by number of objects, *Psychological Science*, 15, 106–111, 2004.)

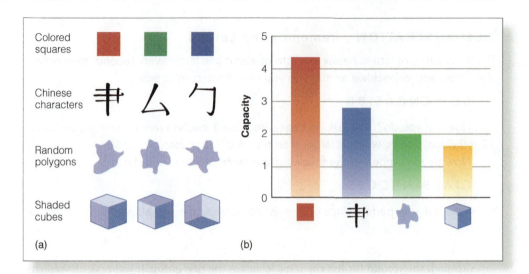

that was either the same as the first one or in which one of the cubes was different. The participant's task was to indicate whether the two displays were the same or different.

The result, shown in **Figure 5.9b**, was that participants' ability to make the same/different judgment depended on the complexity of the stimuli. Memory capacity for the colored squares was 4.4, but capacity for the cubes was only 1.6. Based on this result, Alvarez and Cavanagh concluded that the greater the amount of information in an image, the fewer items that can be held in visual short-term memory.

Should short-term memory capacity be measured in terms of "number of items" (Awh et al., 2007; Fukuda et al., 2010; Luck & Vogel, 1997) or "amount of detailed information" (Alvaraz & Cavanagh, 2004; Bays & Husain, 2008; Brady et al., 2011)? There are experiments that argue for both ideas, and the discussion among researchers is continuing. There is, however, agreement that whether considering items or information, there are limits on how much information we can store in short-term memory.

Our discussion of STM up to this point has focused on two properties: how *long* information is held in STM and how *much* information can be held in STM. Considering STM in this way, we could compare it to a container like a leaky bucket that can hold a certain amount of water for a limited amount of time. But as research on STM progressed, it became apparent that the concept of STM as presented in the modal model was too narrow to explain many research findings. The problem was that STM was described mainly as a short-term storage mechanism. As we will see next, more goes on in short-term memory than storage. Information doesn't just sit in STM; it can be manipulated in the service of mental processes such as computation, learning, and reasoning.

TEST YOURSELF 5.1

1. The chapter began with Christine's descriptions of five different types of memory. What are these? Which are of short duration? Of long duration? Why is short-term memory important?

2. Describe Atkinson and Shiffrin's modal model of memory both in terms of its structure (the boxes connected by arrows) and the control processes. Then describe how each part of the model comes into play when you decide you want to order pizza but can't remember the pizzeria's phone number.

3. Describe sensory memory and Sperling's experiment in which he briefly flashed an array of letters to measure the capacity and duration of sensory memory.

4. How did Peterson and Peterson measure the duration of STM? What is the approximate duration of STM?

5. What is the digit span? What does this indicate about the capacity of STM?

6. Describe Luck and Vogel's change detection experiment. What is the capacity of STM according to the results of this experiment?

7. What is chunking? What does it explain?

8. What two proposals have been made about how the capacity of short-term memory should be measured? Describe Alvarez and Cavanagh's experiment and their conclusion.

▶ Working Memory: Manipulating Information

Working memory, which was introduced in a paper by Baddeley and Hitch (1974), is defined as "a limited-capacity system for temporary storage *and manipulation of information for complex tasks such as comprehension, learning, and reasoning.*" The italicized portion of this definition is what makes working memory different from the old modal model conception of short-term memory.

Short-term memory is concerned mainly with storing information for a brief period of time (for example, remembering a phone number), whereas working memory is concerned with the *manipulation of information* that occurs during complex cognition (for example, remembering numbers while reading a paragraph). We can understand the idea that working memory is involved with the manipulation of information by considering a few examples. First, let's listen in on a conversation Rachel is having with the pizza shop:

Rachel: "I'd like to order a large pizza with broccoli and mushrooms."

Reply: "I'm sorry, but we're out of mushrooms. Would you like to substitute spinach instead?

Rachel was able to understand the pizza shop's reply by holding the first sentence, "I'm sorry, but we're out of mushrooms," in her memory while listening to the second sentence, and then making the connection between the two. If she had remembered only "Would you like to substitute spinach instead?" she wouldn't know whether it was being substituted for the broccoli or for the mushrooms. In this example, Rachel's short-term memory is being used not only for storing information but also for active processes like understanding conversations.

Another example of an active process occurs when we solve even simple math problems, such as "Multiply 43 times 6 in your head." Stop for a moment and try this while being aware of what you are doing in your head.

One way to solve this problem involves the following steps:

Visualize: 43×6.

Multiply $3 \times 6 = 18$.

Hold 8 in memory, while carrying the 1 over to the 4.

Multiply $6 \times 4 = 24$.

Add the carried 1 to the 24.

Place the result, 25, next to the 8.

The answer is 258.

It is easy to see that this calculation involves both storage (holding the 8 in memory, remembering the 6 and 4 for the next multiplication step) and active processes (carrying the 1, multiplying 6 × 4) at the same time. If only storage were involved, the problem could not be solved. There are other ways to carry out this calculation, but whatever method you choose involves both *holding* information in memory and *processing* information.

The fact that STM and the modal model do not consider dynamic processes that unfold over time is what led Baddeley and Hitch to propose that the name *working memory*, rather than *short-term memory*, be used for the short-term memory process. Current researchers often use both terms, short-term memory and working memory, when referring to the short-duration memory process, but the understanding is that the function of this process, whatever it is called, extends beyond just storage.

Returning to Baddeley, one of the things he noticed was that under certain conditions it is possible to carry out two tasks simultaneously, as illustrated in the following demonstration.

DEMONSTRATION   Reading Text and Remembering Numbers

Here are four numbers: 7, 1, 4, and 9. Remember them, then cover them and read the following passage while keeping the numbers in your mind.

> Baddeley reasoned that if STM had a limited storage capacity of about the length of a telephone number, filling up the storage capacity should make it difficult to do other tasks that depend on STM. But he found that participants could hold a short string of numbers in their memory while carrying out another task, such as reading or even solving a simple word problem. How are you doing with this task? What are the numbers? What is the gist of what you have just read?

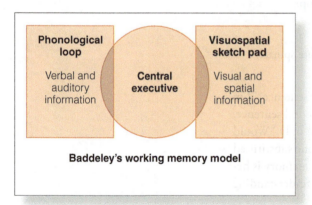

Baddeley's working memory model

➤ **Figure 5.10** Diagram of the three main components of Baddeley and Hitch's (1974; Baddeley, 2000) model of working memory: the phonological loop, the visuospatial sketch pad, and the central executive.

According to Atkinson and Shiffrin's modal model, it should only be possible to perform one of these tasks, which should occupy the entire STM. But when Baddeley did experiments involving tasks similar to those in the previous demonstration, he found that participants were able to read while simultaneously remembering numbers.

What kind of model can take into account both (1) the dynamic processes involved in cognitions such as understanding language and doing math problems and (2) the fact that people can carry out two tasks simultaneously? Baddeley concluded that working memory must be dynamic and must also consist of a number of components that can function separately. He proposed three components: the *phonological loop*, the *visuospatial sketch pad*, and the *central executive* (**Figure 5.10**).

The **phonological loop** consists of two components: the **phonological store**, which has a limited capacity and holds information for only a few seconds, and the **articulatory rehearsal process**, which is responsible for rehearsal that can keep items in the phonological store from decaying. The phonological loop holds verbal and auditory information. Thus, when you are trying to remember a telephone number or a person's name, or to understand what your cognitive psychology professor is talking about, you are using your phonological loop.

The **visuospatial sketch pad** holds visual and spatial information. When you form a picture in your mind or do tasks like solving a puzzle or finding your way around campus, you are using your visuospatial sketch pad. As you can see from the diagram, the phonological loop and the visuospatial sketch pad are attached to the central executive.

The **central executive** is where the major work of working memory occurs. The central executive pulls information from long-term memory and coordinates the activity of the phonological loop and visuospatial sketch pad by focusing on specific parts of a task and deciding how to divide attention between different tasks. The central executive is therefore the "traffic cop" of the working memory system.

To understand this "traffic cop" function, imagine you are driving in a strange city, a friend in the passenger seat is reading you directions to a restaurant, and the car radio is broadcasting the news. Your phonological loop is taking in the verbal directions; your sketch pad is helping you visualize a map of the streets leading to the restaurant; and your central executive is coordinating and combining these two kinds of information (**Figure 5.11**). In addition, the central executive might be helping you ignore the messages from the radio so you can focus your attention on the directions.

We will now describe a number of phenomena that illustrate how the phonological loop handles language, how the visuospatial sketch pad holds visual and spatial information, and how the central executive uses attention to coordinate between the two.

The Phonological Loop

We will describe three phenomena that support the idea of a system specialized for language: the phonological similarity effect, the word length effect, and articulatory suppression.

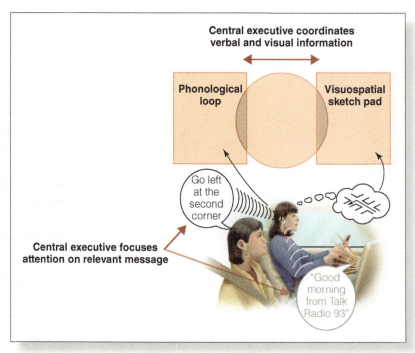

> **Figure 5.11** Tasks processed by the phonological loop (hearing directions, listening to the radio) and the visuospatial sketch pad (visualizing the route) are being coordinated by the central executive. The central executive also helps the driver ignore the messages from the radio so attention can be focused on hearing the directions.

Phonological Similarity Effect The **phonological similarity effect** is the confusion of letters or words that sound similar. In an early demonstration of this effect, R. Conrad (1964) flashed a series of target letters on a screen and instructed his participants to write down the letters in the order they were presented. He found that when participants made errors, they were most likely to misidentify the target letter as another letter that *sounded like* the target. For example, "F" was most often misidentified as "S" or "X," two letters that sound similar to "F," but was not as likely to be confused with letters like "E," that *looked like* the target. Thus, even though the participants *saw* the letters, the mistakes they made were based on the letters' *sounds*.

This result fits with our common experience with telephone numbers. Even though our contact with them is often visual, we usually remember them by repeating their sound over and over rather than by visualizing what the numbers looked like on the computer screen (also see Wickelgren, 1965). In present-day terminology, Conrad's result would be described as a demonstration of the phonological similarity effect, which occurs when words are processed in the phonological store part of the phonological loop.

Word Length Effect The **word length effect** occurs when memory for lists of words is better for short words than for long words. Thus, the word length effect predicts that more words will be recalled from List 1 (below) than from List 2.

List 1: beast, bronze, wife, golf, inn, limp, dirt, star

List 2: alcohol, property, amplifier, officer, gallery, mosquito, orchestra, bricklayer

Each list contains eight words, but according to the word length effect, the second list will be more difficult to remember because it takes more time to pronounce and rehearse longer words and to produce them during recall (Baddeley et al., 1984). (Note, however, that some researchers have proposed that the word length effect does not occur under some conditions; Jalbert et al., 2011; Lovatt et al., 2000, 2002.)

In another study of memory for verbal material, Baddeley and coworkers (1975) found that people are able to remember the number of items that they can pronounce in about 1.5–2.0 seconds (also see Schweickert & Boruff, 1986). Try counting out loud, as fast as you can, for 2 seconds. According to Baddeley, the number of words you can say should be close to your digit span.

Articulatory Suppression   Another way that the operation of the phonological loop has been studied is by determining what happens when its operation is disrupted. This occurs when a person is prevented from rehearsing items to be remembered by repeating an irrelevant sound, such as "the, the, the . . ." (Baddeley, 2000; Baddeley et al., 1984; Murray, 1968).

This repetition of an irrelevant sound results in a phenomenon called **articulatory suppression**, which reduces memory because speaking interferes with rehearsal. The following demonstration, which is based on an experiment by Baddeley and coworkers (1984), illustrates this effect of articulatory suppression.

DEMONSTRATION   Articulatory Suppression

Task 1: Read the following list. Then turn away and recall as many words as you can.

   dishwasher, hummingbird, engineering, hospital, homelessness, reasoning

Task 2: Read the following list while repeating "the, the, the . . ." out loud. Then turn away and recall as many words as you can.

   automobile, apartment, basketball, mathematics, gymnasium, Catholicism

Articulatory suppression makes it more difficult to remember the second list because repeating "the, the, the . . ." overloads the phonological loop, which is responsible for holding verbal and auditory information.

Baddeley and coworkers (1984) found that repeating "the, the, the . . ." not only reduces the ability to remember a list of words, it also eliminates the word length effect (**Figure 5.12a**). According to the word length effect, a list of one-syllable words should be easier to recall than a list of longer words because the shorter words leave more space in the phonological loop for rehearsal. However, eliminating rehearsal by saying "the, the, the . . ." removes this advantage for short words, so both short and long words are lost from the phonological store (**Figure 5.12b**).

The Visuospatial Sketch Pad

The visuospatial sketch pad handles visual and spatial information and is therefore involved in the process of **visual imagery**—the creation of visual images in the mind in the absence of a physical visual stimulus. The following demonstration illustrates an early visual imagery experiment by Roger Shepard and Jacqueline Metzler (1971).

DEMONSTRATION   Comparing Objects

Look at the two pictures in **Figure 5.13a** and decide, as quickly as possible, whether they represent two different views of the same object ("same") or two different objects ("different"). Also make the same judgment for the two objects in **Figure 5.13b**.

When Shepard and Metzler measured participants' reaction time to decide whether pairs of objects were the same or different, they obtained the relationship shown in **Figure 5.14** for objects that were the same. From this function, we can see that when one shape was rotated 40 degrees compared to the other shape (as in Figure 5.13a), it took 2 seconds to decide that a pair was the same shape. However, for a greater difference caused by a rotation of

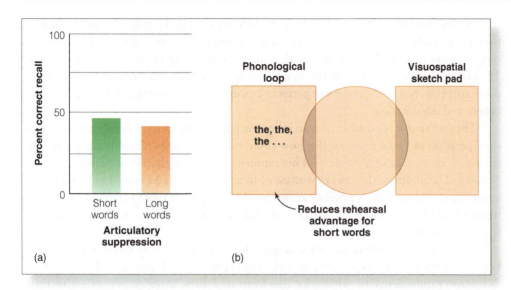

➤ **Figure 5.12** (a) Saying "the, the, the . . ." abolishes the word length effect, so there is little difference in performance for short words and long words (Baddeley et al., 1984). (b) Saying "the, the, the . . ." causes this effect by reducing rehearsal in the phonological loop.

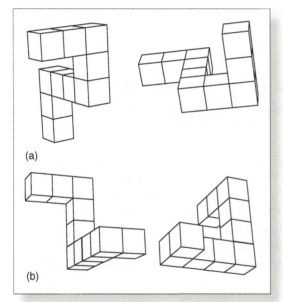

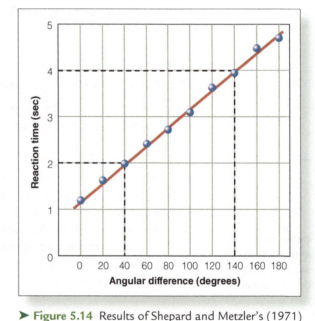

➤ **Figure 5.13** Stimuli for the "Comparing Objects" demonstration. See text for details.

(Source: Based on R. N. Shepard & J. Metzler, Mental rotation of three-dimensional objects, *Science*, 171, Figures 1a & b, 701–703, 1971.)

➤ **Figure 5.14** Results of Shepard and Metzler's (1971) mental rotation experiment.

(Source: Based on R. N. Shepard & J. Metzler, Mental rotation of three-dimensional objects, *Science*, 171, Figures 1a & b, 701–703, 1971.)

140 degrees (as in Figure 5.13b), it took 4 seconds. Based on this finding that reaction times were longer for greater differences in orientation, Shepard and Metzler inferred that participants were solving the problem by rotating an image of one of the objects in their mind, a phenomenon called **mental rotation**. This mental rotation is an example of the operation of the visuospatial sketch pad because it involves visual rotation through space.

Another demonstration of the use of visual representation is an experiment by Sergio Della Sala and coworkers (1999) in which participants were presented with a task like the one in the following demonstration.

DEMONSTRATION   Recalling Visual Patterns

Look at the pattern in **Figure 5.15** for 3 seconds. Then turn the page and indicate which of the squares in **Figure 5.17** need to be filled in to duplicate this pattern.

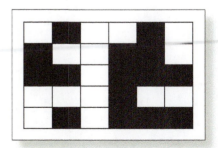

➤ **Figure 5.15** Test pattern for visual recall test. After looking at this for 3 seconds, turn the page.

In this demonstration, the patterns are difficult to code verbally, so completing the pattern depends on visual memory. Della Sala presented his participants with patterns ranging from small (a 2 × 2 matrix with 2 shaded squares) to large (a 5 × 6 matrix with 15 shaded squares), with half of the squares being shaded in each pattern. He found that participants were able to complete patterns consisting of an average of 9 shaded squares before making mistakes.

The fact that it is possible to remember the patterns in Della Sala's matrix illustrates the operation of visual imagery. But how could the participants remember patterns consisting of an average of 9 squares? This number is at the high end of Miller's range of 5 to 9 and is far above the lower estimate of four items for STM from Luck and Vogel's experiment (Figure 5.8). A possible answer to this question is that individual squares can be combined into subpatterns—a form of chunking that could increase the number of squares remembered.

Just as the operation of the phonological loop is disrupted by interference (articulatory suppression, see page 146), so is the visuospatial sketch pad. Lee Brooks (1968) did some experiments in which he demonstrated how interference can affect the operation of the visuospatial sketch pad. The following demonstration is based on one of Brooks's tasks.

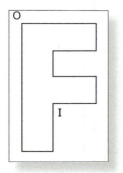

➤ **Figure 5.16** "F" stimulus for Holding a Spatial Stimulus in the Mind demonstration illustrating outside (O) and inside (I) corners. Read the directions in the text, then cover up the F.

(Source: From Brooks, 1968)

DEMONSTRATION   Holding a Spatial Stimulus in the Mind

This demonstration involves visualizing a large "F" like the one in **Figure 5.16**, which has two types of corners, "outside corners" and "inside corners," two of which are labeled.

Task 1: Cover Figure 5.16, and while visualizing F in your mind, start at the upper-left corner (the one marked with the o), and, moving around the outline of the F in a clockwise direction in your mind (no looking at the figure!), *point to* "Out" in **Table 5.2** for an outside corner and "In" for an inside corner. Move your response down one level in Table 5.2 for each new corner.

Task 2: Visualize the F again, but this time, as you move around the outline of the F in a clockwise direction in your mind, *say* "Out" if the corner is an outside corner or "In" if it is an inside corner.

Which was easier, *pointing* to "Out" or "In" or *saying* "Out" or "In"? Most people find that the pointing task is more difficult. The reason is that holding the image of the letter and pointing are both visuospatial tasks, so the visuospatial sketch pad becomes overloaded. In contrast, saying "Out" or "In" is an articulatory task that is handled by the phonological loop, so speaking doesn't interfere with visualizing the F.

The Central Executive

The central executive is the component that makes working memory "work," because it is the control center of the working memory system. Its mission is not to store information but to coordinate how information is used by the phonological loop and visuospatial sketch pad (Baddeley, 1996).

Baddeley describes the central executive as being an *attention controller*. It determines how attention is focused on a specific task, how it is divided between two tasks, and how it is switched between tasks. The central executive is therefore related to *executive attention*, which we introduced in Chapter 4 (p. 123), and it is essential in situations such as when a person is attempting to simultaneously drive and use a cell phone. In this example, the executive would be coordinating phonological loop processes (talking on the phone, understanding the conversation) and sketch-pad processes (visualizing landmarks and the layout of the streets, navigating the car).

One of the ways the central executive has been studied is by assessing the behavior of patients with brain damage. As we will see later in the chapter, the frontal lobe plays a central role in working memory. It is not surprising, therefore, that patients with frontal lobe damage have problems controlling their attention. A typical behavior of patients with frontal lobe damage is **perseveration**—repeatedly performing the same action or thought even if it is not achieving the desired goal.

Consider, for example, a problem that can be easily solved by following a particular rule ("Pick the red object"). A person with frontal lobe damage might be responding correctly on each trial, as long as the rule stays the same. However, when the rule is switched ("Now pick the blue object"), the person continues following the old rule, even when given feedback that his or her responding is now incorrect. This perseveration represents a breakdown in the central executive's ability to control attention.

TABLE 5.2
Use for Demonstration

Corner	Point	
1	OUT	IN
2	OUT	IN
3	OUT	IN
4	OUT	IN
5	OUT	IN
6	OUT	IN
7	OUT	IN
8	OUT	IN
9	OUT	IN
10	OUT	IN

An Added Component: The Episodic Buffer

We have seen that Baddeley's three-component model can explain results such as the phonological similarity effect, the word length effect, articulatory suppression, mental rotation, and how interference affects operation of the visuospatial sketch pad. However, research has shown that there are some things the model can't explain. One of those things is that working memory can hold more than would be expected based on just the phonological loop or visuospatial sketch pad. For example, people can remember long sentences consisting of as many as 15 to 20 words. The ability to do this is related to chunking, in which meaningful units are grouped together (page 140), and it is also related to long-term memory, which is involved in knowing the meanings of words in the sentence and in relating parts of the sentence to each other based on the rules of grammar.

These ideas are nothing new. It has long been known that the capacity of working memory can be increased by chunking and that there is an interchange of information between working memory and long-term memory. But Baddeley decided it was necessary to propose an additional component of working memory to address these abilities. This new component, which he called the **episodic buffer**, is shown in Baddeley's new model of working memory in **Figure 5.18**. The episodic buffer can store information (thereby providing extra capacity) and is connected to LTM (thereby making interchange between working memory and LTM possible). Notice that this model also shows that the visuospatial sketch pad and phonological loop are linked to long-term memory.

The proposal of the episodic buffer represents another step in the evolution of Baddeley's model, which has been stimulating research on working memory for more than 40 years since it was first proposed. If the exact functioning of the episodic buffer seems a little vague, it is because it is a "work in progress." Even Baddeley (Baddeley et al., 2009) states that "the concept of an episodic buffer is still at a very early stage of development" (p. 57). The main

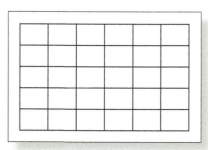

➤ **Figure 5.17** Answer matrix for the visual recall test. Put a check in each square that was darkened in the pattern you just looked at.

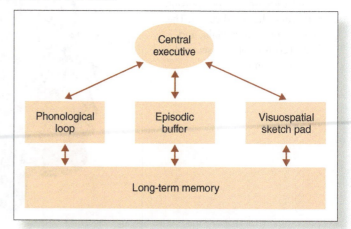

➤ **Figure 5.18** Baddeley's revised working memory model, which contains the original three components plus the episodic buffer.

"take-home message" about the episodic buffer is that it represents a way of increasing storage capacity and communicating with LTM.

Working Memory and the Brain

The history of research on working memory and the brain has been dominated by one structure: the prefrontal cortex (PFC) (see **Figure 5.19**). We will first describe this link between working memory and the PFC and will then consider research that has expanded the "brain map" of working memory to include many additional areas.

The Effect of Damage to the Prefrontal Cortex

The classic example of PFC damage causing changes in behavior is the case of Phineas Gage and the tamping rod (**Figure 5.20a**). The scene takes place on a railroad track in Vermont on September 13, 1848, in which Gage was directing a work crew that was blasting rock from a railway construction project. Unfortunately for Gage, he made a fateful mistake when he jammed a 3-foot 7-inch long, 1.25-inch-wide iron tamping rod into a hole containing gunpowder, and an accidental spark ignited the gunpowder and propelled the tamping rod into this left cheek and out through the top of his head (**Figure 5.20b**), causing damage to his frontal lobe (Ratiu et al., 2004).

Amazingly, Gage survived, but reports from the time noted that the accident had changed Gage's personality from an upstanding citizen to a person with low impulse control, poor ability to plan, and poor social skills. Apparently, there is some uncertainty as to the accuracy of these early descriptions of Gage's behavior (Macmillan, 2002). Nonetheless, reports about Gage, whether accurate or not, gave rise to the idea that the frontal lobes are involved in a variety of mental functions, including personality and planning.

Although Gage's accident and spectacular recovery brought the frontal lobes to people's attention, our present knowledge about the frontal lobe has been deduced from modern neuropsychological case studies and controlled behavioral and neurophysiological

➤ **Figure 5.19** Cross section of the brain showing some key structures involved in memory. The discussion of working memory focuses on the prefrontal cortex and the visual cortex. The hippocampus, amygdala, and frontal cortex will be discussed in Chapters 6 and 7.

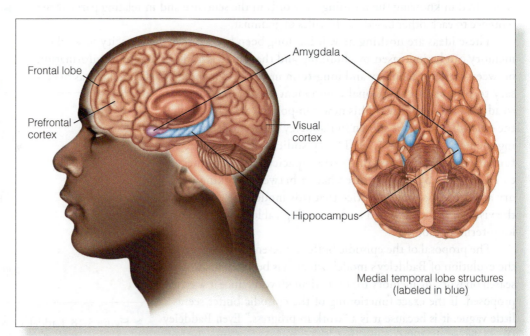

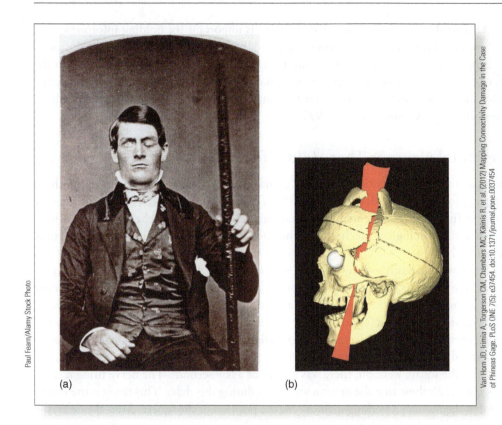

Van Horn JD, Irimia A, Torgerson CM, Chambers MC, Kikinis R, et al. (2012) Mapping Connectivity Damage in the Case of Phineas Gage. PLoS ONE 7(5): e37454. doi:10.1371/journal.pone.0037454

Paul Fearn/Alamy Stock Photo

▶ **Figure 5.20** (a) Phineas Gage posing with the tamping rod. (b) Diagram showing how the tamping rod went through Gage's head.

experiments. We've noted that damage to the frontal lobe causes problems in controlling attention, which is an important function of the central executive.

An example of animal research that explored the effect of frontal lobe damage on memory tested monkeys using the **delayed-response task**, which required a monkey to hold information in working memory during a delay period (Goldman-Rakic, 1990, 1992). **Figure 5.21** shows the setup for this task. The monkey sees a food reward in one of two food wells. Both wells are then covered, a screen is lowered, and then there is a delay before the screen is raised again. When the screen is raised, the monkey must remember which well had the food and uncover the correct food well to obtain a reward. Monkeys can be trained to accomplish this task. However, if their PFC is removed, their performance drops to chance level, so they pick the correct food well only about half of the time.

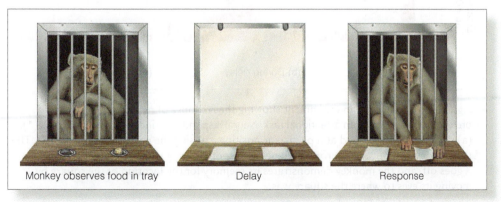

▶ **Figure 5.21** The delayed-response task being administered to a monkey.

This result supports the idea that the PFC is important for holding information for brief periods of time. In fact, it has been suggested that one reason we can describe the memory behavior of very young infants as "out of sight, out of mind" (when an object that the infant can see is then hidden from view, the infant behaves as if the object no longer exists) is that their frontal and prefrontal cortex do not become adequately developed until about 8 months of age (Goldman-Rakic, 1992).

Prefrontal Neurons That Hold Information

An important characteristic of memory is that it involves *delay* or *waiting*. Something happens, followed by a delay, which is brief for working memory; then, if memory is successful, the person remembers what has happened. Researchers, therefore, have looked for physiological mechanisms that hold information about events after they are over.

Shintaro Funahashi and coworkers (1989) conducted an experiment in which they recorded from neurons in a monkey's PFC while the monkey carried out a delayed-response task. The monkey first looked steadily at a fixation point, X, while a square was flashed at one position on the screen (**Figure 5.22a**). In this example, the square was flashed in the upper-left corner (on other trials, the square was flashed at different positions on the screen). This caused a small response in the neuron.

After the square went off, there was a delay of a few seconds. The nerve firing records in **Figure 5.22b** show that the neuron was firing during this delay. This firing is the neural record of the monkey's working memory for the position of the square. After the delay, the fixation X went off. This was a signal for the monkey to move its eyes to where the square

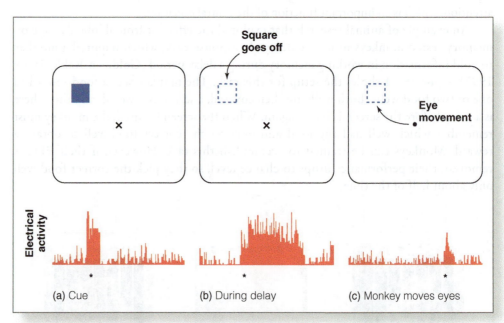

(a) Cue   (b) During delay   (c) Monkey moves eyes

➤ **Figure 5.22** Results of an experiment showing the response of neurons in the monkey's prefrontal cortex during an attentional task. Neural responding is indicated by an asterisk (*). (a) A cue square is flashed at a particular position, causing the neuron to respond. (b) The square goes off, but the neuron continues to respond during the delay. (c) The fixation X goes off, and the monkey demonstrates its memory for the location of the square by moving its eyes to where the square was.

(Source: Adapted from S. Funahashi, C. J. Bruce, & P. S. Goldman-Rakic, Mnemonic coding of visual space in the primate dorsolateral prefrontal cortex, *Journal of Neurophysiology*, 6, 331–349, 1989.)

had been flashed (**Figure 5.22c**). The monkey's ability to do this provides behavioral evidence that it had, in fact, remembered the location of the square.

The key result of this experiment was that Funahashi found neurons that responded only when the square was flashed in a *particular location* and that these neurons *continued responding during the delay*. For example, some neurons responded only when the square was flashed in the upper-right corner and then during the delay; other neurons responded only when the square was presented at other positions on the screen and then during the delay. The firing of these neurons indicates that an object was presented at a particular place, and this information about the object's location remains available for as long as these neurons continue firing (also see Funahashi, 2006).

The Neural Dynamics of Working Memory

The idea that information can be held in working memory by neural activity that continues across a time gap, as in Figure 5.22b, fits with the idea that neural firing transmits information in the nervous system. But some researchers have proposed that information can be held during the delay by a mechanism that doesn't involve continuous firing.

One idea, proposed by Mark Stokes (2015), is that information can be stored by short-term changes in neural networks, as shown in **Figure 5.23**. **Figure 5.23a** shows the *activity state*, in which information to be remembered causes a number of neurons, indicated by the dark circles, to briefly fire. This firing doesn't continue, but causes the *synaptic state*, shown in **Figure 5.23b**, in which a number of connections between neurons, indicated by the darker lines, are strengthened. These changes in connectivity, which Stokes calls **activity-silent working memory**, last only a few seconds, but that is long enough for working memory. Finally, when the memory is being retrieved, the memory is indicated by the pattern of firing in the network, shown by the dark circles in **Figure 5.23c**.

Thus, in Stokes's model, information is held in memory not by continuous nerve firing but by a brief change in the connectivity of neurons in a network. Other researchers have proposed other ways of holding information in working memory that don't require continuous neural firing (Lundquist et al., 2016; Murray et al., 2017). These models are based on experiments and computations too complex to describe here, and all are speculative. But the idea that information can be stored in the nervous system by changes in the

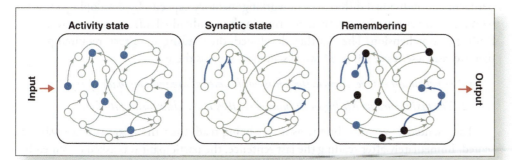

➤ **Figure 5.23** Diagram showing Stokes's (2015) proposal that information can be stored in working memory by changes in the connectivity of a neural network. (a) Activity state, showing that some neurons in the network (blue circles) are activated by the incoming stimulus. (b) Synaptic state, showing connections that have been strengthened between neurons in the network (blue lines). (c) Activity associated with the memory.

(Source: Stokes, M. G, 'Activity-silent' working memory in prefrontal cortex: a dynamic coding framework. Trends in Cognitive Sciences, 19(7), 394–405. Figure 2a, top, p. 397, 2015.)

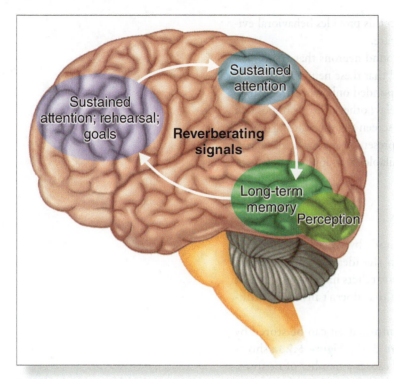

connections in neural networks is one of the "hot" topics of current research on the neural mechanisms of memory (Kaldy & Sigala, 2017).

Another current idea about working memory is that it involves physiological processes that extend beyond the PFC. It isn't hard to see why working memory would involve brain areas in addition to the frontal lobes. Just look back at the woman driving the car in Figure 5.11, who is using her central executive to switch her attention from one thing to another, which involves visual capacities, as she imagines the road layout, and verbal capacities, as she listens to her companion's directions. Working memory, therefore, involves an interplay between a number of areas of the brain. This interplay is symbolized by the interaction between brain areas in **Figure 5.24**, which depicts a network based on the research on a large number of experiments (Curtis & Espisoto, 2003; Ericsson et al., 2015; Lee & Baker, 2016; Riley & Constantinidis, 2016). This idea that a number of areas of the brain are involved in working memory is an example of distributed representation, which we introduced in Chapter 2 (page 43).

➤ **Figure 5.24** Map showing some of the areas of the brain that are involved in working memory. This simplified version of the working memory structures proposed by Ericsson et al. (2015) indicates not only that a number of areas are associated with working memory, but that they communicate with each other.

Source: Ericsson et al., Neurocognitive architecture of working memory, *Neuron* 88, 33–46. Figure 10d, page 35, 2015.)

◆ SOMETHING TO CONSIDER: WHY IS MORE WORKING MEMORY BETTER?

Is working memory the same in different people? The answer to this question—that there are individual differences in the capacity of people's working memory—shouldn't be surprising. After all, people differ in physical capabilities, and it is a common observation that some people have better memory than others. But researchers' interest in individual differences in working memory extends beyond simply demonstrating that differences exist to demonstrating how differences in working memory influence cognitive functioning and behavior.

Meredyth Daneman and Patricia Carpenter (1980) carried out one of the early experiments on individual differences in working memory capacity by developing a test for working memory capacity and then determining how individual differences were related to reading comprehension. The test they developed, the **reading span test**, required participants to read a series of 13- to 16-word sentences such as these:

(1) *When at last his eyes opened, there was no glimmer of strength, no shade of angle.*

(2) *The taxi turned up Michigan Avenue where they had a clear view of the lake.*

Each sentence was seen briefly as it was being read, then the next sentence was presented. Immediately after reading the last sentence, the participant was asked to remember the last word in each sentence in the order that they occurred. The participant's **reading span** was the number of sentences they could read, and then correctly remember all of the last words.

Participants' reading spans ranged from 2 to 5, and the size of the reading span was highly correlated with their performance on a number of reading comprehension tasks and their verbal SAT score. Daneman and Carpenter concluded that working memory capacity is a crucial source of individual differences in reading comprehension. Other research has shown that higher working memory capacity is related to better academic performance

(Best & Miller, 2010; Best et al., 2011), better chance of graduating from high school (Fitzpatrick et al., 2015), the ability to control emotions (Schmeichel et al., 2008), and greater creativity (De Drue et al., 2012).

But what is it about differences in working memory capacity that results in these outcomes? Edmund Vogel and coworkers (2005) focused on one component of working memory: the control of attention by the central executive. They first separated participants into two groups based on their performance on a test of working memory. Participants in the *high-capacity group* were able to hold a number of items in working memory; participants in the *low-capacity group* were able to hold fewer items in working memory.

Participants were tested using the change detection procedure (see Method: Change Detection, page 139). **Figure 5.25a** shows the sequence of stimuli: (1) they first saw a cue indicating whether to direct their attention to the red rectangles on the left side or the red rectangles on the right side of the displays that followed. (2) They then saw a memory display for one-tenth of a second followed by (3) a brief blank screen and then (4) a test display. Their task was to indicate whether the cued red rectangles in the test display had the same or different orientations than the ones in the memory display. While they were making this judgment, a brain response called the *event-related potential* was measured, which indicated how much space was used in working memory as they carried out the task.

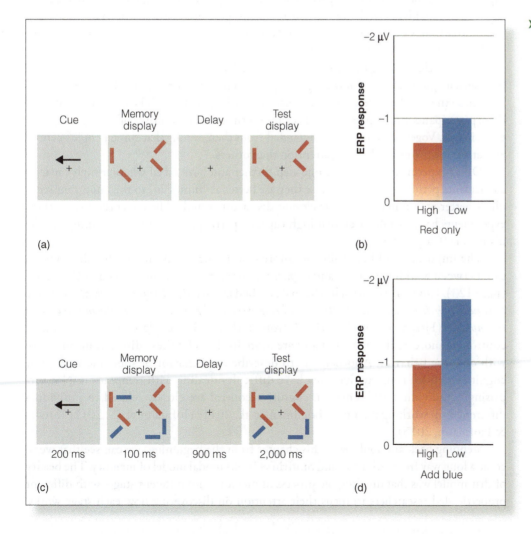

(a)

(b)

(c)

(d)

➤ **Figure 5.25** (a) Sequence for the Vogel et al. (2005) task. The arrow in this example tells the participant to pay attention to the left side of the memory and test displays. The task is to indicate whether the red rectangles on the attended side are the same or different in the two displays. (b) ERP response for low- and high-capacity participants for the task in part (a). (c) Display with blue bars added. These bars are added to distract the participants, who are supposed to be focusing on the red rectangles. (d) ERP response for the task in part (c).

(Source: Based on E. K. Vogel, A. W. McCollough, & M. G. Machizawa, Neural measures reveal individual differences in controlling access to working memory, *Nature*, 438, 500–503, 2005.)

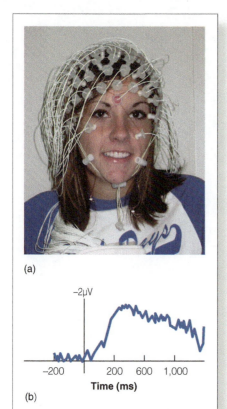

(a)

−2μV

−200   200   600   1,000
Time (ms)

(b)

➤ **Figure 5.26** (a) A person wearing electrodes for recording the event-related potential (ERP). (b) An ERP recorded as a participant is viewing the stimuli.

(Source: Courtesy Natasha Tokowicz.)

METHOD Event-Related Potential

The **event-related potential (ERP)** is recorded with small disc electrodes placed on a person's scalp, as shown in **Figure 5.26a**. Each electrode picks up signals from groups of neurons that fire together. The event-related potential shown in **Figure 5.26b** was recorded as a person was making a judgment in the Vogel experiment. This response had been shown in other experiments to be related to the number of items placed into working memory, so a larger ERP response indicates how much capacity was used.

The graph in **Figure 5.25b** shows the size of the ERP for the red bar only display for the high- and low-working memory groups. This isn't a particularly interesting result, because the size of the ERP is nearly the same for both groups. But Vogel also ran another condition in which he added some extra blue bars, as shown in **Figure 5.25c**. These bars were not relevant to the participant's task so their purpose was to distract the participant's attention. If the central executive is doing its job, these extra bars should have no effect, because attention would remain focused on the red bars. The results in **Figure 5.25d** show that adding blue bars caused an increase in the response of the high-capacity group, but caused a larger increase in the response of the low-capacity group.

The fact that adding the blue bars had only a small effect on the response of the high-capacity group means that these participants were very efficient at ignoring the distractors, so the irrelevant blue stimuli did not take up much space in working memory. Because allocating attention is a function of the central executive, this means that the central executive was functioning well for these participants.

The fact that adding the two blue bars caused a large increase in the response of the low-capacity group means that these participants were not able to ignore the irrelevant blue stimuli, so the blue bars were taking up space in working memory. The central executive of these participants is not operating as efficiently as the central executives of the high-capacity participants. Vogel and coworkers concluded from these results that some people's central executives are better at allocating attention than others'.

Other experiments have gone one step further and have asked whether high-capacity participants performed better because they are better at "tuning in" to the important stimuli or better at "tuning out" the irrelevant distractor stimuli. The conclusion from these experiments has generally been that high-capacity participants are better at tuning out the distractors (Gaspar et al., 2016).

The importance of being able to ignore distracting stimuli highlights the connection between working memory and *cognitive control*, which we introduced in Chapter 4 (page 123). Cognitive control has been described as *a set of functions, which allow people to regulate their behavior and attentional resources, and to resist the temptation to give in to impulses* (Fitzpatrick et al., 2015; Garon et al., 2008). People with poor cognitive control are more easily distracted and are more likely to let these distractions interfere with ongoing behavior. Another way to describe the behavior of someone with poor cognitive control is to say that they have difficulty dealing with temptation. Not surprisingly, individual differences in cognitive control are closely related to individual differences in working memory (Friedman et al., 2011; Hofmann et al., 2012; Kotabe & Hofmann, 2015).

Stepping back and looking at this chapter from the beginning, we can see that we've come a long way from Atkinson and Shiffrin's (1968) modal model of memory. The beauty of that model was that dividing the process of memory into different stages with different properties led researchers to focus their attention on discovering how each stage works.

The story that has unfolded since the modal model was introduced has involved behavioral experiments (which led to proposing more stages, as in Baddeley's model in Figure 5.18), and physiological experiments (which considered how brief memories are stored in the nervous system).

This chapter has been a "warm up" for what is to come. Chapter 6 continues the idea of stages of memory and describes research that zooms in on the long-term memory box of the modal model. We will see how this research distinguished between a number of different types of long-term memory. Chapter 7 then looks at some of the mechanisms involved in getting information into and out of long-term memory and returns to physiology to discuss how neurons can store information for periods ranging from minutes to a lifetime.

TEST YOURSELF 5.2

1. Describe two findings that led Baddeley to begin considering alternatives to the modal model.

2. What are the differences between STM and working memory?

3. Describe Baddeley's three-component model of working memory.

4. Describe the phonological similarity effect, the word length effect, and the effect of articulatory suppression. What do these effects indicate about the phonological loop?

5. Describe the visuospatial sketch pad, the Shepard and Metzler mental rotation task, Della Sala's visual pattern task, and Brooks's "F" task. Be sure you understand what each task indicates about the visuospatial sketch pad.

6. What is the central executive? What happens when executive function is lost because of damage to the frontal lobe?

7. What is the episodic buffer? Why was it proposed, and what are its functions?

8. What is the connection between Phineas Gage and the frontal cortex?

9. The physiology of working memory has been studied (1) by determining how removal of the PFC in monkeys affects memory and (2) by recording neural responses from monkeys. What have these studies taught us about working memory and the brain?

10. How is Stokes's model of working memory a departure from the idea that there has to be continuous neural activity during the delay between presenting a stimulus and remembering it?

11. Describe how Daneman and Carpenter discovered the relationship between working memory capacity, reading comprehension, and verbal SAT scores.

12. Describe Vogel's experiment that measured the event-related potential in participants with high-capacity working memory and those with low-capacity working memory as they were carrying out a change detection task. What does the result of this experiment indicate about how the central executive allocated attention in these two types of participants?

13. Do high-capacity working memory participants perform better because they are better at "tuning in" to relevant stimuli or better at "tuning out" distractors?

14. What is self-control, and why would we expect it to be related to working memory?

CHAPTER SUMMARY

1. Memory is the process involved in retaining, retrieving, and using information about stimuli, images, events, ideas, and skills after the original information is no longer present. Five different types of memory are sensory, short-term, episodic, semantic, and procedural.

2. Atkinson and Shiffrin's modal model of memory consists of three structural features: sensory memory, short-term memory, and long-term memory. Another feature of the model is control processes such as rehearsal and attentional strategies.

3. Sperling used two methods, whole report and partial report, to determine the capacity and time course of visual sensory memory. The duration of visual sensory memory (iconic memory) is less than 1 second, and the duration of auditory sensory memory (echoic memory) is about 2–4 seconds.

4. Short-term memory is our window on the present. Brown and Peterson and Peterson determined that the duration of STM is about 15–20 seconds.

5. Digit span is one measure of the capacity of short-term memory. According to George Miller's classic "Seven, Plus or Minus Two" paper, the capacity of STM is five to nine items. According to more recent experiments, the capacity is about four items. The amount of information held in STM can be expanded by chunking, in which small units are combined into larger, more meaningful units. The memory performance of the runner S.F. provides an example of chunking.

6. It has been suggested that rather than describing short-term memory capacity in terms of number of items, it should be described in terms of amount of information. An experiment by Alvarez and Cavanagh, using stimuli ranging from simple to complex, supports this idea.

7. Baddeley revised the short-term memory component of the modal model in order to deal with dynamic processes that unfold over time and can't be explained by a single short-term process. In this new model, working memory replaces STM.

8. Working memory is a limited-capacity system for storage and manipulation of information in complex tasks. It consists of three components: the phonological loop, which holds auditory or verbal information; the visuospatial sketch pad, which holds visual and spatial information; and the central executive, which coordinates the action of the phonological loop and visuospatial sketch pad.

9. The following effects can be explained in terms of operation of the phonological loop: (a) phonological similarity effect, (b) word-length effect, and (c) articulatory suppression.

10. Shepard and Metzler's mental rotation experiment illustrates visual imagery, which is one of the functions of the visuospatial sketch pad. Della Sala's visual recall task used visual imagery to estimate the capacity of working memory. Brooks's "F" experiment showed that two tasks can be handled simultaneously if one involves the visuospatial sketch pad and the other involves the phonological loop. Performance decreases if one component of working memory is called on to deal with two tasks simultaneously.

11. The central executive coordinates how information is used by the phonological loop and visuospatial sketch pad; it can be thought of as an attention controller. Patients with frontal lobe damage have trouble controlling their attention, as illustrated by the phenomenon of perseveration.

12. The working memory model has been updated to include an additional component called the episodic buffer, which helps connect working memory with LTM and which has a greater capacity and can hold information longer than the phonological loop or the visuospatial sketch pad.

13. Phineas Gage's accident brought some possible functions of the prefrontal cortex to people's attention.

14. Behaviors that depend on working memory can be disrupted by damage to the prefrontal cortex. This has been demonstrated by testing monkeys on the delayed-response task.

15. There are neurons in the prefrontal cortex that fire to presentation of a stimulus and continue firing as this stimulus is held in memory.

16. Current research on the physiology of working memory has introduced the idea that (a) information can be contained in patterns of neural connectivity and (b) working memory involves many areas of the brain.

17. Daneman and Carpenter developed a test to measure working memory capacity called the reading span test. Using this test to determine individual differences in working memory capacity, they found that high-capacity working memory is associated with better reading comprehension and higher SAT scores. Other research has confirmed and extended these findings.

18. Vogel and coworkers used the ERP to demonstrate differences in how the central executive operates for participants with high- and low-capacity working memory and concluded that there are differences in people's ability to allocate attention. Other experiments have shown that people with high-capacity working memory are better at "tuning out" distractors than people with low-capacity working memory.

19. There is a relation between working memory capacity and cognitive control, which is involved in dealing with temptation.

THINK ABOUT IT

1. Analyze the following in terms of how the various stages of the modal model are activated, using Rachel's pizza-ordering experience in **Figure 5.3** as a guide: (1) listening to a lecture in class, taking notes, and reviewing the notes later as you study for an exam; (2) watching a scene in a James Bond movie in which Bond captures the female enemy agent whom he had slept with the night before.

2. Adam has just tested a woman who has brain damage, and he is having difficulty understanding the results. She can't remember any words from a list when she is tested immediately after hearing the words, but her memory gets better when she is tested after a delay. Interestingly enough, when the woman reads the list herself, she remembers well at first, so in that case the delay is not necessary. Can you explain these observations using the modal model? The working memory model? Can you think of a new model that might explain this result better than those two?

KEY TERMS

Activity-silent working memory, 153
Articulatory rehearsal process, 144
Articulatory suppression, 146
Central executive, 144
Change detection, 139
Chunk, 140
Chunking, 140
Control processes, 132
Decay, 137
Delayed partial report method, 136
Delayed-response task, 151
Digit span, 138
Echoic memory, 137

Episodic buffer, 149
Event-related potential (ERP), 156
Iconic memory, 137
Memory, 130
Mental rotation, 147
Modal model of memory, 132
Partial report method, 135
Perseveration, 149
Persistence of vision, 134
Phonological loop, 144
Phonological similarity effect, 145
Phonological store, 144
Reading span, 154

Reading span test, 154
Recall, 138
Rehearsal, 132
Sensory memory, 134
Short-term memory (STM), 137
Structural features, 132
Visual icon, 137
Visual imagery, 146
Visuospatial sketch pad, 144
Whole report method, 135
Word length effect, 145
Working memory, 143

COGLAB EXPERIMENTS   Numbers in parentheses refer to the experiment number in CogLab.

Modality Effect (*17*)
Partial Report (*18*)
Brown-Peterson Task (*20*)
Position Error (*21*)

Sternberg Search (*22*)
Irrelevant Speech Effect (*23*)
Memory Span (*24*)
Operation Span (*25*)

Phonological Similarity Effect (*26*)
Word Length Effect (*27*)
Von Restorff Effect (*32*)
Neighborhood Size Effect (*42*)

Our memories record many different things. This chapter distinguishes between episodic memory—memories that enable us to "relive" in our mind events that have occurred in our lives—and semantic memory—memories for facts that don't depend on remembering specific events. These women may be able to "relive," years later, the experience of taking a "selfie" as well as what the occasion was that brought them together. This is episodic memory. But even if they were to forget taking the selfie and what happened on that particular day, they would likely still remember each other, along with characteristics specific to each person. This is semantic memory. We will see that episodic memory and semantic memory compliment each other and interact to create the richness of our lives.

Long-Term Memory: Structure

6

SOME QUESTIONS WE WILL CONSIDER

▶ How does damage to the brain affect the ability to remember what has happened in the past and the ability to form new memories of ongoing experiences? (170)

▶ How are memories for personal experiences, like what you did last summer, different from memories for facts, like the capital of your state? (172)

▶ How do the different types of memory interact in our everyday experience? (174, 182)

▶ How has memory loss been depicted in popular films? (185)

Christine's memories, from Chapter 5, were varied, ranging from short-lived (a briefly flashed face, a rapidly fading phone number) to longer-lasting (a memorable picnic, the date of a person's birthday, how to ride a bike) (Figure 5.1, page 130) The theme of this chapter is "division and interaction."

Division refers to distinguishing between different types of memory. We introduced this idea in Chapter 5 when we divided Christine's memory into *short-term* and *long-term* and further divided long-term memory into *episodic memory* (memory for specific experiences from the past); *semantic memory* (memory for facts); and *procedural memory* (memory for how to carry out physical actions).

Distinguishing between different types of memory is useful because it divides memory into smaller, easier-to-study components. But this division has to be based on real differences between the components. Thus, one of our goals will be to consider evidence that these different components are based on different mechanisms. We will do this by considering the results of (1) behavioral experiments, (2) neuropsychological studies of the effects of brain damage on memory, and (3) brain imaging experiments. *Interaction* refers to the fact that the different types of memory can interact and share mechanisms. We begin by revisiting short-term memory.

▶ Comparing Short-Term and Long-Term Memory Processes

Long-term memory (LTM) is the system that is responsible for storing information for long periods of time. One way to describe LTM is as an "archive" of information about past events in our lives and knowledge we have learned. What is particularly amazing about this storage is that it stretches from just a few moments ago to as far back as we can remember.

The long time span of LTM is illustrated in **Figure 6.1**, which shows what a student who has just taken a seat in class might be remembering about events that have occurred at various times in the past. His first recollection—that he has just sat down—would be in his

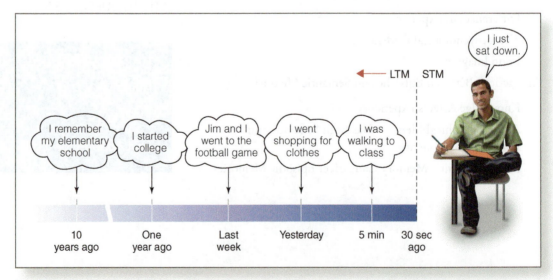

➤ **Figure 6.1** Long-term memory covers a span that stretches from about 30 seconds ago to your earliest memories. Thus, all of this student's memories, except the memory "I just sat down" and anything the student was rehearsing, would be classified as long-term memories.

short-term/working memory (STM/WM) because it happened within the last 30 seconds. But everything before that—from his recent memory that 5 minutes ago he was walking to class, to a memory from 10 years earlier of the elementary school he attended in the third grade—is part of long-term memory.

Let's begin by comparing the two types of memory on either side of the line separating short-term and long-term memory. How are these two types of memory similar, and how are they different?

Our starting point for comparing LTM and STM/WM takes us back to our discussion of STM, when we noted that one of the problems with STM is that most research emphasized its storage function—how much information it can hold and for how long. This led to the proposal of working memory, with its emphasis on dynamic processes that are needed to explain complex cognitions such as understanding language, solving problems, and making decisions.

A similar situation exists for LTM. Although retaining information about the past is an important characteristic of LTM, we also need to understand how this information is used. We can do this by focusing on the dynamic aspects of how LTM operates, including how it interacts with working memory to create our ongoing experience.

Consider, for example, what happens when Tony's friend Cindy says, "Jim and I saw the new James Bond movie last night" (**Figure 6.2**). As Tony's working memory is holding the exact wording of that statement in his mind, it is simultaneously accessing the meaning of words from LTM, which helps him understand the meaning of each of the words that make up the sentence.

Tony's LTM also contains a great deal of additional information about movies, James Bond, and Cindy. Although Tony might not consciously think about all of this information (after all, he has to pay attention to the next thing that Cindy is going to tell him), it is all

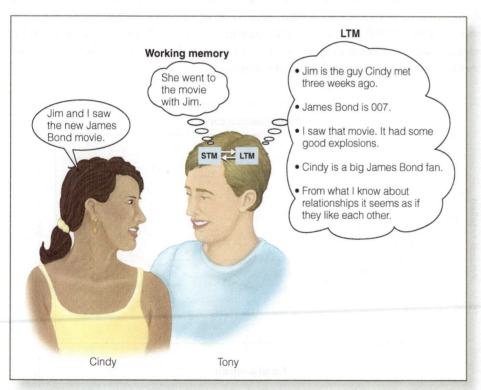

➤ **Figure 6.2** Tony's working memory, which is dealing with the present, and his LTM, which contains knowledge relevant to what is happening, work together as Cindy tells him something.

there in his LTM and adds to his understanding of what he is hearing and his interpretation of what it might mean. LTM therefore provides both an archive that we can refer to when we want to remember events from the past and a wealth of background information that we are constantly consulting as we use working memory to make contact with what is happening at a particular moment.

The interplay between what is happening in the present and information from the past, which we described in the interaction between Tony and Cindy, is based on the distinction between STM/WM and LTM. Beginning in the 1960s, a great deal of research was conducted that was designed to distinguish between short-term and long-term processes. In describing these experiments, we will identify the short-term process as short-term memory (STM) for the early experiments that used that term and as working memory (WM) for more recent experiments that focused on working memory. A classic experiment by B.B. Murdock, Jr. (1962) studied the distinction between STM and LTM by measuring a function called the *serial position curve*.

Serial Position Curve

A **serial position curve** is created by presenting a list of words to a participant, one after another. After the last word, the participant writes down all the words he or she remembers, in any order. The serial position curve in **Figure 6.3**, which plots percentage of a group of participants that recalled each word versus its position in the list, indicates that memory is better for words at the beginning of the list and at the end of the list than for words in the middle (Murdoch, 1962).

The finding that participants are more likely to remember words presented at the beginning of a sequence is called the **primacy effect**. A possible explanation of the primacy effect is that participants had time to rehearse the words at the beginning of the sequence and transfer them to LTM. According to this explanation, participants begin rehearsing the first word right after it is presented; because no other words have been presented, the first word receives 100 percent of the participant's attention. When the second word is presented, attention becomes spread over two words, and so on; as additional words are presented, less rehearsal is possible for later words.

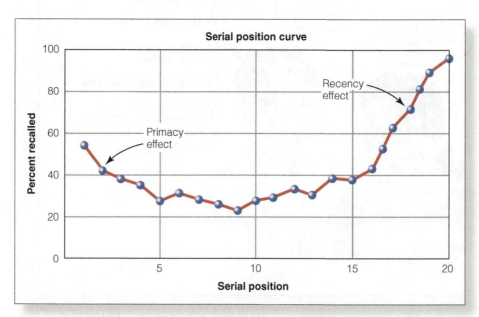

➤ **Figure 6.3** Serial position curve (Murdoch, 1962). Notice that memory is better for words presented at the beginning of the list (primacy effect) and at the end (recency effect).

(Source: B. B. Murdock, Jr., The serial position effect in free recall, Journal of Experimental Psychology, 64, 482–488.)

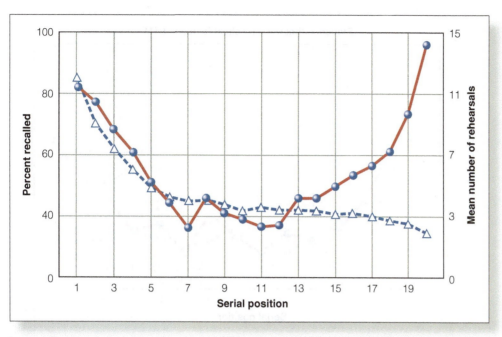

➤ **Figure 6.4** Results of Rundus's (1971) experiment. The solid red line is the usual serial position curve. The dashed blue line indicates how many times the subjects rehearsed (said out loud) each word on the list. Note how the rehearsal curve matches the initial part of the serial position curve.

(Source: D. Rundus, Analysis of rehearsal processes in free recall, Journal of Experimental Psychology, 89, 63–77, Figure 1, p. 66, 1971.)

Dewey Rundus (1971) tested this idea that the primacy effect occurs because participants have more time to rehearse words at the beginning of the list. He first presented a list of 20 words at a rate of 1 word every 5 seconds, and after the last word was presented, he asked his participants to write down all the words they could remember. The resulting serial position curve, which is the red curve in **Figure 6.4**, shows the same primacy effect as Murdoch's curve in Figure 6.3. But Rundus added a twist to his experiment by presenting another list and asking his participants to repeat the words out loud during the 5-second intervals between words. Participants were not told which words to repeat from the list— just that they should keep repeating words during the 5-second intervals between words. The dashed blue curve, which indicates how many times each word was repeated, bears a striking resemblance to the first half of the serial position curve. Words presented early in the list were rehearsed more, and were also more likely to be remembered later. This result supports the idea that the primacy effect is related to the longer rehearsal time available for words at the beginning of the list.

The better memory for the stimuli presented at the end of a sequence is called the **recency effect.** The explanation for the recency effect is that the most recently presented words are still in STM and therefore are easy for participants to remember. To test this idea, Murray Glanzer and Anita Cunitz (1966) first created a serial position curve in the usual way (red curve in **Figure 6.5**). Then, in another experiment, they had participants recall the words after they had counted backwards for 30 seconds right after hearing the last word of the list. This counting prevented rehearsal and allowed time for information to be lost from STM. The result, shown in the blue dashed curve in Figure 6.5, was what we would predict: The delay caused by the counting eliminated the recency effect. Glanzer and Cunitz therefore concluded that the recency effect is due to storage of recently presented items in STM. The serial position results in Figures 6.3, 6.4, and 6.5 are summarized in **Table 6.1**.

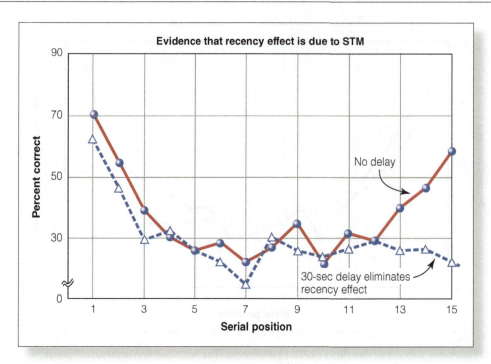

> **Figure 6.5** Results of Glanzer and Cunitz's (1966) experiment. The serial position curve has a normal recency effect when the memory test is immediate (solid red line), but no recency effect occurs if the memory test is delayed for 30 seconds (dashed blue line).

(Source: M. Glanzer & A. R. Cunitz, Two storage mechanisms in free recall, Journal of Verbal Learning and Verbal Behavior, 5, 351–360, Figures 1 & 2. Copyright © 1966 Elsevier Ltd. Republished with permission.)

TABLE 6.1

Serial Position Experiments

Figure	Procedure	Illustrates
Figure 6.3	Participant begins recall immediately after hearing the list of words.	Primacy effect and recency effect.
Figure 6.4	List is presented and participant repeats words out loud in 5-second intervals between words.	Words at the beginning of the list are repeated more, so they are more likely to get into LTM.
Figure 6.5	Participant begins recall after counting backwards for 30 seconds.	Recency effect is eliminated because rehearsal is prevented.

Coding in Short-Term and Long-Term Memory

We can also distinguish between STM and LTM by comparing the way information is *coded* by the two systems. **Coding** refers to the form in which stimuli are represented. For example, as we discussed in Chapter 2, a person's face can be represented by the pattern of firing of a number of neurons (see page 37). Determining how a stimulus is represented by the firing of neurons is a *physiological approach to coding*.

In this section, we will be taking a *mental approach to coding* by asking how a stimulus or an experience is represented in the mind. To compare the way information is represented in the mind in STM and LTM systems, we describe visual coding (coding in the mind in the form of a visual image), auditory coding (coding in the mind in the form of a sound), and semantic coding (coding in the mind in terms of meaning) in both STM and LTM.

Visual Coding in Short-Term and Long-Term Memory   You probably used visual coding in the demonstration "Recalling Visual Patterns" (Chapter 5, page 147), in which you were asked to remember the visual pattern in Figure 5.15. This is visual coding in STM if you remembered the pattern by representing it visually in your mind. You also use visual coding in LTM when you visualize a person or place from the past. For example, if you are remembering your fifth-grade teacher's face, you are using visual coding.

Auditory Coding in Short-Term and Long-Term Memory   Auditory coding in STM is illustrated by Conrad's demonstration of the phonological similarity effect (see page 145), which showed that people often misidentify target letters as another letter that sounds like the target (confusing "F" and "S," for example, which don't look alike but which sound alike). Auditory coding occurs in LTM when you "play" a song in your head.

Semantic Coding in Short-Term Memory: The Wickens Experiment
An experiment by Delos Wickens and coworkers (1976) provides an example of semantic coding in STM. **Figure 6.6** shows the experimental design. On each trial, participants were presented with words related to either (a) fruits (the "Fruits group") or (b) professions (the "Professions group"). Participants in each group listened to three words (for example, *banana, peach, apple* for the Fruits group), counted backward for 15 seconds, and then attempted to recall the three words. They did this for a total of four trials, with different words presented on each trial. Because participants recalled the words so soon after hearing them, they were using their STM.

(a) Fruits group

| Lawyer Firefighter Teacher | Dancer Minister Executive | Grocer Doctor Editor | Orange Cherry Pineapple |
| Trial 1 | Trial 2 | Trial 3 | Trial 4 |

(b) Professions followed by fruits

The basic idea behind this experiment was to create **proactive interference**—the decrease in memory that occurs when previously learned information interferes with learning new information—by presenting words from the same *category* on a series of trials. For example, for the Fruits group, *banana, peach*, and *apple* were presented in trial 1 and *plum, apricot*, and *lime* were presented in trial 2. Proactive interference is illustrated by the falloff in performance on each trial, shown by the blue data points in **Figure 6.7a**.

Evidence that this interference for the Fruits group can be attributed to the *meanings* of the words (all of the words were fruits) is provided by the results for the Professions group shown in **Figure 6.7b**. As for the Professions group, performance is high on trial 1 and then drops on trials 2 and 3 because all of the words are names of professions. But on trial 4, the names of fruits are presented. Because these words are

➤ **Figure 6.6** Stimuli for the Wickens et al. (1976) experiment. (a) Subjects in the Fruits group are presented with the names of three fruits on each trial. After each presentation, subjects counted backwards for 15 seconds and then recalled the names of the fruits. (b) Subjects in the Professions group were presented with the names of three professions on trials 1, 2, and 3, and with the names of three fruits on trial 4. They also counted backwards for 15 seconds before recalling the names on each trial.

(Source: Based on D. D. Wickens, R. E. Dalezman, & F. T. Eggemeier, Multiple encoding of word Attributes in memory, Memory & Cognition, 4, 307–310, 1976.)

from a different category, the proactive interference that built up as the professions were being presented is absent, and performance increases on trial 4. This increase in performance is called **release from proactive interference**.

What does release from proactive interference tell us about coding in STM? The key to answering this question is to realize that the release from proactive interference that occurs in the Wickens experiment depends on the words' *categories* (fruits and professions). Because placing words into categories involves the *meanings* of the words, and because participants were recalling the words 15 seconds after they heard them, this represents an effect of semantic coding in STM.

Semantic Coding in Long-Term Memory: The Sachs Experiment   A study by Jacqueline Sachs (1967) demonstrated semantic coding in LTM. Sachs had participants listen to a tape recording of a passage and then measured their *recognition memory* to determine whether they remembered the exact wording of sentences in the passage or just the general meaning of the passage.

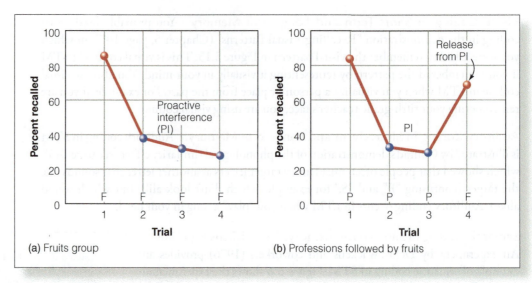

(a) Fruits group   (b) Professions followed by fruits

➤ **Figure 6.7** Results of the Wickens et al. (1976) proactive interference experiment. (a) The Fruits group showed reduced performance on trials 2, 3, and 4, caused at least partially by proactive interference (indicated by blue points). (b) The Professions group showed similarly reduced performance on trials 2 and 3. The increase in performance on trial 4 represents a release from proactive interference because the names of fruits, rather than professions, were presented on trial 4.

(Source: Based on D. D. Wickens, R. E. Dalezman, & F. T. Eggemeier, Multiple encoding of word Attributes in memory, Memory & Cognition, 4, 307–310, 1976.)

METHOD   Measuring Recognition Memory

Recognition memory is the identification of a stimulus that was encountered earlier. The procedure for measuring recognition memory is to present a stimulus during a study period and later to present the same stimulus along with others that were not presented. For example, in the study period, a list of words might be presented that includes the word *house*. Later, in the test, a series of words is presented that includes *house* plus some other words that were not presented, such as *table* and *money*. The participant's task is to answer "Yes" if the word was presented previously (the word *house* in this example) and "No" if it wasn't presented (the words *table* and *money*). Notice that this method is different from testing for *recall* (see Method: Recall, Chapter 5, page 138). In a recall test, the person must *produce* the item to be recalled. An example of a recall test is a fill-in-the-blanks exam question. In contrast, an example of recognition is a multiple-choice exam, in which the task is to pick the correct answer from a number of alternatives. The way Sachs applied recognition to the study of coding in LTM is illustrated in the next demonstration.

DEMONSTRATION   Reading a Passage

Read the following passage:

There is an interesting story about the telescope. In Holland, a man named Lippershey was an eyeglass maker. One day his children were playing with some lenses. They discovered that things seemed very close if two lenses were held about a foot apart. Lippershey began experimenting, and his "spyglass" attracted much attention. He sent a letter about it to Galileo, the great Italian scientist. Galileo at once realized the importance of the discovery and set about building an instrument of his own.

Now cover up the passage and indicate which of the following sentences is identical to a sentence in the passage and which sentences are changed.

He sent a letter about it to Galileo, the great Italian scientist.
Galileo, the great Italian scientist, sent him a letter about it.
A letter about it was sent to Galileo, the great Italian scientist.
He sent Galileo, the great Italian scientist, a letter about it.

Which sentence did you pick? Sentence (1) is the correct answer because it is the only one that is identical to one in the passage. The task facing Sachs's participants was more difficult, because they heard a passage two or three times as long, so there was more material to remember and there was a longer delay between hearing the sentence and being asked to remember it. Many of Sachs's participants correctly identified sentence (1) as being identical and knew that sentence (2) was changed. However, a number of people identified sentences (3) and (4) as matching one in the passage, even though the wording was different. These participants apparently remembered the sentence's meaning but not its exact wording. The finding that specific wording is forgotten but the general meaning can be remembered for a long time has been confirmed in many experiments. This description in terms of meaning is an example of semantic coding in LTM.

Comparing Coding in Short-Term and Long-Term Memory

We have seen that information can be represented in both STM and LTM in terms of vision (visual coding), hearing (auditory coding), and meaning (semantic coding) (Table 6.2). The type of coding that occurs in a particular situation depends largely on the task. Consider, for example, the task of remembering a telephone number that you have just heard. One way of maintaining the number in memory is by repeating it over and over—an example of auditory coding. It is less likely that you would remember the number in terms of either its visual image or the meaning of the phone number. Because of the nature of many STM tasks, auditory coding is the predominant type of coding in STM.

Now consider another example. You finished reading an adventure story last week and are now remembering what you read. It is unlikely that you remember what the words looked like as you were reading them, but you are more likely to remember what happened in the story. Remembering what happened is semantic coding, which often occurs for LTM. If in remembering the story you conjured up images of some of the places you imagined as you read the story (or perhaps saw, if the book included illustrations), this would be an

TABLE 6.2

Examples of Coding in Short-Term and Long-Term Memory

Code	Short-Term Memory	Long-Term Memory
Visual	Holding an image in the mind to reproduce a visual pattern that was just seen (Della Sala et al., 1999.)	Visualizing what the Lincoln Memorial in Washington, D.C., looked like when you saw it last summer
Auditory	Representing the sounds of letters in the mind just after hearing them (Conrad, 1964)	Repeating a song you have heard many times before, over and over in your mind
Semantic	Placing words in an STM task into categories based on their meaning (Wickens et al., 1976)	Recalling the general plot of a novel you read last week (Sachs)

example of visual coding in LTM. Generally, semantic coding is the most likely form of coding for LTM tasks.

Locating Memory in the Brain

At the end of Chapter 5, we saw that the prefrontal cortex and other areas are involved in working memory (Figure 5.19, page 150). Our goal in this section is to describe some experiments that compare where STM and LTM are represented in the brain. We will see that there is evidence that STM and LTM are separated in the brain, but also some evidence for overlap. The strongest evidence for separation is provided by neuropsychological studies.

Neuropsychology   In 1953, Henry Molaison (known as patient HM until his death at the age of 82 in 2008) underwent an experimental procedure designed to eliminate his severe epileptic seizures. The procedure, which involved removal of HM's **hippocampus** (see Figure 5.19) on both sides of his brain, succeeded in decreasing his seizures but had the unintended effect of eliminating his ability to form new long-term memories (Corkin, 2002; Scoville & Milner, 1957).

HM's short-term memory remained intact, so he could remember what had just happened, but he was unable to transfer any of this information into long-term memory. One result of this inability to form new long-term memories was that even though psychologist Brenda Milner tested him many times over many decades, HM always reacted to her arrival in his room as if he were meeting her for the first time. HM's case, although tragic for him personally, led to an understanding of the role of the hippocampus in forming new long-term memories. Furthermore, the fact that his short-term memory remained intact suggested that short-term and long-term memories are served by separate brain regions (also see Suddendorf et al., 2009; Wearing, 2005 for a description of another case of hippocampus damage causing loss of the ability to form long-term memories).

There are also people with a problem opposite to that of HM—that is, they have normal LTM but poor STM. One example is patient KF, who had suffered damage to his parietal lobe in a motorbike accident. KF's poor STM was indicated by a reduced digit span—the number of digits he could remember (see page 138; Shallice & Warrington, 1970). Whereas the typical span is between five and nine digits, KF had a digit span of two; in addition, the recency effect in his serial position curve, which is associated with STM, was reduced. Even though KF's STM was greatly impaired, he had a functioning LTM, as indicated by his ability to form and hold new memories of events in his life.

What's special about these cases together is that because HM had intact STM but wasn't able to form new long-term memories and KF had the opposite problem (intact LTM but a deficient STM), they establish a double dissociation (see Method: Demonstrating a Double Dissociation, page 40) between STM and LTM (**Table 6.3**). This evidence supports the idea that STM and LTM are caused by different mechanisms, which can act independently.

TABLE 6.3

A Double Dissociation for Short-Term and Long-Term Memory

Patient	Short-Term Memory	Long-Term Memory
HM	OK	Impaired
KF	Impaired	OK

The combination of the neuropsychological evidence and the results of behavioral experiments such as those measuring the serial position curve, as well as the proposal of the modal model in which STM and LTM are represented by separate boxes, supports the idea of the separation of STM and LTM. However, some recent brain imaging experiments show that this separation is not so straightforward.

Brain Imaging   Charan Ranganath and Mark D'Esposito (2001) asked whether the hippocampus, which is crucial for forming new long-term memories, might also play a role in holding information for short periods of time. **Figure 6.8a** shows the sequence of stimuli presented to participants as they were having their brain scanned. A sample face was presented for 1 second, followed by a 7-second delay period. Then a test face was presented, and the participant's task was to decide whether it matched the sample face. Participants were run in two conditions. In the "novel face" condition, they were seeing each face for the first time. In the "familiar face" condition, they saw faces that they had seen prior to the experiment.

The results, shown in **Figure 6.8b**, indicate that activity in the hippocampus increases as participants are holding novel faces in memory during the 7-second delay, but activity changes only slightly for the familiar faces. Based on this result, Ranganath and D'Esposito concluded that the hippocampus is involved in maintaining novel information in memory during short delays. Results such as these, plus the results of many other experiments, show that the hippocampus and other medial temporal lobe structures once thought to be involved only in LTM also play some role in STM (Cashdollar et al., 2009; Jonides et al., 2008; Nichols et al., 2006; Ranganath & Blumenfeld, 2005; Rose et al., 2012).

Taking these new results into account, many researchers have concluded that although there is good evidence for the separation of short-term memory and long-term memory, there is also evidence that these functions are not as separated as previously thought, especially for tasks involving novel stimuli. As we now shift our focus to considering only long-term memory, we will focus first on episodic and semantic long-term memory.

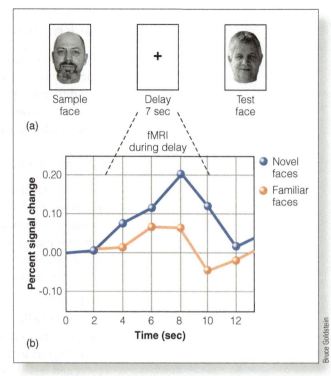

➤ **Figure 6.8** (a) Stimuli presentation for Ranganath and D'Esposito's (2001) experiment. (b) Hippocampus fMRI response increases during the delay for novel faces but only increases slightly for faces people had seen before.

(Source: Based on C. Ranganath & M. D'Esposito, Medial temporal lobe activity associated with active maintenance of novel information, Neuron, 31, 865–873, 2001.)

TEST YOURSELF 6.1

1. Describe how differences between STM and LTM have been determined by measuring serial position curves.

2. What are some examples of visual, auditory, and semantic coding for STM and for LTM?

3. Describe how Wickens and the Sachs experiments provide evidence for semantic coding in STM and LTM. What can we conclude about similarities and differences in STM and LTM based on the way coding occurs in both?

4. What conclusions about the separation of STM and LTM followed from neuropsychology studies involving HM and KF?

5. What do more recent experiments, such as the one by Ranganath and D'Esposito, indicate about the separation between brain mechanisms serving STM and LTM?

Episodic and Semantic Memory

We are now ready to leave short-term memory behind and ask why episodic memory (memory for experiences) and semantic memory (memory for facts) are considered to be two different types of memory. This question has been answered by considering (1) the type of *experience* associated with episodic and semantic memories, (2) how brain damage affects each one, and (3) the fMRI responses to each one.

Distinctions Between Episodic and Semantic Memory

When we say that episodic memory is memory for experiences and that semantic memory is memory for facts, we are distinguishing between two types of memory based on the types of *information* remembered. Endel Tulving (1985), who first proposed that episodic and semantic memories handled different types of information, also suggested that episodic and semantic memory can be distinguished based on the type of *experience* associated with each (also see Gardiner, 2001; Wheeler et al., 1997).

Differences in Experience   According to Tulving, the defining property of the experience of episodic memory is that it involves **mental time travel**—the experience of traveling back in time to reconnect with events that happened in the past. For example, I can travel back 20 years in my mind to remember cresting the top of a mountain near the California coast and seeing the Pacific Ocean far below, as it stretched into the distance. I remember sitting in the car, seeing the ocean, and saying, "Wow!" to my wife, who was sitting next to me. I also remember some of the emotions I was experiencing, and other details, such as the inside of my car, the sun reflecting off the water, and the expectation of what we were going to see on the way down the mountain. In short, when I remember this incident, I feel as if I am *reliving* it. Tulving describes this experience of mental time travel/episodic memory as *self-knowing* or *remembering*.

In contrast to the mental time travel property of episodic memory, the experience of semantic memory involves accessing knowledge about the world that does not have to be tied to remembering a personal experience. This knowledge can be things like facts, vocabulary, numbers, and concepts. When we *experience* semantic memory, we are not traveling back to a specific event from our past, but we are accessing things we are familiar with and know about. For example, I know many facts about the Pacific Ocean—where it is located, that it is big, that if you travel west from San Francisco you end up in Japan—but I can't remember exactly when I learned these things. The various things I know about the Pacific Ocean are semantic memories. Tulving describes the experience of semantic memory as *knowing*, with the idea that knowing does not involve mental time travel.

Neuropsychological Evidence   Just as neuropsychological evidence was used to distinguish between STM and LTM, it has also been used to distinguish between episodic and semantic memory. We first consider the case of KC, who at the age of 30 rode his motorcycle off a freeway exit ramp and suffered severe damage to his hippocampus and surrounding structures (Rosenbaum et al., 2005). As a result of this injury, KC lost his episodic memory—he can no longer relive any of the events of his past. He does, however, know that certain things happened, which would correspond to semantic memory. He is aware of the fact that his brother died 2 years ago but remembers nothing about personal experiences such as how he heard about his brother's death or what he experienced at the funeral. KC also remembers facts like where the eating utensils are located in the kitchen and the difference between a strike and a spare in bowling. Thus, KC has lost the episodic part of his memory, but his semantic memory is largely intact. (Also see Palombo et al., 2015 for more case histories of people who have no episodic memory but good semantic memory.)

TABLE 6.4

A Double Dissociation for Semantic and Episodic Memory

Patient	Semantic Memory	Episodic Memory
KC	OK	Poor
LP	Poor	OK

A person whose brain damage resulted in symptoms opposite to those experienced by KC is LP, an Italian woman who was in normal health until she suffered an attack of encephalitis at the age of 44 (DeRenzi et al., 1987). The first signs of a problem were headaches and a fever, which were later followed by hallucinations lasting for 5 days. When she returned home after a 6-week stay in the hospital, she had difficulty recognizing familiar people; she had trouble shopping because she couldn't remember the meaning of words on the shopping list or where things were in the store; and she could no longer recognize famous people or recall facts such as the identity of Beethoven or the fact that Italy was involved in World War II. All of these are semantic memories.

Despite this severe impairment of memory for semantic information, she was still able to remember events in her life. She could remember what she had done during the day and things that had happened weeks or months before. Thus, although she had lost semantic memories, she was still able to form new episodic memories. **Table 6.4** summarizes the two cases we have described. These cases, taken together, demonstrate a double dissociation between episodic and semantic memory, which supports the idea that memory for these two different types of information probably involves different mechanisms.

Although the double dissociation shown in Table 6.4 supports the idea of separate mechanisms for semantic and episodic memory, interpretation of the results of studies of brain-damaged patients is often tricky because the extent of brain damage often differs from patient to patient. In addition, the method of testing patients may differ in different studies. It is important, therefore, to supplement the results of neuropsychological research with other kinds of evidence. This additional evidence is provided by brain imaging experiments. (See Squire & Zola-Morgan, 1998, and Tulving & Markowitsch, 1998, for further discussion of the neuropsychology of episodic and semantic memory.)

Brain Imaging   Brian Levine and coworkers (2004) did a brain imaging experiment in which they had participants keep diaries on audiotape describing everyday personal events (example: "It was the last night of our Salsa dance class. . . . People were dancing all different styles of Salsa. . . .") and facts drawn from their semantic knowledge ("By 1947, there were 5,000 Japanese Canadians living in Toronto"). When the participants later listened to these audiotaped descriptions while in an fMRI scanner, the recordings of everyday events elicited detailed episodic autobiographical memories (people remembered their experiences), while the other recordings simply reminded people of semantic facts.

Figure 6.9 shows brain activation in a cross-section of the brain. The yellow areas represent brain regions associated with episodic memories; the blue areas represent brain regions associated with semantic, factual knowledge (personal and nonpersonal). These results and others indicate that although there can be overlap between activation caused by episodic and semantic memories, there are also major differences (also see Cabeza & Nyberg, 2000; Duzel et al., 1999; Nyberg et al., 1996).

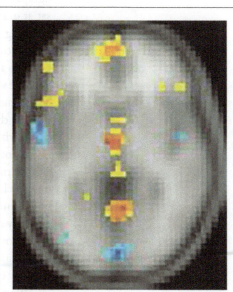

© B.Levine,G.R. Turner,D. Tisserand, S. J Hevenor, S.J Graham,& A.R.McIntosh, The functional neuroanatomy of episodic and semantic autobiographical remembering: A prospective functional MRI study. Journal of Cognitive Neuroscience, 16, 1633–1646,2004. MIT Press Journals.

▶ **Figure 6.9** Brain showing areas activated by episodic and semantic memories. The yellow areas represent brain regions associated with episodic memories; the blue areas represent regions associated with semantic memories. (Source: Levine et al., 2004)

The fact that we can draw distinctions between episodic and semantic memory doesn't mean, however, that they operate totally separately from one another. In keeping with this chapter's theme of *division and interaction*, we will now see that there is a great deal of interaction between these two systems.

Interactions Between Episodic and Semantic Memory

In real life, episodic and semantic memories are often intertwined. Two examples are (1) how knowledge (semantic) affects experience (episodic) and (2) the makeup of autobiographical memory.

Knowledge Affects Experience   We bring a vast store of knowledge with us as we are having the experiences we will later remember. For example, I recently was watching a baseball game with a friend who was British and had never been to a baseball game, so his knowledge was limited to the basic principle that the point of the game is to hit the ball, run the bases, and score runs. As we sat watching the game together, I soon realized that I knew many things about the game that I take for granted. At one point in the game, when there was a man on first and one out, I was anticipating the possibility that a ground ball might result in a double play. Then, when the batter hit a ground ball to the third baseman, I immediately looked to second base, where the third baseman threw the ball for one out, and then to first, where the second baseman threw for the second out. Meanwhile, my British friend's reaction was "What happened?" Clearly, my knowledge of the game influenced what I paid attention to and how I experienced the game. Our knowledge (semantic memory) guides our experience, and this, in turn, influences the episodic memories that follow from that experience.

Autobiographical Memory Has Both Semantic and Episodic Components   The interplay between episodic and semantic memory also occurs when we consider **autobiographical memory**—memory for specific experiences from our life, which can include both episodic and semantic components. For example, consider the following autobiographical memory: "When I met Gil and Mary at the Le Buzz coffee shop yesterday, we sat at our favorite table, which is located near the window, but which is hard to get in the morning when Le Buzz is busy."

Notice that this description contains episodic components (meeting Gil and Mary yesterday is a specific experience) and semantic components (Le Buzz is a coffee shop; the table near the window is our favorite one; that table is difficult to get in the morning are all facts). The semantic components of this description are called **personal semantic memories** because they are facts associated with personal experiences (Renoult et al., 2012). **Table 6.5** summarizes the characteristics of episodic, semantic, and autobiographical memories.

Another interaction between episodic and semantic memory has been demonstrated in an experiment by Robyn Westmacott and Morris Moscovitch (2003), which showed that people's knowledge about public figures, such as actors, singers, and politicians, can include both semantic and episodic components. For example, if you know some facts about Oprah Winfrey and that she had a television program, your knowledge would be mainly semantic. But if you can remember watching some of her television shows, or, better yet, were in the studio audience during one of her shows, your memory for Oprah Winfrey would have episodic components.

Westmacott and Moscovitch call semantic memories involving personal episodes *autobiographically significant* semantic memories. When they tested people's ability to remember the names of public figures, they found that recall was better for names of people who had higher autobiographical significance. Thus, you would be more likely to recall the name of a popular singer (semantic information) if you had attended one of his or her concerts (episodic experience) than if you just knew about the singer because he or she was a famous person.

TABLE 6.5

Types of Long-Term Memory

Type	Definition	Example
Episodic	Memory for specific personal experiences, involving mental time travel back in time to achieve a feeling of reliving the experience.	I remember going to get coffee at Le Buzz yesterday morning and talking with Gil and Mary about their bike trip.
Semantic	Memory for facts.	There is a Starbucks down the road from Le Buzz.
Autobiographical	People's memories for experiences from their own lives. These memories have both episodic components (relived specific events) and semantic components (facts related to these events). These semantic components of autobiographical memory are *personal semantic memories*.	I met Gil and Mary at Le Buzz yesterday morning. We sat at our favorite table near the window, which is often difficult to get in the morning when the coffee shop is busy.

What this means is that experiences related to episodic memories can aid in accessing semantic memories. Interestingly, when Westmacott and coworkers (2003) ran the same experiment on people with brain damage who had lost their episodic memory, there was no enhanced memory for autobiographically significant names. Thus, when episodic memory is present, semantic memory for "facts" (like a person's name) is enhanced. But when episodic memory is absent, this advantage created by personally relevant facts vanishes—another example of the interrelatedness of episodic and semantic memory.

This connection between episodic and semantic memory becomes even more interesting when we ask what happens to long-term memories with the passage of time. Remember that STM lasts only about 15 seconds (unless information is held there by rehearsal), so events we remember from an hour, a day, or a year ago are all remembered from LTM. However, as we will now see, not all long-term memories are created equal. We are more likely to remember the details of something that happened yesterday than something that happened a year ago, and we may later forget something that happened yesterday while still remembering what happened a year ago!

What Happens to Episodic and Semantic Memories as Time Passes?

One procedure for determining what happens to memory as time passes is to present stimuli and then, after some time passes, ask a participant to recall stimuli, as in the serial position curve experiments (page 164) or recognition experiments in which participants are asked to recognize a sentence from a passage they had read (page 168). The typical result of these experiments is that participants forget some of the stimuli, with forgetting increasing at longer time intervals. But when we consider the process of forgetting in more detail, we see that forgetting is not always an "all-or-nothing" process. For example, consider the following situation: A friend introduces you to Roger at the coffee shop on Monday, and you talk briefly. Then later in the week, you see Roger across the street. Some possible reactions to seeing Roger are:

That person looks familiar. What's his name and where did I meet him?
There's Roger. Where did I meet him?
There's Roger, who I met at the coffee shop last Monday. I remember talking with him about football.

It is clear that there are different degrees of forgetting and remembering. The first two examples illustrate *familiarity*—the person seems familiar and you might remember his name, but you can't remember any details about specific experiences involving that person. The last example illustrates *recollection*—remembering specific experiences related to the person. Familiarity is associated with semantic memory because it is not associated with the circumstances under which knowledge was acquired. Recollection is associated with episodic memory because it includes details about what was happening when knowledge was acquired plus an awareness of the event as it was experienced in the past. These two ways of remembering have been measured using the **remember/know procedure**.

> **METHOD**   Remember/Know Procedure
>
> In the remember/know procedure, participants are presented with a stimulus they have encountered before and are asked to respond with (1) *remember* if the stimulus is familiar and they also remember the circumstances under which they originally encountered it; (2) *know* if the stimulus seems familiar but they don't remember experiencing it earlier; or (3) *don't know* if they don't remember the stimulus at all. This procedure has been used in laboratory experiments in which participants are asked to remember lists of stimuli, and has also been used to measure people's memory for actual events from the past. This procedure is important because it distinguishes between the episodic components of memory (indicated by a *remember* response) and semantic components (indicated by a *know* response).

Raluca Petrican and coworkers (2010) determined how people's memory for public events changes over time by presenting descriptions of events that had happened over a 50-year period to older adults (average age = 63 years) and asking them to respond with *remember* if they had a personal experience associated with the event or recollected seeing details about the event on TV or in the newspaper. They were to respond *know* if they were familiar with the event but couldn't recollect any personal experience or details related to media coverage of the event. If they couldn't remember the event at all, they were to respond *don't know*.

The results of this experiment are shown in **Figure 6.10**, which indicates memory for public events that happened within the most recent 10 years, and memory for events that happened 40 to 50 years earlier. (Intermediate delays were also tested in the experiment. We are focusing on the extremes.) As would be expected, complete forgetting increased over time (red bars). But the interesting result is that *remember* responses decreased much more than *know* responses, meaning that memories for 40- to 50-year-old events had lost much of their episodic character. This result illustrates the **semanticization of remote memories**—loss of episodic detail for memories of long-ago events.

This loss of episodic details has been demonstrated both for long-ago events, as in the Petrican experiment, and also for periods as short as 1 week (Addis et al., 2008; D'Argembeau & Van der Linden, 2004; Johnson et al., 1988; Viskontas et al., 2009). This shorter-term semanticization makes sense when we consider personal experiences. You probably remember the details of what you did earlier today or yesterday but fewer details about what happened a week ago (unless what happened a week ago was particularly important).

Another way to appreciate the semanticization of remote memories is to consider how you have acquired the knowledge that makes up your

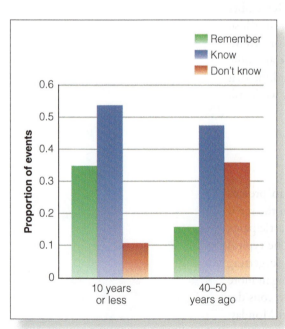

➤ **Figure 6.10** Results of the remember/know experiment that tested older subjects' memory for events over a 50-year period.

(Source: Based on R. Petrican, N. Gopie, L. Leach, T. W. Chow, B. Richards, & M. Moscovitch, Recollection and familiarity for public events in neurologically intact older adults and two brain-damaged patients. Neuropsychologia, 48, 945–960, 2010.)

semantic memories. When you were in the sixth grade, you may have learned that the legislative branch of the U.S. government consists of the Senate and the House of Representatives. Right after learning this, you might have found it easy to remember what was going on in class, including what the classroom looked like, what the teacher was saying, and so on. Remembering all these details about the circumstances of learning comes under the heading of episodic memory. The facts about how the government works is semantic memory.

Many years later, in college, your semantic memory about the structure of the U.S. government remains, but the episodic details about what was happening on the specific day you learned that information are probably gone. Thus, the knowledge that makes up your semantic memories is initially attained through personal experiences that are the basis of episodic memories, but your memory for these experiences often fades, and only semantic memory remains.

▶ Back to the Future

We usually think of memory in terms of bringing back events or facts from the past. But what about imagining what might happen in the future? Is there a connection between the two? William Shakespeare's line, "What's past is prologue," from *The Tempest*, draws a direct connection between the past, the present, and perhaps the future. Steve Jobs, one of the founders of Apple Computer, comments on the connection by noting, "You can't connect the dots looking forward; you can only connect them looking backwards; so you have to trust that the dots will somehow connect in your future" (Jobs, 2005).

Extending the dots into the future has become an important topic of memory research. This research doesn't ask how well we can *predict* the future, but asks how well we can create possible scenarios *about* the future. The reason this has become a topic of research is that there is evidence of a connection between the ability to remember the past and the ability to imagine the future. Evidence for this connection is provided by patients who have lost their episodic memory as a result of brain damage. KC, the motorcyclist we described earlier as having lost his episodic memory because of a head injury, was unable to use his imagination to describe personal events that might happen in the future (Tulving, 1985). Another patient, DB, who had difficulty recalling past events because of damage to his hippocampus, also had difficulty imagining future events. His inability to imagine future events was restricted to things that might happen to him personally; he could still imagine other future events, such as what might happen in politics or other current events (Addis et al., 2007; Hassabis et al., 2007; Klein et al., 2002).

This behavioral evidence for a link between the ability to remember the past and the ability to imagine what might happen in the future led Donna Rose Addis and coworkers (2007) to look for a physiological link by using fMRI to determine how the brain is activated by remembering the past and imagining the future. Brain activation was measured as neurologically normal participants silently thought about either events from the past or events that might happen in the future. The results indicated that all the brain regions that were active while thinking about the past were also active while thinking about the future (Figure 6.11). These results suggest that similar neural mechanisms are involved in remembering the past and predicting the future (Addis et al., 2007, 2009; Schacter & Addis, 2009). Based on these results, Schacter and Addis (2007, 2009) proposed the **constructive episodic simulation hypothesis**, which states that episodic memories are extracted and recombined to construct simulations of future events.

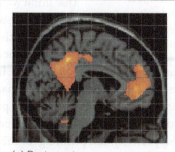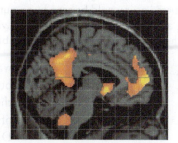

(a) Past events   (a) Future events

© D.R. Addis, A.T. Wong, & D.L. Schacter, Remembering the past and imagining the future: Common and distinct neural substrates during event construction and elaboration, Neuropsychologia, 45, 1363–1337, Figure 2 2007. With Permission from Elsevier.

▶ **Figure 6.11** Brain activation caused by (a) thinking about past events and (b) imagining future events. (Source: Addis et al., 2007)

(a) First-person perspective

(b) Third-person perspective

➤ **Figure 6.12** Two ways of visually remembering an event: (a) First-person perspective. Event is remembered as it would have been seen by the person doing the remembering. (b) Third-person perspective. Event is remembered as it would be seen by an outside observer looking at the event. In this third-person view, the person doing the remembering is the woman in black.

The idea that there is a connection between imagining the past and predicting the future is also supported by an experiment by Eleanor McDermott and coworkers (2016), in which participants were asked to remember an event from the past or to imagine a similar event that might happen in the future. Participants were also told to describe what they were seeing as they remembered or imagined, and to notice whether their observation was from a first-person perspective (what they would see if they were a participant in the event, as in **Figure 6.12a**) or from a third-person perspective (what they would see if they were an outside observer watching the event happen, as in **Figure 6.12b**). When compared in this way, both remembered and imagined events were more likely to be "seen" from a third-person perspective, although there were slightly fewer third-person perceptions for the remembered past (71 percent) than for the imagined future (78 percent).

McDermott also noted the visual viewpoint of her participant's reports. These results, in **Figure 6.13**, show that there are some differences, with more below eye-level and fewer eye-level responses for the imagined future condition. But the above eye-level responses and the distances were the same. Based on the overlap between the results for memories and imagined futures, McDermott concluded that it is likely that common processes are involved in both situations.

Why is it important to be able to imagine the future? One answer to that question is that when the future becomes the present, we need to be able to act effectively. Considered in this way, being able to imagine the future becomes very important, and, in fact, Donna Rose Addis and coworkers (2007) have suggested that perhaps the main role of the episodic memory system is not to remember the past but to enable people to simulate possible future scenarios in order to help anticipate future needs and guide future behavior. This could be useful, for example, in deciding whether to approach or avoid a particular situation, both of which could have implications for effectively dealing with the environment and, perhaps, even for survival (Addis et al., 2007; Schacter, 2012).

The idea that simulating the future might be an adaptive process brings us back to the phenomenon of mind wandering, which we discussed in Chapter 2 (p. 51) and Chapter 4 (p. 114). We saw that mind wandering (1) is associated with activation of the default mode network (DMN), which becomes active when a person isn't focused on a specific task (p. 50) and (2) is extremely prevalent, occurring as much as half the time during waking hours (p. 114). We also noted that mind wandering can cause decreases in performance on tasks that require focused attention (p. 114), but that mind wandering is likely to have positive effects as well.

One hint at a positive role for mind wandering is that when mind wandering occurs, people are more likely to think about the future than about the past or the present (Baird et al., 2011). This has led some researchers to suggest that one of the reasons that the mind wanders is to help people plan for the future by helping create simulations of the future from our episodic memories. And to make this story about mind wandering, DMN activity, and planning for the future even more interesting, recent research has shown that damage to the DMN can cause problems in retrieving autobiographical memories (Philippi et al., 2015), which, as we have seen from the cases KC and DB, is associated with problems in imagining future events.

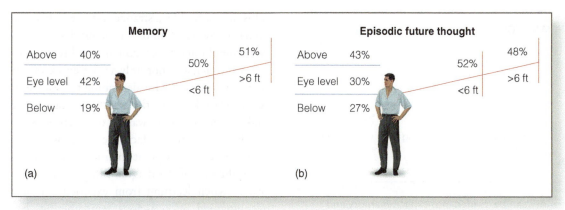

> **Figure 6.13** Points of view for third-person perspectives for (a) memory of a past event; (b) imagining a possible future event. The red numbers indicate percentages of views from above eye level, at eye level, and below eye level. The orange numbers indicate percentages of views that were less than or more than 6 feet away.

(Source: McDermott et al., 2016 Fig. 3, p. 248)

TEST YOURSELF 6.2

1. How have episodic and semantic memory been distinguished from one another? Consider both the definitions and Tulving's idea of mental time travel.
2. Describe neuropsychological evidence for a double dissociation between episodic and semantic memory.
3. Describe Levine's "diary" experiment. What do the brain imaging results indicate about episodic and semantic memory?
4. Describe how knowledge (semantic) can affect experience (episodic).
5. What is autobiographical memory? How does the definition of autobiographical memory incorporate both episodic and semantic memory?
6. Describe how personal significance can make semantic memories easier to remember. What happens to the "personal significance effect" in people who have lost their episodic memories due to brain damage?
7. Describe what happens to memory as time passes. What is the semanticization of episodic memory?
8. What is the remember/know procedure? How does it distinguish between episodic and semantic memories? How has it been used to measure how memory changes over time?
9. Describe the following evidence that indicates overlap between episodic memory for the past and the ability to imagine future events: (1) memory of people who have lost their episodic memory; (2) brain imaging evidence.
10. What is the constructive episodic simulation hypothesis? Describe McDermott's experiment in which she compared the perspectives and viewpoints that people take when remembering the past and imagining the future.
11. What role does Addis and coworkers suggest for episodic memory?

Procedural Memory, Priming, and Conditioning

Figure 6.14 is a diagram of the different types of long-term memory. We have been focusing so far on the two types of memory shown on the left, episodic and semantic, which fall under the heading of *explicit memory*. **Explicit memories** are memories we are aware of.

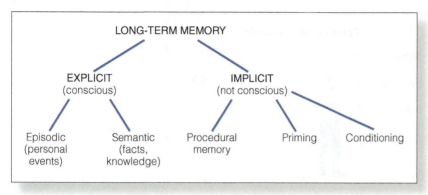

LONG-TERM MEMORY

EXPLICIT
(conscious)

IMPLICIT
(not conscious)

Episodic
(personal
events)

Semantic
(facts,
knowledge)

Procedural
memory

Priming

Conditioning

➤ **Figure 6.14** Long-term memory can be divided into explicit memory and implicit memory. We can also distinguish between two types of explicit memory, episodic and semantic. There are a number of different types of implicit memory. Three of the main types are procedural memory, priming, and conditioning.

This may seem like a strange statement, because aren't we aware of all of our memories? We tell someone about our vacation or give directions to a lost traveler, and not only are we aware of our memories (episodic for describing the vacation; semantic for knowing the directions), but we are making someone else aware of our memories.

But there are, in fact, memories we aren't aware of, called **implicit memories**, shown on the right side of the diagram. Implicit memory occurs when learning from experience is not accompanied by conscious remembering. For example, we do many things without being able to explain how we do them. These abilities come under the heading of *procedural memories*.

Procedural Memory

Procedural memory is also called **skill memory** because it is memory for doing things that usually involve learned skills.

The Implicit Nature of Procedural Memory The implicit nature of procedural memory has been demonstrated in patients like LSJ, a skilled violinist who suffered a loss of episodic memory due to damage to her hippocampus caused by encephalitis, but who could still play the violin (Valtonen et al., 2014). Amnesiac patients can also master new skills even though they don't remember any of the practice that led to this mastery. For example, HM, whose amnesia was caused by having his hippocampus removed (see page 170), practiced a task called *mirror drawing*, which involves copying a picture that is seen in a mirror (**Figure 6.15**). You can appreciate this task by doing the following demonstration.

➤ **Figure 6.15** Mirror drawing. The task is to trace the outline of the star while looking at its image in the mirror.

DEMONSTRATION Mirror Drawing

Draw a star like the one in **Figure 6.15** on a piece of paper. Place a mirror or some other reflective surface (some cell phone screens work) about an inch or two from the star, so that the reflection of the star is visible. Then, while looking at the reflection, trace the outline of the star on the paper (no fair looking at the actual drawing on the paper!). You will probably find that the task is difficult at first but becomes easier with practice.

After a number of days of practice, HM became quite good at mirror drawing, but because his ability to form long-term memories was impaired, he always thought he was practicing mirror drawing for the first time. HM's ability to trace the star in the mirror, even though he couldn't remember having done it before, illustrates the implicit nature of procedural memory. Another example of practice improving performance without any recollection of the practice is the violinist LSJ, mentioned earlier, whose performance improved as she practiced a new piece of music, but who had no memory of practicing the piece (Gregory et al., 2016; Valtonen et al., 2014).

KC provides another example of a person who can't form new long-term memories but who can still learn new skills. After his motorcycle accident, he learned how to sort and stack books in the library. Even though he doesn't remember learning to do this, he can still do it, and his performance improves with practice. The fact that people with amnesia can retain skills from the past and learn new ones has led to an approach to rehabilitating patients with amnesia by teaching them tasks, such as sorting mail or performing repetitive computer-based tasks, that they can become expert at, even though they can't remember their training (Bolognani et al., 2000; Clare & Jones, 2008).

Our examples of implicit memories have so far included motor skills that involve movement and muscle action. You have also developed many purely cognitive skills that qualify as procedural memory. Consider, for example, your ability to have a conversation. Although you may not be able to describe the rules of grammar, that doesn't stop you from having a grammatically correct conversation. Beginning when we are infants, we learn to apply the rules of grammar, without necessarily being able to state the rules (although later, when we are older, we may study them).

Procedural Memory and Attention   The main effect of procedural memories is that they enable us to carry out skilled acts without thinking about what we are doing. For example, consider what happens when a person is learning to play the piano. They may begin by paying close attention to their fingers striking the keys, being careful to play the correct note in the correct sequence. But once they become an expert pianist, their best strategy is to just play, without paying attention to their fingers. In fact, as we noted in Chapter 4, concert pianists report that when they become conscious of how they are moving their fingers while playing a difficult passage, they are no longer able to play the passage.

An interesting outcome of the fact that well-learned procedural memories do not require attention is an effect called **expert-induced amnesia**. Here's how it works: An expert, who is extremely well practiced at a particular skill, carries out the action. It is so well practiced that it happens automatically, much like a concert pianist's fingers move almost magically across the keys. The result of this automatic action is that when asked about what they did in carrying out a skilled action, the expert often has no idea.

An example of expert-induced amnesia in sports happened when the hockey player Sidney Crosby was being interviewed on the ice with a reporter for the TSN hockey network immediately following his overtime goal, which won the 2010 Olympic Gold Medal for Canada in men's ice hockey (**Figure 6.16**). The reporter asked Crosby, "Sid, if you can,

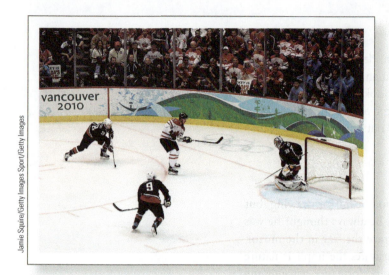

> **Figure 6.16** Sidney Crosby, in white, scoring the winning goal for Canada in the 2010 Olympics.

just take us through how that goal went in." Crosby's reply: "I don't really remember. I just shot it—I think from around here. That's all I really remember. I think it went 5-hole,[1] but um, I didn't really see it to be honest." It is likely that the over 16 million Canadians who watched Crosby's goal could have described what he did in much more detail than Crosby, who, because he was "on automatic" during the play that scored the goal, wasn't sure exactly what happened.

A Connection between Procedural Memory and Semantic Memory   Before leaving procedural memory, let's return to our violin player LSJ. Early research on LSJ noted that she had not only lost her ability to remember past events in her life, but that she had also lost her knowledge of the world. Even though she was a professional artist (in addition to being a violin player), she was unable to identify artists who painted famous works of art like Van Gogh's *Starry Night*. When presented with 62 well-known paintings, art-knowledgeable people in a control group named 71 percent of the paintings correctly, but LSJ named only 2 percent correctly (Gregory et al., 2014).

What does this have to do with procedural memory? It turns out that further testing of LSJ revealed an interesting result: Although she had lost most of her knowledge of the world, she was able to answer questions related to things that involved procedural memory. For example, she could answer questions such as "When you are painting with watercolor, how might you remove excess paint?" or "How is an acrylics brush different from a watercolor brush?" The same result also occurred when LSJ was asked questions about music ("Which instruments usually make up a string orchestra?"), driving ("How many sides does a stop sign have?"), and aviation—she was an expert pilot along with being a musician and an artist! ("What is the landing gear configuration for the Piper Cub?). The fact that LSJ remembers facts about how to do things demonstrates a link between semantic memory and memory involving motor skills like painting, playing music, driving, and piloting a plane.

What does this link between procedural and semantic memory remind you of? Earlier in this chapter we discussed interactions between semantic memory and episodic memory. You are more likely to recall the name of a popular singer (semantic information) if you had attended one of his or her concerts (episodic experience) (page 174). Similarly, the case of LSJ shows how knowledge about different fields (semantic information) is linked to the ability to carry out various skills (procedural memory). Although we can draw diagrams like Figure 6.14, which differentiate between different types of memory, it is also important to realize that these types of memory interact with each other.

Priming

Priming occurs when the presentation of one stimulus (the priming stimulus) changes the way a person responds to another stimulus (the test stimulus). One type of priming, **repetition priming**, occurs when the test stimulus is the same as or resembles the priming stimulus. For example, seeing the word *bird* may cause you to respond more quickly to a later presentation of the word *bird* than to a word you have not seen, even though you may not remember seeing *bird* earlier. Repetition priming is called implicit memory because the priming effect can occur even though participants may not remember the original presentation of the priming stimuli.

---

[1]"5-hole" in hockey is the name for the space between the goalie's legs. So saying the shot went 5-hole means Crosby thought his shot went between the goalie's legs.

One way to ensure that a person doesn't remember the presentation of the priming stimulus is to test patients with amnesia. Peter Graf and coworkers (1985) did this by testing three groups of participants: (1) patients with a condition called Korsakoff's syndrome, which is associated with alcohol abuse and eliminates the ability to form new long-term memories; (2) patients without amnesia who were under treatment for alcoholism; and (3) patients without amnesia who had no history of alcoholism.

The participants' task was to read a 10-word list and rate how much they liked each word (1 = like extremely; 5 = dislike extremely). This caused participants to focus on rating the words rather than on committing the words to memory. Immediately after rating the words, participants were tested in one of two ways: (1) a test of explicit memory, in which they were asked to recall the words they had read; or (2) a word completion test, which is a test of implicit memory. The word completion test contained the first three letters of the 10 words that the participants had seen earlier, plus the first three letters of 10 words they had not seen earlier. For example, the three letters *tab_ _* can be completed to create the word *table*. Participants were presented with three-letter fragments and were asked to add a few letters to create the first word that came into their mind.

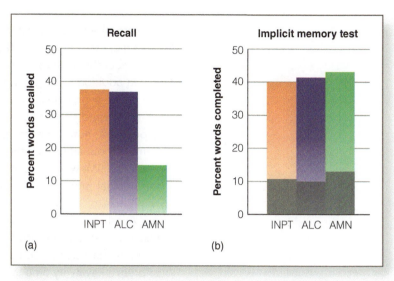

➤ **Figure 6.17** In the Graf et al. (1985) experiment, (a) amnesiac patients (AMN) did poorly on the recall test compared to the medical inpatients (INPT) and the alcoholic controls (ALC). (b) Amnesiac patients did as well as the other patients on the implicit memory test (completing three-letter word stems). The gray areas on each bar indicate performance on words the participants hadn't seen earlier.

(Source: P. Graf, A. P. Shimamura, & L. R. Squire, Priming across modalities and priming across category levels: Extending the domain of preserved function in amnesia, Journal of Experimental Psychology: Learning, Memory, and Cognition, 11, 386–396, 1985.)

The results of the recall experiment, seen in **Figure 6.17a**, show that the amnesiac patients (those with Korsakoff's syndrome) recalled fewer words than the two control groups. This poor recall confirms the poor explicit memory associated with their amnesia. But the results of the word completion test, showing the percentage of primed words that were created (**Figure 6.17b**), indicate that the patients with amnesia performed just as well as the controls. This better performance for words presented previously is an example of priming. What is notable about these results is that the patients with Korsakoff's syndrome performed as well as the two nonamnesiac groups, even though they had poor memory as measured in the recall test.

Although the poor explicit memory of patients with amnesia means that these patients are not remembering the presentation of the priming stimulus, how can we be sure that a participant with normal memory isn't remembering the priming stimulus when responding to the test stimulus? After all, if we present the word *bird* and then later measure how fast a person reacts to another presentation of the word *bird*, couldn't that happen because the person remembers the first time *bird* was presented? If the person did remember the initial presentation of *bird*, then this would be an example of explicit memory, not implicit memory. Researchers have used a number of methods to reduce the chances that a person in a priming experiment will remember the original presentation of the priming stimulus.

METHOD Avoiding Explicit Remembering in a Priming Experiment

One way to minimize the chances that a person with normal memory will remember the presentation of the priming stimulus is to present the priming stimulus in a task that does not appear to be a memory task. For example, if the priming stimuli are the names of animals, participants could be presented with the names and asked to indicate whether each animal would stand more than 2 feet high. This task causes the participant to focus on the task of estimating height and distracts them from trying to remember the animals' names.

In addition to disguising the purpose of the stimulus during the priming part of the experiment, researchers also use testing procedures that do not refer to memory, as in the word completion task in Graf's experiment. Returning to the results of that experiment, notice that the performance on the word completion task for the participants without amnesia is the same as the performance of the patients with Korsakoff's syndrome. We would expect that if the participants without amnesia had remembered the original presentations, their performance would be better than that of patients with Korsakoff's syndrome (Roediger et al.,1994).

Another way of creating a task that won't be recognized as involving a memory test is to measure how accurately or quickly the participant responds to a stimulus. For example, participants could be tested by presenting a list of words and asking them to press a key every time they see a word that has four letters. Priming would be indicated by faster or more accurate responding to four-letter words that corresponded to priming stimuli that participants had seen earlier. The key characteristic of this test is speed. Requiring a rapid response decreases the chances that the participants will take the time to consciously recollect whether they have previously seen the word.

Using methods such as these, researchers have demonstrated implicit memory not only in amnesiac patients but in normal participants as well (Graf et al., 1982; Roediger, 1990; Roediger et al., 1994; Schacter, 1987).

As I was discussing repetition priming in class, a student asked whether we are always being primed in everyday life. That's a good question, and the answer is that it is likely that repetition priming does occur in our everyday experience, although we may not be aware of it. An example of a situation in which implicit memory may affect our behavior without our awareness is when we are exposed to advertisements that extol the virtues of a product or perhaps just present the product's name. Although we may believe that we are unaffected by some advertisements, they can have an effect just because we are exposed to them.

This idea is supported by the results of an experiment by T. J. Perfect and C. Askew (1994), who had participants scan articles in a magazine. Each page of print was faced by an advertisement, but participants were not told to pay attention to the advertisements. When they were later asked to rate a number of advertisements on various dimensions, such as how appealing, eye-catching, distinctive, and memorable they were, they gave higher ratings to the ones they had been exposed to than to other advertisements that they had never seen. This result qualifies as an effect of implicit memory because when the participants were asked to indicate which advertisements had been presented at the beginning of the experiment, they recognized only an average of 2.8 of the original 25 advertisements. This result is related to the **propaganda effect**, in which participants are more likely to rate statements they have read or heard before as being true, simply because they have been exposed to them before. This effect can occur even when the person is told that the statements are false when they first read or hear them (Begg et al., 1992). The propaganda effect involves implicit memory because it can operate even when people are not aware that they have heard or seen a statement before, and may even have thought it was false when they first heard it. This is related to the *illusory truth effect,* which is discussed in Chapter 8 (page 238).

Classical Conditioning

Classical conditioning occurs when the following two stimuli are paired: (1) a neutral stimulus that initially does not result in a response and (2) a conditioning stimulus (more commonly called an unconditioned stimulus) that does result in a response (see page 10).

An example of classical conditioning from the laboratory is presenting a tone to a person followed by a puff of air to the eye that causes the person to blink. The tone initially does not cause an eyeblink, but after a number of pairings with the puff of air, the person blinks in response to the tone. This is implicit memory because it can occur even if the person has forgotten about the original pairing of the tone and the air puff.

Conditioning in real life is often linked to emotional reactions. I remember, for example, the bad feeling I had when, as I was driving along a country road, I saw the flashing red lights of a police car in my rearview mirror. I wasn't happy about receiving a speeding ticket, but the incident did provide an example of classical conditioning, because when I passed that spot on the road later, I reexperienced the emotions that had been triggered by the police car's flashing lights. This example illustrates the classical conditioning of emotions but doesn't illustrate implicit memory, because I was aware of what was causing my conditioned response.

An example of classical conditioning causing implicit memory is provided by a situation we described earlier (page 175), in which you meet someone who seems familiar but you can't remember how you know him or her. Have you ever had this experience and also felt positively or negatively about the person, without knowing why? If so, your emotional reaction was an example of implicit memory.

Now that we have described how cognitive psychologists have distinguished between different types of memory, we will close this chapter by considering how memory has been described by another group—people who make movies.

▶ SOMETHING TO CONSIDER

Memory Loss in the Movies

On September 18, 1993, Kim and Krickett Carpenter, who had been married just 10 weeks earlier, were involved in a car crash. Krickett's head injury erased her memory of her romance with her husband, Kim, and left her thinking he was a complete stranger. The 2012 movie *The Vow*, which is based on the book Kim and Krickett wrote describing their lives after the car crash, accurately describes memory loss because it is based on an actual case. However, this movie is the exception. The accuracy of most movies that describe memory loss ranges from depictions that resemble types of memory loss that actually occur to completely fictional types of memory loss that have never occurred. Sometimes, even when the memory loss in a movie resembles actual cases, it is described using incorrect terminology. We will describe some examples of fact-based memory loss, fictional memory loss, and the use of incorrect terminology in movies.

In some movies, characters lose their memory for everything in their past, including their identity, but are able to form new memories. This is what happened to Jason Bourne, the character played by Matt Damon in *The Bourne Identity* (2002) and other films in the *Bourne* series. In *The Bourne Identity*, the unconscious and badly wounded Bourne is plucked out of the water by a fishing boat. When he regains consciousness, he has no memory of his identity. As he searches for his previous identity, he realizes people are out to kill him, but, because of his memory loss, he doesn't know why. Although Bourne has lost his episodic memories of his past, his semantic memory appears to be intact, and, most interesting of all, he has lost none of his procedural memories from his training as a CIA agent, including ways to outsmart, outrun, and eliminate his adversaries.

Bourne's situation is related to a rare condition called *psychogenic fugue*. Symptoms of this condition include traveling away from where the person lives and a lack of memory for the past, especially personal information such as name, relationships, place of residence, and occupation. In the few cases that have been reported, a person vanishes from his or her normal life situation, often travels far away, and takes on a new identity unrelated to the previous one (Coons & Milstein, 1992; Loewenstein, 1991).

A number of other movies revolve around a central character who loses his or her identity or takes on a new one. In *Who Am I?* (1998), Jackie Chan plays a top-secret soldier who loses his memory in a helicopter crash, triggering a quest to recover his identity. In *Dead Again* (1991), a mystery woman played by Emma Thompson can't remember anything about her life. In *The Long Kiss Goodnight* (1996), Geena Davis plays a suburban homemaker who begins remembering events from her previous life as a secret agent after suffering a blow to her head.

In other movies, the main character has trouble forming new memories. For example, Lenny, the character played by Guy Pearce in *Memento* (2000), continually forgets what has just happened to him. This situation is based on cases such as HM, who was unable to form new memories and was therefore only able to remember the current 1 or 2 minutes of his life. Lenny's problem is apparently not as debilitating as in these real-life cases, because he is able to function in the outside world, although with some difficulty. To compensate for his inability to form new memories, Lenny records his experiences with a Polaroid camera and has key facts tattooed on his body.

The use of terminology in movies that is not the same as that used by psychologists is illustrated in *Memento*, where Lenny's problem is identified as a loss of short-term memory. This reflects a common belief (at least among those who have not taken a cognitive psychology course) that forgetting things that have happened within the last few minutes or hours is a breakdown in short-term memory. Cognitive psychologists, in contrast, identify short-term memory as memory for what has happened in the last 15 or 20 to 30 seconds (or longer, if the events are rehearsed). According to that definition, Lenny's short-term memory was fine, because he could remember what had just happened to him. His problem was that he couldn't form new long-term memories, so, like HM, he could remember the immediate present but forgot everything that had happened more than a few minutes previously.

Another movie character who has problems in making new long-term memories is Dory, the forgetful fish in the animated films *Finding Nemo* and *Finding Dory*, who has Ellen DeGeneres's voice (**Figure 6.18**). Dory's symptoms are similar to HM's. She can't form new long-term memories, so she has only short-term memories, which last only 20 to 30 seconds. But Dory's diagnosis of her condition makes the same mistake movies like *Memento* do when she says, "I suffer from short-term memory loss. I forget things almost instantly."

Although some movies, like the ones already mentioned, are based at least loosely on actual memory disorders, some stray farther into fiction. Douglas Quaid, the character played by Arnold Schwarzenegger in *Total Recall* (1990), lives in a future world in which it is possible to implant memories. Quaid makes the mistake of having an artificial memory of a holiday on Mars implanted, which triggers a series of nightmarish events.

The reverse of *creating* specific memories is selectively *forgetting* specific events. This occasionally occurs, as when memories for particularly traumatic events are lost (although sometimes the opposite happens, so traumatic events stand out in memory; Porter & Birt, 2001). But the characters in *The Eternal Sunshine of the Spotless Mind* (2004) take the idea of

> ➤ **Figure 6.18** Dory (right), the forgetful fish in *Finding Nemo* and *Finding Dory*. Dory thinks she has a problem with short-term memory, but her real problem is that she can't form new long-term memories.

Collection Christophel/Alamy Stock Photo

selective forgetting to an extreme, by purposely undergoing a high-tech procedure to selectively eliminate their memory for a previous relationship. First Clementine (played by Kate Winslet) has her memory for her ex-boyfriend, Joel (played by Jim Carrey), erased. When Joel discovers she has done this, he decides to have Clementine erased from his memory by undergoing the same procedure. The aftermath of this procedure, which I won't reveal in case you want to see the movie, is both thought provoking and entertaining!

The movie *50 First Dates* (2004) is an example of a memory movie based on a condition created by the imagination of the filmmaker. Lucy, played by Drew Barrymore, remembers what is happening to her on a given day (so her short-term and long-term memory are fine during the day), but every morning she contracts a case of amnesia, which has wiped out her memory for what happened the day before. The fact that her memory "resets" every morning seems not to bother Henry, played by Adam Sandler, who falls in love with her. Henry's problem is that because Lucy wakes up each morning with no memory for the previous day, she doesn't remember him, thus the title *50 First Dates*.

When the film was released in 2004, there were no known cases of anyone with a memory disorder in which their memory from a day vanishes during a night of sleep. However, a recent report documents the case of FL, a 51-year-old woman who was treated for a head injury from an automobile accident; after she returned home, she reported that every time she awoke she had no memory for the previous day—just like Lucy in *50 First Dates* (Smith et al., 2010)! But testing in the laboratory revealed something interesting: FL performed well on materials she had learned on the same day and exhibited no memory for material she knew had been presented on the previous day. But if, without FL's knowledge, material learned on the previous day was intermixed with new material, she was able to remember the old material. Based on a number of other tests, the researchers concluded that FL was not intentionally making believe she had amnesia, but suggested that her symptoms may have been influenced by her knowledge of how amnesia was depicted in *50 First Dates*, which was released 15 months before FL reported her symptoms—an interesting example, if true, of life imitating film!

TEST YOURSELF 6.3

1. Distinguish between explicit memory and implicit memory.

2. What is procedural memory? Describe the mirror drawing experiment and other examples from the chapter. Why is procedural memory considered a form of implicit memory?

3. What do recent experiments studying LSJ tell us about connections between procedural memory and semantic memory?

4. What is expert-induced amnesia, and how does it relate to an important property of procedural memory?

5. What is priming? Repetition priming? Describe the Graf experiment, including the results and how they support the idea that priming is a form of implicit memory.

6. What precautions are taken to be sure that people with normal memory do not use episodic memory in an experiment that is designed to test implicit memory?

7. Describe the Perfect and Askew advertising experiment. What is the propaganda effect, and why could it be considered a form of priming?

8. What is classical conditioning? Why is it a form of implicit memory?

9. Describe how memory loss is depicted in movies. How accurate are these depictions?

CHAPTER SUMMARY

1. This chapter is about *division*—distinguishing between different types of memory—and *interaction*—how the different types of memory interact.

2. Long-term memory is an "archive" of information about past experiences in our lives and knowledge we have learned. LTM coordinates with working memory to help create our ongoing experience.

3. The primacy and recency effects that occur in the serial position curve have been linked to long-term memory and short-term memory, respectively.

4. Visual and auditory coding can occur in both STM and LTM.

5. Semantic coding has been demonstrated in STM by Wickens, by demonstrating release from proactive interference.

6. Semantic coding has been demonstrated in LTM by Sachs, using a recognition memory procedure.

7. Auditory coding is the predominant type of coding in STM. Semantic coding is the predominant type in LTM.

8. Neuropsychological studies have demonstrated a double dissociation between STM and LTM, which supports the idea that STM and LTM are caused by different independent mechanisms.

9. The hippocampus is important for forming new long-term memories. Brain imaging experiments have shown that the hippocampus is also involved in holding novel information over short delays.

10. According to Tulving, the defining property of the experience of episodic memory is that it involves mental time travel (self-knowing or remembering). The experience of semantic memory (knowing) does not involve mental time travel.

11. The following evidence supports the idea that episodic and semantic memory involve different mechanisms: (1) double dissociation of episodic and semantic memory in patients with brain damage; (2) brain imaging, which indicates that overlapping but different areas are activated by episodic and semantic memories.

12. Even though episodic and semantic memories are served by different mechanisms, they are connected in the following ways: (1) Knowledge (semantic memory) can influence the nature of experiences that become episodic memories. (2) Autobiographical memories include both episodic and semantic components.

13. Personal semantic memories are semantic memories that are associated with personal experiences. These personal experiences can enhance the recall of semantic information, except not in people who have lost their episodic memories due to brain damage.

14. The remember/know procedure is based on the idea that recollection is associated with episodic memory, and familiarity is associated with semantic memory.

15. Over time, memories lose their episodic nature. This is called the semanticization of remote memories.

16. There is a link between the ability to remember the past and the ability to imagine the future. This has been demonstrated in both neuropsychological and brain imaging experiments and has led to the proposal that a function of episodic memory is to help anticipate future needs and guide future behavior, both of which can be important for survival.

17. Explicit memories, such as episodic and semantic memories, are memories we are aware of. Implicit memory occurs when learning from experience is not accompanied by conscious remembering. Procedural memory, priming, and classical conditioning involve implicit memory.

18. Procedural memory, also called skill memory, has been studied in patients with amnesia. They are able to learn new skills, although they do not remember learning them. Procedural memory is a common component of many of the skills we learn. One outcome of the automatic character of procedural memories is expert-induced amnesia.

19. There is evidence, based on testing a brain-damaged woman, that there is a connection between procedural memory and semantic memories related to motor skills.

20. Priming occurs when the presentation of a stimulus affects a person's response to the same or a related stimulus when it is presented later. The implicit nature of priming has been demonstrated in both patients with amnesia and participants without amnesia. Priming is not just a laboratory phenomenon but also occurs in real life. The propaganda effect is one example of real-life implicit memory.

21. Classical conditioning occurs when a neutral stimulus is paired with a stimulus that elicits a response, so that the neutral stimulus then elicits the response. Classically conditioned emotions occur in everyday experience.

22. Memory loss has been depicted in movies in a number of ways, some of which bear at least a resemblance to actual cases of amnesia, and some of which are totally fictional conditions.

THINK ABOUT IT

1. What do you remember about the last 5 minutes? How much of what you are remembering is in your STM while you are remembering it? Were any of these memories ever in LTM?

2. Not all long-term memories are alike. There is a difference between remembering what you did 10 minutes ago, 1 year ago, and 10 years ago, even though all of these memories are called "long-term memories." How would you expand on the research described in the chapter to demonstrate the properties of these different long-term memories?

3. Untrue information presented repeatedly on social media is sometimes accepted as being factual. How is this phenomenon, which has been called "fake news," related to the propaganda effect?

4. Can you remember how you learned to tie your shoes? How is that process similar to how learning to play the piano was described in the text?

5. View movies such as *Memento, 50 First Dates*, or others that depict memory loss. (Search the Internet for "Movies amnesia" to find films in addition to those mentioned in the book.) Describe the kinds of memory loss depicted in these movies, and compare the characters' problems with the cases of memory loss described in this chapter. Determine how accurately depictions of memory loss in movies reflect memory loss that occurs in actual cases of trauma or brain damage. You may have to do some additional research on memory loss to answer this question.

KEY TERMS

Autobiographical memory, 174

Classical conditioning, 184

Coding, 166

Expert-induced amnesia, 181

Explicit memory, 179

Hippocampus, 170

Implicit memory, 180

Long-term memory (LTM), 162

Mental time travel, 172

Personal semantic memory, 174

Primacy effect, 164

Priming, 182

Proactive interference, 167

Procedural memory, 180

Propaganda effect, 184

Recency effect, 165

Recognition memory, 168

Release from proactive interference, 167

Remember/know procedure, 176

Repetition priming, 182

Semanticization of remote memory, 176

Serial position curve, 164

Skill memory, 180

COGLAB EXPERIMENTS   Numbers in parentheses refer to the experiment number in CogLab.

Suffix Effect (*19*)
Serial Position (*31*)

Remember-Know (*36*)

Implicit Learning (*45*)

This student is engaging in an activity crucial to her success in college—studying—which involves taking in information and being able to remember it later. This chapter describes encoding—how to get information into memory—and retrieval—how to get it out later. Encoding and retrieval can be described in terms of both psychological and physiological processes. Research on these processes has resulted in insights about ways to study more effectively.

LTM: Encoding, Retrieval, and Consolidation

7

You may have heard the phrase "living in the moment." It is perhaps good advice when applied to dealing with life, because what it means is to be conscious of the present moment without dwelling on the past or being concerned or anxious about the future.

But while this prescription may work as a way to get more out of daily life, the reality is that living just in the moment isn't really living at all, as illustrated by cases such as that of HM (p. 170), who couldn't remember anything that happened more than 30 to 60 seconds in his past. He was literally living only in the moment, and so was unable to function independently.

While HM may be an extreme example, the fact is that even when you are "living in the moment," that moment is influenced by what's happened to you in the past and perhaps even your expectation of what is going to happen in the future. Our knowledge of the past, it turns out, is essential for our survival. We use knowledge about the immediate past (what just happened), and knowledge accumulated through years of experiences to deal with the environment (finding our way, keeping appointments, avoiding dangerous situations); relationships (knowing things about other people); work and school (facts and procedures necessary for succeeding in occupations or taking exams); and anticipating and planning for the future (see page 172).

In this chapter, we continue our consideration of long-term memory (LTM) by focusing on how to get information into LTM and how to get it out. We will focus on two processes: **encoding** (the process of acquiring information and transferring it to LTM) and **retrieval** (bringing information into consciousness by transferring it from LTM to working memory).

We introduced encoding in Chapter 5, when we described how Rachel stored a phone number in her LTM as she was ordering pizza. Notice that the term *encoding* is similar to the term *coding* that we discussed in relation to STM and LTM in Chapter 6. Some authors use these terms interchangeably. We have used the term *coding* to refer to the *form* in which information is represented. For example, a word can be coded visually or by its sound or by its meaning. We will use the term *encoding* to refer to the *process* used to get information into LTM. For example, a word can be encoded by repeating it over and over, by thinking of other words that rhyme with it, or by using it in a sentence. One of the main messages in this chapter is that some methods of encoding are more effective than others.

You can appreciate the importance of retrieval by imagining you just finished studying for an exam and are pretty sure you have encoded the material that is likely to be on the exam into your LTM. But the moment of truth occurs when you are in the exam and you have to remember some of this information to answer a question. No matter how much information you've encoded, it won't help you do well on the exam unless you can retrieve it, and interestingly enough, one of the main factors that determines whether you can retrieve information from LTM is the way that information was encoded when you learned it. In the next section, we will focus on how information is encoded into LTM. We will then consider retrieval and how it relates to encoding.

Encoding: Getting Information into Long-Term Memory

There are a number of ways of getting information into long-term memory, some of which are more effective than others. One example is provided by different ways of rehearsing information. Consider, for example, holding a phone number in your memory by repeating it over and over. If you do this without any consideration of meaning or making connections with other information, you are engaging in **maintenance rehearsal**. Typically, this type of rehearsal results in little or no encoding and therefore poor memory, so you don't remember the number when you want to call it again later.

But what if, instead of mindlessly repeating the phone number, you find a way to relate it to something meaningful. As it turns out, the first three numbers are the same as your phone number, and the last four just happen to be the year you were born! Coincidence as this may be, it provides an example of being able to remember the number by considering meaning or making connections to other information. When you do that, you are engaging in **elaborative rehearsal**, which results in better memory than maintenance rehearsal.

This contrast between maintenance rehearsal and elaborative rehearsal is one example of how encoding can influence the ability to retrieve memories. We will now consider a number of other examples, many of which show that better memory is associated with encoding that is based on meaning and making connections.

Levels of Processing Theory

An early idea linking the type of encoding to retrieval, proposed by Fergus Craik and Robert Lockhart (1972), is called **levels of processing theory**. According to levels of processing theory, memory depends on the **depth of processing** that an item receives. Depth of processing distinguishes between *shallow processing* and *deep processing*. **Shallow processing** involves little attention to meaning, as when a phone number is repeated over and over or attention is focused on a word's physical features such as whether it is printed in lowercase or capital letters. **Deep processing** involves close attention and elaborative rehearsal that focuses on an item's meaning and its relationship to something else. According to levels of processing theory, deep processing results in better memory than shallow processing (Craik, 2002).

In an experiment testing memory following different levels of processing, Craik and Endel Tulving (1975) presented words to participants and asked them three different types of questions:

1. A question about the physical features of the word. For example, participants see the word *bird* and are asked whether it is printed in capital letters (**Figure 7.1a**).

2. A question about rhyming. For example, participants see the word *train* and are asked if it rhymes with the word *pain*.

3. A fill-in-the-blanks question. For example, participants see the word *car* and are asked if it fits into the sentence "He saw a _____ on the street."

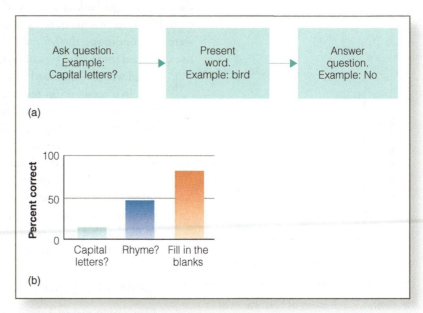

▶ **Figure 7.1** (a) Sequence of events in Craik and Tulving's (1975) experiment. (b) Results of this experiment. Deeper processing (fill-in-the-blanks question) is associated with better memory.

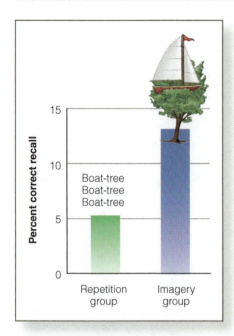

The three types of questions were designed to create different levels of processing: (1) physical features = shallow processing; (2) rhyming = deeper processing; (3) fill in the blanks = deepest processing. After participants responded to these three types of questions, they were given a memory test to see how well they recalled the words. The results, shown in **Figure 7.1b**, indicate that deeper processing is associated with better memory.

The basic idea behind levels of processing theory—that memory retrieval is affected by how items are encoded—has led to a great deal of research that has demonstrated this relationship. For example, research at about the same time that levels of processing theory was proposed showed that forming images can improve memory for word pairs.

> **Figure 7.2** Results of the Bower and Winzenz (1970) experiment. Participants in the repetition group repeated word pairs. Participants in the imagery group formed images representing the pairs.

Forming Visual Images

Gordon Bower and David Winzenz (1970) decided to test whether using visual imagery—generating images in your head to connect words visually—can enhance memory. They used a procedure called **paired-associate learning**, in which a list of word pairs is presented. Later, the first word of each pair is presented, and the participant's task is to remember the word it was paired with.

Bower and Winzenz presented a list of 15 pairs of nouns, such as *boat–tree*, to participants for 5 seconds each. One group was told to silently repeat the pairs as they were presented, and another group was told to form a mental picture in which the two items were interacting. When participants were later given the first word and asked to recall the second one for each pair, the participants who had created images remembered more than twice as many words as the participants who had just repeated the word pairs (**Figure 7.2**).

Linking Words to Yourself

Another example of how memory is improved by encoding is the **self-reference effect**: Memory is better if you are asked to relate a word to yourself. Eric Leshikar and coworkers (2015) demonstrated the self-reference effect by having participants in the study phase of their experiment look at a series of adjectives presented on a screen for about 3 seconds each. Examples of adjectives are *loyal, happy, cultural, talkative, lazy,* and *conformist*. There were two conditions, the *self condition*, in which participants indicated whether the adjective described themselves (yes or no), and the *common condition*, in which participants indicated whether the word was commonly used (yes or no).

In a recognition test that immediately followed the study phase, participants were presented with words from the study phase plus words that weren't presented and were told to indicate whether they remembered the words from before. The results, shown in **Figure 7.3**, show that memory was better for the self condition than the common condition.

Why are participants more likely to remember words they connect to themselves? One possible explanation is that the words become linked to something the participants know well—themselves. Generally, statements that result in richer, more detailed representations in a person's mind result in better memory (also see Rogers et al., 1977; Sui & Humphreys, 2015).

Generating Information

Generating material yourself, rather than passively receiving it, enhances learning and retention. Norman Slameka and Peter Graf (1978) demonstrated this effect, called the **generation effect**, by having participants study a list of word pairs in two different ways:

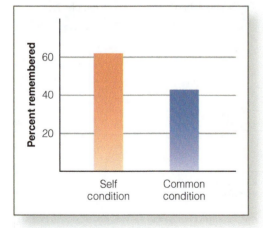

> **Figure 7.3** Results of Leshikar et al.'s (2015) self-reference experiment. Recognition was better for words that the participants had associated with themselves.

1. *Read group*: Read these pairs of related words. king–crown; horse–saddle; lamp–shade; etc.

2. *Generate group*: Fill in the blank with a word that is related to the first word. king–cr _____; horse–sa _____; lamp–sh _____; etc.

After either reading the pairs of words (read group) or generating the list of word pairs based on the word and first two letters of the second word (generate group), participants were presented with the first word in each pair and were told to indicate the word that went with it. Participants who had *generated* the second word in each pair were able to reproduce 28 percent more word pairs than participants who had just *read* the word pairs. You might guess that this finding has some important implications for studying for exams. We will return to this idea in the next section.

Organizing Information

Folders on your computer's desktop, computerized library catalogs, and tabs that separate different subjects in your notebook are all designed to organize information so it can be accessed more efficiently. The memory system also uses organization to access information. This has been shown in a number of ways.

DEMONSTRATION   Remembering a List

Get paper and pen ready. Read the following words, then cover them and write down as many as you can.

apple, desk, shoe, sofa, plum, chair, cherry, coat, lamp, pants, grape, hat, melon, table, gloves

STOP! Cover the words and write down the ones you remember, before reading further.

Look at the list you created and notice whether similar items (for example, *apple, plum, cherry; shoe, coat, pants*) are grouped together. If they are, your result is similar to the result of research that shows that participants spontaneously organize items as they recall them (Jenkins & Russell, 1952). One reason for this result is that remembering words in a particular category may serve as a **retrieval cue**—a word or other stimulus that helps a person remember information stored in memory. In this case, a word in a particular category, such as fruits, serves as a retrieval cue for other words in that category. So, remembering the word *apple* is a retrieval cue for other fruits, such as *grape* or *plum*, and therefore creates a recall list that is more organized than the original list that you read.

If words presented randomly become organized in the mind, what happens when words are presented in an organized way during encoding? Gordon Bower and coworkers (1969) answered this question by presenting material to be learned in an "organizational tree," which organized a number of words according to categories. For example, one tree organized the names of different minerals by grouping together precious stones, rare metals, and so on (**Figure 7.4**).

One group of participants studied four separate trees for minerals, animals, clothing, and transportation for 1 minute each and were then asked to recall as many words as they could from all four trees. In the recall test, participants tended to organize their responses in the same way the trees were organized, first saying "minerals," then "metals," then "common," and so on. Participants in this group recalled an average of 73 words from all four trees.

Another group of participants also saw four trees, but the words were randomized, so that each tree contained a random assortment of minerals, animals, clothing, and

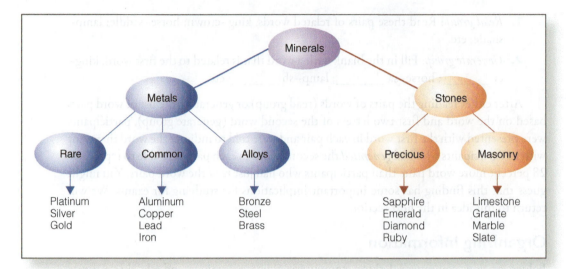

> **Figure 7.4** The organized "tree" for minerals used in Bower et al.'s (1969) experiment on the effect of organization on memory.

(Source: G. H. Bower et al., Hierarchical retrieval schemes in recall of categorized word lists, Journal of Verbal Learning and Verbal Behavior, 8, 323–343, Figure 1. Copyright © 1969 Elsevier Ltd. Republished with permission.)

transportation. These participants were able to remember only 21 words from all four trees. Thus, organizing material to be remembered results in substantially better recall. Perhaps this is something to keep in mind when creating study materials for an exam. You might, for example, find it useful to organize material you are studying for your cognitive psychology exam in trees like the one in **Figure 7.5**.

If presenting material in an organized way improves memory, we might expect that *preventing* organization from happening would *reduce* the ability to remember. This effect was illustrated by John Bransford and Marcia Johnson (1972), who asked their participants to read the following passage:

> If the balloons popped, the sound wouldn't be able to carry since everything would be too far away from the correct floor. A closed window would also prevent the sound from carrying, since most buildings tend to be well insulated. Since the whole operation depends on the steady flow of electricity, a break in the middle of the wire would also cause problems. Of course, the fellow could shout, but the human voice is

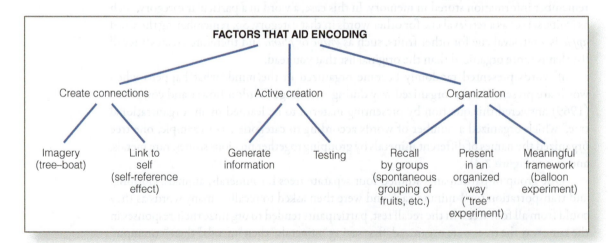

> **Figure 7.5** An organized tree for some of the material about encoding presented in this section of the chapter.

not loud enough to carry that far. An additional problem is that the string could break on the instrument. Then there would be no accompaniment to the message. It is clear that the best situation would involve less distance. Then there would be fewer potential problems. With face to face contact, the least number of things could go wrong. (p. 719)

What was that all about? Although each sentence makes sense, it was probably difficult to picture what was happening, based on the passage. Bransford and Johnson's participants not only found it difficult to picture what was going on, but they also found it extremely difficult to *remember* this passage.

To make sense of this passage, look at **Figure 7.6** on page 198 and then reread the passage. When you do this, the passage makes more sense. Bransford and Johnson's (1972) participants who saw this picture *before* they read the passage remembered twice as much from the passage as participants who did not see the picture or participants who saw the picture *after* they read the passage. The key here is organization. The picture provides a mental framework that helps the reader link one sentence to the next to create a meaningful story. The resulting organization makes this passage easier to comprehend and much easier to remember later. This example illustrates once again that the ability to remember material depends on how that material is programmed into the mind.

Relating Words to Survival Value

James Nairne (2010) proposes that we can understand how memory works by considering its function, because, through the process of evolution, memory was shaped to increase the ability to survive, especially in situations experienced by our ancestors, who were faced with basic survival challenges such as finding food and evading predators. In an experiment designed to test this idea, Nairne had participants imagine that they were stranded on the grassland of a foreign country without any basic survival materials. As they were imagining this, they were presented with a list of words. Their task was to rate each word based on how relevant it would be for finding supplies of food and water and providing protection from predators.

Later, participants were given a surprise memory test that showed that carrying out this "survival" task while reading the words resulted in better memory than other elaborative encoding procedures we have described, such as forming visual images, linking words to yourself, or generating information. Based on this result, Nairne concluded that "survival processing" is a powerful tool for encoding items into memory.

Other researchers, have, however, shown that memory is also enhanced by relating words to situations that our ancestors didn't experience, such as being attacked by zombies, either in the grasslands or in a modern city (Soderstrom & McCabe, 2011), or planning for an upcoming camping trip (Klein et al., 2010, 2011). Because of results such as these, some researchers question the idea that our memory systems are tuned to respond to survival situation faced by our ancient ancestors. There is no question, however, that situations that involve survival can enhance memory.

Retrieval Practice

All of the previous examples have shown that the way material is *studied* can affect memory for the material, with elaborative processing resulting in better memory. But the elaboration that results in better memory can also be achieved by *testing* memory, or, to put it another way, to practice *memory retrieval*.

The **retrieval practice effect** was demonstrated in an experiment by Jeffrey Karpicke and Henry Roediger (2008). In their experiment, participants studied a list

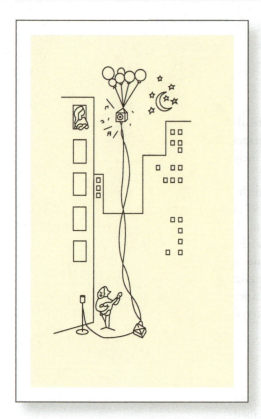

➤ **Figure 7.6** Picture used by Bransford and Johnson (1972) to illustrate the effect of organization on memory.

of 40 Swahili–English word pairs, such as *mashua*–boat, and then saw one of the words in each pair and were asked to remember the other word.

The design of the experiment is shown in **Table 7.1**. There were three groups. In the "first study and test" phase of the experiment (Column 1) all three groups studied all of the pairs and then were tested on all of the pairs. When tested, they recalled some pairs and didn't recall others. In the "repeat study and test" phase of the experiment (Column 2) the three groups had different study and test experiences.

Group 1 continued the original procedure. In each study-test session they studied all pairs and were tested on all pairs until their performance reached 100 percent. For Group 2 the study part of the study-test sequence was changed. Once a pair was recalled correctly in a test, it was no longer *studied* in next study sessions. However, all of the pairs were tested during each test session until performance reached 100 percent. This group therefore *studied* less of the pairs as the experiment progressed. For Group 3 the test part of the study-test sequence was changed. Once a pair was recalled correctly, it was no longer *tested* during the next test sessions. This group was therefore *tested* on less of the pairs as the experiment progressed.

When tested a week later, Groups 1 and 2 recalled 81 percent of the pairs, but Group 3 only recalled 36 percent of the pairs. This result shows that *being tested* is important for learning because when testing was stopped for Group 3 once items were recalled correctly, performance decreased. In contrast, the results for Group 2 show that cessation of studying did not affect performance. The enhanced performance due to retrieval practice is called the **testing effect**. It has been demonstrated in a large number of experiments, both in the laboratory and in classroom settings (Karpicke et al., 2009). For example, testing resulted in better performance than rereading for eighth-grade students' performance on a history test (Carpenter et al., 2009) and for college students' performance on an exam in a brain and behavior course (McDaniel et al., 2007).

All of the above examples of different conditions that aid encoding provide an important message for students studying for exams: When studying, use techniques that result in elaborative processing, and keep testing yourself, even after the material is "learned," because testing provides a way of elaborating the material.

TABLE 7.1

Design and Results of Karpicke and Roediger (2008) Experiment

	First Study and Test Session		Repeat Study and Test Sessions		Test After One Week
	STUDY	TEST	STUDY	TEST	% Correct
Group 1	All pairs	All pairs	All pairs	All pairs	81
Group 2 (less studying)	All pairs	All pairs	Only pairs NOT recalled in previous tests	All pairs	81
Group 3 (less testing)	All pairs	All pairs	All pairs	Only pairs NOT recalled in previous tests	36

TEST YOURSELF 7.1

1. What is encoding? Retrieval? Why is each necessary for successful memory?

2. What is the difference between elaborative rehearsal and maintenance rehearsal in terms of (a) the procedures associated with each type of rehearsal and (b) their effectiveness for creating long-term memories?

3. What is levels of processing theory? Be sure you understand depth of processing, shallow processing, and deep processing. What would levels of processing theory say about the difference between maintenance rehearsal and elaborative rehearsal?

4. Give examples of how memory for a word can be increased by (a) forming visual images, (b) linking words to yourself, (c) generating the word during acquisition, (d) organizing information, (e) rating the word in terms of survival, and (f) practicing retrieval. What do these procedures have in common?

5. What is the testing effect?

6. What do the results of the procedures in question 5 indicate about the relationship between encoding and retrieval?

▶ Effective Studying

How do you study? Students have developed numerous techniques, which vary depending on the type of material to be studied and what works for a particular student. When students are asked to describe their study techniques, the most popular are highlighting material in text or notes (Bell & Limber, 2010; Gurung et al., 2010) and rereading text or notes (Carrier, 2003; Karpicke et al., 2009; Wissman et al., 2012). Unfortunately, research has generally found that these popular techniques are not very effective (Dunlosky et al., 2013). Apparently, students use highlighting and rereading because they are easy to use, and because they are not aware of more effective methods. We will describe a number of ways of learning material that have been shown to be effective. Even if you think highlighting and rereading work for you, you might want to consider also using one or more of the following techniques the next time you study.

Elaborate

A process that helps transfer the material you are reading into long-term memory is elaboration—thinking about what you are reading and giving it meaning by relating it to other things that you know. This becomes easier as you learn more because what you have learned creates a structure on which to hang new information.

Techniques based on association, such as creating images that link two things, as in Figure 7.2, often prove useful for learning individual words or definitions. For example, there is a memory effect called *proactive interference*, which occurs when previously learned information interferes with learning new information. The effect of proactive interference is illustrated by what might happen when learning French vocabulary words makes it more difficult to learn a list of Spanish words a little later. How can you remember the term *proactive interference*? My solution was to think of a "pro" football player smashing everything in his path as he runs forward in time, to remind me that proactive interference is the past influencing the present. I no longer need this image to remember what proactive interference is, but it was helpful when I was first learning this concept.

Generate and Test

The results of research on the generation effect (page 194) indicate that devising situations in which you take an active role in creating material is a powerful way to achieve strong encoding and good long-term retrieval. And research on retrieval practice and the testing effect (page 197) indicates that repeatedly testing yourself on material you are studying pays dividends in improved memory.

Testing is actually a form of generation, because it requires active involvement with the material. If you were going to test yourself, how would you get the test questions? One way would be to use the questions that are sometimes provided in the book or study guide, such as the Test Yourself questions in this book. Another way is to make up questions yourself. Because making up the questions involves active engagement with the material, it strengthens encoding of the material. Research has shown that students who read a text with the idea of *making up* questions did as well on an exam as students who read a text with the idea of *answering* questions later, and both groups did better than a group of students who did not create or answer questions (Frase, 1975).

Research has shown that many students believe that reviewing the material is more effective than testing themselves on it, but when they do test themselves, it is usually to determine how they are doing, not as a tool to increase learning (Kornell & Son, 2009). As it turns out, self-testing accomplishes two things: It indicates what you know *and* increases your ability to remember what you know later.

Organize

The goal of organizing material is to create a framework that helps relate some information to other information to make the material more meaningful and therefore strengthen encoding. Organization can be achieved by making "trees," as in Figure 7.5, or outlines or lists that group similar facts or principles together.

Organization also helps reduce the load on your memory. We can illustrate this by looking at a perceptual example. If you see the black and white pattern in Figure 3.17 (page 72) as unrelated black and white areas, it is extremely difficult to describe what it is. However, once you've seen this pattern as a Dalmatian, it becomes meaningful and therefore much easier to describe and to remember (Wiseman & Neisser, 1974). Organization relates to the phenomenon of chunking that we discussed in Chapter 5. Grouping small elements into larger, more meaningful ones increases memory. Organizing material is one way to achieve this.

Take Breaks

Saying "Take breaks" is another way of saying "Study in a number of shorter study sessions rather than trying to learn everything at once," or "Don't cram." There are good reasons to say these things. Research has shown that memory is better when studying is broken into a number of short sessions, with breaks in between, than when it is concentrated in one long session, even if the total study time is the same. This advantage for short study sessions is called the **spacing effect** (Reder & Anderson, 1982; Smith & Rothkopf, 1984).

Another angle on taking breaks is provided by research that shows that memory performance is enhanced if sleep follows learning (page 214). Although sleeping to avoid studying is probably not a good idea, sleeping soon after studying can improve a process called consolidation (which we will discuss later in this chapter) and which results in stronger memories.

Avoid "Illusions of Learning"

One of the conclusions of both basic memory research and research on specific study techniques is that some study techniques favored by students may *appear* to be more effective than they actually are. For example, one reason for the popularity of rereading as a study technique is that it can create the illusion that learning is occurring. This happens because reading and rereading material results in greater *fluency*—that is, repetition causes the reading to become easier and easier. But although this enhanced ease of reading creates the illusion that the material is being learned, increased fluency doesn't necessarily translate into better memory for the material.

Another mechanism that creates the illusion of learning is the *familiarity effect*. Rereading causes material to become familiar, so when you encounter it a second or third time, there is a tendency to interpret this familiarity as indicating that you know the material. Unfortunately, recognizing material that is right in front of you doesn't necessarily mean that you will be able to remember it later.

Finally, beware of highlighting. A survey by Sarah Peterson (1992) found that 82 percent of students highlight study material, and most of them do so while they are reading the material for the first time. The problem with highlighting is that it seems like elaborative processing (you're taking an active role in your reading by highlighting important points), but it often becomes automatic behavior that involves moving the hand, but with little deep thinking about the material.

When Peterson compared comprehension for a group of students who highlighted and a group who didn't, she found no difference between the performance of the two groups when they were tested on the material. Highlighting may be a good first step for some people, but it is usually important to go back over what you highlighted using techniques such as elaborative rehearsal or generating questions in order to get that information into your memory.

Be An "Active" Note-Taker

The preceding study suggestions are about how to study course material, which typically means studying a textbook, course readings, and lecture notes. In addition to following these suggestions, another way to improve course learning is to think about how you go about creating your lecture notes. Do you take notes by writing them out by hand or by typing them into your laptop?

A majority of students report that they take notes on their laptop (Fried, 2008; Kay & Lauricella, 2011). When asked why they do this, their response is usually that typing notes on the laptop is more efficient, and that they can take more complete notes (Kay & Lauricella, 2011). Many professors, however, feel that taking notes on the laptop isn't a good idea because the laptop creates the temptation to engage in distracting activities like surfing the web or sending texts or emails. But in addition to this distraction argument against laptops, there is another argument against computer note taking: Computer note taking can result in shallower processing of the material, and therefore poorer performance on exams.

Empirical support for this idea has been provided by Pam Mueller and Daniel Oppenheimer (2014) in a paper titled "The Pen is Mightier Than the Keyboard: Advantages of Longhand Over Laptop Note Taking." They ran a number of experiments in which they had students listen to lectures and take notes either by longhand or by using their laptop. Laptop note-takers took more notes, because laptop note taking is easier and faster than note taking by hand. In addition, there were two other differences. The laptop notes contained more word-for-word transcription of the lecture, and students in the laptop group performed worse than the longhand group when tested on the lecture material.

Why did the laptop note-takers perform more poorly on the exam? Answering this question takes us back to the principle that memory for material depends on how it is encoded, and specifically that generating material yourself results in deeper processing and therefore better memory. According to Mueller and Oppenheimer, the shallow processing associated with simply transcribing what the professor is saying works against learning.

In contrast, creating hand-written notes are more likely to involve synthesizing and summarizing the lecture, which results in deeper encoding and better learning. The bottom-line message of the Mueller and Oppenheimer paper is that "active" and "involved" note taking is better than "mindless transcribing."

Adam Putnam and coworkers (2016), in a paper titled "Optimizing Learning in College: Tips from Cognitive Psychology," make many valuable suggestions regarding ways to succeed in college courses. Two of their suggestions, which are based on Mueller and Oppenheimer's results, are that in lecture courses, (1) "leave your laptop at home," to avoid the distraction of the Internet and social media, and (2) "write your notes instead of typing them," because handwriting encourages more reflective, deeper processing. Of course, Mueller and Oppenheimer are just one source, so before writing off computer note taking, it might be best to wait for the results of more research. But whatever mechanism you use to take notes, do your best to take notes in your own words, without simply copying what the lecturer is saying.

The message of all of these study hints is that there are ways to improve your learning by taking cues from the results of cognitive psychology research. The Putnam and coworkers, (2016) paper provides a concise summary of research-based conclusions about studying, and a paper by John Dunlosky and coworkers (2013) provides a more in-depth discussion, which ends by concluding that practice testing (see the upcoming section "Generate and Test") and distributed practice (see the preceding section "Take Breaks") are the two most effective study techniques.

▶ Retrieval: Getting Information Out of Memory

We've already seen how retrieval can strengthen memory. But how can we increase the chances that something will be retrieved? The process of retrieval is extremely important because many of our failures of memory are failures of retrieval—the information is "in there," but we can't get it out. For example, you've studied hard for an exam but can't come up with an answer when you're taking the exam, only to remember it later after the exam is over. Or you unexpectedly meet someone you have previously met and can't recall the person's name, but it suddenly comes to you as you are talking (or, worse, after the person leaves). In both of these examples, you have the information you need but can't retrieve it when you need it.

Retrieval Cues

When we discussed how remembering the word *apple* might serve as a retrieval cue for *grape* (page 195), we defined *retrieval cues* as words or other stimuli that help us remember information stored in our memory. As we now consider these cues in more detail, we will see that they can be provided by a number of different sources.

An experience I had as I was preparing to leave home to go to class illustrates how *location* can serve as a retrieval cue. While I was in my office at home, I made a mental note to be sure to take the DVD on amnesia to school for my cognitive psychology class. A short while later, as I was leaving the house, I had a nagging feeling that I was forgetting something, but I couldn't remember what it was. This wasn't the first time I'd had this problem, so I knew exactly what to do. I returned to my office, and as soon as I got there I remembered that I was supposed to take the DVD. Returning to the place where I had originally thought about taking the disk helped me to retrieve my original thought. My office was a retrieval cue for remembering what I wanted to take to class.

You may have had similar experiences in which returning to a particular place stimulated memories associated with that place. The following description by one of my students illustrates retrieval of memories of childhood experiences:

When I was 8 years old, both of my grandparents passed away. Their house was sold, and that chapter of my life was closed. Since then I can remember general things about being there as a child, but not the details. One day I decided to go for a drive. I went to my grandparents' old house and I pulled around to the alley and parked. As I sat there and stared at the house, the most amazing thing happened. I experienced a vivid recollection. All of a sudden, I was 8 years old again. I could see myself in the backyard, learning to ride a bike for the first time. I could see the inside of the house. I remembered exactly what every detail looked like. I could even remember the distinct smell. So many times I tried to remember these things, but never so vividly did I remember such detail. (Angela Paidousis)

My experience in my office and Angela's experience outside her grandparents' house are examples of retrieval cues that are provided by returning to the location where memories were initially formed. Many other things besides location can provide retrieval cues. Hearing a particular song can bring back memories for events you might not have thought about for years. Or consider smell. I once experienced a musty smell like the stairwell of my grandparents' house and was instantly transported back many decades to the experience of climbing those stairs as a child. The operation of retrieval cues has also been demonstrated in the laboratory using a technique called *cued recall*.

METHOD Cued Recall

We can distinguish two types of recall procedures. In **free recall**, a participant is simply asked to recall stimuli. These stimuli could be words previously presented by the experimenter or events experienced earlier in the participant's life. We have seen how this has been used in many experiments, such as the serial position curve experiment (page 164). In **cued recall**, the participant is presented with retrieval cues to aid in recall of the previously experienced stimuli. These cues are typically words or phrases. For example, Endel Tulving and Zena Pearlstone (1966) did an experiment in which they presented participants with a list of words to remember. The words were drawn from specific categories such as birds (*pigeon, sparrow*), furniture (*chair, dresser*), and professions (*engineer, lawyer*), although the categories were not specifically indicated in the original list. For the memory test, participants in the free recall group were asked to write down as many words as they could. Participants in the cued recall group were also asked to recall the words but were provided with the names of the categories, such as "birds," "furniture," and "professions."

The results of Tulving and Pearlstone's experiment demonstrate that retrieval cues aid memory. Participants in the free recall group recalled 40 percent of the words, whereas participants in the cued recall group who had been provided with the names of categories recalled 75 percent of the words.

One of the most impressive demonstrations of the power of retrieval cues was provided by Timo Mantyla (1986), who presented his participants with a list of 504 nouns, such as *banana, freedom*, and *tree*. During this study phase, participants were told to write three words they associated with each noun. For example, three words for *banana* might be *yellow, bunches*, and *edible*. In the test phase of the experiment, these participants were presented with the three words they had generated (self-generated retrieval cues) for half the nouns, or with three words that someone else had generated (other-person-generated retrieval cues) for the other half of the nouns. Their task was to remember the noun they had seen during the study phase.

The results indicated that when the self-generated retrieval cues were presented, participants remembered 91 percent of the words (top bar in **Figure 7.7**), but when the

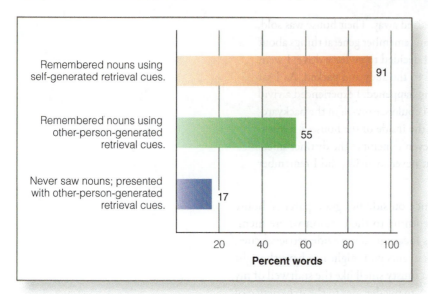

Remembered nouns using self-generated retrieval cues. **91**

Remembered nouns using other-person-generated retrieval cues. **55**

Never saw nouns; presented with other-person-generated retrieval cues. **17**

20   40   60   80   100

Percent words

➤ **Figure 7.7** Results of Mantyla's (1986) experiment. Memory was best when retrieval cues were created by the participant (top bar), and not as good when retrieval cues were created by someone else (middle bar). Control participants who tried to guess the words based on retrieval cues generated by someone else did poorly (bottom bar).

other-person-generated retrieval cues were presented, participants remembered only 55 percent of the words (second bar in Figure 7.7).

You might think it would be possible to guess *banana* from three properties like *yellow, bunches,* and *edible*, even if you had never been presented with the word *banana*. But when Mantyla ran another control group in which he presented the cue words generated by someone else to participants who had never seen the 504 nouns, these participants were able to determine only 17 percent of the nouns. The results of this experiment demonstrate that retrieval cues (the three words) provide extremely effective information for retrieving memories, but that *retrieval cues are significantly more effective when they are created by the person whose memory is being tested.* (Also see Wagenaar, 1986, which describes a study in which Wagenaar was able to remember almost all of 2,400 diary entries he kept over a 6-year period by using retrieval cues.)

Matching Conditions of Encoding and Retrieval

The retrieval cues in the two experiments we just described were verbal "hints"—category names like "furniture" in the Tulving and Pearlstone experiment and three-word descriptions created by the participants in the Mantyla experiment. But we have also seen another kind of "hint" that can help with retrieval: returning to a specific location, such as Angela's grandparents' house or my office.

Let's consider what happened in the office example, in which I needed to return to my office to retrieve my thought about taking a DVD to class. The key to remembering the DVD was that I retrieved the thought "Bring the DVD" by returning to the place where I had originally encoded that thought. This example illustrates the following basic principle: *Retrieval can be increased by matching the conditions at retrieval to the conditions that existed at encoding.*

We will now describe three specific situations in which retrieval is increased by matching conditions at retrieval to conditions at encoding. These different ways to achieve matching are (1) encoding specificity—matching the *context* in which encoding and retrieval occur; (2) state-dependent learning—matching the *internal mood* present during encoding and retrieval; and (3) transfer-appropriate processing—matching the *task* involved in encoding and retrieval.

Encoding Specificity   The principle of **encoding specificity** states that we encode information along with its context. For example, Angela encoded many experiences within the context of her grandparents' house. When she reinstated this context by returning to the house many years later, she remembered many of these experiences.

A classic experiment that demonstrates encoding specificity is D. R. Godden and Alan Baddeley's (1975) "diving experiment." In this experiment, one group of participants put on diving equipment and studied a list of words underwater, and another group studied the words on land (**Figure 7.8a**). These groups were then divided so that half the participants in the land and water groups were tested for recall on land and half were tested underwater. The results, indicated by the numbers, show that the best recall occurred when encoding and retrieval occurred in the same location.

The results of the diving study, and many others, suggest that a good strategy for test taking would be to study in an environment similar to the environment in which you will be tested. Although this doesn't mean you necessarily have to do all of your studying in the classroom where you will be taking the exam, you might want to duplicate in your study situation some of the conditions that will exist during the exam.

This conclusion about studying is supported by an experiment by Harry Grant and coworkers (1998), using the design in **Figure 7.8b**. Participants read an article on psychoimmunology while wearing headphones. The participants in the "quiet" condition heard nothing in the headphones. Participants in the "noise" condition heard a tape of background noise recorded during lunchtime in a university cafeteria (which they were told to ignore). Half the participants in each group were then given a short-answer test on the article under the quiet condition, and the other half were tested under the noise condition.

The results, shown in Figure 7.8b, indicate that participants did better when the testing condition matched the study condition. Because your next cognitive psychology exam will take place under quiet conditions, it might make sense to study under quiet conditions. (Interestingly, a number of my students report that having outside stimulation such as music or television present helps them study. This idea clearly violates the principle of encoding specificity. Can you think of some reasons that students might nonetheless say this?)

State-Dependent Learning   Another example of how matching the conditions at encoding and retrieval can influence memory is **state-dependent learning**—learning that is associated with a particular *internal state*, such as mood or state of awareness. According to the principle of state-dependent learning, memory will be better when a person's internal state (mood or awareness) during retrieval matches his or her internal state during encoding. For example, Eric Eich and Janet Metcalfe (1989) demonstrated that memory is better when a person's mood during retrieval matches his or her mood during encoding. They did this by asking participants to think positive thoughts while listening to "merry" or happy music, or depressing thoughts while listening to "melancholic" or sad music (**Figure 7.8c**). Participants rated their mood while listening to the music, and the encoding part of the experiment began when their rating reached "very pleasant" or "very unpleasant." Once this occurred, usually within 15 to 20 minutes, participants studied lists of words while in their positive or negative mood.

After the study session ended, the participants were told to return in 2 days (although those in the sad group stayed in the lab a little longer, snacking on cookies and chatting with the experimenter while happy music played in the background, so they wouldn't leave the laboratory in a bad mood). Two days later, the participants returned, and the same procedure was used to put them in a positive or negative mood. When they reached the mood, they were given a memory test for the words they had studied 2 days earlier. The results,

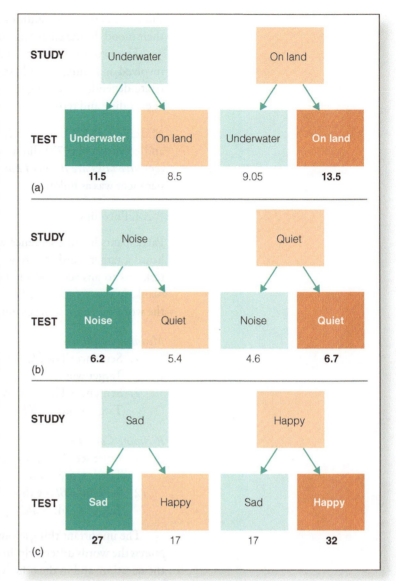

> **Figure 7.8** Design and results for (a) Godden and Baddeley's (1975) "diving" experiment; (b) Grant et al.'s (1998) "studying" experiment; (c) Eich and Metcalfe's (1989) "mood" experiment. Results for each test condition are indicated by the number directly under that condition. The matching colors (light green to dark green, and light orange to dark orange) indicate situations in which study and test conditions matched.

shown in Figure 7.8c, indicate that they did better when their mood at retrieval matched their mood during encoding (also see Eich, 1995).

The two ways of matching encoding and retrieval that we have described so far have involved matching the physical situation (encoding specificity) or an internal feeling (state-dependent learning). Our next example involves matching the type of *cognitive task* at encoding and retrieval.

Matching the Cognitive Task: Transfer-Appropriate Processing   Donald Morris and coworkers (1977) did an experiment that showed that retrieval is better if *the same cognitive tasks are involved during both encoding and retrieval*. The procedure for their experiment was as follows:

Part I. Encoding

Participants heard a sentence with one word replaced by "blank," and 2 seconds later they heard a target word. There were two encoding conditions. In the *meaning condition*, the task was to answer "yes" or "no" based on the *meaning* of the word when it filled in the blank. In the *rhyming condition*, participants answered "yes" or "no" based on the *sound* of the word. Here are some examples:

Meaning Condition
1. Sentence: The *blank* had a silver engine.
   Target word: *train*   Correct answer: "yes"
2. Sentence: The *blank* walked down the street.
   Target word: *building*   Correct answer: "no"

Rhyming Condition
1. Sentence: *Blank* rhymes with pain.
   Target word: *Train*   Correct answer: "yes"
2. Sentence: *Blank* rhymes with car.
   Target word: *Building*   Correct answer: "no"

The important thing about these two groups of participants is that they were asked to *process* the words differently. In one case, they had to focus on the word's meaning to answer the question, and in the other case they focused on the word's sound.

Part II. Retrieval

The question Morris was interested in was how the participants' ability to retrieve the target words would be affected by the way they had processed the words during the encoding part of the experiment. There were a number of different conditions in this part of the experiment, but we are going to focus on what happened when participants were required to process words in terms of their sounds.

Participants in both the meaning group and the rhyming group were presented with a series of test words, one by one. Some of the test words rhymed with target words presented during encoding; some did not. Their task was to answer "yes" if the test word rhymed with one of the target words and "no" if it didn't. In the examples below, notice that the test words were always different from the target word.

Test word: *rain*   Answer: "yes" (because it rhymes with the previously presented target word *train*)

Test word: *street*   Answer: "no" (because it doesn't rhyme with any of the target words that were presented during encoding)

The key result of this experiment was that the participants' retrieval performance depended on whether the retrieval task matched the encoding task. As shown in

Figure 7.9, participants who had focused on rhyming during encoding remembered more words in the rhyming test than participants who had focused on meaning. Thus, participants who had focused on the word's *sound* during the first part of the experiment did better when the test involved focusing on sound. This result—better performance when the *type of processing* matches in encoding and retrieval—is called **transfer-appropriate processing**.

Transfer-appropriate processing is like encoding specificity and state-dependent learning because it demonstrates that matching conditions during encoding and retrieval improves performance. But, in addition, the result of this experiment has important implications for the levels of processing theory discussed earlier. Remember that the main idea behind levels of processing theory is that deeper processing leads to better encoding and, therefore, better retrieval. Levels of processing theory would predict that participants who were in the meaning group during encoding would experience "deeper" processing, so they should perform better. Instead, the rhyming group performed better. Thus, in addition to showing that matching the tasks at encoding and retrieval is important, Morris's experiment shows that deeper processing at encoding does not always result in better retrieval, as proposed by levels of processing theory.

Our approach to encoding and retrieval has so far focused on behavioral experiments that consider how conditions of encoding and retrieval affect memory. But there is another approach to studying encoding and retrieval that focuses on physiology. In the rest of this chapter, we will look "under the hood" of memory to consider how physiological changes that occur during encoding influence our ability to retrieve memory for an experience later.

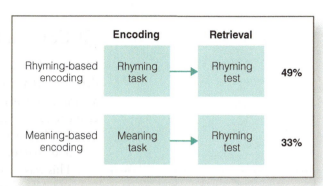

▶ **Figure 7.9** Design and results for the Morris et al. (1977) experiment. Participants who did a rhyming-based encoding task did better on the rhyming test than participants who did a meaning-based encoding task. This result would not be predicted by levels of processing theory but is predicted by the principle that better retrieval occurs if the encoding and retrieval tasks are matched.

TEST YOURSELF 7.2

1. Describe the following five ways of improving the effectiveness of studying: (1) elaborate; (2) generate and test; (3) organize; (4) take breaks; (5) avoid "illusions of learning." How does each technique relate to findings about encoding and retrieval?

2. What does it mean to be an "active" learner? How is this question related to the difference between taking notes by hand versus note taking on a laptop?

3. Retrieval cues are a powerful way to improve the chances that we will remember something. Why can we say that memory performance is better when you use a word in a sentence, create an image, or relate it to yourself, which are all techniques involving retrieval cues?

4. What is cued recall? Compare it to free recall.

5. Describe the Tulving and Pearlstone cued recall experiment and Mantyla's experiment in which he presented 600 words to his participants. What was the procedure and what was the result for each experiment, and what does each tell us about retrieval?

6. What is encoding specificity? Describe Baddeley and Godden's "diving" experiment and Grant's studying experiment. What does each one illustrate about encoding specificity? About cued recall?

7. What is state-dependent learning? Describe Eich and Metcalf's experiment about mood and memory.

8. Describe Morris's transfer-appropriate processing experiment. What aspect of encoding and retrieval was Morris studying? What implications do the results of this experiment have for matching encoding and retrieval? For levels of processing theory?

► Consolidation: Establishing Memories

Memories have a history. Right after an event or learning has occurred, we remember many details of what happened or what we have learned. But with the passage of time and the accumulation of additional experiences, some of these memories are lost, some change their character, and some might end up being different than what actually happened.

Another observation about memory is that while every experience creates the potential for a new memory, new memories are fragile and can therefore be disrupted. This was first demonstrated experimentally by German psychologists Georg Müller and Alfons Pilzecker (1900; also see Dewar et al., 2007), who did an experiment in which two groups of participants learned lists of nonsense syllables. The "immediate" group learned one list and then immediately learned a second list. The "delay" group learned the first list and then waited for 6 minutes before learning the second list (**Figure 7.10**). When recall for the first list was measured, participants in the delay group remembered 48 percent of the syllables, but participants in the immediate (no delay) group remembered only 28 percent. Apparently, immediately presenting the second list to the "no delay" group interrupted the forming of a stable memory for the first list. Based on this result, Müller and Pilzecker proposed the term **consolidation**, which is defined as *the process that transforms new memories from a fragile state, in which they can be disrupted, to a more permanent state, in which they are resistant to disruption.*

In the more than 100 years since Müller and Pilzecker's pioneering experiment, researchers have discovered a great deal about the mechanisms responsible for consolidation and have distinguished two types, based on mechanisms that involve both synapses and neural circuits. Remember from Chapter 2 that synapses are the small spaces between the end of one neuron and the cell body or dendrite of another neuron (see Figure 2.4, page 29), and that when signals reach the end of a neuron, they cause neurotransmitters to be released onto the next neuron. Neural circuits are interconnected groups of neurons. **Synaptic consolidation**, which takes place over minutes or hours, involves structural changes at synapses. **Systems consolidation**, which takes place over months or even years, involves the gradual reorganization of neural circuits within the brain (Nader & Einarsson, 2010).

The fact that synaptic consolidation is relatively fast and systems consolidation is slower doesn't mean that we should think of them as two stages of a process that occur one after the other, like short-term memory and long-term memory in the modal model of memory (Figure 5.2, page 132). It is more accurate to think of them as occurring together, as shown in **Figure 7.11**, but at different speeds and at different levels of the nervous system. When something happens, a process is triggered that causes changes at the synapse. Meanwhile, a longer-term process begins that involves reorganization of neural circuits. Thus, synaptic and systems consolidation are processes that occur simultaneously—one that works rapidly, at the level of the synapse, and another that works more slowly, at the level of neural circuits.

Synaptic Consolidation: Experience Causes Changes at the Synapse

According to an idea first proposed by the Canadian psychologist Donald Hebb (1948), learning and memory are represented in the brain by physiological changes that

► **Figure 7.10** Procedure for Müller and Pilzecker's experiment. (a) In the immediate (no delay) condition, participants used the first list (1) and then immediately learned the second list (2). (b) In the delay condition, the second list was learned after a 6-minute delay. Numbers on the right indicate the percentage of items from the first list recalled when memory for that list was tested later.

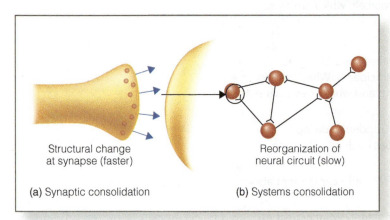

► **Figure 7.11** Synaptic and systems consolidation. (a) Synaptic consolidation involves changes at the synapses. (a) Systems consolidation involves reorganization of neural connections and takes place over a longer time span.

take place at the synapse. Let's assume that a particular experience causes nerve impulses to travel down the axon of neuron A in **Figure 7.12a**, and when these impulses reach the synapse, neurotransmitter is released onto neuron B. Hebb's idea was that repeated activity can strengthen the synapse by causing structural changes, greater transmitter release, and increased firing (**Figures 7.12b** and **7.12c**). Hebb also proposed that changes that occur in the hundreds or thousands of synapses that are activated around the same time by a particular experience provide a neural record of the experience. For example, your experience of last New Year's Eve, according to this idea, is represented by the pattern of structural changes that occur at many synapses.

Hebb's proposal that synaptic changes provide a record of experiences became the starting point for modern research on the physiology of memory. Researchers who followed Hebb's lead determined that activity at the synapse causes a sequence of chemical reactions, which result in the synthesis of new proteins that cause structural changes at the synapse like those shown in Figure 7.12c (Chklovskii et al., 2004; Kida et al., 2002).

One of the outcomes of structural changes at the synapse is a strengthening of synaptic transmission. This strengthening results in a phenomenon called **long-term potentiation (LTP)**—enhanced firing of neurons after repeated stimulation (Bliss & Lomo, 1973; Bliss et al., 2003; Kandel, 2001). Long-term potentiation is illustrated by the firing records in Figure 7.12. The first time that neuron A is stimulated, neuron B fires slowly (Figure 7.12a). However, after repeated stimulation (Figure 7.12b), neuron B fires much more rapidly to the same stimulus (Figure 7.12c).

Results such as these indicate how experiences can cause changes at the synapse. Memories for an experience cause changes in many thousands of synapses, and a specific experience is probably represented by the pattern of firing across this group of neurons. This idea of memories being represented by a pattern of firing is similar to the idea of population coding we introduced in Chapter 2 (see page 36).

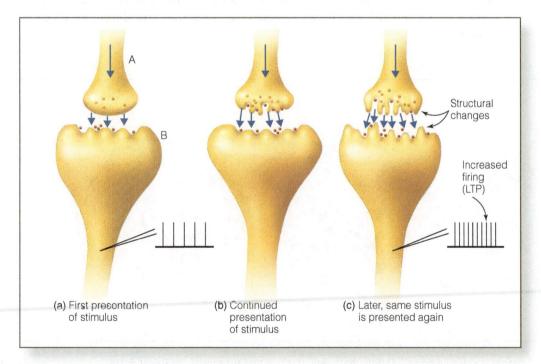

(a) First presentation of stimulus

(b) Continued presentation of stimulus

(c) Later, same stimulus is presented again

➤ **Figure 7.12** What happens at a synapse as (a) a stimulus is first presented. The record next to the electrode indicates the rate of firing recorded from the axon of neuron B. (b) As the stimulus is repeated, structural changes are beginning to occur. (c) After many repetitions, more complex connections have developed between the two neurons, which causes an increase in the firing rate, even though the stimulus is the same one that was presented in (a).

Early research, inspired by Hebb's pioneering work on the role of the synapse in memory, focused on synaptic consolidation. More recent research has focused on systems consolidation, investigating the role of the hippocampus and cortical areas in the formation of memories.

Systems Consolidation: The Hippocampus and the Cortex

The case of HM, who lost his ability to form new memories after his hippocampus was removed (Chapter 6, page 170), indicates the importance of the hippocampus in forming new memories. Once it became clear that the hippocampus is essential for forming new memories, researchers began determining exactly how the hippocampus responds to stimuli and how it participates in the process of systems consolidation. One outcome of this research was the proposal of different models, which focus on the role of the hippocampus in memory.

The Standard Model of Consolidation   The **standard model of consolidation** proposes that memory unfolds according the sequence of steps shown in **Figure 7.13,** in which the hippocampus, shown in red, is involved in encoding new memories, and makes connections with higher cortical areas (blue arrows in **Figure 7.13a**). However, with the passage of time, connections between the hippocampus and cortical areas weaken (dashed blue arrows in **Figure 7.13b**), and connections between cortical areas strengthen (solid green arrows), until, eventually, the HC is no longer involved in those memories (**Figure 7.13c**).

According to this model, the participation of the hippocampus is crucial during early stages of memory, as it is replaying the neural activity associated with a memory and sending this information to the cortex. This process, which is called **reactivation**, helps form direct connections between the various cortical areas. This way of thinking about the interaction between the hippocampus and the cortex pictures the hippocampus as acting like a "glue" that binds together the representations of memory from different cortical areas, but which then becomes unnecessary once the cortical representations are formed.

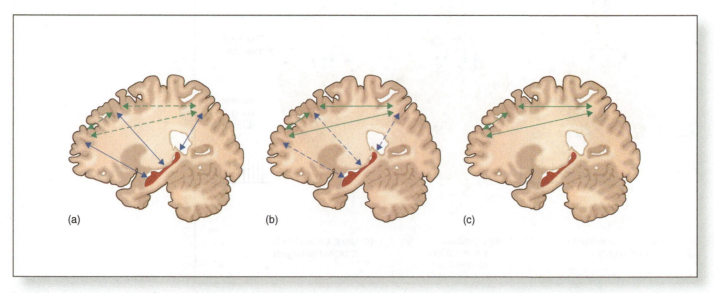

(a)   (b)   (c)

➤ **Figure 7.13** Sequence of events that occur during consolidation, according to the standard model of consolidation. (a) Connections between the cortex and the hippocampus (blue) are initially strong and connections between cortical areas are weak (dashed green). The activity between the hippocampus and cortex is called reactivation. (b) As time passes, connections between the hippocampus and cortex weaken (dashed blue) and connections between cortical areas become stronger (green). (c) Eventually, only intercortical connections remain. (Source: From Maguire, 2014.)

This standard model was based partially on observations of memory loss caused by trauma or injury. It is well known that head trauma, as might be experienced by a football player taking a hard hit as he runs downfield, can cause a loss of memory. Thus, as the player is sitting on the bench after the impact, he might not be aware of what happened during the seconds or minutes before getting hit. This loss of memory for events that occurred before the injury, called **retrograde amnesia**, can extend back minutes, hours, or even years, depending on the nature of the injury.

Figure 7.14 illustrates a characteristic of retrograde amnesia called **graded amnesia**—the amnesia tends to be most severe for events that happened just before the injury and to become less severe for earlier events. This gradual decrease in amnesia corresponds, according to the standard model, to the changes in connections between the hippocampus and cortical areas shown in Figures 7.13b and 7.13c; as time passes after an event, the cortical representation becomes stronger.

Most researchers accept that both the hippocampus and the cortex are involved in consolidation. There is, however, some disagreement regarding whether the hippocampus is important only at the beginning of consolidation, as depicted in Figure 7.13, or whether the hippocampus continues to be important, even for remote memories. One alternative to the standard model, called the *multiple trace model*, proposes a continuing role for the hippocampus, even for remote memories.

The Multiple Trace Model of Consolidation

The **multiple trace model of consolidation** proposes that early in consolidation, the hippocampus communicates with cortical areas, as in **Figure 7.15a**. However, in contrast to the standard model, the multiple trace model proposes that the hippocampus remains in active communication with the cortical areas, even for remote memories, as in **Figure 7.15b** (Nadel & Moskovitch, 1997).

Evidence for this idea comes from experiments like one by Asaf Gilboa and coworkers (2004), who elicited recent and remote episodic memories by showing participants photographs of themselves engaging in various activities that were taken at times ranging from very recently to the distant past, when they were 5 years old. The results of this experiment showed that the hippocampus was activated during retrieval of both recent and remote episodic memories.

But this doesn't mean that the hippocampus is involved in all aspects of memory retrieval. Indre Viskontas and coworkers (2009) demonstrated that the response of the hippocampus can change over time. These researchers had participants view pairs of stimuli, such as the alligator and the candle in **Figure 7.16a**, while undergoing fMRI in a scanner. Participants were told to imagine the items in each pair interacting with each other. Then 10 minutes later and 1 week later, participants saw the original pairs plus some others they had not

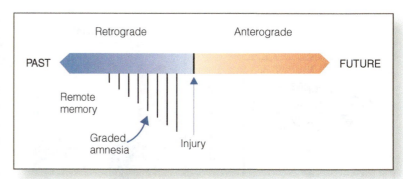

> **Figure 7.14** Anterograde amnesia is amnesia for events that occur after an injury (the inability to form new memories). Retrograde amnesia is amnesia for events that happened before the injury (the inability to remember information from the past). The vertical lines, which symbolize the amount of retrograde amnesia, indicate that amnesia is more severe for events or learning that were closer in time leading up to the injury. This is the graded nature of retrograde amnesia.

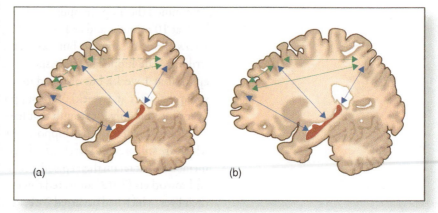

> **Figure 7.15** Sequence of events that occur during consolidation, according to the multiple trace model of consolidation. (a) As with the standard model, connections between the hippocampus and cortex are initially strong (blue) and intercortical connections are weak (dashed green). (b) As time passes, intercortical connections strengthen (green) and hippocampus–cortical connections remain. (Source: From Maguire, 2014.)

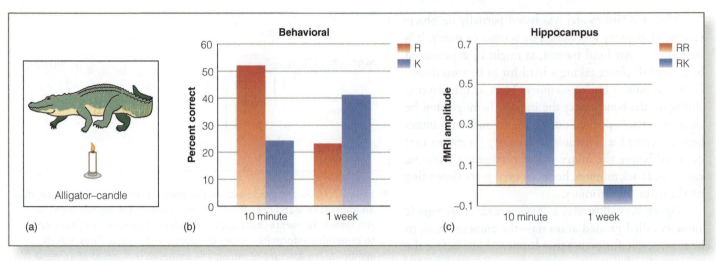

➤ **Figure 7.16** Stimulus and results for the Viskontas et al. (2009) experiment. (a) Subjects saw picture pairs like this one while being scanned. (b) When asked to remember the pairs, the remember response, which corresponds to episodic memory, was high at 10 minutes, but decreased after 1 week. (c) Activity of the hippocampus remained the same for pictures that were remembered at both 10 minutes and 1 week (RR), but decreased for pictures for which the remember response was absent at 1 week (RK).

(Source: Adapted from I. V. Viskontas, V. A. Carr, S. A. Engel, & B. J. Kowlton, The neural correlates of recollection: Hippocampal activation declines as episodic memory fades, Hippocampus, 19, 265–272, Figures 1, 3, & 6, 2009.)

seen and were told to respond to each pair in one of three ways: (1) *remember* (R), meaning "I remember seeing the pair when it was originally presented"; (2) *know* (K), meaning "The pair definitely looks familiar, but I don't remember when I was originally seeing it"; or (3) *don't*, meaning "I don't remember or know the stimuli." As we saw in Chapter 6, when we described the remember/know procedure (see Method, page 176), *remember* responses indicate episodic memory and *know* responses indicate semantic memory.

The behavioral results, shown in **Figure 7.16b**, show that there were more *remember* (episodic) responses than *know* (semantic) responses after 10 minutes, but that only half of the *remember* responses remained after 1 week. This is exactly what we would expect from other research showing that memories lose their episodic character over time, which we described in Chapter 6 (page 176) as the semanticization of remote memories.

But what's happening in the brain as the episodic memories are being lost? Viskontas determined the hippocampus's response for pairs to which participants responded *remember* both at 10 minutes and at 1 week (RR pairs) and for pairs to which participants responded *remember* at 10 minutes but *know* at 1 week (RK pairs). The results, in **Figure 7.16c**, are striking: The hippocampus response remained high for RR pairs (the ones that remained episodic at 1 week), but dropped to near zero for RK pairs (the ones that had lost their episodic character at 1 week). This supports the idea that the hippocampus response changes over time, but only for stimuli that have lost their episodic character.

Viskontas found that hippocampus responding is connected with episodic memories, which are still present a week after learning pairs of pictures. But what about autobiographical memories that retain their episodic character even after many years have passed? Heidi Bonnici and coworkers (2012) answered this question by having participants recollect recent events in their lives, which had occurred 2 weeks earlier, and remote events, which had occurred 10 years earlier. They were told to report only events that they remembered very clearly and vividly, so when remembering, they felt as if they were re-experiencing the event. These instructions were given to be sure participants were recollecting rich episodic memories.

One week later, participants, now in the brain scanner, were asked to recall three of their recent memories and three of their remote memories. Their brain was scanned as they recalled each memory, and afterwards they were asked to rate the vividness of the memory on a scale of 1 to 5, where 5 is the most vivid. The fMRI responses associated with the most vivid memories (ratings of 4 or 5) were then analyzed using the technique of *multivoxel pattern analysis*.

METHOD   Multivoxel Pattern Analysis (MVPA)

The procedure for most fMRI experiments is to present a task to the participant and determine the activity of voxels in the brain (see Method: Brain Imaging, on page 41). An example of the result of such an experiment is shown in Figure 2.18 (page 42), which indicates the areas of the brain that show increased activation for places and for bodies.

Multivoxel pattern analysis (MVPA) goes beyond just determining which areas are activated. It determines the pattern of voxel activation within various structures. For example, the hypothetical data in **Figure 7.17** show how 7 voxels might respond to perception of an apple and a pear. Notice that the patterns are slightly different.

The first step in an MVPA experiment is to train a **classifier**, a computer program designed to recognize patterns of voxel activity. The classifier is trained by having a person look at apples and pears and feeding the voxel patterns for each object into the classifier (**Figure 7.18a**). This is repeated for many trials, so the classifier can learn which pattern goes with each object. Once the classifier is trained, it is ready to be put to the test. The question is, can the classifier tell which object was presented based on the pattern of voxels that is activated (**Figure 7.18b**)? Because MVPA is a relatively new technique, these predictions are often not perfect, but are far above chance.

Bonnici and coworkers presented their classifier with a task more difficult than identifying apples or pears. They trained their classifier to determine the voxel patterns when participants were recalling each of their six memories (three recent and three remote). They found that the classifier was able to predict which recent memories *and* which remote memories were being recalled based on activity in the hippocampus, plus the prefrontal cortex and other cortical structures. This result indicates that recalling memories activates a number of structures, and, most important for the purposes of the multiple trace model, the hippocampus is activated, even for remote memories.

To make this result even more interesting, Bonnici found that (1) more information about remote memories compared to recent memories

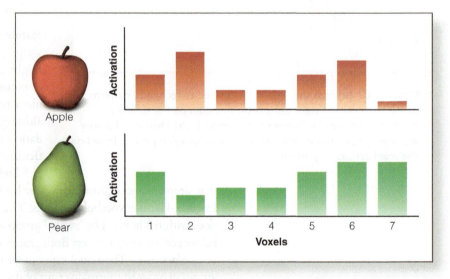

➤ **Figure 7.17** Hypothetical pattern of activation for 7 voxels generated by looking at an apple or a pear.

was contained in the prefrontal cortex, and (2) information about both recent and remote memories was represented throughout the hippocampus, with the posterior hippocampus containing more information about remote memories (**Figure 7.19**). Taken together, these results show that remote memories are richly represented in the cortex, as proposed by both the standard and multiple trace models, and that both recent and remote memories are represented in the hippocampus as well, as proposed by the multiple trace model. In addition to research on different models of consolidation, another active area of research is concerned with the relationship between consolidation and sleep.

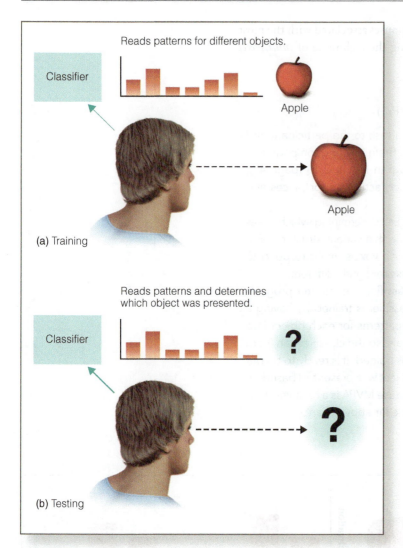

Reads patterns for different objects.

Classifier

Apple

Apple

(a) Training

Reads patterns and determines which object was presented.

Classifier

?

?

(b) Testing

➤ **Figure 7.18** (a) First the classifier is trained to recognize patterns associated with different objects (in this example) or different recalled memories (in Bonnici's experiment). (b) Then the classifier attempts to determine which object (or memory) is present based on the voxel activation pattern.

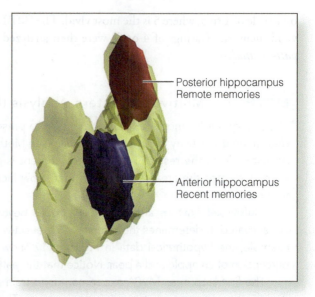

Posterior hippocampus
Remote memories

Anterior hippocampus
Recent memories

➤ **Figure 7.19** Three-dimensional representation of the hippocampus, showing location of voxels associated with recent autobiographical memories (blue) and remote autobiographical memories (red), as determined by Bonnici et al., 2012, using MVPA.

(Source: Bonnici et al., *Journal of Neuroscience* 32(47) 16982–16991, Fig 4, page 16978, Lower left figure only, 2012.)

Consolidation and Sleep: Enhancing Memory

Hamlet says, in his "To be or not to be" soliloquy, "To sleep, perchance to dream." But memory researchers might modify that statement to read "To sleep, perchance to consolidate memory." Not as poetic as Hamlet's statement perhaps, but recent research supports the idea that although the reactivation process associated with consolidation may begin as soon as a memory is formed, it is particularly strong during sleep.

Steffan Gais and coworkers (2006) tested the idea that sleep enhances consolidation by having high school students learn a list of 24 pairs of English–German vocabulary words. The "sleep" group studied the words and then went to sleep within 3 hours. The "awake" group studied the words and remained awake for 10 hours before getting a night's sleep. Both groups were tested within 24 to 36 hours after studying the vocabulary lists. (The actual experiment involved a number of different "sleep" and "awake" groups in order to control for time of day and other factors we aren't going to consider here.) The results of the experiment, shown in **Figure 7.20**, indicate that students in the sleep group forgot much less material than students in the awake group. Why does going to sleep shortly after learning enhance memory? One reason is that going to sleep eliminates environmental stimuli that might interfere with consolidation. Another reason is that consolidation appears to be enhanced during sleep. (See Maurer et al., 2015 and Mazza et al., 2016 for some recent research that demonstrates enhanced learning due to sleep-dependent memory consolidation.)

Interestingly, not only is there evidence that consolidation is enhanced during sleep, but there is also evidence that some memories are more likely to be consolidated than others. This was demonstrated in an experiment by Ines Wilhelm and coworkers (2011) in which participants learned a task and were then told either that they would be tested on the task later or that they would be tested on a different task later. After a night's sleep, participants in both groups were tested on the task to determine if what they *expected* had any effect on consolidation. (In some experiments, some participants were tested after staying awake. The memory of participants in these groups was worse than the memory of those of the sleep groups, as was expected from the results of experiments like the one by Gais, described earlier. We will focus here on what happened for the participants who went to sleep.)

One of the tasks in Wilhelm's experiment was a card memory task similar to the game Concentration. Participants would see an array of "cards" on the computer screen, with two turned over to reveal one pair of pictures (**Figure 7.21a**). Participants saw each card pair twice and then learned the locations by practicing. One card would be "turned over" on the screen, and they indicated where they thought the matching card was located. After receiving the correct answer, they continued practicing until they were able to answer correctly 60 percent of the time. After their training, they were told either that they would be tested on this task 9 hours later (the *expected group*) or that they would be tested on another task (the *unexpected group*).

Memory performance after a night's sleep, shown in **Figure 7.21b**, indicates that the expected group performed significantly better than the unexpected group. Thus, even though both groups had the same training and received the same amount of sleep, memory for the task was stronger if participants expected they would be tested. Results such as this suggest that when we sleep after learning, memories that are more important are more likely to be strengthened by consolidation (see also Fischer & Born, 2009; Payne et al., 2008, 2012; Rauchs et al., 2011; Saletin et al., 2011; van Dongen et al., 2012). Thus, we sleep, perchance to selectively consolidate memories for things that might be most useful to remember later!

We have come a long way from Müller and Pilzecker's demonstration of consolidation. But there is one more twist to this story, which involves returning to our original definition of consolidation. Consolidation, according to our definition, is *the process that transforms new memories from a fragile state, in which they can be disrupted, to a more permanent state, in which they are resistant to disruption* (page 208). This definition implies that once memories

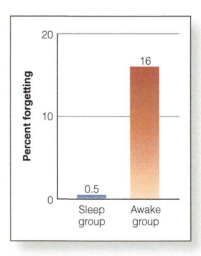

➤ **Figure 7.20** Results of the Gais et al. (2006) experiment in which memory for word pairs was tested for two groups. The sleep group went to sleep shortly after learning a list of word pairs. The awake group stayed awake for quite a while after learning the word pairs. Both groups did get to sleep before testing, so they were equally rested before being tested, but the performance of the sleep group was better.

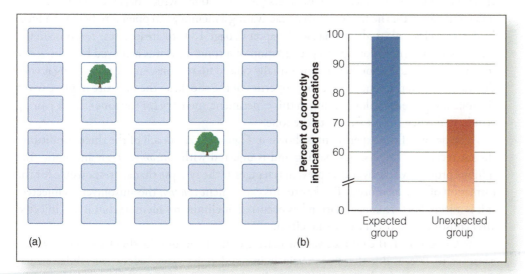

➤ **Figure 7.21** Stimuli and results for the Wilhelm et al. (2011) experiment. (a) The participant's task was to remember where each pair of pictures was located. One pair is shown turned over here. (b) After sleeping, the performance of the group that had expected to be tested on the task was better than the performance of the group that did not expect to be tested. This illustrates preferential consolidation for the material that participants expected would be tested.

(Source: From I. Wilhelm, S. Diekelmann, I. Molzow, A. Ayoub, M. Molle, & J. Born, Sleep selectively enhances memory expected to be of future relevance, *Journal of Neuroscience*, 31, 1563–1569, Figure 3a, 2011.)

are consolidated, they become more permanent. As it turns out, this idea of truly permanent memories has been questioned by research that shows that retrieving a memory can cause that memory to become fragile, just as it was when it was first formed.

 # Reconsolidation: The Dynamics of Memory

Consider the following situation: You are visiting your childhood home. Driving along the roads that lead to your parents' house seems almost automatic, because the route is strongly stamped into your memory. But as you turn onto a street that was part of your old route, you are surprised to find that it is now a dead end. Construction that happened while you were gone has blocked your old route. Eventually, you discover a new route to reach your destination, and—this is the important part—you *update your memory* to form a new map of the route to your parents' home (Bailey & Balsam, 2013).

This example of updating your memory is not unique. It happens all the time. We are constantly learning new things and modifying information stored in memory in order to deal with new circumstances. Thus, although it is useful to be able to remember the past, it is also useful to be able to adapt to new situations. Recent research, first on rats and then on humans, has suggested a possible mechanism for updating memories called *reconsolidation*.

Reconsolidation: A Famous Rat Experiment

Reconsolidation is the idea that when a memory is retrieved (remembered), it becomes fragile, like it was when it was originally formed, and that when it is in this fragile state, it needs to be consolidated again—a process called *reconsolidation*. This is important because when the memory has become fragile again, and before it has been reconsolidated, it can be modified or eliminated. According to this idea, retrieving a memory not only puts us in touch with something that happened in the past, but it also opens the door for either modifying or forgetting the original memory.

The possibility that retrieved memories can become fragile was demonstrated in a rat experiment by Karim Nader and coworkers (2000a, 2000b), which became famous because it demonstrated, for the first time, that reactivating a memory can open it to being changed. Nader used classical conditioning (see Chapter 6, page 184) to create a fear response in the rat of "freezing" (not moving) to presentation of a tone. This was achieved by pairing the tone with a shock. Although the tone initially caused no response in the rat, pairing it with the shock caused the tone to take on properties of the shock, so the rat froze in place when the tone was presented alone. Thus, in this experiment, memory for the tone–shock pairing is indicated when the rat freezes to the tone.

The design of the experiment is shown in **Figure 7.22**. In each of the three conditions, the rat receives a tone–shock pairing and is injected with *anisomycin*, an antibiotic that inhibits protein synthesis and so prevents changes at the synapse that are responsible for the formation of new memories. The key to this experiment is *when* the anisomycin is injected. If it is injected before consolidation has occurred, it eliminates memory, but if it is injected after consolidation occurs, it has no effect.

In Condition 1, the rat receives the pairing of the tone and the shock on Day 1, which causes it to freeze. But the anisomycin is injected right away, before consolidation has occurred (**Figure 7.22a**). The fact that the drug has prevented consolidation is indicated by the fact that when the tone is presented on Day 3, the rat doesn't freeze to the tone. That is, it behaves as if it never received the tone–shock pairing.

In Condition 2, the rat receives the pairing of the tone and shock on Day 1, as before, but doesn't receive anisomycin until Day 2, after consolidation has occurred. Thus, when the tone is presented on Day 3, the rat remembers the tone–shock pairing, as indicated by the fact that it freezes to the tone (**Figure 7.22b**).

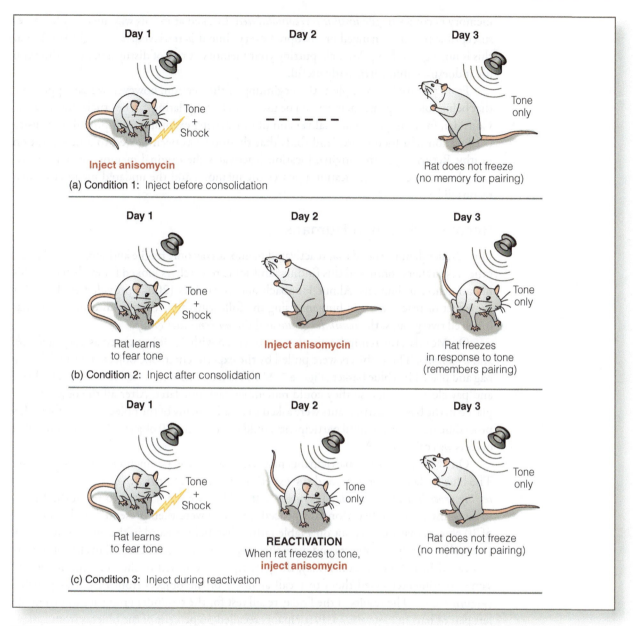

➤ Figure 7.22 The Nader et al. (2000a) experiment on how injecting anisomycin affects fear conditioning.
(a) Anisomycin is injected on Day 1, before consolidation, so memory for the tone-shock pairing is not formed.
(b) Anisomycin is injected on Day 2, after consolidation, so memory for the tone-shock pairing remains.
(c) Anisomycin is injected after reactivation on Day 2, so memory for the tone-shock pairing is eliminated.

Condition 3 is the crucial condition, because it creates a situation in which injecting the drug on Day 2 (which had no effect in Condition 2) can eliminate the memory of the tone–shock pairing. This situation is created by presenting the tone on Day 2 to reactivate the rat's memory for the tone–shock pairing. The rat freezes (indicating that memory has occurred) and then the anisomycin is injected. Because the memory was reactivated by presenting the tone, the anisomycin now has an effect. This is indicated by the fact that the rat doesn't freeze when the tone is presented on Day 3.

This result shows that when a memory is reactivated, it becomes fragile, just as it was immediately after it was first formed, and the drug can prevent reconsolidation. Thus, just as the original memory is fragile *until it is consolidated for the first time*, a reactivated memory becomes fragile *until it is reconsolidated*. Looked at in this way, memory becomes susceptible to being changed or disrupted every time it is retrieved. You might think that this is not a good thing. After all, putting your memory at risk of disruption every time you use it doesn't sound particularly useful.

From the driving example at the beginning of this section, however, we can appreciate that being able to update memory can be useful. In fact, updating can be crucial for survival. Consider, for example, an animal version of our driving example: A chipmunk returns to the location of a food source and finds that the food has been moved to a new location nearby. Returning to the original location reactivates the original memory, new information about the change in location updates the memory, and the updated memory is then reconsolidated.

Reconsolidation in Humans

Once Nader demonstrated that reactivated memories become fragile and subject to change, other researchers confirmed this finding, and some researchers looked for evidence for this phenomenon in humans. Almut Hupbach and coworkers (2007) provided evidence for the effect of reactivation in humans using the following procedure in an experiment that involved two groups: the *reminder group* and the *no-reminder group*.

On Monday, the reminder group was presented with 20 objects, such as a *cup*, a *watch*, and a *hammer*. These objects were pulled by the experimenter, one object at a time, from a bag and placed in a blue basket (**Figure 7.23a**). Participants were asked to name each object and pay close attention so they could remember each one later. After all the objects were placed in the basket, participants were asked to recall as many of the objects as possible. This procedure was repeated until participants could list 17 of the 20 objects. This list of recalled objects was called List A.

On Wednesday, these participants met with the same experimenter in the same room. The blue basket was present, and the experimenter *asked the participants to remember the testing procedure from Monday* (**Figure 7.23b**). They were not asked to recall the List A items—just to remember Monday's procedure. They were then presented with a new set of 20 objects that were set out on a table rather than being placed in the blue basket. They were told to study the objects and were then tested on them, as before. This list of objects was called List B. Finally, on Friday, the participants returned to the same room and the same experimenter asked them to recall as many of the objects from List A as possible (**Figure 7.23c**). The results of the Friday recall test for the reminder group are shown in the left pair of bars in **Figure 7.24**. Participants recalled 36 percent of the objects from List A, but also mistakenly recalled 24 percent of the objects from List B.

The procedure for the no-reminder group was the same on Monday (**Figure 7.23d**), but on Wednesday, they met with a different experimenter in a different room, with no blue basket present. They *were not asked to remember the testing from Monday*; they just saw the 20 new objects and were then tested on them (**Figure 7.23e**). Finally, on Friday, they were tested on List A in the first room they had been in (**Figure 7.23f**). The results of the Friday recall test for the no-reminder group are shown by the right pair of bars in Figure 7.24. Participants recalled 45 percent of the objects from List A, and they mistakenly recalled only 5 percent of the objects from List B.

According to Hupbach, when the reminder group thought back to the original List A training session on Wednesday, that made List A vulnerable to being changed (Figure 7.23b). Because participants immediately learned List B, some of these new objects became integrated into their memory for List A. That is why they mistakenly recalled 24 percent of the objects from List B on Friday when their task was just to recall List A. Another way to express this idea is to say that the reminder reactivated memory for List A and "opened the door" for List B objects to be added to the participants' memory for that list. Thus, the

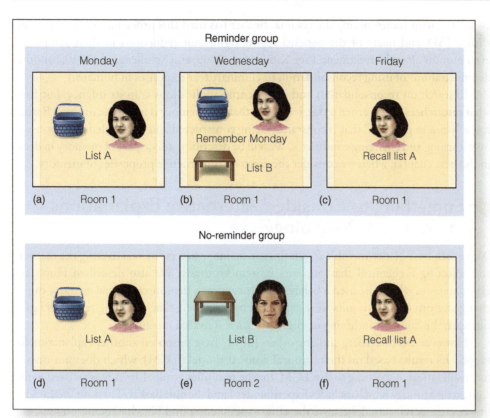

> **Figure 7.23** Design of the Hupbach et al. (2007) experiment. *Reminder Group*: (a) Monday: An experimenter, shown here, shows participants 20 objects one by one and places them in a blue basket. Participants then recall these objects, creating List A. (b) Wednesday: Participants remember Monday's procedure and are presented with 20 new objects on a table. They learn these objects, which creates List B. (c) Friday: Participants are asked to recall all the objects in List A. *Non-Reminder Group*: (d) Monday: Same procedure as (a). (e) Wednesday: Participants see and are tested on new objects (List B) in a different room by a different experimenter and the blue basket is not present. This creates a new context. (f) Friday: Participants are asked to recall List A in the original room with the original experimenter.

original memory was not eliminated, but it was changed. This idea that memories can be changed, has led to practical applications designed to treat conditions such as posttraumatic stress disorder (PTSD), a condition that occurs when, following a traumatic experience, a person experiences "flashbacks" of the experience, often accompanied by extreme anxiety and physical symptoms.

A Practical Outcome of Reconsolidation Research

Alain Brunet and coworkers (2008) tested the idea that reactivation of a memory followed by reconsolidation can help alleviate the symptoms of PTSD. The basic method involved is to reactivate the person's memory for the traumatic event and then administer the drug *propranolol*. This drug blocks activation of stress hormone receptors in the amygdala, a part of the brain important for determining the emotional components of memory. This procedure might be equivalent to the administration of anisomycin on Day 2 in Condition 3 of Nader's experiment (**Figure 7.22c**).

Brunet ran two groups. One group of PTSD patients listened to a 30-second recording describing the circumstances of their traumatic experience and received propranolol. Another group listened to the recording describing their experience but received a placebo, which had no active ingredients.

One week later, both groups were told to imagine their traumatic experience while again listening to the 30-second recording. To determine their reaction to imagining their experience, Brunet measured their blood pressure and skin conductance. He found that the propranolol group experienced much smaller increases in heart rate and skin conductance than the placebo group. Apparently, presenting propranolol when the memory was reactivated a week earlier blocked the stress response in the amygdala, and this reduced the emotional reaction

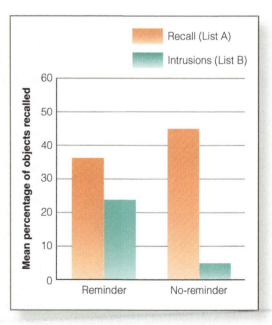

> **Figure 7.24** Results of Hupbach et al.'s (2007) experiment. Hupbach explains the greater intrusions that occurred for the Reminder group as being caused by reactivation and reconsolidation of memories.
> (Source: Based on A. Hupbach, R. Gomez, O. Hardt, & L. Nadel, Reconsolidation of episodic memories: A subtle reminder triggers integration of new information, *Learning and Memory*, 14, 47–53, 2007.)

associated with remembering the trauma. Brunet has used this procedure to treat patients with PTSD, and many of the patients report significant reductions in their symptoms, even months after the treatment. (See Kindt et al., 2009, and Schiller et al., 2010, for other demonstrations of using reconsolidation to eliminate fear responses in humans.)

Research on reconsolidation and its potential applications is in its infancy, but from what researchers have learned so far, it appears that our memory is not static or fixed. Rather, it is a "work in progress" that is constantly being constructed and remodeled in response to new learning and changing conditions. We will be describing this aspect of memory in detail in the next chapter, when we consider the creative, constructive properties of memory.

▶ Something to Consider: Alternative Explanations in Cognitive Psychology

We've seen how Nader was able to eliminate a memory in a rat by reactivating the memory and injecting a chemical that prevents protein synthesis. We also described Hupbach's experiment, in which she used a behavioral procedure to demonstrate how memory can be changed. Both of these results were explained by proposing that blocking reconsolidation can open the door to modifying or eliminating a reactivated memory.

However, Per Sederberg and coworkers (2011) have proposed another explanation for Hupbach's results based on the **temporal context model** (**TCM**), which does not involve reconsolidation. According to the TCM, for the reminder group, List A is associated with a context on Monday, which includes Experimenter 1 and the blue basket. Then, on Wednesday, this context is reinstated, because the same experimenter and blue basket are present, and the participant is also asked to remember Monday's testing procedure. Then, when List B is learned within this List A context, items from List B become associated with the List A context. Because of this association, participants incorrectly recall some List B items when they are tested on Friday. This result does not occur for the no-reminder group, because List B is never associated with the List A context.

These two explanations interpret Hupbach's results in different ways. The reconsolidation hypothesis focuses on re-storage mechanisms that change an existing memory by insertion of new material. The temporal context model focuses on the context within which learning and retrieval occur and assumes that old contexts can become associated with new memories, without changing the content of existing memories. When cued with the old context, both the existing and the new memory will be recalled. Thus, the reconsolidation explanation proposes that what is stored about the old memory has changed, whereas the TCM explanation proposes that considering storage is unnecessary because Hupbach's result can be explained by contextual associations.

We are faced with a conundrum. Two mechanisms have been proposed, each of which could be correct. How to choose? The answer is that at the present time, it is difficult to choose, because the operation of the mind, as we've known since the early experiments by Donders in 1868, can't be determined directly, but must be inferred from the results of behavioral or physiological experiments (page 7). Research is continuing to determine which explanation is correct.

TEST YOURSELF 7.3

1. How did Müller and Pilzecker demonstrate consolidation?

2. What is synaptic consolidation? Systems consolidation? How are they related to each other?

3. Describe how the standard model of consolidation explains systems consolidation. What is some evidence for the standard model?

4. Describe the multiple trace model of consolidation and some evidence for this model. Be sure you understand the Viskontis and the Bonnicci experiments.

5. Describe the connection between sleep and consolidation. Be sure you understand the Gais and Wilhelm experiments.

6. What is reconsolidation? Describe how Nader's rat experiment and Hupbach's human experiment provide evidence that memories can be changed by interfering with reconsolidation.

7. What are the practical implications of the results of experiments that demonstrate reconsolidation?

8. Describe the two explanations that have been proposed to explain the Hupbach's results. Why has it been difficult to determine which explanation is correct?

CHAPTER SUMMARY

1. Encoding is the process of acquiring information and transferring it into LTM. Retrieval is transferring information from LTM into working memory.

2. Some mechanisms of encoding are more effective than others in transferring information into LTM. Maintenance rehearsal helps maintain information in STM but is not an effective way of transferring information into LTM. Elaborative rehearsal is a better way to establish long-term memories.

3. Levels of processing theory states that memory depends on how information is encoded or programmed into the mind. According to this theory, shallow processing is not as effective as deep elaborative processing. An experiment by Craik and Tulving showed that memory was better following deep processing than following shallow processing.

4. Evidence that encoding influences retrieval includes research looking at the effect of (1) forming visual images, (2) linking words to yourself, (3) generating information (the generation effect), (4) organizing information, (5) relating words to survival value, and (6) practicing retrieval (the retrieval practice effect or the testing effect).

5. Five memory principles that can be applied to studying are (1) elaborate, (2) generate and test, (3) organize, (4) take breaks, and (5) avoid "illusions of learning."

6. There is evidence that note taking by hand results in better test performance than note taking by laptop. This can be explained by deeper encoding for handwritten note taking.

7. Retrieving long-term memories is aided by retrieval cues. This has been determined by cued recall experiments and experiments in which participants created retrieval cues that later helped them retrieve memories.

8. Retrieval can be increased by matching conditions at retrieval to conditions that existed at encoding. This is illustrated by encoding specificity, state-dependent learning, and matching type of processing (transfer-appropriate processing).

9. The principle of encoding specificity states that we learn information along with its context. Godden and Baddeley's diving experiment and Grant's studying experiment illustrate the effectiveness of encoding and retrieving information under the same conditions.

10. According to the principle of state-dependent learning, a person's memory will be better when his or her internal state during retrieval matches the state during encoding. Eich's mood experiment supports this idea.

11. Matching types of processing refers to the finding that memory performance is enhanced when the type of coding that occurs during acquisition matches the type of retrieval that occurs during a memory test. The results of an experiment by Morris support this idea, which is called transfer-appropriate processing.

12. Consolidation is the process that transforms new memories from a fragile state into a more permanent state. Müller and Pilzecker carried out an early experiment that illustrated how memory is decreased when consolidation is disrupted.

13. Synaptic consolidation involves structural changes at synapses. Systems consolidation involves the gradual reorganization of neural circuits.

14. Hebb introduced the idea that the formation of memories is associated with structural changes at the synapse. These structural changes are then translated into enhanced nerve firing, as indicated by long-term potentiation.

15. The standard model of consolidation proposes that memory retrieval depends on the hippocampus during consolidation but that after consolidation is complete, retrieval involves the cortex, with the hippocampus no longer being involved.

16. The multiple trace model states that the hippocampus is involved both when memories are being established and during the retrieval of remote episodic memories.

17. There is evidence supporting the standard model, but recent research indicates that retrieval of episodic memories can involve the hippocampus, which supports the multiple trace model.

18. Consolidation is facilitated by sleep. There is also evidence that material people expect they will be asked to remember later is more likely to be consolidated during sleep.

19. Recent research indicates that memories can become susceptible to disruption when they are reactivated by retrieval. After reactivation, these memories must be reconsolidated.

20. There is evidence for the usefulness of reconsolidation therapy in treating conditions such as posttraumatic stress disorder.

21. Two explanations have been proposed to explain the results of Hupbach's experiments in which human memories were reactivated. One explanation involves reconsolidation, the other involves considering the context in which learning takes place.

THINK ABOUT IT

1. Describe an experience in which retrieval cues led you to remember something. Such experiences might include returning to a place where your memory was initially formed, being somewhere that reminds you of an experience you had in the past, having someone else provide a "hint" to help you remember something, or reading about something that triggers a memory.

2. How do you study? Which study techniques that you use should be effective, according to the results of memory research? How could you improve your study techniques by taking into account the results of memory research? (Also see Preface to Students, pages xxix–xxx.)

KEY TERMS

Classifier, 213

Consolidation, 208

Cued recall, 203

Deep processing, 193

Depth of processing, 193

Elaborative rehearsal, 193

Encoding, 192

Encoding specificity, 204

Free recall, 203

Generation effect, 194

Graded amnesia, 211

Levels of processing theory, 193

Long-term potentiation (LTP), 209

Maintenance rehearsal, 193

Multiple trace model of consolidation, 211

Multivoxel pattern analysis (MVPA), 213

Paired-associate learning, 194

Reactivation, 210

Reconsolidation, 216

Retrieval, 192

Retrieval cue, 195

Retrograde amnesia, 211

Self-reference effect, 194

Shallow processing, 193

Spacing effect, 200

Standard model of consolidation, 210

State-dependent learning, 205

Synaptic consolidation, 208

Systems consolidation, 208

Temporal context model (TCM), 220

Testing effect, 198

Transfer-appropriate processing, 207

COGLAB EXPERIMENTS   Numbers in parentheses refer to the experiment number in CogLab.

Encoding Specificity (*28*)

Levels of Processing (*29*)

Production Effect (*30*)

Von Restorff Effect (*32*)

Songquan Deng/Shutterstock.com

These towers of light evoke the memory of the terrorist attack on the World Trade Center on September 11, 2001. This date is etched into the American consciousness, and the events of that day are etched into many people's memories. This chapter considers research on memory for exceptional events such as 9/11, as well as memory for more routine everyday events. This research shows that our memories are not like photographs, accurate and unchanging, but are more like "works in progress," affected not only by the event to be remembered but also by stored knowledge and things that happen after the event.

Everyday Memory and Memory Errors

8

What? Another chapter on memory? Yes, another chapter, because there's still more to explain, especially about how memory operates in everyday life. But before embarking on this final chapter on memory, let's look back at how we got here and what remains to be explained.

▶ The Journey So Far

We began our investigation of memory in Chapter 5 by asking what memory is and what it does, and by describing Atkinson and Shiffrin's information-processing model of memory, which proposed three types of memory (sensory, short-term, and long-term) (Figure 5.2). Although primitive compared to present-day concepts of memory, this model captured the idea that memory is a process that unfolds in steps. This was important not only because it began identifying what happens to information on its way to either becoming a memory or being forgotten, but also because it provided a way to focus on different stages of the process of memory.

The original three-stage model of memory led to the idea that memory is a dynamic process involving not just storage, but also the manipulation of information. Picturing memory as a dynamic information-processing system provided a good entry point for the realization, described in Chapter 6, that remembering the trip you took last summer and that Lady Gaga is a well-known singer who wears outrageous costumes are served by different systems—episodic memory and semantic memory, respectively, which operate separately but which also interact. By the end of Chapter 6, you probably realized that cognition—and certainly memory—is all about interconnectedness between structures and processes.

But after describing how memory deals with different types of information, another question remained: What *processes* are involved in (a) transferring incoming information into memory and (b) retrieving that information when we want to remember it? As we considered these questions in Chapter 7, we described neural mechanisms responsible for the process of consolidation, which strengthens memories, making them more permanent.

But as sometimes happens when you're telling a story, there's a twist to what appears to be a predictable plot, and the rat experiment described at the end of Chapter 7 showed that memories that were originally thought to be firmly consolidated can become fragile and changeable. And just to make this plot twist more interesting, it turns out that when established memories are remembered, they undergo a process called *reconsolidation*, during which they can be changed.

But some people might be tempted to say, in response to this description of once-solid memories becoming fragile, that the laboratory-based research on rats on which this finding is based may not translate to real-life memories in humans. After all, they might say, our experience teaches us that we often remember things accurately. This idea that memories are generally accurate is consistent with the finding of a nationwide poll in which 63 percent of people agreed with the statement "Human memory works like a video camera, accurately recording the events we see and hear so we can review and interpret them later." In the same survey, 48 percent agreed that "once you have experienced an event and formed a memory of it, that memory does not change" (Simons & Chabris, 2011). Thus, a substantial proportion of people believe memories are recorded accurately, as if by a video camera, and that once recorded, the memory does not change.

As we will see in this chapter, these views are erroneous. Everything that happens is not necessarily recorded accurately in the first place, and even if it is, there is a good chance that what you remember may not accurately reflect what actually happened.

But the most important thing about this chapter is not just that it demonstrates limits to our ability to remember, but that it illustrates a basic property of memory: Memories are created by a process of construction, in which what actually happened, other things that happened later, and our general knowledge about how things usually happen are combined to create our memory of an event.

We will illustrate this process of construction by shifting our focus from experiments in which participants are asked to remember lists of words or short passages to experiments in which participants are asked to remember events that have occurred in their lives.

▶ Autobiographical Memory: What Has Happened in My Life

Autobiographical memory is memory for specific experiences from our life, which can include both episodic and semantic components (see Chapter 6, page 172). For example, an autobiographical memory of a childhood birthday party might include images of the cake, people at the party, and games being played (episodic memory); it might also include knowledge about when the party occurred, where your family was living at the time, and your general knowledge about what usually happens at birthday parties (semantic memory) (Cabeza & St. Jacques, 2007). Two important characteristics of autobiographical memories are (1) they are multidimensional and (2) we remember some events in our lives better than others.

The Multidimensional Nature of Autobiographical Memory

Think about a memorable moment in your life—an event involving other people or a solitary memorable experience. Whatever experience you remember, it is pretty certain that there are many components to your memory: visual—what you see when you transport yourself back in time; auditory—what people are saying or other sounds in the environment; and perhaps smells, tastes, and tactile perceptions as well. But memories extend beyond vision, hearing, touch, taste, and smell. They also have spatial components, because events usually take place in a three-dimensional environment. And perhaps most important of all, memories often involve thoughts and emotions, both positive and negative.

All this is a way of saying that memories are multidimensional, with each dimension playing its own, often important, role in the memory. The importance of individual components is illustrated by the finding that patients who have lost their ability to recognize or visualize objects, because of damage to the visual area of their cortex, can experience a loss of autobiographical memory (Greenberg & Rubin, 2003). This may have occurred because visual stimuli were not available to serve as retrieval cues for memories. But even memories not based on visual information are lost in these patients. Apparently, visual experience plays an important role in autobiographical memory. (It would seem reasonable that for blind people, auditory experience might take over this role.)

A brain-scanning study that illustrates a difference between autobiographical memory and laboratory memory was done by Roberto Cabeza and coworkers (2004). Cabeza measured the brain activation caused by two sets of stimulus photographs—one set that the participant took and another set that was taken by someone else (**Figure 8.1**). We will call the photos taken by the participant own-photos, and the ones taken by someone else lab-photos.

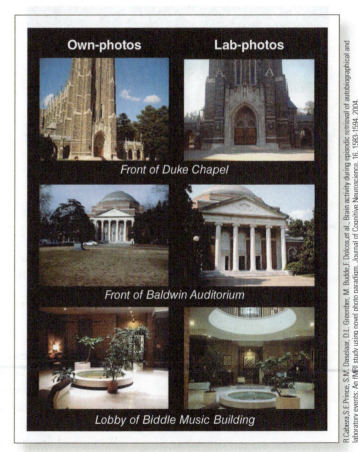

R.Cabeza,S.E.Prince, S.M. Daselaar, D.L. Greenber, M. Budde,F. Dolcos,et al. Brain activity during episodic retrieval of autobiographical and laboratory events: An fMRI study using novel photo paradigm. Journal of Cognitive Neuroscience, 16, 1583-1594, 2004.

> **Figure 8.1** Photographs from Cabeza and coworkers' (2004) experiment. Own-photos were taken by the participant; lab-photos were taken by someone else. (Source: Cabeza et al., 2004)

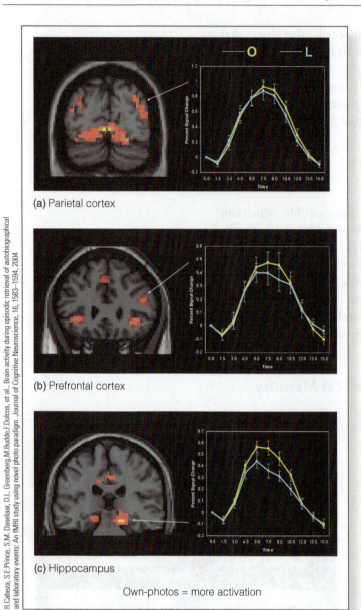

R.Cabeza, S.E.Prince, S.M. Daselaar, D.L. Greenberg,M.Budde, F.Dolcos, et al., Brain activity during episodic retrieval of autobiographical and laboratory events: An fMRI study using novel photo paradigm. Journal of Cognitive Neuroscience, 16, 1583–1594, 2004

(a) Parietal cortex

(b) Prefrontal cortex

(c) Hippocampus

Own-photos = more activation

➤ **Figure 8.2** (a) fMRI response of an area in the parietal cortex showing time-course and amplitude of response caused by own-photos (yellow) and lab-photos (blue) in the memory test. The graph on the right indicates that activation is the same with the own-photos and lab-photos. The response to own-photos is larger in (b) the prefrontal cortex and (c) the hippocampus. (Source: Cabeza et al., 2004)

The photos were created by giving 12 Duke University students digital cameras and telling them to take pictures of 40 specified campus locations over a 10-day period. After taking the photos, participants were shown their own-photos and a lab-photo of each location. A few days later they saw the own-photos and the lab-photos they had seen before, along with some new lab-photos they had never seen. As participants indicated whether each stimulus was an own-photo, a lab-photo they had seen before, or a new lab-photo, their brain activity was measured in an fMRI scanner.

The brain scans showed that own-photos and lab-photos activated many of the same structures in the brain—mainly ones like the medial temporal lobe (MTL) that are associated with episodic memory, as well as an area in the parietal cortex involved in processing scenes (**Figure 8.2a**). But in addition, the own-photos caused more activation in the prefrontal cortex, which is associated with processing information about the self (**Figure 8.2b**), and in the hippocampus, which is involved in recollection (memory associated with "mental time travel") (**Figure 8.2c**).

Thus, the pictures of a particular location that people took themselves elicited memories presumably associated with taking the picture and, therefore, activated a more extensive network of brain areas than pictures of the same location that were taken by someone else. This activation reflects the richness of experiencing autobiographical memories. Other studies have also found that autobiographical memories can elicit emotions, which activates another area of the brain (which we will describe shortly) called the amygdala (see Figure 5.19, page 150).

Memory Over the Life Span

What determines which particular life events we will remember years later? Personal milestones such as graduating from college or receiving a marriage proposal stand out, as do highly emotional events such as surviving a car accident (Pillemer, 1998). Events that become significant parts of a person's life tend to be remembered well. For example, going out to dinner with someone for the first time might stand out if you ended up having a long-term relationship with that person, but the same dinner date might be far less memorable if you never saw the person again.

A particularly interesting result occurs when participants over 40 are asked to remember events in their lives. As shown in **Figure 8.3** for a 55-year-old, events are remembered for all years between ages 5 and 55, but memory is better for recent events and for events occurring between the ages of about 10 and 30 (Conway, 1996; Rubin et al., 1998). The enhanced memory for adolescence and young adulthood found in people over 40 is called the **reminiscence bump**.

Why are adolescence and young adulthood special times for encoding memories? We will describe three hypotheses, all based on the idea that special life events happen during adolescence and young adulthood. The **self-image hypothesis** proposes that memory is enhanced for events that occur as a person's self-image or life identity is being formed (Rathbone et al., 2008). This idea is based on the results of an experiment in which participants with an average age of 54 created "I am" statements, such as "I am a mother" or "I am a psychologist," that they felt defined them as a person. When they then indicated when each statement had become a significant part of their identity, the average age they assigned to the origin of these statements was 25, which is within the span of the reminiscence bump. When participants also listed events that were connected with each statement (such as "I gave birth to my first child" or "I started graduate school in psychology"), most of the events occurred during the time span associated with the reminiscence bump. Development of the self-image therefore brings with it numerous memorable events, most of which happen during adolescence or young adulthood.

Another explanation for the reminiscence bump, called the **cognitive hypothesis**, proposes that periods of rapid change that are followed by stability cause stronger encoding of memories. Adolescence and young adulthood fit this description because the rapid changes, such as going away to school, getting married, and starting a career, that occur during these periods are followed by the relative stability of adult life. One way this hypothesis has been tested is by finding people who have experienced rapid changes in their lives that occurred at a time later than adolescence or young adulthood. The cognitive hypothesis would predict that the reminiscence bump should occur later for these people. To test this idea, Robert Schrauf and David Rubin (1998) determined the recollections of people who had emigrated to the United States either in their 20s or in their mid-30s. **Figure 8.4**, which shows the memory curves for two groups of immigrants, indicates that the reminiscence

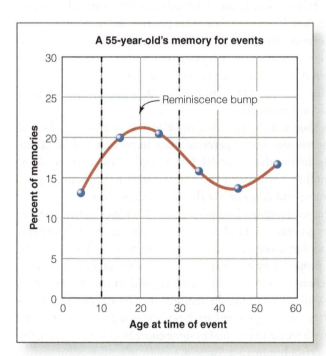

➤ Figure 8.3 Percentage of memories from different ages recalled by a 55-year-old, showing the reminiscence bump, which occurs for events experienced between about 10 and 30 years of age (dashed lines).

(Source: R. W. Schrauf & D. C. Rubin, Bilingual autobiographical memory in older adult immigrants: A test of cognitive explanations of the reminiscence bump and the linguistic encoding of memories, *Journal of Memory and Language*, 39, 437–457. Copyright © 1998 Elsevier Ltd. Republished with permission.)

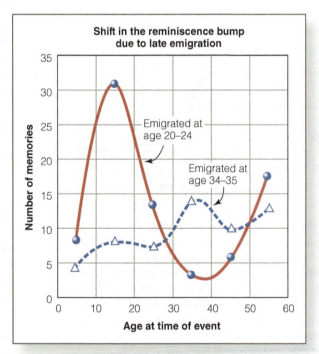

➤ Figure 8.4 The reminiscence bump for people who emigrated at age 34 or 35 is shifted toward older ages, compared to the bump for people who emigrated between the ages of 20 and 24.

(Source: R. W. Schrauf & D. C. Rubin, Bilingual autobiographical memory in older adult immigrants: A test of cognitive explanations of the reminiscence bump and the linguistic encoding of memories, *Journal of Memory and Language*, 39, 437–457. Copyright © 1998 Elsevier Ltd. Republished with permission.)

bump occurs at the normal age for people who emigrated at age 20 to 24 but is shifted to later for those who emigrated at age 34 or 35, just as the cognitive hypothesis would predict.

Notice that the normal reminiscence bump is missing for the people who emigrated later. Schrauf and Rubin explain this by noting that the late emigration eliminates the stable period that usually occurs during early adulthood. Because early adulthood isn't followed by a stable period, no reminiscence bump occurs, as predicted by the cognitive hypothesis.

Finally, the **cultural life script hypothesis** distinguishes between a person's life story, which is all of the events that have occurred in a person's life, and a **cultural life script**, which is the culturally expected events that occur at a particular time in the life span. For example, when Dorthe Berntsen and David Rubin (2004) asked people to list when important events in a typical person's life usually occur, some of the more common responses were falling in love (16 years), college (22 years), marriage (27 years), and having children (28 years). Interestingly, a large number of the most commonly mentioned events occur during the period associated with the reminiscence bump. This doesn't mean that events in a specific person's life always occur at those times, but according to the cultural life script hypothesis, events in a person's life story become easier to recall when they fit the cultural life script for that person's culture.

Related to the cultural life script hypothesis is a phenomenon Jonathan Koppel and Dorthe Berntsen (2014) call the **youth bias**—the tendency for the most notable public events in a person's life to be perceived to occur when the person is young. They reached this conclusion by asking people to imagine a typical infant of their own culture and gender, and by posing the following question: "... throughout this person's life many important public events will take place, both nationally and internationally, such as wars, the deaths of public figures, and sporting events. How old do you think this person is most likely to be when the event that they consider to be the *most* important public event of their lifetime takes place?"

As shown in **Figure 8.5**, most of the responses indicated that the person would perceive most important public events to occur before they were 30. Interestingly, this result occurred when polling both young and older people, and the curves peak in the teens and 20s, just like the reminiscence bump.

The reminiscence bump is a good example of a phenomenon that has generated a number of explanations, many of them plausible and supported by evidence. It isn't surprising that the crucial factors proposed by each explanation—formation of self-identity, rapid changes followed by stability, and culturally expected events—all occur during the reminiscence bump, because that is what they are trying to explain. It is likely that each of the mechanisms we have described makes some contribution to creating the reminiscence bump. (See **Table 8.1**.)

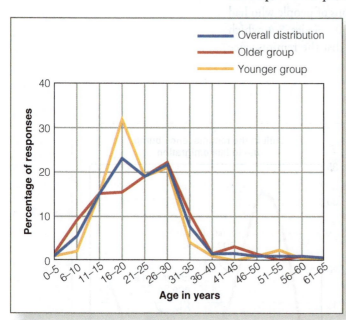

➤ **Figure 8.5** Results of Koppel and Berntsen's (2014) "youth bias" experiment in which participants were asked to indicate how old a hypothetical person would be when the event that they consider to be the most important public event of their lifetime takes place. Notice that the distribution of responses is similar for both younger participants and older participants.

(Source: Koppel and Berntsen, *Quarterly Journal of Experimental Psychology*, 67(3), Figure 1, page 420, 2014.)

TABLE 8.1

Explanations for the Reminiscence Bump

Explanation	Basic Characteristic
Self-image	Period of assuming person's self-image
Cognitive	Encoding is better during periods of rapid change
Cultural life script	Culturally shared expectations structure recall

▶ Memory for "Exceptional" Events

It is clear that some events in a person's life are more likely to be remembered than others. A characteristic of most memorable events is that they are significant and important to the person and, in some cases, are associated with emotions. For example, think about some of the memorable things you remember from your first year in college. When upperclass students were asked to remember events from their first year of college, many of the events that stand out were associated with strong emotions (Pillemer, 1998; Pillemer et al., 1996; Talarico, 2009).

Memory and Emotion

Emotions and memory are intertwined. Emotions are often associated with "special" events, such as beginning or ending relationships or events experienced by many people simultaneously, like the 9/11 terrorist attacks. The idea that emotions are associated with better memory has some support. In one experiment on the association between emotion and enhanced memory, Kevin LaBar and Elizabeth Phelps (1998) tested participants' ability to recall arousing words (for example, profanity and sexually explicit words) and neutral words (such as *street* and *store*), and observed better memory for the arousing words (**Figure 8.6a**). In another study, Florin Dolcos and coworkers (2005) tested participants' ability to recognize emotional and neutral pictures after a 1-year delay and observed better memory for the emotional pictures (**Figure 8.6b**).

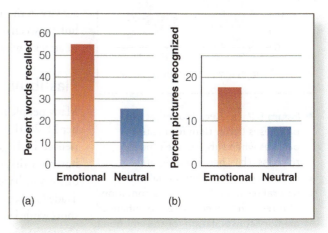

➤ **Figure 8.6** (a) Percent of emotional and neutral words recalled immediately after reading a list of words. (b) Percent of emotional and neutral pictures recognized 1 year after viewing the pictures.
(Source: Part a: LaBar & Phelps, 1998; Part b: Dolcos et al., 2005.)

When we look at what is happening physiologically, one structure stands out: the **amygdala** (see Figure 5.19, page 150). The importance of the amygdala has been demonstrated in a number of ways. For example, in the experiment by Dolcos and coworkers described above, brain scans using fMRI as people were remembering revealed that amygdala activity was higher for the emotional pictures (also see Cahill et al., 1996; Hamann et al., 1999).

The link between emotions and the amygdala was also demonstrated by testing a patient, B.P., who had suffered damage to his amygdala. When participants without brain damage viewed a slide show about a boy and his mother in which the boy is injured halfway through the story, these participants had enhanced memory for the emotional part of the story (when the boy is injured). B.P.'s memory was the same as that of the non-brain-damaged participants for the first part of the story, but it was not enhanced for the emotional part (Cahill et al., 1995). It appears, therefore, that emotions may trigger mechanisms in the amygdala that help us remember events associated with the emotions.

Emotion has also been linked to improved memory consolidation, the process that strengthens memory for an experience and takes place over minutes or hours after the experience (see Chapter 7, pages 208–215) (LaBar & Cabeza, 2006; Tambini et al., 2017). The link between emotion and consolidation was initially suggested by animal research, mainly in rats, that showed that central nervous system stimulants administered shortly after training on a task can enhance memory for the task. Research then determined that hormones such as the stimulant cortisol are released during and after emotionally arousing stimuli like those used in the testing task. These two findings led to the conclusion that stress hormones released after an emotional experience increase consolidation of memory for that experience (McGaugh, 1983; Roozendaal & McGaugh, 2011).

Larry Cahill and coworkers (2003) carried out an experiment that demonstrated this effect in humans. They showed participants neutral and emotionally arousing pictures; then

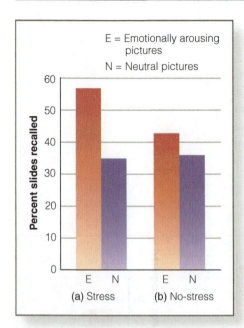

➤ **Figure 8.7** (a) Recall for emotional pictures is better than for neutral pictures when subjects are exposed to stress. (b) There is no significant difference between emotional and neutral recall in the no-stress condition. This result has been related to enhanced memory consolidation for the emotional pictures. (Source: Cahill et al., 2003)

they had some participants (the stress group) immerse their arms in ice water, which causes the release of cortisol, and other participants (the no-stress group) immerse their arms in warm water, which is a nonstressful situation that doesn't cause cortisol release. When asked to describe the pictures a week later, participants who had been exposed to stress recalled more of the emotionally arousing pictures than the neutral pictures (**Figure 8.7a**). There was no significant difference between the neutral and emotionally arousing picture for the no-stress group (**Figure 8.7b**).

What is particularly interesting about these results is that the cortisol enhances memory for the emotional pictures but not for the neutral pictures. Results such as these have led to the conclusion that hormone activation that occurs after arousing emotional experiences enhances memory consolidation in humans (also see Phelps & Sharot, 2008). This increased consolidation associated with emotion has also been linked to increased activity in the amygdala (Ritchey et al., 2008). As we will see in the next section, there is a link between emotion and memory for highly memorable events, such as the 9/11 terrorist attacks, which cause memories that have been called *flashbulb memories*.

Flashbulb Memories

Many people have memories of when they learned about the terrorist attacks of September 11, 2001. Research on memories for public events such as this, which have been experienced by large numbers of people, often ask people to remember where they were and how they first learned of the event. I remember walking into the psychology department office and having a secretary tell me that someone had crashed a plane into the World Trade Center. At the time, I pictured a small private plane that had gone off course, but a short while later, when I called my wife, she told me that the first tower of the World Trade Center had just collapsed. Shortly after that, in my cognitive psychology class, my students and I discussed what we knew about the situation and decided to cancel class for the day.

Brown and Kulik Propose the Term "Flashbulb Memory" The memories I have described about how I heard about the 9/11 attack, and the people and events directly associated with finding out about the attack, are still vivid in my mind more than 16 years later. Is there something special about memories such as this that are associated with unexpected, emotionally charged events? According to Roger Brown and James Kulik (1977), there is. They proposed that memories for the circumstances surrounding learning about events such as 9/11 are special. Their proposal was based on an earlier event, which occurred on November 22, 1963. President John F. Kennedy was sitting high up in an open-top car, waving to people as his motorcade drove down a parade route in Dallas, Texas. As his car was passing the Texas School Book Depository building, three shots rang out. President Kennedy slumped over. The motorcade came to a halt, and Kennedy was rushed to the hospital. Shortly after, the news spread around the world: President Kennedy had been assassinated.

In referring to the day of President Kennedy's assassination, Brown and Kulik stated that "for an instant, the entire nation and perhaps much of the world stopped still to have its picture taken." This description, which likened the process of forming a memory to the taking of a photograph, led them to coin the term **flashbulb memory** to refer to a person's memory for the circumstances surrounding shocking, highly charged events. It is important to emphasize that the term *flashbulb memory* refers to memory for the circumstances surrounding how a person *heard about* an event, not memory *for the event itself*. Thus, a flashbulb memory for 9/11 would be memory for where a person was and what they were doing when they found out about the terrorist attack. Therefore, flashbulb memories give importance to events that otherwise would be unexceptional. For example, although I had talked with the secretary in the psychology department hundreds of times over the years, the one time that stands out is when she told me that a plane had crashed into the World Trade Center.

Brown and Kulik argued that there is something special about the mechanisms responsible for flashbulb memories. Not only do they occur under highly emotional circumstances, but they are remembered for long periods of time and are especially vivid and detailed. Brown and Kulik described the mechanism responsible for these vivid and detailed memories as a "Now Print" mechanism, as if these memories are like a photograph that resists fading.

Flashbulb Memories Are Not Like Photographs   Brown and Kulik's idea that flashbulb memories are like a photograph was based on their finding that people were able to describe in some detail what they were doing when they heard about highly emotional events like the assassinations of John F. Kennedy and Martin Luther King, Jr. But the procedure Brown and Kulik used was flawed because their participants weren't asked what they remembered until years after the events had occurred. The problem with this procedure is that there was no way to determine whether the reported memories were accurate. The only way to check for accuracy is to compare the person's memory to what actually happened or to memory reports collected immediately after the event. The technique of comparing later memories to memories collected immediately after the event is called repeated recall.

METHOD   Repeated Recall

The idea behind repeated recall is to determine whether memory changes over time by testing participants a number of times after an event. The person's memory is first measured immediately after a stimulus is presented or something happens. Even though there is some possibility for errors or omissions immediately after the event, this report is taken as being the most accurate representation of what happened and is used as a baseline. Days, months, or years later, when participants are asked to remember what happened, their reports are compared to this baseline. This use of a baseline provides a way to check the consistency of later reports.

Over the years since Brown and Kulik's "Now Print" proposal, research using the repeated recall task has shown that flashbulb memories are not like photographs. Unlike photographs, which remain the same for many years, people's memories for how they heard about flashbulb events change over time. In fact, one of the main findings of research on flashbulb memories is that although people report that memories surrounding flashbulb events are especially vivid, they are often inaccurate or lacking in detail. For example, Ulric Neisser and Nicole Harsch (1992) did a study in which they asked participants how they had heard about the explosion of the space shuttle *Challenger*. Back in 1986, space launches were still considered special and were often highly anticipated. The flight of the *Challenger* was special because one of the astronauts was New Hampshire high school teacher Christa McAuliffe, who was the first member of NASA's Teacher in Space project. The blastoff from Cape Canaveral on January 28, 1986, seemed routine. But 77 seconds after liftoff, Challenger broke apart and plummeted into the ocean, killing the crew of seven (**Figure 8.8**). Participants in Neisser and Harsch's experiment filled out a questionnaire within a day after the explosion, and then filled out the same questionnaire 2 1/2 to 3 years later. One participant's response, a day after the explosion, indicated that she had heard about it in class:

> I was in my religion class and some people walked in and started talking about [it]. I didn't know any details except that it had exploded and the schoolteacher's students had all been

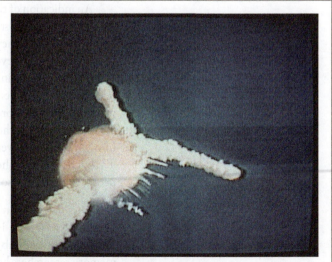

▶ **Figure 8.8** Neisser and Harsch (1992) studied people's memories for the day they heard about the explosion of the space shuttle *Challenger*.

watching, which I thought was so sad. Then after class I went to my room and watched the TV program talking about it, and I got all the details from that.

Two and a half years later, her memory had changed to the following:

When I first heard about the explosion I was sitting in my freshman dorm room with my roommate, and we were watching TV. It came on a news flash, and we were both totally shocked. I was really upset, and I went upstairs to talk to a friend of mine, and then I called my parents.

Responses like these, in which participants first reported hearing about the explosion in one place, such as a classroom, and then later remembered that they had first heard about it on TV, were common. Right after the explosion, only 21 percent of the participants indicated that they had first heard about it on TV, but 2 1/2 years later, 45 percent of the participants reported that they had first heard about it on TV. Reasons for the increase in TV memories could be that the TV reports become more memorable through repetition and that TV is a major source of news. Thus, memory for hearing about the Challenger explosion had a property that is also a characteristic of memory for less dramatic, everyday events: It was affected by people's experiences following the event (people may have seen accounts of the explosion) and their general knowledge (people often first hear about important news on TV).

The idea that memory can be affected by what happens after an event is the basis of Ulric Neisser and coworkers (1996) **narrative rehearsal hypothesis**, which states that we may remember events like those that happened on 9/11 not because of a special mechanism but because we rehearse these events after they occur.

The narrative rehearsal hypothesis makes sense when we consider the events that followed 9/11. Pictures of the planes crashing into the World Trade Center were replayed endlessly on TV, and the event and its aftermath were covered extensively for months afterward in the media. Neisser argues that if rehearsal is the reason for our memories of significant events, then the flashbulb analogy is misleading.

Remember that the memory we are concerned with is the characteristics surrounding how people first heard about 9/11, but much of the rehearsal associated with this event is rehearsal for events that occurred after hearing about it. Seeing TV replays of the planes crashing into the towers, for example, might result in people focusing more on those images than on who told them about the event or where they were, and eventually they might come to believe that they originally heard about the event on TV, as occurred in the *Challenger* study.

An indication of the power of TV to "capture" people's memory is provided by the results of a study by James Ost and coworkers (2002), who approached people in an English shopping center and asked if they would be willing to participate in a study examining how well people can remember tragic events. The target event involved Princess Diana and her companion Dodi Fayed, whose deaths in a car crash in Paris on August 31, 1997, were widely covered on British television. Participants were asked to respond to the following statement: "Have you seen the paparazzi's video-recording of the car crash in which Diana, Princess of Wales, and Dodi Fayed lost their lives?" Of the 45 people who responded to this question, 20 said they had seen the film. This was, however, impossible, because no such film exists. The car crash was reported on TV, but not actually shown. The extensive media coverage of this event apparently caused some people to remember something—seeing the film—that didn't actually occur.

Are Flashbulb Memories Different from Other Memories?　The large number of inaccurate responses in the *Challenger* study suggests that perhaps memories that are supposed to be flashbulb memories decay just like regular memories. In fact, many flashbulb memory researchers have expressed doubt that flashbulb memories are much different from regular memories (Schmolck et al., 2000). This conclusion is supported by an experiment in which a group of college students were asked a number of questions on September 12, 2001, the day after the terrorist attacks involving the World Trade Center, the Pentagon, and Flight 93 in Pennsylvania (Talarico & Rubin, 2003). Some of these questions were about the terrorist attacks ("When did you first hear the news?"). Others were similar questions about an everyday event in the person's life that occurred in the days just preceding the attacks. After picking the everyday event, the participant created a two- or three-word description that could serve as a cue for that event in the future. Some participants were retested 1 week later, some 6 weeks later, and some 32 weeks later by asking them the same questions about the attack and the everyday event.

One result of this experiment was that the participants remembered fewer details and made more errors at longer intervals after the events, with little difference between the results for the flashbulb and everyday memories (**Figure 8.9a**). Thus, details fade for flashbulb memories, just as they do for everyday memories. So why do people think flashbulb memories are special? The results shown in **Figure 8.9b** and **8.9c** may hold the answer. People's memories for flashbulb events remain *more vivid* than everyday memories (Figure 8.9b), and people *believe* that flashbulb memories remain accurate, while everyday memories don't (Figure 8.9c).

Thus, we can say that flashbulb memories are both special (vivid; likely to be remembered) and ordinary (may not be accurate) at the same time. Another way of noting the specialness of flashbulb memories is that people *do* remember them—even if inaccurately— whereas less noteworthy events are less likely to be remembered.

Memory researchers are still discussing the exact mechanism responsible for memory of flashbulb events (Berntsen, 2009; Luminet & Curci, 2009; Talarico & Rubin, 2009). However, whatever mechanism is involved, one important outcome of the flashbulb memory research is that it has revealed that what people believe they remember accurately may not, in fact, be accurate at all. The idea that people's memories for an event can be determined by factors in addition to actually experiencing the event has led many researchers to propose that what people remember is a "construction" that is based on what actually happened plus additional influences. We will discuss this idea in the next section.

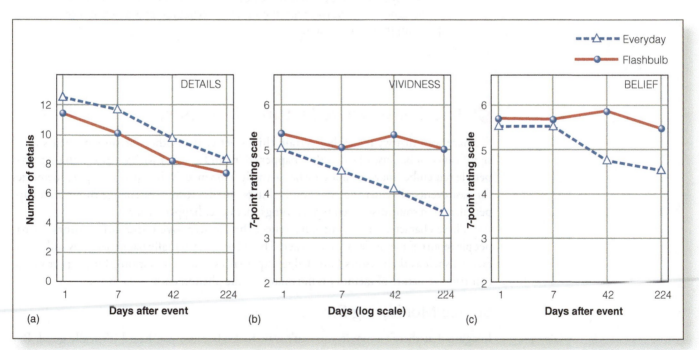

▶ **Figure 8.9** Results of Talarico and Rubin's (2003) flashbulb memory experiment: (a) details remembered; (b) vividness ratings; and (c) belief in accuracy. Details remembered decreased for both flashbulb and everyday memories. Belief in accuracy and vividness also decreased for everyday memories but remained high for flashbulb memories.

(Source: J. M. Talarico & D. C. Rubin, Confidence, not consistency, characterizes flashbulb memories, *Psychological Science*, 14, 455–461, Figures 1 & 2. Copyright © 2003 American Psychological Society. Reproduced by permission.)

TEST YOURSELF 8.1

1. How did people in a nationwide poll respond to the statement about how memory operates like a video camera? How accurate was their response?

2. What is autobiographical memory? What does it mean to say that it includes both episodic and semantic components?

3. What does it mean to say that autobiographical memories are multidimensional? How did Cabeza's photography experiment provide evidence for this idea?

4. What types of events are often the most memorable? What would a plot of "events remembered" versus "age" look like for a 50-year-old person? What theories have been proposed to explain the peak that occurs in this function?

5. What is the evidence that emotionally charged events are easier to remember than nonemotional events? Describe the role of the amygdala in emotional memory, including brain scan (fMRI) and neuropsychological (patient B.P.) evidence linking the amygdala and memory, and the experiment showing that emotion enhances consolidation.

6. What is the youth bias, and which explanation of the reminiscence bump is it associated with?

7. Why did Brown and Kulik call memory for public, emotional events, like the assassination of President Kennedy, "flashbulb memories"? Was their use of the term *flashbulb* correct?

8. Describe the results of repeated recall experiments. What do these results indicate about Brown and Kulik's "Now Print" proposal for flashbulb memories?

9. What is the narrative rehearsal hypothesis? How is the result of the Princess Diana study related to the effect of media coverage on memory?

10. In what ways are flashbulb memories different from other autobiographical memories and in what ways are they similar? What are some hypotheses explaining these differences?

▶ The Constructive Nature of Memory

We have seen that we remember certain things better than others because of their special significance or because of when they happened in our lives. But we have also seen that what people remember may not match what actually happened. When people report memories for past events, they may not only omit things but also distort or change things that happened, and in some cases even report things that never happened at all.

These characteristics of memory reflect the **constructive nature of memory**—what people report as memories are constructed based on what actually happened plus additional factors, such as the person's knowledge, experiences, and expectations. One aspect of the constructive nature of memory is illustrated by the phenomenon of *source monitoring*.

Source Monitoring Errors

Imagine that there's a movie you can't wait to see because you heard it's really good. But when you try to remember what first turned you on to the movie, you're uncertain. Was it the review you read online? That conversation you had with a friend? The billboard you passed on the road? Can you remember the initial *source* that got you interested in the movie? This is the problem of **source monitoring**—the process of determining the origins of our memories, knowledge, or beliefs (Johnson et al., 1993). In searching your memory for when you first heard about the movie, if you decided it was the review you read online but in reality you first heard about it from your friend, you would have committed a **source monitoring error**—misidentifying the source of a memory.

Source monitoring errors are also called **source misattributions** because the memory is attributed to the wrong source. Source monitoring provides an example of the constructive nature of memory because when we remember something, we retrieve the memory ("I remember becoming interested in seeing that movie") and then determine where that memory came from ("It was that review I read online") (Mitchell & Johnson, 2000).

Source monitoring errors are common, and we are often unaware of them. Perhaps you have had the experience of remembering that one person told you about something but later realizing you had heard it from someone else—or the experience of claiming you had said something you had only thought ("I'll be home late for dinner") (Henkel, 2004). In the 1984 presidential campaign, President Ronald Reagan, running for reelection, repeatedly related a story about a heroic act by a U.S. pilot, only to have it revealed later that his story was almost identical to a scene from a 1940s war movie, *A Wing and a Prayer* (Johnson, 2006; Rogin, 1987). Apparently, the source of the president's reported memory was the film rather than an actual event.

Some of the more sensational examples of source monitoring errors are cases of **cryptomnesia**, unconscious plagiarism of the work of others. For example, Beatle George Harrison was sued for appropriating the melody from the song "He's So Fine" (originally recorded by the 1960s group the Chiffons) for his song "My Sweet Lord." Although Harrison claimed he had used the tune unconsciously, he was successfully sued by the publisher of the original song. Harrison's problem was that he thought he was the source of the melody, when the actual source was someone else.

An experiment by Larry Jacoby and coworkers (1989) titled "Becoming Famous Overnight" demonstrated a connection between source monitoring errors and familiarity by testing participants' ability to distinguish between famous and nonfamous names. In the acquisition part of the experiment, Jacoby had participants read a number of made-up nonfamous names like Sebastian Weissdorf and Valerie Marsh (**Figure 8.10**). For the immediate test group, participants were tested immediately after seeing the list of nonfamous names. They were told to pick out the names of famous people from a list containing (1) the nonfamous names they had just seen, (2) new nonfamous names that they had never seen before, and (3) famous names, like Minnie Pearl (a country singer) or Roger Bannister (the first person to run a 4-minute mile), that many people might have recognized in 1988, when the experiment was conducted. Just before this test, participants were reminded that all of the names they had seen in the first part of the experiment were nonfamous. Because the test was given shortly after the participants had seen the first list of nonfamous names,

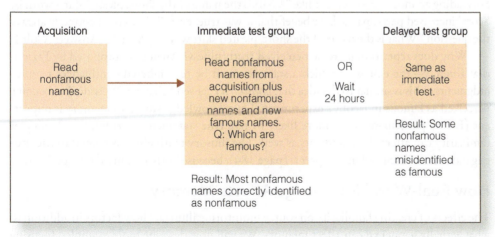

➤ **Figure 8.10** Design of Jacoby et al.'s (1989) "Becoming Famous Overnight" experiment.

they correctly identified most of the old nonfamous names (like Sebastian Weissdorf and Valerie Marsh) as being nonfamous.

The interesting result occurred for participants in the delayed test group, who were tested 24 hours after first seeing the names and, as for the other group, were told that the names they had seen in the first part of the experiment were nonfamous. When tested after this delay, participants were more likely to identify the old nonfamous names as being famous. Thus, waiting 24 hours before testing increased the chances that Sebastian Weissdorf would be labeled as famous.

How did Sebastian Weissdorf become famous overnight? To answer this question, put yourself in the place of one of Jacoby's participants. It is 24 hours since you saw the first list of nonfamous names, and you now have to decide whether Sebastian Weissdorf is famous or nonfamous. How do you make your decision? Sebastian Weissdorf doesn't pop out as someone you know of, but the name is familiar. You ask yourself the question, "Why is this name familiar?" This is a source monitoring problem, because to answer this question you need to determine the source of your familiarity. Are you familiar with the name Sebastian Weissdorf because you saw it 24 hours earlier or because it is the name of a famous person? Apparently, some of Jacoby's participants decided that the familiarity was caused by fame, so the previously unknown Sebastian Weissdorf became famous!

Later in the chapter, when we consider some of the issues involved in determining the accuracy of eyewitness testimony, we will see that situations that create a sense of familiarity can lead to source monitoring errors, such as identifying the wrong person as having been at the scene of a crime. Another demonstration of familiarity causing errors is the *illusory truth effect*.

The Illusory Truth Effect

Is the following sentence true or false? "Chemosynthesis is the name of the process by which plants make their food." If you said "false" you were right. ("Photosynthesis" is the actual process.) But one way to increase the chances that you might incorrectly state that the chemosynthesis statement is true is to have you read it once, and then again later. The enhanced probability of evaluating a statement as being true upon repeated presentation is called the **illusory truth effect** (Begg et al., 1992).

Lisa Fazio and coworkers (2015) presented both true and false statements to participants and then asked them to rate how *interesting* they were. Then, in the second part of the experiment, they asked participants to indicate whether the statements they had read previously, plus a number of new statements, were true or false. The results showed that new statements that were correct were rated "true" 56 percent of the time, but repeated statements that were correct were rated true 62 percent of the time. Similar results occurred for statements that were incorrect. Repetition increased perceived truth, even if the person knew the correct answer. So, reading an incorrect statement like "A Sari is the name of the short, pleated skirts worn by Scots" increased participants' later belief that it was true, even if they could correctly answer the question "What is the name of the short, pleated skirt worn by Scots?" (Answer: A kilt.)

Why does repetition increase perceived truthfulness? An answer proposed by Fazio is that **fluency**—the ease with which a statement can be remembered—influences people's judgments. This is similar to the idea that *familiarity* caused Sebastian Weissdorf to become perceived as famous in Jacoby's experiment. Thus, knowledge stored in memory is important (Fazio's participants were more likely to rate true statements as true), but fluency or familiarity can affect the judgments as well. The illusory truth effect is related to the propaganda effect discussed in Chapter 6 (page 184), because both are caused by repetition.

How Real-World Knowledge Affects Memory

The effects of creating familiarity on source monitoring illustrate how factors in addition to what actually happened can affect memory. We will now describe more examples, focusing on how our knowledge of the world can affect memory. A classic study that illustrates the effect of knowledge on memory was conducted before the first World War and was published in 1932 by Frederick Bartlett.

Bartlett's "War of the Ghosts" Experiment   In this classic study, which was one of the first to suggest that memory was constructive, Bartlett had his participants read the following story from Canadian Indian folklore.

> The War of the Ghosts
>
> One night two young men from Egulac went down to the river to hunt seals, and while they were there it became foggy and calm. Then they heard war cries, and they thought: "Maybe this is a war party." They escaped to the shore and hid behind a log. Now canoes came up, and they heard the noise of paddles and saw one canoe coming up to them. There were five men in the canoe, and they said:
>
> "What do you think? We wish to take you along. We are going up the river to make war on the people."
>
> One of the young men said: "I have no arrows." "Arrows are in the canoe," they said. "I will not go along. I might be killed. My relatives do not know where I have gone. But you," he said, turning to the other, "may go with them."
>
> So one of the young men went, but the other returned home. And the warriors went on up the river to a town on the other side of Kalama. The people came down to the water, and they began to fight, and many were killed. But presently the young man heard one of the warriors say: "Quick, let us go home; that Indian has been hit." Now he thought: "Oh, they are ghosts." He did not feel sick, but they said he had been shot.
>
> So the canoes went back to Egulac, and the young man went ashore to his house and made a fire. And he told everybody and said: "Behold I accompanied the ghosts, and we went to fight. Many of our fellows were killed, and many of those who attacked us were killed. They said I was hit, and I did not feel sick."
>
> He told it all, and then he became quiet. When the sun rose, he fell down. Something black came out of his mouth. His face became contorted. The people jumped up and cried. He was dead. (Bartlett, 1932, p. 65)

After his participants had read this story, Bartlett asked them to recall it as accurately as possible. He then used the technique of **repeated reproduction**, in which the participants tried to remember the story at longer and longer intervals after they had first read it. This is similar to the repeated recall technique used in the flashbulb memory experiments (see Method: Repeated Recall, page 233).

One reason Bartlett's experiment is considered important is because it was one of the first to use the repeated reproduction technique. But the main reason the "War of the Ghosts" experiment is considered important is the nature of the errors Bartlett's participants made. At longer times after reading the story, most participants' reproductions of the story were shorter than the original and contained many omissions and inaccuracies. But what was most significant about the remembered stories is that they tended to reflect the participant's own culture. The original story, which came from Canadian folklore, was transformed by many of Bartlett's participants to make it more consistent with the culture of Edwardian England, to which they belonged. For example, one participant remembered the two men who were out hunting seals as being involved in a sailing expedition, the "canoes" as "boats," and the man who joined the war party as a fighter that any good Englishman would be proud of—ignoring his wounds, he continued fighting and won the admiration of the natives.

One way to think about what happened in Bartlett's experiment is that his participants created their memories from two sources. One source was the original story, and the other was what they knew about similar stories in their own culture. As time passed, the participants used information from both sources, so their reproductions became more like what would happen in Edwardian England. This idea that memories can be comprised of details from various sources is related to source monitoring, discussed earlier.

Making Inferences Memory reports can be influenced by inferences that people make based on their experiences and knowledge. In this section, we will consider this idea further. But first, do this demonstration.

DEMONSTRATION Reading Sentences

For this demonstration, read the following sentences, pausing for a few seconds after each one.

1. The children's snowman vanished when the temperature reached 80.
2. The flimsy shelf weakened under the weight of the books.
3. The absent minded professor didn't have his car keys.
4. The karate champion hit the cinder block.
5. The new baby stayed awake all night.

Now that you have read the sentences, turn to *Demonstration: Reading Sentences (Continued)* on page 258 and follow the directions.

How do your answers from the fill-in-the-blank exercise on page 258 compare to the words that you originally read in the Demonstration? William Brewer (1977) and Kathleen McDermott and Jason Chan (2006) presented participants with a similar task, involving many more sentences than you read, and found that errors occurred for about a third of the sentences. For the sentences above, the most common errors were as follows: (1) *vanished* became *melted*; (2) *weakened* became *collapsed*; (3) *didn't have* became *lost*; (4) hit became *broke* or *smashed*; and (5) *stayed awake* became *cried*.

These wording changes illustrate a process called **pragmatic inference**, which occurs when reading a sentence leads a person to expect something that is not explicitly stated or implied by the sentence (Brewer, 1977). These inferences are based on knowledge gained through experience. Thus, although reading that a baby stayed awake all night does not include any information about crying, knowledge about babies might lead a person to infer that the baby was crying (Chan & McDermott, 2006).

Here is the scenario used in another memory experiment, which was designed specifically to elicit inferences based on the participants' past experiences (Arkes & Freedman, 1984):

In a baseball game, the score is tied 1 to 1. The home team has runners on first and third, with one out. A ground ball is hit to the shortstop. The shortstop throws to second base, attempting a double play. The runner who was on third scores, so it is now 2–1 in favor of the home team.

After hearing a story similar to this one, participants were asked to indicate whether the sentence "The batter was safe at first" was part of the passage. From looking at the story, you can see that this sentence was never presented, and most of the participants who didn't know much about baseball answered correctly. However, participants who knew the rules of baseball were more likely to say that the sentence had been presented. They based this judgment on their knowledge that if the runner on third had scored, then the double play must have failed, which means that the batter safely reached first. Knowledge, in this example, resulted in a correct inference about what probably happened in the ball game but an incorrect inference about the sentence that was presented in the passage.

Schemas and Scripts The preceding examples illustrate how people's memory reports can be influenced by their knowledge. A **schema** is a person's knowledge about some aspect of the environment. For example, a person's schema of a bank might include what banks often look like from the outside, the row of teller windows inside the bank, and the services a bank provides. We develop schemas through our experiences in different situations, such as making a deposit at a bank, going to a ball game, or listening to lectures in a classroom.

In an experiment that studied how memory is influenced by people's schemas, participants who had come to participate in a psychology experiment were asked to wait in an office (**Figure 8.11**) while the experimenter checked "to make sure that the previous hour's participant had completed the experiment." After 35 seconds, the participants were called into another room and were told that the purpose of the experiment was to test their memory for the office and that their task was to write down what they had seen while they were sitting in the office (Brewer & Treyens, 1981). The participants responded by writing down many of the things they remembered seeing, but they also included some things that were not there but that fit into their "office schema." For example, although there were no books in the office, 30 percent of the participants reported having seen books. Thus, the information in schemas can provide a guide for making inferences about what we remember. In this particular example, the inference turned out to be wrong.

Other examples of how schemas can lead to erroneous decisions in memory experiments have involved a type of schema called a script. A **script** is our conception of *the sequence of actions* that usually occurs during a particular experience. For example, your coffee shop script might be waiting in line, ordering a drink and pastry from the barista, receiving the pastry, paying, and waiting near "pickup" for your drink.

Scripts can influence our memory by setting up expectations about what usually happens in a particular situation. To test the influence of scripts, Gordon Bower and coworkers (1979) did an experiment in which participants were asked to remember short passages like the following.

W.F.Brewer&J.C.Treyens, Role of schemata in memory for places, Cognitive Psychology, 13,207–230.Copyright 1981,with permission from Elsevier

➤ **Figure 8.11** Office where Brewer and Treyens's (1981) subjects waited before being tested on their memory for what was present in the office.

The Dentist

Bill had a bad toothache. It seemed like forever before he finally arrived at the dentist's office. Bill looked around at the various dental posters on the wall. Finally the dental hygienist checked and x-rayed his teeth. He wondered what the dentist was doing. The dentist said that Bill had a lot of cavities. As soon as he'd made another appointment, he left the dentist's office. (Bower et al., 1979, p. 190)

The participants read a number of passages like this one, all of which were about familiar activities such as going to the dentist, going swimming, or going to a party. After a delay period, the participants were given the titles of the stories they had read and were told to write down what they remembered about each story as accurately as possible. The participants created stories that included much material that matched the original stories, but they also included material that wasn't presented in the original story but is part of the script for the activity described. For example, for the dentist story, some participants reported reading that "Bill checked in with the dentist's receptionist." This statement is part of most people's "going to the dentist" script, but it was not included in the original story. Thus, knowledge of the dentist script caused the participants to add information that wasn't originally presented. Another example of a link between knowledge and memory is provided by the following demonstration.

DEMONSTRATION   Memory for a List

Read the following list at a rate of about one item per second; then cover the list and write down as many of the words as possible. In order for this demonstration to work, it is important that you cover the words and write down the words you remember before reading past the demonstration.

bed, rest, awake, tired, dream
wake, night, blanket, doze, slumber
snore, pillow, peace, yawn, drowsy

False Recall and Recognition   The demonstration you just did is based on experiments by James Deese (1959) and Henry Roediger and Kathleen McDermott (1995), which were designed to illustrate false recall of items that were not actually presented. Does your list of remembered words include any words that are not on the preceding list? When I present this list to my class, there are always a substantial number of students who report that they remember the word "sleep." Remembering sleep is a false memory because it isn't on the list. This false memory occurs because people associate sleep with other words on the list. This is similar to the effect of schemas, in which people create false memories for office furnishings that aren't present because they associate these office furnishings with what is usually found in offices. Again, constructive processes have created an error in memory.

The crucial thing to take away from all of these examples is that false memories arise from the same constructive process that produces true memories. Thus, construction can cause memory errors, while at the same time providing the creativity that enables us to do things like understand language, solve problems, and make decisions. This creativity also helps us "fill in the blanks" when there is incomplete information. For example, when a person says "we went to the ball game," you have a pretty good idea of many of the things that happened in addition to the game (hot dogs or other ballpark food was likely involved, for example), based on your experience of going to a ball game.

What Is It Like to Have "Exceptional" Memory?

"OK," you might say, "the process of construction may help us do many useful things, but it certainly seems to cause trouble when applied to memory. Wouldn't it be great to have such exceptional memory that construction wouldn't be necessary?"

As it turns out, there are some people who have such good memory that they make few errors. One such person was the Russian memory expert Shereshevskii (S.), whose exceptional memory enabled him to make a living by demonstrating his memory powers on stage. After extensively studying S., Russian psychologist Alexandria Luria (1968) concluded that S.'s memory was "virtually limitless" (though Wilding & Valentine, 1997, pointed out that S. did occasionally make mistakes). But Luria also reported some problems: When S. performed a memory feat, he had trouble forgetting what he had just remembered. His mind was like a blackboard on which everything that happened was written and couldn't be erased. Many things flit through our minds briefly and then we don't need them again; unfortunately for S., these things stayed there even when he wished they would go away. He also was not good at reasoning that involved drawing inferences or "filling in the blanks" based on partial information. We do this so often that we take it for granted, but S.'s ability to record massive amounts of information, and his inability to erase it, may have hindered his ability to do this.

Recently, new cases of impressive memory have been reported; they are described as cases of **highly superior autobiographical memory** (LePort et al., 2012). One, a woman we will call A.J., sent the following email to UCLA memory researcher James McGaugh:

> I am 34 years old and since I was eleven I have had this unbelievable ability to recall
> my past. . . . I can take a date between 1974 and today, and tell you what day it falls on,
> what I was doing that day and if anything of great importance . . . occurred on that day
> I can describe that to you as well. . . . Whenever I see a date flash on the television (or
> anywhere else for that matter) I automatically go back to that day and remember where
> I was, what I was doing, what day it fell on and on and on and on and on. It is non-stop,
> uncontrollable and totally exhausting. . . . I run my entire life through my head every
> day and it drives me crazy!!! (Parker et al., 2006, p. 35)

A.J. describes her memories as happening automatically and not being under her conscious control. When given a date she would, within seconds, relate personal experiences and also special events that occurred on that day, and these recollections proved to be accurate when checked against a diary of daily events that A.J. had been keeping for 24 years (Parker et al., 2006).

A.J.'s excellent memory for personal experiences differed from S.'s in that the contents that she couldn't erase were not numbers or names from memory performances, but the details of her personal life. This was both positive (recalling happy events) and negative (recalling unhappy or disturbing events). But was her memory useful to her in areas other than remembering life events? Apparently, she was not able to apply her powers to help her remember material for exams, as she was an average student. And testing revealed that she had impaired performance on tests that involved organizing material, thinking abstractly, and working with concepts—skills that are important for thinking creatively. Following the discovery of A.J., a study of 10 additional participants confirmed their amazing powers of autobiographical memory recall, but they also performed at levels similar to normal control participants on most standard laboratory memory tests. Their skill therefore, seems to be specialized to remembering autobiographical memories (LaPort et al., 2012).

What the cases of S. and A.J. illustrate is that it is not necessarily an advantage to be able to remember everything; in fact, the mechanisms that result in superior powers of memory may work against the constructive processes that are an important characteristic not only of memory but of our ability to think creatively. Moreover, storing everything that is experienced is an inefficient way for a system to operate because too much storage can overload the system. To avoid this "overload," our memory system is designed to selectively remember things that are particularly important to us or that occur often in our environment (Anderson & Schooler, 1991). Although the resulting system does not record everything we experience, it has operated well enough to enable humans to survive as a species.

TEST YOURSELF 8.2

1. Source monitoring errors provide an example of the constructive nature of memory. Describe what source monitoring and source monitoring errors are and why they are considered "constructive."

2. Describe the "Becoming Famous Overnight" experiment. What does this experiment suggest about one cause of source monitoring errors?

3. Describe the illusory truth effect. Why does it occur?

4. Describe the following examples of how memory errors can occur because of a person's knowledge of the world: (1) Bartlett's "War of the Ghosts" experiment; (2) making inferences (pragmatic inference; baseball experiment); (3) schemas and scripts (office experiment; dentist experiment); (4) false recall and recognition ("sleep" experiment).

5. What is the evidence from clinical case studies that "super memory" may have some disadvantages? What are some advantages of constructive memory?

The Misinformation Effect

We've seen that our memory system is prone to error for a number of reasons. This section continues this theme, as we look at the **misinformation effect**—misleading information presented after a person witnesses an event can change how the person describes that event later. This misleading information is referred to as **misleading postevent information (MPI)**.

METHOD   Presenting Misleading Postevent Information

The usual procedure in an experiment in which MPI is presented is to first present the stimulus to be remembered. For example, this stimulus could be a list of words or a film of an event. The MPI is then presented to one group of participants before their memory is tested and is not presented to a control group. MPI is often presented in a way that seems natural, so it does not occur to participants that they are being misled. However, even when participants are told that postevent information may be incorrect, presenting this information can still affect their memory reports. The effect of MPI is determined by comparing the memory reports of participants who received this misleading information to the memory reports of participants who did not receive it.

An experiment by Elizabeth Loftus and coworkers (1978) illustrates a typical MPI procedure. Participants saw a series of slides in which a car stops at a stop sign and then turns the corner and hits a pedestrian. Some of the participants then answered a number of questions, including ones like, "Did another car pass the red Ford while it was stopped at the stop sign?" For another group of participants (the MPI group), the words "yield sign" replaced "stop sign" in the question. Participants were then shown pictures from the slide show plus some pictures they had never seen. Those in the MPI group were more likely to say they had seen the picture of the car stopped at the yield sign (which, in actuality, they had never seen) than were participants who had not been exposed to MPI. This shift in memory caused by MPI demonstrates the misinformation effect.

Presentation of MPI can alter not only what participants report they saw, but their conclusions about other characteristics of the situation. For example, Loftus and Steven Palmer (1974) showed participants films of a car crash (**Figure 8.12**) and then asked either (1) "How fast were the cars going when they smashed into each other?" or (2) "How fast were the cars going when they hit each other?" Although both groups saw the same event, the average speed estimate by participants who heard the word "smashed" was 41 miles per hour, whereas the estimates for participants who heard "hit" averaged 34 miles per hour. Even more interesting for the study of memory are the participants' responses to the question "Did you see any broken glass?" which Loftus asked 1 week after they had seen the film. Although there was no broken glass in the film, 32 percent of the participants who heard "smashed" before estimating the speed reported seeing broken glass, whereas only 14 percent of the participants who heard "hit" reported seeing the glass (see Loftus, 1993a, 1998).

One explanation for the misinformation effect is based on the idea of source monitoring. From the source monitoring perspective, a person incorrectly concludes that the source of his or her memory for the incorrect event (yield sign) was the slide show, even though the actual source was the experimenter's statement after the slide show.

The following experiment by Stephen Lindsay (1990) investigated source monitoring and MPI by asking whether participants who are exposed to MPI really believe they saw something that was only suggested to them. Lindsay's participants first saw a sequence of

➤ Figure 8.12 Participants in the Loftus and Palmer (1974) experiment saw a film of a car crash, with scenes similar to the picture shown here, and were then asked leading questions about the crash.

slides showing a maintenance man stealing money and a computer (**Figure 8.13**). This slide presentation was narrated by a female speaker, who simply described what was happening as the slides were being shown. The participants were then divided into two groups.

Participants in the *difficult condition* heard a misleading narrative shortly after seeing the slide presentation. This narrative was read by the same female speaker who had described the slide show. For example, when participants viewed the slide show, they saw Folgers coffee, but the misleading narrative said the coffee was Maxwell House. Two days later, participants returned to the lab for a memory test on the slide show. Just before the test, they were told that there were errors in the narrative story that they heard right after the slide show and that they should ignore the information in the story when taking the memory test.

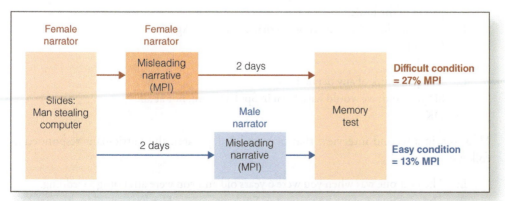

➤ Figure 8.13 Experimental design and results for Lindsay and coworkers' (1990) experiment.

Participants in the *easy condition* also heard the misleading story, but it was delayed for 2 days after the slide presentation, being presented right before they took the memory test. In addition, the story was read by a male speaker. As with the difficult group, these participants were also told to ignore the information presented in the misleading narrative.

The procedure for the difficult condition made it easy to confuse the misleading narrative and the narrated slide show because they occurred one after the other and were both read by the female. The results indicated that 27 percent of the responses of participants in the difficult condition matched the incorrect information that was presented in the misleading narrative. However, in the easy condition, it was easy to separate the misleading narrative from the slide show because they occurred 2 days apart and were read by different speakers. Only 13 percent of the responses for participants in the easy condition matched the misleading narrative. Source monitoring errors (including information from the misleading narrative) were therefore larger in the condition in which it was more difficult to tell the difference between the information presented in the slide show and the misleading narrative.

The experiments we've just described show that an experimenter's suggestion can influence people's memory reports for recently presented events (Loftus's "car crash" film; Lindsay's slide presentation of a robbery). But some of the most dramatic demonstrations of the effect of experimenter suggestion are situations in which suggestion causes people to "remember" events that occurred early in their lives, even though these events never happened.

Creating Memories for Events in People's Lives

A number of experiments have demonstrated how suggestion can influence memory for childhood events.

Creating Childhood Memories

Imagine that a person is in an experiment in which he or she is told about events that happened in his or her childhood. The experimenter provides brief descriptions of events that happened to the person long ago and asks the person to elaborate on each event. It isn't surprising that the person recognizes the events because the descriptions were provided to the experimenters by the person's parents. The person is therefore able to describe what they remember about the event, and sometimes also provide additional details.

But suddenly the person is stumped because the experimenter has described an event they don't remember. For example, here is a conversation that occurred in an experiment by Ira Hyman Jr. and coworkers (1995), in which a bogus event—one that never happened—was presented by the experimenter (E) to the participant (P):

E. At age 6 you attended a wedding reception, and while you were running around with some other kids you bumped into a table and turned a punch bowl over on a parent of the bride.

P: I have no clue. I have never heard that one before. Age 6?

E: Uh-huh.

P: No clue.

E: Can you think of any details?

P: Six years old; we would have been in Spokane, um, not at all.

E: OK.

However, in a second interview that occurred 2 days later, the participant responded as follows:

E: The next one was when you were 6 years old and you were attending a wedding.

P: The wedding was my best friend in Spokane, T___. Her brother, older brother, was getting married, and it was over here in P___, Washington, 'cause that's where her family was from, and it was in the summer or the spring because it was really hot outside, and it was right on the water. It was an outdoor wedding, and I think we were running around and knocked something over like the punch bowl or something and um made a big mess and of course got yelled at for it.

E: Do you remember anything else?

P: No.

E: OK.

What is most interesting about this participant's response is that he didn't remember the wedding the first time but did remember it the second time. Apparently, hearing about the event and then waiting caused the event to emerge as a false memory. This can be explained by familiarity. When questioned about the wedding the second time, the participant's familiarity with the wedding from the first exposure caused him to accept the wedding as having actually happened.

In another childhood memory experiment, Kimberley Wade and coworkers (2002) showed participants photographs obtained from family members that showed the participant involved in various events like birthday parties or vacations when they were 4 to 8 years old. They also saw a photograph created in Photoshop that showed them in an event that never happened—taking a hot air balloon ride (**Figure 8.14**). They were shown the photo and asked to describe what they remembered about the event. If they couldn't remember the event, they were told to close their eyes and picture participating in the event.

Participants easily recalled the real events but initially didn't recall taking the hot air balloon ride. After picturing the event in their minds and further questioning, however, 35 percent of the participants "remembered" the balloon ride, and after two more interviews, 50 percent of the participants described their experience while riding in the balloon. This result is similar to the experiment described earlier in which participants were told that they had turned over a punch bowl at a wedding reception. These studies, and many others, have shown that people can be led to believe that they experienced something in their childhood that never actually happened (see Nash et al., 2017; Scorbia et al., 2017).

Legal Implications of False Memory Research

In the 1990s a number of highly publicized trials took place in which women who were being treated by therapists experienced a return of what has been called a **repressed childhood memory**—memories that have been pushed out of the person's consciousness. The

➤ **Figure 8.14** How the stimulus for Wade and coworkers (2002) hot air balloon experiment was created. The image on the left was Photoshopped onto the balloon so it appeared that the child and his father went on a balloon ride.

hypothesis proposed by some therapists is that this repressed childhood memory can cause psychological problems and that the way to treat the patient's problem is to get them to retrieve the repressed memory. This accomplished using various techniques—hypnosis, guided imagery, strong suggestion—designed to "bring the memory back."

One such case involved 19-year-old Holly, who in the course of therapy for an eating disorder received a suggestion from her therapist that her disorder may have been caused by sexual abuse. After further therapy, which included additional suggestions from the therapist, Holly became convinced that her father had repeatedly raped her when she was a child. Holly's accusations caused her father, Gary Romona, to lose his $400,000-a-year executive job, his reputation, his friends, and contact with his three daughters.

Romona sued Holly's therapists for malpractice, accusing them of implanting memories in his daughter's mind. At the trial, Elizabeth Loftus and other cognitive psychologists described research on the misinformation effect and implanting false memories to demonstrate how suggestion can create false memories for long-ago events that never actually happened (Loftus, 1993b). Romona won a $500,000 judgment against the therapists. As a result of this case, which highlighted how memory can be influenced by suggestion, a number of criminal convictions based on "recovered memory" evidence have since been reversed.

The issues raised by cases like the Gary Romona case are complicated and disturbing. Child sexual abuse is a serious problem, which should not be minimized. But it is also important to be sure accusations are based on accurate information. According to a paper by the American Psychological Association (APA) Working Group on Investigation of Memories of Childhood Abuse, (1) most people who were sexually abused as children remember all or part of what happened to them; (2) it is possible for memories of abuse that have been forgotten for a long time to be remembered; and (3) it is also possible to construct convincing pseudomemories for events that never occurred. What's needed, suggests the APA and other researchers, is to educate both therapists and people in the criminal justice system about these research findings and make them aware of the sometimes tenuous relationship between what is remembered and what actually happened (Howe, 2013; Lindsay & Hyman, 2017; Nash et al., 2017).

▶ Why Do People Make Errors in Eyewitness Testimony?

Continuing our theme of how memory research intersects with the criminal justice system, we now consider the issue of **eyewitness testimony**—testimony by someone who has witnessed a crime. Eyewitness testimony is, in the eyes of jury members, an extremely important source of evidence, because it is provided by people who were present at the crime scene and who are assumed to be doing their best to accurately report what they saw.

The acceptance of eyewitness testimony is based on two assumptions: (1) the eyewitness was able to clearly see what happened; and (2) the eyewitness was able to remember his or her observations and translate them into an accurate description of the perpetrator and what happened. The question then is, how accurate are witnesses' descriptions and identifications? What do you think the answer to this question is, based on what you know about perception, attention, and memory? The answer is that witness descriptions are often not very accurate, unless carried out under ideal conditions. Unfortunately, "ideal conditions" don't always occur, and there is a great deal of evidence that many innocent people have been convicted based on erroneous eyewitness identification.

Errors of Eyewitness Identification

In the United States, 300 people per day become criminal defendants based on eyewitness testimony (Goldstein et al., 1989). Unfortunately, there are many instances in which errors of eyewitness testimony have resulted in the conviction of innocent people. As of 2014, the use of DNA evidence had exonerated 349 people in the United States who had been wrongly convicted of crimes and served an average of 13 years in prison (Innocence Project, 2012; Time Special Edition, 2017). Seventy-five percent of these convictions involved eyewitness testimony (Quinlivan et al., 2010; Scheck et al., 2000).

To put a human face on the problem of wrongful convictions due to faulty eyewitness testimony, consider the case of David Webb, who was sentenced to up to 50 years in prison for rape, attempted rape, and attempted robbery based on eyewitness testimony. After serving 10 months, he was released after another man confessed to the crimes. Charles Clark went to prison for murder in 1938, based on eyewitness testimony that, 30 years later, was found to be inaccurate. He was released in 1968 (Loftus, 1979). Ronald Cotton was convicted of raping Jennifer Thompson in 1984, based on her testimony that she was extremely positive that he was the man who had raped her. Even after Cotton was exonerated by DNA evidence that implicated another man, Thompson still "remembered" Cotton as being her attacker. Cotton was released after serving 10 years (Wells & Quinlivan, 2009).

The disturbing thing about these examples is not only that they occurred, but that they suggest that many other innocent people are currently serving time for crimes they didn't commit. Many of these miscarriages of justice and others, some of which will undoubtedly never be discovered, are based on the assumption, made by jurors and judges, that people see and report things accurately.

This assumption about the accuracy of testimony is based on the popular conception that memory works like a camera or video recorder, as demonstrated by the results of the nationwide survey described at the beginning of this chapter (page 226). Jurors carry these misconceptions about the accuracy of memory into the courtroom, and many judges and law enforcement officials also share these misconceptions about memory (Benton et al., 2006; Howe, 2013). So, the first problem is that jurors don't understand the basic facts about memory. Another problem is that the observations on which witnesses base their testimony are often made under the less than ideal conditions that occur at a crime scene, and then afterward, when they are talking with the police. We will now consider a few of the situations that can create errors.

Errors Associated with Perception and Attention

Witness reports will, of course, be inaccurate if the witness doesn't perceive what happened in the first place. There is ample evidence that identifications are difficult even when participants in laboratory experiments have been instructed to pay close attention to what is happening. A number of experiments have presented participants with films of actual crimes or staged crimes and then asked them to pick the perpetrator from a photo spread (photographs of a number of faces, one of which could be the perpetrator). In one study, participants viewed a security videotape in which a gunman was in view for 8 seconds and then were asked to pick the gunman from photographs. Every participant picked someone they thought was the gunman, even though his picture was not included in the photo spread (Wells & Bradfield, 1998; also see Kneller et al., 2001).

Studies such as this show how difficult it is to accurately identify someone after viewing a videotape of a crime and how strong the inclination is to pick someone. But things become even more complicated when we consider some of the things that happen during actual crimes. Emotions often run high during commission of a crime, and this can affect what a person pays attention to and what they remember later.

In a study of **weapons focus**, the tendency to focus attention on a weapon that results in a narrowing of attention, Claudia Stanny and Thomas Johnson (2000) determined how well participants remembered details of a filmed simulated crime. They found that participants were more likely to recall details of the perpetrator, the victim, and the weapon in the "no-shoot" condition (a gun was present but not fired) than in the "shoot" condition (the

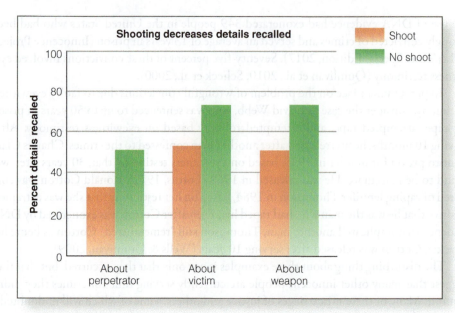

➤ **Figure 8.15** Results of Stanny and Johnson's (2000) weapons focus experiment. Presence of a weapon that was fired is associated with a decrease in memory about the perpetrator, the victim, and the weapon.

gun was fired; **Figure 8.15**). Apparently, the presence of a weapon that was fired distracted attention from other things that were happening (also see Tooley et al., 1987).

Misidentifications Due to Familiarity

Crimes not only involve a perpetrator and a victim but often include innocent bystanders (some of whom, as we will see, may not even be near the scene of the crime). These bystanders add yet another dimension to the testimony of eyewitnesses because there is a chance that a bystander could be mistakenly identified as a perpetrator because of familiarity from some other context. In one case of mistaken identification, a ticket agent at a railway station was robbed and subsequently identified a sailor as being the robber. Luckily for the sailor, he was able to show that he was somewhere else at the time of the crime. When asked why he identified the sailor, the ticket agent said that he looked familiar. The sailor looked familiar not because he was the robber, but because he lived near the train station and had purchased tickets from the agent on a number of occasions. This was an example of a source monitoring error. The ticket agent thought the source of his familiarity with the sailor was seeing him during the holdup; in reality, the source of his familiarity was seeing him when he purchased tickets. The sailor had become transformed from a ticket buyer into a holdup man by a source monitoring error (Ross et al., 1994).

Figure 8.16a shows the design for a laboratory experiment on familiarity and eyewitness testimony (Ross et al., 1994). Participants in the experimental group saw a film of a male teacher reading to students; participants in the control group saw a film of a female teacher reading to students. Participants in both groups then saw a film of the female teacher being robbed and were asked to pick the robber from a photo spread. The photographs did not include the actual robber, but did include the male teacher, who resembled the robber. The results indicate that participants in the experimental group, who had seen the male reading to the students, were three times more likely to pick the male teacher than were participants in the control group (**Figure 8.16b**). Even when the actual robber's face was included in the photo spread, 18 percent of participants in the experimental group picked the teacher, compared to 10 percent in the control group (**Figure 8.16c**). This is another example of how familiarity can result in errors of memory (see pages 238, 247).

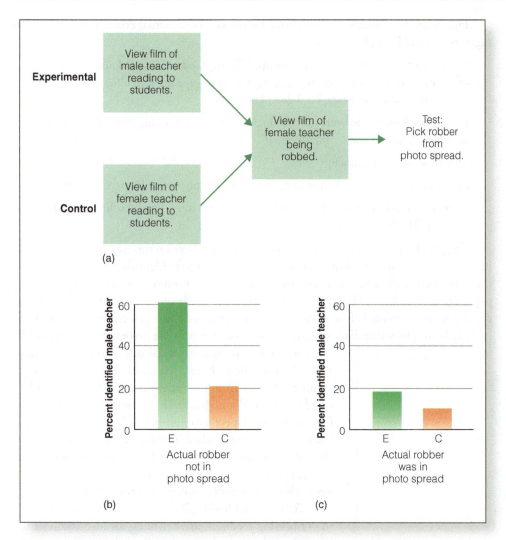

➤ **Figure 8.16** (a) Design of Ross et al.'s (1994) experiment on the effect of familiarity on eyewitness testimony. (b) When the actual robber was not in the photo spread, subjects in the experimental group erroneously identified the male teacher as the robber 60 percent of the time. (c) When the actual robber was in the photo spread, the male teacher was identified 18 percent of the time.

Errors Due to Suggestion

From what we know about the misinformation effect, it is obvious that a police officer asking a witness "Did you see the white car?" could influence the witness's later testimony about what he or she saw. But suggestibility can also operate on a more subtle level. Consider the following situation: A witness to a crime is looking through a one-way window at a lineup of six men standing on a stage. The police officer says, "Which one of these men did it?" What is wrong with this question?

The problem with the police officer's question is that it implies that the perpetrator is in the lineup. This suggestion increases the chances that the witness will pick someone, perhaps using the following type of reasoning: "Well, the guy with the beard looks more like the robber than any of the other men, so that's probably the one." Of course, looking like the robber and actually being the robber may be two different things, so the result may be identification of an innocent man. A better way of presenting the task is to let the witness know that the crime suspect may or may not be in the lineup.

Here is another situation, taken from a transcript of an actual criminal case, in which suggestion could have played a role.

Eyewitness to a crime on viewing a lineup: "Oh, my God.... I don't know.... It's one of those two ... but I don't know..... Oh, man .. the guy a little bit taller than number two.... It's one of those two, but I don't know."

Eyewitness 30 minutes later, still viewing the lineup and having difficulty making a decision: "I don't know ... number two?"

Officer administering lineup: "Okay."

Months later ... at trial: "You were positive it was number two? It wasn't a maybe?"

Answer from eyewitness: "There was no maybe about it.... I was absolutely positive." (Wells & Bradfield, 1998)

The problem with this scenario is that the police officer's response of "okay" may have influenced the witness to think that he or she had correctly identified the suspect. Thus, the witness's initially uncertain response turns into an "absolutely positive" response. In a paper titled "Good, You Identified the Suspect," Gary Wells and Amy Bradfield (1998) had participants view a video of an actual crime and then asked them to identify the perpetrator from a photo spread that did not actually contain a picture of the perpetrator (**Figure 8.17**).

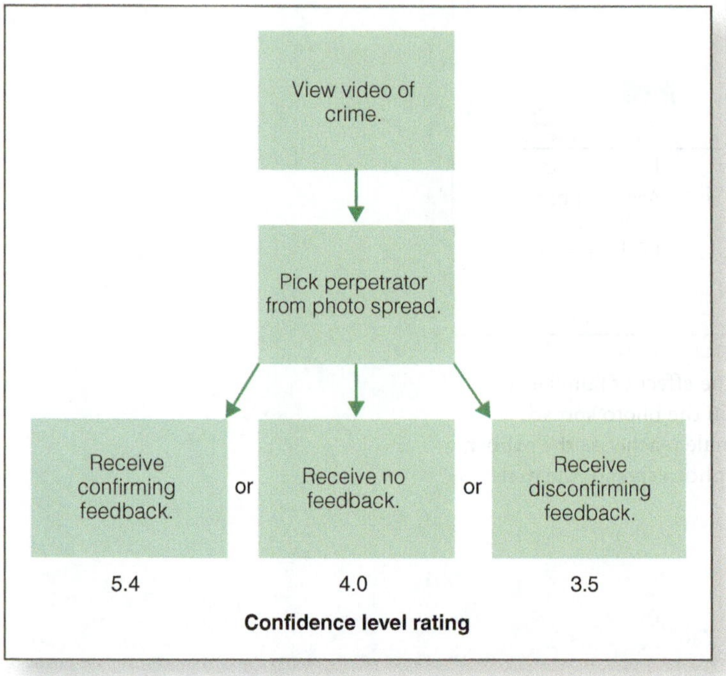

All of the participants picked one of the photographs, and following their choice, witnesses received either confirming feedback from the experimenter ("Good, you identified the suspect"), no feedback, or disconfirming feedback ("Actually, the suspect was number —"). A short time later, the participants were asked how confident they were about their identification. The results, shown at the bottom of the figure, indicate that participants who received the confirming feedback were more confident of their choice.

Wells and Bradfield call this increase in confidence due to confirming feedback after making an identification the **post-identification feedback effect**. This effect creates a serious problem in the criminal justice system, because jurors are strongly influenced by how confident eyewitnesses are about their judgments. Thus, faulty eyewitness judgments can result in picking the wrong person, and the post-identification feedback effect can then increase witnesses' confidence that they made the right judgment (Douglass et al., 2010; Luus & Wells, 1994; Quinlivan et al., 2010; Wells & Quinlivan, 2009).

The fact that memories become more susceptible to suggestion during questioning means that every precaution needs to be taken to avoid making suggestions to the witness. This is often not done, but some steps have been taken to help improve the situation.

> **Figure 8.17** Design and results of Wells and Bradfield's (1998) "Good, You Identified the Suspect" experiment. The type of feedback from the experimenter influenced subjects' confidence in their identification, with confirming feedback resulting in the highest confidence.

What Is Being Done to Improve Eyewitness Testimony?

The first step toward correcting the problem of inaccurate eyewitness testimony is to recognize that the problem exists. This has been achieved, largely through the efforts of memory researchers and attorneys and investigators for unjustly convicted people. The next step is to propose specific solutions. Cognitive psychologists have made suggestions about lineup procedures and interviewing procedures.

Lineup Procedures   Lineups are notorious for producing mistaken identifications. Here are some of the recommendations that have been made:

Recommendation 1: When asking a witness to pick the perpetrator from a lineup, inform the witness that the perpetrator may not be in the particular lineup he or she is viewing. This is important because when a witness assumes that the perpetrator is in the lineup, this increases the chances that an innocent person who looks similar to the perpetrator will be selected. In one experiment, telling participants that the perpetrator may not be present in a lineup caused a 42 percent decrease in false identifications of innocent people (Malpass & Devine, 1981).

Recommendation 2: When constructing a lineup, use "fillers" who are similar to the suspect. When R. C. L. Lindsay and Gary Wells (1980) had participants view a tape of a crime scene and then tested them using high-similarity and low-similarity lineups, they obtained the results shown in **Figure 8.18**. When the perpetrator was in the lineup, increasing similarity did decrease identification of the perpetrator, from 0.71 to 0.58 (**Figure 8.18a**). But when the perpetrator was not in the lineup, increasing similarity caused a large decrease in incorrect identification of an innocent person, from 0.70 to 0.31 (**Figure 8.18b**). Thus, increasing similarity does result in missed identification of some guilty suspects but substantially reduces the erroneous identification of innocent people, especially when the perpetrator is not in the lineup (also see Charman et al., 2011).

Recommendation 3: Use a "blind" lineup administrator—someone who doesn't know who the suspect is. This reduces the chances that the expectations of the person administering the lineup will bias the outcome.

Recommendation 4: Have witnesses rate their confidence immediately—as they are making their identification. Research shows that high confidence measured at the time of identification is associated with more accurate identifications (Wixted et al., 2015, but that confidence at the time of the trial is not a reliable predictor of eyewitness accuracy (National Academy of Sciences, 2014).[1]

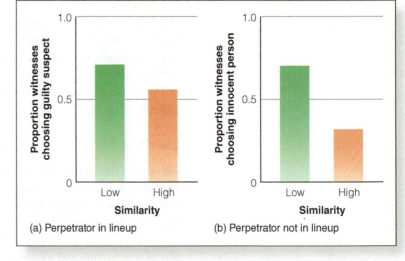

➤ **Figure 8.18** Results of Lindsay and Wells's (1980) experiment, showing that (a) when the perpetrator was in the lineup, increasing similarity decreased identification of the perpetrator, but (b) when the perpetrator was not in the lineup, increasing similarity caused an even greater decrease in incorrect identification of innocent people.

Interviewing Techniques   We have already seen that making suggestions to the witness ("Good, you identified the suspect") can cause errors. To avoid this problem, cognitive psychologists have developed an interview procedure called the **cognitive interview**, which involves letting the witness talk with a minimum of interruption and also uses techniques that help witnesses recreate the situation present at the crime scene by having them place themselves back in the scene and recreate things like emotions they were feeling, where they were looking, and how the scene might have appeared when viewed from different perspectives (Memon et al., 2010).

---

[1] In the last edition of this book, an additional recommendation was listed: Use sequential lineups (where the witness views the lineup photographs one by one) rather than the more traditional simultaneous lineup (when all of the people in the lineup are viewed together). This recommendation was based on research that showed that sequential presentation lessened the chances of misidentifying an innocent person when the perpetrator isn't present. However, further experiments have led to the conclusion that it is unclear whether the sequential procedure is, in fact, better (National Academy of Sciences, 2014; Wells, 2015).

An important feature of the cognitive interview technique is that it decreases the likelihood of any suggestive input by the person conducting the interview. Comparisons of the results of cognitive interviews to routine police questioning have shown that the cognitive interview results in a large increase in reports of correct details. A disadvantage of the cognitive interview is that it takes longer than standard interviewing procedures. To deal with this problem, shorter versions have been developed (Fisher et al., 2013; Geiselman et al., 1986; Memon et al., 2010).

Eliciting False Confessions

We've seen that suggestion can influence the accuracy of what a witness reports as having happened in a crime scene. But let's take this a step further and ask whether suggestion can influence how someone who is suspected of committing a crime might respond to questioning about the crime. Let's begin with a laboratory experiment.

Robert Nash and Kimberley Wade (2009) took videos of participants as they played a computerized gambling game. Participants were told that on a trial in which they won their gamble, a green check would appear on the screen and they should take money from the bank, but when they lost, a red cross would appear and they should give money back to the bank. After participants had played the game, they were shown a doctored video in which the green check was replaced by the red cross to make them appear to be cheating by taking money when they were supposed to be giving it to the bank (**Figure 8.19**). When confronted with the video "evidence," some participants expressed surprise, but all confessed to cheating. In another group, who were told there was a video of them cheating (but who didn't see the video), 73 percent of the participants confessed.

False confessions such as this have also been demonstrated in other experiments, including one by Julia Shaw and Stephen Porter (2015) in which student participants were made to believe that they had committed a crime that involved contact with the police. Like the experiment in which participants were presented with true events that had happened in childhood, plus a false event like tipping over a punch bowl at a wedding reception (p. 246), participants in Shaw and Porter's experiment were presented with a true event that had occurred when they were between 11 and 14 years old, and a false event that they had not experienced. The false event involved committing a crime such as assault, assault with a weapon, or theft, which resulted in police contact.

When first presented with information about the true and false events, participants reported that they remembered the true event, but that they didn't remember committing

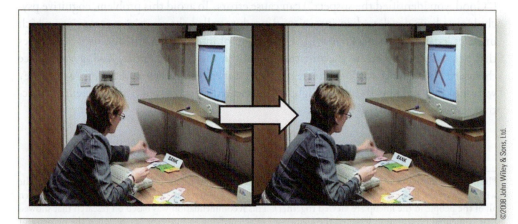

▶ **Figure 8.19** Stills from the video used by Nash and Wade (2009). The left panel is from the original video. The right panel is from the doctored video.

a crime. To induce creation of false memories for committing a crime, the interviewer used social pressure (statements like, "most people can retrieve lost memories if they try hard enough"), and provided instructions for a guided imagery procedure for visualizing the crime, which participants were told to practice every night at home.

When interviewed one- and two-weeks later, 70 percent of the participants reported that they did, in fact, remember the false event, and many reported details such as descriptions of the police officers. Thus, participants ended up believing they had committed a crime, and could provide details about the event, even though it never happened.

But it is one thing to admit to cheating or committing a crime in a laboratory experiment, and another thing to admit to a real crime, which might send you to jail. Flashback to a spring night in 1989, when a 28-year-old white woman was brutally raped and almost murdered while jogging through Central Park in New York. When five black and Hispanic teenage boys were brought in as suspects and were interrogated, all five eventually confessed to the crime. The boys came to be known as "The Central Park Five," and the case generated a huge amount of publicity. Although the police produced no physical evidence linking the boys to the crime, they were found guilty based on their confessions (which they had recanted shortly after being released from interrogation). They ended up spending a cumulative 41 years in prison. The only problem was that the boys were innocent.

Later, a convicted rapist and murderer, who was serving a life term, confessed to the crime—a confession that was backed up by DNA evidence found at the crime scene. The Central Park Five had their convictions vacated, and in 2003 they were awarded $41 million in compensation by New York City.

But, you might say, why would anyone confess to a crime they didn't commit, and, even more perplexing, why would five people confess to a crime they didn't commit? The answer to this question begins to emerge when we remember the laboratory "false confession" experiments we described above. In these experiments, participants confessed after rather mild suggestions from the experimenter, and some of them actually came to believe that they were "guilty."

But the confessions of the Central Park Five occurred after 14 to 30 hours of aggressive interrogation, in which the boys were presented with false evidence indicating they were guilty. According to Saul Kassin, who has studied false confessions for over 35 years, most false confessions involve fake evidence presented to the suspect by the police (Nesterack, 2014). In response to research by Kassin and others, the Department of Justice now requires that interrogations by recorded. Additionally, Kassin argues that police should be prohibited from presenting suspects with false evidence. This recommendation remains to be acted on (see Kassin et al., 2010; Kassin, 2012, 2015).

▶ SOMETHING TO CONSIDER

Music- and Odor-Elicited Autobiographical Memories

Walking along, not thinking about anything in particular, you enter a restaurant when—Bam!—out of the blue, a song playing in the background transports you back to a concert you attended over 10 years ago and also brings back memories about what was happening in your life when the song was popular. But in addition to just eliciting an autobiographical memory, the song also elicits emotions. Sometimes the memories elicited by music create a feeling called **nostalgia**, where nostalgia is defined as a memory that involves a sentimental affection for the past (Barrett et al., 2010). Memories elicited by hearing music are called **music-enhanced autobiographical memories (MEAMS)**.

These MEAMS are often experienced as being *involuntary memories*, because they occur as an automatic response to a stimulus (Berntsen & Rubin, 2008). This is in contrast to memories that require a conscious retrieval process, as might occur if you were asked to

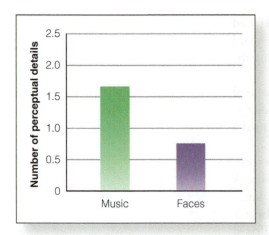

➤ **Figure 8.20** The average number of perceptual details in memories reported by Belfi et al.'s (2016) participants for memories elicited by listening to music and memories elicited by looking at pictures of faces.

(Source: Belfi et al., *Memory,* 24 (7), Figure 3, page 984, 2016.)

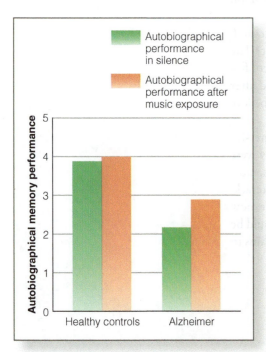

➤ **Figure 8.21** The results of El Haj et al.'s (2013) experiment, which showed normal control participants (left pair of bars) had better autobiographical memory than Alzheimer's patients (right pair of bars), and that the Alzheimer's patients' autobiographical memory was enhanced by listening to music that was meaningful to them.

(Source: El Haj et al., *Journal of Neurolinguistics,* 26, Fig 1, page 696, 2013.)

think back to your earliest memory or to remember what happened on the day you first arrived at college (Jack & Hayne, 2007; Janata et al., 2007).

The power of sensory experiences to elicit autobiographical memories was made famous in literature by Marcel Proust's (1922/1960) description, in his novel *Remembrance of Things Past,* of an experience after eating a small lemon cookie called a madeleine:

> "The sight of the little madeleine had recalled nothing to my mind before I tasted it … as soon as I had recognized the taste of the piece of madeleine soaked in her decoction of lime-blossom which my aunt used to give me … immediately the old grey house upon the street, where her room was, rose up like a stage set to attach itself to the little pavilion opening on to the garden which had been built out behind it for my parents … and with the house the … square where I used to be sent before lunch, the streets along which I used to run errands, the country roads we took when it was fine.

Proust's description of how taste and olfaction unlocked memories he hadn't thought of for years, now called the **Proust effect,** is not an uncommon experience, and it has also been observed in the laboratory. Rachel Herz and Jonathan Schooler (2002) had participants describe a personal memory associated with items like Crayola crayons, Coppertone suntan lotion, and Johnson's baby powder. After describing their memory associated with the objects, they were presented with an object either in visual form (a color photograph) or in odor form (smelling the object's odor) and were asked to think about the event they had described and to rate it on a number of scales. The result was that participants who smelled the odor rated their memories as more emotional than participants who saw the picture. They also had a stronger feeling than the visual group of "being brought back" to the time the memory occurred (also see Chu & Downes, 2002; Larsson & Willander, 2009; Reid et al., 2015; Toffolo et al., 2012).

High emotionality and detail have also been observed for music-elicited autobiographical memories. For example, Amy Belfi and coworkers (2016) demonstrated that music evokes vivid autobiographical memories. Their participants either listened to musical excerpts of songs popular when the participant was 15 to 30 years old or looked at pictures of faces of famous people who were popular during that age span. This range was picked because it corresponds to the reminiscence bump, which is when autobiographical memories are most likely (see page 228).

For songs and pictures that participants rated as being "autobiographical," the memories they described tended to be more vivid and detailed for the memories elicited by music than for the memories elicited by faces (**Figure 8.20**). In addition to eliciting detailed memories, MEAMS tend to elicit strong emotions (El Haj et al., 2012; Janeta et al., 2007).

The power of music to evoke memories has also been demonstrated in people with memory impairments caused by Alzheimer's disease. Mohamad El Haj and coworkers (2013) asked healthy control participants and participants with Alzheimer's to respond to the instruction "describe in detail an event in your life" after (1) two minutes of silence or (2) two minutes of listening to music that they had chosen. The healthy controls were able to describe autobiographical memories equally well in both conditions, but the memory of Alzheimer's patients was better after listening to the music (**Figure 8.21**).

The ability of music to elicit autobiographical memories in Alzheimer's patients inspired the film *Alive Inside* (Rossato-Bennett, director, 2014), which won the audience award at the 2014 Sundance Film Festival. This film documents the work of a nonprofit organization called Music & Memory (musicandmemory.org),

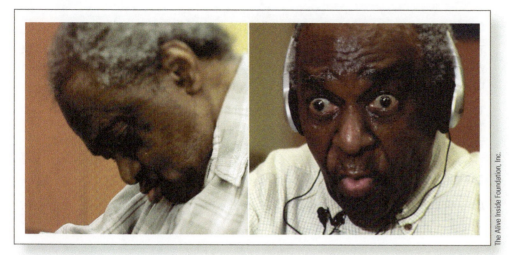

The Alive Inside Foundation, Inc.

➤ **Figure 8.22** Stills from the film *Alive Inside*. (a) Henry in his usual unresponsive state. (b) Henry listening and singing along with music that was meaningful to him. Listening to music also enhanced Henry's ability to talk with his caregivers.

which has distributed iPods to hundreds of long-term care facilities for use by Alzheimer's patients. In a memorable scene, Henry, who suffers from severe dementia, is shown immobile and unresponsive to questions and what is going on around him (**Figure 8.22a**). But when the therapist puts earphones on Henry and turns on the music, he comes alive. He starts moving to the beat. He sings along with the music. And, most important of all, memories that had been locked away by Henry's dementia are released, and he becomes able to talk about some things he remembers from his past (**Figure 8.22b**).

TEST YOURSELF 8.3

1. Describe experiments showing that memory can be affected by suggestion, which led to the proposal of the misinformation effect.

2. Describe Lindsay's experiment involving a maintenance man stealing. What does this experiment suggest about one of the causes of the misinformation effect?

3. How has it been shown that suggestion can influence people's memories for early childhood events?

4. Describe the idea of repressed childhood memory. How has it led to legal cases? What does the American Psychological Association's "white paper" say about repressed memories?

5. What is the evidence, both from "real life" and from laboratory experiments, that eyewitness testimony is not always accurate? Describe how the following factors have been shown to lead to errors in eyewitness testimony: weapons focus, familiarity, leading questions, feedback from a police officer, and postevent questioning.

6. What procedures have cognitive psychologists proposed to increase the accuracy of (a) lineups and (b) interviewing techniques?

7. Describe two laboratory experiments that elicited false confessions from participants.

8. Describe the case of the "Central Park Five." What implications does this case have for criminal interrogation procedures?

9. Describe examples of how odor and music can enhance autobiographical memories. How have music-enhanced autobiographical memories been used with Alzheimer's patients?

DEMONSTRATION   Reading Sentences (Continued)

The sentences below are the ones you read in the demonstration on page 240 but with one or two words missing. Without looking back at the original sentences, fill in the blanks with the words that were in the sentences you initially read.

The flimsy shelf _____ under the weight of the books.
The children's snowman _____ when the temperature reached 80.
The absentminded professor _____ his car keys.
The new baby _____ all night.
The karate champion _____ the cinder block.

After doing this, return to page 240 and read the text that follows the demonstration.

CHAPTER SUMMARY

1. A nationwide poll has shown that a substantial proportion of people have erroneous conceptions about the nature of memory.

2. Autobiographical memory has been defined as memory for specific experiences from our life. It consists of both episodic and semantic components.

3. The multidimensional nature of autobiographical memory has been studied by showing that people who have lost their visual memory due to brain damage experience a loss of autobiographical memory. Also supporting the multidimensional nature of autobiographical memory is Cabeza's experiment, which showed that a person's brain is more extensively activated when viewing photographs taken by the person himself or herself than when viewing photographs taken by someone else.

4. When people are asked to remember events over their lifetime, transition points are particularly memorable. Also, people over age 40 tend to have good memory for events they experienced from adolescence to early adulthood. This is called the *reminiscence bump*.

5. The following hypotheses have been proposed to explain the reminiscence bump: (1) self-image, (2) cognitive, and (3) cultural life script.

6. Emotions are often associated with events that are easily remembered. The amygdala is a key structure for emotional memories, and emotion has been linked to improved memory consolidation.

7. Brown and Kulik proposed the term *flashbulb memory* to refer to a person's memory for the circumstances surrounding hearing about shocking, highly charged events. They proposed that these flashbulb memories are vivid and detailed, like photographs.

8. A number of experiments indicate that it is not accurate to equate flashbulb memories with photographs because, as time passes, people make many errors when reporting flashbulb memories. Studies of memories for hearing about the *Challenger* explosion showed that people's responses became more inaccurate with increasing time after the event.

9. Talarico and Rubin's study of people's memory for when they first heard about the 9/11 terrorist attack indicates that memory errors increased with time, just as for other memories, but that the 9/11 memories were more vivid and people remained more confident of the accuracy of their 9/11 memory.

10. The narrative rehearsal hypothesis proposes that enhanced memory for significant events may be caused by rehearsal. This rehearsal is often linked to TV coverage, as illustrated by the results of the Princess Diana study.

11. According to the constructive approach to memory, originally proposed by Bartlett based on his "War of the Ghosts" experiment, what people report as memories are constructed based on what actually happened plus additional factors such as the person's knowledge, experiences, and expectations.

12. Source monitoring is the process of determining the origins of our memories, knowledge, or beliefs. A source monitoring error occurs when the source of a memory is misidentified. Cryptomnesia (unconscious plagiarism) is an example of a source monitoring error.

13. The results of Jacoby's "Becoming Famous Overnight" experiment show how familiarity can lead to a source monitoring error.

14. The illusory truth effect occurs when repetition increases the perceived truth of a statement.

15. General world knowledge can cause memory errors. This is illustrated by Bartlett's "War of the Ghosts" experiment, pragmatic inference, schemas and scripts, and false recall and recognition.

16. Our knowledge about what is involved in a particular experience is a schema for that experience. The experiment in which participants were asked to remember what was in an office illustrates how schemas can cause errors in memory reports.

17. A *script* is a type of schema that involves our conception of the sequence of actions that usually occur during a particular experience. The "dentist experiment," in which a participant is asked to remember a paragraph about going to the dentist, illustrates how scripts can result in memory errors.

18. The experiment in which people were asked to recall a list of words related to sleep illustrates how our knowledge about things that belong together (for example, that *sleep* belongs with *bed*) can result in reporting words that were not on the original list.

19. Although people often think that it would be an advantage to have a photographic memory, the cases of S. and A.J. show that it may not be an advantage to be able to remember everything perfectly. The fact that our memory system does not store everything may even add to the survival value of the system.

20. Memory experiments in which misleading postevent information (MPI) is presented to participants indicate that memory can be influenced by suggestion. An example is Loftus's traffic accident experiment. Source monitoring errors have been proposed to explain the errors caused by misleading postevent information. Lindsay's experiment provides support for the source monitoring explanation.

21. An experiment by Hyman, in which he created false memories for a party, showed that it is possible to create false memories for early events in a person's life. False memories may have been involved in some cases of "recovered memories" of childhood abuse.

22. There is a great deal of evidence that innocent people have been convicted of crimes because of errors of eyewitness testimony. Some of the reasons for errors in eyewitness testimony are (1) not paying attention to all relevant details because of the emotional situation during a crime (weapons focus is one example of such an attentional effect); (2) errors due to familiarity, which can result in misidentification of an innocent person due to source monitoring error; (3) errors due to suggestion during questioning about a crime; and (4) increased confidence due to postevent feedback (the post-identification feedback effect).

23. Cognitive psychologists have suggested a number of ways to decrease errors in eyewitness testimony. These suggestions focus on improving procedures for conducting lineups and interviewing witnesses.

24. False confessions have been elicited from participants in laboratory experiments and in actual criminal cases. False confessions in criminal cases are often associated with strong suggestion combined with harsh interrogation procedures.

25. Autobiographical memories can be elicited by odors and by music. These rapid, often involuntary, autobiographical memories are often more emotional and vivid than memories created by a thoughtful retrieval process.

26. Music has been used to help Alzheimer's patients retrieve autobiographical memories.

THINK ABOUT IT

1. What do you remember about what you did on the most recent major holiday (Thanksgiving, Christmas, New Year's, etc.) or your birthday? What do you remember about what you did on the same day 1 year earlier? How do these memories differ in terms of (a) how difficult they were to remember, (b) how much detail you can remember, and (c) the accuracy of your memory? (How would you know if your answer to part c is correct?)

2. There have been a large number of reports of people unjustly imprisoned because of errors in eyewitness testimony, with more cases being reported every day, based on DNA evidence. Given this situation, how would you react to the proposal that eyewitness testimony no longer be admitted as evidence in courts of law?

3. Interview people of different ages regarding what they remember about their lives. How do your results fit with the results of autobiographical memory experiments, especially regarding the idea of a reminiscence bump in older people?

KEY TERMS

COGLAB EXPERIMENTS   Numbers in parentheses refer to the experiment number in CogLab.

False Memory (*33*)   Forgot It All Along (*34*)   Memory Judgement (*35*)

This scene, which occurred one morning as the sun was rising in Venice, may not be something you're used to seeing. Nonetheless, you are able to understand it, because of your vast knowledge of categories. Some of the categories that you can identify in this scene are people, lamps, buildings, statues, sidewalk pavers, sunlight and shadows. This chapter describes how people place things in specific categories, what placing something in a category indicates about that thing, and how things in the same category can be different. For example, the large buildings that line the walkway on the left and the small structure that the man and woman are walking towards can both be categorized as "buildings," even though they are very different. The people are all "humans," but some are males and some are females. As you will see, the study of categorization has been approached in a number of different ways, ranging from conducting behavioral experiments, to creating network models, to physiological research.

Conceptual Knowledge

9

SOME QUESTIONS WE WILL CONSIDER

▶ Why is it difficult to decide if a particular object belongs to a particular category, such as "chair," by looking up its definition? (267)

▶ How are the properties of various objects "filed away" in the mind? (276)

▶ How is information about different categories stored in the brain? (285)

What do you think about when you think about knowledge? Facts you need to know for the cognitive psychology exam? The names of people you know? The location of that favorite hard-to-find restaurant? What a black hole is? The list of what you know is vast, because you know about a lot of things. This way of thinking about knowledge is consistent with dictionary definitions of knowledge, such as the following:

Acquaintance with facts, truths, or principles, as from study or investigation.

—**Dictionary.com**

Familiarity, awareness, or understanding of someone or something, such as facts, information, descriptions or skills, which is acquired through experience or education by perceiving, discovering, or learning.

—**Wikipedia**

Definitions such as these capture most people's commonsense idea of what knowledge is. It is, in brief, what we *know*. But as indicated by the title of this chapter, we will be considering a narrower conception of knowledge, which cognitive psychologists call **conceptual knowledge**—knowledge that enables us to recognize objects and events and to make inferences about their properties.

Conceptual knowledge involves answering questions such as the following:

➤ When we encounter a new item or event in the world, how do we come to know what kind of thing it is?

➤ How do we tell which items in our environment are horses, bicycles, trees, lakes, newspapers?

➤ How do we tell dolphins from sharks, or planets from stars? What makes a lemon a lemon?

➤ What are the various kinds of 'things' in the world?" (Rogers & Cox, 2015).

We answer questions such as these all the time, usually without even realizing it. For example, imagine that you find yourself in an unfamiliar town, where you have never been before. As you walk down the street, you notice that many things are not exactly the same as what you would encounter if you were in your own town. On the other hand, there are many things that seem familiar. Cars pass by, there are buildings on either side of the street and a gas station on the corner, and a cat dashes across the street and makes it safely to the other side. Luckily, you know a lot about cars, buildings, gas stations, and cats, so you have no trouble understanding what is going on.

This chapter is about the conceptual knowledge that enables you to recognize and understand the objects in the street scene and the world. This knowledge exists in the form of *concepts*. **Concepts** have been defined in a number of ways, including "the mental representation of a class or individual" (Smith, 1989) and "categories of objects, events, and abstract ideas" (Kiefer & Pulvermüller, 2012). To express this in concrete terms, we can say that the concept "cat" is the answer to the question "What is a cat?" If your answer is that a cat is an animal that is furry, meows, can be petted, moves, and catches mice, you will have described some aspects of the concept "cat" (Kiefer & Pulvermüller, 2012).

Because we are interested in our knowledge about the world, we need to go beyond cats! When we start expanding our scope to dogs, automobiles, can openers, radishes, and roses, things start to become both more complicated and more interesting, because the question then becomes "How are all of these things organized in the mind?" One way we organize concepts is in terms of *categories*.

A **category** includes all possible examples of a particular concept. Thus, the category "cats" includes tabbies, Siamese cats, Persian cats, wildcats, leopards, and so on. Looked at in this way, concepts provide the rules for creating categories. Thus, the mental representation for "cat" would affect what animals we place in the "cat" category. Because concepts provide rules for sorting objects into categories, concepts and categories are often discussed together, and a great deal of research has focused on the process of **categorization**—the process by which things are placed in categories.

Categorization is something we do every time we place an object into a category, and once we have assigned an object to a category, we know a lot about it. For example, being able to say that the furry animal across the street is a "cat" provides a great deal of information about it (**Figure 9.1**). Categories have therefore been called "pointers to knowledge" (Yamauchi & Markman, 2000). Once you know that something is in a category, whether "cat," "gas station," or "impressionist painting," you can focus your energy on specifying what's special about this particular object (see Solomon et al., 1999).

Categorization not only helps understand what is happening in the environment, it also plays an essential role in enabling us to take action. For example, to spread jam on bread, you must recognize the jam jar, the bread, and the knife; realize their relevant properties (bread is soft unless it is toasted; knives are rigid, and jam is sticky); and know how to grasp the knife handle with the right grip to scrape the jam from its jar (Lambon Ralph et al., 2017).

Being able to place things in categories can also help us understand behaviors that we might otherwise find baffling. For example, if we see a man with the left side of his face painted black and the right side painted gold, we might wonder what is going on. However, once we note that the person is heading toward the football stadium and it is Sunday afternoon, we can categorize the person as a "Pittsburgh Steelers fan." Placing him in that

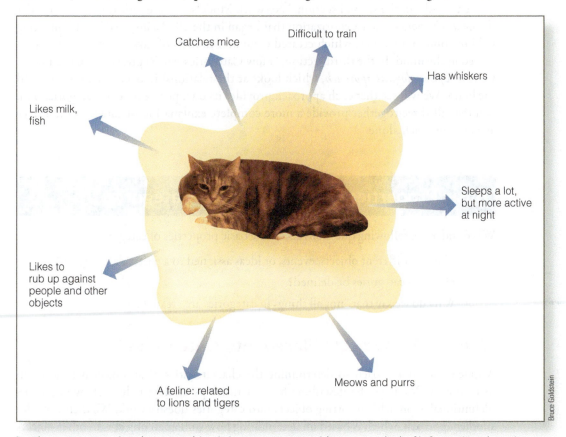

➤ **Figure 9.1** Knowing that something is in a category provides a great deal of information about it.

category explains his painted face and perhaps other strange behaviors that happen to be normal on game day in Pittsburgh (Solomon et al., 1999).

These various uses of categories testify to their importance in everyday life. It is no exaggeration to say that if there were no such thing as categories, we would have a very difficult time dealing with the world. Consider what it would mean if every time you saw a different object, you knew nothing about it other than what you could find out by investigating it individually. Clearly, life would become extremely complicated if we weren't able to rely on the knowledge provided to us by categories.

Yes, categories are important. But what do we need to know in order to understand categories? The answer to this question isn't obvious, because we routinely categorize things, so it seems like an automatic process. It's obvious that there's a *cat* sitting in a *chair*, across the *room*—*cat*, *chair*, and *room* being different categories. These things, and thousands of others, are so easy to categorize that there seems to be no problem to solve.

But as with other cognitive abilities, just because it's easy doesn't mean it's simple. Categorization becomes more difficult if you encounter something unfamiliar. "What is that over there? An aardvark? Very strange." Or things become even more difficult when a person suffers a brain injury that makes it difficult to identify different objects or know what they are used for. Once we understand that there are situations in which categorization becomes difficult, things become more interesting, because recognizing and understanding these difficulties is the first step to uncovering the mechanisms of categorization.

This chapter considers, in three major sections, the difficulties of categorization and the mechanisms involved in day-to-day categorization. Each of the three sections tells a story that involves a different approach to categorization. First, in the section "Basic Properties of Concepts and Categories," we consider a *behavioral approach* that originated with a series of experiments begun in the 1970s, which have helped us understand how we place objects in different categories and which have shown that "not all objects are created equal." In the second section, "Network Models of Categorization," we consider the *network approach* to categorization that began in the 1960s, inspired by the emerging field of computer science, which created computer models of how categories are represented in the mind. In the third section, "How Categories Are Represented in the Brain," we take a *physiological approach*, which looks at the relationship between categories and the brain. We will see that each approach provides its own perspective on categorization, and that all three together provide a more complete explanation of categorization than any one approach alone.

Basic Properties of Concepts and Categories

We consider the following questions about the basic properties of categories:

> ➤ How are different objects, events, or ideas assigned to a particular category?
> ➤ How can categories be defined?
> ➤ Why do we say that "not all things in categories are created equal"?

▶ How Are Objects Placed into Categories?

A time-honored approach to determining the characteristics of an object is to look up its definition. We begin by describing how cognitive psychologists have shown that this "definitional approach" to sorting objects into categories doesn't work. We then consider another approach, which is based on determining how similar an object is to other objects in a category.

Why Definitions Don't Work for Categories

According to the **definitional approach to categorization**, we can decide whether something is a member of a category by determining whether a particular object meets the definition of the category. Definitions work well for some things, such as geometric objects. Thus, defining a square as "a plane figure having four equal sides, with all internal angles the same" works. However, for most natural objects (such as birds, trees, and plants) and many human-made objects (like chairs), definitions do not work well at all.

The problem is that not all of the members of everyday categories have the same features. So, although the dictionary definition of a chair as "a piece of furniture consisting of a seat, legs, back, and often arms, designed to accommodate one person" may sound reasonable, there are objects we call "chairs" that don't meet that definition. For example, although the objects in **Figures 9.2a** and **9.2b** would be classified as chairs by this definition, the ones in **Figures 9.2c** and **9.2d** would not. Most chairs may have legs and a back, as specified in the definition, but most people would still call the disc-shaped furniture in Figure 9.2c a chair, and might go so far as to say that the rock formation in Figure 9.2d is being used as a chair.

The philosopher Ludwig Wittgenstein (1953) noted this problem with definitions and offered a solution:

> Consider for example the proceedings we call "games." I mean board-games, card-games, ball-games, Olympic games, and so on. For if you look at them you will not see something in common to all, but similarities, relationships, and a whole series of them at that. I can think of no better expression to characterize these similarities than "family resemblances."

(a)   (b)

(c)   (d)

Bruce Goldstein

➤ **Figure 9.2** Different objects, all possible "chairs."

Wittgenstein proposed the idea of **family resemblance** to deal with the problem that definitions often do not include all members of a category. Family resemblance refers to the idea that things in a particular category resemble one another in a number of ways. Thus, instead of setting definite criteria that every member of a category must meet, the family resemblance approach allows for some variation within a category. Chairs may come in many different sizes and shapes and may be made of different materials, but every chair does resemble other chairs in some way. Looking at category membership in this way, we can see that the chair in Figure 9.2a and the chair in Figure 9.2c do have in common that they offer a place to sit, a way to support a person's back, and perhaps a place to rest the arms while sitting.

In a series of experiments beginning in the 1970s, Eleanor Rosch and coworkers used the idea of family resemblance as a jumping off point for experiments that investigated the basic nature of categories. One of the early ideas to emerge from these experiments is the idea of prototypes.

The Prototype Approach: Finding the Average Case

According to the **prototype approach to categorization**, membership in a category is determined by comparing the object to a prototype that represents the category. A **prototype** is a "typical" member of the category.

What is a typical member of a category? Eleanor Rosch (1973) proposed that the "typical" prototype is based on an average of members of a category that are commonly experienced. For example, the prototype for the category "birds" might be based on some of the birds you usually see, such as sparrows, robins, and blue jays, but doesn't necessarily look exactly like any one of them. Thus, the prototype is not an actual member of the category but is an "average" representation of the category (**Figure 9.3**).

Of course, not all birds are like robins, blue jays, or sparrows. Owls, buzzards, and penguins are also birds. Rosch describes these variations within categories as representing differences in **typicality**. High typicality means that a category member closely resembles the category prototype (it is like a "typical" member of the category). Low typicality means that the category member does not closely resemble a typical member of the category. Rosch (1975a) quantified this idea by presenting participants with a category title, such as "bird" or "furniture," and a list of about 50 members of the category. The participants' task was to rate the extent to which each member represented the category title on a 7-point scale, with a rating of 1 meaning that the member is a very good example of what the category is, and a rating of 7 meaning that the member fits poorly within the category or is not a member at all.

▶ **Figure 9.3** Three real birds—a sparrow, a robin, and a blue jay—and a "prototype" bird that is the average representation of the category "birds."

Results for some of the objects in two different categories are shown in **Figure 9.4**. The 1.18 rating for sparrow reflects the fact that most people consider a sparrow to be a good example of a bird (**Figure 9.4a**). The 4.53 rating for penguin and 6.15 rating for bat reflect the fact that penguins and bats are not considered good examples of birds. Similarly, chair and sofa (rating = 1.04) are considered very good examples of furniture, but mirror (4.39) and telephone (6.68) are poor examples (**Figure 9.4b**). The idea that a sparrow is a better example of "bird" than a penguin or a bat is not very surprising. But Rosch went beyond this obvious result by doing a series of experiments that demonstrated differences between good and bad examples of a category.

Prototypical Objects Have High Family Resemblance

How well do good and poor examples of a category compare to other items within the category? The following demonstration is based on an experiment by Rosch and Carolyn Mervis (1975).

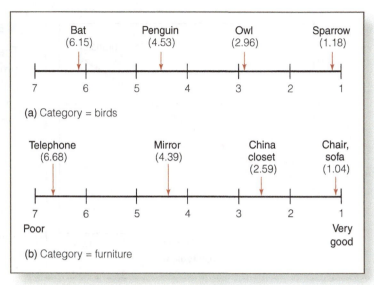

➤ **Figure 9.4** Results of Rosch's (1975a) experiment, in which participants judged objects on a scale of 1 (good example of a category) to 7 (poor example): (a) ratings for birds; (b) ratings for furniture.

DEMONSTRATION   Family Resemblance

Rosch and Mervis's (1975) instructions were as follows: For each of the following common objects, list as many characteristics and attributes as you can that you feel are common to these objects. For example, common characteristics for bicycles are two wheels, pedals, handlebars, you ride on them, they don't use fuel, and so on. Give yourself about a minute to write down the characteristics for each of the following items:

1. chair
2. mirror
3. sofa
4. telephone

If you responded like Rosch and Mervis's participants, you assigned many of the same characteristics to chair and sofa. For example, chairs and sofas share the characteristics of having legs, having backs, you sit on them, they can have cushions, and so on. When an item's characteristics have a large amount of overlap with the characteristics of many other items in a category, this means that the family resemblance of these items is high. But when we consider mirror and telephone, we find that there is far less overlap, even though they were both classified by Rosch and Mervis as "furniture" (Figure 9.4b). Little overlap with other members of a category means the family resemblance is low.

Rosch and Mervis concluded from their results that there is a strong relationship between family resemblance and prototypicality. Thus, good examples of the category "furniture," such as chair and sofa, share many attributes with other members of this category; poor examples, like mirror and telephone, do not. In addition to the connection between prototypicality and family resemblance, researchers have determined a number of other connections between prototypicality and behavior.

Statements About Prototypical Objects Are Verified Rapidly

Edward Smith and coworkers (1974) used a procedure called the **sentence verification technique** to determine how rapidly people could answer questions about an object's category.

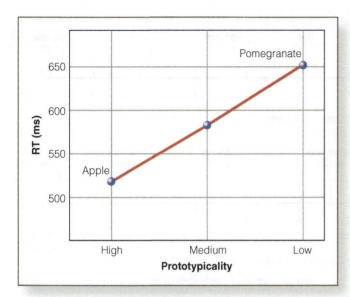

➤ **Figure 9.5** Results of E. E. Smith et al.'s (1974) sentence verification experiment. Reaction time (RT) was faster for objects rated higher in prototypicality.

METHOD Sentence Verification Technique

The procedure for the sentence verification technique is simple. Participants are presented with statements and are asked to answer "yes" if they think the statement is true and "no" if they think it isn't. Try this yourself for the following two statements:

An apple is a fruit.

A pomegranate is a fruit.

When Smith and coworkers (1974) used this technique, they found that participants responded faster for objects that are high in prototypicality (like apple for the category "fruit") than they did for objects that are low in prototypicality (like pomegranate; **Figure 9.5**). This ability to judge highly prototypical objects more rapidly is called the **typicality effect**.

Prototypical Objects Are Named First   When participants are asked to list as many objects in a category as possible, they tend to list the most prototypical members of the category first (Mervis et al., 1976). Thus, for "birds," sparrow would be named before penguin.

Prototypical Objects Are Affected More by Priming   **Priming** occurs when presentation of one stimulus facilitates the response to another stimulus that usually follows closely in time (see Chapter 6, page 182). Rosch (1975b) demonstrated that prototypical members of a category are more affected by a priming stimulus than are nonprototypical members. The procedure for Rosch's experiment is shown in **Figure 9.6**. Participants first heard the prime, which was the name of a color, such as "green." Two seconds later they saw a pair of colors side by side and indicated, by pressing a key as quickly as possible, whether the two colors were the same or different.

The side-by-side colors that participants saw after hearing the prime were paired in three different ways: (1) colors were the same and were good examples of the category (primary reds, blues, greens, etc.; **Figure 9.6a**); (2) colors were the same but were poor examples of the category (less rich versions of the good colors, such as light blue, light green, etc.; **Figure 9.6b**); (3) colors were different, with the two colors coming from different categories (for example, pairing red with blue; **Figure 9.6c**).

The most important result occurred for the two "same" groups. In this condition, priming resulted in faster "same" judgments for the prototypical (good) colors (reaction time, RT = 610 ms) than for the nonprototypical (poor) colors (RT = 780 ms). Thus, when participants heard the word *green*, they judged two patches of primary green as being the same more rapidly than two patches of light green.

Rosch explains this result as follows: When participants hear the word *green*, they imagine a "good" (highly prototypical) green (**Figure 9.7a**). The principle behind priming is that the prime will facilitate the participants' response to a stimulus if it contains some of the information needed to respond to the stimulus. This apparently occurs when the good greens are presented in the test (**Figure 9.7b**), but not when the poor greens are presented (**Figure 9.7c**). Thus, the results of the priming experiments support the idea that participants create images of prototypes in response to color names. **Table 9.1** summarizes the various ways that prototypicality affects behavior.

The prototype approach to categorization, and in particular Rosch's pioneering research, represented a great advance over the definitional approach because it provided a

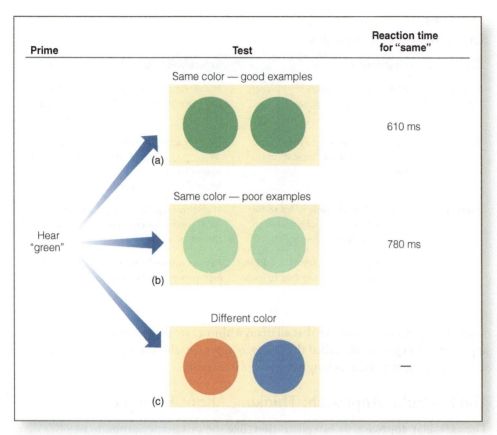

➤ **Figure 9.6** Procedure for Rosch's (1975b) priming experiment. Results for the conditions when the test colors were the same are shown on the right. (a) The person's "green" prototype matches the good green but (b) is a poor match for the light green; (c) shows the condition in which colors were different.

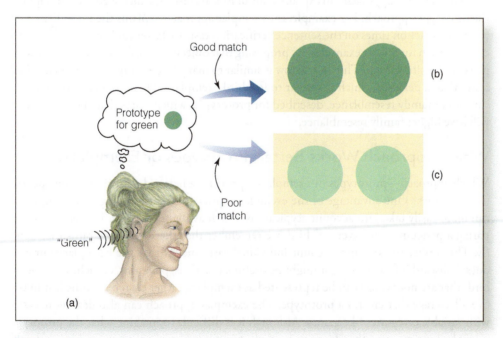

➤ **Figure 9.7** How Rosch explains the finding that priming resulted in faster "same" judgments for prototypical colors than for nonprototypical colors.

TABLE 9.1

Some Effects of Prototypicality

Effect	Description	Experimental Result
Family resemblance	Things in a category resemble each other in a number of ways.	Higher ratings for high-prototypical items when people rate how "good" a member of the category it is (Rosch, 1975a).
Typicality	People react rapidly to members of a category that are "typical" of the category.	Faster reaction time to statements like "A _____ is a bird" for high-prototypical items (like robin) than for low-prototypical items (like ostrich) (Smith et al., 1974).
Naming	People are more likely to list some objects than others when asked to name objects in a category.	High-prototypical items are named first when people list examples of a category (Mervis et al., 1976).
Priming	Presentation of one stimulus affects responses to a stimulus that follows.	Faster same–different color judgments for high-prototypical items (Rosch, 1975b).

wealth of experimental evidence that all items within a category are not the same. Another approach to categorization, called the *exemplar approach*, also takes into account the wide variation among items that belong to a particular category.

The Exemplar Approach: Thinking About Examples

The **exemplar approach to categorization**, like the prototype approach, involves determining whether an object is similar to other objects. However, whereas the standard for the prototype approach is a single "average" member of the category, the standard for the exemplar approach involves many examples, each one called an exemplar. **Exemplars** are actual members of the category that a person has encountered in the past. Thus, if a person has encountered sparrows, robins, and blue jays in the past, each of these would be an exemplar for the category "birds."

The exemplar approach can explain many of Rosch's results, which were used to support the prototype approach. For example, the exemplar approach explains the typicality effect (in which reaction times on the sentence verification task are faster for better examples of a category than for poorer examples) by proposing that objects that are like more of the exemplars are classified faster. Thus, a sparrow is similar to many bird exemplars, so it is classified faster than a penguin, which is similar to few bird exemplars. This is basically the same as the idea of family resemblance, described for prototypes, which states that "better" objects will have higher family resemblance.

Which Approach Works Better: Prototypes or Exemplars?

Which approach—prototypes or exemplars—provides a better description of how people use categories? One advantage of the exemplar approach is that by using real examples, it can more easily take into account atypical cases such as flightless birds. Rather than comparing a penguin to an "average" bird, we remember that there are some birds that don't fly. This ability to take into account individual cases means that the exemplar approach doesn't discard information that might be useful later. Thus, penguins, ostriches, and other birds that are not typical can be represented as exemplars, rather than becoming lost in the overall average that creates a prototype. The exemplar approach can also deal more easily with variable categories like games. Although it is difficult to imagine what the prototype might be for a category that contains football, computer games, solitaire, marbles, and golf, the exemplar approach requires only that we remember some of these varying examples.

Some researchers have concluded that people may use both approaches. It has been proposed that as we initially learn about a category, we may average exemplars into a prototype; then, later in learning, some of the exemplar information becomes stronger (Keri et al., 2002; Malt, 1989). Thus, early in learning, we would be poor at taking into account "exceptions" such as ostriches or penguins, but later, exemplars for these cases would be added to the category. We know generally what cats are—the prototype—but we know our own specific cat the best—an exemplar (Minda & Smith, 2001; Smith & Minda, 2000). A recent survey considering the virtues of both prototypes and exemplars ends with the following conclusion: "The two kinds of information work together to produce our rich store of conceptual knowledge allowing each kind of knowledge to explain the tasks that are most suited for it" (Murphy, 2016).

► Is There a Psychologically "Basic" Level of Categories?

As we have considered the prototype and exemplar approaches, we have used examples of categories such as "furniture," which contains members such as beds, chairs, and tables. But, as you can see in **Figure 9.8a**, the category "chairs" can contain smaller categories such as kitchen chairs and dining room chairs. This kind of organization, in which larger, more general categories are divided into smaller, more specific categories, creating a number of levels of categories, is called a **hierarchical organization.**

One question cognitive psychologists have asked about this organization is whether there is a "basic" level that is more psychologically basic or important than other levels. The research we will describe indicates that although it is possible to demonstrate that there is a basic level of categories with special psychological properties, the basic level may not be the same for everyone. We begin by describing Rosch's research, in which she introduced the idea of basic level categories.

Rosch's Approach: What's Special About Basic Level Categories?

Rosch's research starts with the observation that there are different levels of categories, ranging from general (like "furniture") to specific (like "kitchen table"), as shown in Figure 9.8, and that when people use categories, they tend to focus on one of these levels. She distinguished three levels of categories: (1) the **superordinate level**, which we will call the **global level** (for example, "furniture"); (2) the **basic level** (for example, "table"); and (3) the **subordinate level**, which we will call the **specific level** (for example, "kitchen table"). The following demonstration illustrates some characteristics of the different levels.

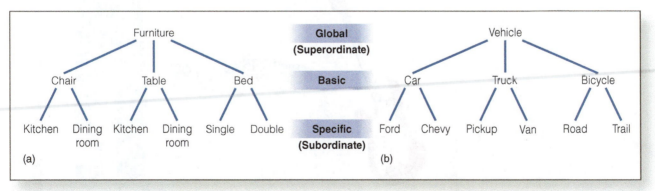

► **Figure 9.8** Levels of categories for (a) furniture and (b) vehicle. Rosch provided evidence for the idea that the basic level is "psychologically privileged."

LEVEL	EXAMPLE	NUMBER OF COMMON FEATURES	
Global	Furniture	3	Lose a lot of information.
Basic	Table	9	Gain just a little information.
Specific	Kitchen table	10.3	

➤ **Figure 9.9** Category levels, examples of each level, and average number of common features listed by participants in Rosch et al.'s (1976) experiment.

If you responded like the participants in the Rosch and coworkers' (1976) experiment, who were given the same task, you listed only a few features that were common to all furniture but many features that were shared by all tables and by all kitchen tables. Rosch's participants listed an average of 3 common features for the global level category "furniture," 9 for basic level categories such as "table," and 10.3 for specific level categories such as "kitchen table" (**Figure 9.9**).

Rosch proposed that the basic level is psychologically special because going above it (to global) results in a large loss of information (9 features at the basic versus 3 at the global level) and going below it (to specific) results in little gain of information (9 features versus 10.3). Here is another demonstration that is relevant to the idea of a basic level.

What names did you assign to each object? When Rosch and coworkers (1976) did a similar experiment, they found that people tended to pick a basic level name. They said *guitar* (basic level) rather than *musical instrument* (global) or *rock guitar* (specific), *fish* rather than *animal* or *trout*, and *pants* rather than *clothing* or *jeans*.

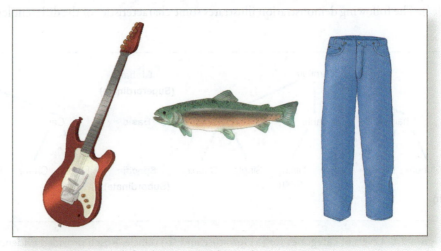

➤ **Figure 9.10** Stimuli for the Naming Things demonstration.

In another experiment, Rosch and coworkers showed participants a category label, such as *car* or *vehicle*, and then, after a brief delay, presented a picture. The participants' task was to indicate, as rapidly as possible, whether the picture was a member of the category. The results showed that they accomplished this task more rapidly for basic level categories (such as car) than for global level categories (such as vehicle). Thus, they would respond "yes" more rapidly when the picture of an automobile was preceded by the word *car* than when the picture was preceded by the word *vehicle*.

How Knowledge Can Affect Categorization

Rosch's experiments, which were carried out on college undergraduates, showed that there is a category level, which she called "basic," that reflects college undergraduates' everyday experience. This has been demonstrated by many researchers in addition to Rosch. Thus, when J. D. Coley and coworkers (1997) asked Northwestern University undergraduates to name, as specifically as possible, 44 different plants on a walk around campus, 75 percent of the responses used labels like "tree," rather than more specific labels like "oak."

But instead of asking college undergraduates to name plants, what if Coley had taken a group of horticulturalists around campus? Do you think they would have said "tree" or "oak"? An experiment by James Tanaka and Marjorie Taylor (1991) asked a similar question for birds. They asked bird experts and nonexperts to name pictures of objects. There were objects from many different categories (tools, clothing, flowers, etc.), but Tanaka and Taylor were interested in how the participants responded to the four bird pictures.

The results (**Figure 9.11**) show that the experts responded by specifying the birds' species (robin, sparrow, jay, or cardinal), but the nonexperts responded by saying "bird." Apparently, the experts had learned to pay attention to features of birds that nonexperts were unaware of. Thus, in order to fully understand how people categorize objects, we need to consider not only the properties of the objects but also the learning and experience of the people perceiving those objects (also see Johnson & Mervis, 1997).

From the result of Tanaka's bird experiment, we can guess that a horticulturist walking around campus would be likely to label plants more specifically than people who had little specific knowledge about plants. In fact, members of the Guatemalan Itzaj culture, who live in close contact with their natural environment, call an oak tree an "oak," not a "tree" (Coley et al., 1997).

Thus, the level that is "special"—meaning that people tend to focus on it—is not the same for everyone. Generally, people with more expertise and familiarity with a particular category tend to focus on the more specific information that Rosch associated with the specific level. This result isn't surprising, because our ability to categorize is learned from experience and depends on which objects we typically encounter and what characteristics of these objects we pay attention to.

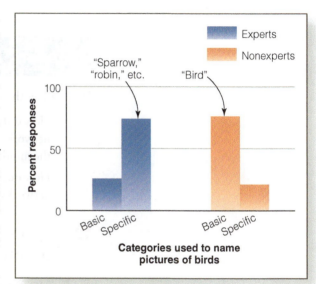

▶ **Figure 9.11** Results of Tanaka and Taylor's (1991) "expert" experiment. Experts (left pair of bars) used more specific categories to name birds, whereas nonexperts (right pair of bars) used more basic categories.

TEST YOURSELF 9.1

1. Why is the use of categories so important for our day-to-day functioning?

2. Describe the definitional approach to categories. Why does it initially seem like a good way of thinking about categories, but it then becomes troublesome when we consider the kinds of objects that can make up a category?

Network Models of Categorization

We consider the following questions about the network approach to categorization:

➤ How did an early network approach called the semantic network approach use networks of connected concepts to explain how these concepts are organized in the mind?

➤ How does a more modern network approach called connectionism describe how networks can be "trained" to recognize specific objects?

▶ Representing Relationships Among Categories: Semantic Networks

We have seen that categories can be arranged in a hierarchy of levels, from global (at the top) to specific (at the bottom). In this section, our main concern is to explain an approach to categories that focuses on how categories or concepts are organized in the mind. The approach we will be describing, called the **semantic network approach**, proposes that concepts are arranged in networks.

Introduction to Semantic Networks: Collins and Quillian's Hierarchical Model

One of the first semantic network models was based on the pioneering work of Ross Quillian (1967, 1969), whose goal was to develop a computer model of human memory. We will describe Quillian's approach by looking at a simplified version of his model proposed by Allan Collins and Quillian (1969).

Figure 9.12 shows Collins and Quillian's network. The network consists of nodes that are connected by links. Each node represents a category or concept, and concepts are placed in the network so that related concepts are connected. In addition, a number of properties are indicated for each concept.

The links connecting the concepts indicate how they are related to each other in the mind. Thus, the model shown in Figure 9.12 indicates that there is an association in the mind between *canary* and *bird*, and between *bird* and *animal* (indicated by the dashes along the links in Figure 9.12). It is a **hierarchical model**, because it consists of levels arranged so that more specific concepts, such as "canary" and "salmon," are at the bottom, and more general concepts are at higher levels.

We can illustrate how this network works, and how it proposes that knowledge about concepts is organized in the mind, by considering how we would retrieve the properties of canaries from the network. We start by entering the network at the concept node for "canary." At this node, we obtain the information that a canary can sing and is yellow.

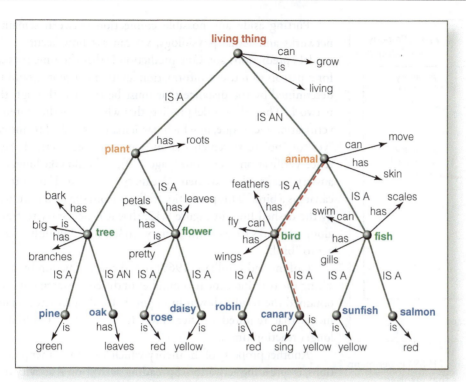

➤ **Figure 9.12** Collins and Quillian's (1969) semantic network. Specific concepts are indicated in color. Properties of concepts are indicated at the nodes for each concept. Additional properties of a concept can be determined by moving up the network, along the lines connecting the concepts. For example, moving from "canary" up to "bird" indicates that canaries have feathers and wings and can fly. The dashed lines indicate the distance in the network from canary to bird and from bird to animal.

(Source: Adapted from T. T. Rogers & J. L. McClelland, 2004)

To access more information about "canary," we move up the link and learn that a canary is a bird and that a bird has wings, can fly, and has feathers. Moving up another level, we find that a canary is also an animal, which has skin and can move, and finally we reach the level of living things, which tells us it can grow and is living.

You might wonder why we have to travel from "canary" to "bird" to find out that a canary can fly. That information could have been placed at the canary node, and then we would know it right away. But Collins and Quillian proposed that including "can fly" at the node for every bird (canary, robin, vulture, etc.) was inefficient and would use up too much storage space. Thus, instead of indicating the properties "can fly" and "has feathers" for every kind of bird, these properties are placed at the node for "bird" because this property holds for most birds. This way of storing shared properties just once at a higher-level node is called **cognitive economy**.

Although cognitive economy makes the network more efficient, it does create a problem because not all birds fly. To deal with this problem while still achieving the advantages of cognitive economy, Collins and Quillian added exceptions at lower nodes. For example, the node for "ostrich," which is not shown in this network, would indicate the property "can't fly."

How do the elements in this semantic network correspond to the actual operation of the brain? The links and nodes we have been describing do not necessarily correspond to specific nerve fibers or locations in the brain. The Collins and Quillian model is not meant to mirror physiology but to indicate how concepts and their properties are associated in the mind, and to make predictions about how we retrieve properties associated with a concept.

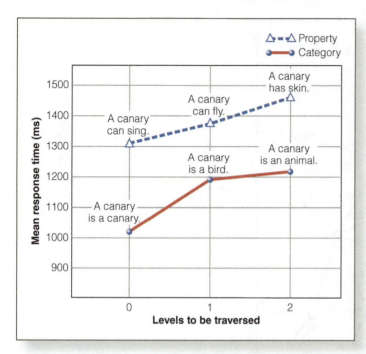

➤ **Figure 9.13** Results of Collins and Quillian's (1969) experiment that measured reaction times to statements that involved traversing different distances in the network. Greater distances are associated with longer reaction times, when verifying statements both about properties of canaries (top) and about categories of which the canary is a member (bottom).

(Source: A. M. Collins et al., 1969)

Putting aside any possible connection between semantic networks and actual physiology, we can ask how accurate the model's predictions are. One prediction is that the time it takes for a person to retrieve information about a concept should be determined by the distance that must be traveled through the network. Thus, the model predicts that when using the sentence verification technique, in which participants are asked to answer "yes" or "no" to statements about concepts (see Method: Sentence Verification Technique, page 270), it should take longer to answer "yes" to the statement "A canary is an animal" than to "A canary is a bird." This prediction follows from the fact, indicated by the dashed lines in Figure 9.12, that it is necessary to travel along two links to get from "canary" to "animal" but only one to get to "bird."

Collins and Quillian (1969) tested this prediction by measuring the reaction time to a number of different statements and obtained the results shown in **Figure 9.13**. As predicted, statements that required further travel from "canary" resulted in longer reaction times.

Another property of the theory, which leads to further predictions, is spreading activation. **Spreading activation** is activity that spreads out along any link that is connected to an activated node. For example, moving through the network from "robin" to "bird" activates the node at "bird" and the link we use to get from robin to bird, as indicated by the colored arrow in **Figure 9.14**. But according to the idea of spreading activation, this activation also spreads to other nodes in the network, as indicated by the dashed lines. Thus, activating the canary-to-bird pathway activates additional concepts that are connected to "bird," such as "animal" and other types of birds. The result of this spreading activation is that the additional concepts that receive this activation become "primed" and so can be retrieved more easily from memory.

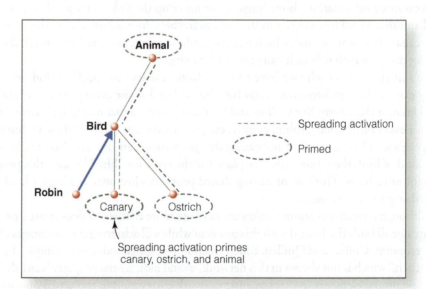

➤ **Figure 9.14** How activation can spread through a network as a person searches from "robin" to "bird" (blue arrow). The dashed lines indicate activation that is spreading from the activated bird node. Circled concepts, which have become primed, are easier to retrieve from memory because of the spreading activation.

The idea that spreading activation can influence priming was studied by David Meyer and Roger Schvaneveldt (1971) in a paper published shortly after Collins and Quillian's model was proposed. They used a method called the *lexical decision task*.

METHOD   Lexical Decision Task

In the **lexical decision task**, participants read stimuli, some of which are words and some of which are not words. Their task is to indicate as quickly as possible whether each entry is a word or a nonword. For example, the correct responses for *bloog* would be "no" and for *bloat* would be "yes."

Meyer and Schvaneveldt used a variation of the lexical decision task by presenting participants with pairs of words, one above the other, as shown below:

Pair 1	Pair 2	Pair 3	Pair 4
Fundt	Bleem	Chair	Bread
Glurb	Dress	Money	Wheat

The participants' task was to press, as quickly as possible, the "yes" key when both items were words or the "no" key when at least one item in the pair was a nonword. Thus, pairs 1 and 2 would require a "no" response, and pairs 3 and 4 would require a "yes" response.

The key variable in this experiment was the association between the pairs of real words. In some trials, the words were closely associated (like bread and wheat), and in some trials, they were weakly associated (chair and money). The result, shown in **Figure 9.15**, was that reaction time was faster when the two words were associated. Meyer and Schvaneveldt proposed that this might have occurred because retrieving one word from memory triggered a spread of activation to other nearby locations in a network. Because more activation would spread to words that were related, the response to the related words was faster than the response to unrelated words.

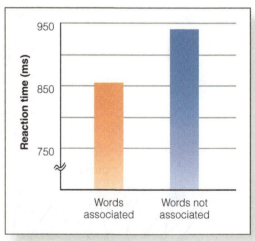

➤ **Figure 9.15** Results of Meyer and Schvaneveldt's (1971) experiment. Participants responded faster for words that were more closely associated (left bar).

Criticism of the Collins and Quillian Model

Although Collins and Quillian's model was supported by the results of a number of experiments, such as their reaction time experiment (Figure 9.13) and Meyer and Schvaneveldt's priming experiment, it didn't take long for other researchers to call the theory into question. They pointed out that the theory couldn't explain the *typicality effect*, in which reaction times for statements about an object are faster for more typical members of a category than for less typical members (see page 270; Rips et al., 1973). Thus, the statement "A canary is a bird" is verified more quickly than "An ostrich is a bird," but the model predicts equally fast reaction times because "canary" and "ostrich" are both one node away from "bird."

Researchers also questioned the concept of cognitive economy because of evidence that people may, in fact, store specific properties of concepts (like "has wings" for "canary") right at the node for that concept (Conrad, 1972). In addition, Lance Rips and coworkers (1973) obtained sentence verification results such as the following:

A pig is a mammal. RT = 1,476 ms

A pig is an animal. RT = 1,268 ms

"A pig is an animal" is verified more quickly, but as we can see from the network in **Figure 9.16**, the Collins and Quillian model predicts that "A pig is a mammal" should be

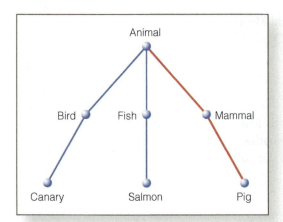

> ➤ **Figure 9.16** Semantic network that shows that "pig" is closer to "mammal" than to "animal."

verified more quickly because a link leads directly from "pig" to "mammal," but we need to travel one link past the "mammal" node to get to "animal." Sentence verification results such as these, plus the other criticisms of the theory, led researchers to look for alternative ways to using networks to describe how concepts are organized (Glass & Holyoak, 1975; Murphy et al., 2012) and eventually, in the 1980s, to the proposal of a new approach to networks, called *connectionism*.

▶ The Connectionist Approach

Criticism of semantic networks, combined with advances in understanding how information is represented in the brain, led to the emergence of a new approach to explaining how knowledge is represented in the mind. In two volumes, both titled *Parallel Distributed Processing: Explorations in the Microstructure of Cognition* (McClelland & Rumelhart, 1986; Rumelhart & McClelland, 1986), James McClelland and David Rumelhart proposed a new approach called *connectionism*. This approach has gained favor among many researchers because (1) it is inspired by how information is represented in the brain; and (2) it can explain a number of findings, including how concepts are learned and how damage to the brain affects people's knowledge about concepts.

What Is a Connectionist Model?

Connectionism is an approach to creating computer models for representing cognitive processes. We will focus on connectionist models designed to represent concepts. These models are also called **parallel distributed processing (PDP)** models because, as we will see shortly, they propose that concepts are represented by activity that is distributed across a network.

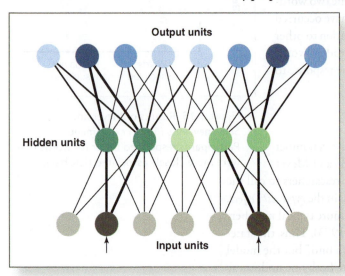

An example of a simple **connectionist network** is shown in **Figure 9.17**. The circles are **units**. These units are inspired by the neurons found in the brain. As we will see, concepts and their properties are represented in the network by the pattern of activity across these units.

The lines are connections that transfer information between units and are roughly equivalent to axons in the brain. Like neurons, some units can be activated by stimuli from the environment, and some can be activated by signals received from other units. Units activated by stimuli from the environment (or stimuli presented by the experimenter) are **input units**. In the simple network illustrated here, input units send signals to **hidden units**, which send signals to **output units**.

An additional feature of a connectionist network is connection weights. A **connection weight** determines how signals sent from one unit either increase or decrease the activity of the next unit. These weights correspond to what happens at a synapse that transmits signals from one neuron to another (Figure 2.4, page 29). In Chapter 7 we saw that some synapses can transmit signals more strongly than others and therefore cause a high firing rate in the next neuron (Figure 7.12, page 209). Other synapses can cause a decrease in the firing rate of the next neuron. Connection weights in a connectionist network operate in the same way. High connection weights result in a strong tendency to excite the next unit, lower weights cause less excitation, and negative weights can decrease excitation or inhibit activation of the receiving unit.

> ➤ **Figure 9.17** A parallel distributed processing (PDP) network showing input units, hidden units, and output units. Incoming stimuli, indicated by the arrows, activate the input units, and signals travel through the network, activating the hidden and output units. Activity of units is indicated by shading, with darker shading and heavier connector lines indicating more activity. The patterns of activity that occur in the hidden and output units are determined both by the initial activity of the input units and by the connection weights that determine how strongly a unit will be activated by incoming activity. Connection weights are not shown in this figure.

Activation of units in a network therefore depends on two things: (1) the signal that origi-nates in the input units and (2) the connection weights throughout the network.

In the network of Figure 9.17, two of the input units are receiving stimuli. Activation of each of the hidden and output units is indicated by the shading, with darker shading indicating more activation. These differences in activation, and the pattern of activity they create, are responsible for a basic principle of connectionism: A stimulus pre-sented to the input units is represented by the *pattern of activity* that is *distributed across the other units*. If this sounds familiar, it is because it is similar to the distributed representations in the brain we described in Chapters 2 (page 43) and 5 (page 154), Now that we have used the simple network in Figure 9.17, we will consider how some specific concepts are represented in the more complex connectionist network shown in **Figure 9.18**.

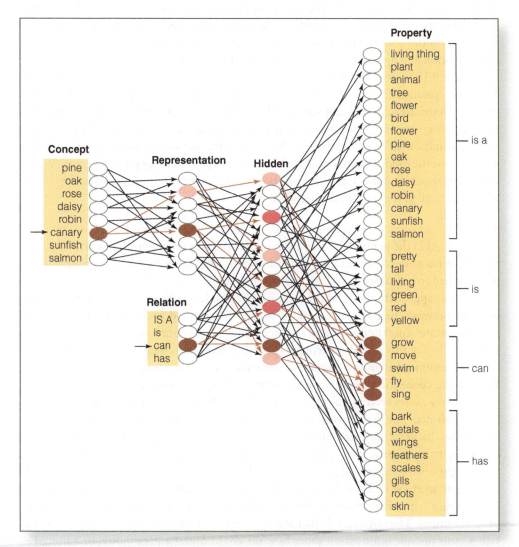

➤ **Figure 9.18** A connectionist network. Activation of an item unit ("canary") and a relation unit (*can*) causes activity to travel through the network that eventually results in activation of the property units *grow, move, fly,* and *sing,* associated with "canary can." Shading indicates the activity of the units, with darker shading indicating more activity. Note that only a few of the units and connections that would be activated by "canary" and *can* are shown as being activated. In the actual network, many more units and connections would be activated.

(Source: T. T. Rogers & J. L. McClelland, 2004)

How Are Concepts Represented in a Connectionist Network?

The model in Figure 9.18 was described by James McClelland and Timothy Rogers (2003) to show how different concepts and their properties can be represented in a connectionist network. Although this model is more complex than the one in Figure 9.17, it has similar components: units, links, and connection weights (although the connection weights are not shown).

Representing a Canary   Let's first compare this model to the Collins and Quillian hierarchical model in Figure 9.12. The first thing to notice is that both models are dealing with the same concepts. Specific concepts, such as "canary" and "salmon," shown in blue in Figure 9.12, are represented on the far left as concept items in Figure 9.18. Also notice that the properties of the concepts are indicated in both networks by the following four relation statements: "is a" (A canary is a bird); "is" (A canary is yellow); "can" (A canary can fly); and "has" (A canary has wings). But whereas the hierarchical network in Figure 9.12 represents these properties at the network's nodes, connectionist networks indicate these properties by activity in the attribute units on the far right, and also by the pattern of activity in the representation and hidden units in the middle of the network.

Figure 9.18 shows that when we activate the concept "canary" and a relation unit, *can,* activation spreads along the connections from "canary" and *can* so that some of the representation units are activated and some of the hidden units are activated. The connection weights, which are not shown, cause some units to be activated strongly and others more weakly, as indicated by the shading of the units. If the network is working properly, this activation in the hidden units activates the *grow, move, fly,* and *sing* property units. What's important about all of this activity is that the concept "canary" is represented by the pattern of activity in all of the units in the network.

Training a Network   According to the above description, the answer to "A canary can ..." is represented in the network by activation of the property units plus the pattern of activation of the network's representation and hidden units. But according to connectionism, this network had to be trained in order to achieve this result.

We can appreciate the need for training by considering **Figure 9.19**, which indicates how the network might have responded before training had occurred. In the untrained network, stimulating the *canary* and *can* units sends activity out to the rest of the network, with the effect of this activation depending on the connection weights between the units.

Let's assume that in our untrained network, all of the connection weights are 1.0. Because the connection weights are the same, activity spreads throughout the network, and property nodes such as flower, pine, and bark, which have nothing to do with canaries, are activated. For the network to operate properly, the connection weights have to be adjusted so that activating the concept unit "canary" and the relation unit *can* activates only the property units *grow, move, fly,* and *sing.* This adjustment of weights is achieved by a learning process. The learning process occurs when the erroneous responses in the property units cause an **error signal** to be sent back through the network, by a process called **back propagation** (since the signals are being sent *backward* in the network starting from the property units). The error signals that are sent back to the hidden units and the representation units provide information about how the connection weights should be adjusted so that the correct property units will be activated.

To explain the idea behind activation and back propagation, let's consider a behavioral example. A young child is watching a robin sitting on a branch, when suddenly the robin flies away. This simple observation, which strengthens the association between "robin" and *can fly,* would involve activation. But if the child were to see a canary and say "robin," the child's parent might correct her and say "That is a canary" and "Robins have red breasts." The information provided by the parent is similar to the idea of feedback provided by back propagation.

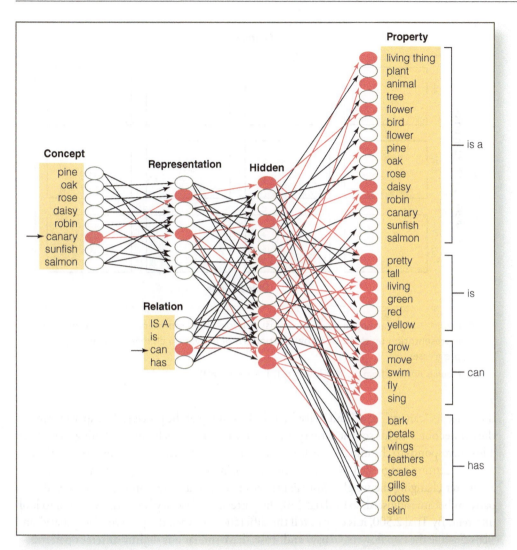

➤ **Figure 9.19** How the connectionist network in Figure 9.18 might respond before training, when all of the connection weights are 1.0. See text for details.

Thus, a child's learning about concepts begins with little information and some incorrect ideas, which are slowly modified in response both to observation of the environment and to feedback from others. Similarly, the connectionist network's learning about concepts begins with incorrect connection weights that result in the activation shown in Figure 9.19, which are slowly modified in response to error signals to create the correctly functioning network in Figure 9.18.

Although this "educated" network might work well for canaries, what happens when a robin flies by and alights on the branch of a pine tree? To be useful, this network needs to be able to represent not just canaries but also robins and pine trees. Thus, to create a network that can represent many different concepts, the network is not trained just on "canary." Instead, presentations of "canary" are interleaved with presentations of "robin," "pine tree," and so on, with small changes in connection weights made after each presentation.

We can appreciate how this learning process occurs over many trials by looking at the results of a computer simulation (McClelland & Rogers, 2003). The network in Figure 9.18 was presented with a number of different concepts and relation statements, one after another, and the activity of the units and connection weights between units were calculated by the computer. **Figure 9.20** indicates the activation of the eight representation units in response to

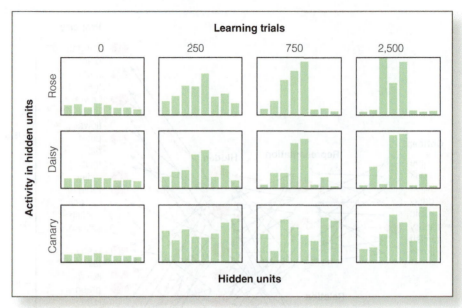

> **Figure 9.20** Learning in a connectionist network. Bars represent activity in the eight representation units. Notice how the pattern of activation changes as learning progresses.
(Source: Adapted from J. L. McClelland & T. T. Rogers, 2003)

the concepts "canary," "rose," and "daisy." At the beginning of the process, the experimenter set the connection weights so that activity was about the same in each unit (Learning trials = 0). This corresponds to the initially weak and undifferentiated activation we discussed earlier.

As learning progressed, with each concept being presented one after another and the computer changing the weights just slightly after each trial in response to error signals, the patterns became adjusted, so by Trial 250, the patterns for "canary" and "daisy" begin to look different. By Trial 2,500, it is easy to tell the difference between the patterns for "canary" and "daisy," while the two flowers, "daisy" and "rose," have similar but slightly different patterns.

Although our description has been based on one particular connectionist network, most networks have similar properties. Connectionist networks are created by a learning process that shapes the networks so information about each concept is contained in the distributed pattern of activity across a number of units.

Notice how different this operation of the connectionist network is from the operation of Collins and Quillian's hierarchical network, in which concepts and their properties are represented by activation of different nodes. Representation in a connectionist network is far more complex, involving many more units for each concept, but it is also much more like what happens in the brain.

Because of the resemblance between connectionist networks and the brain, and the fact that connectionist networks have been developed that can simulate normal cognitive functioning for processes such as language processing, memory, and cognitive development (Rogers & McClelland, 2004; Seidenberg & Zevin, 2006), many researchers believe that the idea that knowledge is represented by distributed activity holds great promise. The following results also support the idea of connectionism:

1. *The operation of connectionist networks is not totally disrupted by damage.* Because information in the network is distributed across many units, damage to the system does not completely disrupt its operation. This property, in which disruption of performance occurs only gradually as parts of the system are damaged, is called **graceful degradation**. It is similar to what often happens in actual cases of brain damage, in which damage to the brain causes only a partial loss of functioning.

Some researchers have suggested that studying the way networks respond to damage may suggest strategies for rehabilitation of human patients (Farah et al., 1993; Hinton & Shallice, 1991; Olson & Humphreys, 1997; Plaut, 1996).

2. *Connectionist networks can explain generalization of learning.* Because similar concepts have similar patterns, training a system to recognize the properties of one concept (such as "canary") also provides information about other, related concepts (such as "robin" or "sparrow"). This is similar to the way we actually learn about concepts because learning about canaries enables us to predict properties of different types of birds we've never seen (see McClelland et al., 1995).

While active research on connectionism continues in many laboratories, some researchers point out that there are limits to what connectionist networks can explain. Whatever the final verdict on connectionism, this approach has stimulated a great deal of research, some of which has added to our understanding of both normal cognition and how brain damage affects cognition. In the next section, we will focus even more directly on the brain by considering neuropsychological and brain imaging research on how concepts are represented in the brain.

TEST YOURSELF 9.2

1. What is the basic idea behind Collins and Quillian's semantic network approach? What is the goal of this approach, and how did the network created by Collins and Quillian accomplish this goal?
2. What is the evidence for and against the Collins and Quillian model?
3. What is a connectionist network? Describe how a connectionist network learns, considering specifically what happens to connection weights.
4. How does the way information is represented in a connectionist network differ from the way it is represented in a semantic network?
5. How are connectionist networks affected by damage? How is this similar to what happens in cases of brain damage?
6. How do connectionist networks explain generalization of learning?

How Concepts Are Represented in the Brain

We consider the following questions about how categories are represented in the brain:

➤ What do the results of neuropsychological research tell us about where different categories are represented in the brain?

➤ How has this neuropsychological research led to a number of different models that explain how categories are organized in the brain?

➤ What does brain imaging research tell us about how and where different categories are represented in the brain?

▶ Four Proposals About How Concepts Are Represented in the Brain

Early research on how concepts are represented in the brain was based on studying patients whose brain damage caused them to lose the ability to understand specific types of concepts. This research led to the proposal of the *sensory-functional hypothesis*.

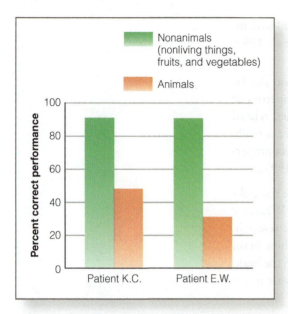

➤ **Figure 9.21** Performance on a naming task for patients K.C. and E.W., both of whom had category-specific memory impairment. They were able to correctly name pictures of nonliving things (such as car and table) and fruits and vegetables (such as tomato and pear) but performed poorly when asked to name pictures of animals.

(Source: B. Z. Mahon & A. Caramazza, 2009)

The Sensory-Functional Hypothesis

In one of the classic papers in neuropsychology, Elizabeth Warrington and Tim Shallice (1984) reported on four patients who had suffered memory loss from encephalitis. These patients had a **category-specific memory impairment**—an impairment in which they had lost the ability to identify one type of object but retained the ability to identify other types of objects. Specifically, these patients were able to identify nonanimals, like furniture and tools, as well as fruits and vegetables, but had impaired ability to identify animals (**Figure 9.21**). (As we discuss various cases next, we will use the term *artifacts* to refer to non-living things, which would include furniture and tools.)

To explain why this selective impairment occurred, Warrington and Shallice considered properties that people use to distinguish between artifacts and living things. They noted that distinguishing living things depends on perceiving their sensory features. For example, distinguishing between a tiger and a leopard depends on perceiving stripes and spots. Artifacts, in contrast, are more likely to be distinguished by their function. For example, a screwdriver, chisel, and hammer are all tools but are used for different purposes (turning screws, scraping, and pounding nails) (**Table 9.2**).

The observation that living things are distinguished by sensory properties and artifacts by functions led to the **sensory-functional (S-F) hypothesis**, which states that our ability to differentiate living things and artifacts depends on a memory system that distinguishes sensory attributes and a system that distinguishes functions.

While the S-F hypothesis explained the behavior of Warrington and Shallice's patients, plus dozens of other patients, researchers began describing cases that couldn't be explained by this hypothesis. For example, Matthew Lambon Ralph and coworkers (1998) studied a patient who had a sensory deficit—she performed poorly on perceptual tests—yet she was better at identifying animals than artifacts, which is the opposite of what the S-F hypothesis predicts. In addition, there are patients who are able to identify mechanical devices even if they perform poorly for other types of artifacts. For example, Hoffman and Lambon Ralph describe patients who have poor comprehension of small artifacts like tools but better knowledge of larger artifacts, such as vehicles (Cappa et al., 1998; Hillis et al., 1990; Warrington & McCarthy, 1987). Thus, "artifacts" are not a single homogeneous category as hypothesized by the S-F hypothesis. Results such as these have led many researchers to conclude that many effects of brain damage can't be explained by the simple distinction between sensory and function (Hoffman & Lambon, 2013).

TABLE 9.2

The Sensory-Functional Hypothesis

Relevant Information	Relevant to ...	Deficit in ability to process relevant information causes...
Sensory	Living things (Ex: a tiger has stripes)	Problems identifying living things
Functional	Artifacts (Ex: A hammer hits nails)	Problems identifying artifacts

The Multiple-Factor Approach

The idea of distributed representation is a central feature of the **multiple-factor approach**, which has led to searching for factors beyond sensory and functional that determine how concepts are divided within a category. We can appreciate this approach by posing the

TABLE 9.3

Sample Stimuli and Question Used in the Hoffman and Lambon Ralph (2013) Experiment

A. A Few of the 160 Items Presented to Subjects		
Mammal	Machine	Clothing
Pet	Vehicle	Weapon
Bird	Furniture	Tool
Door	Fish	Fruit

B. Question for Subjects	
How much do you associate (insert item from list above) with a particular . . .	
Color	Taste
Visual form	Smell
Motion	Tactile (Touch)
Sound	Performed action (in which you interact with the object)

following question: Assume that we start with a large number of items selected from lists of different types of animals, plants, and artifacts. If you wanted to arrange them in terms of how similar they are to each other, how would you do it? You could arrange them by shape, but then items like a pencil, a screwdriver, a person's finger, and a breakfast sausage might be grouped together. Or considering just color, you could end up placing fir trees, leprechauns, and Kermit the Frog together. Although it is true that members of specific categories do share similar perceptual attributes, it is also clear that we need to use more than just one or two features when grouping objects in terms of similarity.

Taking this idea as their starting point, researchers picked a number of different features and had participants rate a large number of items with regard to these features. This was the idea behind an experiment by Paul Hoffman and Matthew Lambon Ralph (2013), who used 160 items like the ones shown in **Table 9.3a**. The participants' task was to rate each item on the features shown in **Table 9.3b**. For example, for the concept "door," the participant would be asked "How much do you associate door with a particular color (or form, or motion, etc.)?" Participants assigned a rating of 7 for "very strongly" to 1 for "not at all."

The results, shown in **Figure 9.22**, indicate that animals were more highly associated with motion and color compared to artifacts, and artifacts were more highly associated with performed actions (actions associated with using or interacting with an object). This result conforms to the S-F hypothesis, but when Hoffman and Lambon Ralph looked at the groupings more closely, they found some interesting results. Mechanical devices such as machines, vehicles, and musical instruments overlapped with both artifacts (involving performed actions) and animals (involving sound and motion). For example, musical instruments are associated with specific actions (how you play them), which goes with artifacts, and are also associated with sensory properties (their visual form and the sounds they create), which goes with animals. Thus, musical instruments and some mechanical devices occupy a middle ground between artifacts and living things, because they can involve both action knowledge and sensory attributes.

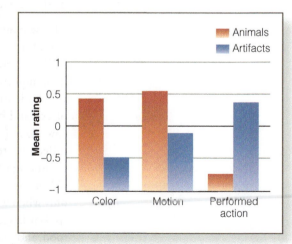

► **Figure 9.22** How participants rated animals and artifacts on color, motion, and performed actions. Animals are rated higher on color and motion; artifacts are rated higher on performed actions.

(Source: Based on data in P. Hoffman & M. A. Lambon Ralph, 2013)

> **Figure 9.23** Some animals and vehicles. Notice that the animals are more similar to each other than are the vehicles. This higher similarity of animals is called crowding.

Another factor that researchers have proposed to differentiate between animals and artifacts is **crowding**, which refers to the fact that animals tend to share many properties (like eyes, legs, and the ability to move). In contrast, artifacts like cars and boats share fewer properties, other than that they are both vehicles (**Figure 9.23**) (Rogers & Cox, 2015; Tyler & Moss 2001). This has led some researches to propose that patients who appear to have category-specific impairments, such as difficulty recognizing living things but not artifacts, don't really have a category-specific impairment at all. They propose that these patients have difficulty recognizing living things because they have difficulty distinguishing between items that share similar features. According to this idea, because animals tend to be more similar then artifacts, these patients find animals harder to recognize (Cree & McRae, 2003; Lambon Ralph et al., 2007).

The Semantic Category Approach

The **semantic category approach** proposes that there are specific neural circuits in the brain for some specific categories. According to Bradford Mahon and Alfonso Caramazza (2011), there are a limited number of categories that are innately determined because of their importance for survival. This idea is based on research that we described in Chapter 2, which identified areas of the brain that respond to specific types of stimuli such as faces, places, and bodies (page 42). In addition, we described an experiment by Alex Huth and coworkers (2012), which resulted in the map in Figure 2.20 (page 43), showing where different categories are represented in the cortex. This "category map" was determined by measuring fMRI responses as participants were viewing films, and determining how individual voxels responded to objects in the films. But semantic categories come into play not only when we look at a scene but also when we listen to someone speaking. Understanding spoken language involves not only knowing about concrete categories like living things, food, and places, but about abstract concepts like feelings, values, and thoughts.

To create a map based on spoken language, Huth and coworkers (2016) used a procedure similar to their earlier experiment, but instead of having their participants view films, they had them listen to more than two hours of stories from *The Moth Radio Hour* broadcast (themoth.org) while in a brain scanner. **Figure 9.24a** shows a map that extends over a large area of the cortex, which indicates were specific words activate the cortex. **Figure 9.24b** zooms in to make some of the words easier to read. **Figure 9.25** shows the

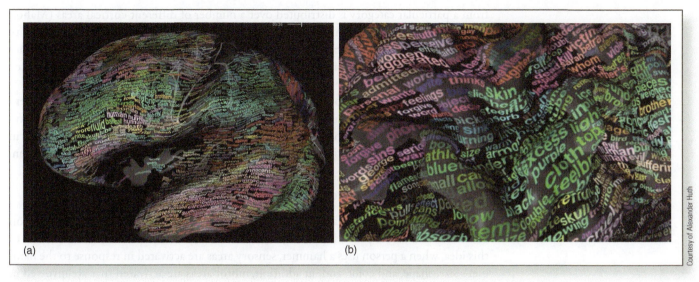

➤ **Figure 9.24** Results of the Huth et al. (2016) experiment in which participants listened to stories in a scanner. (a) Words that activated different places on the cortex. (b) Close-up of a smaller area of cortex. Note that a particular area usually responded to a number of different words, as indicated in Figure 9.25.

cortex color-coded to indicate where different categories of words activate the cortex. For example, the light area in the back of the brain is activated by words associated with violence. The words that activated a single voxel in that area are indicated on the right. Another voxel, which is activated by words associated with visual qualities, is shown in the green area near the top of the brain. An interesting aspect of Huth's results is that the maps were very similar for each of the seven participants.

While the semantic category approach focuses on areas of the brain that are specialized to respond to specific types of stimuli, it also emphasizes that the brain's response to items

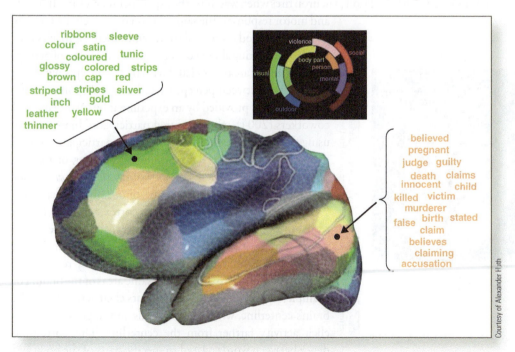

➤ **Figure 9.25** More results from the Huth et al. (2016) experiment. Colors on the cortex indicate where different categories of words caused activation, as indicated on the legend in the upper right. The pink words activated a voxel that responded to words related to violence. The green words activated a voxel that responded to visual qualities.

from a particular category is distributed over a number of different cortical areas (Mahon et al., 2007; Mahon & Caramazza, 2011). Thus, identifying faces may be based on activity in the face area in the temporal lobe (see Chapter 2, page 42), but it also depends on activity in areas that respond to emotions, facial expressions, where the face is looking, and the face's attractiveness (see page 43).

Similarly, the response to a hammer activates visual areas that respond to the hammer's shape and color, but it also causes activity in areas that respond to how a hammer is used and to a hammer's typical motions. This idea that some objects, like hammers, cause activity in areas of the brain associated with actions, brings us to the *embodied approach* to categorization.

The Embodied Approach

The **embodied approach** states that our knowledge of concepts is based on reactivation of sensory and motor processes that occur when we interact with the object. According to this idea, when a person uses a hammer, sensory areas are activated in response to the hammer's size, shape, and color, and, in addition, motor areas are activated that are involved in carrying out actions involved in using a hammer. When we see a hammer or read the word *hammer* later, these sensory and motor areas are reactivated, and it is this information that represents the hammer (Barsalou, 2008).

We can understand the basis of the embodied approach by returning to Chapter 3, where we described how perception and taking action interact, as when Crystal reached across the table to pick up a cup of coffee (page 81). The important message behind that example was that even simple actions involve a back-and-forth interaction between pathways in the brain involved in perception and pathways involved in taking action (see Figure 3.31, page 83) (Almeida et al., 2014).

Also in Chapter 3, we saw how *mirror neurons* in the prefrontal cortex fire both when a monkey performs an action and when the monkey sees the experimenter performing the same action (review pages 85–87; Figure 3.35). What do mirror neurons have to do with concepts? The link between perception (a neuron fires when watching the experimenter pick up the food) and motor responses (the same neuron fires when the monkey picks up the food) is central to the embodied approach's proposal that thinking about concepts causes activation of perceptual and motor areas associated with these concepts. Evidence for this link between perceptual and motor responses in the human brain is provided by an experiment by Olaf Hauk and coworkers (2004), who measured participants' brain activity using fMRI under two conditions: (1) as participants moved their right or left foot, left or right index finger, or tongue; (2) as participants read "action words" such as *kick* (foot action), *pick* (finger or hand action), or *lick* (tongue action).

The results show areas of the cortex activated by the actual movements (**Figure 9.26a**) and by reading the action words (**Figure 9.26b**). The activation is more extensive for actual movements, but the activation caused by reading the words occurs in approximately the same areas of the brain. For example, leg words and leg movements elicit activity near the brain's centerline, whereas arm words and finger movements elicit activity farther from the centerline. This correspondence between words related to specific parts of the body and the location of brain activity is called **semantic somatotopy**.

Although there is convincing evidence linking concepts and activation of motor areas in the brain, some researchers

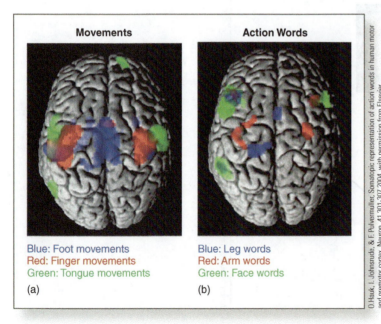

Movements

Action Words

Blue: Foot movements
Red: Finger movements
Green: Tongue movements

(a)

Blue: Leg words
Red: Arm words
Green: Face words

(b)

O. Hauk, I. Johnsrude, & F. Pulvermuller, Somatopic representation of action words in human motor and premotor cortex, Neuron, 41,301-307,2004, with permission from Elsevier.

➤ **Figure 9.26** Hauk et al. (2004) results. Colored areas indicate the areas of the brain activated by (a) foot, finger, and tongue movements; (b) leg, arm, and face words.

(Source: Hauk et al., 2004)

question whether the embodied approach offers a complete explanation of how the brain processes concepts (Almeida et al., 2013; Chatterjee, 2010; Dravida et al., 2013; Goldinger et al., 2016). For example, Frank Garcea and coworkers (2013) tested patient AA, who had suffered a stroke that affected his ability to produce actions associated with various objects. Thus, when AA was asked to use hand motions to indicate how he would use objects such as a hammer, scissors, and a feather duster, he was impaired compared to normal control participants in producing these actions. According to the embodied approach, a person who has trouble producing actions associated with objects should have trouble recognizing the objects. AA was, however, able to identify pictures of the objects. Garcea and coworkers concluded from this result that the ability to represent motor activity associated with actions is not necessary for recognizing objects, as the embodied approach would predict.

Another criticism of the embodied approach is that it isn't well suited to explaining our knowledge of abstract concepts such as "democracy" or "truth." However, proponents of the embodied approach have offered explanations in response to these criticisms (which we won't go into here; see Barsalou, 2005; Chatterjee, 2010).

Summarizing the Approaches

Our survey of how concepts are represented in the brain began with the sensory-functional approach, based on neuropsychological studies begun in the 1980s. But once it became clear that things were more complex than the distinction between sensory and functional, research led in different directions that resulted in more complex hypotheses.

One thing that all of the approaches agree on is that information about concepts is distributed across many structures in the brain, with each approach emphasizing different types of information. The multiple-factor approach emphasizes the role of many different features and properties. The category-specific approach emphasizes specialized areas of the brain and networks connecting these areas, and the embodied approach emphasizes activity caused by the sensory and motor properties of objects. It is likely that, as research on concepts in the brain continues, the final answer will contain elements of each of these approaches (Goldstone et al., 2012).

▶ Something to Consider: The Hub and Spoke Model

The ideas we have been discussing about how concepts are represented in the brain have been based largely on patients with category-specific memory impairments. However, there is another type of problem, called **semantic dementia**, which causes a general loss of knowledge for all concepts. Patients with semantic dementia tend to be equally deficient in identifying living things and artifacts (Patterson et al., 2007).

The generalized nature of the deficits experienced by semantic dementia patients, along with the finding that the **anterior temporal lobe (ATL)** (purple area in **Figure 9.27a**) is generally damaged in these patients, has led some researchers to propose the **hub and spoke model** of semantic knowledge. According to this model, areas of the brain that are associated with specific functions are connected to the ATL, which serves as a hub that integrates the information from these areas. These functions, indicated in Figure 9.27a, include valence—which is weak versus strong (yellow); speech (pink); auditory (red); praxis—which refers to involving manipulation (dark blue); functionality (light blue); and visual (green).

Evidence supporting the idea of a hub with spokes is that damage to one of the specialized brain areas (the spokes) can cause specific deficits, such as an inability to identify artifacts, but damage to the ATL (the hub) causes general deficits, as in semantic dementia (Lambon Ralph et al., 2017; Patterson et al., 2007). This difference between hub and spoke functions has also been demonstrated in non–brain-damaged participants using a technique called **transcranial magnetic stimulation (TMS)**.

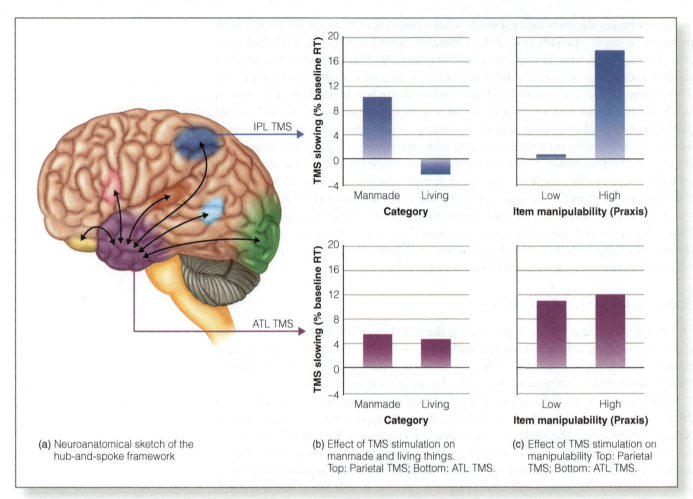

(a) Neuroanatomical sketch of the hub-and-spoke framework

(b) Effect of TMS stimulation on manmade and living things. Top: Parietal TMS; Bottom: ATL TMS.

(c) Effect of TMS stimulation on manipulability Top: Parietal TMS; Bottom: ATL TMS.

➤ **Figure 9.27** (a) The hub and spoke model proposes that areas of the brain specialized for different functions are linked to the anterior temporal lobe (purple), which integrates the information from areas that serve the following functions: Valence (yellow); speech (pink); auditory (red); praxis (dark blue); functionality (light blue); visual (green). The dark blue area is in the parietal cortex. (b) Effect of TMS stimulation on man-made objects versus living things. Top: Parietal stimulation causes more slowing of RT to man-made objects than to living things. Bottom: ATL stimulation causes the same effect on both. (c) Effect of TMS stimulation on low versus high manipulability objects. Top: Parietal stimulation causes more slowing of RT to high manipulability objects compared to low. Bottom: ATL stimulation causes the same effect on both.

(Source: Adapted from Lambon Ralph et al., 2017. Supplementary Figure 5. Based on data from Pobric et al., 2013.)

METHOD   Transcranial Magnetic Stimulation (TMS)

It is possible to temporarily disrupt the functioning of a particular area of the human brain by applying a pulsating magnetic field using a stimulating coil placed over the person's skull (**Figure 9.28**). A series of pulses presented to a particular area of the brain for seconds or minutes temporarily interferes with brain functioning in that area. If a particular behavior is disrupted by the pulses, researchers conclude that the disrupted area of the brain is involved in that behavior.

Gorana Pobric and coworkers (2010) presented pictures of living things and artifacts to participants and measured the response time for naming each picture. They then repeated this procedure while TMS was being applied either to the ATL or to an area in the parietal lobe that is normally activated when a person is manipulating an object. Figure 9.27b indicates that parietal inactivation (top) slowed reaction times for manmade objects but not for living objects, whereas ATL inactivation (bottom) caused the same effect for both manmade and living objects. Figure 9.27c indicates that parietal activation caused a large slowing in reaction time for highly manipulatable objects (like some tools) but not for non-manipulatable objects (like furniture), whereas ATL inactivation affected both types of objects equally. This result—a general effect of stimulating the "hub" (ATL), but a more specific effect of stimulating an area that would be associated with one of the "spokes" (parietal cortex)—supports the idea of a hub with general functions and spokes with more specific functions (Jefferies, 2013; Lambon-Ralph et al., 2017).

Most researchers agree that the ATL plays a role in integrating information from different areas. But it has also been suggested that other structures may be "hubs," or that the most important way concepts are represented is not by "hubs" but by the pattern of connections formed between the "spokes" (Pulvermüller, 2013). Thus, as we noted at the end of the last section, research on how concepts are represented in the brain is still a "work in progress."

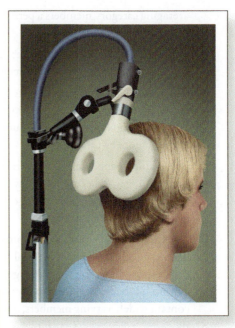

➤ **Figure 9.28** TMS coil positioned to present a magnetic field to a person's head. The coil in this position is stimulating the occipital lobe.

TEST YOURSELF 9.3

1. What is the sensory-functional hypothesis of brain categorization? Describe the neuropsychological evidence that supports this hypothesis.

2. Describe neuropsychological evidence that can't be explained by the S-F hypothesis.

3. What is the multiple-factor approach? How did research on non–brain-damaged participants support this approach?

4. What is crowding?

5. What is the semantic category approach? What do the results of Huth's imaging experiment in which participants had their brain scanned while listening to stories indicate about how concepts are represented in the brain?

6. What is the embodied approach?

7. What are mirror neurons and how are they related to the embodied approach?

8. Describe Hauk's brain imaging experiment that supports the embodied approach and Garcea's neuropsychology study that argues against the embodied approach.

9. What is the hub and spoke model? Where is the hub?

10. How do the results of transcranial magnetic stimulation experiments provide evidence for the hub and spoke model?

CHAPTER SUMMARY

1. Semantic memory is our memory for facts and knowledge.

2. Categories are "pointers to knowledge." Once you know something is in a category, you know a lot of general things about it and can focus your energy on specifying what is special about this particular object.

3. The definitional approach to categorization doesn't work because most categories contain members that do not conform to the definition. The philosopher Wittgenstein proposed the idea of family resemblances to deal with the fact that definitions do not include all members of a category.

4. The idea behind the prototypical approach to categorization is that we decide whether an object belongs to a category by deciding whether it is similar to a standard representative of the category, called a prototype. A prototype is formed by

averaging category members a person has encountered in the past.

5. *Prototypicality* is a term used to describe how well an object resembles the prototype of a particular category.

6. The following is true of high-prototypical objects: (a) they have high family resemblance; (b) statements about them are verified rapidly; (c) they are named first; and (d) they are affected more by priming.

7. The exemplar approach to categorization involves determining whether an object is similar to an exemplar. An exemplar is an actual member of a category that a person has encountered in the past.

8. An advantage to the exemplar approach is that it doesn't discard information about atypical cases within a category, such as penguin in the "bird" category. The exemplar approach can also deal more easily with categories that contain widely varying members, such as games.

9. Researchers have concluded that people use both approaches to categorization. Prototypes may be more important as people initially learn about categories; later, exemplar information may become more important.

10. The kind of organization in which larger, more general categories are divided into smaller, more specific categories is called hierarchical organization. Experiments by Rosch indicate that a basic level of categories (such as guitar, as opposed to musical instrument or rock guitar) is a "basic" level of categorization that reflects people's everyday experience.

11. Experiments in which experts were tested show that the basic level of categorization can depend on a person's degree of expertise.

12. The semantic network approach proposes that concepts are arranged in networks that represent the way concepts are organized in the mind. Collins and Quillian's model is a network that consists of nodes connected by links. Concepts and properties of concepts are located at the nodes. Properties that hold for most members of a concept are stored at higher level nodes. This is called cognitive economy.

13. Collins and Quillian's model is supported by the results of experiments using the sentence verification technique. The spreading activation feature of the model is supported by priming experiments.

14. The Collins and Quillian model has been criticized for several reasons: It can't explain the typicality effect, the idea of cognitive economy doesn't always hold, and it can't explain all results of sentence verification experiments.

15. The connectionist approach proposes that concepts are represented in networks that consist of input units, hidden units, and output units, and that information about concepts is represented in these networks by a distributed activation of these units. This approach is also called the parallel distributed processing (PDP) approach.

16. Connectionist networks learn the correct distributed pattern for a particular concept through a gradual learning process that involves adjusting the weights that determine how activation is transferred from one unit to another.

17. Connectionist networks have a number of features that enable them to reproduce many aspects of human concept formation.

18. Four approaches to explaining how concepts are represented in the brain are the sensory-functional hypothesis, the semantic category approach, the multiple-factor approach, and the embodied approach.

19. The hub and spoke model proposes that different functions in the brain are integrated by the anterior temporal lobe (ATL).

THINK ABOUT IT

1. In this chapter, we have seen how networks can be constructed that link different levels of concepts. In Chapter 7 we saw how networks can be constructed that organize knowledge about a particular topic (see Figure 7.5). Create a network that represents the material in this chapter by linking together things that are related. How is this network similar to or different from the semantic network in Figure 9.12? Is your network hierarchical? What information does it contain about each concept?

2. Do a survey to determine people's conception of "typical" members of various categories. For example, ask several people to name, as quickly as possible, three typical "birds" or "vehicles" or "beverages." What do the results of this survey tell you about what level is "basic" for different people? What do the results tell you about the variability of different people's conception of categories?

3. Try asking a number of people to name the objects pictured in Figure 9.10. Rosch, who ran her experiment in the early 1970s, found that the most common responses were guitar, fish, and pants. Notice whether the responses you receive are the same as or different from the responses reported by Rosch. If they are different, explain why you think this might have occurred.

KEY TERMS

Anterior temporal lobe (ATL), 291

Back propagation, 282

Basic level, 273

Categorization, 265

Category, 265

Category-specific memory impairment, 286

Cognitive economy, 277

Concept, 264

Conceptual knowledge, 264

Connection weight, 280

Connectionism, 280

Connectionist network, 280

Crowding, 288

Definitional approach to categorization, 266

Embodied approach, 290

Error signal, 282

Exemplar, 272

Exemplar approach to categorization, 272

Family resemblance, 268

Global level, 273

Graceful degradation, 284

Hidden units, 280

Hierarchical model, 276

Hierarchical organization, 273

Hub and spoke model, 291

Input units, 280

Lexical decision task, 279

Multiple-factor approach, 286

Output units, 280

Parallel distributed processing (PDP), 280

Priming, 270

Prototype, 268

Prototype approach to categorization, 268

Semantic category approach, 288

Semantic dementia, 291

Semantic network approach, 276

Semantic somatotopy, 290

Sensory-functional (S-F) hypothesis, 286

Sentence verification technique, 269

Specific level, 273

Spreading activation, 278

Subordinate (specific) level, 273

Superordinate (global) level, 273

Transcranial magnetic stimulation (TMS), 291

Typicality, 268

Typicality effect, 270

Unit (in a connectionist network), 280

COGLAB EXPERIMENTS   Numbers in parentheses refer to the experiment number in CogLab.

Lexical Decision (*41*)

Absolute Identification (*44*)

Prototypes (*46*)

dugdax/Shutterstock.com

"Visual imagery" occurs when a person sees in his or her mind something that isn't physically present. This picture symbolizes the finding that although visual perception and visual imagery share many properties, experiences associated with visual imagery can be less detailed and more fragile than experiences associated with visual perception.

Visual Imagery

10

SOME QUESTIONS WE WILL CONSIDER

▶ How do "pictures in your head" created by imagining an object compare to the experience you have when you see the actual object? (300, 312)

▶ How does damage to the brain affect the ability to form visual images? (310)

▶ How can we use visual imagery to improve memory? (312)

▶ How do people differ in their ability to create visual images? (314)

Answer the following questions:

➤ How many windows are there in front of the house or apartment where you live?
➤ How is the furniture arranged in your bedroom?
➤ Are an elephant's ears rounded or pointy?
➤ Is the green of grass darker or lighter than the green of a pine tree?

How did you go about answering these questions? If you experienced visual images when answering these questions, you were experiencing **visual imagery**—seeing in the absence of a visual stimulus (Hegarty, 2010). **Mental imagery**, a broader term that refers to the ability to re-create the sensory world in the absence of physical stimuli, is used to include all of the senses. People have the ability to imagine tastes, smells, and tactile experiences. Most people can imagine melodies of familiar songs in their head, so it is not surprising that musicians often report strong auditory imagery and that the ability to imagine melodies has played an important role in musical composition. Paul McCartney says that the song "Yesterday" came to him as a mental image when he woke up with the tune in his head. Another example of auditory imagery is orchestra conductors' using a technique called the "inner audition" to practice without their orchestras by imagining a musical score in their minds. When they do this, they imagine not only the sounds of the various instruments but also their locations relative to the podium.

Just as auditory imagery has played an important role in the creative process of music, visual imagery has resulted in both scientific insights and practical applications. One of the most famous accounts of how visual imagery led to scientific discovery is the story related by the 19th-century German chemist Friedrich August Kekule. Kekule said that the structure of benzene came to him in a dream in which he saw a writhing chain that formed a circle that resembled a snake, with its head swallowing its tail. This visual image gave Kekule the insight that the carbon atoms that make up the benzene molecule are arranged in a ring.

A more recent example of visual imagery leading to scientific discovery is Albert Einstein's description of how he developed the theory of relativity by imagining himself traveling beside a beam of light (Intons-Peterson, 1993). On a more athletic level, many competitors at the Olympics use mental imagery to visualize downhill ski runs, snowboarding moves, bobsled turns, and speedskating races (Clarey, 2014).

One message of these examples is that imagery provides a way of thinking that adds another dimension to the verbal techniques usually associated with thinking. But what is most important about imagery is that it is associated not just with discoveries by famous people but also with most people's everyday experience. In this chapter, we will focus on visual imagery, because most of the research on imagery has been on this type of imagery. We will describe the basic characteristics of visual imagery and how visual imagery relates to other cognitive processes such as thinking, memory, and perception. This connection between imagery and cognition in general is an important theme in the history of psychology, beginning in the early days of scientific psychology in the 19th century.

▶ Imagery in the History of Psychology

We can trace the history of imagery back to the first laboratory of psychology, founded by Wilhelm Wundt (see Chapter 1, page 7).

Early Ideas About Imagery

Wundt proposed that images were one of the three basic elements of consciousness, along with sensations and feelings. He also proposed that because images accompany thought, studying images was a way of studying thinking. This idea of a link between imagery and thinking gave rise to the **imageless thought debate**, with some psychologists taking up Aristotle's idea that "thought is impossible without an image" and others contending that thinking can occur without images.

Evidence supporting the idea that imagery was not required for thinking was Francis Galton's (1883) observation that people who had great difficulty forming visual images were still quite capable of thinking (also see Richardson, 1994, for more modern accounts of imagery differences between people). Other arguments both for and against the idea that images are necessary for thinking were proposed in the late 1800s and early 1900s, but these arguments and counterarguments ended when behaviorism toppled imagery from its central place in psychology (Watson, 1913; see Chapter 1, page 10). The behaviorists branded the study of imagery as unproductive because visual images are invisible to everyone except the person experiencing them. The founder of behaviorism, John Watson, described images as "unproven" and "mythological" (1928) and therefore not worthy of study. The dominance of behaviorism from the 1920s through the 1950s pushed the study of imagery out of mainstream psychology. However, this situation changed when the study of cognition was reborn in the 1950s.

Imagery and the Cognitive Revolution

The history of cognitive psychology that we described in Chapter 1 recounts events in the 1950s and 1960s that came to be known as the cognitive revolution. One of the keys to the success of this "revolution" was that cognitive psychologists developed ways to measure behavior that could be used to infer cognitive processes. One example of a method that linked behavior and cognition is Alan Paivio's (1963) work on memory. Paivio showed that it was easier to remember concrete nouns, like truck or tree, that can be imaged than it is to remember abstract nouns, like truth or justice, that are difficult to image. One technique Paivio used was paired-associate learning.

METHOD   Paired-Associate Learning

In a **paired-associate learning** experiment, participants are presented with pairs of words, like boat–hat or car–house, during a study period. They are then presented, during the test period, with the first word from each pair. Their task is to recall the word that was paired with it during the study period. Thus, if they were presented with the word boat, the correct response would be hat.

To explain the finding that memory for pairs of concrete nouns is better than memory for pairs of abstract nouns, Paivio (1963, 1965) proposed the **conceptual peg hypothesis**. According to this hypothesis, concrete nouns create images that other words can "hang onto." For example, if presenting the pair boat–hat creates an image of a boat, then presenting the word boat later will bring back the boat image, which provides a number of places on which participants can place the hat in their mind (see Paivio, 2006, for an updating of his ideas about memory).

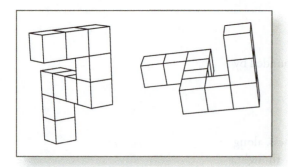

> **Figure 10.1** Stimuli for Shepard and Metzler's (1971) mental rotation experiment.
(Source: Shepard & Metzler, 1971)

Whereas Paivio inferred cognitive processes by measuring memory, Roger Shepard and Jacqueline Metzler (1971) inferred cognitive processes by using **mental chronometry**, determining the amount of time needed to carry out various cognitive tasks. In Shepard and Metzler's experiment, which we described in Chapter 5 (see page 146), participants saw pictures like the ones in **Figure 10.1**. Their task was to indicate, as rapidly as possible, whether the two pictures were of the same object or of different objects. This experiment showed that the time it took to decide that two views were of the same object was directly related to how different the angles were between the two views (see Figure 5.14, page 147). This result was interpreted as showing that participants were mentally rotating one of the views to see whether it matched the other one.

What was important about this experiment was that it was one of the first to apply quantitative methods to the study of imagery and to suggest that imagery and perception may share the same mechanisms. (References to "mechanisms" include both mental mechanisms, such as ways of manipulating perceptual and mental images in the mind, and brain mechanisms, such as which structures are involved in creating perceptual and mental images.)

We will now describe research that illustrates similarities between imagery and perception, and also the possibility that there is a basic difference between how imagery and perception are represented in the mind. As we will see, these comparisons have involved a large number of behavioral and physiological experiments, which demonstrate both similarities and differences between imagery and perception.

▶ Imagery and Perception: Do They Share the Same Mechanisms?

The idea that imagery and perception may share the same mechanisms is based on the observation that although mental images differ from perception in that they are not as vivid or long lasting, imagery shares many properties with perception. Shepard and Metzler's results showed that mental and perceptual images both involve spatial representation of the stimulus. That is, the spatial experience for both imagery and perception matches the layout of the actual stimulus. This idea, that there is a spatial correspondence between imagery and perception, is supported by a number of experiments by Stephen Kosslyn involving a task called **mental scanning**, in which participants create mental images and then scan them in their minds.

Kosslyn's Mental Scanning Experiments

Stephen Kosslyn has done enough research on imagery to fill three books (Kosslyn, 1980, 1994; Kosslyn et al., 2006), and he has proposed some influential theories of imagery based on parallels between imagery and perception. In one of his early experiments, Kosslyn (1973) asked participants to memorize a picture of an object, such as the boat in **Figure 10.2**, and then to create an image of that object in their mind and to focus on one part of the boat, such as the anchor. They were then asked to look for another part of the boat, such as the motor, and to press the "true" button when they found this part or the "false" button when they couldn't find it.

Kosslyn reasoned that if imagery, like perception, is spatial, then it should take longer for participants to find parts that are located farther from the initial point of focus because they would be scanning across the image of the object. This is actually what happened, and Kosslyn took this as evidence for the spatial nature of imagery. But, as often happens in science,

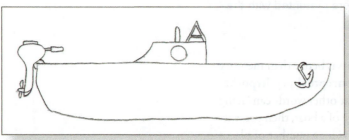

> **Figure 10.2** Stimulus for Kosslyn's (1973) image-scanning experiment.

another researcher proposed a different explanation. Glen Lea (1975) proposed that as participants scanned, they may have encountered other interesting parts, such as the cabin, and this distraction may have increased their reaction time.

To answer this concern, Kosslyn and coworkers (1978) did another scanning experiment, this time asking participants to scan between two places on a map. Before reading about Kosslyn's experiment, try the following demonstration.

METHOD/DEMONSTRATION Mental Scanning

Imagine a map of your state that includes three locations: the place where you live, a town that is far away, and another town that is closer but does not fall on a straight line connecting your location and the far town. For example, for my state, I imagine Pittsburgh, the place where I am now; Philadelphia, all the way across the state (contrary to some people's idea, Pittsburgh is not a suburb of Philadelphia!); and Erie, which is closer than Philadelphia but not in the same direction (**Figure 10.3**).

Your task is to create a mental image of your state and, starting at your location, to form an image of a black speck moving along a straight line between your location and the closer town. Be aware of about how long it took to arrive at this town. Then repeat the same procedure for the far town, again noting about how long it took to arrive.

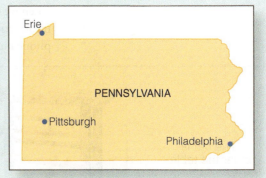

➤ **Figure 10.3** Example of a state map for the Mental Scanning method/demonstration. Use your own state for this method/demonstration.

Kosslyn's participants used the same procedure as you did for the demonstration but were told to imagine an island, like the one in **Figure 10.4a**, that contained seven different locations. By having participants scan between every possible pair of locations (a total of 21 trips), Kosslyn determined the relationship between reaction time and distance shown in **Figure 10.4b**. Just as in the boat experiment, it took longer to scan between greater distances on the image, a result that supports the idea that visual imagery is spatial in nature. As convincing as Kosslyn's results were, however, Zenon Pylyshyn (1973) proposed another

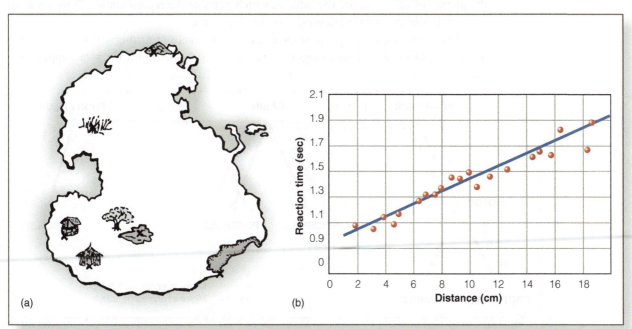

➤ **Figure 10.4** (a) Island used in Kosslyn et al.'s (1978) image-scanning experiment. Participants mentally traveled between various locations on the island. (b) Results of the island experiment.

(Source: Kosslyn, Ball, & Reiser, 1978)

explanation, which started what has been called the **imagery debate**—a debate about whether imagery is based on spatial mechanisms, such as those involved in perception, or on mechanisms related to language, called propositional mechanisms.

The Imagery Debate: Is Imagery Spatial or Propositional?

Much of the research we have described so far in this book is about determining the nature of the mental representations that lie behind different cognitive experiences. For example, when we considered short-term memory (STM) in Chapter 5, we presented evidence that information in STM is often represented in auditory form, as when you rehearse a telephone number you have just looked up.

Kosslyn interpreted the results of his research on imagery as supporting the idea that the mechanism responsible for imagery involves **spatial representations**—representations in which different parts of an image can be described as corresponding to specific locations in space. But Pylyshyn (1973) disagreed, saying that just because we *experience* imagery as spatial, that doesn't mean that the underlying representation is spatial. After all, one thing that is clear from research in cognitive psychology is that we often aren't aware of what is going on in our mind. The spatial experience of mental images, argues Pylyshyn, is an **epiphenomenon**—something that accompanies the real mechanism but is not actually part of the mechanism.

Pylyshyn proposed that, rather than the spatial representations suggested by Kosslyn, the mechanism underlying imagery involves **propositional representations**—representations in which relationships can be represented by abstract symbols, such as an equation, or a statement, such as "The cat is under the table."

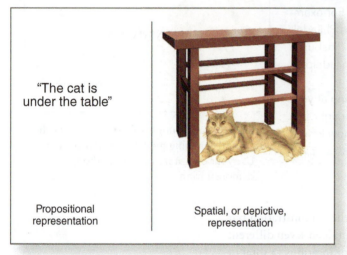

"The cat is under the table"

Propositional representation

Spatial, or depictive, representation

➤ **Figure 10.5** Propositional and spatial, or depictive, representations of "The cat is under the table."

In contrast, a spatial representation would involve a spatial layout showing the cat and the table that could be represented in a picture (**Figure 10.5**). Spatial representations such as the picture of the cat under the table in which parts of the representation correspond to parts of the object are called **depictive representations**.

We can understand the propositional approach better by returning to the depictive representation of Kosslyn's boat in Figure 10.2. **Figure 10.6** shows how the visual appearance

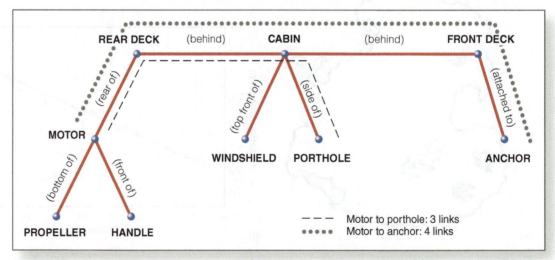

REAR DECK   (behind)   CABIN   (behind)   FRONT DECK

(rear of)

MOTOR

(top front of)   (side of)   (attached to)

WINDSHIELD   PORTHOLE   ANCHOR

(bottom of)   (front of)

PROPELLER   HANDLE

– – – Motor to porthole: 3 links
••••• Motor to anchor: 4 links

➤ **Figure 10.6** How the visual appearance of the boat in Figure 10.2 can be represented propositionally. Paths between motor and porthole (dashed line) and motor and anchor (dotted line) indicate the number of nodes that would be traversed between these parts of the boat.
(Source: Kosslyn et al., 1995)

of this boat can be represented propositionally. The words indicate parts of the boat, the length of the lines indicate the distances between the parts, and the words in parentheses indicate the spatial relations between the parts. A representation such as this would predict that when starting at the motor, it should take longer to scan and find the anchor than to find the porthole because it is necessary to travel across three links to get to the porthole (dashed line) and four links to get to the anchor (dotted line). This kind of explanation proposes that imagery operates in a way similar to the semantic networks we described in Chapter 9 (see page 276).

We've discussed both the spatial and the propositional approaches to imagery because these two explanations provide an excellent example of how data can be interpreted in different ways. (See Chapter 7, Something to Consider: Alternative Explanations in Cognitive Psychology, page 220.) Pylyshyn's criticisms stimulated a large number of experiments that have taught us a great deal about the nature of visual imagery (also see Intons-Peterson, 1983). However, after many years of discussion and experimentation, the weight of the evidence supports the idea that imagery is served by a spatial mechanism and that it shares mechanisms with perception. We will now look at additional evidence that supports the idea of spatial representation.

Comparing Imagery and Perception

We begin by describing another experiment by Kosslyn. This one looks at how imagery is affected by the size of an object in a person's visual field.

Size in the Visual Field   If you observe an automobile from far away, it fills only a portion of your visual field, and it is difficult to see small details such as the door handle. As you move closer, it fills more of your visual field, and you can perceive details like the door handle more easily (**Figure 10.7**). With these observations about perception in mind, Kosslyn wondered whether this relationship between viewing distance and the ability to perceive details also occurs for mental images.

To answer this question, Kosslyn (1978) asked participants to imagine two animals, such as an elephant and a rabbit, next to each other and to imagine that they were standing close enough so that the larger animal filled most of their visual field (**Figure 10.8a**). He then posed questions such as "Does the rabbit have whiskers?" and asked his participants to find that part of the animal in their mental image and to answer as quickly as possible. When he repeated this procedure but told participants to imagine a rabbit and a fly next to each other, participants created larger images of the rabbit, as shown in **Figure 10.8b**. The result of these experiments, shown alongside the pictures, was that participants answered questions about the rabbit more rapidly when it filled more of the visual field.

View from afar   Move closer

▶ **Figure 10.7** Moving closer to an object, such as this car, has two effects: (1) The object fills more of your visual field, and (2) details are easier to see.

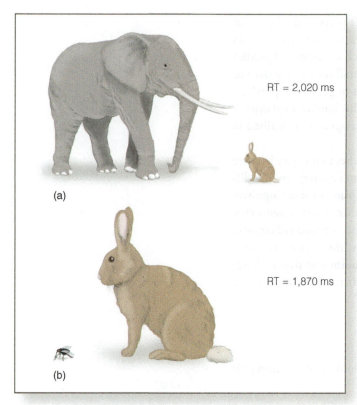

RT = 2,020 ms

(a)

RT = 1,870 ms

(b)

➤ **Figure 10.8** These pictures represent images that Kosslyn's (1978) participants created, which filled different portions of their visual field. (a) Imagine elephant and rabbit, so elephant fills the field. (b) Imagine rabbit and fly, so rabbit fills the field. Reaction times indicate how long it took participants to answer questions about the rabbit.

➤ **Figure 10.9** Participant in Perky's (1910) experiment. Unbeknownst to the participants, Perky was projecting dim images onto the screen.

In addition to asking participants to respond to details in visual images, Kosslyn also asked them to do a **mental walk task**, in which they were to imagine that they were walking toward their mental image of an animal. Their task was to estimate how far away they were from the animal when they began to experience "overflow"—when the image filled the visual field or when its edges started becoming fuzzy. The result was that participants had to move closer for small animals (less than a foot away for a mouse) than for larger animals (about 11 feet away for an elephant), just as they would have to do if they were walking toward actual animals. This result provides further evidence for the idea that images are spatial, just like perception.

Interactions of Imagery and Perception Another way to demonstrate connections between imagery and perception is to show that they interact with one another. The basic rationale behind this approach is that if imagery affects perception, or perception affects imagery, this means that imagery and perception both have access to the same mechanisms.

The classic demonstration of interaction between perception and imagery dates back to 1910, when Cheves Perky did the experiment pictured in **Figure 10.9**. Perky asked her participants to "project" visual images of common objects onto a screen and then to describe these images. Unbeknownst to the participants, Perky was back-projecting a very dim image of this object onto the screen. Thus, when participants were asked to create an image of a banana, Perky projected a dim image of a banana onto the screen. Interestingly, the participants' descriptions of their images matched the images that Perky was projecting. For example, they described the banana as being oriented vertically, just as was the projected image. Even more interesting, not one of Perky's 24 participants noticed that there was an actual picture on the screen. They had apparently mistaken an actual picture for a mental image.

Modern researchers have replicated Perky's result (see Craver-Lemley & Reeves, 1992; Segal & Fusella, 1970) and have demonstrated interactions between perception and imagery in a number of other ways. Martha Farah (1985) instructed her participants to imagine either the letter H or the letter T on a screen (**Figure 10.10a**). Once they had formed a clear image on the screen, they pressed a button that caused two squares to flash, one after the other (**Figure 10.10b**). One of the squares contained a target letter, which was either an H or a T. The participants' task was to indicate whether the letter was in the first square or the second one. The results, shown in **Figure 10.11c**, indicate that the target letter was detected more accurately when the participant had been imagining the same letter rather than the different letter. Farah interpreted this result as showing that perception and imagery share mechanisms; later experiments that have also shown that imagery can affect perception have come to the same conclusion (Kosslyn & Thompson, 2000; Pearson et al., 2008). In the next section, we will consider physiological evidence for connections between imagery and perception.

TEST YOURSELF 10.1

1. Is imagery just a "laboratory phenomenon," or does it occur in real life?

2. Make a list of the important events in the history of the study of imagery in psychology, from the imageless thought debate of the 1800s to the studies of imagery that occurred early in the cognitive revolution in the 1960s and 1970s.

3. How did Kosslyn use the technique of mental scanning (in the boat and island experiments) to demonstrate similarities between perception and imagery?

4. What is the imagery debate? Describe the spatial (or depictive) and propositional explanations of the mechanism underlying imagery. How does the propositional explanation interpret the results of Kosslyn's boat and island image-scanning experiments?

5. Describe experiments by Kosslyn, Perky, and Farah that demonstrate interactions between imagery and perception.

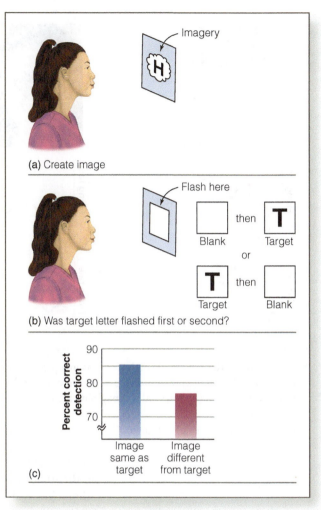

(a) Create image

(b) Was target letter flashed first or second?

(c)

► Figure 10.10 Procedure for Farah's (1985) letter visualization experiment. (a) The participant visualizes H or T on the screen. (b) Then two squares flash, one after the other, on the same screen. As shown on the right, the target letter can be in the first square or in the second one. The participants' task is to determine whether the test letter was flashed in the first square or in the second square. (c) Results showing that accuracy was higher when the letter in (b) was the same as the one that had been imagined in (a). (Source: Farah, 1985)

Imagery and the Brain

As we look at a number of types of physiological experiments, we will see that a great deal of evidence points to a connection between imagery and perception, but the overlap is not perfect. We begin by looking at the results of research that has measured the brain's response to imagery and will then consider how brain damage affects the ability to form visual images.

Imagery Neurons in the Human Brain

Studies in which activity is recorded from single neurons in humans are rare but have been done in situations in which patients are being prepared for brain surgery.

METHOD   Recording from Single Neurons in Humans

The vast majority of single neuron recordings have been carried out on animals. But in a few experiments, single neuron responses have been recorded from humans. In these experiments, the participants were patients with intractable epilepsy that couldn't be controlled by drugs. For these patients, a possible cure is provided by surgery that removes the small area of the brain called the *epileptic focus*, where the seizures originate.

To determine the location of this focus, electrodes are implanted in these patients' brains and are then monitored over a period of a few days in the hope that spontaneous seizures will help pinpoint the location of the focus (Fried et al., 1999). Because the electrodes are implanted, it is possible, with the patients' consent, to record the activity caused by cognitive actions such as perceiving, imagining, and remembering. These experiments make it possible not only to record neural responses to stimuli, as is routinely done in animal experiments, but also to study how these neurons respond when the patients carry out cognitive activities such as imaging and remembering.

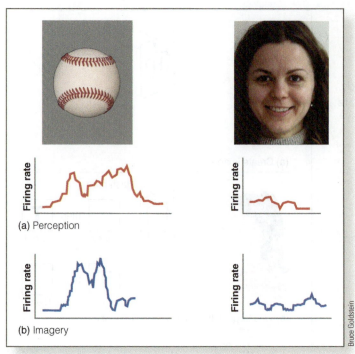

Figure 10.11 Responses of single neurons in a person's medial temporal lobe that (a) respond to perception of a baseball but not of a face, and (b) respond to imagining a baseball but not to imagining a face.

(Source: Kreiman, Koch, & Fried, 2000)

Gabriel Kreiman and coworkers (2000) were able to study patients who had electrodes implanted in various areas in their medial temporal lobe, which includes the hippocampus and the amygdala (see Figure 5.19, page 150). Kreiman found neurons that responded to some objects but not to others. For example, the records in **Figure 10.11a** show the response of a neuron that responded to a picture of a baseball but did not respond to a picture of a face. In addition, **Figure 10.11b** shows that this neuron fired in the same way when the person closed his or her eyes and imagined a baseball (good firing) or a face (no firing). Kreiman called these neurons **imagery neurons.**

Kreiman's discovery of imagery neurons is important, both because it demonstrates a possible physiological mechanism for imagery and because these neurons respond in the same way to perceiving an object and to imagining it, thereby supporting the idea of a close relation between perception and imagery. However, most research on humans has involved not recording from single neurons, but brain imaging that measures brain activity as participants are perceiving objects and were creating visual images of these objects (see Method: Brain Imaging, Chapter 2, page 41).

Brain Imaging

An early study of imagery using brain imaging was carried out by Samuel Le Bihan and coworkers (1993), who demonstrated that both perception and imagery activate the visual cortex. **Figure 10.12** shows how activity in the striate cortex increased both when a person observed presentations of actual visual stimuli (marked "Perception") and when the person was imagining the stimulus ("Imagery").

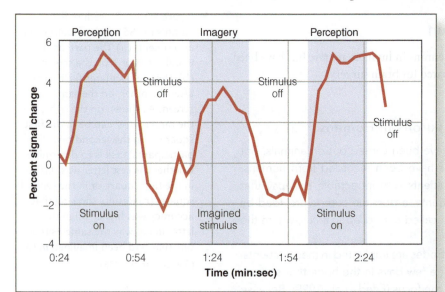

Figure 10.12 Results of Le Bihan et al.'s (1993) study measuring brain activity using fMRI. Activity increases to presentation of a visual stimulus (shaded area marked "Stimulus on") and also increases when participants are imagining the stimulus (area marked "Imagined stimulus"). In contrast, activity is low when there is no actual or imagined stimulus.

(Source: Le Bihan et al., 1993)

In another brain imaging experiment, asking participants to think about questions that involved imagery—for example, "Is the green of the trees darker than the green of the grass?"—generated a greater response in the visual cortex than asking nonimagery questions, such as "Is the intensity of electrical current measured in amperes?" (Goldenberg et al., 1989).

Another imaging experiment, by Stephen Kosslyn and coworkers (1995), made use of the way the visual cortex is organized as a **topographic map,** in which specific locations on a visual stimulus cause activity at specific locations in the visual cortex, and points next to each other on the stimulus cause activity at locations next to each other on the cortex. Research on the topographic map on the visual cortex indicates that looking at a small object causes activity in the back of the visual cortex, as shown by the green area in **Figure 10.13a,** and looking at larger objects causes activity to spread toward the front of the visual cortex, as indicated by the red area.

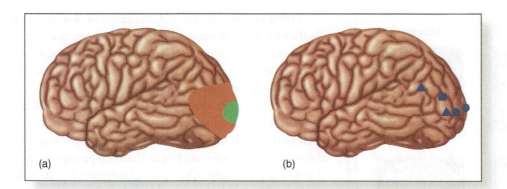

➤ **Figure 10.13** (a) Looking at a small object causes activity in the back of the visual cortex (green). Larger objects cause activity to spread forward (red). (b) Results of Kosslyn et al.'s (1995) experiment. The symbols indicate the most activated location caused by imagery: small image (circle); medium image (square); large image (triangle).
(Source: Kosslyn et al., 1995)

What would happen, Kosslyn wondered, if participants created mental images of different sizes? To answer this question, participants were instructed to create small, medium, and large visual images while they were in a brain scanner. The result, indicated by the symbols in **Figure 10.13b**, is that when participants created small visual images, activity was centered near the back of the brain (circles), but as the size of the mental image increased, activation moved toward the front of the visual cortex (squares and triangles), just as it does for perception. (Notice that one of the triangles representing large images is near the back of the visual cortex. Kosslyn suggests that this could have been caused by activation by internal details of the larger image.) Thus, both imagery and perception result in topographically organized brain activation.

Another approach to studying imagery and the brain has been to determine whether there is overlap between brain areas activated by perceiving an object and those activated by creating a mental image of the object. These experiments have demonstrated an overlap between areas activated by perception and by imagery, but have also found differences. For example, Giorgio Ganis and coworkers (2004) used fMRI to measure activation under two conditions, perception and imagery. For the perception condition, participants observed a drawing of an object, such as the tree in **Figure 10.14**. For the imagery condition, participants were told to imagine a picture that they had studied before, when they heard a tone. For both the perception and imagery tasks, participants had to answer a question such as "Is the object wider than it is tall?"

Results of Ganis's experiment are shown in **Figure 10.15**, which shows activation at three different locations in the brain. **Figure 10.15a** shows that perception and imagery both activate the same areas in the frontal lobe. **Figure 10.15b** shows the same result farther back in the brain. However, **Figure 10.15c**, which shows activation in the visual cortex in the occipital lobe at the back of the brain, indicates that perception activates much more of this area of the brain than does imagery. This greater activity for perception isn't surprising because the visual cortex is where signals from the retina first reach the cortex. Thus, there is almost complete overlap of the activation caused by perception and imagery in the front of the brain, but some difference near the back of the brain.

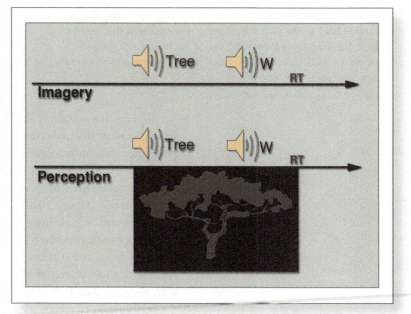

➤ **Figure 10.14** Procedure for Ganis et al.'s (2004) experiment. A trial begins with the name of an object that was previously studied, in this case "tree." In the imagery condition, participants had their eyes closed and had to imagine the tree. In the perception condition, participants saw a faint picture of the object. Participants then heard instructions. The W in this example means they were to judge whether the object was "wider than tall."
(Source: Ganis, Thompson, & Kosslyn, 2004)

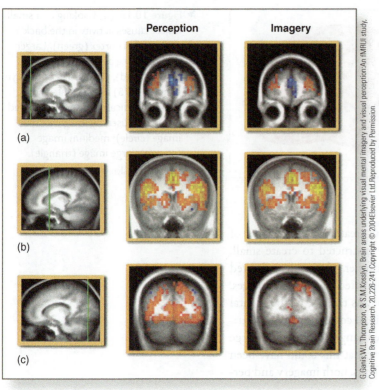

➤ **Figure 10.15** Brain scan results from Ganis et al. (2004). The vertical lines through the brains in the far-left column indicate where activity was being recorded. The columns labeled "Perception" and "Imagery" indicate responses in the perception and imagery conditions. (a) Responses of areas in the frontal lobe. Perception and imagery cause the same activation. (b) Responses farther back in the brain. Activation is the same in this area as well. (c) Responses from the back of the brain, including the primary visual area. There is much more activation in this area in the perception condition.

(Source: Ganis, Thompson, & Kosslyn, 2004)

Other experiments have also concluded that there are similarities but also some differences between brain activation for perception and for imagery. For example, an fMRI experiment by Amir Amedi and coworkers (2005) showed overlap but also found that when participants were using visual imagery, the response of some areas associated with nonvisual stimuli, such as hearing and touch, was decreased. Amedi suggests that the reason for this might be that visual images are more fragile than real perception, and this deactivation helps quiet down irrelevant activity that might interfere with the mental image.

Multivoxel Pattern Analysis

Another way brain imaging has been applied to studying possible links between imagery and perception is multivoxel pattern analysis (MVPA), which we introduced in Chapter 7 (page 213). Remember that the procedure in MVPA is to train a classifier to associate a pattern of voxel activation with particular stimuli, like the apple and pear in Figure 7.17 (page 213), and then to present a stimulus and see if the classifier can identify it, based on the pattern of voxel activity created by the stimulus.

Matthew Johnson and Marcia Johnson (2014) used this procedure to study the relation between imagery and perception by training a classifier by presenting four different kinds of scenes—beach, desert, field, or house—to a person in a scanner (**Figure 10.16a**). After the classifier was trained on these perceptual stimuli, it was time for the test. Voxel activity was recorded as a participant viewed a picture (for example, the beach scene), and the classifier predicted, from two possibilities (say, the beach scene or the house), which picture the person was perceiving (**Figure 10.16b**).

The result was that the classifier predicted the correct picture on 63 percent of the trials, which is above chance accuracy (where chance performance is 50 percent). This "train on perception, test on perception" test showed that the classifier could use the information it had learned during perception training to predict what the participant was seeing. But what if the perception-trained classifier was asked to indicate which of two scenes the participant was *imagining*? (**Figure 10.16c**).

The result of experiments in which voxel activity was measured as participants imagined one of the scenes was 55 percent accuracy—not as good as predicting what the person was perceiving, but still above chance. Clearly, a lot of work remains to be done before classifiers can accurately predict what a person is perceiving or imagining, but identifying with above-chance accuracy what a person is imagining based on activity collected when the person was perceiving is impressive, and other researchers have reported similar results (Albers et al., 2013; Cichy et al., 2012; Horikawa & Kamitani, 2017; Naselaris et al., 2015).

Transcranial Magnetic Stimulation

Another technique used to investigate connections between perception and imagery involves transcranial magnetic stimulation (TMS), which we described in Chapter 9 (see Method: Transcranial Magnetic Stimulation (TMS), page 292).

Measure voxel patterns to four different scenes

(a) Train Classifier on 4 scenes

Present 1 Scene   Classifier predicts which of the two is being perceived

(b) Perception Test

Imagine 1 Scene   Classifier predicts which of the two is being imagined

(c) Imagery Test

➤ **Figure 10.16** Procedure for Johnson and Johnson's (2014) multivoxel pattern analysis experiment. (a) The classifier is calibrated by measuring the pattern of voxel activation to four pictures. (b) Perception test. Participant is presented with one of the pictures, and the perception-calibrated classifier determines, from the pattern of voxel activation, which of two possible pictures was presented. (c) Imagery test. Participant is asked to imagine one of the pictures, and the perception-calibrated classifier determines which of two possible pictures was being imagined.

Stephen Kosslyn and coworkers (1999) presented transcranial magnetic stimulation to the visual cortex while participants were carrying out either a perception task or an imagery task. For the perception task, participants briefly viewed a display like the one in **Figure 10.17** and were asked to make a judgment about the stripes in two of the quadrants. For example, they might be asked to indicate whether the stripes in quadrant 3 were longer than the stripes in quadrant 2. The imagery task was the same, but instead of actually looking at the stripes while answering the questions, the participants closed their eyes and based their judgments on their mental image of the display.

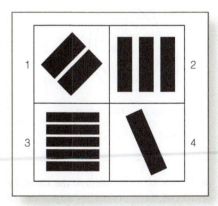

➤ **Figure 10.17** Bar stimuli used for Kosslyn et al.'s (1999) experiment. Participants created visual images of displays such as this and answered questions about the stripes.

Kosslyn measured participants' reaction time to make the judgment, both when transcranial magnetic stimulation was being applied to the visual area of the brain and also during a control condition when the stimulation was directed to another part of the brain. The results indicated that stimulation caused participants to respond more slowly, and that this slowing effect occurred both for perception and for imagery. Based on these results, Kosslyn concluded that brain activity in the visual cortex plays a causal role in both perception and imagery.

Neuropsychological Case Studies

How can we use studies of people with brain damage to help us understand imagery? One approach is to determine how brain damage affects imagery. Another approach is to determine how brain damage affects both imagery and perception, and to note whether both are affected in the same way.

Removing Part of the Visual Cortex Decreases Image Size   Patient M.G.S. was a young woman who was about to have part of her right occipital lobe removed as treatment for a severe case of epilepsy. Before the operation, Martha Farah and coworkers (1993) had M.G.S. perform the mental walk task that we described earlier, in which she imagined walking toward an animal and estimated how close she was when the image began to overflow her visual field. **Figure 10.18** shows that before the operation, M.G.S. felt she was about 15 feet from an imaginary horse before its image overflowed. But when Farah had her repeat this task after her right occipital lobe had been removed, the distance increased to 35 feet. This occurred because removing part of the visual cortex reduced the size of her field of view, so the horse filled up the field when she was farther away. This result supports the idea that the visual cortex is important for imagery.

Problems with Perceiving Are Accompanied by Problems with Imagery   A large number of cases have been studied in which a patient with brain damage has a perceptual problem and also has a similar problem in creating images. For example, people who have lost the ability to see color due to brain damage are also unable to create colors through imagery (DeRenzi & Spinnler, 1967; DeVreese, 1991).

Damage to the parietal lobes can cause a condition called **unilateral neglect**, in which the patient ignores objects in one half of the visual field, even to the extent of shaving just one side of his face or eating only the food on one side of her plate. Edoardo Bisiach and Claudio Luzzatti (1978) tested the imagery of a patient with unilateral neglect by asking him to describe things he saw when imagining himself standing at one end of the Piazza del Duomo in Milan, a place with which he had been familiar before his brain was damaged (**Figure 10.19**).

The patient's responses showed that he neglected the left side of his mental image, just as he neglected the left side of his perceptions. Thus, when he imagined himself standing at A, he neglected the left side and named only objects to his right (small a's). When he imagined himself standing at B, he continued to neglect the left side, again naming only objects on his right (small b's).

The correspondence between the physiology of mental imagery and the physiology of perception, as demonstrated by brain scans in normal participants and the effects of brain damage in participants

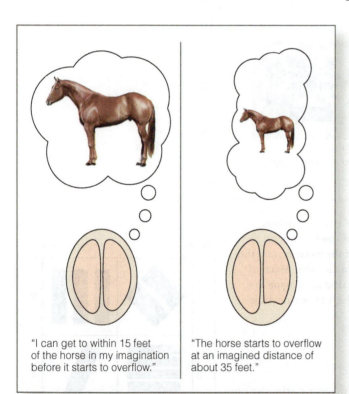

"I can get to within 15 feet of the horse in my imagination before it starts to overflow."

"The horse starts to overflow at an imagined distance of about 35 feet."

➤ **Figure 10.18** Results of the mental walk task for patient M.G.S. Left: Before her operation, she could mentally "walk" to within 15 feet before the image of the horse overflowed her visual field. Right: After removal of the right occipital lobe, the size of the visual field was reduced, and she could mentally approach only to within 35 feet of the horse before it overflowed her visual field.

(Source: Farah, 2000)

with neglect, supports the idea that mental imagery and perception share physiological mechanisms. However, not all physiological results support a one-to-one correspondence between imagery and perception.

Dissociations Between Imagery and Perception   In Chapter 2, we described dissociations between different types of perception, in which some people with brain damage were unable to recognize faces but could recognize objects, and other people had the opposite problem (see Method: Demonstrating a Double Dissociation, Chapter 2, page 40). Cases have also been reported of dissociations between imagery and perception. For example, Cecilia Guariglia and coworkers (1993) studied a patient whose brain damage had little effect on his ability to perceive but caused neglect in his mental images (his mental images were limited to only one side, as in the case of the man imagining the piazza in Milan).

Another case of normal perception but impaired imagery is the case of R.M., who had suffered damage to his occipital and parietal lobes (Farah et al., 1988). R.M. was able to recognize objects and to draw accurate pictures of objects that were placed before him. However, he was unable to draw objects from memory, a task that requires imagery. He also had trouble answering questions that depend on imagery, such as verifying whether the sentence "A grapefruit is larger than an orange" is correct.

Dissociations have also been reported with the opposite result, so that perception is impaired but imagery is relatively normal. For example, Marlene Behrmann and coworkers (1994) studied C.K., a 33-year-old graduate student who was struck by a car as he was jogging. C.K. suffered from visual agnosia, the inability to visually recognize objects. Thus, he labeled the pictures in **Figure 10.20a** as a "feather duster" (the dart), a "fencer's mask" (the tennis racquet), and a "rose twig with thorns" (the asparagus). These results show that C.K. could recognize parts of objects but couldn't integrate them into a meaningful whole. But despite his inability to name pictures of objects, C.K. was able to draw objects from memory, a task that depends on imagery (**Figure 10.20b**). Interestingly, when he was shown his own drawings after enough time had passed so he had forgotten the actual drawing experience, he was unable to identify the objects he had drawn.

These neuropsychological dissociations, in which perception is normal but imagery is poor (Guariglia's patient and R.M.), or perception is poor but imagery is normal (C.K.), present a paradox. On one hand, evidence for a double dissociation between imagery and perception (**Table 10.1**) is usually interpreted to mean that the two functions are served by different mechanisms (see page 40). However, this conclusion contradicts the other evidence we have presented that shows that imagery and perception share mechanisms.

This apparent paradox highlights the difficulty in interpreting neuropsychological results. For one thing, the damage in individual cases varies greatly between individuals and usually isn't restricted to the borders between areas in anatomical diagrams. In addition, it is important to bear in mind that much of the research that presents evidence for an overlap between perception and imagery also acknowledges that the overlap is only partial.

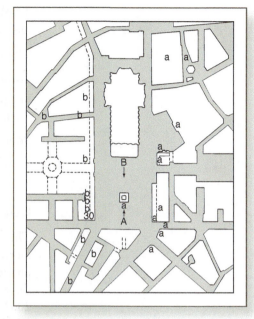

▶ **Figure 10.19** Piazza del Duomo in Milan. When Bisiach and Luzzatti's (1978) patient imagined himself standing at A, he could name objects indicated by a's. When he imagined himself at B, he could name objects indicated by b's.

(Source: Bisiach & Luzzatti, 1978)

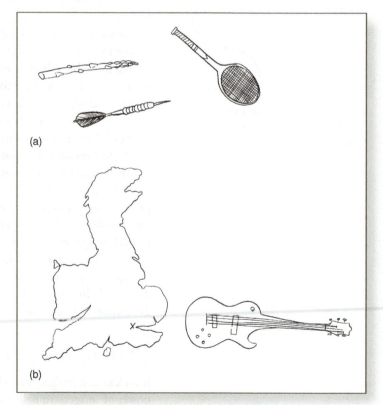

▶ **Figure 10.20** (a) Pictures incorrectly labeled by C.K., who had visual agnosia. (b) Drawings from memory by C.K.

(Source: Behrmann et al., 1994)

TABLE 10.1

Dissociations Between Perception and Imagery

Case	Perception	Imagery
Guariglia (1993)	OK	Neglect (image limited to one side).
Farah et al. (1993) (R.M.)	OK. Recognizes objects and can draw pictures.	Poor. Can't draw from memory or answer questions based on imagery.
Behrmann et al. (1994) (C.K.)	Poor. Visual agnosia so can't recognize objects.	OK. Can draw object from memory.

Conclusions from the Imagery Debate

The imagery debate provides an outstanding example of a situation in which a controversy motivated a large amount of research. Most psychologists, looking at the behavioral and physiological evidence, have concluded that imagery and perception are closely related and share some (but not all) mechanisms (Pearson & Kosslyn, 2015; but see Pylyshyn, 2001, 2003, who disagrees).

The idea of shared mechanisms follows from all of the parallels and interactions between perception and imagery. The idea that not all mechanisms are shared follows from some of the fMRI results, which show that the overlap between brain activation is not complete; some of the neuropsychological results, which show dissociations between imagery and perception; and also from differences between the experience of imagery and perception. For example, perception occurs automatically when we look at something, but imagery needs to be generated with some effort. Also, perception is stable—it continues as long as you are observing a stimulus—but imagery is fragile—it can vanish without continued effort.

Another example of a difference between imagery and perception is that it is harder to manipulate mental images than images that are created perceptually. This was demonstrated by Deborah Chalmers and Daniel Reisberg (1985), who asked their participants to create mental images of ambiguous figures such as the one in **Figure 10.21**, which can be seen as a rabbit or a duck. Perceptually, it is fairly easy to "flip" between these two perceptions. However, Chalmers and Reisberg found that participants who were holding a mental image of this figure were unable to flip from one perception to another.

Other research has shown that people can manipulate simpler mental images. For example, Ronald Finke and coworkers (1989) showed that when participants followed instructions to imagine a capital letter D, and then rotate it 90 degrees to the left and place a capital letter J at the bottom, they reported seeing an umbrella. Also, Fred Mast and Kosslyn (2002) showed that people who were good at imagery were able to rotate mental images of ambiguous figures if they were provided with extra information such as drawings of parts of the images that are partially rotated. So, the experiments on manipulating images lead to the same conclusion as all of the other experiments we have described: Imagery and perception have many features in common, but there are also differences between them.

▶ Using Imagery to Improve Memory

It is clear that imagery can play an important role in memory. But how can you harness the power of imagery to help you remember things better? In Chapter 7, we saw that encoding is aided by forming connections with other information and described an experiment (Bower & Winzenz, 1970) in which participants who created images based on two paired

▶ **Figure 10.21** What is this, a rabbit (facing right) or a duck (facing left)?

words (like boat and tree) remembered more than twice as many words as participants who just repeated the words (see Figure 7.2, page 194). Another principle of memory we described in Chapter 7 was that organization improves encoding. The mind tends to spontaneously organize information that is initially unorganized, and presenting information that is organized improves memory performance. We will now describe a method based on these principles, which involves placing images at locations.

Placing Images at Locations

The power of imagery to improve memory is tied to its ability to create organized locations at which memories for specific items can be placed. An example of the organizational function of imagery from ancient history is provided by a story about the Greek poet Simonides. According to legend, 2,500 years ago Simonides presented an address at a banquet, and just after he left the banquet the roof of the hall collapsed, killing most of the people inside. To compound this tragedy, many of the bodies were so severely mutilated that they couldn't be identified. But Simonides realized that as he had looked out over the audience during his address, he had created a mental picture of where each person had been seated at the banquet table. Based on this image of people's locations around the table, he was able to determine who had been killed.

What is important about this rather gory example is that Simonides realized that the technique he had used to help him remember who was at the banquet could be used to remember other things as well. He found that he could remember things by imagining a physical space, like the banquet table, and placing, in his mind, items to be remembered in the seats surrounding the table. This feat of mental organization enabled him to later "read out" the items by mentally scanning the locations around the table, just as he had done to identify people's bodies. Simonides had invented what is now called the **method of loci**—a method in which things to be remembered are placed at different locations in a mental image of a spatial layout. The following demonstration illustrates how to use the method of loci to remember something from your own experience.

> **DEMONSTRATION**   Method of Loci
>
> Pick a place with a spatial layout that is very familiar to you, such as the rooms in your house or apartment, or the buildings on your college campus. Then pick five to seven things that you want to remember—either events from the past or things you need to do later today. Create an image representing each event, and place each image at a location in the house or on campus. If you need to remember the events in a particular order, decide on a path you would take while walking through the house or campus, and place the images representing each event along your walking path so they will be encountered in the correct order. After you have done this, retrace the path in your mind, and see if encountering the images helps you remember the events. To really test this method, try mentally "walking" this path a few hours from now.

Placing images at locations can help with retrieving memories later. For example, to help me remember a dentist appointment later in the day, I could visually place a huge pair of teeth in my living room. To remind myself to go to the gym and work out, I could imagine a treadmill on the stairs that lead from the living room to the second floor, and to represent the *This Is Us* TV show that I want to watch later tonight, I could imagine one of the characters on the show sitting on the landing at the top of the stairs.

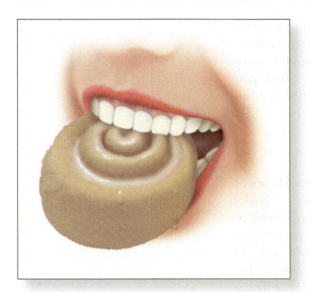

➤ **Figure 10.22** An image used by the author to remember a dentist appointment, using the pegword technique.

Associating Images with Words

The **pegword technique** involves imagery, as in the method of loci, but instead of visualizing items in different locations, you associate them with concrete words. The first step is to create a list of nouns, like the following: one–bun; two–shoe; three–tree; four–door; five–hive; six–sticks; seven–heaven; eight–gate; nine–mine; ten–hen. It's easy to remember these words in order because they were created by rhyming them with the numbers. Also, the rhyming provides a retrieval cue (see page 202) that helps remember each word. The next step is to pair each of the things to be remembered with a pegword by creating a vivid image of your item-to-be-remembered together with the object represented by the word.

Figure 10.22 shows an image I created for the dentist appointment. For the other items I wanted to remember, I might picture an elliptical trainer inside a shoe, and the word US in a tree. The beauty of this system is that it makes it possible to immediately identify an item based on its order on the list. So, if I want to identify the third thing I need to do today, I go straight to tree, which translates into my image of the word US dangling in a tree, and this reminds me to watch the program *This is Us* on TV.

Imagery techniques like the ones just described are often the basis behind books that claim to provide the key to improving your memory (see Crook & Adderly, 1998; Lorayne & Lucas, 1996; Treadeau, 1997). Although these books do provide imagery-based techniques that work, people who purchase these books in the hope of discovering an easy way to develop "photographic memory" are often disappointed. Although imagery techniques work, they do not provide easy, "magical" improvements in memory, but rather require a great deal of practice and perseverance (Schacter, 2001).

➤ SOMETHING TO CONSIDER

Individual Differences in Visual Imagery

People differ in how they perceive things and how well they can maintain their attention, remember things, and solve problems. So it isn't surprising that there are differences between people in terms of imagery as well. One person might remember a birthday party by seeing a birthday cake with candles flickering on a table. But someone else might remember the party more in terms of where people were standing and the layout of the room (Sheldon et al., 2017).

The idea that people differ in imaging was suggested in the 19th century by Francis Galton, who noted that there are "different degrees of vividness with which different persons have the faculty of recalling familiar scenes under the form of mental pictures" (Galton, 1880, p. 306). Modern researchers have confirmed Galton's idea of differences in people's imaging and have added important details to the story.

Maria Kozhevnikov and coworkers (2005) did an experiment in which they first presented a questionnaire designed to determine participants' preference for using imagery versus verbal-logical strategies when solving problems. This questionnaire involved solving different kinds of problems and indicating the strategies used to solve these problems. Kozhevnikov classified the participants as visualizers or verbalizers, so this initial result indicated that some people use imagery to solve problems and some

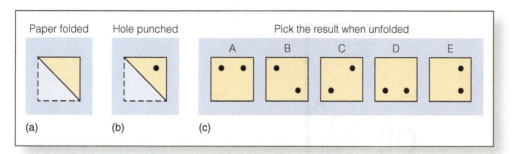

➤ **Figure 10.23** One trial from the paper folding test. (a) A piece of paper is folded and then pierced by a pencil to create a hole. (b) The participant's task is to determine which of five alternatives is what the paper will look like when unfolded.

people don't. We will describe the results of Kozhevnikov's experiments, focusing on the visualizers.

The visualizers were given tests designed to measure two types of imagery: spatial imagery and object imagery. **Spatial imagery refers** to the ability to image spatial relations, such as the layout of a garden. **Object imagery refers** to the ability to image visual details, features, or objects, such as a rose bush with bright red roses in the garden (Sheldon et al., 2017).

The **paper folding test (PFT)** is designed to measure spatial imagery. Participants saw a piece of paper being folded and then pierced by a pencil (**Figure 10.23a**). Their task was to pick from five choices what the paper would look like when unfolded (**Figure 10.23b**).

The **vividness of visual imagery questionnaire (VVIQ)** was designed to measure object imagery. Participants rated, on a 5-point scale, the vividness of mental images they were asked to create. A typical item: "The sun is rising above the horizon into a hazy sky."

The results of the tests, shown in **Figure 10.24**, demonstrate differences between participants with a low score on the PFT (low spatial imagery) and participants with a high score (high spatial imagery). Sixty-two percent of the low spatial imagers had high scores on the VVIQ, meaning they had high object imagery, whereas 51 percent of the high spatial imagers had low scores on the VVIQ, meaning they had low object imagery.

In another experiment, participants were presented with the *degraded pictures task* and a *mental rotation task*. The **degraded pictures task** consisted of a number of degraded line drawings like the one in **Figure 10.25**. Can you determine what it is? (See **Figure 10.27** on page 316 for the answer.) The **mental rotation task** required participants to judge whether pictures like the ones in **Figure 10.1** (page 300) were two views of the same object or mirror-image objects. Which type of imagers do you think did better on each task?

The answer: Spatial imagers did better in the mental rotation task, and object imagers did better on the degraded pictures task, thus providing more evidence distinguishing between spatial and object imagers.

In a study designed to determine how well participants with different levels of spatial imagery performed on physics problems, Kozhevnikov and coworkers (2007) presented the picture in **Figure 10.26** with the following

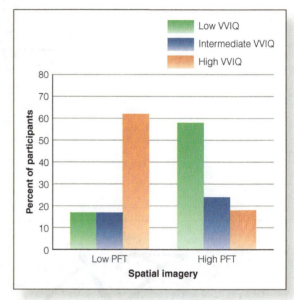

➤ **Figure 10.24** Results of the vividness of visual imagery questionnaire (VVIQ) for participants in Kozhevnikov et al.'s (2005) experiment who were classified as low and high spatial imagery based on results of the paper folding test (PFT).

(Source: Kozhevnikov, Kosslyn, & Shephard, 2005)

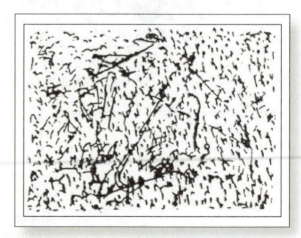

➤ **Figure 10.25** One of the degraded picture stimuli used by Kozhevnikov et al. (2005). What does the hidden line drawing depict?

(Source: Kozhevnikov, Kosslyn, & Shephard, 2005)

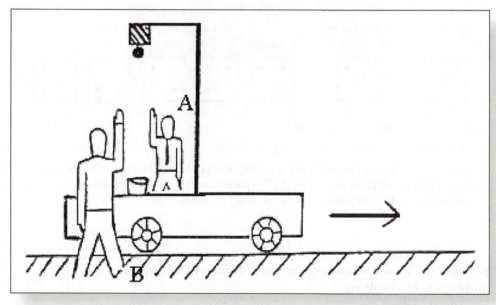

> **Figure 10.26** Picture for the frame of reference problem presented in the Kozhevnikov et al. (2007) experiment.

(Source: Kozhevnikov, Motes, & Hegarty, 2007)

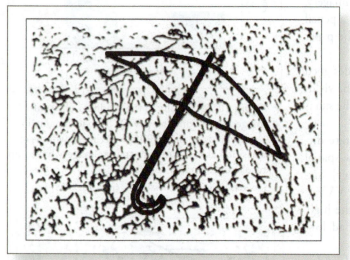

> **Figure 10.27** Answer to the degraded picture problem in Figure 10.25.

(Source: Kozhevnikov, Kosslyn, & Shephard, 2005)

text and questions to a group of students who had not taken any physics courses in high school or college.

Frame of Reference Problem

A small metal ball is being held by a magnet attached to a post on a cart. A cup is on the cart directly below the ball. The cart is moving at a constant speed as shown by the arrow in the figure. Suppose the ball falls off the magnet while the cart is in motion. Observer A stands in the cart, and observer B stands on the road, directly opposite the post of the cart at the moment of ball releasing.

Which of the reports described below corresponds to observer A's view of the falling ball:

(a) The falling ball moves straight down.
(b) The falling ball moves forward.
(c) The falling ball moves backward.

Which of the reports described below corresponds to observer B's view of the falling ball:

(a) The falling ball moves straight down.
(b) The falling ball moves forward.
(c) The falling ball moves backward.

Spoiler alert! Answer before reading further.

The answer: Observer A is in the cart, moving along with the ball, so he will see the ball as moving straight down into the cup. Because observer B is standing outside the cart, he will see the falling ball move down and forward before falling into the cup.

Half of the students correctly answered that observer A would see the ball move straight down into the cup. Focusing on the students who answered correctly for observer A, Kozhevnikov and coworkers (2007) found that 70 percent of students who were high spatial imagers correctly answered that observer B would see the ball moving down and forward, but only 18 percent of the low spatial imagers came up with the correct answer. From these results, and the results for additional physics problems, Kozhevnikov concluded that spatial ability is related to solving many types of physics problems.

The results of experiments like the ones above confirm Galton's idea that people vary in their experience of visual imagery, and we now know that people who are good at imagery are often good at one kind of imagery—spatial or object—but not as good at the other kind. And, yes, there are also some people who are good at both!

TEST YOURSELF 10.2

1. Describe how experiments using the following physiological techniques have provided evidence of parallels between imagery and perception: (a) recording from single neurons in the human brain; (b) brain imaging; (c) multivoxel pattern analysis; (d) deactivation of part of the brain; and (e) neuropsychology

2. What are some differences between imagery and perception? What have most psychologists concluded about the connection between imagery and perception?

3. Under what conditions does imagery improve memory? Describe techniques that use imagery as a tool to improve memory. What is the basic principle that underlies these techniques?

4. What is the evidence for individual differences in imagery? What is the difference between spatial visualizers and object visualizers?

CHAPTER SUMMARY

1. Mental imagery is experiencing a sensory impression in the absence of sensory input. Visual imagery is "seeing" in the absence of a visual stimulus. Imagery has played an important role in the creative process and as a way of thinking in addition to purely verbal techniques.

2. Early ideas about imagery included the imageless thought debate and Galton's work with visual images, but imagery research stopped during the behaviorist era. Imagery research began again in the 1960s with the advent of the cognitive revolution.

3. Kosslyn's mental scanning experiments suggested that imagery shares the same mechanisms as perception (that is, creates a depictive representation in the person's mind), but these results and others were challenged by Pylyshyn, who stated that imagery is based on a mechanism related to language (that is, it creates a propositional representation in a person's mind).

4. The following experiments demonstrated parallels between imagery and perception: (a) size in the visual field (visual walk task); (b) interaction between perception and imagery (Perky's 1910 experiment; Farah's experiment in which participants imagined H or T); and (c) physiological experiments.

5. Parallels between perception and imagery have been demonstrated physiologically by the following methods: (a) recording from single neurons (imagery neurons); (b) brain imaging (demonstrating overlapping activation in the brain); (c) multivoxel pattern analysis; (d) transcranial magnetic stimulation experiments (comparing the effect of brain inactivation on perception and imagery); and (e) neuropsychological case studies (removal of visual cortex affects image size; unilateral neglect).

6. There is also physiological evidence for differences between imagery and perception. This evidence includes

(a) differences in areas of the brain activated and (b) brain damage causing dissociations between perception and imagery.

7. Most psychologists, taking all of the above evidence into account, have concluded that imagery is closely related to perception and shares some (but not all) mechanisms.

8. The use of imagery can improve memory in a number of ways: (a) visualizing interacting images; (b) organization

using the method of loci; and (c) associating items with nouns using the pegword technique.

9. There is variability in people's ability to use imagery and what they experience when they create images. Some people prefer using verbal-logical reasoning to solve problems, and others are more comfortable using imagery. Among people who are "imagers," there are spatial imagers and object imagers. Kozhevnikov found that students with high spatial imagery tend to perform better on physics problems.

THINK ABOUT IT

1. Look at an object for a minute; then look away, create a mental image of it, and draw a sketch of the object based on your mental image. Then draw a sketch of the same object while you are looking at it. What kinds of information about the object in the imagery drawing were omitted, compared to the sketch you made while looking at the object?

2. Write a description of an object as you are looking at it. Then compare the written description with the information you can obtain by looking at the object or at a picture of the object. Is it true that "a picture is worth a thousand

words"? How does your comparison of written and visual representations relate to the discussion of propositional versus depictive representations in this chapter?

3. Try using one of the techniques described at the end of this chapter to create images that represent things you have to do later today or during the coming week. Then, after some time passes (anywhere from an hour to a few days), check to see whether you can retrieve the memories for these images and if you can remember what they stand for.

KEY TERMS

Conceptual peg hypothesis, 299

Degraded pictures task, 315

Depictive representation, 302

Epiphenomenon, 302

Imageless thought debate, 299

Imagery debate, 302

Imagery neuron, 306

Mental chronometry, 300

Mental imagery, 298

Mental rotation task, 315

Mental scanning, 300

Mental walk task, 304

Method of loci, 313

Object imagery, 315

Paired-associate learning, 299

Paper folding task (PFT), 315

Pegword technique, 314

Propositional representation, 302

Spatial imagery, 315

Spatial representation, 302

Topographic map, 306

Unilateral neglect, 310

Visual imagery, 298

Vividness of visual imagery questionnaire (VVIQ), 315

COGLAB EXPERIMENTS   Numbers in parentheses refer to the experiment number in CogLab.

Link Word (*37*)

Mental Rotation (*38*)

It is clear that there is communication going on between this father and his son. We can't tell what they are talking about, but we do know that they are using language. As we will see, not only is language used by all humans, but the study of how people use and understand language teaches us a great deal about how the mind operates.

Language

11

This chapter tells a story that begins with how we perceive and understand words; then considers how strings of words create meaningful sentences; and ends by considering how we use language to communicate in text, stories, and conversation.

Throughout this story, we will encounter the recurring themes of how readers and listeners use inference and prediction to create meaning. This chapter therefore follows in the footsteps of previous chapters that have discussed the role of inference and prediction in cognition. For example, in Chapter 3, Perception, we described Helmholtz's theory of unconscious inference, which proposed that to deal with the ambiguity of the visual stimulus (see page 65), we unconsciously infer which of a number of possible alternatives is most likely to be what is "out there" in the environment (page 70).

We have also seen how, as we scan a scene by making a series of eye movements, these eye movements are partially guided by our knowledge of where important objects are likely to be in the scene (page 105). And in Chapter 6, Long-Term Memory, we saw how memories for past experiences are used to predict what might be likely to occur in the future (page 177).

You may wonder how inference and prediction are involved in language. You will see that some things you may think are simple, like understanding the words in a conversation, actually pose challenges that must be solved by bringing to bear knowledge from your past experience with language. And then there are those constructions called sentences, which are created by strings of words, one after the other. While you might think that understanding a sentence is just a matter of adding up the meanings of the words, you will see that the meanings of the words are just the beginning, because the order of the words also matters, some of the words may have multiple meanings, and two sentences that are identical can have different meanings. Just as every other type of cognition you've encountered so far has turned out to be more complicated than you may have thought it would be, the same thing holds for language. You routinely use inference and prediction to understand language, just as you are doing right now, as you are reading this, probably without even realizing it.

▶ What is Language?

The following definition of language captures the idea that the ability to string sounds and words together opens the door to a world of communication: **Language** is *a system of communication using sounds or symbols that enables us to express our feelings, thoughts, ideas, and experiences.*

But this definition doesn't go far enough, because it conceivably could include some forms of animal communication. Cats "meow" when their food dish is empty; monkeys have a repertoire of "calls" that stand for things such as "danger" or "greeting"; bees perform a "waggle dance" at the hive that indicates the location of flowers. But as impressive as some animal communication is, it is much more rigid than human language. Animals use a limited number of sounds or gestures to communicate about a limited number of things that are important for survival. In contrast, humans use a wide variety of signals, which can be combined in countless ways. One of the properties of human language is, therefore, creativity.

The Creativity of Human Language

Human language provides a way of arranging a sequence of signals—sounds for spoken language, letters and written words for written language, and physical signs for sign language—to transmit, from one person to another, things ranging from the simple and commonplace

("My car is over there") to messages that have perhaps never been previously written or uttered in the entire history of the world ("My trip with Zelda, my cousin from California who lost her job in February, was on Groundhog Day").

Language makes it possible to create new and unique sentences because it has a structure that is both hierarchical and governed by rules. The **hierarchical nature of language** means that it consists of a series of small components that can be combined to form larger units. For example, words can be combined to create phrases, which in turn can create sentences, which themselves can become components of a story. The **rule-based nature of language** means that these components can be arranged in certain ways ("What is my cat saying?" is permissible in English), but not in other ways ("Cat my saying is what?" is not). These two properties—a hierarchical structure and rules—endow humans with the ability to go far beyond the fixed calls and signs of animals to communicate whatever we want to express.

The Universal Need to Communicate with Language

Although people do "talk" to themselves, as when Hamlet wondered, "To be or not to be," or when you daydream in class, language is primarily used for communication, whether it be conversing with another person or reading what someone has written. This need to communicate using language has been called "universal" because it occurs wherever there are people. For example, consider the following:

➤ People's need to communicate is so powerful that when deaf children find themselves in an environment where nobody speaks or uses sign language, they invent a sign language themselves (Goldin-Meadow, 1982).

➤ All humans with normal capacities develop a language and learn to follow its complex rules, even though they are usually not aware of these rules. Although many people find the study of grammar to be very difficult, they have no trouble using language.

➤ Language is universal across cultures. There are more than 5,000 different languages, and there isn't a single culture without language. When European explorers first set foot in New Guinea in the 1500s, the people they discovered, who had been isolated from the rest of the world for eons, had developed more than 750 languages, many of them quite different from one another.

➤ Language development is similar across cultures. No matter what the culture or the particular language, children generally begin babbling at about 7 months, a few meaningful words appear by their first birthday, and the first multiword utterances occur at about age 2 (Levelt, 2001).

➤ Even though a large number of languages are very different from one another, we can describe them as being "unique but the same." They are unique in that they use different words and sounds, and they may use different rules for combining these words (although many languages use similar rules). They are the same in that all languages have words that serve the functions of nouns and verbs, and all languages include a system to make things negative, to ask questions, and to refer to the past and present.

Studying Language

Language has fascinated thinkers for thousands of years, dating back to the ancient Greek philosophers Socrates, Plato, and Aristotle (350–450 BCE), and before. The modern scientific study of language traces its beginnings to the work of Paul Broca (1861) and Carl Wernicke (1874). Broca's study of patients with brain damage led to the proposal that an area in the frontal lobe (Broca's area) is responsible for the production of language. Wernicke proposed that an area in the temporal lobe (Wernicke's area) is responsible for comprehension. We described Broca's and Wernicke's observations in Chapter 2 (see page 39), and also noted that modern research has shown that the situation is quite a bit more complicated than just two language areas in the brain (see page 44).

In this chapter, we will focus not on the connection between language and the brain, but on behavioral research on the cognitive mechanisms of language. We take up the story of behavioral research on language in the 1950s when behaviorism was still the dominant approach in psychology (see page 10). In 1957, B. F. Skinner, the main proponent of behaviorism, published a book called *Verbal Behavior*, in which he proposed that language is learned through reinforcement. According to this idea, just as children learn appropriate behavior by being rewarded for "good" behavior and punished for "bad" behavior, children learn language by being rewarded for using correct language and punished (or not rewarded) for using incorrect language.

In the same year, linguist Noam Chomsky (1957) published a book titled *Syntactic Structures*, in which he proposed that human language is coded in the genes. According to this idea, just as humans are genetically programmed to walk, they are also programmed to acquire and use language. Chomsky concluded that despite the wide variations that exist across languages, the underlying basis of all language is similar. Most important for our purposes, Chomsky saw studying language as a way to study the properties of the mind and therefore disagreed with the behaviorist idea that the mind is not a valid topic of study for psychology.

Chomsky's disagreement with behaviorism led him to publish a scathing review of Skinner's *Verbal Behavior* in 1959. In his review, he presented arguments against the behaviorist idea that language can be explained in terms of reinforcements and without reference to the mind. One of Chomsky's most persuasive arguments was that as children learn language, they produce sentences that they have never heard and that have never been reinforced. (A classic example of a sentence that has been created by many children and that is unlikely to have been taught or reinforced by parents is "I hate you, Mommy.") Chomsky's criticism of behaviorism was an important event in the cognitive revolution and began changing the focus of the young discipline of **psycholinguistics**, the field concerned with the psychological study of language.

The goal of psycholinguistics is to discover the psychological processes by which humans acquire and process language (Clark & Van der Wege, 2002; Gleason & Ratner, 1998; Miller, 1965). The four major concerns of psycholinguistics are as follows:

1. Comprehension. How do people understand spoken and written language? This includes how people process language sounds; how they understand words, sentences, and stories expressed in writing, speech, or sign language; and how people have conversations with one another.

2. Representation. How is language represented in the mind? This includes how people group words together into phrases to create meaningful sentences and how they make connections between different parts of a story.

3. Speech production. How do people produce language? This includes the physical processes of speech production and the mental processes that occur as a person creates speech.

4. Acquisition. How do people learn language? This includes not only how children learn language but also how people learn additional languages, either as children or later in life.

Because of the vast scope of psycholinguistics, we are going to restrict our attention to the first two of these concerns, describing research on comprehension and representation, which together explain how we understand language. The plan is to start with words, then look at how words are combined to create sentences, then how sentences create "stories" that we read, hear, or create ourselves as we have conversations with other people.

▶ Understanding Words: A Few Complications

We begin our discussion of words by defining a few terms. Our **lexicon** is all of the words we know, which has also been called our "mental dictionary." **Semantics** is the meaning of language. This is important for words, because each word has one or more meanings. The meaning of words is called **lexical semantics**. Our goal in this section is to consider how we determine the meanings of words. You might think that determining a word's meaning is simple: We just look it up in our lexicon. But determining word meaning is more complicated than a single "look up." We will now consider a number of factors that pose challenges to perceiving and understanding words.

Not All Words Are Created Equal: Differences in Frequency

Some words occur more frequently than others in a particular language. For example, in English, *home* occurs 547 times per million words, and *hike* occurs only 4 times per million words. The frequency with which a word appears in a language is called **word frequency**, and the **word frequency effect** refers to the fact that we respond more rapidly to high-frequency words like *home* than to low-frequency words like *hike*. The reason this is important is because a word's frequency influences how we process the word.

One way to illustrate processing differences between high- and low-frequency words is to use a **lexical decision task** in which the task is to decide as quickly as possible whether strings of letters are words or nonwords. Try this for the following four words: *reverie, cratily, history, garvola*. Note that there were two real words, *reverie*, which is a low-frequency word, and *history*, which is a high-frequency word. Research using the lexical decision task has demonstrated slower responding to low-frequency words (Carrol, 2004; also see Chapter 9, page 279 for a description of another way the lexical decision task has been used).

The slower response for low-frequency words has also been demonstrated by measuring people's eye movements while reading. Keith Rayner and Susan Duffy (1986) measured participants' eye movements and the durations of the fixations that occur as the eye pauses at a particular place (see Chapter 4, page 103) while they read sentences that contained either a high-frequency or a low-frequency target word, where frequency refers to how often a word occurs in normal language usage. The average frequencies were 5.1 times per million for the low-frequency words and 122.3 times per million for the high-frequency words. For example, the low-frequency target word in the sentence "The slow waltz captured their attention" is *waltz*, and replacing *waltz* with the high-frequency word *music* creates the sentence "The slow *music* captured their attention." The duration of the first fixation on the words, shown in **Figure 11.1a**, was 37 msec longer for low-frequency words compared to high-frequency words. (Sometimes a word might be fixated more than once, as when the person reads a word and then looks back at it in response to what the person has read later in the sentence.) **Figure 11.1b** shows that the total gaze duration—the sum of all fixations made on a word, was 87 msec longer for low-frequency words than for high-frequency words. One reason for these longer fixations on low-frequency words could be that the readers needed more time to access the meaning of the low-frequency words. The word frequency effect, therefore, demonstrates how our past experience with words influences our ability to access their meaning.

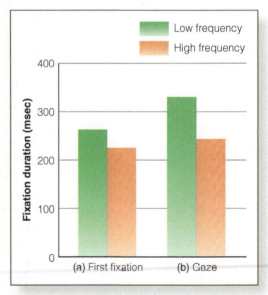

▶ **Figure 11.1** Fixation durations on low-frequency and high-frequency words in sentences measured by Rayner and Duffy (1986). (a) First fixation durations; (b) Total gaze duration. In both cases, fixation times are longer for low-frequency words.

(Source: Based on data from Rayner and Duffy, 1986, Table 2, p. 195)

The Pronunciation of Words Is Variable

Another problem that makes understanding words challenging is that not everyone pronounces words in the same way. People talk with different accents and at different speeds, and, most important, people often take a relaxed approach to pronouncing words when they are speaking naturally. For example, if you were talking to a friend, how would you say "Did you go to class today?" Would you say "Did you" or "Di-joo"? You have your own ways of producing various words and phonemes, and other people have theirs. For example, analysis of how people actually speak has determined that there are 50 different ways to pronounce the word *the* (Waldrop, 1988).

So how do we deal with this? One way is to use the context within which the word appears. The fact that context helps is illustrated by what happens when you hear a word taken out of context. Irwin Pollack and J. M. Pickett (1964) showed that words are more difficult to understand when taken out of context and presented alone, by recording the conversations of participants who sat in a room waiting for the experiment to begin. When the participants were then presented with recordings of single words taken out of their own conversations, they could identify only half the words, even though they were listening to their own voices! The fact that the people in this experiment were able to identify words as they were talking to each other, but couldn't identify the same words when the words were isolated, illustrates that their ability to perceive words in conversations is aided by the context provided by the words and sentences that make up the conversation.

There Are No Silences Between Words in Normal Conversation

The fact that the sounds of speech are easier to understand when we hear them spoken in a sentence is particularly amazing when we consider that unlike the words you are now reading that are separated by spaces, words spoken in a sentence are usually not separated by silence. This is not what we might expect, because when we listen to someone speak we usually hear the individual words, and sometimes it may seem as if there are silences that separate one word from another. However, remember our discussion in Chapter 3 (page 68) in which we noted that a record of the physical energy produced by conversational speech reveals that there are often no physical breaks between words in the speech signal or that breaks can occur in the middle of words (see Figure 3.12).

In Chapter 3 we described an experiment by Jennifer Saffran and coworkers (2008), which showed that infants are sensitive to statistical regularities in the speech signal—the way that different sounds follow one another in a particular language and how knowing these regularities helps infants achieve **speech segmentation**—the perception of individual words even though there are often no pauses between words. (see page 68).

We use the statistical properties of language all the time without realizing it. For example, we have learned that certain sounds are more likely to follow one another within a word, and some sounds are more likely to follow each other in different words. Consider the words *pretty baby*. In English, it is likely that *pre* and *ty* will follow each other in the same word (*pre-ty*) and that *ty* and *ba* will be separated in two different words (pre*ty ba*by).

Another thing that aids speech segmentation is our knowledge of the meanings of words. In Chapter 3 we pointed out that when we listen to an unfamiliar foreign language, it is often difficult to distinguish one word from the next, but if we know a language, individual words stand out (see page 68). This observation illustrates that knowing the meanings of words helps us perceive them. Perhaps you have had the experience of hearing individual words that you happen to know in a foreign language seem to "pop out" from what appears to be an otherwise continuous stream of speech.

Another example of how meaning is responsible for organizing sounds into words is provided by these two sentences:

Jamie's mother said, "Be a big girl and eat your vegetables."

The thing Big Earl loved most in the world was his car.

"Big girl" and "Big Earl" are both pronounced the same way, so hearing them differently depends on the overall meaning of the sentence in which these words appear. This example is similar to the familiar "I scream, you scream, we all scream for ice cream" that many people learn as children. The sound stimuli for "I scream" and "ice cream" are identical, so the different organizations must be achieved by the meaning of the sentence in which these words appear.

So our ability to hear and understand spoken words is affected by (1) how frequently we have encountered a word in the past; (2) the context in which the words appear; (3) our knowledge of statistical regularities of our language; and (4) our knowledge of word meanings. There's an important message here—all of these things involve knowledge achieved by learning/experience with language. Sound familiar? Yes, this continues the theme of the importance of knowledge that occurs throughout this chapter as we consider how we understand sentences, stories, and conversations. But we aren't through with words yet, because just to make things more interesting, many words have multiple meanings.

▶ Understanding Ambiguous Words

Words can often have more than one meaning, a situation called **lexical ambiguity**. For example, the word *bug* can refer to an insect, a hidden listening device, or to annoying someone, among other things. When ambiguous words appear in a sentence, we usually use the context of the sentence to determine which definition applies. For example, if Susan says, "My mother is bugging me," we can be pretty sure that *bugging* refers to the fact that Susan's mother is annoying her, as opposed to sprinkling insects on her or installing a hidden listening device in her room (although we might need further context to totally rule out this last possibility).

Accessing Multiple Meanings

The examples for *bug* indicate that context often clears up ambiguity so rapidly that we are not aware of its existence. But research has shown that something interesting happens in the mind right after a word is heard. Michael Tanenhaus and coworkers (1979) showed that people briefly access multiple meanings of ambiguous words before the effect of context takes over. They did this by presenting participants with a tape recording of short sentences such as *She held the rose*, in which the target word *rose* is a noun referring to a flower, or *They all rose*, in which *rose* is a verb referring to people standing up.

Tanenhaus and coworkers wanted to determine what meanings of *rose* occurred in a person's mind for each of these sentences. To do this, they used a procedure called *lexical priming*.

METHOD   Lexical Priming

Remember from Chapter 6 (page 182) that priming occurs when seeing a stimulus makes it easier to respond to that stimulus when it is presented again. This is called *repetition priming*, because priming occurs when the same word is repeated. The basic principle behind priming is that the first presentation of a stimulus activates a representation of the stimulus, and a person can respond more rapidly if this activation is still present when the stimulus is presented again.

Lexical priming is priming that involves the meaning of words. Lexical priming occurs when a word is followed by another word with a similar meaning. For example, presenting the word *rose* and then the word *flower* can cause a person to respond faster to the word *flower* because the meanings of *rose* and *flower* are related. This priming effect does not, however, occur if the word *cloud* is presented before flower because their meanings are not related. The presence of a lexical priming effect therefore indicates whether two words, like *rose* and *flower*, have similar meanings in a person's mind.

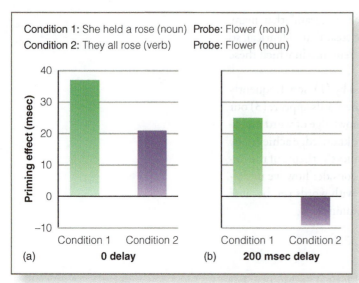

Condition 1: She held a rose (noun) Probe: Flower (noun)
Condition 2: They all rose (verb) Probe: Flower (noun)

➤ Figure 11.2 (a) Priming effect (decrease in response time compared to the control condition) at zero delay between word and probe. Condition 1: Noun (Example: She held a rose) followed by noun probe (flower). Condition 2: Verb (They all rose) followed by noun probe (flower). (b) Priming effect for the same conditions at 200 msec delay.

(Source: Based on data from Tanenhaus et al., 1979).

Tanenhaus and coworkers measured lexical priming using two conditions: (1) The noun-noun condition: a word is presented as a noun followed by a noun probe stimulus; and (2) The verb-noun condition: a word is presented as a verb followed by a noun probe stimulus. For example, in Condition 1, participants would hear a sentence like *She held a rose*, in which *rose* is a noun (a type of flower), followed immediately by the probe word *flower*. Their task was to read the probe word as quickly as possible. The time that elapsed between the end of the sentence and when the participant began saying the word is the reaction time.

To determine if presenting the word *rose* caused faster responding to *flower*, a control condition was run in which a sentence like *She held a post* was followed by the same probe word, *flower*. Because the meaning of *post* is not related to the meaning of *flower*, priming would not be expected, and this is what happened. As shown in the left bar in **Figure 11.2a**, the word *rose*, used as a flower, resulted in a 37 msec faster response to the word *flower* than in the control condition. This is what we would expect, because *rose*, the flower, is related to the meaning of the word *flower*.

Tanenhaus's results become more significant when we consider Condition 2, when the sentence was *They all rose*, in which *rose* is a verb (people getting up) and the probe word was still *flower*. The control for this sentence was *They all touched*. The result, shown in the right bar in **Figure 11.3a**, shows that priming occurred in this condition as well. Even though *rose* was presented as a verb, it still caused a faster response to flower!

What this means is that the "flower" meaning of *rose* is activated immediately after hearing *rose*, whether it is used as a noun or a verb. Tanenhaus also showed that the verb meaning of *rose* is activated whether it is used as a noun or a verb, and concluded from these results that all of an ambiguous word's meanings are activated immediately after the word is heard.

To make things even more interesting, when Tanenhaus ran the same experiment but added a delay of 200 msec between the end of the sentences and the probe word, the result changed. As shown in **Figure 11.2b**, priming still occurs for Condition 1—*rose* the noun primes *flower*—but no longer occurs for Condition 2—*rose* the verb does not prime *flower*. What this means is that by 200 msec after hearing the word *rose* as a verb, the flower meaning of *rose* is gone. Thus, the context provided by a sentence helps determine the meaning of a word, but context exerts its influence after a slight delay during which other meanings of a word are briefly accessed (also see Swinney, 1979, for a similar result and Lucas, 1999, for more on how context affects the meaning of words.)

Frequency Influences Which Meanings Are Activated

While context helps determine the appropriate meaning of words in a sentence, there's another factor at work: how frequently different meanings occur, with meanings that occur more frequently being more likely. As Matthew Traxler (2012) puts it, "Many words have multiple meanings, but these meanings are not all created equal." For example, consider the word *tin*. The most frequent meaning of *tin* is a type of metal, while a less-frequent meaning is a small metal container. The relative frequency of the meanings of ambiguous words is described in terms of **meaning dominance**. Words such as *tin*, in which one meaning (a type of metal) occurs more often than the other (a small metal container), is an example of **biased dominance**. Words such as *cast*, in which one meaning (members of a play) and the other meaning (plaster cast) are equally likely, is an example of **balanced dominance**.

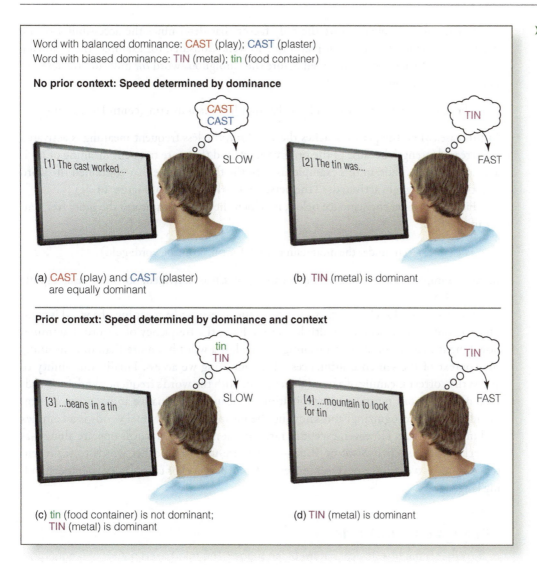

Word with balanced dominance: CAST (play); CAST (plaster)
Word with biased dominance: TIN (metal); tin (food container)

No prior context: Speed determined by dominance

[1] The cast worked...   CAST CAST   SLOW

[2] The tin was...   TIN   FAST

(a) CAST (play) and CAST (plaster) are equally dominant

(b) TIN (metal) is dominant

Prior context: Speed determined by dominance and context

[3] ...beans in a tin   tin TIN   SLOW

[4] ...mountain to look for tin   TIN   FAST

(c) tin (food container) is not dominant; TIN (metal) is dominant

(d) TIN (metal) is dominant

➤ **Figure 11.3** Accessing the meaning of ambiguous words while reading a sentence is determined by the word's dominance and the context created by the sentence. If there is no prior context: (a) competition between equally likely meanings of a word with balanced dominance results in slow access; (b) activation of only the most frequent meaning of a word with biased dominance results in fast access. If there is context before a word with biased dominance: (c) activation of both the less frequent and most frequent meanings results in slow access; (d) activation of only the most frequent meaning results in fast access. See text for examples.

This difference between biased and balanced dominance influences the way people access the meanings of words as they read them. This has been demonstrated in experiments in which researchers measure eye movements as participants read sentences and note the fixation time for an ambiguous word and also for a control word with just one meaning that replaces the ambiguous word in the sentence. Consider the following sentence, in which the ambiguous word *cast* has balanced dominance.

The *cast* worked into the night. (control word: *cook*)

As a person reads the word cast, both meanings of cast are activated, because cast (member of a play) and cast (plaster cast) are equally likely. Because the two meanings compete for activation, the person looks longer at *cast* than at the control word *cook*, which has only one meaning as a noun. Eventually, when the reader reaches the end of the sentence, the meaning becomes clear (Duffy et al., 1988; Rayner & Frazier, 1989; Traxler, 2012) (Figure 11.3a).

But consider the following, with the ambiguous word *tin*:

The *tin* was bright and shiny. (control word: *gold*)

In this case, people read the biased ambiguous word *tin* just as quickly as the control word, because only the dominant meaning of *tin* is activated, and the meaning of tin as a metal is accessed quickly (**Figure 11.3b**).

But meaning frequency isn't the only factor that determines the accessibility of the meaning of a word. Context can play a role as well. Consider, for example, the following sentence, in which the context added before the ambiguous word *tin* indicates the less-frequent meaning of tin:

The miners went to the store and saw that they had beans in a tin. (control word: cup)

In this case, when the person reaches the word *tin*, the less frequent meaning is activated at increased strength because of the prior context, and the more frequent meaning of *tin* is activated as well. Thus, in this example, as with the first sentence that contained the word *cast*, two meanings are activated, so the person looks longer at *tin* (**Figure 11.3c**).

Finally, consider the sentence below, in which the context indicates the more frequent meaning of *tin*:

The miners went under the mountain to look for tin. (control word: gold)

In this example, only the dominant meaning of *tin* is activated, so *tin* is read rapidly (**Figure 11.3d**).

We've seen in this chapter that the process of accessing the meaning of a word is complicated and is influenced by multiple factors. First, the frequency of a word determines how long it takes to process its meaning. Second, if a word has more than one meaning, the context of the sentence influences which meaning we access. Finally, our ability to access the correct meaning of a word depends on both the word's frequency and, for words with more than one meaning, a combination of meaning dominance and context. So simply identifying, recognizing, and knowing the meaning of individual words is a complex and impressive feat. However, except in rare situations in which words operate alone—as in exclamations such as *Stop*! or *Wait*!—words are used with other words to form sentences, and, as we will see next, sentences add another level of complexity to understanding language.

TEST YOURSELF 11.1

1. What is the hierarchical nature of language? The rule-based nature of language?
2. Why has the need to communicate been called universal?
3. What events are associated with the beginning of the modern study of language in the 1950s?
4. What is psycholinguistics? What are its concerns, and what part of psycholinguistics does this chapter focus on?
5. What is semantics? The lexicon?
6. How does word frequency affect our processing of words? Describe the eye movement experiment that illustrates an effect of word frequency.
7. What is the evidence that context helps people deal with the variability of word pronunciation?
8. What is speech segmentation and why is it a problem? What are some of the factors that help us achieve speech segmentation?
9. What is lexical ambiguity? Describe the experiment that used lexical priming to show that (a) all of the multiple meanings of a word are accessed immediately after the word is heard; and (b) context determines the appropriate meaning of an ambiguous word within about 200 msec.
10. What is meaning dominance? Biased dominance? Balanced dominance?
11. How do frequency and context combine to determine the correct meaning of ambiguous words?

▶ Understanding Sentences

When we considered words, we saw how sentences create context, which makes it possible to (1) deal with the variability of word pronunciations, (2) perceive individual words in a continuous stream of speech, and (3) determine the meanings of ambiguous words. But now we are going to go beyond just considering how sentences help us understand words, by asking how combining words into sentences creates meaning.

To understand how we determine the meaning of a sentence, we need to consider **syntax**—the structure of a sentence—and the study of syntax involves discovering cues that languages provide that show how words in a sentence relate to one another (Traxler, 2012). To start, let's think about what happens as we hear a sentence. Speech unfolds over time, with one word following another. This sequential process is central to understanding sentences, because one way to think about sentences is meaning unfolding over time.

What mental processes are occurring as a person hears a sentence? A simple way to answer this question would be to picture the meaning as being created by adding up the meanings of each word as they occur. But this idea runs into trouble right away when we consider that some words have more than one meaning and also that a sequence of words can have more than one meaning. The key to determining how strings of words create meaning is to consider how meaning is created by the grouping of words into phrases—a process called **parsing**.

Parsing: Making Sense of Sentences

Understanding the meaning of a sentence is a feat of mental pyrotechnics that involves understanding each word as it occurs (some of which may be ambiguous) and parsing words into phrases (**Figure 11.4**). To introduce parsing, let's look at some sentences. Consider, for example, a sentence that begins:

After the musician played the piano ...

What do you think comes next? Some possibilities are:

a. ... she left the stage.

b. ... she bowed to the audience.

c. ... the crowd cheered wildly.

All of these possibilities, which create sentences that are easy to understand and that make sense, involving grouping the words as follows: [After the musician played the piano] [the crowd cheered wildly]. But what if the sentence continued by stating

d. ... was wheeled off of the stage.

Reading the sentence ending in (d) as a whole, *After the musician played the piano was wheeled off of the stage*, might take you by surprise because the grouping of [After the musician played the piano] isn't correct. The correct grouping is [After the musician played] [the piano was wheeled off of the stage.]. When written, adding a comma makes the correct parsing of this sentence clear: *After the musician played, the piano was wheeled off the stage.*

Sentences like this one, which begin appearing to mean one thing but then end up meaning something else, are called **garden path sentences** (from the phrase "leading a person down the garden path," which means misleading the person). Garden path sentences illustrate **temporary ambiguity**, because first one organization is adopted and then—when the error is realized—the person shifts to the correct organization.

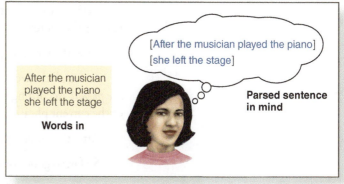

▶ **Figure 11.4** Parsing is the process that occurs when a person hears or reads a string of words (*Words in*) and groups these words into phrases in their mind (*Parsed sentence in mind*). The way the words are grouped in this example indicates that the person has interpreted the sentence to mean that the musician played the piano and then left the stage.

The Garden Path Model of Parsing

Language researchers have used sentences with temporary ambiguity to help understand the mechanisms that operate during parsing. One of the early proposals to explain parsing, and garden path sentences in particular, is called the **garden path model of parsing**. This approach, proposed by Lynn Frazier (1979, 1987), states that as people read a sentence, their grouping of words into phrases is governed by a number of processing mechanisms called **heuristics**. As we will see when we discuss reasoning and decision making, a heuristic is a rule that can be applied rapidly to make a decision. The decisions involved in parsing are decisions about the structure of a sentence as it unfolds in time.

Heuristics have two properties: On the positive side, they are fast, which is important for language, which occurs at about 200 words per minute (Traxler, 2012). On the negative side, they sometimes result in the wrong decision. These properties become apparent in a sentence like *After the musician played the piano was wheeled off the stage*, in which the initial parse of the sentence turns out to be incorrect. The garden path model proposes that when this happens, we reconsider the initial parse and make appropriate corrections.

The garden path model specifies not only that rules are involved in parsing, but that these rules are based on syntax—the structural characteristic of language. We will focus on one of these syntax-based principles, which is called late closure. The principle of **late closure** states that when a person encounters a new word, the person's parsing mechanism assumes that this word is part of the current phrase, so each new word is added to the current phrase for as long as possible (Frazier, 1987).

Let's return to sentence about the musician to see how this works. The person begins reading the sentence:

After the musician played ...

So far, all the words are in the same phrase. But what happens when we reach the words *the piano*? According to late closure, the parsing mechanism assumes that *the piano* is part of the current phrase, so the phrase now becomes

After the musician played the piano ...

So far, so good. But when we reach *was*, late closure adds this to the phrase to create

After the musician played the piano was ...

And then, when *wheeled* is added to create an even longer phrase, it becomes obvious that something is wrong. Late closure has led us astray (down the garden path!) by adding too many words to the first phrase. We need to reconsider, taking the meaning of the sentence into account, and reparse the sentence so "the piano" is not added to the first phrase. Instead, it becomes part of the second phrase to create the grouping

[After the musician played] [the piano was wheeled off the stage].

The garden path model generated a great deal of research, which resulted in support for the model (Frazier, 1987). However, some researchers questioned the proposal that syntactic rules like late closure operate alone to determine parsing until it becomes obvious that a correction is needed (Altmann et al., 1992; Tanenhaus & Trueswell, 1995). These researchers have provided evidence to show that factors in addition to syntax can influence parsing right from the beginning.

The Constraint-Based Approach to Parsing

The idea that information in addition to syntax participates in processing as a person reads or hears a sentence is called the **constraint-based approach to parsing**. As we consider some examples that show how parsing can be influenced by factors in addition to syntax, we will encounter a theme we introduced at the beginning of the chapter: Information contained in the words of a sentence, and in the context within which a sentence occurs, is used to make *predictions* about how the sentence should be parsed (Kuperberg & Jaeger, 2015).

Influence of Word Meaning   Here are two sentences that illustrate how the meaning of words in a sentence can influence parsing right from the beginning. They differ in how hard they are to figure out because of the meanings of the second words in each sentence.

1. The defendant examined by the lawyer was unclear.
2. The evidence examined by the lawyer was unclear.

Which one was easier to figure out as you were reading along? The process that occurs as sentence (1) is unfolding is illustrated in **Figure 11.5a**. After reading *The defendant examined*, two possibilities present themselves: (1) the defendant could be examining something or (2) the defendant could be being examined by someone else. It's only after reading the rest of the sentence *by the attorney* that it is possible to definitely determine that the defendant is being examined.

In contrast, only one possibility presents itself after reading *The evidence examined* in sentence (2) because it is unlikely that the evidence will be doing any examining. (**Figure 11.5b**).

Here are two more examples:

1. The dog buried in the sand was hidden.
2. The treasure buried in the sand was hidden.

Which one of these is more likely to initially lead to the wrong conclusion, and why?

Influence of Story Context   Consider the following sentence proposed by Thomas Bever (1970), which has been called the most famous garden path sentence because of the confusion it causes:

The horse raced past the barn fell

Whoa! What's going on here? For many people, everything is fine until they hit *fell*. Readers are often confused, and may even accuse the sentence of being ungrammatical. But let's look at the sentence in the context of the following story:

There were two jockeys who decided to race their horses. One raced his horse along the path that went past the garden. The other raced his horse along the path that went past the barn. The horse raced past the barn fell.

Of course, the confusion could have been avoided by simply stating that the horse *that was* raced past the barn fell, but even without these helpful words, context wins the day and we parse the sentence correctly!

Influence of Scene Context   Parsing of a sentence is influenced not only by the context provided by stories but also by context provided by scenes. To investigate how observing objects in a scene can influence how we interpret a sentence, Michael Tanenhaus and coworkers (1995) developed a technique called the **visual world paradigm**, which involves determining how information in a scene can influence how a sentence is processed. Participants' eye movements were measured as they saw objects on a table, as in

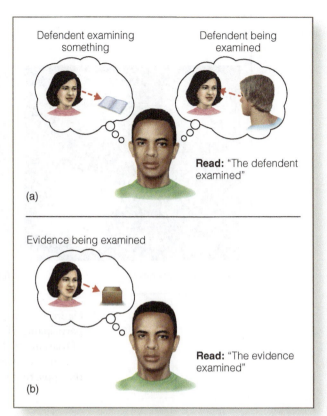

➤ **Figure 11.5** (a) Two possible predictions that could be made after reading or hearing *The defendant examined* in sentence (1) The defendant is going to either examine something (top) or be examined by someone else (bottom). (b) The only possible reading of *The evidence examined* in sentence (2) is that the evidence is examined by someone. The possibility that the evidence was going to examine something is highly unlikely.

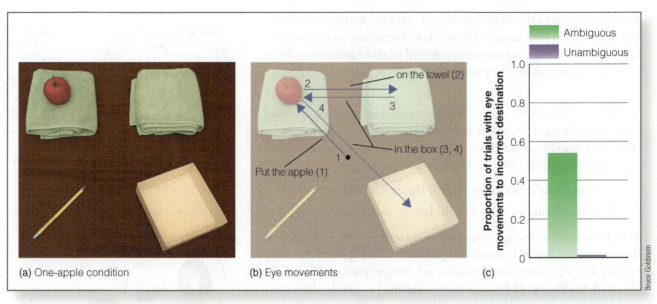

(a) One-apple condition   (b) Eye movements   (c)

> **Figure 11.6** (a) One-apple scene similar to the one viewed by Tanenhaus et al.'s (1995) participants. (b) Eye movements made while comprehending the task. (c) Proportion of trials in which eye movements were made to the towel on the right for the ambiguous sentence. (Place the apple on the towel in the box) and the unambiguous sentence (Place the apple that's on the towel in the box).

Figure 11.6a. As participants looked at this display, they were told to carry out the following instructions:

Place the apple on the towel in the box.

When participants heard the phrase *Place the apple*, they moved their eyes to the apple, then hearing *on the towel*, they looked at the other towel (**Figure 11.6b**). They did this because at this point in the sentence they were assuming that they were being told to put the apple on the other towel. Then, when they heard *in the box,* they realized that they were looking at the wrong place and quickly shifted their eyes to the box.

The reason participants looked first at the wrong place was that the sentence is ambiguous. First it seems like *on the towel* means where the apple should *be placed*, but then it becomes clear that *on the towel* is referring to where the apple *is located*. When the ambiguity was removed by changing the sentence to *Move the apple that's on the towel to the box*, participants immediately focused their attention on the box. **Figure 11.6c** shows this result. When the sentence was ambiguous, participants looked at the other towel on 55 percent of the trials; when it wasn't ambiguous, participants didn't look at the other towel.

Tanenhaus also ran another condition in which he presented the two-apple display like the one in **Figure 11.7a**. Because there are two apples, participants interpreted *on the towel* to be indicating *which* apple they should move, and so looked at the apple and then at the box (**Figure 11.7b**). **Figure 11.7c** shows that participants looked at the other towel on only about 10 percent of the trials for both *place the apple on the towel* (the ambiguous sentence) and *place the apple that's on the towel* (the non-ambiguous sentence) when looking at this display. The fact that the eye movement patterns were the same for the ambiguous and non-ambiguous sentences means that in this context the participants were not led down the garden path.

The important result of this study is that the participants' eye movements occur as they are reading the sentence and are influenced by the contents of the scene. Tanenhaus therefore showed that participants take into account not only information provided by the syntactic structure of the sentence, but also by what Tanenhaus calls *non-linguistic information—* in this case, information provided by the scene. This result argues against the idea proposed

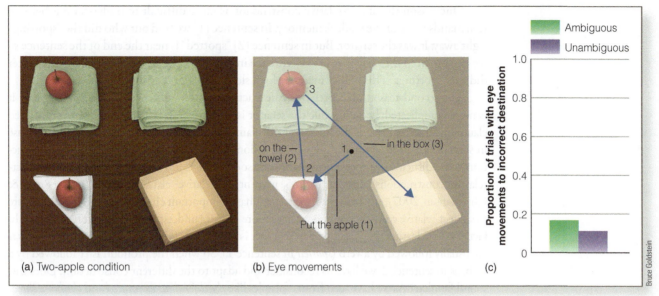

(a) Two-apple condition   (b) Eye movements   (c)

➤ **Figure 11.7** (a) Two-apple scene similar to the one viewed by Tanenhaus et al.'s (1995) subjects. (b) Eye movements while comprehending the task. (c) Proportion of trials in which eye movements were made to the towel on the right for the ambiguous sentence (Place the apple on the towel in the box) and the unambiguous sentence (Place the apple that's on the towel in the box).

by the garden path model that syntactic rules are the only thing taken into account as a sentence is initially unfolding.

Influence of Memory Load and Prior Experience with Language   Consider these two sentences:

1. The senator who spotted the reporter shouted

2. The senator who the reporter spotted shouted

These sentences have the same words, but they are arranged differently to create different constructions. Sentence (2) is more difficult to understand, as indicated by research that shows that readers spend longer looking at the part of the sentence following *who* in sentences with structures like sentence (2) (Traxler et al., 2002).

To understand why sentence (2) is more difficult to understand, we need to break these sentences down into clauses. Sentence (1) has two clauses:

Main clause: The senator shouted.

Embedded clause: The senator spotted the reporter.

The embedded clause is called embedded, because *who spotted the reporter* is inside the main clause. The senator is the subject of both the main clause and the embedded clause. This construction is called a **subject-relative construction.**

Sentence [2] also contains two clauses:

Main clause: The senator shouted.

Embedded clause: The reporter spotted the senator.

In this case, the senator is the subject of the main clause, as before, and is also replaced by *who* in the embedded clause, but is the object in this clause. The senator is the object because he is the target who was spotted. (The reporter is the subject of this clause, because he did the spotting.) This construction is called an **object-relative construction.**

One reason the object-relative construction is more difficult to understand is because it demands more of the reader's memory. In sentence [1] we find out who did the "spotting" right away. It was the senator. But in sentence [2] "spotted" is near the end of the sentence so we need to hold the early part of the sentence in memory until we find out that the reporter did the "spotting." This higher memory load slows down processing.

The second reason object-relative construction is more difficult to understand is that it is more complicated, because while the senator is the subject in both the main and embedded clauses in sentence [1], it is the subject of the main clause and the object of the embedded clause in sentence [2]. This more complex construction not only makes the object-relative construction more difficult to process, it may be a reason that it is less prevalent in English. Subject-relative constructions account for 65 percent of relative clause constructions (Reali & Christiansen, 2007), and being more prevalent has an important effect—we have more exposure to subject-relative constructions, so we have more practice understanding these constructions. In fact, we have learned to expect that in sentences of this type, pronouns like *who*, *which*, or *that* are usually followed by a verb (*spotted* in sentence 1). So when the pronoun isn't followed by a verb, as in sentence 2, we have to reconsider and adapt to the different construction. Does this sound familiar? As we have seen from examples like *the defendant examined* and *the horse raced*, making predictions during a sentence that turn out to be wrong slows down sentence processing.

Prediction, Prediction, Prediction...

The examples we've considered so far—the defendant being examined, the falling horse, the apple on the towel, and the shouting senator—all have something in common. They illustrate how people make predictions about what is likely to happen next in a sentence. We predict that *The defendant examined* means that the defendant is going to examine something but instead it turns out that the defendant is *being* examined! Oops! Our incorrect prediction has led us down the garden path. Similarly, we predict that *The horse raced* is going to say something about how the horse raced (*The horse raced faster than it ever had before*), but instead we find that *raced* refers to which horse was racing. We predict that we are being asked to place the apple on the other towel, but it turns out to be otherwise.

But even though incorrect predications can temporarily throw us off track, most of the time prediction is our friend. We are constantly making predictions about what is likely to happen next in a sentence, and most of the time these predictions are correct. These correct predictions help us deal with the rapid pace of language. And prediction becomes even more important when language is degraded, as in a poor phone connection, or is heard in a noisy environment, or when you are trying to understand someone with a foreign accent.

Gerry Altmann and Yuki Kamide (1999) did an experiment that showed that the participants were making predictions as they were reading a sentence by measuring their eye movements. **Figure 11.8** shows a picture similar to one from the experiment. Participants heard either *The boy will move the cake* or *The boy will eat the cake* while viewing this scene. For both of these sentences, *cake* is the target object.

Participants were told to indicate whether the sentence they read could be applied to the pictures. Altmann and Kamide didn't care how they responded in this task. What they did care about was how they were processing the information as they were hearing the sentences.

Let's consider what might be happening as the sentences unfold: First, *The boy will move ...* What do you think the boy is

➤ **Figure 11.8** A picture similar to one used in Altman and Kamide's (1999) experiment in which they measured eye movements that occurred as participants heard a sentence while looking at the picture.

going to move? The answer isn't really clear, because the boy could move the car, the train, the ball, or even the cake. Now consider *The boy will eat ...* This one is easy. The boy will eat the cake.

Measurement of participants' eye movements as they were hearing these sentences indicated that eye movements toward the target object (*cake* in this example) occurred 127 msec *after* hearing the word *cake* for the *move* sentences and 87 msec *before* hearing the word *cake* for the *eat* sentences. Thus, hearing the word *eat* causes the participant to begin looking toward the cake before he or she even hears the word. *Eat* leads to the prediction that *cake* will be the next word.

This kind of prediction is likely occurring constantly as we hear or read sentences. As we will see in the next sections, predictions also play an important role in understanding stories and having conversations.

TEST YOURSELF 11.2

1. What is syntax?
2. What is parsing? What are garden path sentences?
3. Describe the garden path model of parsing. Be sure you understand what a heuristic is and the principle of late closure.
4. Describe the constraint-based approach to parsing. How does it differ from the garden path approach?
5. Describe the following lines of evidence that support the constraint-based approach to parsing:
   ➤ How meanings of words in a sentence affect parsing.
   ➤ How story context affects parsing.
   ➤ How scene context affects processing. Be sure you understand the visual world paradigm.
   ➤ How memory load and predictions based on knowledge of language structure affect parsing. Be sure you understand the difference between subject-relative and object-relative constructions and why object-relative constructions are harder to understand.
6. How can garden path sentences be related to prediction?
7. How is prediction important for understanding sentences?

▶ Understanding Text and Stories

Just as sentences are more than the sum of the meanings of individual words, stories are more than the sum of the meanings of individual sentences. In a well-written story, sentences in one part of the story are related to sentences in other parts of the story. The reader's task is to use these relationships between sentences to create a coherent, understandable story.

An important part of the process of creating a coherent story is making **inferences**—determining what the text means by using our knowledge to go beyond the information provided by the text. We have seen how unconscious inference is involved in perception (Chapter 3, page 70), and when we described the constructive nature of memory in Chapter 8, we saw that we often make inferences, often without realizing it, as we retrieve memories of what has happened in the past (page 240).

Making Inferences

An early demonstration of inference in language was an experiment by John Bransford and Marcia Johnson (1973), in which they had participants read passages and then tested them to determine what they remembered. One of the passages Bransford and Johnson's participants read was

> John was trying to fix the birdhouse. He was pounding the nail when his father came out to watch him and help him do the work.

After reading that passage, participants were likely to indicate that they had previously seen the following passage: "John was using a hammer to fix the birdhouse when his father came out to watch him and help him do the work." They often reported seeing this passage, even though they had never read that John was using a hammer, because they inferred that John was using a hammer from the information that he was pounding the nail. People use a similar creative process to make a number of different types of inferences as they are reading a text.

One role of inference is to create connections between parts of a story. This process is typically illustrated with excerpts from narrative texts. **Narrative** refers to texts in which there is a story that progresses from one event to another, although stories can also include flashbacks of events that happened earlier. An important property of any narrative is **coherence**—the representation of the text in a person's mind that creates clear relations between parts of the text and between parts of the text and the main topic of the story. Coherence can be created by a number of different types of inference. Consider the following sentence:

> Riffifi, the famous poodle, won the dog show. She has now won the last three shows she has entered.

What does *she* refer to? If you picked Riffifi you are using **anaphoric inference**—inference that involves inferring that both *she*s in the second sentence refer to Riffifi. In the previous "John and the birdhouse" example, knowing that *He* in the second sentence refers to John is another example of anaphoric inference.

We usually have little trouble making anaphoric inferences because of the way information is presented in sentences and our ability to make use of knowledge we bring to the situation. But the following quote from a *New York Times* interview with former heavyweight champion George Foreman (also known for lending his name to a popular line of grills) puts our ability to create anaphoric inference to the test.

> … we really love to … go down to our ranch. …I take the kids out and we fish. And then, of course, we grill them. (Stevens, 2002)

From just the structure of the sentences, we might conclude that the kids were grilled, but we know the chances are pretty good that the fish were grilled, not George Foreman's children! Readers are capable of creating anaphoric inferences even under adverse conditions because they add information from their knowledge of the world to the information provided in the text.

Here's another opportunity to use your powers of inference. What do you picture upon reading the sentence, "William Shakespeare wrote Hamlet while he was sitting at his desk"? It is likely that from what you know about the time Shakespeare lived that he was probably using a quill pen (not a laptop computer!) and that his desk was made of wood. This is an example of **instrument inference**. Similarly, inferring from the passage about John and the birdhouse that he is using a hammer to pound the nails would be an instrument inference.

Here's another one:

> Sharon took an aspirin. Her headache went away.

You probably inferred that *Her* was referring to Sharon, but what caused her headache to go away? Nowhere in these two sentences is that question answered, *unless* you engage in

causal inference, in which you infer that the events described in one clause or sentence were caused by events that occurred in a previous sentence, and infer that taking the aspirin made her headache go away (Goldman et al., 1999; Graesser et al., 1994; Singer et al., 1992; van den Broek, 1994). But what can you conclude from the following two sentences?

Sharon took a shower. Her headache went away.

You might conclude, from the fact that the headache sentence directly follows the shower sentence, that the shower had something to do with eliminating Sharon's headache. However, the causal connection between the shower and the headache is weaker than the connection between the aspirin and the headache in the first pair of sentences. Making the shower–headache connection requires more work from the reader. You might infer that the shower relaxed Sharon, or perhaps her habit of singing in the shower was therapeutic. Or you might decide there actually isn't much connection between the two sentences. Going back to our discussion of how information in stories can aid in parsing, we can also imagine that if we had been reading a story about Sharon, which previously had described how Sharon loved taking showers because they took away her tension, then you might be more likely to give the shower credit for eliminating her headache.

Inferences create connections that are essential for creating coherence in texts, and making these inferences can involve creativity by the reader. Thus, reading a text involves more than just understanding words or sentences. It is a dynamic process that involves transformation of the words, sentences, and sequences of sentences into a meaningful story. Sometimes this is easy, sometimes harder, depending on the skill and intention of both the reader and the writer (Goldman et al., 1999; Graesser et al., 1994; van den Broek, 1994).

We have been describing the process of text comprehension so far in terms of how people bring their knowledge to bear to infer connections between different parts of a story. Another approach to understanding how people understand stories is to consider the nature of the mental representation that people form as they read a story.

Situation Models

What do we mean when we say people form mental representations as they read a story? One way to answer this question is to think about what's happening in your mind as you read. For example, *the runner jumped over the hurdle* probably brings up an image of a runner on a track, jumping a hurdle. This image goes beyond information about phrases, sentences, or paragraphs; instead, it is a representation of the situation in terms of the people, objects, locations, and events being described in the story (Barsalou, 2008, 2009; Graesser & Wiemer-Hastings, 1999; Zwaan, 1999).

This approach to how we understand sentences proposes that as people read or hear a story, they create a **situation model**, which simulates the perceptual and motor (movement) characteristics of the objects and actions in a story. This idea has been tested by having participants read a sentence that describes a situation involving an object and then indicate as quickly as possible whether a picture shows the object mentioned in the sentence. For example, consider the following two sentences.

1. He hammered the nail into the wall.
2. He hammered the nail into the floor.

In **Figure 11.9a**, the horizontal nail matches the orientation that would be expected for sentence (1), and the vertical nail matches the orientation for sentence (2). Robert Stanfield and Rolf Zwaan (2001) presented these sentences, followed by either a matching picture or

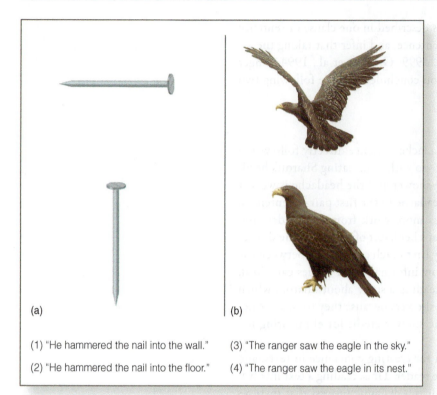

(a)

(1) "He hammered the nail into the wall."

(2) "He hammered the nail into the floor."

(b)

(3) "The ranger saw the eagle in the sky."

(4) "The ranger saw the eagle in its nest."

➤ **Figure 11.9** Stimuli similar to those used in (a) Stanfield and Zwaan's (2001) "orientation" experiment and (b) Zwaan et al.'s (2002) "shape" experiment. Subjects heard sentences and were then asked to indicate whether the picture was the object mentioned in the sentence

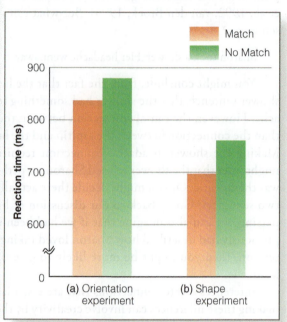

➤ **Figure 11.10** Results of Stanfield and Zwaan's (2001) and Zwaan et al.'s (2002) experiments. Subjects responded "yes" more rapidly for the orientation, in (a), and the shape, in (b), that was more consistent with the sentence.

a nonmatching picture. Because the pictures both show nails and the task was to indicate whether the picture shows the object mentioned in the sentence, the correct answer was "yes" no matter which nail was presented. However, participants responded "yes" more rapidly when the picture's orientation matched the situation described in the sentence (**Figure 11.10a**).

The pictures for another experiment, involving object shape, are shown in **Figure 11.9b**. The sentences for these pictures are

1. The ranger saw the eagle in the sky.
2. The ranger saw the eagle in its nest.

In this experiment, by Zwaan and coworkers (2002), the picture of an eagle with wings outstretched elicited a faster response when it followed sentence (1) than when it followed sentence (2). Again, reaction times were faster when the picture matched the situation described in the sentence. This result, shown in **Figure 11.10b**, matches the result for the orientation experiment, and both experiments support the idea that the participants created perceptions that matched the situation as they were reading the sentences.

Another study that demonstrates how situations are represented in the mind was carried out by Ross Metusalem and coworkers (2012), who were interested in how our knowledge about a situation is activated in our mind as we read a story. Metusalem measured the event-related potential (ERP), which we introduced in Chapter 5 (see page 156) as participants were reading a story. The ERP has a number of different components. One of these components is called the N400 wave because it is a negative response that occurs about 400 msec after a word is heard or read. One of the characteristics of the N400 response is that the response is larger when a word in a sentence is unexpected. This is shown in **Figure 11.11**. The blue record shows the N400 response to *eat* in the sentence *The cat* *won't eat.* But if the sentence is changed to *The cat won't bake*, then the unexpected word *bake* elicits a larger response.

Metusalem recorded the ERP as participants read scenarios such as the following:

CONCERT SCENARIO

The band was very popular and Joe was sure the concert would be sold out. Amazingly, he was able to get a seat down in front. He couldn't believe how close he was when he saw the group walk out onto the (stage/guitar/barn) and start playing.

Three different versions of each scenario were created, using each of the words shown in parentheses. Each participant read one version of each scenario.

If you were reading this scenario, which word would you predict to follow "he saw the group walk out onto the …"? *Stage* is the obvious choice, so it was called the "expected" condition. *Guitar* doesn't fit the passage, but since it is related to concerts and bands, it is called the "event-related" word. *Barn* doesn't fit the passage and is also not related to the topic, so it is called the "event-unrelated" word.

Figure 11.12 shows the average ERPs recorded as participants read the target words. *Stage* was the expected word, so there is only a small N400 response to this word. The interesting result is the response to the other two words. *Barn* causes a large N400, because it isn't related to the passage. *Guitar*, which doesn't fit the passage either but is related to "concerts," generates a smaller N400 than *barn*.

We would expect *stage* to generate little or no N400 response, because it fits the meaning of the sentence. However, the fact that *guitar* generates a smaller N400 than *barn* means that this word is at least slightly activated by the concert scenario. According to Metusalem, our knowledge about different situations is continually being accessed as we read a story, and if *guitar* is activated, it is also likely that other words related to concerts, such as *drums*, *vocalist*, *crowds*, and *beer* (depending on your experience with concerts), would also be activated.

The idea that many things associated with a particular scenario are activated is connected with the idea that we create a situation model while we are reading. What the ERP results show is that as we read, models of the situation are activated that include lots of details based on what we know about particular situations (also see Kuperberg, 2013; Paczynski & Kuperberg, 2012). In addition to suggesting that we are constantly accessing our world knowledge as we read or listen to a story, results like these also indicate that we access this knowledge rapidly, within fractions of a second after reading a particular word.

Another aspect of the situation model approach is the idea that a reader or listener simulates the motor characteristics of the objects in a story. According to this idea, a story that involves movement will result in simulation of this movement as the person is comprehending the story. For example, reading a story about a bicycle elicits not only the perception of what a bicycle looks like but also properties associated with movement, such as how a bicycle is propelled (by peddling) and the physical exertion involved in riding the bicycle under different conditions (climbing hills, racing, coasting). This corresponds to the idea introduced in Chapter 9 that knowledge about a category goes beyond simply identifying a typical object in that category: It also includes various properties of the object, such as how the object is used, what it does, and sometimes even emotional responses it elicits. This way of looking at the reader's response adds a richness to events in a story that extends beyond simply understanding what is going on (Barsalou, 2008; Fischer & Zwaan, 2008).

We saw in Chapter 9 (page 290) how Olaf Hauk and coworkers (2004) determined the link between movement, action words, and brain activation by measuring brain activity using fMRI under two conditions: (1) as participants moved their right or left foot, left

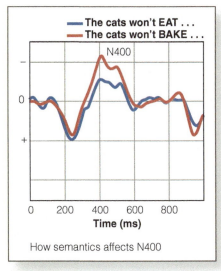

> **Figure 11.11** The N400 wave of the ERP is affected by the meaning of the word. It becomes larger (red line) when the meaning of the word does not fit the rest of the sentence.
> (Source: Osterhout et al., 1997)

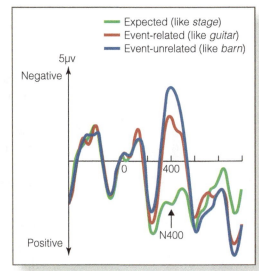

> **Figure 11.12** Results of Metusalem et al.'s (2012) experiment for the concert scenario. The key result is that the N400 response to an event-related word like *guitar* (red curve) is smaller than the response to an event-unrelated word like *barn* (blue curve). This suggests that even though *guitar* doesn't fit in the sentence, the person's knowledge that guitars are associated with concerts is activated.

or right index finger, or tongue; (2) as participants read "action words" such as *kick* (foot action), *pick* (finger or hand action), or *lick* (tongue action).

Hauk's results show areas of the cortex activated by the actual movements (Figure 9.26a, page 290) and by reading the action words (Figure 9.26b). The activation is more extensive for actual movements, but the activation caused by reading the words occurs in approximately the same areas of the brain. For example, leg words and leg movements elicit activity near the brain's center line, whereas arm words and finger movements elicit activity farther from the center line. This link between action words and activation of action areas in the brain suggests a physiological mechanism that may be related to creating situation models as a person reads a story.

The overall conclusion from research on how people comprehend stories is that understanding a text or story is a creative and dynamic process. Understanding stories involves understanding sentences by determining how words are organized into phrases; then determining the relationships between sentences, often using inference to link sentences in one part of a story to sentences in another part; and finally, creating mental representations or simulations that involve both perceptual and motor properties of objects and events in the story. As we will now see, a creative and dynamic process also occurs when two or more people are having a conversation.

▶ Having Conversations

Although language can be produced by a single person talking alone, as when a person recites a monologue or gives a speech, the most common form of language production is conversation—two or more people talking with one another. Conversation, or dialogue, provides another example of a cognitive skill that seems simple but contains underlying complexities.

Having a conversation is often easy, especially if you know the person you are talking with and have talked with them before. But sometimes conversations can become more difficult, especially if you're talking with someone for the first time. Why should this be so? One answer is that when talking to someone else, it helps if you have some awareness of what the other person knows about the topic you're discussing. Even when both people bring similar knowledge to a conversation, it helps if speakers take steps to guide their listeners through the conversation. One way of achieving this is by following the *given–new contract*.

The Given–New Contract

The **given–new contract** states that a speaker should construct sentences so that they include two kinds of information: (1) given information—information that the listener already knows; and (2) new information—information that the listener is hearing for the first time (Haviland & Clark, 1974). For example, consider the following two sentences.

Sentence 1. Ed was given an alligator for his birthday.

Given information (from previous conversation): Ed had a birthday.

New information: He got an alligator.

Sentence 2. The alligator was his favorite present.

Given information (from sentence [1]): Ed got an alligator.

New information: It was his favorite present.

Notice how the new information in the first sentence becomes the given information in the second sentence.

Susan Haviland and Herbert Clark (1974) demonstrated the consequences of not following the given–new contract by presenting pairs of sentences and asking participants to press a button when they thought they understood the second sentence in each pair. They found that it took longer for participants to comprehend the second sentence in pairs like this one:

We checked the picnic supplies.

The beer was warm.

than it took to comprehend the second sentence in pairs like this one:

We got some beer out of the trunk.

The beer was warm.

The reason comprehending the second sentence in the first pair takes longer is that the given information (that there were picnic supplies) does not mention beer. Thus, the reader or listener needs to make an inference that beer was among the picnic supplies. This inference is not required in the second pair because the first sentence includes the information that there is beer in the trunk.

The idea of given and new captures the collaborative nature of conversations. Herbert Clark (1996) sees collaboration as being central to the understanding of language. Describing language as "a form of joint action," Clark proposes that understanding this joint action involves considering not only providing given and new information but also taking into account the knowledge, beliefs, and assumptions that the other person brings to the conversation, a process called establishing *common ground* (Isaacs & Clark, 1987).

Common Ground: Taking the Other Person into Account

Common ground is the mental knowledge and beliefs shared among conversational parties (Brown-Schmidt & Hanna, 2011). The key word in this definition is *shared*. When two people are having a conversation, each person may have some idea of what the other person knows about what they are discussing, and as the conversation continues, the amount of shared information increases. What's especially important about this sharing of information is that each person is not only accumulating information about the topic at hand (like knowing in our discussion of *given–new* that the beer was in the trunk), but they are also accumulating information about what the other person knows. Having a conversation is, after all, about you *and* the other person, and conversations go more smoothly if you know as much as possible about the other person.

One example of how having a successful conversation depends on understanding what the other person knows is how doctors who communicate well with patients usually assume that their patients have limited knowledge of physiology and medical terminology. Taking this into account, these doctors use lay terminology, such as heart attack rather than myocardial infarction. However, if the doctor realizes that the patient is also a doctor, he or she knows that it is permissible to use medical terminology (Issacs & Clark, 1987).

Establishing Common Ground

Going beyond knowing how much knowledge people bring to a conversation, a great deal of research on common ground considers how people establish common ground *during* a conversation. One way this is studied is to analyze transcripts of conversations. The following example is a conversation among three students who are trying to recall a scene from the movie *The Secret of Roan Inish* (Brennan et al., 2010):

Leah: um … then he gets punished or whatever?

Dale: what was that, a wreath or—

Leah: yeah it was some kind of browny—

Adam: yeah it was some kind of straw thing or something

Leah: mhm

Dale: around his neck

Leah: so that everybody knew what he did or something?

Adam: straw wreath

Dale: yeah

One thing this conversation reveals is that people often talk not in whole sentences but in fragments. It also illustrates how a conversation unfolds in an orderly way, as the conversation reconstructs the events the people are talking about. In the end, they come to a conclusion that everyone shares.

Another way of studying how common ground is established is through the **referential communication task**, a task in which two people are exchanging information in a conversation, when this information involves *reference*—identifying something by naming or describing it (Yule, 1997). An example of a referential communication task is provided by an experiment by P. Stellman and Susan Brennan (1993; described in Brennan et al., 2010) in which two partners, A (the director) and B (the matcher), had identical sets of 12 cards with pictures of abstract geometrical objects. A arranged the cards in a specific order. B's task was to arrange her cards in the same order. Because B couldn't see A's cards, she had to determine the identity of each card through conversation. Here is an example of a conversation that resulted in B understanding the identity of one of A's cards.

Trial 1:

A: ah boy this one ah boy alright it looks kinda like on the right top there's a square that looks diagonal

B: uh huh

A: and you have sort of another like rectangle shape, the—like a triangle, angled, and on the bottom it's ah I don't know what that is, glass shaped

B: alright I think I got it

A: it's almost like a person kind of in a weird way

B: yeah like like a monk praying or something

A: right yeah good great

B: alright I got it. (they go on to the next card)

After all of the cards are identified and placed in the correct order, A rearranges the cards and the partners repeat the task two more times. Trials 2 and 3, shown below, indicate that the conversations for these trials are much briefer:

Trial 2:

B: 9 is that monk praying

A: yup (they go on to the next card)

Trial 3:

A: number 4 is the monk

B: ok (they go on to the next card)

What this means is that the partners have established common ground. They know what each other knows and can refer to the cards by the

"A bat"
"The candle"
"The anchor"
"The rocket ship"
"The Olympic torch"
"The Canada symbol"
"The symmetrical one"
"Shapes on top of shapes"
"The one with all the shapes"
"The bird diving straight down"
"The airplane flying straight down"
"The angel upside down with sleeves"
"The man jumping in the air with bell bottoms on"

➤ **Figure 11.13** An abstract picture used by Stellman and Brennan (1993) to study common ground. Each description was proposed by a different pair of participants in a referential communication task.

(Source: From Brannan, Galati and Kuhlen, 2010. Originally from Stellmann and Brennan, 1993.)

names they have created. **Figure 11.13** shows another of the geometrical objects used in this task (not the "monk" object) and the descriptive names established by 13 different A–B pairs. It is clear that it doesn't matter what the object is called, just so both partners have the same information about the object. And once common ground is established, conversations flow much more smoothly.

The process of creating common ground results in **entrainment**—synchronization between the two partners. In this example, synchronization occurs in the naming of the objects on the cards. But entrainment also occurs in other ways as well. Conversational partners can establish similar gestures, speaking rate, body positions, and sometimes pronunciation (Brennan et al., 2010). We now consider how conversational partners can end up coordinating their grammatical constructions—an effect called **syntactic coordination**.

Syntactic Coordination

When two people exchange statements in a conversation, it is common for them to use similar grammatical constructions. Kathryn Bock (1990) provides the following example, taken from a recorded conversation between a bank robber and his lookout, which was intercepted by a ham radio operator as the robber was removing the equivalent of $1 million from a bank vault in England.

Robber: "... *you've got to hear* and witness it *to realize how bad it is*."

Lookout: "*You have got to experience exactly* the same position as me, mate, *to understand how I feel*." (from Schenkein, 1980, p. 22)

Bock has added italics to illustrate how the lookout copied the form of the robber's statement. This copying of form reflects a phenomenon called **syntactic priming**—hearing a statement with a particular syntactic construction increases the chances that a sentence will be produced with the same construction. Syntactic priming is important because it can lead people to coordinate the grammatical form of their statements during a conversation. Holly Branigan and coworkers (2000) illustrated syntactic priming by using the following procedure to set up a give-and-take between two people.

METHOD Syntactic Priming

In a syntactic priming experiment, two people engage in a conversation, and the experimenter determines whether a specific grammatical construction used by one person causes the other person to use the same construction. In Branigan's experiment, participants were told that the experiment was about how people communicate when they can't see each other. They thought they were working with another participant who was on the other side of a screen (the person on the left in **Figure 11.14a**). In reality, person A, on the left, was working with the experimenter, and person B, on the right, was the participant in the experiment.

Person A began the experiment by making a priming statement, as shown on the left of **Figure 11.14a**. This statement was in one of the following two forms:

The girl gave the book to the boy.
or
The girl gave the boy the book.

The participant responded by locating, among the cards laid out on the table, the matching card that corresponded to the confederate's statement, as shown on the right in **Figure 11.14a**. The participant then picked the top card from the response pile on

The girl gave the boy a book.

Matching cards

Participant picks matching card that matches statement.

Confederate reads statement.

(a)

The father gave his daughter a present.

Response cards

Participant picks response card and describes picture to confederate.

Confederate listening

(b)

➤ **Figure 11.14** The Branigan et al. (2000) experiment. (a) The subject (right) picks, from the cards laid out on the table, a card with a picture that matches the statement read by the confederate (left). (b) The participant then takes a card from the pile of response cards and describes the picture on the response card to the confederate. This is the key part of the experiment, because the question is whether the participant on the right will match the syntactic construction used by the confederate on the left.

the corner of the table, looked at the picture on the card, and described it to the confederate. The question is: How does B phrase his or her description? Saying "The father gave his daughter a present" to describe the picture in **Figure 11.14b** matches A's syntax in this example. Saying "The father gave a present to his daughter" would not match the syntax. If the syntax does match, as in the example in Figure 11.14b, we can conclude that syntactic priming has occurred.

Branigan found that on 78 percent of the trials, the form of B's description matched the form of A's priming statement. This supports the idea that speakers are sensitive to the linguistic behavior of other speakers and adjust their behaviors to match. This coordination of syntactic form between speakers reduces the computational load involved in creating a conversation because it is easier to copy the form of someone else's sentence than it is to create your own form from scratch.

Let's summarize what we have said about conversations: Conversations are dynamic and rapid, but a number of processes make them easier. On the semantic side, people take other people's knowledge into account and help establish common ground if necessary. On the syntactic side, people coordinate or align the syntactic form of their statements. This makes speaking easier and frees up resources to deal with the task of alternating between understanding and producing messages that is the hallmark of successful conversations.

But this discussion illustrates just a few things about conversations and grounding. There are lots of things going on. Think about what a person has to do to maintain a conversation. First, the person has to plan what he or she is going to say, while simultaneously taking in the other person's input and doing what is necessary to understand it. Part of understanding what the other person means involves **theory of mind**, the ability to understand what others feel, think, or believe (Corballis, 2017), and also the ability to interpret and react to the person's gestures, facial expressions, tone of voice, and other things that provide cues to meaning (Brennan et al., 2010; Horton & Brennan, 2016). Finally, just to make things even more interesting, each person in a conversation has to anticipate when it is appropriate to enter the conversation, a process called "turn taking" (Garrod & Pickering, 2015; Levinson, 2016). Thus, communication by conversation goes beyond simply analyzing strings of words or sequences of sentences. It also involves all of the complexities inherent in social interactions, yet somehow, we are able to do it, often effortlessly.

▶ SOMETHING TO CONSIDER

Music and Language

Diana Deutsch (2010) relates a story about an experience she had while testing tape loops for a lecture on music and the brain. As she was doing something, with the taped phrase "sometimes I behave so strangely" repeating over and over in the background, she was suddenly surprised to hear a strange woman singing. After determining that no one else was there, she realized that she was hearing her own voice from the tape loop, but the repeating words on the tape had morphed into song in her mind. Deutsch found that other people also experienced this speech to song effect, and concluded that there is a close connection between song and speech.

Music and Language: Similarities and Differences

Connections between music and language extend beyond song and speech to music and language in general. Emotion is a central player in both. Music has been called the "language of emotion," and people often state that emotion is one of the main reasons they listen to music. Emotion in language is often created by **prosody**—the pattern of intonation and rhythm in spoken language (Banziger & Scherer, 2005; Heffner & Slevc, 2015). Orators and actors create emotions by varying the pitch of their voice and the cadence of their words, speaking softly to express tenderness or loudly to emphasize a point or to capture the audience's attention.

But emotion also illustrates a difference between music and language. Music creates emotion through sounds that in themselves have no meaning. But listening to a film score leaves no doubt that these meaningless sounds can create meaning, with emotions following close behind (Boltz, 2004). Language, on the other hand, creates emotions using meaningful words, so the emotions elicited by *I hate you* and *I love you* are caused directly by the meanings of the words *hate* and *love*. Recently the introduction of

➤ **Figure 11.15** Examples of emojis, which, like words, are used to indicate emotions in language. The emoji on the right, "face with tears of joy," was named Word of the Year by the Oxford English Dictionary. While words and pictures can *indicate* emotions to someone hearing or reading language, sounds *elicit* emotions in a person who is listening to music.

➤ **Figure 11.16** The first line of "*Twinkle, twinkle, little star.*"

(Source: From Goldstein, Sensation and Perception 10e, Figure 12.24, page 305)

emoji's—pictographs like the ones in **Figure 11.15**, have provided another way of indicating emotions in written language (Evans, 2017). The emoji on the far right, which is called "face with tears of joy," was named the "Word of the Year" for 2015 by the Oxford English Dictionary.

An important similarity between music and language is that they both combine elements—tones for music and words for language—to create structured sequences. These sequences are organized into phrases and are governed by syntax—rules for arranging these components (Deutsch, 2010). Nonetheless, it is obvious that there are differences between creating phrases in response to instrumental music and creating phrases when reading a book or having a conversation. Although music and language both unfold over time and have syntax, the rules for combining notes and words are very different. Notes are combined based on their sound, with some sounds going together better than others. But words are combined based on their meanings. There are no analogues for nouns and verbs in music, and there is no "who did what to whom" in music (Patel, 2013).

More items could be added to both the "similarities" and "differences" lists, but the overall message is that although there are important differences in the outcomes and mechanisms associated with music and language, they are also similar in many respects. We will explore two of these areas of overlap in more detail: expectations and brain mechanisms.

Expectations in Music and Language

We have discussed the role of expectations in language by describing how readers and listeners are constantly making predictions about what might be coming next as a sentence unfolds. A similar situation exists in music.

To illustrate expectation in music, let's consider how the notes of a melody are organized around the note associated with the composition's key, which is called the **tonic** (Krumhansl, 1985). For example, C is the tonic for the key of C and its associated scale: C, D, E, F, G, A, B, C. Organizing pitches around a tonic creates a framework within which a listener generates expectations about what might be coming next. One common expectation is that a song that begins with the tonic will end on the tonic. This effect, which is called **return to the tonic**, occurs in "Twinkle, Twinkle, Little Star," which begins and ends on a C in the example in **Figure 11.16**. To illustrate this, try singing the first line of "Twinkle, Twinkle, Little Star," but stop at "you," just before the song has returned to the tonic. The effect of pausing just before the end of the phrase, which could be called a violation of musical syntax, is unsettling and has us longing for the final note that will bring us back to the tonic.

Another violation of musical syntax occurs when an unlikely note or chord is inserted that doesn't seem to "fit" in the tonality of the melody. Aniruddh Patel and coworkers (1998) had participants listen to a musical phrase like the one in **Figure 11.17**,

➤ **Figure 11.17** (a) The musical phrase heard by participants in Patel and coworkers' (1998) experiment. The location of the target chord is indicated by the downward-pointing arrow. The chord in the music staff is the "In key" chord. The other two chords were inserted in that position for the "Nearby key" and "Distant key" conditions. (b) ERP responses to the target chord. Solid = in-key; Dotted = near-key; Dashed = far-key.

(Source: From Goldstein, Sensation and Perception, 10e, Fig. 12.28, p. 307)

which contained a target chord, indicated by the arrow above the music. There were three different targets: (1) an "In key" chord, that fit the piece, shown on the musical staff; (2) a "Nearby key" chord, that didn't fit as well; and (3) a "Distant key" chord that fit even less well. In the behavioral part of the experiment, listeners judged the phrase as acceptable 80 percent of the time when it contained the in-key chord; 49 percent when it contained the nearby-key chord; and 28 percent when it contained the distant-key chord. One way of stating this result is that listeners were judging how "grammatically correct" each version was.

In the physiological part of the experiment, Patel used the event-related potential (ERP) to measure the brain's response to violations of syntax. When we discussed the ERP in connection with the "Concert Scenario" experiment on page 341, we saw that the N400 component of the ERP became larger in response to words that didn't fit into a sentence, like *bake* in *The cat won't bake*. Patel focused on another component of the ERP, called the P600, because it is a positive response that occurs 600 msec after the onset of a word. One of the properties of P600 is that it becomes larger in response to violations of syntax. For example, the blue curve in **Figure 11.18** shows the response that occurs after the word *eat* in the sentence *The cats won't eat* (blue curve). The response to this grammatically correct word shows no P600 response. However, the red curve, elicited by the word *eating*, which is grammatically incorrect in the sentence *The cats won't eating*, has a large P600 response.

Patel measured large P600 responses when his participants listened to sentences that contained violations of grammar, as in the example in Figure 11.18. He then measured the ERP response to each of the three musical targets in Figure 11.17. Figure 11.17b shows that there is no P600 response when the phrase contained the in-key chord (black record), but that there are P600 responses for the two other chords, with the bigger response for the more out-of-key chord (red record). Patel concluded from this result that music, like language, has a syntax that influences how we react to it. Other studies following Patel's have also found that electrical responses like P600 occur to violations of musical syntax (Koelsch, 2005; Koelsch et al., 2000; Maess et al., 2001; Vuust et al., 2009).

Looking at the idea of musical syntax in a larger context, we can assume that as we listen to music, we are focusing on the notes we are hearing, while (without thinking about it) we have expectations about what is going to happen next. You can demonstrate your ability to predict what is going to happen by listening to a song, preferably instrumental and not too fast. As you listen, try guessing what notes or phrases are coming next. This is easier for some compositions, such as ones with repeating themes, but even when there isn't repetition, what's coming usually isn't a surprise. What's particularly compelling about this exercise is that it often works even for music you are hearing for the first time. Just as our perception of visual scenes we are seeing for the first time is influenced by our past experiences in perceiving the environment, our perception of music we are hearing for the first time can be influenced by our history of listening to music.

Do Music and Language Overlap in the Brain?

Patel's demonstration of similar electrical responses to violations of musical syntax and language syntax shows that both music and language involve similar processes. But we can't say, based on this finding alone, that music and language involve overlapping areas of the brain.

Early research on brain mechanisms of music and language involved studying patients with brain damage due to stroke. Patel and coworkers (2008) studied a group of stroke patients who had **Broca's aphasia**—difficulty in understanding sentences with complex syntax (see page 39). These patients and a group of controls were given (1) a language task that involved understanding syntactically complex sentences; and (2) a music task that involved detecting the off-key chords in a sequence of chords. The results of these tests, shown in **Figure 11.19**, indicate that the patients performed very poorly on the language task compared to the controls

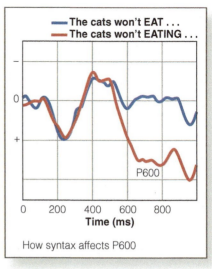

➤ **Figure 11.18** The P600 wave of the ERP is affected by grammar. It becomes larger (red line) when a grammatically incorrect form is used.

(Source: Osterhout et al., 1997)

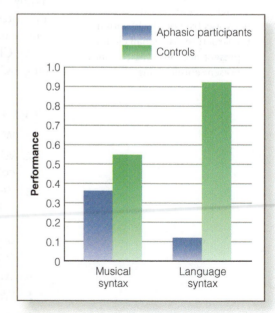

➤ **Figure 11.19** Performance on language syntax tasks and musical syntax tasks for aphasic participants and control participants.

(Source: From Patel et al., 2008)

(right pair of bars), and that the patients also performed more poorly on the music task (left pair of bars). Two things that are noteworthy about these results is that (1) there is a connection between poor performance on the language task and poor performance on the music task, which suggests a connection between the two; and (2) the deficits in the music task for aphasia patients were small compared to the deficits in the language tasks. These results support a connection between brain mechanisms involved in music and language, but not necessarily a strong connection.

Other neuropsychological studies have provided evidence that different brain mechanisms are involved in music and language. For example, patients who are born having problems with music perception—a condition called **congenital amusia**—have severe problems with tasks such as discriminating between simple melodies or recognizing common tunes. Yet these individuals often have normal language abilities (Patel, 2013).

Cases have also been observed that demonstrate differences in the opposite direction. Robert Slevc and coworkers (2016) tested a 64-year-old woman who had Broca's aphasia caused by a stroke. She had trouble comprehending complex sentences and had great difficulty putting words together into meaningful thoughts. Yet she was able to detect out-of-key chords in sequences like those presented by Patel (Figure 11.16a). Neuropsychological research therefore provides evidence for separate brain mechanisms for music and language (also see Peretz & Hyde, 2003).

Brain mechanisms have also been studied using neuroimaging. Some of these studies have shown that different areas are involved in music and language (Fedorenko et al., 2012). Other studies have shown that music and language activate overlapping areas of the brain. For example, Broca's area, which is involved in language syntax, is also activated by music (Fitch & Martins, 2014; Koelsch, 2005, 2011; Peretz & Zatorre, 2005).

It has also been suggested that even if neuroimaging identifies an area that is activated by both music and language, this doesn't necessarily mean that music and language are activating the same neurons within that area. There is evidence that music and language activation can occur within an area but involve different neural networks (**Figure 11.20**) (Peretz et al., 2015).

The conclusion from all of these studies—both behavioral and physiological—is that while there is evidence for the separateness of music and language in the brain, especially from neuropsychological studies, there is also evidence for overlap between music and language, mostly from behavioral and brain scanning studies. Thus, it seems that music and language are related, but the overlap isn't complete, as might be expected when you consider the difference between reading your cognitive psychology textbook and listening to your favorite music. Clearly, our knowledge of the relation between music and language is still a "work in progress," which, as it continues, will add to our understanding of both music and language.

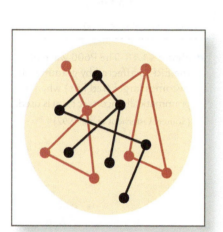

➤ **Figure 11.20** Illustration of the idea that two different capacities, such as language and music, might activate the same structure in the brain (indicated by the circle), but when looked at closely, each capacity could activate different networks (red or black) within the structure. The small circles represent neurons, and the lines represent connections.

TEST YOURSELF 11.3

1. What does the "fixing the birdhouse" experiment indicate about inference?

2. What is coherence? Describe the different types of inference that help achieve coherence.

3. What is the assumption behind a situation model? Describe what the following evidence tells us about this approach to understanding stories: (a) reaction times for pictures that match or don't match the orientations or shapes of objects in a story; (b) brain activation for action words compared to actual action; (c) predictions based on the situation.

4. What is the given–new contract?

5. What is common ground? How is it established in a conversation?

6. What does the "abstract picture" experiment tell us about how common ground is established?

7. Once common ground is established, what happens?

8. What is syntactic coordination? Describe the syntactic priming experiment that was used to demonstrate syntactic coordination.

9. What are some similarities and differences between music and language?

10. What is the tonic? What does return to the tonic say about expectation in music?

11. Describe Patel's experiment in which he measured the P600 response of the ERP to syntactic violations. What does his result say about connections between music and language?

12. What is the evidence for and against the idea that music and language activate overlapping areas of the brain?

13. If music and language both activate the same brain area, can we say with certainty that they share neural mechanisms?

CHAPTER SUMMARY

1. Language is a system of communication that uses sounds or symbols that enable us to express our feelings, thoughts, ideas, and experiences. It is hierarchical and rule-based.

2. Modern research in the psychology of language blossomed in the 1950s and 1960s, with the advent of the cognitive revolution. One of the central events in the cognitive revolution was Chomsky's critique of Skinner's behavioristic analysis of language.

3. All the words a person knows are his or her *lexicon*. *Semantics* is the meaning of language.

4. The ability to understand words in a sentence is influenced by word frequency. This has been demonstrated using the lexical decision task and by measuring eye movements.

5. The pronunciation of words is variable, which can make it difficult to perceive words when they are heard out of context.

6. There are often no silences between words during normal speech, which gives rise to the problem of speech segmentation. Past experience with words, the word's context, statistical properties of language, and knowledge of the meanings of words help solve this problem.

7. *Lexical ambiguity* refers to the fact that a word can have more than one meaning. Tanenhaus used the lexical priming technique to show that (1) multiple meanings of ambiguous words are accessed immediately after they are heard, and (2) the "correct" meaning for the sentence's context is identified within 200 msec.

8. The relative frequency of the meanings of ambiguous words is described in terms of meaning dominance. Some words

have biased dominance, some have balanced dominance. The type of dominance, combined with the word's context, influences which meaning is accessed.

9. Syntax is the structure of a sentence. Parsing is the process by which words in a sentence are grouped into phrases. Grouping into phrases is a major determinant of the meaning of a sentence. This process has been studied by using garden path sentences that illustrate the effect of temporary ambiguity.

10. Two mechanisms proposed to explain parsing are (1) the garden path model and (2) the constraint-based approach. The garden path model emphasizes how syntactic principles such as late closure determine how a sentence is parsed. The constraint-based approach states that semantics, syntax, and other factors operate simultaneously to determine parsing. The constraint-based approach is supported by (a) the way words with different meanings affect the interpretation of a sentence, (b) how story context influences parsing, (c) how scene context, studied using the visual world paradigm, influences parsing, and (d) how the effect of memory load and prior experience with language influences understandability.

11. Coherence enables us to understand stories. Coherence is largely determined by inference. Three major types of inference are anaphoric, instrumental, and causal.

12. The situation model approach to text comprehension states that people represent the situation in a story in terms of the people, objects, locations, and events that are being described in the story.

13. Measurements of brain activity have demonstrated how similar areas of the cortex are activated by reading action words and by actual movements.

14. Experiments that measure the ERP response to passages show that many things associated with the passage are activated as the passage is being read.

15. Conversations, which involve give-and-take between two or more people, are made easier by procedures that involve cooperation between participants in a conversation. These procedures include the given–new contract and establishing common ground.

16. Establishing common ground has been studied by analyzing transcripts of conversations. As common ground is established, conversations become more efficient.

17. The process of creating common ground results in entrainment—synchronization between the people in the conversation. One demonstration of entrainment is provided by syntactic coordination—how people's grammatical constructions become coordinated.

18. Music and language are similar in a number of ways. There is a close relation between song and speech, music and language both cause emotion, and both consist of organized sequences.

19. There are important differences between music and language. They create emotions in different ways, and rules for combining tones and words are different. The most important difference is based on the fact that words have meanings.

20. Expectation occurs in both music and language. These parallel effects have been demonstrated by experiments using the ERP to assess the effect of syntactic violations in both music and language.

21. There is evidence for separateness and overlap of music and language in the brain.

THINK ABOUT IT

1. How do the ideas of coherence and connection apply to some of the movies you have seen lately? Have you found that some movies are easy to understand whereas others are more difficult? In the movies that are easy to understand, does one thing appear to follow from another, whereas in the more difficult ones, some things seem to be left out? What is the difference in the "mental work" needed to determine what is going on in these two kinds of movies? (You can also apply this kind of analysis to books you have read.)

2. The next time you are able to eavesdrop on a conversation, notice how the give-and-take among participants follows (or does not follow) the given–new contract. Also, notice how people change topics and how that affects the flow of the conversation. Finally, see if you can find any evidence of syntactic priming. One way to "eavesdrop" is to be part of a conversation that includes at least two other people. But don't forget to say something every so often!

3. One of the interesting things about languages is the use of "figures of speech," which people who know the language understand but nonnative speakers often find baffling. One example is the sentence "He brought everything but the kitchen sink." Can you think of other examples? If you speak a language other than English, can you identify figures of speech in that language that might be baffling to English-speakers?

4. Newspaper headlines are often good sources of ambiguous phrases. For example, consider the following actual headlines: "Milk Drinkers Are Turning to Powder," "Iraqi Head Seeks Arms," "Farm Bill Dies in House," and "Squad Helps Dog Bite Victim." See if you can find examples of ambiguous headlines in the newspaper, and try to figure out what it is that makes the headlines ambiguous.

5. People often say things in an indirect way, but listeners can often still understand what they mean. See if you can detect these indirect statements in normal conversation. (Examples: "Do you want to turn left here?" to mean "I think you should turn left here"; "Is it cold in here?" to mean "Please close the window.")

6. It is a common observation that people are more irritated by nearby cell phone conversations than by conversations between two people who are physically present. Why do you think this occurs? (See Emberson et al., 2010, for one answer.)

KEY TERMS

COGLAB EXPERIMENTS   Numbers in parentheses refer to the experiment number in CogLab.

People solve problems in many different ways. We will see that sometimes solving a problem involves hard word and methodological analysis, while other times solutions to problems can appear to happen in a flash of insight. We will also see that sometimes letting your mind "rest," perhaps to wander or daydream, as this woman might be doing as she sits by the canal, can play an important role in leading to creative solutions to problems.

The following is a story about physicist Richard Feynman, who received the Nobel Prize in Physics for his work in nuclear fission and quantum dynamics and who had a reputation as a scientific genius.

> A physicist working at the California Institute of Technology in the 1950s is having trouble deciphering some of Feynman's notes. He asks Murray Gell-Mann, a Nobel Laureate and occasional collaborator of Feynman, "What are Feynman's methods?" Gell-Mann leans coyly against the blackboard and says—"Dick's method is this. You write down the problem. You think very hard." [Gell-Mann shuts his eyes and presses his knuckles periodically to his forehead.] "Then you write down the answer." (adapted from Gleick, 1992, p. 315)

This is an amusing way of describing Feynman's genius, but it leaves unanswered the question of what was really going on inside his head while he was thinking "very hard." Although we may not know the answer to this question for Feynman, research on problem solving has provided some answers for people in general. In this chapter, we will explore some of the ways cognitive psychologists have described the mental processes involved in solving problems and being creative. We begin by focusing on problems.

▶ What Is a Problem?

What problems have you had to solve lately? When I ask students in my cognitive psychology class this question, I get answers such as the following: problems for math, chemistry, or physics courses; getting writing assignments in on time; dealing with roommates, friends, and relationships in general; deciding what courses to take, what career to go into; whether to go to graduate school or look for a job; how to pay for a new car. Many of these things fit the following definition: A **problem** occurs when there is an obstacle between a present state and a goal and it is not immediately obvious how to get around the obstacle (Duncker, 1945; Lovett, 2002). Thus, a problem, as defined by psychologists, is a situation in which you need to accomplish a goal and the solution is not immediately obvious.

We begin by considering the approach of the Gestalt psychologists, who introduced the study of problem solving to psychology in the 1920s.

▶ The Gestalt Approach

We introduced the Gestalt psychologists in Chapter 3 by describing their laws of perceptual organization (page 71). The Gestalt psychologists were interested not only in perception but also in learning, problem solving, and even attitudes and beliefs (Koffka, 1935). But even as they considered other areas of psychology, they still took a perceptual approach. Problem solving, for the Gestalt psychologists, was about (1) how people represent a problem in their mind and (2) how solving a problem involves a reorganization or restructuring of this representation.

Representing a Problem in the Mind

What does it mean to say that a problem is "represented" in the mind? One way to answer this question is to begin with how problems are presented. Consider, for example, a crossword puzzle (**Figure 12.1**). This type of problem is represented on the page by a diagram and clues about how to fill in the open squares. How this problem is represented in the mind is probably different for different people, but it is likely to differ from how it is represented on the page. For example, as people try to solve this problem, they may choose to represent only a small part of the puzzle at a time. Some people might focus on filling in horizontal words and then use these words to help determine the vertical words. Others might pick one corner of the puzzle and search in their mind for both verticals and horizontals that fit together. Each of these ways of going about solving the problem involves a different way of representing it in the mind.

One of the central ideas of the Gestalt approach is that success in solving a problem is influenced by how it is represented in the person's mind. This idea—that the solution to a problem depends on how it is represented—is illustrated by the problem in **Figure 12.2**. This problem, which was posed by Gestalt psychologist Wolfgang Kohler (1929), asks us to determine the length of the segment marked *x* if the radius of the circle has a length *r*. Try this problem before reading the next paragraph.

One way to describe how this problem is represented on the page is "a circle with thin vertical and horizontal lines that divide the circle into quarters, and darker lines that create a small triangle in the upper left quadrant." The key to solving this problem is to change the last part of the representation to "a small rectangle in the upper left quadrant, with *x* being the diagonal between the corners." Once *x* is recognized as the diagonal of the rectangle, the representation can be reorganized by creating the rectangle's other diagonal (**Figure 12.3**). Once we realize that this diagonal is the radius of the circle, and that both diagonals of a rectangle are the same length, we can conclude that the length of *x* equals the length of the radius, *r*.

What is important about this solution is that it doesn't require mathematical equations. Instead, the solution is obtained by first perceiving the object and then representing it in a different way. The Gestalt psychologists called the process of changing the problem's representation **restructuring**.

The Idea of Insight

In addition to identifying restructuring as being important in problem solving, the Gestalt psychologists also noted that restructuring is often the outcome of a process called insight (Weisberg & Alba, 1981). **Insight** has been defined as *any sudden comprehension, realization, or problem solution that involves a reorganization of a person's mental representation of a stimulus, situation, or event to yield an interpretation that was not initially obvious* (adapted from Kounios & Beeman, 2014). This definition contains the central ideas behind the Gestalt approach. "Reorganization of a person's mental representation" corresponds to restructuring, and "sudden comprehension" corresponds to the Gestalt emphasis on suddenly realizing the problem's solution (Dunbar, 1998).

This sudden realization property of insight is illustrated by an experiment by Janet Metcalfe and David Wiebe (1987) that was designed to distinguish between insight problems and noninsight problems. They hypothesized that there should be a difference in how participants feel they are progressing toward a solution in insight problems versus noninsight problems. They predicted that participants working on an insight problem, in which the answer appears suddenly, should not be very good at predicting how near they are to a solution. Participants working on a noninsight problem, which involves a more methodical process, would be more likely to know when they are getting closer to the solution.

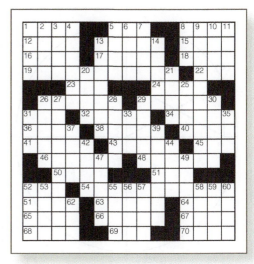

► **Figure 12.1** This is a picture of how a crossword puzzle is represented on the page. In addition, there are clues for filling in the horizontal and vertical words.

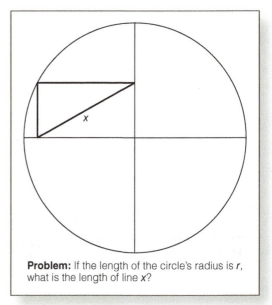

Problem: If the length of the circle's radius is *r*, what is the length of line *x*?

► **Figure 12.2** Circle problem. See Figure 12.3, page 358, for the solution.

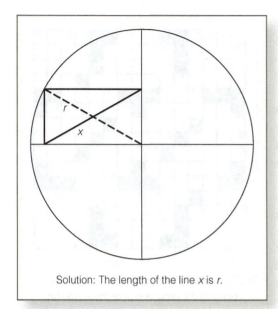

Solution: The length of the line *x* is *r*.

▶ **Figure 12.3** Solution to the circle problem. Note that the length of *x* is the same as the radius, *r*, because *x* and *r* are both diagonals of the rectangle.

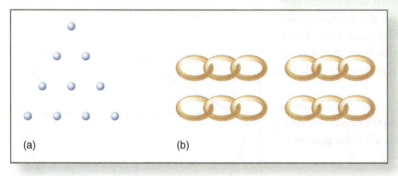

(a)   (b)

▶ **Figure 12.4** (a) Triangle problem and (b) chain problem for "Two Insight Problems" demonstration. See page 389 for solutions.

To test this hypothesis, Metcalfe and Wiebe gave participants insight problems, as in the following demonstration, and noninsight problems and asked them to make "warmth" judgments every 15 seconds as they were working on the problems. Ratings closer to "hot" (7 on a 7-point scale) indicated that they believed they were getting close to a solution; ratings closer to "cold" (1 on the scale) indicated that they felt that they were far from a solution. Here are two examples of insight problems that Metcalfe and Wiebe used.

DEMONSTRATION   Two Insight Problems

Triangle Problem The triangle shown in **Figure 12.4a** points to the top of the page. Show how you can move three of the dots to get the triangle to point to the bottom of the page. (For the answer, see **Figure 12.31** on page 389.)

As you work on this problem, see whether you can monitor your progress. Do you feel as though you are making steady progress toward a solution until eventually it all adds up to the answer, or as though you are not really making much progress but then suddenly experience the solution as an "Aha!" experience? Once you have tried the triangle problem, try the following problem and monitor your progress in the same way.

Chain Problem A woman has four pieces of chain. Each piece is made up of three links, as shown in **Figure 12.4b**. She wants to join the pieces into a single closed loop of chain. It costs 2 cents to open a link, and it costs 3 cents to close a link. She only has 15 cents. How does she do it? (For the answer, see Figure 12.32 on page 389.)

For noninsight problems, Metcalfe and Wiebe used algebra problems like the ones following, which were taken from a high school mathematics text. These problems are also called **analytically based problems** because they are solved by a process of systematic analysis, often using techniques based on past experience.

Solve for x: $(1/5)x + 10 = 25$
Factor $16y^2 - 40yz + 25z^2$

The results of their experiment are shown in **Figure 12.5**, which indicates the warmth ratings for all of the participants during the minute just before they solved the two kinds of problems.

For the insight problems (solid line), warmth ratings began at 2 and then didn't change much, until all of a sudden they jumped from 3 to 7 at the end. Thus, 15 seconds before the solution, the median rating was a relatively cold 3 for the insight problems, meaning at this point participants didn't feel they were close to a solution. In contrast, for the algebra problems (dashed line), the ratings began at 3 and then gradually increased until the problem was solved. Thus, Metcalfe and Wiebe demonstrated that solutions for problems that have been called insight problems do, in fact, occur suddenly, as measured by people's reports of how close they feel they are to a solution.

Modern researchers have debated whether the process involved in insight problem solving is always different than the process involved in analytical, noninsight problem solving.

For example, Jessica Fleck and Robert Weisberg (2013) have presented evidence, which we won't go into here, supporting the idea that solving an insight problem (that involves an "Aha" experience) can involve analytical processes (also see Weisberg, 2015). Whatever mechanisms are involved, there is no question that people often experience sudden "insightful" realizations of problem solutions (Bowden et al., 2005; Kounios et al., 2008).

Functional Fixedness and Mental Set

In addition to highlighting the phenomenon of insight, the Gestalt psychologists also described various obstacles to problem solving. One of the major obstacles to problem solving, according to the Gestalt psychologists, is **fixation**—people's tendency to focus on a specific characteristic of the problem that keeps them from arriving at a solution. One type of fixation that can work against solving a problem, focusing on familiar functions or uses of an object, is called **functional fixedness** (Jansson & Smith, 1991).

An example of functional fixedness is provided by the **candle problem**, which was first described by Karl Duncker (1945). In his experiment, he asked participants to use various objects to complete a task. The following demonstration asks you to try to solve Duncker's problem by imagining that you have the specified objects.

The solution to the problem occurs when the person realizes that the matchbox can be used as a support rather than as a container. When Duncker did this experiment, he presented one group of participants with small cardboard boxes containing the materials (candles, tacks, and matches) and presented another group with the same materials, but outside the boxes, so the boxes were empty. When he compared the performance of the two groups, he found that the group that had been presented with the boxes

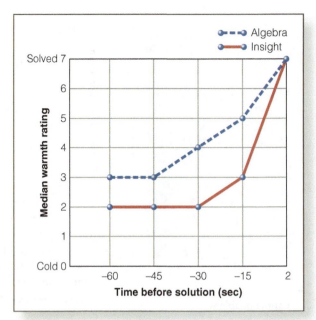

> **Figure 12.5** Results of Metcalfe and Wiebe's (1987) experiment showing participants' judgments of how close they were to solving insight problems and algebra problems during the minute just before solving the problem.

(Source: Based on J. Metcalfe & D. Wiebe, 1987)

DEMONSTRATION The Candle Problem

You are in a room with a vertical corkboard mounted on the wall. You are given the materials shown in **Figure 12.6**—some candles, matches in a matchbox, and some tacks. Your task is to mount a candle on the corkboard so it will burn without dripping wax on the floor. Try to figure out how you would solve this problem before reading further; then check your answer in **Figure 12.7** on page 360.

> **Figure 12.6** Objects for Duncker's (1945) candle problem.

(Source: Based on K. Duncker, 1945)

➤ **Figure 12.7** Solution to the candle problem.

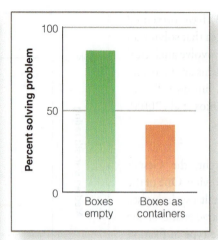

➤ **Figure 12.8** Results of Adamson's (1952) replication of Duncker's candle problem.

(Source: Based on R. E. Adamson, 1952)

as containers found the problem more difficult than did the group presented with empty boxes. Robert Adamson (1952) repeated Duncker's experiment and obtained the same result: Participants who were presented with empty boxes were twice as likely to solve the problem as participants who were presented with boxes that were being used as containers (**Figure 12.8**).

The fact that seeing the boxes as containers inhibited using them as supports is an example of functional fixedness. Another demonstration of functional fixedness is provided by Maier's (1931) **two-string problem**, in which the participants' task was to tie together two strings that were hanging from the ceiling. This was difficult because the strings were so far apart that it was impossible to reach one of them while holding the other (**Figure 12.9**). Other objects available for solving this problem were a chair and a pair of pliers.

To solve this problem, participants needed to tie the pliers to one of the strings to create a pendulum, which could then be swung to within the person's reach. This is an example of functional fixedness because people usually think of using pliers as a tool, not as a weight at the end of a pendulum. Thus, 37 of the 60 participants did not solve the problem because they focused on the usual function of pliers.

When the majority of the participants were unable to solve the problem within 10 minutes, Maier provided a "hint" when he set the string in motion by "accidentally" brushing against it. Once the participants saw the string moving, 23 of the 37 who hadn't solved the problem solved it within 60 seconds. Seeing the string swinging from side to side led to the idea that the pliers could be used as a weight to create a pendulum. In Gestalt terms, the solution to the problem occurred once the participants restructured their representation of how to achieve the solution (get the strings to swing from side to side) and changed their representation of the function of the pliers (they can be used as a weight to create a pendulum).

Both the candle problem and the two-string problem were difficult because of people's preconceptions about the uses of objects. These preconceptions are a type of **mental set**, a preconceived notion about how to approach a problem, which is determined by a person's experience of what has worked in the past. In these experiments, mental set was created by people's knowledge about the usual uses of objects.

The Gestalt psychologists also showed how mental set can arise out of the situation created as a person solves a problem. An example is provided by the Luchins **water jug problem**, in which participants were told that their task was to figure out on paper how to obtain a required volume of water, given three empty jars for measures. Luchins (1942) presented the first example to his participants, in which the three jugs had the following capacities: A = 21 quarts, B = 127 quarts, C = 3 quarts, and the desired volume was 100 quarts. This is Problem 1 in **Figure 12.10a**. After giving his participants some time to solve the problem, Luchins provided the following solution:

1. Fill jug B with 127 quarts, and pour from B to fill A, so 21 quarts are subtracted from B. This leaves 106 quarts in B (**Figure 12.10b**).

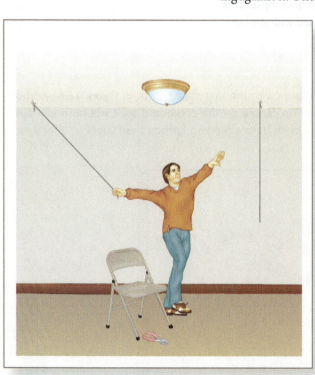

➤ **Figure 12.9** Maier's (1931) two-string problem. As hard as the participant tries, he can't grab the second string. How can he tie the two strings together? (Note: Just using the chair doesn't work!)

(Source: Based on N. R. F. Maier, 1931)

2. Pour from jug B to fill jug C, so 3 quarts are subtracted from B, leaving 103 quarts (**Figure 12.10c**).

3. Pour from jug B again into C, so 3 more quarts are subtracted, leaving 100 quarts (**Figure 12.10d**).

The solution for Problem 1 can be stated as *Desired amount = B − A − 2C*. After demonstrating how to solve Problem 1 (but without mentioning this formula), Luchins had his participants solve Problems 2–8, all of which could be solved by applying the same formula. (Some textbook descriptions of the Luchins experiment state that participants were given water jugs of different capacities and were asked to measure out the specified amounts. If this were the case, participants would have had to be very strong, since jug A, with 127 quarts of water, would weigh more than 250 pounds! Luckily for the participants, they were just required to solve the problem on paper.)

Luchins was interested in how his participants solved Problems 7 and 8, which could be solved by the B − A − 2C formula, but which also could be solved more simply as follows:

Problem 7: Desired quantity = A + C (Fill A and C and pour into B.)

Problem 8: Desired quantity = A − C (Fill A and pour into C.)

The question Luchins asked was: How will participants solve Problems 7 and 8 with and without mental set? He determined this by running two groups:

Mental set group: Using the procedure described above, he presented Problem 1 first as a demonstration, then had participants solve Problems 2–8, beginning with Problem 2. This established a mental set for using the B − A − 2C procedure.

No mental set group: Participants just solved Problems 7 and 8, beginning with 7. In this case, participants weren't exposed to the B − A − 2C procedure.

The result was that only 23 percent of the participants in the *mental set group* used the simpler solutions for Problems 7 and 8, but all of the participants in the *no mental set group* used the simpler solutions. Thus, mental set can influence problem solving both because of preconceptions about the functions of an object (candle and two-string problems) and because of preconceptions about the way to solve a problem (water jug problem).

Between about 1920 and 1950, the Gestalt psychologists described numerous problems illustrating how mental set can influence problem solving and how solving a problem often involves creating a new representation. This idea that problem solving depends on how the problem is represented in the mind is one of the enduring contributions of Gestalt psychology. Modern research has taken this idea as a starting point for the information-processing approach to the study of problem solving.

Problem	Jug A	Jug B	Jug C	Desired quantity
1	21	127	3	100
2	14	163	25	99
3	18	43	10	5
4	9	42	6	21
5	20	59	4	31
6	20	50	3	24
7	15	39	3	18
8	28	59	3	25

Capacities (quarts)

➤ **Figure 12.10** (a) The Luchins (1942) water jug problem. Each problem specifies the capacities of jugs A, B, and C and a final desired quantity. The task is to figure out how to use the jugs with these capacities to measure out the desired quantity. (b) The first step in solving Problem 1; (c) the second step; (d) the third step. All of the other problems can be solved using the same pattern of pourings, indicated by the equation *Desired quantity = B − A − 2C*, but there are more efficient ways to solve Problems 7 and 8.

(Source: Based on A. S. Luchins, 1942)

▶ The Information-Processing Approach

In our description of the history of cognitive psychology in Chapter 1, we noted that in 1956 there were two important conferences, one at the Massachusetts Institute of Technology and one at Dartmouth University, that brought together researchers from many disciplines to discuss new ways to study the mind. At both of these conferences, Alan Newell and Herbert Simon described their "logic theorist" computer program that was designed to simulate human problem solving. This marked the beginning of a research program that described problem solving as a process that involves search. That is, instead of just considering the initial structure of a problem and then the new structure achieved when the problem is solved, Newell and Simon described problem solving as a search that occurs between the posing of the problem and its solution.

The idea of problem solving as a search is part of our language. People commonly talk about problems in terms of "searching for a way to reach a goal," "getting around roadblocks," "hitting a dead end," and "approaching a problem from a different angle" (Lakoff & Turner, 1989). We will introduce Newell and Simon's approach by describing the **Tower of Hanoi problem**.

Newell and Simon's Approach

Newell and Simon (1972) saw problems in terms of an **initial state**—conditions at the beginning of the problem—and a **goal state**—the solution of the problem. **Figure 12.11a** shows the initial state of the Tower of Hanoi problem as three discs stacked on the left peg, and the goal state as these discs stacked on the right peg. In addition to specifying initial and goal states of a problem, Newell and Simon also introduced the idea of **operators**—actions that take the problem from one state to another. For the Tower of Hanoi problem, the operators are moving the disc to another peg. The rules in the demonstration specify which actions are allowed and which are not (see **Figure 12.11b**). Try solving this problem by following the instructions in the demonstration.

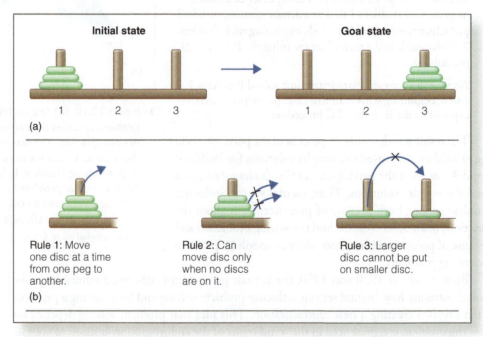

▶ **Figure 12.11** (a) Initial and goal states for the Tower of Hanoi problem. (b) The rules for actions allowed when solving the problem.
(Source: Based on K. Kotovsky, J. R. Hayes, & H. A. Simon, 1985)

DEMONSTRATION   The Tower of Hanoi Problem

Move the discs from the left peg to the right peg, as shown in Figure 12.11a, following these rules:

1. Discs are moved one at a time from one peg to another.

2. A disc can be moved only when there are no discs on top of it.

3. A larger disc can never be placed on top of a smaller disc.

As you try solving this problem, count the number of moves it takes to get from the initial to the goal state.

This problem is called the Tower of Hanoi problem because of a legend that there are monks in a monastery near Hanoi who are working on this problem. Their version of it, however, is vastly more complex than ours, with 64 discs on peg 1. According to the legend, the world will end when the problem is solved. Luckily, this will take close to a trillion years to accomplish even if the monks make one move every second and every move is correct (Raphael, 1976).

As you tried solving the problem, you may have realized that there were a number of possible ways to move the discs as you tried to reach the goal state. Newell and Simon conceived of problem solving as involving a sequence of choices of steps, with each action creating an **intermediate state**. Thus, a problem starts with an initial state, continues through a number of intermediate states, and finally reaches the goal state. The initial state, goal state, and all the possible intermediate states for a particular problem make up the **problem space**. (See **Table 12.1** for a summary of the terms used by Newell and Simon.)

TABLE 12.1

Key Terms for Newell-Simon Approach to Problem Solving

Term	Description	Example From Tower of Hanoi
Initial state	Conditions at the beginning of a problem	All three discs are on the left peg.
Goal state	Solution to the problem	All three discs are on the right peg.
Intermediate state	Conditions after each step is made toward solving a problem	After the smallest disc is moved to the right peg, the two larger discs are on the left peg and the smallest one is on the right.
Operators	Actions that take the problem from one state to another Operators are usually governed by rules	Rule: A larger disc can't be placed on a smaller one.
Problem space	All possible states that could occur when solving a problem	See Figure 12.12.
Means–end analysis	A way of solving a problem in which the goal is to reduce the difference between the initial and goal states	Establish subgoals, each of which moves the solution closer to the goal state.
Subgoals	Small goals that help create intermediate states that are closer to the goal. Occasionally, a subgoal may appear to increase the distance to the goal state, but in the long run can result in the shortest path to the goal.	Subgoal 4: To free up the medium-sized disc, you need to move the small disc from the middle peg back to the peg on the left.

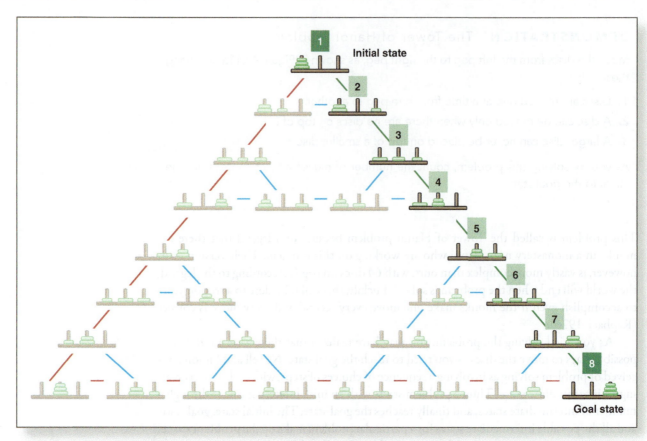

Figure 12.12 Problem space for the Tower of Hanoi problem. The green lines indicate the shortest path between the initial state (1) and the goal state (8). The red lines indicate a longer path.

(Source: Based on Dunbar, 1998)

The problem space for the Tower of Hanoi problem is shown in **Figure 12.12**. The initial state is marked 1 and the goal state is marked 8. All of the other possible configurations of discs on pegs are intermediate states. There are a number of ways to get from the initial state to the goal state. One possibility, indicated by the red lines, involves making 14 moves. The best solution, indicated by the green lines, requires only 7 moves.

Given all of the possible ways to reach the goal, how can we decide which moves to make, especially when starting out? It is important to realize that the problem-solver does not have a picture of the problem space, like the one in Figure 12.12, when trying to solve the problem. According to Newell and Simon, the person has to search the problem space to find a solution, and they proposed that one way to direct the search is to use a strategy called **means–end analysis**. The primary goal of means–end analysis is to reduce the difference between the initial and goal states. This is achieved by creating **subgoals**—intermediate states that are closer to the goal.

Our overall goal in applying means–end analysis to the Tower of Hanoi problem is to reduce the size of the difference between initial and goal states. An initial goal would be to move the large disc that is on the left over to the peg on the right. However, if we are to obey the rules, we can't accomplish this in just one step, because we can move only one disc at a time and can't move a disc if another disc is on top of it. To solve the problem we therefore set a series of subgoals, some of which may involve a few moves:

Subgoal 1:   Free up the large disc so we can move it onto peg 3. Do this by (a) removing the small disc and placing it on the third peg (**Figure 12.13a**; this is state 2 in the problem space in Figure 12.12). (b) Remove the medium disc and place it on the second peg (**Figure 12.13b**; state 3 in the problem space). This completes the subgoal of freeing up the large disc.

Subgoal 2:   Free up the third peg so we can move the large disc onto it. Do this by moving the small disc onto the medium one (**Figure 12.13c**; state 4 in the problem space).

Subgoal 3:   Move the large disc onto peg 3 (**Figure 12.13d**; state 5 in the problem space).

Subgoal 4:   Free up the medium disc.

Now that we have reached state 5 in the problem space, let's stop and decide how to achieve subgoal 4, freeing up the medium disc. We can move the small disc either onto peg 3 or onto peg 1. These two possible choices illustrate that to find the shortest path to the goal, we need to look slightly ahead. When we do this, we can see that we should not move the small disc to peg 3, even though it appears to reduce the difference between the initial and goal states. Moving to peg 3 is the wrong move, because that would block moving the medium disc there, which would be our next subgoal. Thus, we move the disc back to peg 1 (state 6), which makes it possible to move the medium disc to peg 3 (state 7), and we have almost solved the problem! This procedure of setting subgoals and looking slightly ahead often results in an efficient solution to a problem.

Why is the Tower of Hanoi problem important? One reason is that it illustrates means–end analysis, with its setting of subgoals, and this approach can be applied to real-life situations. For example, I recently had to plan a trip from Pittsburgh to Copenhagen. Remember that in Newell and Simon's terminology, an operator is the action to get from one state to another. The operator for getting from Pittsburgh to Copenhagen is to take a plane, and there are two rules governing this operator:

1. If there isn't a direct flight (there isn't!), it is important to have enough time between flights to ensure that passengers and baggage can get from the first flight to the second one.

2. The cost of the flights has to be within my budget.

My first subgoal was to try to reduce the distance between myself and Copenhagen. One way to achieve this was to take a flight from Pittsburgh to Paris, and then transfer to a flight to Copenhagen (**Figure 12.14**). But the plane schedule showed that there was only 70 minutes between flights, which violated rule 1, and waiting for a later flight to Copenhagen increased the fare, which violated rule 2. The failure of the Pittsburgh to Paris idea led me to create a new subgoal: Find a flight to a city with a number of low-cost connecting flights to Copenhagen. I eventually determined that flying from Pittsburgh to Atlanta satisfied this subgoal. So the problem was solved. Notice that the solution involved setting a subgoal that involved initially traveling away

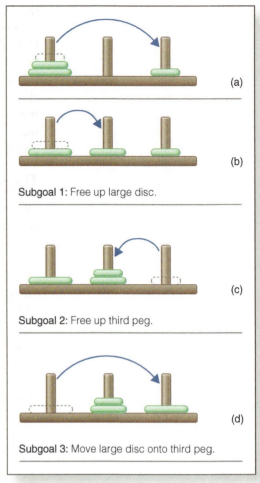

Subgoal 1: Free up large disc.

Subgoal 2: Free up third peg.

Subgoal 3: Move large disc onto third peg.

➤ **Figure 12.13** Initial steps in solving the Tower of Hanoi problem, showing how the problem can be broken down into subgoals.

(Source: Based on K. Kotovsky, J. R. Hayes, & H. A. Simon, 1985)

➤ **Figure 12.14** Two possible routes from Pittsburgh to Copenhagen. The route through Paris (black line) immediately reduces the distance to Copenhagen, but doesn't satisfy the rules of the problem. The route through Atlanta (dashed red line) involves some backtracking but works because it satisfies the rules.

from Copenhagen. Just as for subgoal 4 in the Tower of Hanoi example, in which we had to move a disc away from the right peg to eventually get it there, I had to first fly away from Copenhagen to position myself to achieve my goal.

One of the main contributions of Newell and Simon's approach to problem solving is that it provided a way to specify the possible pathways from the initial to goal states. They also demonstrated how people solve some problems in a stepwise manner using subgoals. But research has shown that there is more to problem solving than specifying the problem space and subgoals. As we will see in the next section, this research has shown that two problems with the same problem space can vary greatly in difficulty.

The Importance of How a Problem Is Stated

How a problem is stated can affect its difficulty. We can appreciate this by considering the *mutilated checkerboard problem.*

DEMONSTRATION   The Mutilated Checkerboard Problem

A checkerboard consists of 64 squares, which can be completely covered by placing 32 dominos on the board so that each domino covers two squares. The **mutilated checkerboard problem** asks the following question: If we eliminate two corners of the checkerboard, as shown in **Figure 12.15**, can we now cover the remaining squares with 31 dominos? See whether you can solve this problem before reading further. A solution would be either a "yes" or "no" answer plus a statement of the rationale behind your answer.

▶ Figure 12.15 Mutilated checkerboard problem. See demonstration for instructions.

Remember the Gestalt idea that adopting the correct problem representation is a key to successful problem solving. The key to solving the mutilated checkerboard problem is understanding the principle that each domino covers two squares and that these squares must be of different colors, so removing the two corner squares with the same color makes it impossible to solve the problem. Starting with this idea, Craig Kaplan and Herbert Simon (1990) hypothesized that versions of the mutilated checkerboard problem that were more likely to lead participants to become aware of this principle would be easier to solve. To test this idea, they created the following four version of the checkerboard, shown in **Figure 12.16**:

1. Blank: a board with all blank squares
2. Color: alternating black and pink squares as might appear on a regular checkerboard
3. The words *black* and *pink* on the board
4. The words *bread* and *butter* on the board

All four versions of the checkerboard problem have the same board layout and the same solution. What is different is the information on the boards (or lack of information on the blank board) that can be used to provide participants with the insight that a domino covers two squares and that these squares must be of different colors. Not surprisingly, participants who were presented boards that emphasized the difference between adjoining squares found the problem easier to solve. The bread-and-butter condition emphasized the difference the most, because bread and butter are very different but are also associated with each other. The blank board had no information about the difference, because all the squares were the same.

Participants in the bread-and-butter group solved the problem twice as fast as those in the blank group and required fewer hints, which the experimenter provided when participants appeared to be at a "dead end." The bread-and-butter group required an average of

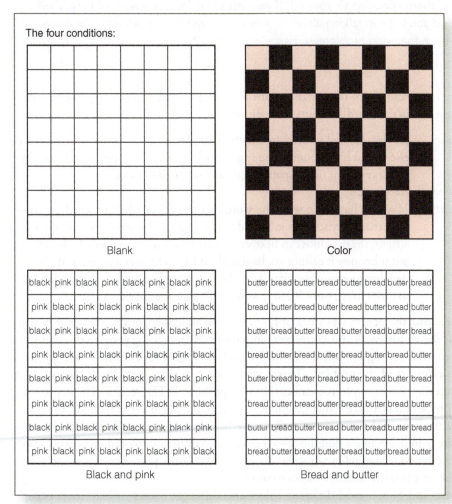

➤ **Figure 12.16** Conditions in Kaplan and Simon's (1990) study of the mutilated checkerboard problem.

(Source: C. A. Kaplan & H. A. Simon, 1990)

1 hint; the blank group required an average of 3.14 hints. The performance of the color and the black-and-pink groups fell between these two. This result shows that solving a problem becomes easier when information is provided that helps point people toward the correct representation of the problem.

To achieve a better understanding of participants' thought processes as they were solving the problem, Kaplan and Simon used a technique introduced by Simon called the *think-aloud protocol*.

METHOD   Think-Aloud Protocol

In the **think-aloud protocol** procedure, participants are asked to say out loud what they are thinking while solving a problem. They are instructed not to describe what they are doing, but to verbalize new thoughts as they occur. One goal of a think-aloud protocol is to determine what information the person is attending to while solving a problem. The following is an example of the instructions given to a participant:

> In this experiment we are interested in what you say to yourself as you perform some tasks that we give you. In order to do this we will ask you to talk aloud as you work on the problems. What I mean by talk aloud is that I want you to say out loud everything that you say to yourself silently. Just act as if you are alone in the room speaking to yourself. If you are silent for any length of time, I will remind you to keep talking aloud. ... Any questions? Please talk aloud while you solve the following problem. (Ericsson & Simon, 1993)

Here is an example of the verbalizations from Kaplan and Simon's experiment. This participant was in the bread-and-butter condition.

Participant: Just by trial and error I can only find 30 places. ... I dunno, maybe someone else would have counted the spaces and just said that you could fit 31, but if you try it out on the paper, you can only fit 30. (Pause)

Experimenter: Keep trying.

Participant: Maybe it has to do with the words on the page? I haven't tried anything with that. Maybe that's it. OK, dominos, umm, the dominos can only fit ... alright, the dominos can fit over two squares, and no matter which way you put it because it cannot go diagonally, it has to fit over a butter and a bread. And because you crossed out two breads, it has to leave two butters left over so it doesn't ... only 30, so it won't fit. Is that the answer?

Notice that the person was stuck at first and then suddenly got the answer after realizing that the words *bread* and *butter* were important. By recording people's thought processes as they are solving a problem, the think-aloud protocol reveals a shift in how a person perceives elements of the problem. This is very similar to the Gestalt psychologists' idea of restructuring. For example, remember the circle problem in Figure 12.2. The key to solving that problem was realizing that the line *x* was the same length as the radius of the circle. Similarly, the key to solving the mutilated checkerboard problem is realizing that adjoining squares are paired, because a domino always covers two different-colored squares on a normal checkerboard. Thus, in Gestalt terms, we could say that the person creates a representation of the problem that makes it easier to solve.

Kaplan and Simon used different colors and different names to help their participants realize that pairing of adjacent squares is important. But this has also been achieved in another way—by telling the following story, which has parallels to the checkerboard problem.

The Russian Marriage Problem

In a small Russian village, there were 32 bachelors and 32 unmarried women. Through tireless efforts, the village matchmaker succeeded in arranging 32 highly satisfactory marriages. The village was proud and happy. Then one drunken night, two bachelors, in a test of strength, stuffed each other with pierogies and died. Can the matchmaker, through some quick arrangements, come up with 31 heterosexual marriages among the 62 survivors? (Adapted from Hayes, 1978, p. 180.)

The answer to this problem is obvious. Losing two males leaves 30 men and 32 women, making it impossible to arrange 31 heterosexual marriages. Of course, this is exactly the situation in the mutilated checkerboard problem, except instead of males and females being paired up, light and dark squares are. People who read this story are usually able to solve the mutilated checkerboard problem if they realize the connection between the couples in the story and the alternating squares on the checkerboard. This process of noticing connections between similar problems and applying the solution for one problem to other problems is called *analogical transfer*. In the next section, we will look more closely at how the process of analogical transfer has been used in problem solving.

TEST YOURSELF 12.1

1. What is the psychological definition of a problem?

2. What is the basic principle behind the Gestalt approach to problem solving? Describe how the following problems illustrate this principle, and also what else these problems demonstrate about problem solving: the circle problem; the candle problem; the two-string problem; the water jug problem. Be sure you understand functional fixedness.

3. What is insight, and what is the evidence that insight does, in fact, occur as people are solving a problem?

4. Describe Newell and Simon's approach to problem solving, in which "search" plays a central role. How does means–end analysis as applied to the Tower of Hanoi problem illustrate this approach? What is the think-aloud protocol?

5. How does the mutilated checkerboard experiment illustrate that the way a problem is stated can affect a person's ability to solve the problem? What are the implications of this research for Newell and Simon's "problem space" approach?

▶ Using Analogies to Solve Problems

A person is faced with a problem and wonders how to proceed. Questions such as "What move should I make?" or "How should I begin thinking about this problem?" arise. One tactic that is sometimes helpful is to consider whether another problem that the person has solved before is similar to the new problem and ask "Can I apply the same methods to solving this problem?" This technique of using an **analogy**—that is, using the solution to a similar problem to guide solution of a new problem—is called **analogical problem solving**.

Using the Russian marriage problem to help solve the mutilated checkerboard problem is an example of an effective use of analogy to solve a problem. Research on analogical problem solving has considered some of the conditions in which using analogies to solve problems is effective or ineffective.

Analogical Transfer

The starting point for much of the research on analogical problem solving has been to first determine how well people can transfer their experience from solving one problem to solving another, similar problem. This transfer from one problem to another is called **analogical transfer**. Two key terms that are used in research on analogical transfer are **target problem**, which is the problem the participant is trying to solve, and **source problem**, which is another problem that shares some similarities with the target problem and that illustrates a way to solve the target problem.

For the mutilated checkerboard problem, the checkerboard problem is the target problem, and the Russian marriage problem is the source problem. Evidence that analogical transfer has occurred is provided when presentation of the Russian marriage problem enhances the ability to solve the mutilated checkerboard problem. We saw that analogical transfer occurs in this example, because participants readily see that the principle governing the solution of the Russian marriage problem is similar to the principle that needs to be applied to solve the checkerboard problem. However, as we will now see, good analogical transfer does not always occur.

A problem that has been widely used in research on analogical problem solving is Karl Duncker's **radiation problem**.

DEMONSTRATION   Duncker's Radiation Problem

Try solving the following problem: Suppose you are a doctor faced with a patient who has a malignant tumor in his stomach. It is impossible to operate on the patient, but unless the tumor is destroyed the patient will die. There is a kind of ray that can be used to destroy the tumor. If the ray reaches the tumor at a sufficiently high intensity, the tumor will be destroyed. Unfortunately, at this intensity the healthy tissue that the ray passes through on the way to the tumor will also be destroyed. At lower intensities the ray is harmless to healthy tissue, but it will not affect the tumor either. What type of procedure might be used to destroy the tumor and at the same time avoid destroying the healthy tissue (Gick & Holyoak, 1980)?

If after thinking about this problem for a while, you haven't come up with a suitable answer, you are not alone. When Duncker (1945) originally posed this problem, most of his participants could not solve it, and Mary Gick and Keith Holyoak (1980, 1983) found that only 10 percent of their participants arrived at the correct solution, shown in **Figure 12.17a**. The solution is to bombard the tumor with a number of low-intensity rays from different directions, which destroys the tumor without damaging the tissue the rays are passing through. The solution to this problem is actually the procedure used in modern radiosurgery, in which a tumor is bombarded with 201 gamma ray beams that intersect at the tumor (Tarkan, 2003; **Figure 12.17b**).

Notice how the radiation problem and its solution fit with the Gestalt idea of representation and restructuring. The initial representation of the problem is a single ray that destroys the tumor but also destroys healthy tissue. The restructured solution involves dividing the single ray into many smaller rays.

After confirming Duncker's finding that the radiation problem is extremely difficult, Gick and Holyoak (1980, 1983) had another group of participants read and memorize the fortress story below, giving them the impression that the purpose was to test their memory for the story.

FORTRESS STORY

A small country was ruled from a strong fortress by a dictator. The fortress was situated in the middle of the country, surrounded by farms and villages. Many roads led to the fortress through the countryside. A rebel general vowed to capture the fortress. The general knew that an attack by his entire army would capture the fortress. He gathered his army at the head of one of the roads, ready to launch a full-scale direct attack. However, the general then learned that the dictator had planted mines on each of the roads. The mines were set so that small bodies of men could pass over them safely, since the dictator needed to move his troops and workers to and from the fortress. However, any large force would detonate the mines. Not only would this blow up the road, but it would also destroy many neighboring villages. It therefore seemed impossible to capture the fortress.

However, the general devised a simple plan. He divided his army into small groups and dispatched each group to the head of a different road. When all was ready he gave the signal and each group marched down a different road. Each group continued down its road to the fortress so that the entire army arrived together at the fortress at the same time. In this way, the general captured the fortress and overthrew the dictator. (See **Figure 12.17c.**)

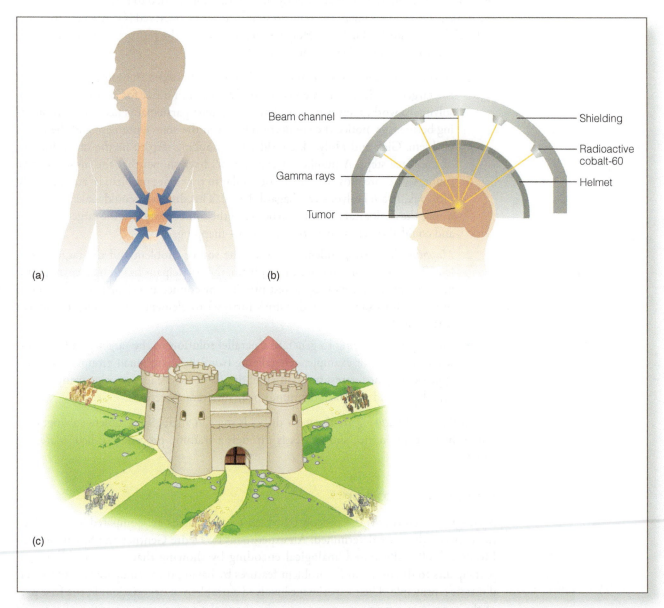

➤ **Figure 12.17** (a) Solution to the radiation problem. Bombarding the tumor, in the center, with a number of low-intensity rays from different directions destroys the tumor without damaging the tissue it passes through. (b) Radiosurgery, a modern medical technique for irradiating brain tumors with a number of beams of gamma rays, uses the same principle. The actual technique uses 201 gamma ray beams. (c) How the general solved the fortress problem.

The fortress story is analogous to the radiation problem: The dictator's fortress corresponds to the tumor, and the small groups of soldiers sent down different roads correspond to the low-intensity rays that can be directed at the tumor. After Gick and Holyoak's participants read the story, they were told to begin work on the radiation problem. Thirty percent of the people in this group were able to solve the radiation problem, an improvement over the 10 percent who solved the problem when it was presented alone. However, what is significant about this experiment is that 70 percent of the participants were still unable to solve the problem, even after reading an analogous source story. This result highlights one of the major findings of research on using analogies as an aid to problem solving: Even when exposed to analogous source problems, most people do not make the connection between the source problem and the target problem.

However, when Gick and Holyoak's participants were told to think about the story they had read, their success rate more than doubled, to 75 percent. Since no new information was given about the story, apparently the information needed to recognize the analogy was available in people's memories but had simply not been retrieved (Gentner & Colhoun, 2010). These results led Gick and Holyoak to propose that the process of analogical problem solving involves the following three steps:

1. *Noticing* that there is an analogous relationship between the source problem and the target problem. This step is obviously crucial in order for analogical problem solving to work. However, as we have seen, most participants need some prompting before they notice the connection between the source problem and the target problem. Gick and Holyoak consider this noticing step to be the most difficult of the three steps. A number of experiments have shown that the most effective source stories are those that are most similar to the target problem (Catrambone & Holyoak, 1989; Holyoak & Thagard, 1995). This similarity could make it easier to notice the analogical relationship between the source story and the target problem, and could also help achieve the next step—mapping.

2. *Mapping* the correspondence between the source problem and the target problem. To use the story to solve the problem, the participant has to map corresponding parts of the story onto the test problem by connecting elements of the source problem (for example, the dictator's fortress) to elements of the target problem (the tumor).

3. *Applying* the mapping to generate a parallel solution to the target problem. This would involve, for example, generalizing from the many small groups of soldiers approaching the fortress from different directions to the idea of using many weaker rays that would approach the tumor from different directions.

Noticing and *mapping* are the most difficult steps in analogical problem solving. One way to help people notice similarities is through a training procedure called *analogical encoding*.

Analogical Encoding

Analogical encoding is the process by which two problems are compared and similarities between them are determined. An experiment by Dedre Gentner and Susan Goldin-Meadow (2003) illustrated analogical encoding by showing that it is possible to get participants to discover similar problem features by having them compare two cases that illustrate a principle. Their experiment involved a problem in negotiation. In the first part of the experiment, participants were taught about the negotiation strategies of *trade-off* and *contingency*.

The **trade-off strategy** refers to a negotiating strategy in which one person says to another, "I'll give you A, if you'll give me B." This is illustrated by two sisters who are quarreling over who should get an orange. Eventually, they reach a trade-off solution when they realize that one wants the juice and the other wants just the peel, so one takes the juice and the other takes the peel. (This example is attributed to management consultant Mary Parker Follet in Gentner & Goldin-Meadow, 2003.)

The **contingency strategy** refers to a negotiating strategy in which a person gets what he or she wants if something else happens. This is illustrated by a situation in which an author wants 18 percent royalties, but the publisher wants to pay only 12 percent. The contingent solution would be to tie royalties to sales: "You can have 18 percent if sales are high, but less if sales are low."

After being familiarized with these negotiating strategies, one group of participants received two sample cases, both of which described trade-off solutions. The participants' task was to compare these two cases to arrive at a successful negotiation. Another group did the same thing, but their examples involved the contingency principle. Then both groups were given a new case, which potentially could be solved by either negotiating principle.

The results of this experiment are shown in **Figure 12.18**. When presented with the new test problem, participants tended to use the negotiating strategy that had been emphasized in the sample cases. Gentner concluded from these results that having people compare source stories is an effective way to achieve analogical encoding because it forces them to pay attention to problem features that enhance their ability to solve other problems.

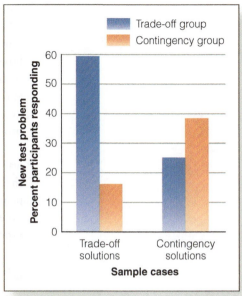

➤ **Figure 12.18** Results of Gentner and Goldin-Meadow's (2003) study of negotiating strategies. In the test case, participants who had compared trade-off examples were more apt to find trade-off solutions, whereas those who had compared contingency examples were more apt to find contingency solutions.

(Source: Based on D. Gentner & S. Goldin-Meadow, 2003)

Analogy in the Real World

So far, our examples of analogy problems have involved laboratory research. But what about the use of analogy in the real world? Many real-world examples of analogical problem solving illustrate what Kevin Dunbar (2001) has called the **analogical paradox**: While it is difficult to apply analogies in laboratory research, people routinely use analogies in real-world settings. Dunbar studied the use of analogies in real-world settings using a technique called *in-vivo problem-solving research*.

METHOD   In Vivo Problem-Solving Research

In vivo problem-solving research involves observing people to determine how they solve problems in real-world situations (Dunbar, 2002). This method has been used to study the use of analogy in a number of different settings, including laboratory meetings of a university research group and brainstorming sessions in which the goal was to develop a new product. Discussions recorded during these meetings have been analyzed for statements indicating that analogy is being used to help solve a problem. The advantage of the in vivo approach is that it captures thinking in naturalistic settings. A disadvantage is that it is time-consuming, and, as with most observational research, it is difficult to isolate and control specific variables.

When Dunbar and coworkers (Dunbar, 1999; Dunbar & Blanchette, 2001) videotaped molecular biologists and immunologists during their lab meetings, they found that researchers used analogies from 3 to 15 times in a 1-hour laboratory meeting. An example of an analogy from these laboratory meetings is the statement "If *E. coli* works like this, maybe your gene is doing the same thing." Similarly, Bo Christensen and Christian Schunn (2007) recorded meetings of design engineers who were creating new plastic products for medical applications. The engineers were trying to figure out how to create a container that would hold small amounts of liquid for a few minutes before falling apart. Christensen and Schunn found that the engineers proposed an analogy about every 5 minutes. When one engineer suggested that the container could be like a paper envelope, the group took off from this suggestion and eventually proposed a solution based on using paper. Thus, analogies play an important role both in solving scientific problems and in designing new products. When we discuss creativity later in this chapter, we will describe some examples of how analogical thinking has led to the development of useful products.

Although we understand some of the mental processes that occur as a person works toward the solution to a problem, what actually happens is still unclear. We do know, however, that one factor that can sometimes make problem solving easier is practice or training. Some people can become very good at solving certain kinds of problems because they become experts in an area. We will now consider what it means to be an expert and how being an expert affects problem solving.

► How Experts Solve Problems

Experts are people who, by devoting a large amount of time to learning about a field and practicing and applying that learning, have become acknowledged as being extremely knowledgeable or skilled in that particular field. For example, by spending 10,000–20,000 hours playing and studying chess, some chess players have reached the rank of grand master (Chase & Simon, 1973a, 1973b). Not surprisingly, experts tend to be better than nonexperts at solving problems in their field. Research on the nature of expertise has focused on determining differences between the way experts and nonexperts go about solving problems.

Differences Between How Experts and Novices Solve Problems

Experts in a particular field usually solve problems faster with a higher success rate than do novices (people who are beginners or who have not had the extensive training of experts; Chi et al., 1982; Larkin et al., 1980). But what is behind this faster speed and greater success? Are experts smarter than novices? Are they better at reasoning in general? Do they approach problems in a different way? Cognitive psychologists have answered these questions by comparing the performance and methods of experts and novices, and have reached the following conclusions.

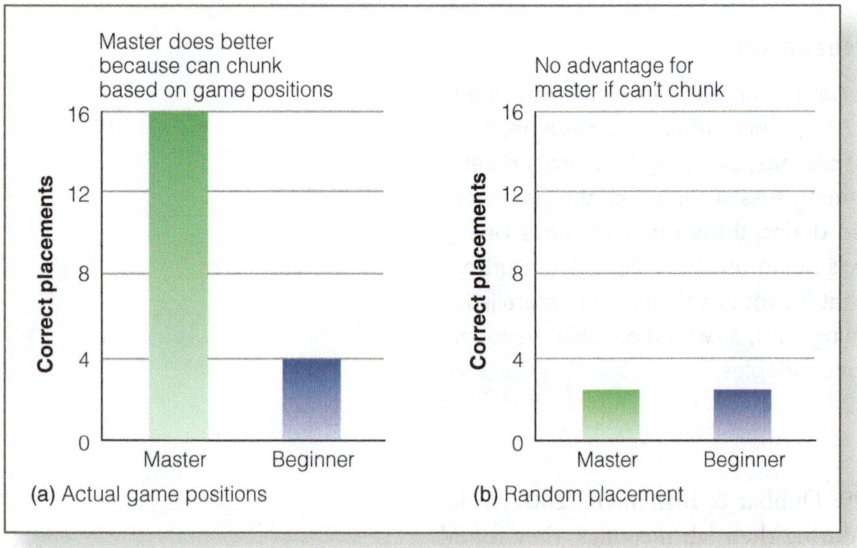

Experts Possess More Knowledge About Their Fields An experiment by William Chase and Herbart Simon (1973a, 1973b) compared how well a chess master with more than 10,000 hours of experience and a beginner with fewer than 100 hours of experience were able to reproduce the positions of pieces on a chessboard after looking at an arrangement for 5 seconds. The results showed that experts excelled at this task when the chess pieces were arranged in actual game positions (**Figure 12.19a**) but were no better than the beginners when the pieces were arranged randomly (**Figure 12.19b**). The reason for the experts' superior performance with actual

► **Figure 12.19** Results of Chase and Simon's (1973a, 1973b) chess memory experiment. (a) The chess master is better at reproducing actual game positions. (b) The master's performance drops to the level of the beginner's when the pieces are arranged randomly.
(Source: Based on W. G. Chase & H. A. Simon, 1973)

positions is that the chess masters had stored many of the patterns that occur in real games in their long-term memory, so they saw the layout of chess pieces not in terms of individual pieces but in terms of four to six chunks, each made up of a group of pieces that formed familiar, meaningful patterns. When the pieces were arranged randomly, the familiar patterns were destroyed, and the chess masters' advantage vanished (also see DeGroot, 1965; Gobet et al., 2001). We will now see that in addition to the fact that experts possess more knowledge than novices, experts also organize this knowledge differently.

Experts' Knowledge Is Organized Differently Than Novices'   The difference in organization between experts and novices is illustrated by an experiment by Michelene Chi and coworkers (1982; also see Chi et al., 1981). They presented 24 physics problems to a group of experts (physics professors) and a group of novices (students with one semester of physics) and asked them to sort the problems into groups based on their similarities. **Figure 12.20** shows diagrams of problems that were grouped together by an expert and by a novice. We don't need a statement of the actual problems to see from the diagrams that the novice sorted the problems based on characteristics such as how similar the objects in the problem were. Thus, two problems that included inclined planes were grouped together, even though the physical principles involved in the problems were quite different.

The expert, in contrast, sorted problems based on general principles of physics. The expert perceived two problems as similar because they both involved the principle of conservation of energy, even though the diagrams indicate that one problem involved a spring and another an inclined plane. Thus, novices categorized problems based on what the objects looked like and the experts categorized them based on the underlying principles involved. As it turns out, organizing based on principles results in more effective problem solving, and experts' ability to organize knowledge has been found to be important not only for chess masters and physics professors but for experts in many other fields as well (Egan & Schwartz, 1979; Reitman, 1976).

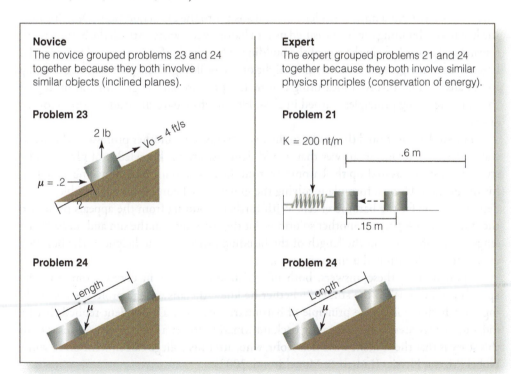

➤ **Figure 12.20** The kinds of physics problems that were grouped together by novices (left) and experts (right).

(Source: Based on M. T. H. Chi, P. J. Feltovich, & R. Glaser, 1981)

Experts Spend More Time Analyzing Problems   Experts often get off to what appears to be a slow start on a problem, because they spend time trying to understand the problem rather than immediately trying to solve it (Lesgold, 1988). Although this may slow them down at the beginning, this strategy usually pays off in a more effective approach to the problem.

Expertise Is Only an Advantage in the Expert's Specialty

Although there are many differences between experts and novices, it appears that these differences hold only when problems are within an expert's field. When James Voss and coworkers (1983) posed a real-world problem involving Russian agriculture to expert political scientists, expert chemists, and novice political scientists, they found that the expert political scientists performed best and that the expert chemists performed as poorly as the novice political scientists. In general, experts are experts only within their own field and perform like anyone else outside of their field (Bedard & Chi, 1992). This makes sense when we remember that the superior performance of experts occurs largely because they possess a larger and better organized store of knowledge about their specific field.

Before leaving our discussion of expertise, we should note that being an expert is not always an advantage. One disadvantage is that knowing about the established facts and theories in a field may make experts less open to new ways of looking at problems. This may be why younger and less-experienced scientists in a field are often the ones responsible for revolutionary discoveries (Kuhn, 1970; Simonton, 1984). Thus, it has been suggested that being an expert may be a disadvantage when confronting a problem that requires flexible thinking—a problem whose solution may involve rejecting the usual procedures in favor of other procedures that might not normally be used (Frensch & Sternberg, 1989).

Creative Problem Solving

There's a story about a physics student who, in answer to the exam question "Describe how the height of a building can be measured using a barometer," wrote "Attach the barometer to a string and lower it from the top of the building. The length of string needed to lower the barometer to the ground indicates the height of the building." The professor was looking for an answer that involved measuring barometric pressure on the ground and on top of the building, using principles learned in class. He therefore gave the student a zero for his answer.

The student protested the grade, so the case was given to another professor, who asked the student to provide an answer that would demonstrate his knowledge of physics. The student's answer was to drop the barometer from the roof and measure how long it took to hit the ground. Using a formula involving the gravitational constant would enable one to determine how far the barometer fell. With further prodding from the appeals professor, the student also suggested another solution: Put the barometer in the sun and measure the length of its shadow and the length of the building's shadow. The height of the building could then be determined using proportions.

Upon hearing these answers, both of which could result in correct solutions, the appeals professor asked the student whether he knew the answer the professor was looking for, which involved the principle of barometric pressure. The student replied that he did, but he was tired of just repeating back information to get a good grade. A footnote to this story is that the student was Niels Bohr, who, after his college career, went on to win a Nobel Prize in Physics (Lubart & Mouchiroud, 2003).

This story illustrates that being too creative can get you into trouble. But it also poses a question. Was the student being creative? The answer is "yes" if we define creativity as producing original answers or as being able to come up with multiple solutions to a problem.

But some creativity researchers have proposed definitions of creativity that go beyond originality.

What Is Creativity?

Many examples of creativity focus on **divergent thinking**—thinking that is open-ended, involving a large number of potential "solutions" (although some proposals might work better than others; see Guilford, 1956; Ward et al., 1997). James Kaufman (2009), in his book *Creativity 101*, notes that divergent thinking is the cornerstone of creativity, but it is not all that creativity can be. Kaufman proposes that in addition to being original, a creative response to a problem must be useful (Simonton, 2012). This approach to creativity is captured in the definition of creativity as "anything made by people that is in some way novel and has potential value or utility" (Smith et al., 2009). This definition works well, especially when considering creativity in designing products for people to use. It doesn't do as well in describing the creativity involved in creating visual art, music, or theater. Is a Picasso painting, a Beethoven symphony, or a play by Shakespeare creative? Most people would say yes, without any consideration of "usefulness." (Although it could be argued that great visual art, music, and theater are, in fact, useful, as they meet basic human needs for aesthetic experience.) For the purposes of our discussion, we will begin by considering some examples of how some practical products were invented.

Practical Creativity

Many examples of how inventions were created involve analogical problem solving, in which observing a phenomenon has led to a new, novel, and useful solution to a practical problem. A famous example of an invention that resulted from analogical problem solving is the story of George de Mestral, who in 1948 went for a nature hike with his dog and returned home with burrs covering his pants and the dog's fur. To discover why the burrs were clinging so tenaciously, de Mestral inspected the burrs under a microscope. What he saw were many tiny hook like structures, which led him to design a fabric fastener with many small hooks on one side and soft loops on the other side. In 1955 he patented his design and called it Velcro!

A more recent example of a creative idea based on analogical thinking is the case of Jorge Odón, an Argentine car mechanic, who designed a device to deal with the life-threatening situation of a baby stuck in the mother's birth canal during delivery. The beginnings of Odón's design can be traced to viewing a YouTube video that demonstrated how to remove a cork that had been pushed inside a wine bottle (see Dvorak Uncensored, 2007). The procedure involves slipping a plastic bag into the bottle, and blowing up the bag until it pushes the cork to the side of the bottle (**Figure 12.21a**). When the bag is pulled out, the cork comes with it.

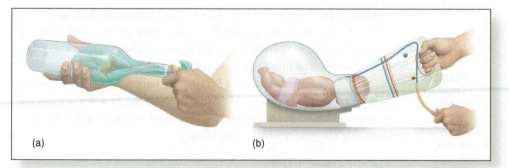

(a)   (b)

➤ **Figure 12.21** (a) How to get a cork out of a bottle without breaking the bottle. A bag is pushed into the bottle and inflated; when it is removed, the cork comes with it. (b) The prototype of Odón's device for getting a stuck baby out of the birth canal. For the prototype, Odón used a doll for the baby and a glass container to represent the womb.

The jump from the "removing a cork from a bottle trick" on YouTube to a way to save a baby stuck in the birth canal came to Odón as he slept. He woke at 4 AM with an idea for a device using the same principle: Inflate a bag inside the uterus and pull the bag out, bringing the baby with it. The process of translating this idea into a working model took years. Odón started by building a prototype device in his kitchen, using a glass jar for the womb, a doll for the baby, and a fabric bag as the extraction device. Eventually, after many different prototypes and numerous consultations with obstetricians, the Odón device was born! A plastic bag inside a lubricated sleeve is placed around the baby's head, the bag is inflated, and the bag is pulled out, bringing the baby with it (**Figure 12.21b**; McNeil, 2013; Venema, 2013).

The Odón device has been endorsed by the World Health Organization and has the potential for saving babies in poor countries and to reduce cesarean section births in rich ones. It is an example of analogical thinking applied to creative problem solving that resulted in a truly useful product (and also demonstrates that watching YouTube videos can be productive!).

The examples of Velcro and the Odón device not only illustrate creative problem solving but also demonstrate that most creative problem solving includes far more than just getting an idea. It also involves a lengthy period of trial-and-error development to turn the idea into a useful device. Odón's device took years to develop, and although de Mestral observed the burrs sticking to his dog in 1948, he didn't patent Velcro until 1955.

Many researchers have proposed the idea that creative problem solving involves a *process*. One proposal, illustrated in **Figure 12.22**, conceives of creative problem solving as a four-stage process that begins with generation of the problem and ends with implementation of the solution (Basadur et al., 2000). As we will see later when we discuss brain networks and creativity, some research has focused on two steps in this process, *generating* ideas (which corresponds to problem finding) and *evaluating* the idea (evaluation and selection). If one thinks of problem solving in this way, then one of the most important steps is realizing that there is a problem in the first place, which then leads to ideas, which are evaluated and eventually turned into a product (also see Finke, 1990; Mumford et al., 2012).

Another example of problem solving that involved a long process was the Wright brothers' invention of the airplane (Weisberg, 2009). Their design, which culminated in a successful flight at Kitty Hawk in December 1903, was the culmination of 4 years of effort in which they had to focus on how to design each component of the airplane, with special emphasis on developing a mechanism to steer the plane.

The Wright brothers example also illustrates that problem solving is not simply about getting an idea in a flash of insight, although that may happen, but about having a base of knowledge that eventually leads to a solution. The Wright brothers were successful because their knowledge of physics and mechanics, plus their extensive experience with bicycles in their bicycle repair shop, provided a basis for their creative ideas about how to combine a number of components to create an airplane.

Although generating ideas is only one part of the creative process, ideas are a crucial first step. We will now consider how some principles of cognition have been applied to understanding some of the factors responsible for generating creative ideas.

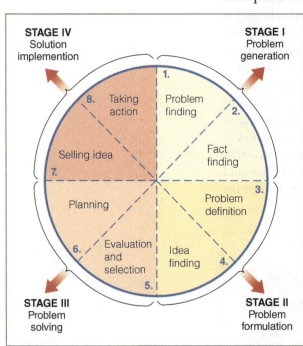

➤ **Figure 12.22** Problem solving process proposed by Basadur et al. (2000). Basadur proposes four steps, each of which is divided into two processes. For example, Stage II, problem formulation, consists of two steps: defining the problem and finding ideas.

(Source: Based on M. Basadur, M. Runco, & L. A. Vega, 2000)

Generating Ideas

When Linus Pauling, who won the Nobel Prize in Chemistry in 1914, was asked how he got ideas, he replied, "If you want to have good ideas you must have many ideas. Most of them will be wrong, and what you have to learn is which ones to throw away" (Crick, 1995). This answer emphasizes the importance of ideas for scientific discovery, as well as the importance of what occurs after ideas happen.

The question "What leads to ideas?" is difficult to answer because so many different factors are involved. The example of the Wright brothers illustrates that ideas depend on having a base of knowledge. And de Mestral, who was an engineer, knew enough to look at the burrs that his dog brought home under a microscope in order to reveal the hook like structure that led to the idea for Velcro.

But as important as knowledge is, sometimes too much knowledge can hinder creative problem solving. We noted at the end of the section on expertise that being an expert in a field may be a disadvantage when working on a problem that requires thinking flexibly and rejecting accepted procedures. This is exactly what happened in the case of Odón's invention. Although he had patented a number of inventions, they were for devices related to automobiles, like stabilization bars and car suspensions. It may be no coincidence that an auto mechanic, and not a doctor, developed a device for birthing. As one of the doctors who had worked with Odón said, "Doctors are very structured in their thinking and Jorge is a free mind, he can think of new things" (Venema, 2013). It is perhaps fortunate that Odón didn't have too much knowledge about medicine.

How too much knowledge can be a bad thing was demonstrated in an experiment by Steven Smith and coworkers (1993), who showed that providing examples to people before they solve a problem can influence the nature of their solutions. Smith's participants were given the task of inventing, sketching, labeling, and describing new and creative toys, or new life forms that might evolve on a planet like Earth. One group of participants was presented with three examples before they began working on the problem. For the life-form-generation task, all three examples had four legs, an antenna, and a tail.

Compared with the life forms created by a control group that had not seen any examples, the designs generated by the example group incorporated many more of the example features (**Figure 12.23a**). **Figure 12.23b** indicates the proportion of the designs that included example features (antennae, tail, and four legs) for the two groups. The greater use of these features by the example group is related to the idea of functional fixedness, described earlier in the chapter. Sometimes preconceptions can inhibit creativity (see Chrysikou & Weisberg 2005).

The idea that preconceptions can inhibit creativity led Alex Osborn (1953) to propose the technique of **group brainstorming**. The purpose of this technique is to encourage people to freely express ideas that might be useful in solving a particular problem. Instructions given to participants in brainstorming groups emphasize that they should just say whatever ideas come into their mind, without being critical of their own ideas or of the ideas of others in the group. The basis of these instructions is to increase creativity by opening people to "think outside the box."

This proposal has led to the widespread use of brainstorming in organizations. However, research has shown that placing people in groups to share ideas results in fewer ideas than adding up the ideas generated by the same number of people asked to think of ideas individually

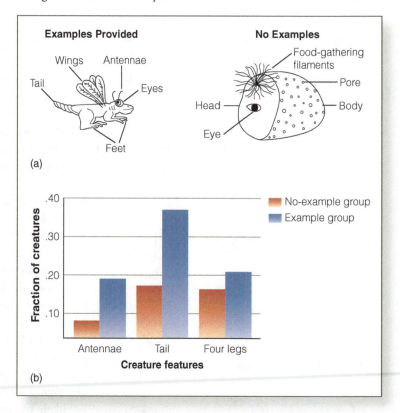

(a)

(b)

► **Figure 12.23** Two life forms created by participants in the Smith et al. (1993) experiment. (a) Participants who were provided with examples designed life forms that had characteristics that were included in the examples. (b) Proportion of life forms with antennae, tails, and four legs. Participants in the example group were more likely to include these features.

(Source: Based on S. M. Smith, A. Kerne, E. Koh, & J. Shah, 2009)

(Mullen et al., 1991). This occurs for a number of reasons. In groups, some people may dominate the discussion so others aren't able to participate. Also, despite the instructions to express any idea that comes to mind, being in a group can inhibit some people from expressing their ideas, possibly because they are afraid they will be judged. People also may be paying attention to others in the group, which keeps them from coming up with ideas of their own. Brainstorming in groups therefore turns out not to be a good way to generate ideas. Individual brainstorming to generate ideas, however, can be effective.

One method of individual idea generation that does work has been proposed by Ronald Finke, who developed a technique called **creative cognition** to train people to think creatively. The following demonstration illustrates Finke's technique.

DEMONSTRATION   Creating an Object

Figure 12.24 shows 15 object parts and their names. Touch the page three times without looking at the objects to randomly pick three of the object parts. After reading these instructions, take 1 minute to construct a new object using these three parts. The object should be interesting-looking and possibly useful, but try to avoid making your object correspond to a familiar object, and don't worry what it might be used for. You can vary the size, position, orientation, and material of the parts, as long as you don't alter the basic shape (except for the wire and the tube, which can be bent). Once you come up with something in your mind, draw a picture of it.

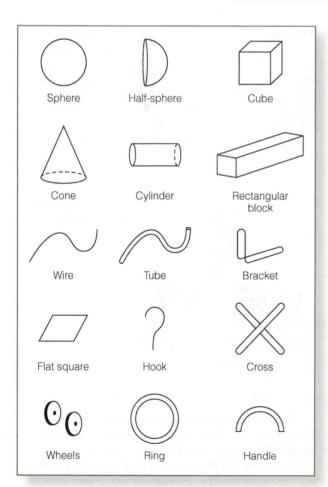

► **Figure 12.24** Objects used by Finke (1990, 1995).
(Source: R. A. Finke, 1995)

This exercise is patterned after one devised by Finke (1990, 1995), who randomly selected three of the object parts from Figure 12.24 for his participants. After the participants had created an object, they were provided with the name of one of the object categories from **Table 12.2** and were given 1 minute to interpret their object. For example, if the category was tools and utensils, the person had to interpret his or her form as a screwdriver, a spoon, or some other tool or utensil. To do this for your form, pick a category, and then decide what your object could be used for and describe how it functions. **Figure 12.25** shows how a single form that was constructed from the half-sphere, wire, and hook could be interpreted in terms of each of the eight categories in Table 12.2.

Finke called these "inventions" **preinventive forms** because they are ideas that precede the creation of a finished creative product. Just as it took de Mestral years to develop Velcro after his initial insight, preinventive forms need to be developed further before becoming useful "inventions."

Finke demonstrated not only that you don't have to be an "inventor" to be creative, but also that many of the processes that occur during creative cognition are similar to cognitive process from other areas of cognitive psychology. For example, Finke found that people were more likely to come up with creative uses for preinventive objects that they had created themselves than for objects created by other people. This occurred even though participants were instructed not to consider uses for the forms as they were creating them. This result is similar to the generation effect we discussed in Chapter 7: People remember material better when they generate it themselves (page 194). This advantage for self-generated material also occurs for retrieval cues (page 195).

TABLE 12.2

Object Categories in Preinventive Form Studies

Categories	Examples
Furniture	Chairs, tables, lamps
Personal items	Jewelry, glasses
Scientific instruments	Measuring devices
Appliances	Washing machines, toasters
Transportation	Cars, boats
Tools and utensils	Screwdrivers, spoons
Toys and games	Baseball bats, dolls
Weapons	Guns, missiles

Source: Adapted from R. A. Finke, Creative insight and preinventive forms, in R. J. Sternberg & J. E. Davidson (Eds.), *The nature of insight,* pp. 255–280 (Cambridge, MA: MIT Press, 1995).

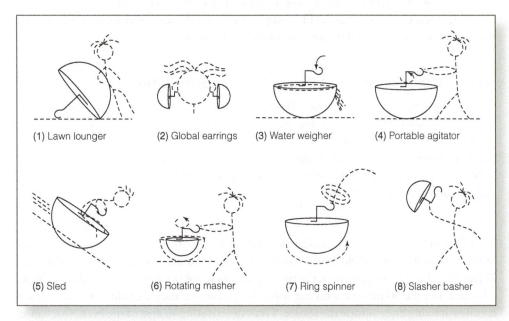

➤ **Figure 12.25** How a preinventive form that was constructed from the half-sphere, wire, and hook can be interpreted in terms of each of the eight categories in Table 12.2. (Source: R. A. Finke, 1995)

The research on creativity we've considered so far has focused on behavioral experiments. But other research has considered what is happening in the brain during the creative process.

▶ Creativity and the Brain

Many approaches have been taken to researching creativity and the brain. We will describe experiments designed to answer three different questions: (1) Will deactivating an area in the brain that might inhibit our openness to creative thinking increase creativity? (2) Are there different brain states that favor insightful versus analytical problem solving? (3) What is the connection between brain networks and creativity?

➤ **Figure 12.26** Display for the nine-dot problem. See text for instructions.

Opening the Mind to Think "Outside the Box"

Here's a problem, called the **nine-dot problem**: Draw four straight lines that pass through all nine dots in **Figure 12.26** without lifting your pen from the paper or retracing a line. After you've tried to solve this problem, see **Figure 12.28** on page 384 for the answer.

If you solved the problem, you are in the minority, because most people perceive the nine dots as a square and do not consider the possibility of extending the lines outside the square. Why is this problem so difficult? One reason has to do with our tendency, described in Chapter 3, to perceive individual elements as grouped together (see the Chapter 3 section, *The Gestalt Principles of Organization*, pages 71–73). Thus, when we look up at the night sky, we group individual stars into constellations. When applied to the nine-dot problem, when we look at the nine dots we see a square, so we don't consider the possibility of extending the lines outside the square.

Richard Chi and Alan Snyder (2012) considered the results of previous experiments that showed that the left anterior temporal lobe (ATL; see page 291) is associated with grouping lower level information into meaningful patterns, just as individual stars are grouped into constellations, and the nine dots in Figure 12.26 are grouped into a square. Chi and Snyder wondered whether deactivating the left ATL might open up people's thinking about patterns like the nine-dot problem. To test this idea, they deactivated the left ATL and activated the right ATL using **transcranial direct current stimulation** while their participants attempted to solve the nine-dot problem.

> **METHOD**   Transcranial Direct Current Stimulation
>
> This is a procedure for stimulating the brain in which two electrodes are placed on a person's head. These electrodes are connected to a battery-powered device that delivers direct current. One of the electrodes is the cathodal electrode, which is negatively charged and decreases the excitability of neurons under the electrode. The other is the anodal electrode, which is positively charged and increases the excitability of neurons under the electrode.

Chi and Snyder placed a cathodal electrode over the left ATL, to decrease excitability of this area, and an anodal electrode over the right ATL, to increase excitability of this area. When they did this, 40 percent of the participants were able to solve the nine-dot problem. This matches the 40 percent who can solve the problem if they are told that the solution involves drawing lines outside the square. Thus, deactivating an area of the brain that causes us to interpret the world in certain ways can help us to think "outside the box" (or "outside the square" in this case).

Brain "Preparation" for Insight and Analytical Problem Solving

What is happening in the brain just before we solve a problem or make a creative discovery? The answer to this question has implications for the way the problem is solved. We've seen that having an insight or "Aha" moment involves a sudden realization of the solution. In contrast, noninsight problems are usually solved more gradually, using an analytical process that gradually approaches the solution (page 358).

John Kounios and coworkers (2006), in a paper titled "The Prepared Mind," showed that whether a problem is solved by an insight-driven process or an analytical process is associated with the state the brain is in just before the problem is presented. Participants in their experiment were fitted with electrodes, as shown in Figure 5.26, page 156, which measured the **electroencephalogram (EEG)**. The EEG is a response like the one in **Figure 12.27a**, recorded from the thousands of neurons under the electrodes.

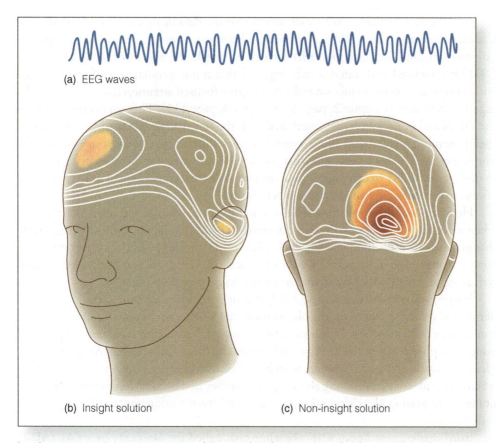

> **Figure 12.27** (a) EEG response. This record is about 4 seconds of responding. (b) The colored area indicates high EEG activation in the frontal lobe prior to an insight solution. (c) The colored area indicates high EEG activation in the occipital lobe prior to a non-insight (analytical) solution.

(Source: From Kounios et al., 2006. Adapted from Figure 2a, page 884)

The EEG was measured for two seconds, followed by presentation of a **compound remote-associate problem**, in which three words are presented, such as *pine*, *crab*, and *sauce*, and the task is to determine one word that, when combined with each of these words, forms a new word or a phrase (*pineapple*, *crabapple*, and *applesauce*, in this example). This type of problem can be solved both by insight or analytically.

Participants solved about 50 percent of the problems within 30 seconds, and immediately after solving each problem indicated whether their solution was by insight (56 percent of the solutions) or noninsight (44 percent) The results in Figure 12.27 show that EEG activity increased in the frontal lobe just before the insight solutions (**Figure 12.27b**) and increased in the occipital lobe just before the noninsight solutions (**Figure 12.27c**).

Because these differences in activity occurred *before* the participants had seen the problems, Kounios concluded that "neural activity during a preparatory interval before subjects saw verbal problems predicted which problems they would subsequently solve with . . . self-reported insight." In other words, the status of your brain before you begin a problem can influence the approach you take to solving the problem.

Networks Associated with Creativity

The experiments we've described, in which a brain area was deactivated before solving a problem and in which brain activity was measured before seeing a problem, both indicate that there is a relationship between the state of the brain and creative problem solving. We now continue this story by looking at how two brain networks are involved in creativity.

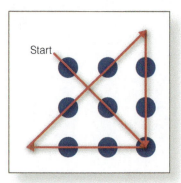

➤ **Figure 12.28** Solution to the nine-dot problem.

Default Mode Network   When we introduced the default mode network (DMN) in Chapter 2, we noted that DMN activity *decreases* when a person is involved in a specific task and *increases* when attention isn't focused on a task. We also saw that activity in the DMN is associated with mind wandering, and that mind wandering is often associated with a decrease in performance on tasks that require focused attention like reading or solving math problems (Chapter 2, page 51; Chapter 4, page 115). This connection between the DMN and mind wandering, combined with the fact that people spend almost half of their time mind wandering (Killingsworth & Gilbert, 2010), raised a question: What is the purpose of the DMN? Could it be that its purpose is to create mind wandering in order to disrupt our ability to carry out important tasks? This certainly seemed unlikely, but the answer to this question had to await further research.

Hope for a positive role for the DMN and mind wandering appeared in Chapter 6 when we saw that mind wandering is often involved in thinking about the future, suggesting that perhaps one of its functions is to help plan for the future (page 177). And now, as we consider mind wandering and the DMN again, we will see that there is evidence that mind wandering and the DMN play an important role in creative thinking.

Benjamin Baird and coworkers (2012) did an experiment that connected mind wandering and creativity, based on the observation that when a person is working on a problem but can't solve it, the solution sometimes "appears" after they have put the problem aside. This phenomenon has been noted by scientific thinkers, including Albert Einstein, Henri Poincaré, and Isaac Newton, who have described having moments of inspiration when they had stopped thinking about a problem they had been trying to solve. The phenomenon of getting ideas after taking a "time-out" from working on a problem is called **incubation**.

Baird's experiment began with a baseline task, called the **alternate uses task** (**AUT**; also called the unusual uses task), in which participants had 2 minutes to think of unusual uses for common objects. For example, how many unusual uses can you think of for bricks? (A few examples: use as a weapon, a paperweight, a steppingstone, as a weight for an anchor.)

The baseline AUT task was followed by a 12-minute incubation period, during which participants carried out a difficult task, which resulted in a low rate of mind wandering, or an easy task, which resulted in a higher rate of mind wandering. When participants then repeated the AUT task for the same objects they had considered before, the results were clear-cut: Following the easy task, which was accompanied by a high rate of mind wandering, performance on the repeat AUT tasks increased by 40 percent compared with the baseline. Following the hard task, performance was unchanged. Mind wandering, concluded Baird, facilitates creative incubation.

The blue arrows in **Figure 12.29** indicate the relationships between mind wandering and DMN activity and between mind wandering and creativity that we have discussed so far. But is there a connection between DMN activity and creativity? Naama Mayseless and coworkers (2015) studied this question by presenting participants with a task based on the alternate uses task. Mayseless's participants were presented with an object and were instructed to propose one possible use for the object that was different than its usual use, with an emphasis on being novel and unique. Participants' brain activity (fMRI) was measured in a scanner as they were doing the task.

The key variable in this experiment was the originality of the proposed uses. For example, proposing "to stab" as a use for a pencil was rated low in originality, because a number of people proposed that use. However, proposing that a pencil could be "used as a rolling pin" was rated high in originality, because no one else proposed that use.

The result of this experiment was that higher originality ratings were associated with higher activity of structures in the DMN. This result enables us to add the

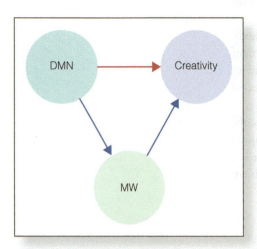

➤ **Figure 12.29** Relationships between mind wandering (MW), default mode network (DMN) activity, and creativity. See text for details.

relation shown by the red arrow in Figure 12.29, between DMN activity and creativity. This relation between DMN activity and creativity has been confirmed by the results of a number of experiments (Beaty et al., 2014; Ellamil et al., 2012). However, the connection between brain networks and creativity is more complex than the diagram in Figure 12.29, because networks in addition to the DMN are also involved in creativity. One of the most important networks is the executive control network.

Executive Control Network   The **executive control network (ECN)**, which is involved in directing attention as a person is carrying out tasks (page 48), plays a crucial role in creativity. An experiment by Melissa Ellamil and coworkers (2012) supports a link between the ECN and creativity. Participants carried out the creative task of designing book covers while in a scanner that used fMRI to determine which areas of the brain were activated. An important feature of this experiment is that participants were instructed to create their book cover design in two phases: After reading a description of what the book was about, they were told to *generate* ideas for the cover. Then, after a short break, they were told to shift their thinking to *evaluating* the designs that they had generated.

This sequence—generating followed by evaluating—is often used to describe the process involved in creativity (see Figure 12.22). Ellamil found that regions of the DMN and ECN were both more strongly activated during idea evaluation than during generation. Based on this result, they concluded that activity of the DMN and ECN was coordinated during creative evaluation.

Taking the idea of coordinated activity a step further, when Ellamil measured the functional connectivity between the DMN and ECN using the resting state fMRI method (see pages 46–48), she found that the DMN and ECN were functionally connected during both the generation and evaluation stages of the creative process. Functional connectivity between the DMN and ECN was also determined by Roger Beaty and coworkers (2014) by measuring connectivity in people who were high and low in creativity, as determined by their scores on a battery of creativity tests. As they expected, the functional connectivity between the DMN and ECN was stronger in the high-creative group.

The idea that the DMN and ECN networks work together during creative thinking is especially interesting because these two networks are usually thought to oppose each other. Because the ECN is involved with regulating attention, its activity increases when people are involved in tasks that require attention. But focusing attention during tasks shuts down the DMN. Conversely, ECN activity usually decreases under conditions in which the DMN would be expected to be active.

What's going on here? How can two networks that oppose each other work together? Researchers are still working to answer this question. But if we set aside the facts that these networks normally respond in opposite ways, the connection between mind wandering and creativity makes sense when we consider how the spontaneous nature of mind wandering creates a flow of thoughts and ideas. And it also makes sense that creativity often requires a "traffic cop," which is where the ECN comes in, by guiding thinking in original directions. For example, the ECN might direct attention away from unoriginal responses to the alternate uses task (such as "to build a house" as a use for "brick"), so more original uses can be explored. Beaty and coworkers (2014), who found that the DMN and ECN were more strongly connected in highly creative people, put it this way: "increased functional connectivity ... may correspond to a greater ability of creative individuals to govern their imagination by executing complex search processes, inhibiting task-irrelevant information, and selecting ideas among a large set of competing alternatives." This striking cooperation between one network associated with imagination (DMN) and the other with attention (ECN), even though they have an antagonistic relation with each other, highlights the special nature of creative thinking (Christoff et al., 2009).

▶ **SOMETHING TO CONSIDER**

Wired to Create: Things Creative People Do Differently

Picasso creating a painting, Einstein formulating the theory of relativity, Charlotte and Emily Brontë writing Jayne Eyre (Charlotte) and Wuthering Heights (Emily): What can we learn about creativity from these famous people that we can apply to our own creative process? That is the question Scott Barry Kaufman and Carolyn Gregoire ask in their book, *Wired to Create: Unraveling the Mysteries of the Creative Mind* (2015). This highly readable book brings together insights from the lives of creative people and current research in cognitive psychology to create the "Ten things highly creative people do differently," described in **Table 12.3**.

One of the things that makes each chapter interesting is stories about the specific techniques that have helped famous people be more creative. We see how activities such as taking a hike, finding a place to be alone, engaging in hobbies outside their field, and meditating have been practiced by creative people such as Alice Walker, who wrote *The Color Purple*, scientists Charles Darwin and Louis Pasteur, innovator Steve Jobs, and musicians Yo-Yo Ma and Michael Jackson.

While these stories about well-known people are interesting, what is most important about each chapter is what it tells us about things we can do to enhance our own creativity. We briefly describe some of the ideas in Chapters 3 (Daydreaming), 4 (Solitude), and 7 (Mindfulness), and highlight some actions you can take that may lead to greater creativity.

Daydreaming

Daydreaming is something we've already discussed, because it is another name for mind wandering. One of the keys to using daydreaming to enhance creativity is to know how

TABLE 12.3

Ten Things That Highly Creative People Do Differently

Chapter	Characteristic	Description
1	Imaginative Play	Children's engagement in imaginative play enables them to experiment with different types of experience. Carried into adulthood, this playfulness supports innovation.
2	Passion	Focusing on a particular pursuit that the person loves and wants to devote his or her life to
3	Daydreaming	Mind wandering that occurs when a person's attention shifts from the external environment to internally generated, often involuntary, thoughts (see pages 114, 384)
4	Solitude	Solitary reflection that is facilitated by being alone in order to avoid distractions
5	Intuition	Intuitive thoughts, or insights, arriving from unconscious information-processing systems. These often occur unexpectedly, although they are often preceded by unconscious mental activity.
6	Openness to Experience	The drive for cognitive exploration of one's inner mind and the outer world.
7	Mindfulness	Paying attention to what is happening in our mind and in the environment. Has been associated with some types of meditation.
8	Sensitivity	Heightened awareness of the environment and processes occurring in the mind
9	Turning Adversity into Advantage	Creativity arising out of loss, suffering, or trauma. Both good and bad life events are potential sources of inspiration and motivation.
10	Thinking Differently	Rejection of traditional ways of thinking. Being open to new paradigms (see page 13).

to harness its power. One way to do this is to take a break from what you are doing and purposely let your mind wander, an activity which we've seen has been linked to creativity (Baird et al., 2010). The act of choosing to disengage from external tasks in order to pursue an internal stream of thought that might have positive outcomes is called **volitional daydreaming** (McMillan et al., 2013).

Kaufman and Gregoire describe how some creative people have engaged in activities that may foster mind wandering. One of the activities they describe is taking a shower, which is one of the main activities associated with mind wandering (Killingsworth, 2011). Or consider walking. Philosopher Immanuel Kant took an hour-long walk every day, along a street in Konigsberg, Germany, which later was named "Philosopher's Walk." Charles Darwin, Henry David Thoreau, Sigmund Freud, and many others used walking to help them create, and the philosopher Friedrich Nietzsche stated that "all truly great thoughts are conceived by walking" (Nietzsche, 1889).

More than daydreaming might be going on during walking, but the result—increased creativity—is what's important. And you don't have to be famous to benefit from walking. Marily Oppezzo and Daniel Schwartz (2014) showed that walking resulted in an increase of 60 percent in the number of uses proposed in the alternate uses task (see page 384) in a group of undergraduate students who walked compared with a group who remained seated for the same amount of time.

Actions you can take:

➤ Take a break.

➤ Take a shower.

➤ Take a walk.

➤ Pay attention to your mind wanderings.

Solitude

In our discussion of daydreaming we saw that solitary experiences such as being alone in the shower or taking a walk have been used as ways to increase creativity. But solitude goes beyond finding ways to enhance daydreaming. Solitude can also enhance analytical thinking that requires focused attention.

One obvious benefit of solitude is that it can help avoid distractions. (Note that being alone with your cell phone doesn't count as solitude!) But Kaufman and Gregoire say that "solitude isn't just about avoiding distractions; it's about giving the mind the space it needs to reflect, make new connections and find meaning." Although the chapter on solitude has few references to psychological research on solitude, it contains many examples of how solitude has been embraced by creative individuals.

Numerous writers have reported taking steps to insure solitude. Thoreau wrote *Walden or a Life in the Woods* (1854) while living alone for over 2 years at Walden Pond; writer Zadie Smith said she thought it was important to have a private work space away from other people (Smith, 2010); and writer Jonathan Franzen wrote his best-selling novel *The Connections* in his studio with the curtains drawn and lights off (Currey, 2013). But solitude works for non-writers as well. Steve Wozniack, cofounder of Apple computer, advised would-be innovators to "work alone" (Wozniack & Smith, 2007); the inventor Thomas Edison stated that "the best thinking has been done in solitude," and Nikola Tesla, the inventor of alternating current, wrote, "Be alone, that is the secret of invention; be alone, that is when ideas are born."

At the end of their chapter on solitude, Kaufman and Gregoire note that eventually, ideas that were created while in solitude are shared with others, and that "the key to creativity is the balance of focus on the self and focus on others." Thus, while solitude is one step in the creative process, it is also necessary to share creative output and collaborate with others to translate creative ideas into useful products. For example, remember the process involved in Jorge Odón's development of the Odón device for birthing, in which translating his idea into a working device involved much trial and error and working in consultation with obstetricians.

Actions:

➤ Have a place to be alone, away from distractions.
➤ Stay there for long enough to give your mind space to create ideas.

Mindfulness

Mindfulness has been described as "the simple process of actively noticing new things" and "paying attention to the present moment" (Langer, 2014). Another, more extensive, definition of mindfulness is "paying attention on purpose, in the present moment, and nonjudgmentally, to the unfolding of experience moment to moment." (Kabat-Zinn, 2003, p. 145). One of the paragons of mindfulness is the fictional detective Sherlock Holmes, who had an uncanny ability to solve cases using clues based on his close observation of small details (Konnikova, 2013).

But if you're not Sherlock Holmes, what is the best way to achieve mindfulness? One pathway that has been proposed to achieve mindfulness is **meditation**. But just saying "meditation" isn't enough, because there are numerous types of mediation. One type, which has become extremely prevalent in recent decades, is called **focused attention (FA) meditation**. The basic procedure for FA mediation is to focus on one thing, like the in and out of your breath, and when your mind wanders, as it inevitability will, to bring your attention back to your breath (Brewer et al., 2011). This procedure quiets the mind, and experienced practitioners often experience a decrease in mind wandering. This procedure has been used to reduce stress and has been shown to have health benefits and to alter the structure of the brain in a positive way (Fox et al., 2014).

But you might notice that this description creates a paradox. FA meditation decreases mind wandering, which decreases distractions (good), but which also may decrease creativity (bad). Because decreasing mind wandering may cause a decrease in creativity, another type of meditation, called **open monitoring (OM) meditation**, may be preferable. OM meditation, which involves simply paying attention to whatever comes into the mind, and to follow this thought until something else comes along, does not decrease mind wandering (Brewer et al., 2011; Xu et al., 2014).

Lorenza Colzato and coworkers (2012) compared FA and OM mind wandering in an experiment that involved three groups of participants, one that practiced FA meditation before being presented with the alternate uses task, one that practiced OM meditation, and a control group in which participants visualized household activities like giving a dinner party or cooking. They found that both meditation groups did better on the alternate uses task than the control group, but that the OM meditation group thought of more uses and had more original ideas than the FA meditation group (**Figure 12.30**). Also, Jian Xu and coworkers (2014) found that OM meditation caused greater activation of the DMN than FA meditation. Based on results such as these, Kaufman and Gregoire recommend OM meditation for enhancing creativity.

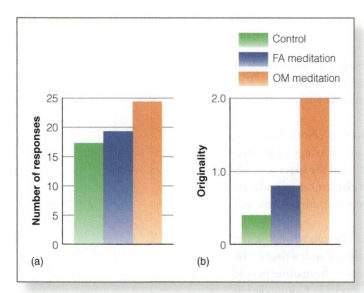

➤ **Figure 12.30** Results of Colzato et al.'s (2012) experiment showing performance on the alternate uses task for the control group, the focused attention (FA) meditation group, and the open-monitoring (OM) meditation group. (a) Number of uses proposed. (b) Originality. Originality for each response was scored as follows: Responses given by only 5 percent of the group = 1 point; Responses given by only 1 percent of the group = 2 points. The score achieved by the OM meditation group is therefore the maximum possible score.
(Source: From Colzato et. al., 2010. Based on data in Table 1.)

Action:

> ➤ Meditate regularly. Open monitoring is best for creativity.

All of the ways to enhance creativity we have described suggest concrete steps that anyone can take. For more suggestions, as well as stories about many highly creative people, see Kaufman and Gregoire's book. If you read this book, you will encounter things that we discussed in the section "Networks Associated With Creativity" (page 383), because the book has many references to the default mode network, which Kaufman and Gregoire call the **imagination network**. Kaufman and Gregoire also consider how the default mode network and the executive attention network work together. This material on networks, which is mentioned throughout the book, is one reason the book is titled *Wired to Create*.

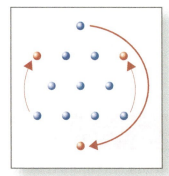

➤ **Figure 12.31** Solution to the triangle problem. Arrows indicate movement; colored circles indicate new positions.

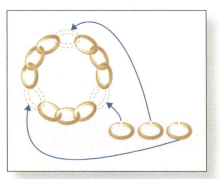

➤ **Figure 12.32** Solution to the chain problem. All the links in one chain are cut and separated (3 cuts @ 2 cents = 6 cents). The separated links are then used to connect the other three pieces and then closed (3 closings @ 3 cents = 9 cents). Total = 15 cents.

TEST YOURSELF 12.2

1. What is the basic idea behind analogical problem solving? What is the source problem? The target problem? How effective is it to present a source problem and then the target problem, without indicating that the two are related?

2. Describe Duncker's radiation problem. What is the solution, and how have researchers used this problem to illustrate analogical problem solving?

3. What are the three steps in the process of analogical problem solving? Which of the steps appears to be the most difficult to achieve?

4. What is analogical encoding? What two strategies have been described that help people discover similar problem features?

5. What is the analogical paradox? How has analogical problem solving been studied in the real world?

6. What is an expert? What are some differences between the way experts and nonexperts go about solving problems? How good are experts at solving problems outside of their field?

7. What is divergent thinking? How is it related to connectivity? How does the definition of creativity extend beyond originality?

8. Describe analogical problem solving as illustrated by de Mestral's invention of Velcro and Odón's invention of a birthing device.

9. What does it mean to say that problem solving is a process?

10. Discuss the factors involved in generating ideas, including the role of knowledge, the use of brainstorming, and the creative cognition approach.

11. Why would deactivating the left anterior temporal lobe be expected to increase creativity? Describe Chi and Snyder's experiment.

12. Describe Kounios and coworkers' (2006) experiment, which showed that different brain states precede insight or noninsight problem solving.

13. What is the evidence that the default mode network and the executive control network are both involved in creativity? Why is their joint involvement in creativity called a paradox?

14. Describe the actions of daydreaming and solitude, as practiced by highly creative people.

15. What is the difference between focused attention meditation and open monitoring meditation? Which one has been shown to result in greater creativity?

CHAPTER SUMMARY

1. A problem occurs when there is an obstacle between a present state and a goal and it is not immediately obvious how to get around the obstacle.

2. The Gestalt psychologists focused on how people represent a problem in their mind. They devised a number of problems to illustrate how solving a problem involves a restructuring of this representation and to demonstrate factors that pose obstacles to problem solving.

3. The Gestalt psychologists introduced the idea that reorganization is associated with insight—a sudden realization of a problem's solution. Insight has been demonstrated experimentally by tracking how close people feel they are to solving insight and non-insight problems.

4. Functional fixedness is an obstacle to problem solving that is illustrated by Duncker's candle problem and Maier's two-string problem. Situationally produced mental set is illustrated by the Luchins water jug problem.

5. Alan Newell and Herbert Simon were early proponents of the information-processing approach to problem solving. They saw problem solving as the searching of a problem space to find the path between the statement of the problem (the initial state) and the solution to the problem (the goal state). This search is governed by operators and is usually accomplished by setting subgoals. The Tower of Hanoi problem has been used to illustrate this process.

6. Research on the mutilated checkerboard problem also illustrates the importance of how a problem is presented.

7. Newell and Simon developed the technique of think-aloud protocols to study participants' thought process as they are solving a problem.

8. Analogical problem solving occurs when experience with a previously solved source problem or a source story is used to help solve a new target problem. Research involving Duncker's radiation problem has shown that even when people are exposed to analogous source problems or stories, most people do not make the connection between the source problem or story and the target problem.

9. The analogical paradox is that, while it is difficult to apply analogies in laboratory research, analogical problem solving is often used in real-world settings.

10. Experts are better than novices at solving problems in their field of expertise. They have more knowledge of the field, organize this knowledge based more on deep structure than on surface features, and spend more time analyzing a problem when it is first presented.

11. Creative problem solving is associated with divergent thinking. We have only a limited understanding of the processes involved in creative problem solving and creativity in general. The examples of George de Mestral and Jorge Odón illustrate how analogy has been used to create practical inventions.

12. Creative problem solving has been described as a process that begins with generation of the problem and ends with implementation of the solution, with ideas happening in between.

13. The question of what leads to generation of ideas is a complicated one. Knowledge is often essential for generating ideas, but sometimes too much knowledge can be a bad thing, as illustrated by Smith's experiment showing that providing examples can inhibit creative design.

14. The technique of brainstorming has been proposed as a way to increase creativity, but generating ideas in groups is generally not as effective as generating ideas individually and combining them. The creative cognition technique has been successfully used to create innovative designs.

15. Recent research has shown that deactivating the left ATL can increase creativity; that different brain states, measured with the EEG, are associated with insight-based and analytical-based problem solving; and that the default mode and executive control networks work together during creative thinking.

16. Kaufman and Gregoire's book *Wired to Create* lists ten things that highly creative people do differently.

THINK ABOUT IT

1. Pick a problem you have had to deal with, and analyze the process of solving it into subgoals, as is done in means–end analysis.

2. Have you ever experienced a situation in which you were trying to solve a problem but stopped working on it because you couldn't come up with the answer? Then, after a while, when you returned to the problem, you got the answer right away? What do you think might be behind this process?

3. On August 14, 2003, a power failure caused millions of people in the northeastern and midwestern United States and eastern Canada to lose their electricity. A few days later, after most people had their electricity restored, experts still did not know why the power failure had occurred and said it would take weeks to determine the cause. Imagine that you are a member of a special commission that has the task of solving this problem, or some other major problem. How could the processes described in this chapter be applied to finding a solution? What would the shortcomings of these processes be for solving this kind of problem?

4. Think of some examples of situations in which you overcame functional fixedness and found a new use for an object.

KEY TERMS

Alternate uses task (AUT), 384

Analogical encoding, 372

Analogical paradox, 373

Analogical problem solving, 369

Analogical transfer, 370

Analytically based problem, 358

Analogy, 369

Candle problem, 359

Compound remote-association problem, 383

Contingency strategy, 373

Creative cognition, 380

Daydreaming, 386

Divergent thinking, 377

Electroencephalogram (EEG), 382

Executive control network (ECN), 385

Expert, 374

Fixation, 359

Focused attention (FA) meditation, 388

Functional fixedness, 359

Goal state, 362

Group brainstorming, 379

Imagination network, 389

In vivo problem-solving research, 373

Incubation, 384

Initial state, 362

Insight, 357

Intermediate states, 363

Means–end analysis, 364

Meditation, 388

Mental set, 360

Mindfulness, 388

Mutilated checkerboard problem, 366

Nine-dot problem, 382

Open monitoring (OM) meditation, 388

Operators, 362

Preinventive forms, 380

Problem space, 363

Problem, 356

Radiation problem, 370

Restructuring, 357

Source problem, 370

Subgoals, 364

Target problem, 370

Think-aloud protocol, 368

Tower of Hanoi problem, 362

Trade-off strategy, 372

Transcranial direct current stimulation, 382

Two-string problem, 360

Volitional daydreaming, 387

Water jug problem, 360

Here's something to think about: One male is selected randomly from the population of the United States. That male, Robert, wears glasses, speaks quietly, and reads a lot. Is it more likely that Robert is a librarian or a farmer? This is one of the questions posed in an experiment we will discuss in this chapter. The way participants answered this question, plus the results of many other experiments in which people were asked to make judgments, has helped us understand the mental processes involved in making judgments. This chapter also considers the mental processes involved in the closely related topics of decision making and reasoning.

Judgment, Decisions, and Reasoning

By Laura Cacciamani and Bruce Goldstein

In the 2007 draft of the National Basketball Association (NBA), there was a 22-year-old, 7′1″ player by the name of Marc Gasol. According to mathematical models predicting player success, Gasol was expected to do very well and be a positive addition to any team. However, upon seeing Gasol shirtless, the scouts for the Houston Rockets noticed that he didn't quite look like their typical NBA player: he appeared out of shape and not very muscular, especially when compared to other players. Based on the scouts' past experiences, players with bodies that looked like that were less likely to be successful. So, the scouts reasoned that Gasol would not be successful either, and when Houston's 26th pick came up, they passed on Gasol—a decision made based on a judgment of his appearance rather than his mathematically predicted success. Gasol ended up signing with the Memphis Grizzlies where he was highly successful, winning the NBA Defensive Player of the Year Award and ultimately becoming a three-time NBA All-Star, and the Houston Rockets were left kicking themselves in regret (Lewis, 2016).

Although you might not be recruiting NBA players on a daily basis, this example demonstrates the use of judgments, reasoning, and decision making and shows how these processes can sometimes result in errors. In the case of Marc Gasol, the Houston Rockets made a **judgment** about his appearance and athleticism ("He looks out of shape"). They then relied on **reasoning**—the process of drawing conclusions—to determine that Gasol would not be successful based on prior evidence ("In the past, players who looked out of shape were not successful"). This allowed the Rockets staff to make a **decision**—the process of choosing between alternatives—to not draft Gasol. In this case, their judgments and reasoning led to an erroneous conclusion, which resulted in a poor decision.

We've been devoting a lot of attention to Marc Gasol to make a point: Even though we can distinguish between making judgments, reasoning based on evidence, and making decisions, they are all related. Decisions are based on judgments we make, and applying these judgments can involve various reasoning processes. We could, in fact, have called this chapter "Thinking," although that is too general because it also applies to material in many other chapters in this book. Our strategy in this chapter will be to describe judgments, reasoning, and decision making separately, while keeping in mind that they overlap and interact. We will also see how and why these processes can sometimes result in errors, as in Marc Gasol's situation.

▶ Inductive Reasoning: Making Judgments from Observations

We are constantly making judgments about things in our environment, including people, events, and behaviors. One of the primary mechanisms involved in making judgments is **inductive reasoning**, which is the process of drawing general conclusions based on specific observations and evidence. One of the characteristics of inductive reasoning is that the conclusions we reach are *probably*, but not *definitely*, true. For example, concluding that John cares about the environment based on the observation that he is wearing a Sierra Club jacket makes sense. But it is also possible that he bought the jacket because he liked its style or color, or that he borrowed it from his brother. Thus, the conclusions we reach from inductive reasoning are suggested with various degrees of certainty but do not definitely follow from the observations. This is illustrated by the following two inductive arguments.

> *Observation*: All the crows I've seen in Pittsburgh are totally black. When I visited my brother in Washington, DC, the crows I saw there were black too.
>
> *Conclusion*: All crows are black.
>
> *Observation*: Ever since I can remember, the sun has risen every morning here in Tucson.
>
> *Conclusion*: The sun is going to rise in Tucson tomorrow.

Notice there is a certain logic to each argument, but the second argument is more convincing than the first. Remember that inductive arguments lead to what is *probably* true, not what is *definitely* true. Strong inductive arguments result in conclusions that are more likely to be true, and weak arguments result in conclusions that are not as likely to be true. A number of factors can contribute to the strength of an inductive argument. Among them are the following:

➤ *Representativeness of observations.* How well do the observations about a particular category represent all of the members of that category? Clearly, the crows example suffers from a lack of representativeness because it does not consider crows from other parts of the country or the world.

➤ *Number of observations.* The argument about the crows is made stronger by adding the Washington, DC, observations to the Pittsburgh observations. However, further research reveals that the hooded crow, found in Europe, is gray with black wings and tail, and the home crow, from Asia, is gray and black. So it turns out that the conclusion "All crows are black" is not true. In contrast, the conclusion about the sun rising in Tucson is extremely strong because it is supported by a very large number of observations.

➤ *Quality of the evidence.* Stronger evidence results in stronger conclusions. For example, although the conclusion "The sun will rise in Tucson" is extremely strong because of the number of observations, it becomes even stronger when we consider scientific descriptions of how the earth rotates on its axis and revolves around the sun. Thus, adding the observation "Scientific measurements of the rotation of the earth indicate that every time the earth rotates the sun will appear to rise" strengthens the conclusion even further.

Although our examples of inductive reasoning have been "academic" in nature, we often use inductive reasoning in everyday life, usually without even realizing it. For example, Sarah observed in a course she took with Professor X that he asked a lot of multiple-choice questions on his exams. Based on this specific observation, Sarah makes the general conclusion that all of his exams probably have multiple-choice questions, which can help her know what to expect when she takes another of Professor X's courses. In another example, Sam has bought merchandise from Internet company Y before and gotten good service, so he places more orders based on the prediction that he will continue to get good service. Anytime we make a prediction about what *will happen* based on our observations about what *has happened* in the past, we are using inductive reasoning.

It makes sense that we make predictions and choices based on past experiences, especially when those experiences are highly familiar and frequent, such as studying for an exam or buying merchandise over the Internet. We make so many assumptions about the world based on past experience that we are using inductive reasoning constantly, often without realizing it. For example, did you run a stress test on the chair you are sitting in to be sure it wouldn't collapse when you sat down? Probably not. You assumed, based on your past experience with chairs, that it would not collapse. This kind of inductive reasoning is so automatic that you are not aware that any kind of "reasoning" is happening at all. Think about how time-consuming it would be if you had to approach every experience as if you were having it for the first time. Inductive reasoning provides the mechanism for using past experience to guide present behavior.

The above chair example shows that when we use past experience to guide present behavior, we often use shortcuts to help us reach conclusions rapidly. After all, we don't have the time or energy to stop and gather every bit of information that we need to be 100 percent certain that every conclusion we reach is correct. These shortcuts take the form of **heuristics**—"rules of thumb" that are likely to provide the correct answer to a problem but are not foolproof. For example, in the Marc Gasol situation described at the beginning of this chapter, the recruiters relied on a heuristic to help them choose basketball players, but this didn't work out as planned.

We have been discussing in this section how inductive reasoning goes from *specific observations* to *general conclusions*; heuristics provide us with shortcuts to help us generalize from specific experiences to broader judgments and conclusions. People use a number of heuristics in reasoning that often lead to the correct conclusion but importantly, sometimes do not. We will now describe two of these heuristics: the *availability heuristic* and the *representativeness heuristic*.

The Availability Heuristic

The following demonstration introduces the availability heuristic.

DEMONSTRATION   Which Is More Prevalent?

Answer the following questions:

➤ Which are more prevalent in English, words that begin with the letter *r* or words in which *r* is the third letter?

➤ Some possible causes of death are listed below in pairs. Within each pair, which cause of death do you consider to be more likely for people in the United States? That is, if you randomly picked someone in the United States, would that person be more likely to die next year from cause A or cause B?

Cause A	Cause B
Homicide	Appendicitis
Auto–train collision	Drowning
Botulism	Asthma
Asthma	Tornado
Appendicitis	Pregnancy

Our behaviors and judgments are often guided by what we remember from the past. The **availability heuristic** states that events that more easily come to mind are judged as being more probable than events that are less easily recalled (Tversky & Kahneman, 1973). Consider, for example, the problems posed in the demonstration. When participants were asked to judge whether there are more words with *r* in the first position or the third, 70 percent responded that more words begin with *r*, even though in reality three times more words have *r* in the third position (Tversky & Kahneman, 1973; but see also Gigerenzer & Todd, 1999).

Table 13.1 shows the results of an experiment in which participants were asked to judge the relative prevalence of various causes of death (Lichtenstein et al., 1978). For

TABLE 13.1

Causes of Death

More Likely	Less Likely	Percent of Participants Picking Less Likely
Homicide (20)	Appendicitis	9
Drowning (5)	Auto-train collision	34
Asthma (920)	Botulism	41
Asthma (20)	Tornado	58
Appendicitis (2)	Pregnancy	83

Source: Adapted from S. Lichtenstein, P. Slovic, B. Fischoff, M. Layman, & B. Combs, Judged frequency of lethal events, *Journal of Experimental Psychology: Human Learning and Memory, 4*, 551–578 (1978).

each pair, the more likely cause of death is listed in the left column. The number in parentheses indicates the relative frequency of the more likely cause compared to the less likely cause. For example, 20 times more people die of homicide than die of appendicitis. The number on the right indicates the percentage of participants who picked the less likely alternative. For example, 9 percent of participants thought it was more likely that a person would die from appendicitis than from homicide. In this case, therefore, a large majority of people, 91 percent, correctly picked homicide as causing more deaths. However, for the other causes of death, a substantial proportion of participants misjudged their relative likelihood. In these cases, large numbers of errors were associated with causes that had been publicized by the media. For example, 58 percent thought that more deaths were caused by tornados than by asthma, when in reality, 20 times more people die from asthma than from tornados. Particularly striking is the finding that 41 percent of participants thought botulism caused more deaths than asthma, even though 920 times more people die of asthma.

The explanation for these misjudgments appears linked to availability. When you try to think of words that begin with *r* or that have *r* in the third position, it is much easier to think of words that begin with *r* (*run, rain, real*) than words that have *r* in their third position (*word, car, arranged*). When people die of botulism or in a tornado, it is front-page news, whereas deaths from asthma are not as publicized and therefore go virtually unnoticed by the general public (Lichtenstein et al., 1978).

These examples illustrate how the availability heuristic can mislead us into reaching the wrong conclusion when less frequently occurring events stand out in our memory. The availability heuristic doesn't always lead to errors, though; there are many situations in which the events that most easily come to mind actually *do* occur frequently. For example, you might know from past observations that when it is cloudy and there is a certain smell in the air, it is likely going to rain. You have made these observations many times, so, thanks to the availability heuristic, the conclusion "it's going to rain" easily comes to mind, and now you know to grab your umbrella. As another example, you may have noticed that your boss is more likely to grant your requests when he or she is in a good mood—another case in which the availability heuristic can help you arrive at reasonable conclusions.

Although observing correlations between events can be useful, sometimes people fall into the trap of creating illusory correlations. **Illusory correlations** occur when a relationship between two events appears to exist, but in reality, there is no relationship or the relationship is much weaker than it is assumed to be. Illusory correlations can occur when we expect two things to be related; for instance, you may make an illusory correlation between wearing your "lucky" shirt and your team winning the game, so now you always wear that shirt to games, even though no relationship actually exists. This example shows how we can fool ourselves into thinking two events are related even when they are not.

Illusory correlations can also result in **stereotypes**—an oversimplified generalization about a group or class of people that often focuses on the negative. A stereotype about the characteristics of a particular group may lead people to pay particular attention to behaviors associated with that stereotype, and this attention creates an illusory correlation that reinforces the stereotype. For example, a person who lives in a rural area might adopt the stereotype that people who live in big cities are rude. This conclusion could be based on a few interactions with big city people, or perhaps images from the media. But the problem with stereotypes is that they can lead to the conclusion that all people in a group have a particular quality, when that may be far from the case. Many big city people can, in fact, be quite friendly! This phenomenon is related to the availability heuristic because selective attention to the stereotypical behaviors makes these behaviors more "available" (Chapman & Chapman, 1969; Hamilton, 1981).

The Representativeness Heuristic

Whereas the availability heuristic involves making judgments based on how easily an event comes to mind, the *representativeness heuristic* involves making judgments based on how much an event resembles other events.

Making Judgments Based on Resemblance   When making judgments about an event or instance, it can be helpful to try to place that event in the same category as similar events that we know more about. That way, we can draw conclusions based on not just the event in question, but based on the properties of the larger group. This shortcut is known as the **representativeness heuristic**, which states that the likelihood that an instance is a member of a larger category depends on how well that instance resembles properties we typically associate with that category. To put this in more concrete terms, consider the following demonstration.

> **DEMONSTRATION**   Judging Occupations
>
> We randomly pick one male from the population of the United States. That male, Robert, wears glasses, speaks quietly, and reads a lot. Is it more likely that Robert is a librarian or a farmer?

When Amos Tversky and Daniel Kahneman (1974) presented this question in an experiment, more people guessed that Robert was a librarian. Apparently, the description of Robert as wearing glasses, speaking quietly, and reading a lot matched these people's image of a typical librarian (see illusory correlations, above, and the chapter opening illustration on page 392). Thus, they were influenced by the fact that the description of Robert matches their conception of what a librarian is like. However, they were ignoring another important source of information—the base rates of farmers and librarians in the population. The **base rate** is the relative proportion of different classes in the population. In 1972, when this experiment was carried out, there were many more male farmers than male librarians in the United States, so if Robert was randomly chosen from the population, it is much more likely that he was a farmer. (Note that this base rate difference still holds. In 2016, according to the U.S. Bureau of Labor Statistics, there were more than 20 times as many male farmers as male librarians.)

One reaction to the farmer–librarian problem might be that perhaps the participants were not aware of the base rates for farmers and librarians, so they didn't have the information they needed to make a correct judgment. The effect of knowing the base rate has been demonstrated by presenting participants with the following problem:

> In a group of 100 people, there are 70 lawyers and 30 engineers. What is the chance that if we pick one person from the group at random that the person will be an engineer?

Participants given this problem correctly guessed that there would be a 30 percent chance of picking an engineer. However, for some participants, the following description of the person who was picked was added to the above statement about base rate information:

> Jack is a 45-year-old man. He is married and has four children. He is generally conservative, careful, and ambitious. He shows no interest in political and social issues and spends most of his free time on his many hobbies, which include home carpentry, sailing, and mathematical puzzles.

Adding this description caused participants to greatly increase their estimate of the chances that the randomly picked person (Jack, in this case) was an engineer. Apparently, when only base rate information is available, people use that information to make their estimates. However, when any descriptive information is also available, people disregard the available base rate information, and this can potentially lead to errors in reasoning. Note, however, that the right kind of descriptive information can increase the accuracy of a judgment. For example, if the description of Jack also noted that his last job involved determining the structural characteristics of a bridge, then this would greatly increase the chances that he was, in fact, an engineer. Thus, just as it is important to pay attention to base rate information, the information provided by descriptions can also be useful if it is relevant to the instance that you are judging. When such information is available, then applying the representativeness heuristic can help us make correct judgments.

Making Judgments Without Considering the Conjunction Rule   The following demonstration illustrates another characteristic of the representativeness heuristic.

DEMONSTRATION   Description of a Person

Linda is 31 years old, single, outspoken, and very bright. She majored in philosophy. As a student, she was deeply concerned with issues of discrimination and social justice, and she also participated in antinuclear demonstrations. Which of the following alternatives is more probable?

➤ Linda is a bank teller.
➤ Linda is a bank teller and is active in the feminist movement.

The correct answer to this problem is that Statement 1 has a greater probability of being true, but when Tversky and Kahneman (1983) posed this problem to their participants, 85 percent picked Statement 2. It is easy to see why they did this. The participants were influenced by the representativeness heuristic, because the description of Linda fits people's idea of a typical feminist. However, in doing this, they violated the **conjunction rule**, which states that the probability of a conjunction of two events (A and B) cannot be higher than the probability of the single constituents (A alone or B alone). Because there are more bank tellers (A) than feminist bank tellers (A and B), stating that Linda is a bank teller *includes* the possibility that she is a feminist bank teller (**Figure 13.1**).

People tend to violate the conjunction rule even when it is clear that they understand it. The culprit is the representativeness heuristic. In the example just cited, the participants saw Linda's characteristics as more representative of "feminist bank teller" than "bank teller."

Incorrectly Assuming that Small Samples Are Representative   When using the representativeness heuristic to help draw conclusions, people can also

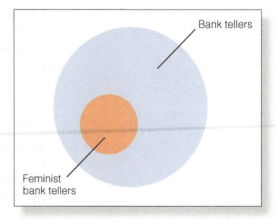

➤ Figure 13.1 Because feminist bank tellers are a subset of bank tellers, it is always more likely that someone is a bank teller than a feminist bank teller.

make errors by ignoring the importance of the size of the sample on which observations are based. The following demonstration illustrates the effect of sample size.

DEMONSTRATION   Male and Female Births

A certain town is served by two hospitals. In the larger hospital, about 45 babies are born each day, and in the smaller hospital, about 15 babies are born each day. As you know, about 50 percent of all babies are boys. However, the exact percentage varies from day to day. Sometimes it may be higher than 50 percent, sometimes lower. For a period of 1 year, each hospital recorded the days on which more than 60 percent of the babies born were boys. Which hospital do you think recorded more such days?

The larger hospital?
The smaller hospital?
About the same

When participants were asked this question in an experiment (Tversky & Kahneman, 1974), 22 percent picked the larger hospital, 22 percent picked the smaller hospital, and 56 percent stated that there would be no difference. The group that thought there would be no difference was presumably assuming that the birthrate for males and females in both hospitals would be representative of the overall birthrate for males and females. However, the correct answer is that there would be more days with over 60 percent male births in the small hospital. (And if the question had been about girls, there would also be more days with over 60 percent female births in the small hospital.)

We can understand why this is the case by considering a statistical rule called the **law of large numbers**, which states that the larger the number of individuals that are randomly drawn from a population, the more representative the resulting group will be of the entire population. Conversely, samples of small numbers of individuals will be less representative of the population. Thus, in the hospital problem, it is more likely that the percentage of boys or girls born on any given day will be closer to 50 percent in the large hospital and farther from 50 percent in the small hospital. To make this conclusion clear, imagine that there is a very small hospital that records only one birth each day. Over a period of a year there will be 365 births, with about 50 percent being boys and 50 percent being girls. However, on any given day, there will be either 100 percent boys or 100 percent girls—clearly percentages that are not representative of the overall population. People often assume that representativeness holds for small samples, and this can result in errors in reasoning. When there are a small number of observations, we should always be skeptical of the conclusions that are drawn. (See Gigerenzer & Hoffrage, 1995; Gigerenzer & Todd, 1999, for additional perspectives on how statistical thinking and heuristics operate in reasoning.)

Attitudes Can Affect Judgment

So far, we've seen that in inductive reasoning, heuristics can be used to help us quickly and easily make general judgments based on specific observations. Although these "shortcuts" are often useful and can lead to accurate conclusions, heuristics can also result in faulty conclusions by causing us to ignore some evidence. In addition to heuristics, the attitudes that we bring to the situation can also influence our judgments.

The Myside Bias   Charles Lord and coworkers (1979) demonstrated how people can evaluate evidence in a way that is biased toward their own opinions and attitudes, an effect called the **myside bias**. (McKenzie, 2004; Stanovich et al., 2013; Taber & Lodge, 2006). Lord used a questionnaire to identify one group of participants in favor of capital punishment and another group against it. Each participant was then presented with descriptions of research studies on capital punishment. Some of the studies provided evidence that capital punishment had a deterrent effect on murder; others provided evidence that capital punishment had no deterrent effect.

When the participants reacted to the studies, their responses reflected the attitudes they had at the beginning of the experiment. For example, an article presenting evidence that supported the deterrent effect of capital punishment was rated as "convincing" by proponents of capital punishment and "unconvincing" by those against capital punishment. Apparently, people's prior beliefs may have caused them to attend to information that corresponded with their beliefs and to disregard information that didn't.

The Confirmation Bias   The myside bias is a type of **confirmation bias**, which occurs when people look for information that conforms to their hypothesis and ignore information that refutes it. The confirmation bias is broader than the myside bias because it holds for any situation (not just for opinions or attitudes) in which information is favored that confirms a hypothesis. Peter C. Wason (1960) demonstrated how the confirmation bias can affect how people approach solving a problem by presenting participants with the following instructions:

> You will be given three numbers which conform to a simple rule that I have in mind.… Your aim is to discover this rule by writing down sets of three numbers together with your reasons for your choice of them. After you have written down each set, I shall tell you whether your numbers conform to the rule or not. When you feel highly confident that you have discovered the rule, you are to write it down and tell me what it is. (p. 131)

After Wason presented the first set of numbers, 2, 4, and 6, the participants began creating their own sets of three numbers, and for each set received feedback from Wason regarding whether their series of three numbers fit his rule. Note that Wason told participants only whether their numbers fit *his* rule. The participants did not find out whether *their* rationale for creating the three numbers was correct until they felt confident enough to actually announce their rule. The most common initial hypothesis was "increasing intervals of two." But because the actual rule was "three numbers in increasing order of magnitude," the rule "increasing intervals of two" is incorrect even though it creates sequences that satisfy Wason's rule.

The reason why many people settled on an incorrect rule is because they were only seeking evidence that *confirmed* their hypothesis, not evidence that *refuted* it—that is, they were guilty of confirmation bias. The secret to determining the correct rule is to overcome confirmation bias by trying to create sequences that *don't* satisfy the person's current hypothesis but *do* satisfy Wason's rule. Thus, determining that the sequence 2, 4, 5 is correct allows us to reject our "increasing intervals of two" hypothesis and formulate a new one. The few participants whose rule was correct on their first guess followed the strategy of testing a number of hypotheses themselves before giving their answer, by creating sequences that were designed to *disconfirm* their current hypothesis. In contrast, participants who didn't guess the rule correctly on their first try tended to keep creating sequences that *confirmed* their current hypothesis.

The confirmation bias acts like a pair of blinders—we see the world according to rules we think are correct and are never dissuaded from this view because we seek out only evidence that confirms our rule. As we saw in the Lord experiment, these blinders created by our attitudes can influence our judgment in ways that extend beyond how we go about solving a problem.

Evaluating False Evidence

"True opinions can prevail only if the facts to which they refer are known; if they are not known, false ideas are just as effective as true ones, if not a little more effective."

Walter Lippmann, *Liberty and the News* (1920)

We have described various ways in which you could arrive at incorrect conclusions if there are errors in your reasoning. However, even if your reasoning is error-free, you could *still* arrive at incorrect conclusions if your facts are wrong to begin with. At this point, you might be asking yourself, "wait, why would my facts be wrong? Aren't 'facts' inherently true?" There has been a lot of public discussion recently on what is a "fact" and what isn't. For example, how do you know that information that you read online is accurate? It's not always easy to tell. This is why it's important to critically evaluate any evidence and information that you encounter, especially if you're drawing conclusions from that evidence, as we often do.

A recent initiative by the Italian government is exploring ways to better educate youths on how to identify false information online (Horowitz, 2017). This initiative includes curriculum updates focused on media literacy, such as how to recognize spoofed web addresses, verify the source of information, reach out to experts in the field, and even how to show others how they identified a story as fake—skills that are particularly important in Italy where conspiracy theories are common. This program has been rolled out in 8,000 Italian high schools as of October 2017 with the hope of encouraging students to become more critical consumers of information and evaluators of evidence in the digital age.

The Italian initiative is important because recent research in the area of media literacy has shown that people aren't always diligent about evaluating evidence and instead sometimes rely on inaccurate information. For example, Sam Wineburg and coworkers (2016) assessed high school students' ability to critically evaluate information that they find online. The students were shown a real post from a photo-sharing website. The post consisted of a picture of malformed daisies with the claim that the flowers had "nuclear birth defects" from Japan's Fukushima Daiichi nuclear disaster, but provided no sources or anything else to back up the claim. When asked if the post provided strong evidence of the radioactive conditions near the nuclear plant, only 20 percent of students said "no" and were critical of the post. The remaining 80 percent of students were more inclined to believe the evidence, even though nothing was known about the photo's source or the credibility of the person who posted it. As it turns out, the photo *was* taken near Fukushima, but there was no evidence that the flowers' appearance was due to radiation, which makes the post's claim inaccurate.

Why might people be so quick to believe information that they read online or in the news, as in Wineburg's study? Maybe they just don't have access to (or don't seek out) the resources to know whether the information is inaccurate, so they take it at face value without evaluating it further. According to this explanation, if people *did* have the resources to know that the information was inaccurate, then they would no longer trust it or draw conclusions from it.

Surprisingly, though, this is not always the case. Research has shown that people do sometimes trust information that they were told was wrong. A study by Nyhan and Reifler (2010) assessed this using a real news situation from 2003: the misperception that Iraq was hiding weapons of mass destruction (WMDs)—a statement disseminated by the Bush administration in order to justify the subsequent U.S. invasion of Iraq. Participants were given a mock news story suggesting that there were WMDs in Iraq. One group of participants was then provided with a correction stating that, in fact, no such weapons had ever been found. All of the participants were then asked to what extent they agreed with the following statement: "Immediately before the U.S. invasion, Iraq had an active weapons of mass destruction program, the ability to produce these weapons, and large stockpiles of

WMDs, but Saddam Hussein was able to hide or destroy these weapons right before U.S. forces arrived."

The results showed that among participants who described themselves as very liberal, those who received the correction were more likely to disagree with the above statement than those who did not receive the correction, indicating that the correction effectively reduced WMD misperceptions. For moderate-liberal and centrist participants, the correction had no effect on WMD misperceptions; these participants still believed the WMD misperception just as much as the people who did not receive the correction. Interestingly, moderate-conservative and very conservative participants were actually *more* likely to believe the misperception that Iraq had WMDs after being told that that information was false.

The finding that an individual's support for a particular viewpoint could actually become stronger when faced with corrective facts opposing their viewpoint has been called the **backfire effect**. This might be why conversations between people with strong opposing views (as in politics) can sometimes seem counterproductive—because with each new fact presented by one side, the other often clings even closer to their own beliefs. Due to these tightly held beliefs and preconceptions, it can be difficult to objectively evaluate evidence, which can lead to errors in conclusions drawn from that evidence.

We have now seen how inductive reasoning can lead to incorrect conclusions due to errors in the reasoning process, the effect of people's attitudes, and problems in evaluating evidence. Table 13.2 summarizes these potential sources of errors in inductive reasoning.

TABLE 13.2

Potential Sources of Errors in Judgments

Page	Source	Description	Error occurs when
396	Availability heuristic	Events that are more easily remembered are judged as more probable.	Easily remembered event is less probable.
397	Illusory correlation	Strong correlation between two events appears to exist but doesn't.	There is no correlation, or it is weaker than it appears to be.
398	Representativeness heuristic	Probability that A is a member of class B is determined by how well properties of A resemble properties usually associated with B.	Presence of similar properties doesn't predict membership in class B.
398	Base rate	Relative proportions of different classes in the population.	Base rate information is not taken into account.
399	Conjunction rule	Probability of conjunction of two events (A and B) cannot be higher than the probability of single constituents.	Higher probability is assigned to the conjunction.
400	Law of large numbers	The larger the number of individuals drawn from a population, the more representative the group will be of the entire population.	It is assumed that a small number of individuals accurately represents the entire population.
401	Myside bias	Tendency for people to generate and evaluate evidence and test their hypotheses in a way that is biased toward their own opinions and attitudes; the myside bias is a type of confirmation bias.	People let their own opinions and attitudes influence how they evaluate evidence needed to make decisions.
401	Confirmation bias	Selectively looking for information that conforms to a hypothesis and overlooking information that argues against it.	There is a narrow focus only on confirming information.
403	Backfire effect	Person's support for a particular viewpoint becomes stronger when presented with facts opposing their viewpoint.	Person holds to their beliefs in the face of contradictory evidence.

Although you might get the impression from this discussion that most of our judgments are in error, this isn't actually the case. For instance, we have seen that the availability heuristic and representativeness heuristic can be helpful and quick shortcuts. Additionally, if we understand the base rate principle, conjunction rule, and the law of large numbers, we are more likely to arrive at accurate conclusions. Finally, by being aware of the effects of our own preconceptions and beliefs, such as the myside and confirmation biases, we can try to avoid the errors that can arise from them.

TEST YOURSELF 13.1

1. What is inductive reasoning? What factors contribute to the strength of an inductive argument?

2. How is inductive reasoning involved in everyday experience?

3. Describe how the following can cause errors in reasoning: availability heuristic; illusory correlations; representativeness heuristic.

4. How can failure to take into account base rates cause errors in reasoning? Be sure you understand how the judging occupations experiment relates to the representative heuristic and base rates.

5. What is the conjunction rule? Describe the experiment involving Linda the bank teller and indicate how it relates to both the representativeness heuristic and the conjunction rule.

6. Describe the male and female births experiment. How do the results of this experiment relate to the law of large numbers?

7. What is the myside bias? Describe Lord's experiment on attitudes about capital punishment.

8. What is the confirmation bias? Describe Wason's experiment on sequences of numbers.

9. Describe Wineburg's experiment on how people sometimes fail to critically evaluate evidence. What is the backfire effect, and how might it lead to incorrect conclusions?

▶ Deductive Reasoning: Syllogisms and Logic

So far, we have considered inductive reasoning, which is drawing conclusions based on observations. In **deductive reasoning**, we determine whether a conclusion *logically follows* from statements. To help us understand the difference between these two types of reasoning, we can consider the scope of the information being processed. Inductive reasoning starts with *specific* cases and generalizes to *broad* principles. For example, in the case of Marc Gasol described at the beginning of the chapter, the NBA recruiters relied on specific instances of non-muscular players being unsuccessful to generalize that all non-muscular players would be unsuccessful. In contrast, deductive reasoning starts with *broad* principles to make logical predictions about *specific* cases. For example, we could start with the broad principle that "all NBA players are humans," and then consider that "Marc Gasol is an NBA player," in order to logically conclude that "Marc Gasol is a human." Let's now consider how logic is used to arrive at conclusions in deductive reasoning.

Categorical Syllogisms

The father of deductive reasoning is Aristotle, who introduced the basic form of deductive reasoning called the **syllogism**. A syllogism consists of two broad statements, or **premises,** followed by a third statement called the conclusion. We will first consider

categorical syllogisms, in which the premises and conclusion are statements that begin with *All, No*, or *Some*. An example of a categorical syllogism is the following:

Syllogism 1

Premise 1: All birds are animals. (All A are B)

Premise 2: All animals eat food. (All B are C)

Conclusion: Therefore, all birds eat food. (All A are C)

Notice that the syllogism is stated both in terms of birds, animals, and food, and A, B, and C. We will see that the A, B, C format is a useful way to compare the forms of different syllogisms. Look at this syllogism and decide, before reading further, whether the conclusion follows from the two premises.

What was your answer? If it was "yes," you were correct, but what does it mean to say that the conclusion follows from the premises? The answer to this question involves considering the difference between *validity* and *truth* in syllogisms.

The word *valid* is often used in everyday conversation to mean that something is true or might be true. For example, saying "Susan has a valid point" could mean that what Susan is saying is true, or possibly that her point should be considered further. However, when used in conjunction with syllogisms, the term **validity** has a different meaning: A syllogism is valid when the *form* of the syllogism indicates that its conclusion follows *logically* from its two premises. Notice that nowhere in this meaning does it say anything about the conclusion being "true." We will return to this in a moment.

Let's now consider another syllogism that has exactly the same form as the first one.

Syllogism 2

All birds are animals. (All A are B)

All animals have four legs. (All B are C)

All birds have four legs. (All A are C)

From the A, B, C notation we can see that this syllogism has the same form as Syllogism 1. Because the syllogism's form is what determines its validity, and we saw that Syllogism 1 is valid, we can therefore conclude that the conclusion of Syllogism 2 follows from the premises, so it is also valid.

At this point you may feel that something is wrong. How can Syllogism 2 be valid when it is obvious that the conclusion is wrong, because birds don't have four legs? This brings us back to the fact that nowhere in our definition of validity does the word "truth" appear. Validity is about whether the conclusion *logically follows* from the premises based on the form or structure of the syllogism. If it does, *and* the premises are true, as in Syllogism 1, then the conclusion will be true as well. But if one or both of the premises are not true, the conclusion may not be true, even though the syllogism's reasoning is valid. Returning to Syllogism 2, we see that "All animals have four legs" is not true; that is, it is not consistent with what we know about the world. It is no coincidence, then, that the conclusion, "All birds have four legs," is not true either, even though the syllogism is valid.

The difference between validity and truth can make it difficult to judge whether reasoning is "logical" or not, because not only can valid syllogisms result in false conclusions, as in Syllogism 2, but syllogisms can also be invalid even though each of the premises and the conclusion could be true. In other words, a syllogism can have validity but not truth (as in Syllogism 2) or can have truth but not validity, as in Syllogism 3 below, in which each of the premises could be true and the conclusion could be true.

Syllogism 3

All of the students are tired. (All A are B)

Some tired people are irritable. (Some C are D)

Some of the students are irritable. (Some A are D)

You may have found that this syllogism is more difficult than Syllogisms 1 and 2 because two of the statements start with *Some*. This syllogism is not valid—the conclusion does not follow from the two premises. Students often have a hard time accepting this. After all, they probably know tired and irritable students (maybe including themselves, especially around exam time), and students are people, all of which suggests that it is possible that some students are irritable. One way to appreciate that the conclusion doesn't logically follow from the premises is to consider Syllogism 4, in which the wording is different but the form is the same.

Syllogism 4

All of the students live in Tucson. (All A are B)

Some people who live in Tucson are millionaires. (Some C are D)

Some of the students are millionaires. (Some A are D)

Using this new wording, while keeping the form the same, makes it easier to see that the people in the second premise do not have to include students. I happen to know, from living in Tucson myself, that most students do not live in the same part of town as the millionaires. Of course, there could be some millionaire students on campus, but we can't say for sure. It is, in fact, *possible* that no students are millionaires.

One reason that people think Syllogism 3 is valid can be traced to the **belief bias**—the tendency to think a syllogism is valid if its conclusion is believable. For Syllogism 3, the idea that some students are irritable is believable. But when we change the wording to create Syllogism 4, the new conclusion, "Some of the students are millionaires," isn't as believable. Thus, the belief bias is less likely to operate for Syllogism 4. The belief bias also works the other way, as in valid Syllogism 2, in which an unbelievable conclusion makes it more likely the syllogism will be considered invalid.

Figure 13.2 shows the results of an experiment in which participants read valid and invalid syllogisms that had either believable or unbelievable conclusions (Evans et al., 1983; Morley et al., 2004). The participants' task was to indicate whether the conclusion was valid. The left pair of bars illustrates the belief bias; when the syllogism was valid, participants accepted its conclusion 80 percent of the time if it was believable but only 56 percent of the time if it was unbelievable. But the most interesting result is on the right, which shows that invalid syllogisms that had believable conclusions were judged as valid 71 percent of the time. The belief bias therefore can cause faulty reasoning to be accepted as valid, especially if the conclusion of an invalid syllogism is believable.

If you've decided at this point that it is not easy to judge the validity of a syllogism, you're right. Unfortunately, there is no easy procedure to determine validity or lack of validity, especially for complex syllogisms. The main message to take away from our discussion is that "good reasoning" and "truth" are not the same thing, and this can have important implications for examples of reasoning that you might encounter. Consider, for example, the following statement:

> Listen to me. I know for a fact that all of the members of Congress from New York are against that new tax law. And I also know that some members of Congress who are against that tax law are taking money from special interest groups. What this means, as far as I can tell, is that some of the members of Congress from New York are taking money from special interest groups.

What is wrong with this argument? You can answer this yourself by putting the argument into syllogism form and then using the A, B, C, D notation. When you do this, you will see that the resulting syllogism has exactly the same form as Syllogism 3, and as with Syllogism 3, it doesn't logically follow: just because all of the members of Congress from New York are against the new tax, and some members of Congress who are against the new tax law are taking money from special interest groups, this doesn't mean that some

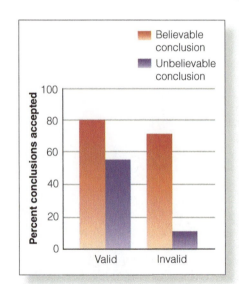

▶ Figure 13.2 The results of the Evans et al. (1983) experiment that demonstrated the effect of belief bias in judging the validity of syllogisms. The left pair of bars indicates that a valid syllogism with an unbelievable conclusion is less likely to be judged as valid than is a valid syllogism with a believable conclusion. The right pair of bars indicates that the tendency to judge an invalid syllogism as valid is high if the conclusion is believable.

(Source: Based on Evans et al., 1983)

members of Congress from New York are taking money from special interest groups. Thus, even though syllogisms may seem "academic," people often use syllogisms to "prove" their point, often without realizing that their reasoning is sometimes invalid. It is therefore important to realize that it is easy to fall prey to the belief bias, and that even conclusions that might sound true are not necessarily the result of good reasoning.

Now that we have discussed how to judge the conclusions reached by deductive reasoning, we can think back to the first part of the chapter and compare this to judgments reached by inductive reasoning. In inductive reasoning, we saw that conclusions reached are *probably true*, but not *definitely true*, because the conclusions drawn are based on generalizations from specific observations that are not always representative of the broader principle or population. For example, our initial conclusion about all crows being black, which was based on observations made in Pittsburgh and Washington, DC, turned out to be wrong when we expanded our observations to Europe and Asia. In deductive reasoning, the conclusions reached can be *definitely* true, but *only* if both premises are definitely true *and* if the form of the syllogism is valid. In this way, there can be more certainty in the conclusions drawn by deductive reasoning than inductive reasoning. However, as we've seen in this section, judging the truth and validity of syllogisms is not always easy. Luckily, as we'll discuss next, there are methods that we can use to help us.

Mental Models of Deductive Reasoning

To aid in judging the validity of syllogisms, Phillip Johnson-Laird (1999a, 1999b) has suggested an approach called the **mental model approach**. To illustrate the use of a mental model, Johnson-Laird (1995) posed a problem similar to this one (try it):

> On a pool table, there is a black ball directly above the cue ball. The green ball is on the right side of the cue ball, and there is a red ball between them. If I move so the red ball is between me and the black ball, the cue ball is to the _____ of my line of sight.

How did you go about solving this problem? Johnson-Laird points out that the problem can be solved by applying logical rules, but that most people solve it by imagining the way the balls are arranged on the pool table. The idea that people can imagine situations is the basis of Johnson-Laird's proposal that people use mental models to solve deductive reasoning problems.

A **mental model** is a specific situation represented in a person's mind that can be used to help determine the validity of syllogisms in deductive reasoning. The basic principle behind mental models is that people create a model, or an imagined representation of the situation, for a reasoning problem. They generate a tentative conclusion based on this model and then look for exceptions that might falsify the model. If they do find an exception, they modify the model. Eventually, if they can find no more exceptions and their current model matches the conclusion, they can conclude that the syllogism is valid. We can illustrate how this would work for a categorical syllogism by using the following example (from Johnson-Laird, 1999b):

> None of the artists are beekeepers.
>
> All of the beekeepers are chemists.
>
> Some of the chemists are not artists.

To help us create a model based on this syllogism, we will imagine that we are visiting a meeting of the Artists, Beekeepers, and Chemists Society (the ABC Society, for short). We know that everyone who is eligible to be a member must be an artist, a beekeeper, or a chemist, and that they must also abide by the following rules, which correspond to the first two premises of the syllogism above:

> Rule 1: No artists can be beekeepers.
>
> Rule 2: All of the beekeepers must be chemists.

(a) Artists (b) Beekeepers (c) Chemists

➤ **Figure 13.3** Types of hats worn by artists, beekeepers, and chemists attending the ABC convention.

Our task is made easier because we can tell what professions people have by what hats they are wearing. As shown in **Figure 13.3**, artists are wearing berets, beekeepers are wearing protective beekeepers' veils, and chemists are wearing molecule hats. According to the rules, no artists can be beekeepers, so people wearing berets can never wear beekeepers' veils. Also, the fact that all beekeepers must be chemists means that everyone wearing a beekeeper's veil must also be wearing a molecule hat.

In considering just the two rules and these imaginary hats, we can create a mental model of the premises and try to draw our own conclusions about what this means for the connection between chemists and artists. At the ABC meeting, let's say we meet Alice and see that she is an artist because of her beret, and we also notice she is following rule 1: no artists can be beekeepers (**Figure 13.4a**). Then we meet Beechem, who is wearing a combination beekeeper-molecule getup, in line with rule 2: all beekeepers must be chemists (**Figure 13.4b**). Remember that the conclusion, "some of the chemists are not artists" has to do with chemists and artists. Based on our observation of the artist Alice (who is not a chemist) and chemist Beechem (who is not an artist), we can formulate our first model: *No chemists are artists.* According to this model, no one wearing a beret (like Alice) should be wearing a molecule hat and no one wearing molecule hat (like Beechem) should also be wearing a beret.

But we aren't through, because once we have proposed our first model, we need to look for possible exceptions to the model. Specifically, to falsify this model, we would have to find chemists who are artists, without breaking the two rules. So, we mill around in the crowd until we meet artist Cyart, who is both an artist and chemist as indicated by his beret and molecule hat (**Figure 13.4c**). We note that he is not violating the two rules, so we now know that our first model, "No chemists are artists," cannot be true, and, thinking back to Beechem, the beekeeper-chemist, we revise our model to "Some of the chemists are not artists."

We then look for an exception that falsifies our new model, but find only Clara, who is only a chemist, which is also allowed by the rules (**Figure 13.4d**). This case does not refute our new model, and after more searching, we can't find anyone else in the room whose existence would refute this syllogism's conclusion, so we accept it. This example illustrates the basic principle behind the mental model theory: A conclusion is valid only if it cannot be refuted by any model of the premises.

The mental model theory is attractive because it can be used to assess a syllogism's validity without training in the rules of logic and because it makes predictions that can be tested. For example, the theory predicts that syllogisms that require more complex models will be more difficult to solve, and this prediction has been confirmed in experiments (Buciarelli & Johnson-Laird, 1999).

There are also other proposals about how people might assess validity in syllogisms (see Rips, 1995, 2002), but there isn't agreement among researchers regarding the correct approach. We have presented the mental model theory because it is supported by the results of a number of experiments and

(a) Alice (a) Beechem

(c) Cyart (d) Clara

➤ **Figure 13.4** Different types of people attending the ABC convention, all wearing hats that obey the rules for the syllogism that has the conclusion "Some of the chemists are not artists." This procedure, which is based on the mental models approach to reasoning, indicates that the syllogism is valid, because case (c) is a chemist who is an artist, but (b) and (d) are chemists who are not artists.

because it is one of the models that is easiest to apply and explain. However, a number of challenges face researchers who are trying to determine how people evaluate syllogisms. These problems include the fact that people use a variety of different strategies in reasoning, and that some people are much better at solving syllogisms than others (Buciarelli & Johnson-Laird, 1999). Thus, the question of how people go about determining validity in syllogisms remains to be answered.

But we aren't through with syllogisms yet. In addition to categorical syllogisms, which have premises and conclusions that begin with *All, Some,* or *No,* there is another type of syllogism, called the *conditional syllogism,* in which the first premise has the form "*If … then.*"

Conditional Syllogisms

Conditional syllogisms have two premises and a conclusion like categorical syllogisms, but the first premise has the form "If … then." This kind of deductive reasoning is common in everyday life. For example, let's say that you lent your friend Steve $20, but he has never paid you back. Knowing Steve, you might say to yourself that you knew this would happen. Stated in the form of a syllogism, your reasoning might look like this: *If* I lend Steve $20, *then* I won't get it back. I lent Steve $20. Therefore, I won't get my $20 back. As in categorical syllogisms, if both of the premises are true and the syllogism is valid, then the conclusion is definitely true. However, also like in categorical syllogisms, assessing a syllogism's validity can be tricky depending on its form and content, as we'll see in the following examples.

There are four major types of conditional syllogisms, which are listed in **Table 13.3** in abstract form (using *p* and *q*). Conditional syllogisms typically use the notations *p* and *q* instead of the *A* and *B* used in categorical syllogisms. To make these syllogisms easier to understand, we will replace the *p*'s and *q*'s in the four types of syllogisms in Table 13.3 with more real-life examples.

> *Conditional Syllogism 1*
> If I study, I'll get a good grade.
> I studied.
> Therefore, I'll get a good grade.

This form of syllogism—called *modus ponens,* which is Latin for (roughly translated) "the way that affirms by affirming"—is valid: The conclusion follows logically from the two premises. When participants are asked to indicate whether the *p* and *q* form of this syllogism is valid, about 97 percent of them correctly classify it as valid (see Table 13.3).

TABLE 13.3

Four Syllogisms That Begin with the Same First Premise

First premise of all syllogisms: If *p*, then *q*.

Syllogism	Second Premise	Conclusion	Is It Valid?	Judged Correctly?
Syllogism 1: Modus ponens	*p*	Therefore, *q*	Yes	97%
Syllogism 2: Modus tollens	Not *q*	Therefore, not *p*	Yes	60%
Syllogism 3	*q*	Therefore, *p*	No	40%
Syllogism 4	Not *p*	Therefore, not *q*	No	40%

Conditional Syllogism 2

If I study, I'll get a good grade.

I didn't get a good grade.

Therefore, I didn't study.

Valid or not valid? The answer is that this type of syllogism, called *modus tollens* (for "the way that denies by denying"), is valid. This form is more difficult to evaluate; only 60 percent get the *p* and *q* version of *modus tollens* correct.

Conditional Syllogism 3

If I study, I'll get a good grade.

I got a good grade.

Therefore, I studied.

The conclusion in this syllogism ("I studied") is not valid because even if you didn't study, it is still possible that you could have received a good grade. Perhaps the exam was easy, or maybe you already knew the material. Only 40 percent of participants correctly classify this syllogism as invalid. Assessing the validity of this type of syllogism can be particularly difficult depending on its content. To demonstrate this, consider the following syllogism, which has the same form but different content.

If I live in Tucson, then I live in Arizona

I live in Arizona.

Therefore, I live in Tucson.

It is much more obvious that the conclusion of this syllogism does not follow from the premises, because if you live in Arizona, there are lots of places other than Tucson that you could live. This shows that the way a problem or a syllogism is stated can influence how easy it is to evaluate it.

Finally, let's consider Syllogism 4.

Conditional Syllogism 4

If I study, then I'll get a good grade.

I didn't study.

Therefore, I didn't get a good grade.

The conclusion of this syllogism (I didn't get a good grade) is not valid. As with Syllogism 3, you can probably think of situations that would contradict the conclusion, in which someone got a good grade even though he or she didn't study. Once again, the fact that this syllogism is invalid becomes more obvious when restated in terms of Tucson and Arizona.

If I live in Tucson, then I live in Arizona.

I don't live in Tucson.

Therefore, I don't live in Arizona.

As with Syllogism 3, the fact that the conclusion (I don't live in Arizona) is not valid becomes more obvious when we change the content. Note from Table 13.3 that only 40 percent of participants correctly evaluate this syllogism as invalid when it is in the *p* and *q* format. In the next section, we will describe a reasoning problem that further supports the idea that the way a syllogism is stated can make it easier to evaluate it correctly.

Conditional Reasoning: The Wason Four-Card Problem

If reasoning from conditional syllogisms depended only on applying rules of formal logic, then it wouldn't matter whether the syllogism was stated in terms of abstract symbols, such as *p* and *q*, or in terms of real-world examples, such as studying or cities. However, research shows that people are often better at judging the validity of syllogisms when real-world examples are substituted for abstract symbols. As we look at this research, we will see that, as with our syllogism examples, some real-world examples are better than others. Our main goal, however, is not simply to show that stating a problem in real-world terms makes it easier, but to consider how researchers have used various ways of stating a problem to propose mechanisms that explain *why* the real-world problems are easier. To study this, many researchers have used a classic reasoning problem called the **Wason four-card problem**.

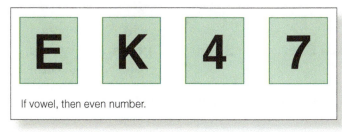

If vowel, then even number.

➤ **Figure 13.5** The Wason four-card problem (Wason, 1966). Follow the directions in the demonstration and try this problem. (Source: Based on Wason, 1966)

DEMONSTRATION   The Wason Four-Card Problem

Four cards are shown in **Figure 13.5**. Each card has a letter on one side and a number on the other side. Your task is to indicate which cards you would need to turn over to test the following rule:

If there is a vowel on one side of the card, then there is an even number on the other side.

When Wason (1966) posed this task (which we will call the abstract version of the task), 53 percent of his participants indicated that the E must be turned over. We can see that this is correct from **Figure 13.6a**, which shows the two possibilities that can result from turning over the E: either an odd number or an even number. Outcomes that conform to Wason's rule are outlined in green, those that don't conform are outlined in red, and those that aren't covered by the rule have no color. Thus, turning over the E and revealing an even number conforms to the rule, but revealing an odd number doesn't conform to the rule. Because finding an odd number on the other side of the E would indicate that the rule is not true, it is necessary to turn over the E to test the rule.

However, another card needs to be turned over to fully test the rule. In Wason's experiment, 46 percent of participants indicated that in addition to the E, the 4 would need to be turned over. But **Figure 13.6b** shows that this tells us nothing, because the rule doesn't mention consonants. Although there's nothing wrong with finding a vowel on the other side of the 4, this provides no information about whether the rule is true other than it works *in this case*. What we're looking for when testing any rule is an example that *doesn't* work. As soon as we find such an example, we can conclude that the rule is false. This is the **falsification principle**: *To test a rule, it is necessary to look for situations that would falsify the rule.*

Returning to Figure 13.6, we can see that whatever happens when turning over the K tells us nothing (it's another irrelevant consonant), but finding a vowel on the other side of the 7 falsifies the rule. Only 4 percent of Wason's participants came up with the correct answer—that the second card that needs to be turned over is the 7.

What Real-world Versions of the Wason Task Tell Us   The Wason task has generated a great deal of research, because it is an "If ... then" conditional

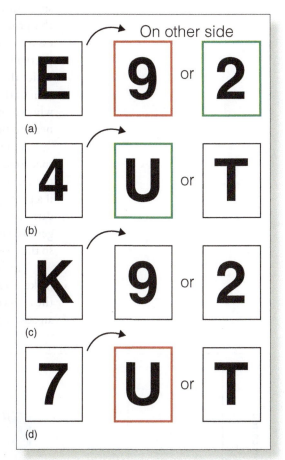

On other side

(a) E → 9 (red) or 2 (green)

(b) 4 → U (green) or T

(c) K → 9 or 2

(d) 7 → U (red) or T

➤ **Figure 13.6** Possible outcomes of turning over cards in the Wason four-card problem from Figure 13.5. Red borders indicate a situation in which turning over the card falsifies the statement "If there is a vowel on one side, then there is an even number on the other side." Green borders indicate a situation in which turning over the card confirms the statement. No color indicates that the outcome is irrelevant to the statement. To test the statement by applying the falsification principle, it is necessary to turn over the E and 7 cards.

> **Figure 13.7** The beer/drinking-age version of the four-card problem.
(Source: Based on Griggs & Cox, 1982)

reasoning task. One of the reasons researchers are interested in this problem is that when the problem is stated in real-world terms, performance improves. For example, Richard Griggs and James Cox (1982) stated the problem as follows:

> Four cards are shown in **Figure 13.7**. Each card has an age on one side and the name of a beverage on the other side. Imagine you are a police officer who is applying the rule "If a person is drinking beer, then he or she must be over 19 years old." (The participants in this experiment were from Florida, where the drinking age was 19 at the time.) Which of the cards in Figure 13.7 must be turned over to determine whether the rule is being followed?

This beer/drinking-age version of Wason's problem is identical to the abstract version except that concrete everyday terms (beer and soda; younger and older ages) are substituted for the letters and numbers. Griggs and Cox found that for this version of the problem, 73 percent of their participants provided the correct response: It is necessary to turn over the "Beer" and the "16 years old" cards. In contrast, none of their participants answered the abstract task correctly (**Figure 13.8**). Why is the concrete task easier than the abstract task? According to Griggs and Cox, the beer/drinking-age version of the task is easier because it involves regulations people are familiar with. Anyone who knows there is a minimum age for drinking knows that if someone looks 16, they need to be checked.

A similar explanation was proposed by Patricia Cheng and Keith Holyoak (1985), who suggested that people think in terms of schemas—their knowledge about rules that govern their thoughts and actions. One of these schemas is a **permission schema**, which states that if a person satisfies a specific condition (being of legal drinking age), then he or she gets to carry out an action (being served alcohol). The permission schema "If you are 19, then you get to drink beer" is something that most of the participants in this experiment had learned, so they were able to apply that schema to the card task.

This idea that people apply a real-life schema like the permission schema to the card task makes it easier to understand the difference between the abstract version of the card task and the real-world beer/drinking-age version. In the abstract task, the goal is to indicate whether an abstract statement about letters and numbers is true. But in the beer/drinking-age task, the goal is to be sure that a person has permission to drink alcohol. Apparently, activating the permission schema helps people focus attention on the card that would test that schema. Participants' attention is attracted to the "16 years old" card because they know that "Beer" on the other side would be violating the rule that a person must be 19 years old to drink.

The research presented in this section of the chapter has shown that it can be easier to understand syllogisms like the Wason task when they are stated in terms of real-world situations. One reason for this may be that people are sensitive to situations in which permissions or regulations are involved (Cheng & Holyoak, 1985), but perhaps it's some other reason. Indeed, other researchers have suggested alternative explanations for the results of the real-world Wason task. For instance, Leda Cosmides and John Tooby (1992) have suggested that real-world versions are easier to solve because people are on the lookout for cheaters. The reasoning behind this explanation is based on the idea that from an evolutionary point of view, being aware of other people's cheating is important for survival.

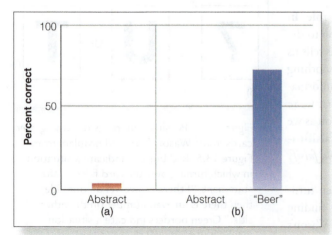

> **Figure 13.8** Performance on different versions of the four-card problem. (a) Abstract version (Wason, 1966), shown in Figure 13.6. (b) Abstract version and beer/drinking-age version (Griggs & Cox, 1982), shown in Figure 13.7.
(Sources: Based on Wason, 1996; Griggs & Cox, 1982)

Each of these explanations—the permissions explanation and cheating explanation— has evidence supporting and refuting it (Johnson-Laird, 1999b; Manktelow, 1999, 2012). Regardless of the explanation, we are left with the important finding that the context within which conditional reasoning occurs makes a big difference. Stating the four-card problem in terms of familiar situations can often generate better reasoning than abstract statements or statements that people cannot relate to. This relates back to our discussion of categorical syllogisms, where we saw that the way the syllogism is stated (i.e., in terms of real-world, familiar situations rather than p and q) can greatly influence our ability to evaluate it.

TEST YOURSELF 13.2

1. What is deductive reasoning? What does it mean to say that the conclusion to a syllogism is "valid"? How can a conclusion be valid but not true? True but not valid?

2. What is a categorical syllogism? What is the difference between validity and truth in categorical syllogisms?

3. What is the belief bias? Be sure you understand the results shown in Figure 13.2.

4. What is the mental model approach to determining the validity of reasoning?

5. What is a conditional syllogism? Which of the four types of syllogisms described in the chapter are valid, which are not valid, and how well can people judge the validity of each type? How does changing the wording, while keeping the form the same, influence the ability to determine whether a syllogism is valid?

6. What is the Wason four-card problem? Describe why the 7 card needs to be turned over in order to solve the problem.

7. What do the results of experiments that have used real-life versions of the Wason four-card problem indicate about how knowledge of regulations and permission schemas and awareness of cheating may be involved in solving this problem? What can we conclude from all of the experiments on the Wason problem?

▶ Decision Making: Choosing Among Alternatives

As we noted at the beginning of the chapter, we make decisions every day, from relatively unimportant ones (what clothes to wear, what movie to see) to those that can have a great impact on our lives (what college to attend, whom to marry, what job to choose). When we discussed the availability and representativeness heuristics, we used examples in which people were asked to make judgments about things like causes of death or people's occupations. As we discuss decision making, our emphasis will be on how people make judgments that involve choices between different *courses of action*. These choices may involve personal decisions, such as what school to attend or whether to fly or drive to a destination, or decisions made in conjunction with a profession, such as "Which advertising campaign should my company run?" or "Which basketball player should we draft?" We begin by considering one of the basic properties of decision making: Decisions involve both benefits and costs.

The Utility Approach to Decisions

Much of the early theorizing on decision making was influenced by **expected utility theory**, which assumes that people are basically rational. According to this theory, if people have all of the relevant information, they will make a decision that results in the maximum expected utility, where **utility** refers to outcomes that achieve a person's goals (Manktelow, 1999; Reber, 1995). The economists who studied decision making thought about utility in terms of monetary value; thus, the goal of good decision making was to make choices that resulted in the maximum monetary payoff.

One of the advantages of the utility approach is that it specifies procedures that make it possible to determine which choice would result in the highest monetary value. For example, if we know the odds of winning when playing a slot machine in a casino and also know the cost of playing and the size of the payoff, it is possible to determine that, in the long run, playing slot machines is a losing proposition. But just because it is possible to predict the optimum strategy doesn't mean that people will follow that strategy. People regularly behave in ways that ignore the optimum way of responding based on probabilities. Even though most people realize that in the long run the casino wins, the huge popularity of gambling indicates that many people have decided to patronize casinos anyway. Observations such as this, as well as the results of many experiments, have led psychologists to conclude that people do not follow the decision-making procedures proposed by expected utility theory.

Here are some additional examples of situations in which people's decisions do not maximize the probability of a good outcome. Veronica Denes-Raj and Seymour Epstein (1994) offered participants the opportunity to earn up to $7 by receiving $1 every time they drew a red jelly bean from a bowl containing red and white jelly beans. When given a choice between drawing from a small bowl containing 1 red and 9 white beans (chances of drawing red = 10 percent; **Figure 13.9a**) or from a larger bowl containing a smaller proportion of red beans (for example, 7 red beans and 93 white beans, chances of drawing red = 7 percent; **Figure 13.9b**), many participants chose the larger bowl with the less favorable probability. When asked to explain, they reported that even though they knew the probabilities were against them, they somehow felt as if they had a better chance if there were more red beans. Apparently seeing more red beans overpowered their knowledge that the probability was lower (they were told how many red and white beans there were on each trial).

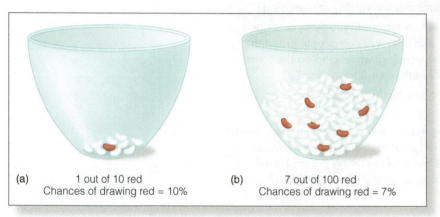

(a)   1 out of 10 red
Chances of drawing red = 10%

(b)   7 out of 100 red
Chances of drawing red = 7%

➤ **Figure 13.9** Denes-Raj and Epstein (1994) gave participants a choice between randomly picking one jelly bean from (a) a bowl with 1 red bean and 9 white beans or (b) a bowl with 7 red beans and 93 white beans (not all of the white beans are shown in this picture). Participants received money if they picked a red bean.
(Source: Based on Denes-Raj & Epstein, 1994)

While deciding which bowl to pick jelly beans from is not a particularly important decision, participants' preference for the lower probability choice shows that they are influenced by considerations other than their knowledge of probabilities. A decision of greater consequence is the real-life decision of whether to travel by car or plane. Although it is well known that the odds are far greater of being killed in a car accident than in a plane crash, a decrease in air travel and an increase in driving occurred following the 9/11 terrorist attacks. According to one calculation, the number of Americans who lost their lives on the road by avoiding the risk of flying was higher than the total number of passengers killed on the four hijacked flights (Gigerenzer, 2004).

The idea that people often ignore probabilities when making decisions is also supported by an analysis of how contestants respond in the TV game show *Deal or No Deal*, which premiered in the United States in 2005. In this show, a contestant is shown a list of 26 amounts of money, ranging from one cent to a million dollars. Each of these amounts is contained in one of 26 briefcases, which are displayed on stage. The game begins when the contestant picks one of these briefcases to be his or her own. The contestant is entitled to whatever amount of money is contained in that briefcase. The problem, however, is that the contestant doesn't know how much is in the briefcase, and the only way to find out is to open the remaining 25 briefcases, one by one, until the contestant's briefcase is the only one left (**Figure 13.10**).

The contestant indicates which of the remaining 25 briefcases to open, one by one. Each time the contestant decides on a briefcase number, the model next to that briefcase opens it and reveals how much money is inside. Each dollar amount that is revealed is taken off the list of 26 values. Thus, by looking at the list of values, the contestant can tell which values are out of play (the values in briefcases that have been opened) and which values are still in play. One of the values still in play will be in the contestant's briefcase, but the contestant doesn't know which one.

After opening 6 briefcases, the contestant is offered a deal by the bank based on the 20 remaining prizes. At this point, the contestant must choose between taking the guaranteed amount offered by the bank (Deal) or continuing the game (No Deal). The only information that can help the contestant decide is the amount the bank is offering and the list of values that are still in play, one of which is in the contestant's briefcase. If the contestant rejects the bank's initial offer, then the contestant opens more briefcases, and the bank will make a new offer. Each time the bank makes an offer, the contestant considers the bank's offer and the values that are still in play and decides whether to take the bank's deal or continue the game.

For example, consider the following situation, shown in Table 13.4, which occurred in an actual game for a contestant we will call contestant X. The amounts in the left column are the values that were inside the 21 briefcases that contestant X had opened. The amounts in the right column are the values inside the 5 briefcases that had not yet been opened. Four of these briefcases were on stage, and the remaining 1 belonged to contestant X. Based on these amounts, the bank made an offer of $80,000. In other words, contestant X had a choice between definitely receiving $80,000 or taking a chance at getting a higher amount listed in the right column. The rational choice would seem to be to take the $80,000, because there was only a 1 in 5 chance of winning $300,000 and all of the other amounts were less than $80,000. Unfortunately, contestant X didn't take the deal, and the next briefcase opened contained $300,000, taking it out of play. Contestant X then accepted the bank's new offer of $21,000, ending the game.

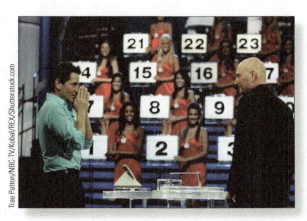

➤ **Figure 13.10** A decision point early in a game on the television show Deal or No Deal. The host, Howie Mandel, on the right, has just asked the contestant whether he wants to accept an offer made by the bank (Deal) or continue the game (No Deal). In the background, models stand next to numbered briefcases that have not yet been opened. Each of these briefcases contains an unknown amount of money. The contestant's briefcase, not shown here, also contains an unknown amount of money.

TABLE 13.4

Deal or No Deal Payoffs

21 Briefcases Opened (No Longer in Play)		5 Briefcases Remaining (Still in Play)
$0.01	$5,000	$100
$1	$10,000	
$5	$25,000	$400
$10	$75,000	
$25	$100,000	$1,000
$50	$200,000	
$75	$400,000	$50,000
$200	$500,000	
$300	$750,000	$300,000
$500	$1,000,000	
$750		

Thierry Post and coworkers (2008) analyzed contestants' responses in hundreds of games and concluded that the contestants' choices are determined not just by the amounts of money left in the briefcases but by what has happened leading up to their decision. Post found that if things are going well for the contestant (they have opened a number of small money briefcases) and the bank begins offering more and more, the contestant is likely to be cautious and accept a deal early. In contrast, when contestants are doing poorly (having opened a number of large denomination briefcases, taking those amounts out of play) and the bank's offers go down, they are likely to take more risks and keep playing. Post suggests that one reason for this behavior of contestants who are doing poorly is that they want to avoid the negative feeling of being a loser. They therefore take more risks in the hope of "beating the odds" and coming out ahead in the end. This is probably what happened to contestant X, with unfortunate results. What seems to be happening here is that contestants' decisions are swayed by their emotions. We will now describe a number of examples of how decision making is influenced by emotions and also by other factors not considered by utility theory.

How Emotions Affect Decisions

Personal emotional qualities have been linked to decision making. For instance, anxious people tend to avoid making decisions that could potentially lead to large negative consequences, a response called *risk avoidance* that we will return to shortly (Maner & Schmidt, 2006; Paulus & Yu, 2012). Another example is the quality of optimism, which is often considered a positive personal quality. However, optimistic people are more likely to ignore negative information and focus on positive information, causing them to base their decisions on incomplete information. Too much optimism can therefore lead to poor decision making (Izuma & Adolphs, 2011; Sharot et al., 2011). We will now consider research that has considered a number of other ways that emotions can affect decisions.

People Inaccurately Predict Their Emotions One of the most powerful effects of emotion on decision making involves **expected emotions**, emotions that people *predict* they will feel for a particular outcome. For example, a *Deal or No Deal* contestant might think about a choice in terms of how good she will feel about accepting the bank's offer of $125,000 (even though she could potentially win $500,000), how great she will feel if she wins the $500,000, but also how bad she will feel if she doesn't accept the bank's offer and finds out there is only $10 in her briefcase.

Expected emotions are one of the determinants of **risk aversion**—the tendency to avoid taking risks. One of the things that increases the chance of risk aversion is the tendency to predict that a particular loss will have a greater impact than a gain of the same size (Tversky & Kahneman, 1991). For example, if people predict that it would be very disturbing to lose $100 but only slightly pleasant to win $100, then this would cause them to decline a bet for which the odds are 50–50, such as flipping a coin (win $100 for heads; lose $100 for tails). In fact, because of this effect, some people are reluctant to take a bet in which there is a 50 percent chance of winning $200 and a 50 percent chance of losing $100, even though in accordance with utility theory, this would be a good bet (Kermer et al., 2006).

Deborah Kermer and coworkers (2006) studied this effect by doing an experiment that compared people's expected emotions with their actual emotions. They gave participants $5 and told them that based on a coin flip they would either win an additional $5 or lose $3. Participants rated their happiness before the experiment started and then predicted how their happiness would change if they won the coin toss (gain $5, so they have $10) or lost it (lose $3, so they have $2). The results of these ratings are indicated by the left pair of bars in **Figure 13.11**. Notice that before the experiment, the participants predicted that the negative effect of losing $3 would be greater than the positive effect of winning $5.

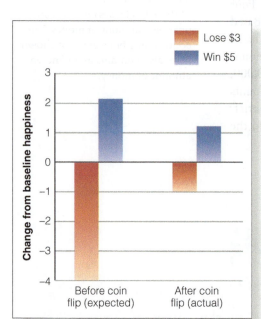

➤ **Figure 13.11** The results of Kermer et al.'s (2006) experiments showing that people greatly overestimate the expected negative effect of losing (left red bar), compared to the actual effect of losing (right red bar). The blue bars indicate that people only slightly overestimate the expected positive effect of winning (left blue bar), compared to the actual effect of winning (right blue bar).

(Source: Based on Kermer et al., 2006)

After the coin flip, in which some participants won and some lost, they carried out a filler task for 10 minutes and then rated their happiness. The bars on the right show that the actual effect of losing was substantially less than predicted, but the positive effect of winning was only a little less than predicted. So, after their gamble, the positive effect of winning and negative effect of losing turned out to be about equal.

Why do people overestimate what their negative feelings will be? One reason is that when making their prediction, they don't take into account the various coping mechanisms they may use to deal with adversity. For example, a person who doesn't get a job he wanted might rationalize the failure by saying "The salary wasn't what I really wanted" or "I'll find something better." In Kermer's experiment, when participants predicted how they would feel if they lost, they focused on losing $5, but after the outcome was determined, participants who actually lost focused on the fact that they still had $2 left.

The results of Kermer's experiment, plus others, show that the inability to correctly predict the emotional outcome of a decision can lead to inefficient decision making (Peters et al., 2006; Wilson & Gilbert, 2003). We will now see how emotions that aren't even related to making the decision can affect the decision.

Incidental Emotions Affect Decisions   **Incidental emotions** are emotions that are not caused by having to make a decision. Incidental emotions can be related to a person's general disposition (the person is naturally happy, for example), something that happened earlier in the day, or the general environment such as background music being played in a game show or the cheers of the game show audience.

How might the fact that you feel happy or sad, or are in an environment that causes positive or negative feelings, affect your decisions? There is evidence that decision making is affected by these incidental emotions, even though they are not directly related to the decision. For example, in a paper titled "Clouds Make Nerds Look Good," Uri Simonsohn (2007) reports an analysis of university admissions decisions in which he found that applicants' academic attributes were more heavily weighted on cloudy days than on sunny days (nonacademic attributes won out on sunny days). In another study, he found that prospective students visiting an academically highly rated university were more likely to enroll if they had visited the campus on a cloudy day (Simonsohn, 2009).

Decisions Can Depend on the Context Within Which They Are Made

Evidence that decisions can be influenced by context comes from experiments that show that adding alternatives to be considered as possible choices can influence decisions. For example, in a study that asked physicians whether they would prescribe arthritis medication to a hypothetical 67-year-old patient, 72 percent opted to prescribe medication when their choice was to prescribe a specific medication or not to prescribe anything. However, when a second possible medication was added, so the choice became whether to prescribe medication 1, medication 2, or nothing, only 53 percent opted to prescribe medication. Apparently, being faced with a more difficult decision can lead to making no decision at all (Redelmeier & Shafir, 1995).

Another example of how context can affect medical decision making is provided by an experiment in which physicians were presented with a hypothetical test case involving a possible candidate for cesarean section (Shen et al., 2010). The decision whether to opt for cesarean section was made under three different contexts: (1) Control: The test case was presented first. (2) Serious previous cases: The test case was preceded by four other cases in which there were serious complications that would usually call for a cesarean section. (3) Not serious previous cases: The test case was preceded by four other cases that were fairly routine and usually wouldn't call for a cesarean section. The results, in

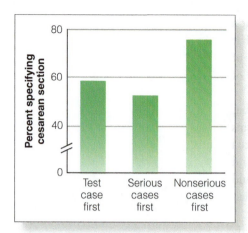

► **Figure 13.12** The effect of context on decision making. The likelihood that physicians would recommend a cesarean section was the same if the test case was presented first (control condition) or if it was preceded by four serious cases that required a cesarean section. However, the likelihood that physicians would recommend a cesarean section was higher if the same test case was preceded by four nonserious cases that didn't require a cesarean section.

(Source: Based on Shen et al., 2010)

Figure 13.12, show that slightly more than half of the physicians in the control and serious conditions recommended a cesarean delivery. However, 75 percent recommended a cesarean when the test case was preceded by the nonserious cases. Apparently, the test case was perceived to be more serious when preceded by uncomplicated cases that didn't require special actions. What this means, if these results were to translate into an actual medical situation, is that a patient's chances of undergoing a cesarean section can be influenced by the immediately prior experiences of the physician.

If the finding that medical decisions may depend on the doctor's immediately prior experiences is a little unsettling, consider the plight of prisoners applying to Israeli parole boards. Shai Danziger and coworkers (2011) studied more than 1,000 judicial rulings on parole requests and found that the probability of a favorable response (parole granted) was 65 percent when judges heard a case just after taking a meal break, but dropped to near zero when heard just before taking a break. This finding that extraneous variables (whether the judge is hungry or tired) can affect judicial decisions lends credibility to a saying coined by Judge Jerome Frank (1930) that "Justice is what the judge had for breakfast."

Although you might not be making major medical or judicial decisions, these examples do show various ways in which context can affect decisions. For a more relatable everyday example, consider the situation of deciding which camera to purchase in a store. Perhaps there are two models on display: a $170 model and a $240 model, each with its own set of features. Which do you choose? In fact, your purchasing decision might be affected by the context of the display. Simonson and Tversky (1992) showed that decisions were split about equally between the $170 and $240 model if those were the only options, but if a third, even more expensive option for $470 was also on display, participants were much more likely to choose the $240 option than the $170 option. This shows that even for everyday decisions like what to purchase, context can play a role—perhaps something to keep in mind the next time you're choosing between products at the store.

Decisions Can Depend on How Choices Are Presented

People's judgments are affected by the way choices are stated. For example, take a decision about whether to become a potential organ donor. Although a poll has found that 85 percent of Americans approve of organ donation, only 28 percent have actually granted permission by signing a donor card. This signing of the card is called an **opt-in procedure** because it requires the person to take an active step (Johnson & Goldstein, 2003).

The low American consent rate for organ donation also occurs in other countries, such as Denmark (4 percent), the United Kingdom (27 percent), and Germany (12 percent). One thing that these countries have in common is that they all use an opt-in procedure. However, in France and Belgium, the consent rate is more than 99 percent. These countries use an **opt-out procedure**, in which everyone is a potential organ donor unless he or she requests not to be.

Related to people's tendency to do nothing when faced with the need to opt in is the **status quo bias**—the tendency to do nothing when faced with making a decision. For example, in some states, drivers have the choice of getting an expensive car insurance policy that protects the driver's right to sue and a cheaper plan that restricts the right to sue. For Pennsylvania drivers, the expensive plan is offered by default, so drivers have to choose the cheaper plan if they want it. However, in New Jersey, the cheaper plan is offered by default, so they have to choose the more expensive plan if they want it. In both cases, most drivers stick with the default option (Johnson et al., 1993). This tendency to stay with the status quo also occurs when people decide to stay with their present electrical service provider, retirement plan, or health plan, even when they are given choices that, in some cases, might be better (Suri et al., 2013).

The examples involving organ donations and car insurance policies have to do with whether a person chooses to make a decision to change. The way a choice is presented is also important when a person is forced to pick one alternative or another. Paul Slovic and coworkers (2000) showed forensic psychologists and psychiatrists a case history of a mental patient, Mr. Jones, and asked them to judge the likelihood that the patient would commit an act of violence within 6 months of being discharged. The key variable in this experiment was the nature of a statement that presented information about previous cases. When they were told that "20 out of every 100 patients similar to Mr. Jones are estimated to commit an act of violence," 41 percent refused to discharge him. However, when told that "patients similar to Mr. Jones are estimated to have a 20 percent chance of committing an act of violence," only 21 percent refused to discharge him. Why did this difference occur? One possibility is that the first statement conjures up images of 20 people being beaten up, whereas the second is a more abstract probability statement that could be interpreted to mean that there is only a small chance that patients like Mr. Jones will be violent.

Here's another example of choosing between two alternatives, for you to try.

DEMONSTRATION   What Would You Do?

Imagine that the United States is preparing for the outbreak of an unusual disease that is expected to kill 600 people. Two alternative programs to combat the disease have been proposed. Assume that the exact scientific estimates of the consequences of the programs are as follows:

If Program A is adopted, 200 people will be saved.

If Program B is adopted, there is a one-third probability that 600 people will be saved, and a two-thirds probability that no people will be saved.

Which of the two programs would you favor?

Now consider the following additional proposals for combating the same disease:

If Program C is adopted, 400 people will die.

If Program D is adopted, there is a one-third probability that nobody will die, and a two-thirds probability that 600 people will die.

Which of these two programs would you pick?

When offered the first pair of proposals, 72 percent of the students in an experiment by Tversky and Kahneman (1981) chose Program A, and the rest picked Program B (**Figure 13.13**). The choice of Program A suggested that participants were using a **risk aversion strategy**. The idea of saving 200 lives with certainty is more attractive than the two-thirds probability that no one will be saved. However, when Tversky and Kahneman presented the descriptions of Programs C and D to another group of students, 22 percent picked Program C and 78 percent picked Program D. This represents a **risk-taking strategy**, because certain death of 400 people is less acceptable than taking a 2 in 3 risk that 600 people will die.

But if we look at the four programs closely, we can see that they are identical pairs (Figure 13.13). Programs A and C both result in 200 people living and 400 people dying. Yet 72 percent of the participants picked Program A and only 22 percent picked Program C. A similar situation occurs if we compare Programs B and D. Both lead to the same number of deaths, yet one was picked by 28 percent of the participants and the other by 78 percent. These results illustrate the **framing effect**—decisions are influenced by how the choices are stated, or *framed*. Tversky and Kahneman concluded that, in general, when a choice is

➤ **Figure 13.13** How framing affects decision making. These pie charts diagram the conditions set forth for Programs A, B, C, and D in the text. Note that the number of deaths and probabilities for Programs A and B are exactly the same as for Programs C and D. The percentages indicate the percentage of participants who picked each program when given choices between A and B or between C and D.

(Source: Based on Tversky & Kahneman, 1981)

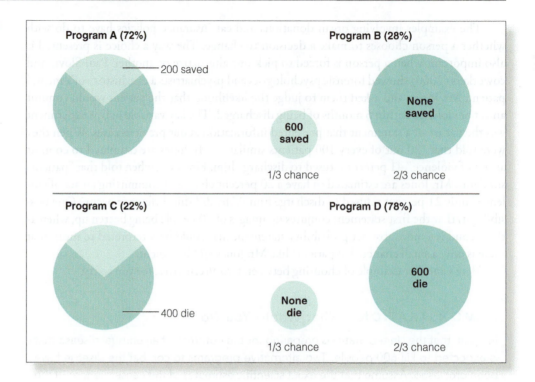

framed in terms of gains (as in the first problem, which is stated in terms of saving lives), people use a risk aversion strategy, and when a choice is framed in terms of losses (as in the second problem, which is stated in terms of losing lives), people use a risk-taking strategy.

One reason people's decisions are affected by framing is that the way a problem is stated can highlight some features of the situation (for example, that people will die) and deemphasize others (Kahneman, 2003). It should not be a surprise that the way a choice is stated can influence cognitive processes, since we already saw evidence of this in the discussion of syllogisms in the deductive reasoning section of this chapter, and also in Chapter 12, where the results of various experiments showed that the way a problem is stated can influence our ability to solve it (page 366).

Neuroeconomics: The Neural Basis of Decision Making

A new approach to studying decision making, called **neuroeconomics**, combines research from the fields of psychology, neuroscience, and economics to study how brain activation is related to decisions that involve potential gains or losses (Lee, 2006; Lee & Seo, 2016; Lowenstein et al., 2008; Sanfey et al., 2006). One outcome of this approach has been research that has identified areas of the brain that are activated as people make decisions while playing economic games. This research shows that decisions are often influenced by emotions, and that these emotions are associated with activity in specific areas of the brain.

To illustrate the neuroeconomics approach, we will describe an experiment by Alan Sanfey and coworkers (2003) in which people's brain activity was measured as they played the ultimatum game. The **ultimatum game** involves two players, one designated as the *proposer* and the other as the *responder*. The proposer is given a sum of money, say $10, and makes an offer to the responder as to how this money should be split between them. If the responder accepts the offer, then the money is split according to the proposal. If the responder rejects the offer, neither player receives anything. Either way, the game is over after the responder makes his or her decision.

According to utility theory, the responder should always accept the proposer's offer as long as it's greater than zero. This is the rational response, because if you accept the offer you get something, but if you refuse it you get nothing (remember that the game is only one trial long, so there is no second chance).

In Sanfey's experiment, participants played 20 separate games as responder: 10 with 10 different human partners and 10 with a computer partner. The offers made by both the human and computer partners were determined by the experimenters, with some being "fair" (evenly split, so the responder received $5) and some "unfair" (the responder received $1, $2, or $3). The results of responders' interactions with their human partners (orange bars in **Figure 13.14**) match the results of other research on the ultimatum game: All responders accept an offer of $5, most accept the $3 offer, and half or more reject the $1 or $2 offers.

Why do people reject low offers? When Sanfey and coworkers asked participants, many explained that they were angry because they felt the offers were unfair. Consistent with this explanation, when participants received exactly the same offers from their computer partner, more accepted "unfair" proposals (turquoise bars in Figure 13.14). Apparently, people are less likely to get angry with an unfair computer than with an unfair person.

In addition to testing people's behavior, Sanfey and coworkers used fMRI to measure brain activity in the responders as they were making their decisions. The results showed that the right anterior insula, an area located deep within the brain between the parietal and temporal lobes, was activated about three times more strongly when responders rejected an offer than when they accepted it (**Figure 13.15a**). Also, participants with higher activation to unfair offers rejected a higher proportion of the offers. The fact that the insula responded during rejection is not surprising when we consider that this area of the brain is connected with negative emotional states, including pain, distress, hunger, anger, and disgust.

What about the prefrontal cortex (PFC), which plays such a large role in complex cognitive behaviors? The PFC was also activated by the decision task, but this activation was the same for offers that were rejected and offers that were accepted (**Figure 13.15b**). Sanfey suggests that the function of the PFC may be to deal with the cognitive demands of the task, which involves weighing the choices to determine which decision is best. This decision-making process can be difficult, as the emotional instinct is to reject unfair offers, but the rational decision is to accept all offers so that at least some money can be gained. The PFC might help to regulate this process and implement the best decision based on one's goals. In the case of an unfair offer, this often means deciding to reject the offer based on the emotional goal of punishing unfairness.

To test this hypothesis, Knoch and colleagues (2006) investigated what would happen to the decision-making process if the PFC was not functioning. In this experiment, participants played the ultimatum game as the responder, but one group of participants had their PFC temporarily deactivated by transcranial magnetic stimulation (TMS; see page 292), while other participants were in the control "sham" condition, which looked and felt indistinguishable from TMS but did not disturb PFC functioning. Participants in both groups rated low offers as equally unfair; however, the participants with their PFC deactivated were significantly more likely to accept those unfair offers (see also van't Wout et al., 2005). This finding indicates that the PFC plays an important role in implementing the cognitively demanding decision to reject unfair offers, such that without a functioning PFC, unfair offers are more likely to be accepted. This study adds to Sanfey's initial fMRI study by providing causal evidence of the role of the PFC in decision making.

The PFC as well as the insula have been shown to be involved not only in *social* decisions—that is, decisions involving other people, as in the ultimatum game—but in individual decisions as well, such as whether to purchase a particular model of camera at the store. Research by Brian Knutson and coworkers (2007) has found that your brain activation when viewing a product can actually predict whether you will purchase it.

► **Figure 13.14** Behavioral results of Sanfey and coworkers' (2003) experiment, showing responders' acceptance rates in response to different offers made by human partners and computer partners.

(Source: Based on Sanfey et al., 2003)

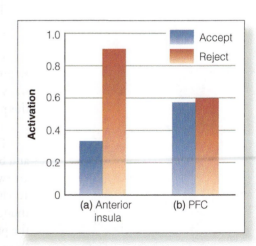

► **Figure 13.15** Response of the insula and prefrontal cortex (PFC) to "fair" and "unfair" offers.

(Source: Based on Sanfey et al., 2006)

Participants in Knutson's study viewed pictures of products and their prices while brain activity was measured using fMRI. The participants' task was to subsequently decide whether they would purchase the item.

Consistent with the other research described in this section, the PFC was shown to be involved in this decision-making task; specifically, increased PFC activation while viewing the product predicted subsequent decisions to purchase that product. Interestingly, the insula also predicted purchase decisions, but in a different way; the insula was particularly active when participants viewed excessively priced items, and this activation predicted decisions *not* to purchase. This makes sense, as you can probably recall a time when you saw an excessively overpriced item at the store that made you feel disgusted, annoyed, or even mildly distressed—all negative emotions that, as we saw in Sanfey's study (Figure 13.15a), involve the insula. Knutson's research furthers our understanding of the underlying neural correlates of those negative feelings and how they can influence everyday decisions.

Although all of this recent research has greatly bolstered our understanding of the neural basis of decision making, there is still a great deal that we don't know. Neuroeconomics is a relatively new area of study, and researchers are continuing to look for links between brain activation, potential payoffs or losses, and other aspects of decision making (Levy & Glimcher, 2013; Lowenstein et al., 2008; Sanfey et al., 2006). Additionally, neuroimaging technology continues to become more advanced, available, and powerful, which can help researchers reach conclusions about what might be happening in the brain.

▶ SOMETHING TO CONSIDER

The Dual Systems Approach to Thinking

One of the things that runs through our discussion of judgments, reasoning, and decisions is that people make mistakes. In making judgments, we are misled by heuristics like availability or representativeness. In reasoning by syllogism, we are good at judging the validity of simple syllogisms but are easily misled by the belief bias for more complex ones. In making decisions, we can be influenced by emotions, context, and how choices are presented, even if these things have nothing to do with the decision and don't optimize gains. We will see that these errors all have something in common, but first quickly solve the following simple puzzle in your head by using your intuition:

> A bat and a ball cost $1.10.
>
> The bat costs one dollar more than the ball.
>
> How much does the ball cost?

Did a number come to your mind? If so, it was probably 10 cents (Frederick, 2005; Kahneman, 2011). This answer, which immediately comes to mind, is wrong, but if that was your answer, you are not alone. More than half of thousands of participants who tried this problem answered 10 cents (Fredrick, 2005). Further thought indicates that the answer is 5 cents ($1.05 + $0.05 = $1.10), but why does 10 cents jump out for many people?

Daniel Kahneman (2011), in his best-selling book *Thinking Fast and Slow*, uses the bat and ball example to illustrate the **dual systems approach** to thinking: the idea that there are two mental systems—a fast, automatic, intuitive system, which Kahneman calls System 1, which may have seduced you into the 10 cent answer, and a slower, more deliberative, thoughtful system called System 2, which you would have used if you had thought about the problem more carefully. Other psychologists, including Keith Stanovich and Richard West (2000; also Stanovich, 1999, 2011), who originally proposed the idea of dual systems, favor the terms Type 1 processing and Type 2 processing. We will use System 1 and System 2 for simplicity, but will return to Type 1 and Type 2 processing at the end of our discussion.

This distinction between two systems or types of processing proposes that the two systems have the following properties (Evans & Stanovich, 2013):

System 1	System 2
Intuitive	Reflective
Fast	Slow
Nonconscious	Conscious
Automatic	Controlled

System 1 is linked to many of the errors we have described in this chapter. For example, the belief bias misleads us about the validity of a syllogism when we take into account the believability or lack of believability of the syllogism's conclusion. This influence of believability is the work of System 1. Evidence that System 1 is involved in the belief bias is that evaluating syllogisms under time pressure increases the belief bias effect (Evans & Curtis-Holmes, 2005). Participants also make more errors in the "Linda the bank teller" problem (page 399) when they are asked to respond quickly (De Neys, 2006).

System 1 might also be using the availability and representativeness heuristics to arrive at conclusions quickly and effortlessly, and might not consider the law of large numbers. In the Wason four-card task, the abstract version involving letters and numbers is out of System 1's league because it involves thoughtful reasoning, but real-world versions (such as the beer and drinking age example) can be easily solved by System 1 using intuition (Evans & Stanovich, 2013). System 1 might also be in play when we quickly evaluate evidence that we see in the news; we see a story that just "makes sense," as in the case of the malformed daisies produced by the nuclear disaster (Wineburg et al., 2016), and just accept it without thinking critically about its source.

But System 2 can intervene. Taking some time to step back and think logically about the situation gives System 2 time to operate. When participants are given instructions that encourage them to take time to focus on the logic behind a syllogism, for instance, System 2 is more likely to operate, and errors go down (Evans & Stanovich, 2013).

But before we condemn System 1 as being completely inept, we need to consider that in our day-to-day lives, System 1 is often running the show. Many of the things we do are automatically controlled by System 1. We perceive things in the environment, react to a loud noise, read emotions in someone's face, or negotiate a curve while driving. All of these things are taken care of by System 1. As we saw when we considered perception and attention, having some things taken care of automatically and without conscious effort is a good thing, because it means we don't have to be monitoring our every thought and move. Kahneman sees System 1 as providing information for System 2—most of which is accurate and is accepted—while System 2 is idling in the background monitoring the information.

However, when the going gets tough, System 2 can take over. Although System 1 may be taking care of routine driving, System 2 takes over when close attention is needed, as when entering a construction zone or passing a large truck at 70 miles an hour. System 2 is also mobilized when a question arises for which System 1 doesn't have an answer. As Kahneman puts it, System 1 automatically calculates $2 + 2 = ?$ (you couldn't keep yourself from saying 4, right?), but can't deal with 27×13. This is a problem for System 2.

This idea of two mental systems is an important one, because it explains many of the mistakes we make in terms of different mental systems or mechanisms. It is important to note, however, that there are many different varieties of dual process theories, which differ in details. Also, some researchers have proposed that two processes aren't necessary and have proposed a single-system approach (Evans & Stanovich, 2013; Gigerenzer, 2011; Keren & Schul, 2009; Kruglanski & Gigerenzer, 2011; Osman, 2004).

To end our discussion of the dual systems approach to thinking, let's return to the issue of terminology. Although we used Kahneman's System 1 and System 2 terminology, there is a reason that many researchers favor using Type 1 processing and Type 2 processing instead. When we talk about two "systems," it almost sounds as though they are two little people in your mind with different characteristics. In fact, in his popular book about dual processing, Kahneman says that you can read about System 1 and System 2 "as a psychodrama with two characters." Although this idea makes for more interesting reading, and maybe one of the reasons the book is so popular (in addition to Kahneman's talent for relating psychological theory to everyday life), it is important to realize that these two systems are, in fact, two different types of processing. They are not characters in your head but are the result of complex, interconnected, and distributed processing that is served by many areas of the brain and results in many different behavioral outcomes.

▶ POSTSCRIPT: DONDERS RETURNS

At the beginning of this book, we described an experiment carried out over 150 years ago by the Dutch physiologist Franciscus Donders. When Donders did his experiment in 1868 it was generally thought that the mind couldn't be studied, because the properties of the mind couldn't be measured. But Donders defied popular wisdom by determining (1) how long it took for a person to push a button when a single light was flashed and (2) how long it took to push one button if a light flashed on the left and another button if a light flashed on the right.

Based on these simple measurements, Donders concluded that it took one-tenth of a second to decide whether a light was presented on the right or on the left. We described this experiment to illustrate the basic principle that the workings of the mind must be inferred from behavioral observations, and then, in the chapters that followed, we described experiments far more complex than Donders' reaction time experiment, and techniques that Donders could never have dreamed of.

But now that you've made it to the end of the book, let's allow ourselves to imagine something magical—Donders is given a chance to visit a 21st-century cognitive psychology laboratory. When Donders walks into the lab, he is amazed by the technology, especially the computers and the brain scanner. But after noting these new developments, he turns to the lab director and says, "Amazing technology, but what I really want to know is have you figured out a way to measure the operation of the mind directly?" The lab director answers, "Well, no. We measure behavior and physiology and infer what is happening in the mind." "Oh," says Donders, "so the technology has changed, but besides that, nothing's different. Studying the mind still involves measuring indirectly, hypothesizing, and inferring." "That's right," says the lab director, "but let me tell you what we've found out since 1868. . . ."

TEST YOURSELF 13.3

1. What is the basic assumption of the expected utility approach to decision making? What are some examples of situations in which people do not behave to maximize the outcome, as the utility approach proposes?

2. Describe what the behavior of contestants on *Deal or No Deal* tells us about what determines their decisions.

3. What are expected emotions? Describe how expected emotions are related to risk aversion. Describe the Kermer experiment in which participants rated their expected happiness before gambling and their actual happiness after the results were known.

4. What is some evidence that incidental emotions affect decisions? Consider the relationship between the weather and university admissions.

5. How does context affect decisions? Describe the prescribing medication experiment, the cesarean delivery experiment, and the parole board study.

6. How does the way choices are presented affect the decisions people make? Describe the examples of organ donations, car insurance policies, and making judgments about the violence of mental patients.

7. Describe the "What Would You Do?" demonstration. Be sure you understand what determines risk aversion and risk taking, as well as the framing effect.

8. What is neuroeconomics? Describe Sanfey's ultimatum game and the effect of TMS. How are the PFC and insula involved in both social and individual decision making?

9. What is the dual systems approach to thinking? Be sure you understand the properties of System 1 and System 2 and how their operation relates to the various phenomena we have described in this chapter.

10. What would Donders learn if he were to visit a modern cognitive psychology laboratory?

CHAPTER SUMMARY

1. In inductive reasoning, conclusions follow not from logically constructed syllogisms but from evidence. Conclusions are *suggested* with varying degrees of certainty. The strength of an inductive argument depends on the representativeness, number, and quality of observations on which the argument is based.

2. Inductive reasoning plays a major role in everyday life because we often make predictions about what we think will happen based on our observations about what has happened in the past.

3. The availability heuristic states that events that are more easily remembered are judged as being more probable than events that are less easily remembered. This heuristic can sometimes lead to correct judgments, and sometimes not. Errors due to the availability heuristic have been demonstrated by having people estimate the relative prevalence of various causes of death.

4. Illusory correlations and stereotypes, which can lead to incorrect conclusions about relationships among things, are related to the availability heuristic, because they draw attention to specific relationships and therefore make them more "available."

5. The representativeness heuristic is based on the idea that people often make judgments based on how much one event resembles other events. Errors due to this heuristic have been demonstrated by asking participants to judge a person's occupation based on descriptive information. Errors occur when the representativeness heuristic leads people to ignore base rate information. In other situations, judgment errors occur when people ignore the conjunction rule and the law of large numbers.

6. The myside bias is the tendency for people to generate and evaluate evidence and test their hypotheses in a way that is biased toward their own opinions and attitudes.

7. The confirmation bias is the tendency to selectively look for information that conforms to a hypothesis and to overlook information that argues against it. Operation of this bias was demonstrated by Wason's number sequence task.

8. Reasoning is a cognitive process in which people start with information and come to conclusions that go beyond that information. Deductive reasoning involves syllogisms and can result in definite conclusions.

9. Categorical syllogisms have two premises and a conclusion that describe the relation between two categories by using statements that begin with *All, No,* or *Some.*

10. A syllogism is valid if its conclusion follows logically from its premises. The validity of a syllogism is determined by its form. This is different from *truth*, which is determined by the content of the statements in the syllogism and has to do with how statements correspond to known facts.

11. Conditional syllogisms have two premises and a conclusion like categorical syllogisms, but the first premise has the form "If … then." People do well at judging the validity of the *modus ponens* syllogism but less well at judging the validity of other forms of conditional syllogisms. Changing the wording of syllogisms while keeping the form the same can help people determine validity.

12. The Wason four-card problem has been used to study how people think when evaluating conditional syllogisms. People make errors in the abstract version because they do not apply the falsification principle.

13. Experiments using real-world versions of the Wason problem, such as the beer/drinking-age version, have demonstrated that the way in which a problem is stated can influence people's performance.

14. The utility approach to decision making is based on the idea that people are basically rational, so when they have all of the relevant information, they will make decisions that result in outcomes that are in their best interest. Evidence that people do not always act in accordance with this approach includes gambling behavior, choosing to drive in the face of evidence that it is more dangerous than flying, and the behavior of contestants on game shows like *Deal or No Deal*.

15. Emotions can affect decisions. Expected emotions are emotions a person predicts will happen in response to the outcome of a decision. There is evidence that people are not always accurate in predicting their emotions. This can lead to risk aversion. An experiment by Kermer demonstrates the difference between predicted emotions and the emotions actually experienced after making a decision.

16. There is a large amount of evidence that incidental emotions can affect decisions. For instance, gloomy weather can influence college admissions.

17. Decisions can depend on the context in which they are made. The number of available choices, the types of decision making that preceded this decision, and hunger or fatigue can all affect decisions.

18. Decisions can depend on how choices are presented, or *framed*. Evidence includes the differences in behavior with opt-in versus opt-out procedures, the results of Slovic's experiment involving decisions about a mental patient,

and people's response to the Tversky and Kahneman lethal disease problem. When a choice is framed in terms of gains, people tend to use a risk aversion strategy, but when the choice is framed in terms of losses, people tend to use a risk-taking strategy.

19. Neuroeconomics studies decision making by combining approaches from psychology, neuroscience, and economics. The results of a neuroeconomics experiment using the ultimatum game have shown that people's emotions can interfere with their ability to make rational decisions. Brain imaging indicates that the anterior insula is associated with the emotions that occur during the ultimatum game, whereas the PFC may be involved in the cognitive demands of the task. A transcranial magnetic stimulation experiment further demonstrates the causal role of the PFC in decision making.

20. The PFC and insula are also involved in purchasing decisions. Activation in the PFC predicts decisions to purchase a product, while activation in the insula predicts decisions not to purchase.

21. The dual systems approach to thinking proposes that there are two mental systems. System 1 (or Type 1 processing) is intuitive, fast, nonconscious, and automatic. System 2 (or Type 2 processing) is reflective, slow, conscious, and controlled. Many of the errors of reasoning discussed in this chapter can be linked to System 1, although this system also provides many valuable functions that do not involve error. System 2 takes over when slower, more thoughtful thinking is necessary.

22. If Donders returned today, he would be amazed at the technology but perhaps not surprised that cognitive psychologists still study the mind indirectly, just as he did.

THINK ABOUT IT

1. From watching the news or reading the paper, what can you conclude about how the availability heuristic can influence our conceptions of the nature of the lives of different groups of people (for example, movie stars; rich people; various racial, ethnic, or cultural groups) and how accurate these conceptions might actually be?

2. Astrology is popular with many people because they perceive a close connection between astrological predictions and events in their lives. Explain factors that might lead to this perception even if a close connection does not, in fact, exist.

3. Johanna has a reputation for being extremely good at justifying her behavior by a process that is often called "rationalization." For example, she justifies the fact that she eats anything she wants by saying, "Ten years ago this food was supposed to be bad for you, and now they are saying it may even have some beneficial effects, so what's the point of listening to the

so-called health experts?" or "That movie actor who was really into red meat lived to be 95." Analyze Johanna's arguments by stating them as inductive or deductive arguments; better yet, do the same for one of your own rationalizations.

4. Think about a decision you have made recently. It can be a minor one, such as deciding which restaurant to go to on Saturday evening, or a more important one, such as choosing an apartment or deciding which college to attend. Analyze this decision, taking into account the processes you went through to arrive at it and how you justified it in your mind as being a good decision.

5. Create deductive syllogisms and inductive arguments that apply to the decision you analyzed in the previous question.

6. Describe a situation in which you made a poor decision because your judgment was clouded by emotion or some other factor.

KEY TERMS

Availability heuristic, 396

Backfire effect, 403

Base rate, 398

Belief bias, 406

Categorical syllogism, 405

Conditional syllogism, 409

Confirmation bias, 401

Conjunction rule, 399

Decision, 394

Deductive reasoning, 404

Dual systems approach, 422

Expected emotion, 416

Expected utility theory, 413

Falsification principle, 411

Framing effect, 419

Heuristics, 396

Illusory correlation, 397

Incidental emotions, 417

Inductive reasoning, 394

Judgment, 394

Law of large numbers, 400

Mental model, 407

Mental model approach, 407

Myside bias, 401

Neuroeconomics, 420

Opt-in procedure, 418

Opt-out procedure, 418

Permission schema, 412

Premise, 404

Reasoning, 394

Representativeness heuristic, 398

Risk aversion, 416

Risk aversion strategy, 419

Risk-taking strategy, 419

Status quo bias, 418

Stereotype, 398

Syllogism, 404

Ultimatum game, 420

Utility, 413

Validity, 405

Wason four-card problem, 411

COGLAB EXPERIMENTS   Numbers in parentheses refer to the experiment number in CogLab.

Decision Making (*50*)

Monty Hall (*51*)

Risky Decisions (*52*)

Typical Reasoning (*53*)

Wason Selection (*54*)

Glossary

Number in parentheses is the chapter in which the term first appears.

Action pathway Neural pathway, extending from the occipital lobe to the parietal lobe, that is associated with neural processing that occurs when people take action. Corresponds to the *where* pathway. *(3)*

Action potential Propagated electrical potential responsible for transmitting neural information and for communication between neurons. Action potentials typically travel down a neuron's axon. *(2)*

Activity-silent working memory Short-term changes in neural network connectivity that has been hypothesized as a mechanism for holding information in working memory. *(5)*

Alternate uses task (AUT) A task used to assess creativity, in which the person's task is to think unusual uses for an object. Also called the unusual uses task. *(12)*

Amygdala A subcortical structure that is involved in processing emotional aspects of experience, including memory for emotional events. *(8)*

Analogical encoding A technique in which people compare two problems that illustrate a principle. This technique is designed to help people discover similar structural features of cases or problems. *(12)*

Analogical paradox People find it difficult to apply analogies in laboratory settings, but routinely use them in real-world settings. *(12)*

Analogical problem solving The use of analogies as an aid to solving problems. Typically, a solution to one problem, the source problem, is presented that is analogous to the solution to another problem, the target problem. *(12)*

Analogical transfer Transferring experience in solving one problem to the solution of another, similar problem. *(12)*

Analogy Making a comparison in order to show a similarity between two different things. *(12)*

Analytic introspection A procedure used by early psychologists in which trained participants described their experiences and thought processes in response to stimuli. *(1)*

Analytically based problem Problem that is solved by a process of systematic analysis, often using techniques based on past experience. *(12)*

Anaphoric inference An inference that connects an object or person in one sentence to an object or person in another sentence. See also **Causal inference; Instrument inference**. *(11)*

Anterior temporal lobe (ATL) Area in the temporal lobe. Damage to the ATL has been connected with semantic deficits in dementia patients and with the savant syndrome. *(9)*

Apparent movement An illusion of movement perception that occurs when stimuli in different locations are flashed one after another with the proper timing. *(3)*

Articulatory rehearsal process Rehearsal process involved in working memory that keeps items in the phonological store from decaying. *(5)*

Articulatory suppression Interference with operation of the phonological loop that occurs when a person repeats an irrelevant word such as "the" while carrying out a task that requires the phonological loop. *(5)*

Artificial intelligence The ability of a computer to perform tasks usually associated with human intelligence. *(1)*

Attention Focusing on specific features, objects, or locations or on certain thoughts or activities. *(4)*

Attentional capture A rapid shifting of attention, usually caused by a stimulus such as a loud noise, bright light, or sudden movement. *(4)*

Attentional warping Occurs when the map of categories on the brain changes to make more space for categories that are being searched for as a person attends to a scene. *(4)*

Attenuation model of attention Anne Treisman's model of selective attention that proposes that selection occurs in two stages. In the first stage, an attenuator analyzes the incoming message and lets through the attended message—and also the unattended message, but at a lower (attenuated) strength. *(4)*

Attenuator In Treisman's model of selective attention, the attenuator analyzes the incoming message in terms of physical characteristics, language, and meaning. Attended messages pass through the attenuator at full strength, and unattended messages pass through with reduced strength. *(4)*

Autobiographical memory Memory for specific events from a person's life, which can include both episodic and semantic components. *(6, 8)*

Automatic processing Processing that occurs automatically, without the person's intending to do it, and that also uses few cognitive resources. Automatic processing is associated with easy or well-practiced tasks. *(4)*

Availability heuristic Events that are more easily remembered are judged to be more probable than events that are less easily remembered. *(13)*

Axon Part of the neuron that transmits signals from the cell body to the synapse at the end of the axon. *(2)*

Backfire effect Occurs when individuals' support for a particular viewpoint becomes stronger when faced with corrective facts opposing their viewpoint. *(13)*

Back propagation A process by which learning can occur in a connectionist network, in which an error signal is transmitted backward through the network. This backward-transmitted error signal provides the information needed to adjust the weights in the network to achieve the correct output signal for a stimulus. *(9)*

Balanced dominance When a word has more than one meaning and all meanings are equally likely. *(11)*

Balint's syndrome A condition caused by brain damage in which a person has difficulty focusing attention on individual objects. *(4)*

Base rate The relative proportions of different classes in a population. Failure to consider base rates can often lead to errors of reasoning. *(13)*

Basic level In Rosch's categorization scheme, the level below the global (superordinate) level (e.g., "table" or "chair" for the superordinate category "furniture"). According to Rosch, the basic level is psychologically special because it is the level above which much information is lost and below which little is gained. See also **Global level; Specific level**. *(9)*

Bayesian inference The idea that our estimate of the probability of an outcome is determined by the prior probability (our initial belief) and the likelihood (the extent to which the available evidence is consistent with the outcome). *(3)*

Behaviorism The approach to psychology, founded by John B. Watson, which states that observable behavior provides the only valid data for psychology. A consequence of this idea is that consciousness and unobservable mental processes are not considered worthy of study by psychologists. *(1)*

Belief bias Tendency to think a syllogism is valid if its conclusion is believable or that it is invalid if the conclusion is not believable. *(13)*

Biased dominance When a word has more than one meaning, and one meaning is more likely. *(11)*

Binding Process by which features such as color, form, motion, and location are combined to create perception of a coherent object. *(4)*

Binding problem The problem of explaining how an object's individual features become bound together. *(4)*

Bottom-up processing Processing that starts with information received by the receptors. This type of processing is also called data-based processing. *(3)*

Brain ablation A procedure in which a specific area is removed from an animal's brain. It is usually done to determine the function of this area by assessing the effect on the animal's behavior. *(3)*

Brain imaging Technique such as functional magnetic resonance imaging (fMRI) that results in images of the brain that represent brain activity. In cognitive psychology, activity is measured in response to specific cognitive tasks. *(2)*

Broca's aphasia A condition associated with damage to Broca's area, in the frontal lobe, characterized by labored ungrammatical speech and difficulty in understanding some types of sentences. *(2, 11)*

Broca's area An area in the frontal lobe associated with the production of language. Damage to this area causes Broca's aphasia. *(2)*

Candle problem A problem, first described by Duncker, in which a person is given a number of objects and is given the task of mounting a candle on a wall so it can burn without dripping wax on the floor. This problem was used to study functional fixedness. *(12)*

Categorical syllogism A syllogism in which the premises and conclusion describe the relationship between two categories by using statements that begin with *All, No,* or *Some*. *(13)*

Categorization The process by which objects are placed in categories. *(9)*

Category Groups of objects that belong together because they belong to the same class of objects, such as "houses," "furniture," or "schools." *(9)*

Category-specific memory impairment A result of brain damage in which the patient has trouble recognizing objects in a specific category. *(9)*

Causal inference An inference that results in the conclusion that the events described in one clause or sentence were caused by events that occurred in a previous clause or sentence. See also **Anaphoric inference; Instrument inference**. *(11)*

Cell body Part of a cell that contains mechanisms that keep the cell alive. In some neurons, the cell body and the dendrites associated with it receive information from other neurons. *(2)*

Central executive The part of working memory that coordinates the activity of the phonological loop and the visuospatial sketch pad. The "traffic cop" of the working memory system. *(5)*

Cerebral cortex The 3-mm-thick outer layer of the brain that contains the mechanisms responsible for higher mental functions such as perception, language, thinking, and problem solving. *(2)*

Change blindness Difficulty in detecting changes in similar, but slightly different, scenes that are presented one after another. The changes are often easy to see once attention is directed to them but are usually undetected in the absence of appropriate attention. *(4)*

Change detection Detecting differences between pictures or displays that are presented one after another. *(4, 5)*

Choice reaction time Time to respond to one of two or more stimuli. For example, in the Donders experiment, subjects had to make one response to one stimulus and a different response to another stimulus. *(1)*

Chunk Used in connection with the idea of chunking in memory. A chunk is a collection of elements that are strongly associated with each other but weakly associated with elements in other chunks. *(5)*

Chunking Combining small units into larger ones, such as when individual words are combined into a meaningful sentence. Chunking can be used to increase the capacity of memory. *(5)*

Classical conditioning A procedure in which pairing a neutral stimulus with a stimulus that elicits a response causes the neutral stimulus to elicit that response. *(1, 6)*

Classifier In multivoxel pattern analysis, the classifier is a computer program designed to recognize patterns of voxel activity. *(7)*

Cocktail party effect The ability to focus on one stimulus while filtering out other stimuli, especially at a party where there are a lot of simultaneous conversations. *(4)*

Coding The form in which stimuli are represented in the mind. For example, information can be represented in visual, semantic, and phonological forms. *(6)*

Cognition The mental processes involved in perception, attention, memory, language, problem solving, reasoning, and decision making. *(1)*

Cognitive control A mechanism involved in dealing with conflicting stimuli. Related to executive function, inhibitory control, and willpower. *(4)*

Cognitive economy A feature of some semantic network models in which properties of a category that are shared by many members of a category are stored at a higher-level node in the network. For example, the property "can fly" would be stored at the node for "bird" rather than at the node for "canary." *(9)*

Cognitive hypothesis An explanation for the reminiscence bump, which states that memories are better for adolescence and early adulthood because encoding is better during periods of rapid change that are followed by stability. *(8)*

Cognitive interview A procedure used for interviewing crime scene witnesses that involves letting witnesses talk with a minimum of interruption. It also uses techniques that help witnesses recreate the situation present at the crime scene by having them place themselves back in the scene and recreate emotions they were feeling, where they were looking, and how the scene may have appeared when viewed from different perspectives. *(8)*

Cognitive map Mental conception of a spatial layout. *(1)*

Cognitive neuroscience Field concerned with studying the neural basis of cognition. *(2)*

Cognitive psychology The branch of psychology concerned with the scientific study of the mental processes involved in perception, attention, memory, language, problem solving, reasoning, and decision making. In short, cognitive psychology is concerned with the scientific study of the mind and mental processes. *(1)*

Cognitive revolution A shift in psychology, beginning in the 1950s, from the behaviorist approach to an approach in which the main thrust was to explain behavior in terms of the mind. One of the outcomes of the cognitive revolution was the introduction of the information-processing approach to studying the mind. *(1)*

Coherence The representation of a text or story in a reader's mind so that information in one part of the text or story is related to information in another part. *(11)*

Common ground Knowledge, beliefs, and assumptions shared between two speakers. *(11)*

Compound remote-association problem A problem in which three words are presented, and the task is to determine one word that when combined with each of these words forms a new word or a phrase. *(12)*

Concept A mental representation of a class or individual. Also, the meaning of objects, events, and abstract ideas. An example of a concept would be the way a person mentally represents "cat" or "house." *(9)*

Conceptual knowledge Knowledge that enables people to recognize objects and events and to make inferences about their properties. *(9)*

Conceptual peg hypothesis A hypothesis, associated with Paivio's dual coding theory, that states that concrete nouns create images that other words can hang on to, which enhances memory for these words. *(10)*

Conditional syllogism Syllogism with two premises and a conclusion, like a categorical syllogism, but whose first premise is an "If … then" statement. *(13)*

Confirmation bias The tendency to selectively look for information that conforms to our hypothesis and to overlook information that argues against it. *(13)*

Congenital amusia A condition, present at birth, in which people have problems with music perception, including tasks such as discriminating between simple melodies or recognizing common tunes. *(11)*

Conjunction rule The probability of the conjunction of two events (such as feminist and bank teller) cannot be higher than the probability of the single constituents (feminist alone or bank teller alone). *(13)*

Conjunction search Searching among distractors for a target that involves two or more features, such as "horizontal" and "green." *(4)*

Connection weight In connectionist models, a connection weight determines the degree to which signals sent from one unit either increase or decrease the activity of the next unit. *(9)*

Connectionism A network model of mental operation that proposes that concepts are represented in networks that are modeled after neural networks. This approach to describing the mental representation of concepts is also called the parallel distributed processing (PDP) approach. See also **Connectionist network**. *(9)*

Connectionist network The type of network proposed by the connectionist approach to the representation of concepts. Connectionist networks are based on neural networks but are not necessarily identical to them. One of the key properties of a connectionist network is that a specific category is represented by activity that is distributed over many units in the network. This contrasts with semantic networks, in which specific categories are represented at individual nodes. *(9)*

Consolidation The process that transforms new memories into a state in which they are more resistant to disruption. See also **Standard model of consolidation**. *(7)*

Constraint-based approach to parsing An approach to parsing that proposes that semantics, syntax, and other factors operate simultaneously to determine parsing. *(11)*

Constructive episodic simulation hypothesis The hypothesis proposed by Schacter and Addis that episodic memories are extracted and recombined to construct simulations of future events. *(6)*

Constructive nature of memory The idea that what people report as memories are constructed based on what actually happened plus additional factors, such as expectations, other knowledge, and other life experiences. *(8)*

Contingency strategy A negotiating strategy in which a person gets what he or she wants if something else happens. *(12)*

Continuity errors In film, changes that occur from one scene to another that do not match, such as when a character reaches for a croissant in one shot, which turns into a pancake in the next shot. *(4)*

Control processes In Atkinson and Shiffrin's modal model of memory, active processes that can be controlled by the person and that may differ from one task to another. Rehearsal is an example of a control process. *(5)*

Cortical equipotentiality The idea, popular in the early 1800s, that the brain operates as an indivisible whole, as opposed to operating based on specialized areas. *(2)*

Covert attention Occurs when attention is shifted without moving the eyes, commonly referred to as seeing something "out of the corner of one's eye." Contrasts with **Overt attention**. *(4)*

Creative cognition A technique developed by Finke to train people to think creatively. *(12)*

Crowding Animals tend to share many properties, such as eyes, legs, and the ability to move. This is relevant to the multiple-factor approach to the representation of concepts in the brain. *(9)*

Cryptomnesia Unconscious plagiarism of the work of others. This has been associated with errors in source monitoring. *(8)*

Cued recall A procedure for testing memory in which a participant is presented with cues, such as words or phrases, to aid recall of previously experienced stimuli. See also **Free recall**. *(7)*

Cultural life script Life events that commonly occur in a particular culture. *(8)*

Cultural life script hypothesis The idea that events in a person's life story become easier to recall when they fit the cultural life script for that person's culture. This has been cited to explain the reminiscence bump. *(8)*

Daydreaming See **Mind wandering**.

Decay Process by which information is lost from memory due to the passage of time. *(5)*

Decisions Making choices between alternatives. *(13)*

Deductive reasoning Reasoning that involves syllogisms in which a conclusion logically follows from premises. See also **Inductive reasoning**. *(13)*

Deep processing Processing that involves attention to meaning and relating an item to something else. Deep processing is usually associated with elaborative rehearsal. See also **Depth of processing; Shallow processing**. *(7)*

Default mode network (DMN) Network of structures that are active when a person is not involved in specific tasks. *(2)*

Definitional approach to categorization The idea that we can decide whether something is a member of a category by determining whether the object meets the definition of the category. See also **Family resemblance**. *(9)*

Degraded pictures task A task in which a line drawing is degraded by omitting parts of the drawing and obscuring it with a visual noise pattern. The person's task is to identify the object. *(10)*

Delayed partial report method Procedure used in Sperling's experiment on the properties of the visual icon, in which participants were instructed to report only some of the stimuli in a briefly presented display. A cue tone that was delayed for a fraction of a second after the display was extinguished indicated which part of the display to report. See also **Partial report method; Whole report method**. *(5)*

Delayed-response task A task in which information is provided, a delay is imposed, and then memory is tested. This task has been used to study short-term memory by testing monkeys' ability to hold information about the location of a food reward during a delay. *(5)*

Dendrites Structures that branch out from the cell body to receive electrical signals from other neurons. *(2)*

Depictive representation Corresponds to spatial representation. So-called because a spatial representation can be depicted by a picture. *(10)*

Depth of processing The idea that the processing that occurs as an item is being encoded into memory can be deep or shallow. Deep processing involves attention to meaning and is associated with elaborative rehearsal. Shallow processing involves repetition with little attention to meaning and is associated with maintenance rehearsal. See also **Levels of processing theory**. *(7)*

Detector   In Broadbent's model of attention, the detector processes the information from the attended message to determine higher-level characteristics of the message, such as its meaning. *(4)*

Dichotic listening   The procedure of presenting one message to the left ear and a different message to the right ear. *(4)*

Dictionary unit   A component of Treisman's attenuation model of attention. This processing unit contains stored words and thresholds for activating the words. The dictionary unit helps explain why we can sometimes hear a familiar word, such as our name, in an unattended message. See also **Attenuation model of attention**. *(4)*

Digit span   The number of digits a person can remember. Digit span is used as a measure of the capacity of short-term memory. *(5)*

Direct pathway model   Model of pain perception that proposes that pain signals are sent directly from receptors to the brain. *(3)*

Distraction   Occurs when one stimulus interferes with attention to or the processing of another stimulus. *(4)*

Distributed representation   Occurs when a specific cognition activates many areas of the brain. *(2)*

Divergent thinking   Thinking that is open-ended, involving a large number of potential solutions. *(12)*

Divided attention   The ability to pay attention to, or carry out, two or more different tasks simultaneously. *(4)*

Dorsal attention network   A network that controls attention based on top-down processing. *(4)*

Dorsal pathway   Pathway that extends from the visual cortex in the occipital lobe to the parietal lobe. This is also known as the *where pathway*. *(3)*

Double dissociation   A situation in which a single dissociation can be demonstrated in one person and the opposite type of single dissociation can be demonstrated in another person (i.e., Person 1: function A is present, function B is damaged; Person 2: function A is damaged, function B is present). *(2)*

Dual systems approach   The idea that there are two mental systems, one fast and the other slower, that have different capabilities and serve different functions. *(13)*

Early selection model   Model of attention that explains selective attention by early filtering out of the unattended message. In Broadbent's early selection model, the filtering step occurs before the message is analyzed to determine its meaning. *(4)*

Echoic memory   Brief sensory memory for auditory stimuli that lasts for a few seconds after a stimulus is extinguished. *(5)*

Effective connectivity   How easily activity can travel along a particular pathway between two structures. *(4)*

Elaborative rehearsal   Rehearsal that involves thinking about the meaning of an item to be remembered or making connections between that item and prior knowledge. Compare to **Maintenance rehearsal**. *(7)*

Electroencephalogram (EEG)   An electrical response recorded from the scalp using disc electrodes. *(12)*

Electrophysiology   Techniques used to measure electrical responses of the nervous system. *(1)*

Embodied approach   Proposal that our knowledge of concepts is based on reactivation of sensory and motor processes that occur when we interact with an object. *(9)*

Emoji   Symbols used in electronic communication and web pages that can indicate emotions, and are also used to represent other things, such as objects, animals, places, and weather. *(11)*

Encoding   The process of acquiring information and transferring it into memory. *(7)*

Encoding specificity   The principle that we learn information together with its context. This means that presence of the context can lead to enhanced memory for the information. *(7)*

Entrainment   Synchronization between partners in a conversation. This can include gestures speaking rate, body position, pronunciation, and grammatical structure. *(11)*

Epiphenomenon   A phenomenon that accompanies a mechanism but is not actually part of the mechanism. An example of an epiphenomenon is lights that flash on a mainframe computer as it operates. *(10)*

Episodic buffer   A component added to Baddeley's original working memory model that serves as a "backup" store that communicates with both long-term memory and the components of working memory. It holds information longer and has greater capacity than the phonological loop or visuospatial sketch pad. *(5)*

Error signal   During learning in a connectionist network, the difference between the output signal generated by a particular stimulus and the output that actually represents that stimulus. *(9)*

Event-related potential (ERP)   An electrical potential, recorded with disc electrodes on a person's scalp, that reflects the response of many thousands of neurons near the electrode that fire together. The ERP consists of a number of waves that occur at different delays after a stimulus is presented and that can be linked to different functions. For example, the N400 wave occurs in response to a sentence that contains a word that doesn't fit the meaning of the sentence. *(5)*

Executive action network   A complex network that is involved in controlling executive functions. *(4)*

Executive control network (ECN)   A brain network that is involved in directing attention as a person is carrying out tasks. *(12)*

Executive functions A number of processes that involve controlling attention and dealing with conflicting responses. *(4)*

Exemplar In categorization, members of a category that a person has experienced in the past. *(9)*

Exemplar approach to categorization The approach to categorization in which members of a category are judged against exemplars—examples of members of the category that the person has encountered in the past. *(9)*

Expected emotion Emotion that a person predicts he or she will feel for a particular outcome of a decision. *(13)*

Expected utility theory The idea that people are basically rational, so if they have all of the relevant information, they will make a decision that results in the most beneficial result. *(13)*

Experience-dependent plasticity A mechanism that causes an organism's neurons to develop so they respond best to the type of stimulation to which the organism has been exposed. *(3)*

Experience sampling A procedure that was developed to answer the question, "what percentage of the time during the day are people engaged in a specific behavior?" One way this has been achieved is by having people report what they are doing when they receive signals at random times during the day. *(4)*

Expert Person who, by devoting a large amount of time to learning about a field and practicing and applying that learning, has become acknowledged as being extremely skilled or knowledgeable in that field. *(12)*

Expert-induced amnesia Amnesia that occurs because well-learned procedural memories do not require attention. *(6)*

Explicit memory Memory that involves conscious recollections of events or facts that we have learned in the past. *(6)*

Extrastriate body area (EBA) An area in the temporal cortex that is activated by pictures of bodies and parts of bodies, but not by faces or other objects. *(2)*

Eyewitness testimony Testimony by eyewitnesses to a crime about what they saw during commission of the crime. *(8)*

Falsification principle The reasoning principle that to test a rule, it is necessary to look for situations that would falsify the rule. *(13)*

Family resemblance In considering the process of categorization, the idea that things in a particular category resemble each other in a number of ways. This approach can be contrasted with the definitional approach, which states that an object belongs to a category only when it meets a definite set of criteria. *(9)*

Feature detectors Neurons that respond to specific visual features, such as orientation, size, or the more complex features that make up environmental stimuli. *(2)*

Feature integration theory An approach to object perception, developed by Anne Treisman, that proposes a sequence of stages in which features are first analyzed and then combined to result in perception of an object. *(4)*

Feature search Searching among distractors for a target item that involves detecting one feature, such as "horizontal." *(4)*

Filter In Broadbent's model of attention, the filter identifies the message that is being attended to based on its physical characteristics—things like the speaker's tone of voice, pitch, speed of talking, and accent—and lets only this attended message pass through to the detector in the next stage. *(4)*

Filter model of attention Model of attention that proposes a filter that lets attended stimuli through and blocks some or all of the unattended stimuli. *(4)*

Fixation In perception and attention, a pausing of the eyes on places of interest while observing a scene. *(4)*

Fixation In problem solving, people's tendency to focus on a specific characteristic of the problem that keeps them from arriving at a solution. See also **Functional fixedness**. *(12)*

Flashbulb memory Memory for the circumstances that surround hearing about shocking, highly charged events. It has been claimed that such memories are particularly vivid and accurate. See **Narrative rehearsal hypothesis** for another viewpoint. *(8)*

Fluency The ease with which a statement can be remembered. *(8)*

Focused attention (FA) meditation A type of meditation in which the basic procedure is to focus on one thing, like the in and out of your breath, and when your mind wanders, to bring your attention back to your breath. *(12)*

Focused attention stage The second stage of Treisman's feature integration theory. According to the theory, attention causes the combination of features into perception of an object. *(4)*

Framing effect Decisions are influenced by how the choices are stated. *(13)*

Free recall A procedure for testing memory in which the participant is asked to remember stimuli that were previously presented. See also **Cued recall**. *(7)*

Frontal lobe The lobe in the front of the brain that serves higher functions such as language, thought, memory, and motor functioning. *(2)*

Functional connectivity The extent to which the neural activity in separate brain areas is correlated with each other. *(2)*

Functional fixedness An effect that occurs when the ideas a person has about an object's function inhibit the person's ability to use the object for a different function. See also **Fixation** (in problem solving). *(12)*

Functional magnetic resonance imaging (fMRI) A brain imaging technique that measures how blood flow changes in response to cognitive activity. *(2)*

Fusiform face area (FFA) An area in the temporal lobe that contains many neurons that respond selectively to faces. *(2)*

Garden path model of parsing A model of parsing that emphasizes syntactic principles as a major determinant of parsing. *(11)*

Garden path sentence A sentence in which the meaning that seems to be implied at the beginning of the sentence turns out to be incorrect, based on information that is presented later in the sentence. *(11)*

Generation effect Memory for material is better when a person generates the material him- or herself, rather than passively receiving it. *(7)*

Gestalt psychologists A group of psychologists who proposed principles governing perception, such as laws of organization, and a perceptual approach to problem solving involving restructuring. *(3)*

Given–new contract In a conversation, a speaker should construct sentences so that they contain both given information (information that the listener already knows) and new information (information that the listener is hearing for the first time). *(11)*

Global level The highest level in Rosch's categorization scheme (e.g., "furniture" or "vehicles"). See also **Basic level; Specific level**. *(9)*

Goal state In problem solving, the condition that occurs when a problem has been solved. *(12)*

Good continuation, principle of Law of perceptual organization stating that points that, when connected, result in straight or smoothly curving lines are seen as belonging together. In addition, lines tend to be seen as following the smoothest path. *(3)*

Good figure, principle of See **Pragnanz, law of**. *(3)*

Graceful degradation Disruption of performance due to damage to a system that occurs only gradually as parts of the system are damaged. This occurs in some cases of brain damage and also when parts of a connectionist network are damaged. *(9)*

Graded amnesia When amnesia is most severe for events that occurred just prior to an injury and becomes less severe for earlier, more remote events. *(7)*

Group brainstorming When people in a problem-solving group are encouraged to express whatever ideas come to mind, without censorship. *(12)*

Heuristic A "rule of thumb" that provides a best-guess solution to a problem. *(11, 13)*

Hidden units Units in a connectionist network that are located between input units and output units. See also **Connectionist network; Input units; Output units**. *(9)*

Hierarchical model As applied to knowledge representation, a model that consists of levels arranged so that more specific concepts, such as canary or salmon, are at the bottom and more general concepts, such as bird, fish, or animal, are at higher levels. *(9)*

Hierarchical nature of language The idea that language consists of a series of small components that can be combined to form larger units. For example, words can be combined to create phrases, which in turn can create sentences, which themselves can become components of a story. *(11)*

Hierarchical organization Organization of categories in which larger, more general categories are divided into smaller, more specific categories. These smaller categories can, in turn, be divided into even more specific categories to create a number of levels. *(9)*

Hierarchical processing Processing that occurs in a progression from lower to higher areas of the brain. *(2)*

High-load task A task that uses most or all of a person's resources and so leaves little capacity to handle other tasks. *(4)*

Highly superior autobiographical memory Autobiographical memory capacity possessed by some people who can remember personal experiences that occurred on any specific day from their past. *(8)*

Hippocampus A subcortical structure that is important for forming long-term memories, and that also plays a role in remote episodic memories and in short-term storage of novel information. *(6)*

Hub and spoke model A model of semantic knowledge that proposes that areas of the brain that are associated with different functions are connected to the anterior temporal lobe, which integrates information from these areas. *(9)*

Iconic memory Brief sensory memory for visual stimuli that lasts for a fraction of a second after a stimulus is extinguished. This corresponds to the sensory memory stage of the modal model of memory. *(5)*

Illusory conjunctions A situation, demonstrated in experiments by Anne Treisman, in which features from different objects are inappropriately combined. *(4)*

Illusory correlation A correlation that appears to exist between two events, when in reality there is no correlation or it is weaker than it is assumed to be. *(13)*

Illusory truth effect Enhanced probability of evaluating a statement as being true upon repeated presentation. *(8)*

Imageless thought debate The debate about whether thought is possible in the absence of images. *(10)*

Imagery debate The debate about whether imagery is based on spatial mechanisms, such as those involved in perception, or on propositional mechanisms that are related to language. *(10)*

Imagery neuron Neurons in the human brain studied by Kreiman, which fire in the same way when a person sees a picture of an object and when a person creates a visual image of the object. *(10)*

Imagination network Kaufman and Gregoire's (2015) name for the default mode network (DMN). *(12)*

Implicit memory Memory that occurs when an experience affects a person's behavior, even though the person is not aware that he or she has had the experience. *(6)*

Inattentional blindness Not noticing something even though it is in clear view, usually caused by failure to pay attention to the object or the place where the object is located. See also **Change blindness.** *(4)*

Inattentional deafness Occurs when inattention causes a person to miss an auditory stimulus. For example, experiments have shown that it is more difficult to detect a tone when engaged in a difficult visual search task. *(4)*

***13Incidental emotions** In a decision-making situation, emotions not directly caused by the act of having to make a decision. *(13)*

Incubation The phenomenon of getting ideas after taking a "time-out" from working on a problem. *(12)*

Inductive reasoning Reasoning in which a conclusion follows from a consideration of evidence. This conclusion is stated as being probably true rather than definitely true, as can be the case for the conclusions from deductive reasoning. *(13)*

Inference In language, the process by which readers create information that is not explicitly stated in the text. *(11)*

Information-processing approach The approach to psychology, developed beginning in the 1950s, in which the mind is described as processing information through a sequence of stages. *(1)*

Inhibitory control A mechanism involved in dealing with conflicting stimuli. Related to executive function, cognitive control and willpower. *(4)*

Initial state In problem solving, the conditions at the beginning of a problem. *(12)*

Input units Units in a connectionist network that are activated by stimulation from the environment. See also **Connectionist network; Hidden units; Output units.** *(9)*

Insight Sudden realization of a problem's solution. *(12)*

Instrument inference An inference about tools or methods that occurs while reading text or listening to speech. See also **Anaphoric inference; Causal inference.** *(11)*

Intermediate states In problem solving, the various conditions that exist along the pathways between the initial and goal states. *(12)*

Inverse projection problem Task of determining the object that caused a particular image on the retina. *(3)*

In vivo problem-solving research Observing people to determine how they solve problems in real-world situations. This technique has been used to study the use of analogy in a number of different settings, including laboratory meetings of a university research group and design brainstorming sessions in an industrial research and development department. *(12)*

Judgment Making a decision or drawing a conclusion. *(13)*

Landmark discrimination problem Problem in which the task is to remember an object's location and to choose that location after a delay. Associated with research on the *where* processing stream. *(3)*

Language A system of communication using sounds or symbols that enables us to express our feelings, thoughts, ideas, and experiences. *(11)*

Late closure In parsing, when a person encounters a new word, the parser assumes that this word is part of the current phrase. *(11)*

Late selection model of attention A model of selective attention that proposes that selection of stimuli for final processing does not occur until after the information in the message has been analyzed for meaning. *(4)*

Law of large numbers The larger the number of individuals that are randomly drawn from a population, the more representative the resulting group will be of the entire population. *(13)*

Law of pragnanz See **Pragnanz, law of.**

Levels of analysis A topic can be understood by studying it at a number of different levels of a system. *(2)*

Levels of processing theory The idea that memory depends on how information is encoded, with better memory being achieved when processing is deep than when processing is shallow. Deep processing involves attention to meaning and is associated with elaborative rehearsal. Shallow processing involves repetition with little attention to meaning and is associated with maintenance rehearsal. *(7)*

Lexical ambiguity When a word can have more than one meaning. For example, *bug* can mean an insect, a listening device, to annoy, or a problem in a computer program. *(11)*

Lexical decision task A procedure in which a person is asked to decide as quickly as possible whether a particular stimulus is a word or a nonword. *(9, 11)*

Lexical priming Priming that involves the meaning of words. For example, *rose* would prime *flower*, because their meanings are related. *(11)*

Lexical semantics The meaning of words. *(11)*

Lexicon A person's knowledge of what words mean, how they sound, and how they are used in relation to other words. *(11)*

Light-from-above assumption The assumption that light is coming from above. This is a heuristic that can influence how we perceive three-dimensional objects that are illuminated. *(3)*

Likelihood In Bayesian inference, the extent to which the available evidence is consistent with the outcome. *(3)*

Likelihood principle Part of Helmholtz's theory of unconscious inference that states that we perceive the object that is *most likely* to have caused the pattern of stimuli we have received. *(3)*

Load theory of attention Proposal that the ability to ignore task-irrelevant stimuli depends on the load of the task the person is carrying out. High-load tasks result in less distraction. *(4)*

Localization of function Location of specific functions in specific areas of the brain. For example, areas have been identified that are specialized to process information involved in the perception of movement, form, speech, and different aspects of memory. *(2)*

Long-term memory (LTM) A memory mechanism that can hold large amounts of information for long periods of time. Long-term memory is one of the stages in the modal model of memory. *(6)*

Long-term potentiation (LTP) The increased firing that occurs in a neuron due to prior activity at the synapse. *(7)*

Low-load task A task that uses few resources, leaving some capacity to handle other tasks. *(4)*

Maintenance rehearsal Rehearsal that involves repetition without any consideration of meaning or making connections to other information. Compare to **Elaborative rehearsal**. *(7)*

Meaning dominance Some meanings of words occur more frequently than others. *(11)*

Means–end analysis A problem-solving strategy that seeks to reduce the difference between the initial and goal states. This is achieved by creating subgoals, intermediate states that are closer to the goal. *(12)*

Meditation A number of different practices for controlling the mind. See **Focused attention (FA) meditation**; **Open monitoring meditation**. *(12)*

Memory The processes involved in retaining, retrieving, and using information about stimuli, images, events, ideas, and skills after the original information is no longer present. *(5)*

Mental chronometry Determining the amount of time needed to carry out a cognitive task. *(10)*

Mental imagery Experiencing a sensory impression in the absence of sensory input. *(10)*

Mental model A specific situation that is represented in a person's mind. *(13)*

Mental model approach In deductive reasoning, determining if syllogisms are valid by creating mental models of situations based on the premises of the syllogism. *(13)*

Mental rotation Rotating an image of an object in the mind. *(5)*

Mental rotation task A task in which a person judges whether two pictures of three-dimensional geometric objects are pictures of the same object rotated in space or are pictures of two mirror-image objects rotated in space. *(10)*

Mental scanning A process of mental imagery in which a person scans a mental image in his or her mind. *(10)*

Mental set A preconceived notion about how to approach a problem based on a person's experience or what has worked in the past. *(12)*

Mental time travel According to Tulving, the defining property of the *experience* of episodic memory, in which a person travels back in time in his or her mind to reexperience events that happened in the past. *(6)*

Mental walk task A task used in imagery experiments in which participants are asked to form a mental image of an object and to imagine that they are walking toward this mental image. *(10)*

Method of loci A method for remembering things in which the things to be remembered are placed at different locations in a mental image of a spatial layout. See also **Pegword technique**. *(10)*

Microelectrodes Small wires that are used to record electrical signals from single neurons. *(2)*

Mind System that creates mental representations of the world and controls mental functions such as perception, attention, memory, emotions, language, deciding, thinking, and reasoning. *(1)*

Mind wandering Thoughts that come from within a person, often unintentionally. In early research this was called daydreaming. *(4)*

Mindfulness Paying attention on purpose, in the present moment, and nonjudgmentally, to the unfolding of experience moment to moment. *(12)*

Mirror neurons Neurons in the premotor cortex, originally discovered in the monkey, that respond both when a monkey observes someone else (usually the experimenter) carrying out an action and when the monkey itself carries out the action. There is also evidence for mirror neurons in humans. *(3)*

Mirror neuron system A network of neurons in the brain that have mirror neuron properties. *(3)*

Misinformation effect Misleading information presented after a person witnesses an event that changes how the person describes that event later. *(8)*

Misleading postevent information (MPI) The misleading information that causes the misinformation effect. *(8)*

Modal model of memory The model proposed by Atkinson and Shiffrin that describes memory as a mechanism that involves processing information through a series of stages, including short-term memory and long-term memory. It is called the *modal model* because it contained features of many models that were being proposed in the 1960s. *(5)*

Multidimensional The multidimensional nature of cognition refers to the fact that even simple experiences involve combinations of different qualities. *(2)*

Multiple-factor approach Seeking to describe how concepts are represented in the brain by searching for multiple factors that determine how concepts are divided up within a category. *(9)*

Multiple trace model of consolidation The idea that the hippocampus is involved in the retrieval of remote memories, especially episodic memories. This contrasts with the standard model of memory, which proposes that the hippocampus is involved only in the retrieval of recent memories. *(7)*

Multivoxel pattern analysis (MVPA) A procedure for determining the *pattern* of voxel activation that is elicited by specific stimuli, within various structures. *(7)*

Music-enhanced autobiographical memories (MEAMS) Autobiographical memories elicited by hearing music. *(8)*

Mutilated checkerboard problem A problem that has been used to study how the statement of a problem influences a person's ability to reach a solution. *(12)*

*13Myside bias Type of confirmation bias in which people generate and test hypotheses in a way that is biased toward their own opinions and attitudes. *(13)*

Narrative A story that progresses from one event to another. *(11)*

Narrative rehearsal hypothesis The idea that we remember some life events better because we rehearse them. This idea was proposed by Neisser as an explanation for "flashbulb" memories. *(8)*

Nerve fiber See **Axon**. *(2)*

Nerve impulse An electrical response that is propagated down the length of an axon (nerve fiber). Also called an **Action potential**. *(2)*

Nerve net A network of continuously interconnected nerve fibers (as contrasted with neural networks, in which fibers are connected by synapses). *(2)*

Neural circuit Group of interconnected neurons that are responsible for neural processing. *(2)*

Neural network Groups of neurons or structures that are connected together. *(2)*

Neural representation, principle of Everything a person experiences is based on representations in the person's nervous system. *(2)*

Neuroeconomics An approach to studying decision making that combines research from the fields of psychology, neuroscience, and economics. *(13)*

Neuron Cell that is specialized to receive and transmit information in the nervous system. *(2)*

Neuron doctrine The idea that individual cells called neurons transmit signals in the nervous system, and that these cells are not continuous with other cells as proposed by nerve net theory. *(2)*

Neuropsychology The study of the behavioral effects of brain damage in humans. *(1, 2)*

Neurotransmitter Chemical that is released at the synapse in response to incoming action potentials. *(2)*

Nine-dot problem A problem involving nine dots, arranged in a square pattern, in which the task is to draw four straight lines that pass through all nine dots without lifting the pen from the paper or retracing a line. *(12)*

Nostalgia A memory that involves a sentimental affection for the past. *(8)*

Object discrimination problem A problem in which the task is to remember an object based on its shape and choose it when presented with another object after a delay. Associated with research on the *what* processing stream. *(3)*

Object-relative construction A sentence construction in which the subject of the main clause is the object in the embedded clause, as in this sentence: *The senator who the reporter spotted shouted*. *(11)*

Object imagery The ability to image visual details, features, or objects. *(10)*

Oblique effect The finding that vertical and horizontal orientations can be perceived more easily than other (slanted) orientations. *(3)*

Occipital lobe The lobe at the back of the brain that is devoted primarily to analyzing incoming visual information. *(2)*

Open monitoring (OM) meditation A type of meditation that involves paying attention to whatever comes into the mind, and to follow this thought until something else comes along. *(12)*

Operant conditioning Type of conditioning championed by B. F. Skinner, which focuses on how behavior is strengthened by presentation of positive reinforcers, such as food or social approval, or withdrawal of negative reinforcers, such as a shock or social rejection. *(1, 4)*

Operators In problem solving, permissible moves that can be made toward a problem's solution. *(12)*

Opt-in procedure Procedure in which a person must take an active step to *choose* a course of action—for example, choosing to be an organ donor. *(13)*

Opt-out procedure Procedure in which a person must take an active step to *avoid* a course of action—for example, choosing not to be an organ donor. *(13)*

Output units Units in a connectionist network that contain the final output of the network. See also **Connectionist network; Hidden units; Input units**. *(9)*

Overt attention Shifting of attention by moving the eyes. Contrasts with **Covert attention**. *(4)*

Paired-associate learning A learning task in which participants are first presented with pairs of words, then one word of each pair is presented and the task is to recall the other word. *(7, 10)*

Paper folding test (PFT) A test in which a piece of paper is folded and then pierced by a pencil to create a hole. The task is to determine, from a number of alternatives, where the holes will be on the unfolded piece of paper. *(10)*

Paradigm A system of ideas, which guide thinking in a particular field. *(1)*

Paradigm shift A shift in thinking from one paradigm to another. *(1)*

Parahippocampal place area (PPA) An area in the temporal lobe that contains neurons that are selectively activated by pictures of indoor and outdoor scenes. *(2)*

Parallel distributed processing (PDP) See **Connectionism; Connectionist network**. *(9)*

Parietal lobe The lobe at the top of the brain that contains mechanisms responsible for sensations caused by stimulation of the skin and also some aspects of visual information. *(2)*

Parsing The mental grouping of words in a sentence into phrases. The way a sentence is parsed determines its meaning. *(11)*

Partial report method Procedure used in Sperling's experiment on the properties of the visual icon, in which participants were instructed to report only some of the stimuli in a briefly presented display. A cue tone immediately after the display was extinguished indicated which part of the display to report. See also **Delayed partial report method; Sensory memory; Whole report method**. *(5)*

Pegword technique A method for remembering things in which the things to be remembered are associated with concrete words. See also **Method of loci**. *(10)*

Perception Conscious experience that results from stimulation of the senses. *(3)*

Perception pathway Neural pathway, extending from the occipital lobe to the temporal lobe, that is associated with perceiving or recognizing objects. Corresponds to the *what* pathway. *(3)*

Perceptual load Related to the difficulty of a task. Low-load tasks use only a small amount of a person's processing capacity. High-load tasks use more of the processing capacity. *(4)*

Perceptual organization, principles of Rules proposed by the Gestalt psychologists to explain how small elements of a scene or a display become perceptually grouped to form larger units. These "laws" are described as "heuristics" in this book. *(3)*

Permission schema A pragmatic reasoning schema that states that if a person satisfies condition A, then they get to carry out action B. The permission schema has been used to explain the results of the Wason four-card problem. *(13)*

Perseveration Difficulty in switching from one behavior to another, which can hinder a person's ability to solve problems that require flexible thinking. Perseveration is observed in cases in which the prefrontal cortex has been damaged. *(5)*

Persistence of vision The continued perception of light for a fraction of a second after the original light stimulus has been extinguished. Perceiving a trail of light from a moving sparkler is caused by the persistence of vision. See also **Iconic memory**. *(5)*

Personal semantic memory Semantic components of autobiographical memories. *(6)*

Phonological loop The part of working memory that holds and processes verbal and auditory information. See also **Central executive; Visuospatial sketch pad; Working memory**. *(5)*

Phonological similarity effect An effect that occurs when letters or words that sound similar are confused. For example, T and P are two similar-sounding letters that could be confused. *(5)*

Phonological store Component of the phonological loop of working memory that holds a limited amount of verbal and auditory information for a few seconds. *(5)*

Physical regularities Regularly occurring physical properties of the environment. For example, there are more vertical and horizontal orientations in the environment than oblique (angled) orientations. *(3)*

Placebo A pill or procedure that patients believe delivers active ingredients (usually pain killers), but which contains no active ingredient. *(3)*

Placebo effect Decrease in pain from a procedure or substance that delivers no active ingredient. *(3)*

Population coding Neural representation of a stimulus by the pattern of firing of a large number of neurons. *(2)*

Post-identification feedback effect An increase in confidence of memory recall due to confirming feedback after making an identification, as in a police lineup. *(8)*

Pragmatic inference Inference that occurs when reading or hearing a statement leads a person to expect something that is not explicitly stated or necessarily implied by the statement. *(8)*

Pragnanz, law of Law of perceptual organization that states that every stimulus pattern is seen in such a way that the resulting structure is as simple as possible. Also called the *law of good figure* and the *law of simplicity*. *(3)*

Preattentive stage The first stage of Treisman's feature integration theory, in which an object is analyzed into its features. *(4)*

Precueing A procedure in which participants are given a cue that will usually help them carry out a subsequent task. This procedure has been used in visual attention experiments in which participants are presented with a cue that tells them where to direct their attention. *(4)*

Preinventive forms Objects created in Finke's "creative cognition" experiment that precede the creation of a finished creative product. *(12)*

Premise The first two statements in a syllogism. The third statement is the conclusion. *(13)*

Primacy effect In a memory experiment in which a list of words is presented, enhanced memory for words presented at the beginning of the list. See also **Recency effect**. *(6)*

Priming A change in response to a stimulus caused by the previous presentation of the same or a similar stimulus. See also **Repetition priming**. *(6, 9)*

Principle(s) of good continuation, good figure, similarity, simplicity See inverted entries (e.g., **Good continuation, principle of**). *(3)*

Prior A person's initial belief about the probability of an outcome. *(3)*

Prior probability See **Prior**. *(3)*

Proactive interference When information learned previously interferes with learning new information. See also **Retroactive interference**. *(5, 6)*

Problem A situation in which there is an obstacle between a present state and a goal state and it is not immediately obvious how to get around the obstacle. *(12)*

Problem of sensory coding The problem of determining the neural representation for the senses. *(2)*

Problem space The initial state, goal state, and all the possible intermediate states for a particular problem. *(12)*

Procedural memory Memory for how to carry out highly practiced skills. Procedural memory is a type of implicit memory because although people can carry out a skilled behavior, they often cannot explain exactly how they are able to do so. *(6)*

Processing capacity The amount of information input that a person can handle. This sets a limit on the person's ability to process information. *(4)*

Propaganda effect People are more likely to rate statements they have read or heard before as being true, just because of prior exposure to the statements. *(6)*

Propositional representation A representation in which relationships are represented by symbols, as when the words of a language represent objects and the relationships between objects. *(10)*

Prosody The pattern of intonation and rhythm in spoken language. *(11)*

Prosopagnosia Condition caused by damage to the temporal lobe that is characterized by an inability to recognize faces. *(2)*

Prototype A standard used in categorization that is formed by averaging the category members a person has encountered in the past. *(9)*

Prototype approach to categorization The idea that we decide whether something is a member of a category by determining whether it is similar to a standard representation of the category, called a prototype. *(9)*

Psycholinguistics The field concerned with the psychological study of language. *(11)*

Radiation problem A problem posed by Duncker that involves finding a way to destroy a tumor by radiation without damaging other organs in the body. This problem has been widely used to study the role of analogy in problem solving. *(12)*

Reaction time The time it takes to react to a stimulus. This is usually determined by measuring the time between presentation of a stimulus and the response to the stimulus. Examples of responses are pushing a button, saying a word, moving the eyes, and the appearance of a particular brain wave. *(1)*

Reactivation A process that occurs during memory consolidation, in which the hippocampus replays the neural activity associated with a memory. During reactivation, activity occurs in the network connecting the hippocampus and the cortex. This activity results in the formation of connections between the cortical areas. *(7)*

Reading span Measure used by Daneman and Carpenter to determine individual differences in working memory. It is the number of 13- to 16-word sentences that a person can read and then correctly remember the last words of all of the sentences. *(5)*

Reading span test The test used by Daneman and Carpenter to measure reading span. *(5)*

Reasoning Cognitive processes by which people start with information and come to conclusions that go beyond that information. See also **Deductive reasoning; Inductive reasoning**. *(13)*

Recall Subjects are asked to report stimuli they have previously seen or heard. *(5)*

Recency effect In a memory experiment in which a list of words is presented, enhanced memory for words presented at the end of the list. See also **Primacy effect**. *(6)*

Receptors Specialized neural structures that respond to environmental stimuli such as light, mechanical stimulation, or chemical stimuli. *(2)*

Recognition memory Identifying a stimulus that was encountered earlier. Stimuli are presented during a study period; later, the same stimuli plus other, new stimuli are presented. The participants' task is to pick the stimuli that were originally presented. *(6)*

Reconsolidation A process proposed by Nader and others that occurs when a memory is retrieved and so becomes reactivated. Once this occurs, the memory must be consolidated again, as it was during the initial learning. This repeat consolidation is reconsolidation. *(7)*

Recording electrode When used to study neural functioning, a very thin glass or metal probe that can pick up electrical signals from single neurons. *(2)*

Reference electrode Used in conjunction with a recording electrode to measure the difference in charge between the two. Reference electrodes are generally placed where the electrical signal remains constant, so any change in charge between the recording and reference electrodes reflects events happening near the tip of the recording electrode. *(2)*

Referential communication task A task in which two people are exchanging information in a conversation, when this information involves reference—identifying something by naming or describing it. *(11)*

Regularities in the environment Characteristics of the environment that occur frequently. For example, blue is associated with open sky, landscapes are often green and smooth, and verticals and horizontals are often associated with buildings. *(3)*

Rehearsal The process of repeating a stimulus over and over, usually for the purpose of remembering it, that keeps the stimulus active in short-term memory. *(5)*

Release from proactive interference A situation in which conditions occur that eliminate or reduce the decrease in performance caused by proactive interference. See the Wickens experiment described in Chapter 6. *(6)*

Remember/know procedure A procedure in which subjects are presented with a stimulus they have encountered before and are asked to indicate *remember*, if they remember the circumstances under which they initially encountered it, or *know*, if the stimulus seems familiar but they don't remember experiencing it earlier. *(6)*

Reminiscence bump The empirical finding that people over 40 years old have enhanced memory for events from adolescence and early adulthood, compared to other periods of their lives. *(8)*

Repeated recall Recall that is tested immediately after an event and then retested at various times after the event. *(8)*

Repeated reproduction A method of measuring memory in which a person is asked to reproduce a stimulus on repeated occasions at longer and longer intervals after the original presentation of the material to be remembered. *(8)*

Repetition priming When an initial presentation of a stimulus affects the person's response to the same stimulus when it is presented later. *(6)*

Representativeness heuristic The probability that an event A comes from class B can be determined by how well A resembles the properties of class B. *(13)*

Repressed childhood memory Memories that have been pushed out of a person's consciousness. *(8)*

Resting potential Difference in charge between the inside and outside of a nerve fiber when the fiber is at rest (no other electrical signals are present). *(2)*

Resting-state fMRI The fMRI response recorded when a person is at rest (not involved in any cognitive tasks) *(2)*

Resting-state functional connectivity A method for determining functional connectivity that involves determining the correlation between the resting-state fMRI in separated structures. *(2)*

Restructuring The process of changing a problem's representation. According to the Gestalt psychologists, restructuring is the key mechanism of problem solving. *(12)*

Retrieval The process of remembering information that has been stored in long-term memory. *(7)*

Retrieval cues Cues that help a person remember information that is stored in memory. *(7)*

Retrieval practice effect When practicing memory retrieval increases elaboration, which increases performance on memory tasks. *(7)*

Retroactive interference When more recent learning interferes with memory for something that happened in the past. See also **Proactive interference**. *(5, 8)*

Retrograde amnesia Loss of memory for something that happened prior to an injury or traumatic event such as a concussion. *(7)*

Return to the tonic In a musical composition, coming back to the tonic note that was at the beginning of the composition. *(11)*

Risk aversion The tendency to make decisions that avoid risk. *(13)*

Risk aversion strategy A decision-making strategy that is governed by the idea of avoiding risk. Often used when a problem is stated in terms of gains. See also **Risk-taking strategy**. *(13)*

Risk-taking strategy A decision-making strategy that is governed by the idea of taking risks. Often used when a problem is stated in terms of losses. See also **Risk aversion strategy**. *(13)*

Rule-based nature of language The idea that there are rules in a language that specify the permissible ways for arranging words and phrases.

Saccadic eye movements Eye movements from one fixation point to another. See also **Fixation** (in perception and attention). *(4)*

Saliency map Map of a scene that indicates the stimulus salience of areas and objects in the scene. *(4)*

Same-object advantage Occurs when the enhancing effect of attention spreads throughout an object, so that attention to one place on an object results in a facilitation of processing at other places on the object. *(4)*

Savings Measure used by Ebbinghaus to determine the magnitude of memory left from initial learning. Higher savings indicate greater memory. *(1)*

Savings curve Plot of savings versus time after original learning. *(1)*

Scene schema A person's knowledge about what is likely to be contained in a particular scene. This knowledge can help guide attention to different areas of the scene. For example, knowledge of what is usually in an office may cause a person to look toward the desk to see the computer. *(3, 4)*

Schema A person's knowledge about what is involved in a particular experience. See also **Script**. *(8)*

Scientific revolution Occurs when there is a shift in thinking from one scientific paradigm to another. *(1)*

Script A type of schema. The conception of the sequence of actions that describe a particular activity. For example, the sequence of events that are associated with going to class would be a "going to class" script. See also **Schema**. *(8)*

Seed location The area of the brain associated with carrying out a specific cognitive or motor task that serves as the reference area the resting-state functional connectivity method. *(2)*

Selective attention The ability to focus on one message and ignore all others. *(4)*

Self-image hypothesis The idea that memory is enhanced for events that occur as a person's self-image or life identity is being formed. This is one of the explanations for the reminiscence bump. *(8)*

Self-reference effect Memory for a word is improved by relating the word to the self. *(7)*

Semantic category approach An approach to describing how semantic information is represented in the brain that proposes that there are specific neural circuits for some specific categories. *(9)*

Semantic dementia Condition in which there is a general loss of knowledge for all concepts. *(9)*

Semantic network approach An approach to understanding how concepts are organized in the mind that proposes that concepts are arranged in networks. *(9)*

Semantic regularities Characteristics associated with the functions carried out in different types of scenes. For example, food preparation, cooking, and perhaps eating occur in a kitchen. *(3)*

Semantic somatotopy Correspondence between words related to specific parts of the body and the location of brain activity associated with that part of the body. *(9)*

Semanticization of remote memory Loss of episodic details for memories of long-ago events. *(6)*

Semantics The meanings of words and sentences. Distinguished from **Syntax**. *(11)*

Sensory code How neural firing represents various characteristics of the environment. *(2)*

Sensory-functional (S-F) hypothesis Explanation of how semantic information is represented in the brain that states that the ability to differentiate living things and artifacts depends on one system that distinguishes sensory attributes and another system that distinguishes function. *(9)*

Sensory memory A brief stage of memory that holds information for seconds or fractions of a second. It is the first stage in the modal model of memory. See also **Iconic memory; Persistence of vision**. *(5)*

Sentence verification technique A technique in which the participant is asked to indicate whether a particular sentence is true or false. For example, sentences like "An apple is a fruit" have been used in studies on categorization. *(9)*

Serial position curve In a memory experiment in which participants are asked to recall a list of words, a plot of the percentage of participants remembering each word against the position of that word in the list. See also **Primacy effect; Recency effect**. *(6)*

Shadowing The procedure of repeating a message out loud as it is heard. Shadowing is commonly used in conjunction with studies of selective attention that use the dichotic listening procedure. *(4)*

Shallow processing Processing that involves repetition with little attention to meaning. Shallow processing is usually associated with maintenance rehearsal. See also **Deep processing; Depth of processing**. *(7)*

Short-term memory (STM) A memory mechanism that can hold a limited amount of information for a brief period of time, usually around 30 seconds, unless there is rehearsal (such as repeating a telephone number) to maintain the information in short-term memory. Short-term memory is one of the stages in the modal model of memory. *(5)*

Similarity, principle of Law of perceptual organization that states that similar things appear to be grouped together. *(3)*

Simple reaction time Reacting to the presence or absence of a single stimulus (as opposed to having to choose between a number of stimuli before making a response). See also **Choice reaction time**. *(1)*

Simplicity, principle of See **Pragnanz, law of**. *(3)*

Situation model A mental representation of what a text is about. *(11)*

Size-weight illusion When a person is presented with two similar objects that are the same weight but different sizes, the larger one seems lighter when they are lifted together. *(3)*

Skill memory Memory for doing things that usually involve learned skills. See **Procedural memory**. *(6)*

Source misattribution Occurs when the source of a memory is misidentified. See **Source monitoring error**. *(8)*

Source monitoring The process by which people determine the origins of memories, knowledge, or beliefs. Remembering that you heard about something from a particular person would be an example of source monitoring. *(8)*

Source monitoring error Misidentifying the source of a memory. See **Source misattribution**. *(8)*

Source problem A problem or story that is analogous to the target problem and which therefore provides information that can lead to a solution to the target problem. See also **Analogical problem solving; Target problem**. *(12)*

Spacing effect The advantage in performance caused by short study sessions separated by breaks from studying. *(7)*

Sparse coding Neural coding based on the pattern of activity in small groups of neurons. *(2)*

Spatial imagery The ability to image spatial relations. *(10)*

Spatial representation A representation in which different parts of an image can be described as corresponding to specific locations in space. See also **Depictive representation**. *(10)*

Specific level In Rosch's categorization scheme, the level below the basic level (e.g., "kitchen table" for the basic category "table"). See also **Basic level; Global level**. *(9)*

Specificity coding The representation of a specific stimulus by the firing of neurons that respond only to that stimulus. An example would be the signaling of a person's face by the firing of a neuron that responds only to that person's face. *(2)*

Speech segmentation The process of perceiving individual words within the continuous flow of the speech signal. *(3, 11)*

Spreading activation Activity that spreads out along any link in a semantic network that is connected to an activated node. *(9)*

Standard model of consolidation Proposes that memory retrieval depends on the hippocampus during consolidation, but that once consolidation is complete, retrieval no longer depends on the hippocampus. *(7)*

State-dependent learning The principle that memory is best when a person is in the same state for encoding and retrieval. This principle is related to encoding specificity. *(7)*

Statistical learning The process of learning about transitional probabilities and about other characteristics of language. Statistical learning also occurs for vision, based on learning about what types of things usually occur in the environment. *(3)*

Status quo bias Tendency to do nothing when faced with making a decision. *(13)*

Stereotype An oversimplified generalization about a group or class of people that often focuses on negative characteristics. See also **Illusory correlation**. *(13)*

Stimulus salience Bottom-up factors that determine attention to elements of a scene. Examples are color, contrast, and orientation. The meaningfulness of the images, which is a top-down factor, does not contribute to stimulus salience. See also **Saliency map**. *(4)*

Stroop effect An effect originally studied by J. R. Stroop, using a task in which a person is instructed to respond to one aspect of a stimulus, such as the color of ink that a word is printed in, and ignore another aspect, such as the color that the word names. The Stroop effect refers to the fact that people find this task difficult when, for example, the word *RED* is printed in blue ink. *(4)*

Structural features (memory models) Types of memory indicated by boxes in models of memory. In the modal model, the types are sensory memory, short-term memory, and long-term memory. *(5)*

Structural features (problem solving) The underlying principle that governs the solution to a problem—for example, in the radiation problem, needing high intensity to fix something surrounded by material that could be damaged by high intensity. Contrast with **Surface features**. *(12)*

Structuralism An approach to psychology that explained perception as the adding up of small elementary units called sensations. *(1)*

Subcortical areas Areas of the brain below the cerebral cortex. Two examples of subcortical structures are the amygdala and the hippocampus. *(2)*

Subgoals In the means–end analysis approach to problem solving, intermediate states that move the process of solution closer to the goal. *(12)*

Subject-relative construction A sentence construction in which the subject of the main clause is also the subject in the embedded clause, as in the sentence, *The senator who spotted the reporter shouted*. *(11)*

Subordinate (specific) level The most specific category level distinguished by Rosch—for example, "kitchen table." *(9)*

Superordinate (global) level The most general category level distinguished by Rosch—for example, "furniture." *(9)*

Syllogism A series of three statements: two premises followed by a conclusion. The conclusion can follow from the premises based on the rules of logic. See also **Categorical syllogism; Conditional syllogism**. *(13)*

Synapse Space between the end of an axon and the cell body or dendrite of the next axon. *(2)*

Synaptic consolidation A process of consolidation that involves structural changes at synapses that happen rapidly, over a period of minutes. See also **Consolidation; Systems consolidation**. *(7)*

Synchronization Occurs when neural responses become synchronized in time, so positive and negative responses occur at the same time and with similar amplitudes. It has been proposed that synchronization is a mechanism responsible for enhanced effective connectivity and enhanced communication between two areas that accompany shifts of attention. *(4)*

Syntactic coordination Process by which people use similar grammatical constructions when having a conversation. *(11)*

Syntactic priming Hearing a statement with a particular syntactic construction increases the chances that a statement that follows will be produced with the same construction. *(11)*

Syntax The rules for combining words into sentences. Distinguished from **Semantics**. *(11)*

Systems consolidation A consolidation process that involves the gradual reorganization of circuits within brain regions and takes place on a long timescale, lasting weeks, months, or even years. See also **Consolidation; Synaptic consolidation**. *(7)*

Target problem A problem to be solved. In analogical problem solving, solution of this problem can become easier when the problem-solver is exposed to an analogous source problem or story. See also **Source problem**. *(12)*

Task-related fMRI The fMRI response that occurs in response to a specific cognitive task. *(2)*

Temporal lobe The lobe on the side of the brain that contains mechanisms responsible for language, memory, hearing, and vision. *(2)*

Temporary ambiguity A situation in which the meaning of a sentence, based on its initial words, is ambiguous because a number of meanings are possible, depending on how the sentence unfolds. "Cast iron sinks quickly rust" is an example of a sentence that creates temporary ambiguity. *(11)*

Test location When measuring resting-state functional connectivity, the activity at the test location is compared to the activity at the seed location to determine the degree of functional connectivity between the two locations. *(2)*

Testing effect Enhanced performance on a memory test caused by being tested on the material to be remembered. *(7)*

Theory of mind The ability to understand what others think, feel or believe. *(11)*

Theory of natural selection Darwin's theory that characteristics that enhance an animal's ability to survive and reproduce will be passed on to future generations. *(3)*

Think-aloud protocol A procedure in which subjects are asked to say out loud what they are thinking while doing a problem. This procedure is used to help determine people's thought processes as they are solving a problem. *(12)*

Time-series response The way the fMRI response changes over time. *(2)*

Top-down processing Processing that involves a person's knowledge or expectations. This type of processing has also been called knowledge-based processing. *(3)*

Tonic The key of a musical composition. The tonic note is the first note of a scale in a particular key. *(11)*

Topographic map Each point on a visual stimulus causes activity at a specific location on a brain structure, such as the visual cortex, and points next to each other on the stimulus cause activity at points next to each other on the structure. *(10)*

Tower of Hanoi problem A problem involving moving discs from one set of pegs to another. It has been used to illustrate the process involved in means–end analysis. *(12)*

Trade-off strategy A negotiating strategy in which one person says to another, "I'll give you A, if you'll give me B." *(12)*

Track-weighted imaging (TWI) A technique for determining connectivity in the brain that is based on detection of how water diffuses along the length of nerve fibers. *(2)*

Transcranial direct current stimulation A procedure for stimulating the brain in which two electrodes, which are connected to a battery-powered device that delivers direct current, are placed on a person's head. *(12)*

Transcranial magnetic stimulation (TMS) A procedure in which magnetic pulses are applied to the skull in order to temporarily disrupt the functioning of part of the brain. *(9)*

Transfer-appropriate processing When the type of task that occurs during encoding matches the type of task that occurs during retrieval. This type of processing can result in enhanced memory. *(7)*

Transitional probabilities In speech, the likelihood that one speech sound will follow another within a word. *(3)*

Two-string problem A problem first described by Maier in which a person is given the task of attaching two strings together that are too far apart to be reached at the same time. This task was devised to illustrate the operation of functional fixedness. *(12)*

Typicality effect The ability to judge the truth or falsity of sentences involving high-prototypical members of a category more rapidly than sentences involving low-prototypical members of a category. See also **Sentence verification technique**. *(9)*

Ultimatum game A game in which a *proposer* is given a sum of money and makes an offer to a *responder* as to how this money should be split between them. The responder must choose to accept the offer or reject it. This game has been used to study people's decision-making strategies. *(13)*

Unconscious inference Helmholtz's idea that some of our perceptions are the result of unconscious assumptions that we make about the environment. See also **Likelihood principle**. *(3)*

Unilateral neglect A problem caused by brain damage, usually to the right parietal lobe, in which the patient ignores objects in the left half of his or her visual field. *(10)*

Units "Neuronlike processing units" in a connectionist network. See also **Hidden units; Input units; Output units**. *(9)*

Utility Outcomes that achieve a person's goals; in economic terms, the maximum monetary payoff. *(13)*

Validity Quality of a syllogism whose conclusion follows logically from its premises. *(13)*

Ventral attention network A network that controls attention based on stimulus salience. *(4)*

Ventral pathway The pathway from the visual cortex in the occipital lobe to the temporal lobe. This is also known as the *what pathway*. *(3)*

Viewpoint invariance The ability to recognize an object seen from different viewpoints. *(3)*

Visual cortex Area in the occipital lobe that receives signals from the eyes. *(2)*

Visual icon See **Iconic memory**. *(5)*

Visual imagery A type of mental imagery involving vision, in which an image is experienced in the absence of a visual stimulus. *(5, 10)*

Visual scanning Movement of the eyes from one location or object to another. *(4)*

Visual search Occurs when a person is looking for one stimulus or object among a number of other stimuli or objects. *(4)*

Visual world paradigm In experiments on language processing, determining how subjects are processing information in a scene as they respond to specific instructions related to the scene. *(11)*

Visuospatial sketch pad The part of working memory that holds and processes visual and spatial information. See also **Central executive; Phonological loop; Working memory.** *(5)*

Vividness of visual imagery questionnaire (VVIQ) A test in which people are asked to rate the vividness of mental images they create. This test is designed to measure object imagery ability. *(10)*

Volitional Daydreaming The act of consciously choosing to disengage from external tasks in order to pursue an internal stream of thought that might have positive outcomes. *(12)*

Voxel Small cube-shaped areas in the brain used in the analysis of data from brain scanning experiments. *(2)*

*Wason four-card problem A conditional reasoning task developed by Wason that involves four cards. Various versions of this problem have been used to study the mechanisms that determine the outcomes of conditional reasoning tasks. *(13)*

Water jug problem A problem, first described by Luchins, that illustrates how mental set can influence the strategies that people use to solve a problem. *(12)*

Weapons focus The tendency for eyewitnesses to a crime to focus attention on a weapon, which causes poorer memory for other things that are happening. *(8)*

Wernicke's aphasia A condition, caused by damage to Wernicke's area, that is characterized by difficulty in understanding language, and fluent, grammatically correct, but incoherent speech. *(2)*

Wernicke's area Area in the temporal lobe associated with understanding language. Damage to this area causes Wernicke's aphasia. *(2)*

What pathway Neural pathway, extending from the occipital lobe to the temporal lobe, that is associated with perceiving or recognizing objects. Corresponds to the perception pathway. *(3)*

Where pathway Neural pathway, extending from the occipital lobe to the parietal lobe, that is associated with neural processing that occurs when people locate objects in space. Roughly corresponds to the action pathway. *(3)*

Whole report method Procedure used in Sperling's experiment on the properties of the visual icon, in which participants were instructed to report all of the stimuli they saw in a brief presentation. See also **Partial report method; Sensory memory.** *(5)*

Willpower A mechanism involved in dealing with conflicting stimuli. Related to executive function, inhibitory control, and cognitive control. *(4)*

Word frequency The relative usage of words in a particular language. For example, in English, *home* has higher word frequency than *hike*. *(11)*

Word frequency effect The phenomenon of faster reading time for high-frequency words than for low-frequency words. *(11)*

Word length effect The notion that it is more difficult to remember a list of long words than a list of short words. *(5)*

Working memory A limited-capacity system for temporary storage and manipulation of information for complex tasks such as comprehension, learning, and reasoning. *(5)*

Youth bias Tendency for the most notable public events in a person's life to be perceived to occur when the person is young. *(8)*

References

Adamson, R. E. (1952). Functional fixedness as related to problem solving. *Journal of Experimental Psychology, 44*, 288–291.

Addis, D. R., Pan, L., Vu, M-A., Laiser, N., & Schacter, D. L. (2009). Constructive episodic simulation of the future and the past: Distinct subsystems of a core brain network mediate imagining and remembering. *Neuropsychologia, 47*, 2222–2238.

Addis, D. R., Wong, A. T., & Schacter, D. L. (2007). Remembering the past and imagining the future: Common and distinct neural substrates during event construction and elaboration. *Neuropsychologia, 45*, 1363–1377.

Addis, D. R., Wong, A. T., & Schacter, D. L. (2008). Age-related changes in the episodic simulation of future events. *Psychological Science, 19*, 33–41.

Adrian, E. D. (1928). *The basis of sensation.* New York: Norton.

Adrian, E. D. (1932). *The mechanism of nervous action.* Philadelphia, PA: University of Pennsylvania Press.

Aguirre, G. K., Zarahn, E., & D'Esposito, M. (1998). An area within human ventral cortex sensitive to "building" stimuli: Evidence and implications. *Neuron, 21*, 373–383.

Albers, A. M., Kok, P., Toni, I, Dijkerman, H. C., & de Lange, F. P. (2013). Shared representations for working memory and mental imagery in early visual cortex. *Current Biology, 22*, 1427–1431.

Almeida, J., Fintzi, A. R., & Mahon, B. Z. (2014). Tool manipulation knowledge is retrieved by way of the ventral visual object processing pathway. *Cortex, 49*, 2334–2344.

Altmann, G. T. M., Garnham, A., & Dennis, Y. (1992). Avoiding the garden path: Eye movements in context. *Journal of Memory and Language, 31*, 685–712.

Altmann, G. T. M., & Kamide, Y. (1999). Incremental interpretation at verbs: restricting the domain of subsequent reference. *Cognition, 73*, 247–264.

Alvarez, G. A., & Cavanagh, P. (2004). The capacity of visual short-term memory is set both by visual information load and by number of objects. *Psychological Science, 15*, 106–111.

Amedi, A., Malach, R., & Pascual-Leone, A. (2005). Negative BOLD differentiates visual imagery and perception. *Neuron, 48*, 859–872.

Anderson, J. R., & Schooler, L. J. (1991). Reflections of the environment in memory. *Psychological Science, 2*, 396–408.

Anton-Erxeleben, K., Stephan, V. M, & Treue, S. (2009). Attention reshapes center-surround receptive field structure in Macaque cortical area MT. *Cerebral Cortex, 19*, 2466–2478.

Appelle, S. (1972). Perception and discrimination as a function of stimulus orientation: The "oblique effect" in man and animals. *Psychological Bulletin, 78*, 266–278.

Arkes, H. R., & Freedman, M. R. (1984). A demonstration of the costs and benefits of expertise in recognition memory. *Memory & Cognition, 12*, 84–89.

Atkinson, R. C., & Shiffrin, R. M. (1968). Human memory: A proposed system and its control processes. In K. W. Spence & J. T. Spence (Eds.), *The psychology of learning and motivation* (Vol. 2, pp. 89–195). New York: Academic Press.

Awh, E., Barton, B., & Vogel, E. K. (2007). Visual working memory represents a fixed number of items regardless of complexity. *Psychological Science, 18*, 622–628.

Baddeley, A. D. (1996). Exploring the central executive. *Quarterly Journal of Experimental Psychology, 49A*, 5–28.

Baddeley, A. D. (2000). Short-term and working memory. In E. Tulving & F. I. M. Craik (Eds.), *The Oxford handbook of memory* (pp. 77–92). New York: Oxford University Press.

Baddeley, A. D., Eysenck, M., & Anderson, M. C. (2009). *Memory.* New York: Psychology Press.

Baddeley, A. D., & Hitch, G. J. (1974). Working memory. In G. A. Bower (Ed.), *The psychology of learning and motivation* (pp. 47–89). New York: Academic Press.

Baddeley, A. D., Lewis, V. F. J., & Vallar, G. (1984). Exploring the articulatory loop. *Quarterly Journal of Experimental Psychology, 36*, 233–252.

Baddeley, A. D., Thomson, N., & Buchanan, M. (1975). Word length and the structure of short-term memory. *Journal of Verbal Learning and Verbal Behavior, 14*, 575–589.

Bailey, M. R., & Balsam, P. D. (2013). Memory reconsolidation: Time to change your mind. *Current Biology, 23*, R243–R245.

Baird, B., Smallwood, J., Mrazek, M. D., Kam, J. W. Y., Franklin, M. S., & Schooler, J. W. (2012). Inspired by distraction Mind wandering facilitates creative incubation. *Psychological Science, 23*, 1117–1122.

Baird, B., Smallwood, J., & Schooler, J. W. (2011). Back to the future: Autobiographical planning and the functionality of mind wandering. *Consciousness and Cognition, 20*, 1604–1611.

Banziger, T., & Scherer, K. R. (2005). The role of intonation in emotional expressions. *Speech Communication, 46*, 252–267.

Barch, D. M. (2013). Brain network interactions in health and disease.

Trends in Cognitive Sciences, 17, 603–605.

Barks, A., Searight, H. R., & Ratwik, S. (2011). Effect of text messaging on academic performance. *Signum Temporis 4,* 4–9.

Baronchelli, A., Ferrer-i-Cancho, R., Pastor-Satorras, R., Chater, N., & Christiansen, M. H. (2013). Networks in cognitive science. *Trends in Cognitive Sciences, 17,* 348–359.

Barrett, F. S., Grimm, K. J., Robins, R. W., Wildschut, T., Sedikides, C., & Janata, P. (2010). Music-evoked nostalgia: Affect, memory, and personality. *Emotion, 10(3),* 390–403.

Barsalou, L. W. (2005). Continuity of the conceptual system across species. *Trends in Cognitive Sciences, 9,* 309–311.

Barsalou, L. W. (2008). Grounded cognition. *Annual Review of Psychology, 59,* 617–645.

Barsalou, L. W. (2009). Simulation, situated conceptualization and prediction. *Philosophical Transactions of the Royal Society B, 364,* 1281–1289.

Bartlett, F. C. (1932). *Remembering: A study in experimental and social psychology.* Cambridge, UK: Cambridge University Press.

Basadur, M., Runco, M., & Vega, L. A. (2000). Understanding how creative thinking skills, attitudes and behaviors work together: A causal process model. *Journal of Creative Behavior, 34,* 77–100.

Bassett, D. S., & Sporns, O. (2017). Network neuroscience. *Nature Neuroscience, 20,* 353–364.

Baylis, G. C., & Driver, J. (1993). Visual attention and objects: Evidence for hierarchical coding of location. *Journal of Experimental Psychology: Human Perception and Performance, 19,* 451–470.

Bays, P. M., & Husain, M. (2008). Dynamic shifts of limited working memory resources in human vision. *Science, 321,* 851–854.

Beaty, R. E., Benedek, M., Wilkins, R. W., Jauk, E., Fink, A., Silvia, P. J., . . . Neubauer, A. C. (2014).

Creativity and the default network: A functional connectivity analysis of the creative brain at rest. *Neuropsychologia, 64,* 92–98.

Bechtel, W., Abrahamsen, A., & Graham, G. (1998). The life of cognitive science. In W. Bechtel & G. Graham (Eds.), *A companion to cognitive science* (pp. 2–104). Oxford, UK: Blackwell.

Bedard, J., & Chi, M. T. H. (1992). Expertise. *Current Directions in Psychological Science, 1,* 135–139.

Beecher, H. K. (1959) *Measurement of subjective responses.* New York: Oxford University Press.

Begg, I. M., Anas, A., & Farinacci, S. (1992). Dissociation of processes in belief: Source recollection, statement familiarity, and the illusion of truth. *Journal of Experimental Psychology: General, 121,* 446–458.

Behrmann, M., Moscovitch, M., & Winocur, G. (1994). Intact visual imagery and impaired visual perception in a patient with visual agnosia. *Journal of Experimental Psychology: Human Perception and Performance, 30,* 1068–1087.

Belfi, A. M., Karlan, B., & Tranel, D. (2016). Music evokes vivid autobiographical memories. *Memory, 24(7),* 979–989.

Bell, K. E., & Limber, J. E. (2010). Reading skill, textbook marking, and course performance. *Literacy Research and Instruction, 49,* 56–67.

Belz, A. (2010, July 16). Lifeguards, camp staff abound as 2 drown in Pella pool. *Des Moines Register.*

Benton, T. R., Ross, D F, Bradshaw, E., Thomas, W. N., & Bradshaw, G. S. (2006). Eyewitness memory is still not common sense: Comparing jurors, judges and law enforcement to eyewitness experts. Applied Cognitive Psychology, 20, 115–129.

Berntsen, D. (2009). Flashbulb memory and social identity. In O. Luminet & A. Curci (Eds.), Flashbulb memories: New issues and new perspectives (pp. 187–205). Hove, UK: Psychology Press.

Berntsen, D., & Rubin, C. (2004). Cultural life scripts structure recall from autobiographical memory. *Memory & Cognition, 32,* 427–442.

Best, J. R., & Miller, P. H. (2010). A developmental perspective on executive function. *Child Development, 81,* 1641–1660.

Best, J. R., Miller, P. H., & Naglieri, J. A. (2011). Relations between executive function and academic achievement from ages 5 to 17 in a large, representative national sample. *Learning and Individual Differences, 21,* 327–336.

Bever, T. G. (1970). The cognitive basis for linguistic structures. In J. R. Hayes (Ed.), *Cognition and the development of language* (pp. 279–362). New York: Wiley.

Bisiach, E., & Luzzatti, G. (1978). Unilateral neglect of representational space. *Cortex, 14,* 129–133.

Biswal, B., Yetkin, F. Z., Haughton, V. M., & Hyde, J. S. (1995). Functional connectivity in the motor cortex of resting human brain using echo-planar MRI. *Magnetic Resonance Medicine, 34,* 537–541.

Blakemore, C., & Cooper, G. G. (1970). Development of the brain depends on the visual environment. *Nature, 228,* 477–478.

Blank, I., Balewski, Z., Mahowald, K., & Fedorenko, E. (2016). Syntactic processing is distributed across the language system. *Neuroimage, 127,* 307–323.

Bliss, T. V. P., & Lomo, T. (1973). Long-lasting potentiation of synaptic transmission in the dentate area of the anaesthetized rabbit following stimulation of the perforant path. *Journal of Physiology (London), 232,* 331–336.

Bliss, T. V. P., Collingridge, G. L., & Morris, R. G. M. (2003). Introduction. *Philosophical Transactions of the Royal Society, Series B: Biological Sciences, 358,* 607–611.

Bock, K. (1990). Structure in language. *American Psychologist, 45,* 1221–1236.

Boden, M. A. (2006). *Mind as machine: A history of cognitive science.* New York: Oxford University Press.

Bolles, R. C., Baker, H., & Marimont, D. H. (1987). *International Journal of Computer Vision, 1,* 7–55.

Bolognani, S. A., Gouvia, P. A., Brucki, S. M., & Bueno, O. F. (2000). Implicit memory and its contribution to the rehabilitation of an amnesic patient: Case study. *Arquiuos de neuro-psiqustria, 58,* 924–930.

Boltz, M. G. (2004). The cognitive processing of film and music soundtracks. *Memory & Cognition, 32,* 1194–1205.

Bonnici, H. M., Chadwick, M. J., Lutti, A., Hasabis, D., Weiskopf, N., & Magurie, E. A. (2012). Detecting representations of recent and remote autobiographical memories in vmPFC and hippocampus. *Journal of Neuroscience, 32,* 16982–16991.

Boring, E. G. (1942). *Sensation and perception in the history of experimental psychology.* New York: Appleton-Century-Crofts.

Bosman, C. A., Schoffelen, J-M., Brunet, N., Oostenveld, R., Bastos, A. M., Womelsdorf, T., et al. (2012). Attentional stimulus selection through selective synchronization between monkey visual areas. *Neuron, 75,* 875–888.

Bowden, E. M., Jung-Beeman, M., Fleck, J., & Kounios, J. (2005). New approaches to demystifying insight. *Trends in Cognitive Sciences, 9,* 322–328.

Bower, G. G., & Winzenz, D. (1970). Comparison of associative learning strategies. *Psychonomic Science, 20,* 119–120.

Bower, G. H., Black, J. B., & Turner, T. J. (1979). Scripts in memory for text. *Cognitive Psychology, 11,* 177–220.

Bower, G. H., Clark, M. C., Lesgold, A. M., & Winzenz, D. (1969). Hierarchical retrieval schemes in recall of categorized word lists. *Journal of Verbal Learning and Verbal Behavior, 8,* 323–343.

Bower, G. H., & Winzenz, D. (1970). Comparison of associative learning strategies. *Psychonomic Science, 20,* 119–120.

Brady, T. F., Konkie, T., & Alvarez, G. A. (2011). A review of visual memory capacity: Beyond individual items and toward structured representations. *Journal of Vision, 11(5),* 1–34.

Branigan, H. P., Pickering, M. J., & Cleland, A. A. (2000). Syntactic co-ordination in dialogue. *Cognition, 75,* B13–B25.

Bransford, J. D., & Johnson, M. K. (1972). Contextual prerequisites for understanding: Some investigations of comprehension and recall. *Journal of Verbal Learning and Verbal Behavior, 11,* 717–726.

Bransford, J. D., & Johnson, M. K. (1973). Consideration of some problems of comprehension. In W. C. Chase (Ed.), *Visual information processing* (pp. 383–438). New York: Academic Press.

Brennan, S. E., Galati, A., & Kuhlen, A. K. (2010). Two minds, one dialog: Coordinating speaking and understanding. *Psychology of Learning and Motivation, 53,* 301–344.

Bressler, S. L., & Menon, V. (2010). Large-scale brain networks in cognition: emerging methods and principles. *Trends in Cognitive Sciences, 14,* 277–290.

Brewer, J. A., Worhunsky, P. D., Gray, J. R., Tang, Y.-Y., Weber, J., & Kober, H. (2011). Meditation experience is associated with differences in default mode network activity and connectivity. *Proceedings of the National Academy of Sciences, 108,* 20254–20259.

Brewer, W. F. (1977). Memory for the pragmatic implication of sentences. *Memory & Cognition, 5,* 673–678.

Brewer, W. F., & Treyens, J. C. (1981). Role of schemata in memory for places. *Cognitive Psychology, 13,* 207–230.

Broadbent, D. E. (1958). *Perception and communication.* London: Pergamon Press.

Broca, P. (1861). Sur le volume et al forme du cerveau suivant les individus et suivant les races. *Bulletin Societé d'Anthropologie Paris, 2,* 139–207, 301–321, 441–446. (See psychclassics.yorku.ca for translations of portions of this paper.)

Brooks, L. (1968). Spatial and verbal components of the act of recall. *Canadian Journal of Psychology, 22,* 349–368.

Brown, J. (1958). Some tests of the decay theory of immediate memory. *Quarterly Journal of Experimental Psychology, 10,* 12–21.

Brown, R., & Kulik, J. (1977). Flashbulb memories. *Cognition, 5,* 73–99.

Brown-Schmidt, S., & Hanna, J. E. (2011). Talking in another person's shoes: Incremental perspective-taking in language processing. *Dialogue and Discourse, 2,* 11–33.

Brunet, A., Orr, S. P., Tremblay, J. Robertson, K., Nader, K., & Pitman, R K. (2008). Effect of post-retrieval propranolol on psychophysiologic responding during subsequent script-driven traumatic imagery in post-traumatic stress disorder. *Journal of Psychiatric Research, 42,* 503–506.

Buciarelli, M., & Johnson-Laird, P. N. (1999). Strategies in syllogistic reasoning. *Cognitive Science, 23,* 247–303.

Buckingham, G., Goodale, M. A., White, J. A., & Westwood, D. A. (2016). Equal-magnitude size-weight illusions experienced within and between object categories. *Journal of Vision, 16,* 1–9.

Buhle, J. T., Stevens, B. L., Friedman, J. J., & Wager, T. D. (2012). Distraction and placebo: Two separate routes to pain control. *Psychological Science, 23,* 246–253.

Burton, A. M., Young, A. W., Bruce, V., Johnston, R. A., & Ellis, A. W. (1991). Understanding covert recognition. *Cognition, 39,* 129–166.

Buschman, T. J. and Kastner, S. (2015). From behavior to neural dynamics: An integrated theory of attention. *Neuron, 88,* 127–144.

Butterworth, B., Shallice, T., & Watson, F. L. (1990). Short-term retention without short-term memory. In G. Vallar & T. Shallice (Eds.), *Neuropsychological impairments of short-term memory* (pp. 187–213). Cambridge, UK: Cambridge University Press.

Cabeza, R., & Nyberg, L. (2000). Imaging cognition II: An empirical review of 275 PET and fMRI studies. *Journal of Cognitive Neuroscience, 12*, 1–47.

Cabeza, R., Prince, S. E., Daselaar, S. M., Greenberg, D. L., Budde, M., Dolcos, F., et al. (2004). Brain activity during episodic retrieval of autobiographical and laboratory events: An fMRI study using novel photo paradigm. *Journal of Cognitive Neuroscience, 16*, 1583–1594.

Cabeza, R., & St. Jacques, P. (2007). Functional neuroimaging of autobiographical memory. *Trends in Cognitive Sciences, 11*, 219–227.

Caggiano, V., Fogassi, L., Rizzolatti, G., Pomper, J. K., Their, P., Giese, M. A., et al. (2011). View-based encoding of actions in mirror neurons of area F5 in Macaque premotor cortex. *Current Biology, 21*, 144–148.

Cahill, L., Babinsky, R., Markowitsch, H. J., & McGaugh, J. L. (1995). The amygdala and emotional memory. *Nature, 377*, 295–296.

Cahill, L., Gorski, L., & Le, K. (2003). Enhanced human memory consolidation with post-learning stress: Interaction with the degree of arousal at encoding. *Learning & Memory, 10*, 270–274.

Cahill, L., Haier, R. J., Fallon, J., Alkire, M. T., Tang, C., Keator, D., et al. (1996). Amygdala activity at encoding correlated with long-term free recall of emotional information. *Proceedings of the National Academy of Sciences, USA, 93*, 8016–8021.

Calamante, F., Masterton, R. A. J., Tournier, J. D., Smith, R. E., Willats, L., Raffelt, D., & Connelly, A. (2013). Track-weighted functional connectivity (TW-FC): A tool for characterizing the structural-functional connections in the brain. *NeuroImage, 70*, 199–210.

Calder, A. J., Beaver, J. D., Winston, J. S., Dolan, R. J., Jenkins, R., Eger, E., et al. (2007). Separate coding of different gaze directions in the superior temporal sulcus and inferior parietal lobule. *Current Biology, 17*, 20–25.

Campbell, F. W., Kulikowski, J. J., & Levinson, J. (1966). The effect of orientation on the visual resolution of gratings. *Journal of Physiology (London), 187*, 427–436.

Cappa, S. F., Frugoni, M., Pasquali, P., Perani, D., & Zorat, F. (1998). Category specific naming impairment for artefacts: A new case. *Neurocase, 4*, 391–397.

Carpenter, S. K., Pashler, H., & Cepeda, N. J. (2009). Using tests to enhance 8th grade students' retention of U.S. History facts. *Applied Cognitive Psychology, 23*, 760–771.

Carrasco, M., Ling, S., & Read, S. (2004). Attention alters appearance. *Nature Neuroscience, 7*, 308–313.

Carrier, L. M. (2003). College students' choices of study strategies. *Perceptual and Motor Skills, 96*, 54–56.

Carroll, D. W. (2004). *Psychology of language* (4th ed.). Belmont, CA: Wadsworth.

Cartwright-Finch, U., & Lavie, N. (2007). The role of perceptual load in inattentional blindness. *Cognition, 102*, 321–340.

Cashdollar, N., Malecki, J., Rugg-Gunn, F. J., Duncan, J. S., Lavie, N., & Duzel E. (2009). Hippocampus-dependent and –independent theta-networks of active maintenance. *Proceedings of the National Academy of Sciences, 106*, 20493–20498.

Caspers, S., Zilles, K., Laird, A. R., & Eickhoff, S. B. (2010). ALE meta-analysis of action observation and imitation in the human brain. *NeuroImage, 50*, 1148–1167.

Castelhano, M. S., & Henderson, J. M. (2008). Stable individual differences across images in human saccadic eye movements. *Canadian Journal of Experimental Psychology, 62*, 1–14.

Catrambone, R., & Holyoak, K. J. (1989). Overcoming contextual limitations on problem-solving transfer. *Journal of Experimental Psychology: Learning, Memory, and Cognition, 15*, 1147–1156.

Cattaneo, L., & Rizzolatti, G. (2009). The mirror neuron system. *Neurological Review, 66*, 557–560.

Chalmers, D., & Reisberg, D. (1985). Can mental images be ambiguous? *Journal of Experimental Psychology: Human Perception and Performance, 11*, 317–328.

Chalupa, L. M. & Werner, J. S. (Eds.) (2003). *The visual neurosciences.* Cambridge, MA: MIT Press.

Chan, J. C. K., & McDermott, K. B. (2006). Remembering pragmatic inferences. *Applied Cognitive Psychology, 20*, 633–639.

Chapman, L. J., & Chapman, J. P. (1969). Genesis of popular but erroneous psychodiagnostic observations. *Journal of Abnormal Psychology, 74*, 272–280.

Charman, S. D., Wells, G. L., & Joy, S. W. (2011). The dud effect: Adding highly dissimilar fillers increases confidence in lineup identifications. *Law and Human Behavior, 35*, 479–500.

Chase, W. G., & Simon, H. A. (1973a). Perception in chess. *Cognitive Psychology, 4*, 55–81.

Chase, W. G., & Simon, H. A. (1973b). The mind's eye in chess. In W. G. Chase (Ed.), *Visual information processing.* New York: Academic Press.

Chatterjee, A. (2010). Disembodying cognition. *Language and Cognition, 2*, 79–116.

Cheng, P. W., & Holyoak, K. J. (1985). Pragmatic reasoning schemas. *Cognitive Psychology, 17*, 391–416.

Cherry, E. C. (1953). Some experiments on the recognition of speech, with one and with two ears. *Journal of the Acoustical Society of America, 25*, 975–979.

Chi, M. T. H., Feltovich, P. J., & Glaser, R. (1981). Categorization and representation of physics problems by experts and novices. *Cognitive Science, 5*, 121–152.

Chi, M. T. H., Glaser, R., & Rees, E. (1982). Expertise in problem solving. In R. J. Sternberg (Ed.), *Advances in the psychology of human intelligence.* Hillsdale, NJ: Erlbaum.

Chi, R. P., & Snyder, A. W., (2012). Brain stimulation enables the solution of an inherently difficult problem. *Neuroscience Letters, 515*, 121–124.

Chklovskii, D. B., Mel, B. W., & Svoboda, K. (2004). Cortical rewiring and information storage. *Nature, 431*, 782–788.

Chomsky, N. (1957). *Syntactic structures.* The Hague, Netherlands: Mouton.

Chomsky, N. (1959). A review of Skinner's *Verbal Behavior. Language, 35*, 26–58.

Christensen, B. T., & Schunn, C. D. (2007). The relationship of analogical distance to analogical function and pre-inventive structure: The case of engineering design. *Memory and* Cognition, 35, 29–38.

Christoff, K., Gordon, A. M., Smallwood, J., Smith, R., & Schooler, J. W. (2009). Experience sampling during fMRI reveals default network and executive system contributions to mind wandering. *Proceedings of the National Academy of Sciences, 106*, 8719–8724.

Chrysikou, E. G., & Weisberg, R. W. (2005). Following the wrong footsteps: Fixation effects of pictorial examples in a design problem-solving task. *Journal of Experimental Psychology: Learning, Memory, and Cognition, 31*, 1134–1148.

Chu, S., & Downes, J. J. (2002). Proust nose best: Odors and better cues of autobiographical memory. *Memory & Cognition, 30(4)*, 511–518.

Cichy, R. M., Heinzle, J., & Haynes, J.-D. (2012). Imagery and perception share cortical representations of content and location. *Cerebral Cortex, 22*, 372–380.

Clare, L., & Jones, R. S. P. (2008). Errorless learning in the rehabilitation of memory impairment: a critical review. *Neuropsychology Review, 18*, 1–23.

Clarey, C. (2014). Their minds have seen the glory. *New York Times,* February 23. Sports Sunday, page 1.

Clark, A. (2013). Whatever next? Predictive brains, situated agents, and the future of cognitive science. *Behavioral and Brain Sciences, 36*, 181–253.

Clark, H. H. (1996). *Using language.* Cambridge: Cambridge University Press.

Clark, H. H., & Van der Wege, M. M. (2002). Psycholinguistics. In H. Pashler & S. Yantis (Eds.), *Stevens' handbook of experimental psychology* (3rd ed., pp. 209–259). New York: Wiley.

Coley, J. D., Medin, D. L., & Atran, S. (1997). Does rank have its privilege? Inductive inferences within folkbiological taxonomies. *Cognition, 64*, 73–112.

Collins, A. M., & Quillian, M. R. (1969). Retrieval time from semantic memory. *Journal of Verbal Learning and Verbal Behavior, 8*, 240–247.

Colloca, L., & Benedetti, F. (2005). Placebos and painkillers: Is mind as real as matter? *Nature Reviews Neuroscience, 6*, 545–552.

Colzato, L. S., Ozturk, A., & Hommel, B. (2012). Meditate to create: the impact of focused-attention and open-monitoring training on convergent and divergent thinking. *Frontiers in Psychology, 3*, Article 116.

Conrad, C. (1972). Cognitive economy in semantic memory. *Journal of Experimental Psychology, 92*, 149–154.

Conrad, R. (1964). Acoustic confusion in immediate memory. *British Journal of Psychology, 55*, 75–84.

Conrad, R. (1964). Acoustic confusion in immediate memory. *British Journal of Psychology, 92*, 149–154.

Conway, M. A. (1996). Autobiographical memory. In E. L. Bjork & R. A. Bjork (Eds.), *Handbook of perception and cognition: Vol. 10. Memory* (2nd ed., pp. 165–194). New York: Academic Press.

Cook, R., Bird, G., Catmur, C., Press, C., Heyes, C. (2014). Mirror neurons: From origin to function. *Behavioral and Brain Sciences, 37*, 177–241.

Coons, P. M., & Milstein, V. (1992). Psychogenic amnesia: A clinical investigation of 25 cases. *Dissociation, 5*, 73–79.

Coppola, D. M., White, L. E., Fitzpatrick, D., & Purves, D. (1998). Unequal distribution of cardinal and oblique contours in ferret visual cortex. *Proceedings of the National Academy of Sciences, 95*, 2621–2623.

Corballis, M. C. (2017). Language evolution: A changing perspective. *Trends in Cognitive Sciences, 21*, 229–236.

Corkin, S. (2002). What's new with the amnesic patient H.M.? (2002). *Nature Reviews Neuroscience, 3*, 1–8.

Cosmides, L., & Tooby, J. (1992). Cognitive adaptations for social exchange. In J. H. Barkow, L. Cosmides, & J. Tooby (Eds.), *The adapted mind* (pp. 179–228). Oxford, UK: Oxford University Press.

Cowan, N. (2001). The magical number 4 in short-term memory: A reconsideration of mental storage capacity. *Behavioral Brain Sciences, 24*, 87–185.

Craik, F. I. M. (2002). Levels of processing: Past, present… and future? *Memory, 10*, 5–6.

Craik, F. I. M., & Lockhart, R. S. (1972). Levels of processing: A framework for memory research. *Journal of Verbal Learning and Verbal Behavior, 11*, 671–684.

Craik, F. I. M., & Tulving, E. (1975). Depth of processing and retention of words in episodic memory. *Journal of Experimental Psychology: General, 104*, 268–294.

Craver-Lemley, C., & Reeves, A. (1992). How visual imagery interferes with vision. *Psychological Review, 99*, 633–649.

Cree, G. S., & McRae, K. (2003). Analyzing the factors underlying the structure and computation of the meaning of *chipmunk, cherry, cheese,* and *cello* (and many other such concrete nouns). *Journal of Experimental Psychology: General, 132,* 163–201.

Crick, F. (1995). The impact of Linus Pauling on molecular biology. *The Pauling Symposium,* Special Collections, The Valley Library, Oregon State University.

Crook, T. H., & Adderly, B. (1998). *The memory cure.* New York: Simon & Schuster.

Cukur, T., Nishimoto, S, Huth, A. G., & Gallant, J. I. (2013). Attention during natural vision warps semantic representation across the human brain. *Nature Neuroscience, 16 (6),* 763–770.

Currey, M. (2013). *Daily rituals: How artists work.* New York: Knopf.

Curtis, C. E., & D'Esposito, M. (2003). Persistent activity in the prefrontal cortex during working memory. *Trends in Cognitive Sciences, 7,* 415–423.

Daneman, M., & Carpenter, P. A. (1980). Individual differences in working memory and reading. *Journal of Verbal Learning and Verbal Behavior, 19,* 450–466.

D'Argembeau, A., & Van der Linden, M. (2004). Phenomenal characteristics associated with projecting oneself back into the past and forward into the future: Influence of valence and temporal distance. *Consciousness and Cognition, 13,* 844–858.

Daneman, M., & Carpenter, P. A. (1980). Individual differences in working memory and reading. *Journal of Verbal Learning and Verbal Behavior, 19,* 450–466.

Danziger, S., Levav, J., & Avanim-Pesso, L. (2011). Extraneous factors in judicial decisions. *Proceedings of the National Academy of Sciences, 108,* 6889–6892.

Darwin, C. J., Turvey, M. T., & Crowder, R. G. (1972). An auditory analogue of the Sperling partial report procedure: Evidence for brief auditory storage. *Cognitive Psychology, 3,* 255–267.

De Dreu, C. K. W., Nijstad, B. A., Bass, M., Wolsink, I., & Roskes, M. (2012). Working memory benefits creative insight, musical improvisation, and original ideation through maintained task-focused attention. *Personality and Social Psychology Bulletin, 38(5),* 656–669.

Deese, J. (1959). On the prediction of occurrence of particular verbal intrusions in immediate recall. *Journal of Experimental Psychology, 58,* 17–22.

DeGroot, A. (1965). *Thought and choice in chess.* The Hague, Netherlands: Mouton

Della Sala, S., Gray, C., Baddeley, A., Allamano, N., & Wilson, L. (1999). Attention span: A tool for unwelding visuo-spatial memory. *Neuropsychologia, 37,* 1189–1199.

Denes-Raj, V., & Epstein, S. (1994). Conflict between intuitive and rational processing: When people behave against their better judgment. *Journal of Personality and Social Psychology, 66,* 819–829.

De Neys, W. (2006). Automatic-heuristic and executive-analytic processing during reasoning: Chronometric and dual-task considerations. *Quarterly Journal of Experimental Psychology, 59,* 1070–1010.

DeRenzi, E., Liotti, M., & Nichelli, P. (1987). Semantic amnesia with preservation of autobiographic memory: A case report. *Cortex, 23,* 575–597.

DeRenzi, E., & Spinnler, H. (1967). Impaired performance on color tasks inpatients with hemispheric lesions. *Cortex, 3,* 194–217.

Deutsch, D. (2010). Speaking in tones. *Scientific American Mind,* July-August, 2010, 36–43.

Deutsch, J. A., & Deutsch, D. (1963). Attention: Some theoretical considerations. *Psychological Review, 70,* 80–90.

DeValois, R. L., Yund, E. W., & Hepler, N. (1982). The orientation and direction selectivity of cells in macaque visual cortex. *Vision Research, 22,* 531–544.

DeVreese, L. P. (1991). Two systems for colour-naming defects: Verbal disconnection vs. colour imagery disorder. *Neuropsychologia, 29,* 1–18.

Dewar, M. T., Cowan, N., & Della Sala, S. (2007). Forgetting due to retroactive interference: A fusion of Muller and Pilecker's (1900) early insights into everyday forgetting and recent research on anterograde amnesia. *Cortex, 43,* 616–634.

Dick, F., Bates, E., Wulfeck, B., Utman, J. A., Dronkers, N., & Gernsbacher, M. A. (2001). Language deficits, localization, and grammar: Evidence for a distributive model of language breakdown in aphasic patients and neurologically intact individuals. *Psychological Review, 108,* 759–768.

Dingus, T. A., Klauer, S. G., Neale, V. L., Petersen, A., Lee, S. E., Sudweeks, J., et al. (2006). *The 100-Car Naturalistic Driving Study: Phase II. Results of the 100-car field experiment* (Interim Project Report for DTNH22-00-C-07007, Task Order 6; Report No. DOT HS 810 593). Washington, DC: National Highway Traffic Safety Administration.

di Pelligrino, G., Fadiga, L., Fogassi, L., Gallese, V., & Rizzolatti, G. (1992). Understanding motor events: a neurophysiological study. *Experimental Brain Research, 91,* 176–180.

Dolcos, F., LaBar, K. S., & Cabeza, R. (2005). Remembering one year later: Role of the amygdala and the medial temporal lobe memory system in retrieving emotional memories. *Proceedings of the National Academy of Sciences, 102,* 2626–2631.

Donders, F. C. (1969). Over de snelheid van psychische processen [Speed of mental processes]. Onderzoekingen gedann in het Psyciologish Laboratorium der Utrechtsche Hoogeschool (W. G. Koster, Trans.). In W. G. Koster (Ed.), Attention and performance II. *Acta Psychologica, 30,* 412–431. (Original work published 1868.)

Douglass, A. B., Neuschatz, J. S., Imrich, J., & Wilkinson, M. (2010). Does post-identification feedback affect evaluations of eyewitness testimony and identification procedures? *Law & Human Behavior, 34,* 282–294.

Downing, P. E., Jiang, Y., Shuman, M., & Kanwisher, N. (2001). Cortical area selective for visual processing of the human body. *Science, 293,* 2470–2473.

Dravida, S., Saxe, R., & Bedny, M. (2013). People can understand descriptions of motion without activating visual motion brain regions. *Frontiers in Psychology, 4,* Article 537, 1–14.

Duffy, S. A., Morris, R. K., & Rayner, K. (1988). Lexical ambiguity and fixation times in reading. *Journal of Memory and Language, 27,* 429–446.

Dunbar, K. (1998). Problem solving. In W. Bechtel & G. Graham (Eds.), *A companion to cognitive science* (pp. 289–298). London: Blackwell.

Dunbar, K. (1999). How scientists build models: Invivo science as a window on the scientific mind. In L. Magnani, N. Nersessian, & P. Thagard (Eds.), *Model-based reasoning in scientific discovery* (pp. 89–98). New York: Plenum.

Dunbar, K. (2001). The analogical paradox: Why analogy is so easy in naturalistic settings yet so difficult in the psychological laboratory. In D. Gentner, K. J. Holyoak, & B. Kokinov (Eds.), *Analogy: Perspectives form cognitive science.* Cambridge, MA: MIT Press.

Dunbar, K. (2002). Science as a category: Implications of *In Vivo* science for theories of cognitive development, scientific discovery, and the nature of science. In P. Caruthers, S. Stich, & M. Siegel (Eds.). *New Directions in Scientific and Technical Thinking.* Hillsdale, NJ: Lawrence Erlbaum.

Dunbar, K., & Blanchette, I. (2001). The *in vivo/in vitro* approach to cognition: The case of analogy. *Trends in Cognitive Sciences, 5,* 334–339.

Duncker, K. (1945). On problem solving. *Psychological Monographs 58(270).*

Dunlosky, J., Rawson, K. A., Marsh, E. J., Nathan, M. J., & Willingham, D. T. (2013). Improving students' learning and comprehension: Promising directions from cognitive and educational psychology. *Psychological Science in the Public Interest, 14,* 4–58.

Duzel, E., Cabeza, R., Picton, T. W., Yonelinas, A. P., Scheich, H., Heinze, H.-J., et al. (1999). Task-related and item-related brain processes of memory retrieval. *Proceedings of the National Academy of Sciences, USA, 96,* 1794–1799.

DvorakUncensored (2007) Removing a cork from inside a wine bottle trick. *You Tube.*

Dyson, F. J. (2012). Is science mostly driven by ideas or by tools? *Science, 338,* 1426–1427.

Ebbinghaus, H. (1913). *Memory: A contribution to experimental psychology* (Henry A. Ruger & Clara E. Bussenius, Trans.). New York: Teachers College, Columbia University. (Original work, *Über das Gedächtnis,* published 1885.)

Egan, D. E., & Schwartz, B. J. (1979). Chunking in recall of symbolic drawings. *Memory and Cognition, 7,* 149–158.

Eich, E. (1995). Searching for mood dependent memory. *Psychological Science, 6,* 67–75.

Eich, E., & Metcalfe, J. (1989). Mood dependent memory for internal vs. external events. *Journal of Experimental Psychology: Learning, Memory and Cognition, 15,* 443–455.

Eklund, A., Nichols, T. E., & Knutsson, H. (2016). Cluster failure: Why fMRI inferences for spatial extent have inflated false-positive rates. *Proceedings of the National Academy of Sciences, 113,* 7900–7905.

El Haj, M., Clement, S., Fasotti, L., & Allain, P. (2013). Effects of music on autobiographical verbal narration in Alzheimer's disease. *Journal of Neurolinguistics, 26,* 691–700.

El Haj, M., Fasotti, L., & Allain, P. (2012). The involuntary nature of music-evoked autobiographical memories in Alzheimer's disease. *Consciousness and Cognition, 21,* 238–246.

Ellamil, M., Dobson, C., Beeman, M., & Christoff, K. (2012). Evaluative and generative modes of thought during the creative process. *Neuroimage, 59,* 1783–1794.

Emberson, L. L., Lupyan, G., Goldstein, M. H., & Spivey, M. J. (2010). Overheard cell-phone conversations: When less speech is more distracting. *Psychological Science, 21,* 1383–1388.

Epstein, R., Harris, A., Stanley, D., & Kanwisher, N. (1999). The parahippocampal place area: Recognition, navigation, or encoding? *Neuron, 23,* 115–125.

Ericsson, J., Vogel, E. K., Lansner, A., Bergstrom, F., & Nyberg, L. (2015). Neurocognitive architecture of working memory. *Neuron, 88,* 33–46.

Ericsson, K. A., Chase, W. G., & Falloon, F. (1980). Acquisition of a memory skill. *Science, 208,* 1181–1182.

Ericsson, K. A., & Simon, H. A. (1993). *Protocol analysis.* Cambridge, MA: MIT Press.

Evans, J. St. B. T., Barston, J., & Pollard, P. (1983). On the conflict between logic and belief in syllogistic reasoning. *Memory and Cognition, 11,* 295–306.

Evans, J. St. B. T., & Curtis-Holmes, J. (2005). Rapid responding increases belief bias: Evidence for the dual-process theory of reasoning *Thinking & Reasoning, 11,* 382–389.

Evans, J. St. B. T., & Stanovich, K. E. (2013). Dual-process theories of higher cognition: Advancing the debate. *Perspectives on Psychological Science, 8,* 223–241.

Evans, V. (2017) *The emoji code.* New York: Picador.

Farah, M. J. (1985). Psychophysical evidence for a shared representational medium for mental images and percepts. *Journal of Experimental Psychology: General, 114,* 91–103.

Farah, M. J. (1988). Is visual imagery really visual? Overlooked evidence from neuropsychology. *Psychological Review, 95,* 307–317.

Farah, M. J. (2000). The neural basis of mental imagery. In M. Gazzaniga (Ed.), *The cognitive neurosciences* (2nd ed., pp. 965–974). Cambridge, MA: MIT Press.

Farah, M. J., Levine, D. N., & Calvanio, R. (1988). A case study of mental imagery deficit. *Brain and Cognition, 8,* 147–164.

Farah, M. J., O'Reilly, R. C., & Vecera, S. P. (1993). Dissociated overt and covert recognition as an emergent property of a lesioned neural network. *Psychological Review, 100,* 571–588.

Fazio, L., Brashier, N. M., Payne, B. K., Marsh, E. J. (2015). Knowledge does not protect against illusory truth. *Journal of Experimental Psychology: General, 144(5),* 993–1002.

Fedorenko, E., Duncan, J., & Kanwisher, N. (2012). Language-selective and domain-general regions lie side by side within Broca's area. *Current Biology, 22,* 2059–2062.

Fedorenko, E., McDermott, J. J., Norman-Haignere, S., & Kanwisher, N. (2012). Sensitivity to musical structure in the human brain. *Journal of Neuropshysiology, 108,* 3289–3300.

Fei-Fei, L. (2015). How we're teaching computers to understand pictures. TED talk video.

Felleman, D. J., & Van Essen, D. C. (1991). Distributed hierarchical processing in the primate cerebral cortex. *Cerebral Cortes, 1,* 1–47.

Finke, R. A. (1990). *Creative imagery: Discoveries and inventions in visualization.* Hillsdale, NJ: Erlbaum.

Finke, R. A. (1995). Creative insight and preinventive forms. In R. J. Sternberg & J. E. Davidson (Eds.), *The nature of insight* (pp. 255–280). Cambridge, MA: MIT Press.

Finke, R. A., Pinker, S., & Farah, M. J. (1989). Reinterpreting visual patterns in visual imagery. *Cognitive Science, 13,* 51–78.

Finn, E. S., Shin, X., Scheinost, D., Rosenberg, M. D., Huang, J., Chun, M. M., Papademetris, X., & Constable, R. T. (2015). Functional connectome fingerprinting: Identifying individuals using patterns of brain connectivity. *Nature Neuroscience, 18,* 1664–1671.

Finniss, D. G., & Benedetti, F. (2005). Mechanisms of the placebo response and their impact on clinical trials and clinical practice. *Pain, 114,* 3–6.

Fischer, M. H., & Zwaan, R. A. (2008). Embodied language: A review of the role of the motor system in language comprehension. *Quarterly Journal of Experimental Psychology, 61,* 825–850.

Fischer, S., & Born, J. (2009). Anticipated reward enhances offline learning during sleep. *Journal of Experimental Psychology: Learning, Memory & Cognition, 35,* 1586–1593.

Fischl, B., & Dale, A. M. (2000). Measuring the thickness of the human cerebral cortex from magnetic resonance images. *Proceedings of the National Academy of Sciences, 97,* 11050–11055.

Fisher, R. P., Schreiber, C., Rivard, J., & Hirn, D. (2013). Interviewing witnesses. In T. Perfect & S. Lindsay (Eds.), *The Sage handbook of applied memory.* London: Sage.

Fitch, W. T., & Martins, M. D. (2014). Hierarchical processing in music, language, and action: Lashley revisited. *Annals of the New York Academy of Sciences, 1316,* 87–104.

Fitzpatrick, C., Archambault, I., Janosz, M., & Pagani, L. S. (2015). Early childhood working memory forecasts high school dropout risk. *Intelligence, 53,* 160–165.

Fleck, J. I., & Weisberg, R. W. (2013). Insight versus analysis: Evidence for diverse methods in problem solving. *Journal of Cognitive Psychology, 25,* 436–463.

Flourens, M. J. P. (1824). Researches experimentales sur les proprieties et les fonctions du systeme nerveux, sans les animaux vertebres. Paris: Chez Crevot, Vol. 26, p. 20.

Forgassi, L., Ferri, P.F., Gesierih, B., Rozzi, S., Chersi, F., & Riizzolatti, G. (2005). Parietal lobe: From action organization to intention understanding. *Science, 308,* 662–667.

Fox, K. C. R., Nijeboer, S., Dixon, M. L., Floman, J. L., Ellamil, M., Rumak, S. P., Sedlmeier, P., & Christoff, K. (2014). Is meditation associated with altered brain structure? A systematic review and meta-analysis of morphometric neuroimaging in meditation practitioners. *Neuroscience and Biobehavioral Reviews, 43,* 48–73.

Fox, P. T. (1993). Human brain mapping: A convergence of disciplines. *Human Brain Mapping, 1,* 1–2.

Frank, J. (1930). *Law and the modern mind.* New York: Brentano's.

Frase, L. T. (1975). Prose processing. In G. H. Bower (Ed.), *The psychology of learning and motivation* (Vol. 9). New York: Academic Press.

Frazier, L. (1979). *On Comprehending Sentences: Syntactic Parsing Strategies.* PhD Thesis. University of Massachusetts. Indiana University Linguistics Club.

Frazier, L. (1987). Sentence processing: A tutorial review. In M. Coltheart (Ed.), *Attention and performance: Vol. XII. The psychology of reading* (pp. 559–586). Hove, UK: Erlbaum.

Fredrick, S. (2005). Cognitive reflection and decision making. *Journal of Economic Perspectives, 19(4),* 25–42.

Frensch, P. A., & Sternberg, R. J. (1989). Expertise and intelligent thinking: When is it worse to know better? In R. J. Sternberg (Ed.), *Advances in the psychology of human intelligence, Vol. 5.* Hillsdale, NJ: Erlbaum.

Fried, C. B. (2008). In-class laptop use and its effects on student learning. *Computers & Education, 50,* 906–914.

Fried, T., Wilson, C., Maidment, N. T., Engel, J., Behnke, E., Fields, T. A., et al. (1999). Cerebral microdialysis combined with single-neuron and electroencephalographic recording in neurosurgical patients. *Journal of Neurosurgery, 91*, 697–705.

Friedman, N. P., Miyake, A., Robinson, J. L., & Hewitt, J. K. (2011). Developmental trajectories in toddlers' self-restraint predict individual differences in executive functions 14 years later: A behavioral genetic analysis. *Developmental Psychology, 47*, 1410–1430.

Friedman-Hill, S. R., Robertson, L. C., & Treisman, A. (1995). Parietal contributions to visual feature binding: Evidence from a patient with bilateral lesions. *Science, 269*, 853–855.

Fukuda, K., Awh, E., & Vogel, E. K. (2010). Discrete capacity limits in visual working memory. *Current Opinion in Neurobiology, 20*, 177–182.

Fuller, S., & Carrasco, M. (2006). Exogenous attention and color perception: Performance and appearance of saturation and hue. *Vision Research, 46*, 4032–4047.

Funahashi, S. (2006). Prefrontal cortex and working memory processes. *Neuroscience, 139*, 251–261.

Funahashi, S., Bruce, C. J., & Goldman-Rakic, P. S. (1989). Mnemonic coding of visual space in the primate dorsolateral prefrontal cortex. *Journal of Neurophysiology, 61*, 331–349.

Furmanski, C. S., & Engel, S. A. (2000). An oblique effect in human primary visual cortex. *Nature Neuroscience, 3*, 535–536.

Gais, S., Lucas, B., & Born, J. (2006). Sleep after learning aids memory recall. *Learning and Memory, 13*, 259–262.

Galison, P. (1997). *Image and logic.* Chicago, IL: University of Chicago Press.

Gallese, V. (2007). Before and below "theory of mind": Embodied simulation and the neural correlates of social cognition. *Philosophical Transactions of the Royal Society B, 362*, 659–669.

Gallese, V., Fadiga, L., Fogassi, L., & Rizzolatti, G. (1996). Action recognition in the premotor cortex. *Brain, 119*, 593–609.

Galton, F. (1880). Statistics of mental imagery. *Mind, 5*, 301–318.

Galton, F. (1883). *Inquiries into human faculty and its development.* London: Macmillan.

Ganis, G., Thompson, W. L., Kosslyn, S. M. (2004). Brain areas underlying visual mental imagery and visual perception: An fMRI study. *Cognitive Brain Research, 20*, 226–241.

Garcea, F. E., Dombovy, M., & Mahon, B. Z. (2013). Preserved tool knowledge in the context of impaired action knowledge: Implications for models of semantic memory. *Frontiers in Human Neuroscience, 7*, Article 120, 1–18.

Gardiner, J. M. (2001). Episodic memory and autonoetic consciousness: A first-person approach. *Philosophical Transactions of the Royal Society of London B, 356*, 1351–1361.

Garon, N., Bryson, S. E., & Smith, I. M. (2008). Executive function in preschoolers: A review using an integrative framework. *Psychological Bulletin, 134*, 31–60.

Garrod, S., & Pickering, M. J. (2015). The use of content and timing to predict turn transitions. *Frontiers in Psychology, 6*, Article 751.

Gaspar, J. M., Christie, G. J., Prime, D. J., Jolicoeur, P., & McDonald, J. J. (2016). Inability to suppress salient distractors predicts low visual working memory capacity. *Proceedings of the National Academy of Science, 113*, 3693–3698.

Gauthier, I., Skudlarski, P., Gore, J. C., & Anderson, A. W. (2000). Expertise for cars and birds recruits brain areas involved in face recognition. *Nature Neuroscience, 3*, 191–197.

Gauthier, I., Tarr, M. J., Anderson, A. W., Skudlarski, P., & Gore, J. C. (1999). Activation of the middle fusiform "face area" increases with expertise in recognizing novel objects. *Nature Neuroscience, 2*, 568–573.

Gazzola, V., van der Worp, H., Muder, T., Wicker, B., Rizzolatti, G., & Keysers, C. (2007). Aplasics born without hands mirror the goal of hand actions with their feet. *Current Biology, 17*, 1235–1240.

Geiselman, R. E., Fisher, R. P., MacKinnon, D. P., & Holland, H. L. (1986). Enhancement of eyewitness memory with the cognitive interview. *American Journal of Psychology, 99*, 385–401.

Geisler, W. S. (2008). Visual perception and statistical properties of natural scenes. *Annual Review of Psychology, 59*, 167–192.

Geisler, W. S. (2011). Contributions of ideal observer theory to vision research. *Vision Research, 51*, 771–781.

Gentner, D., & Colhoun, J. (2010). Analogical processes in human thinking and learning. In B. Glatzeder, V. Goel, & A. von Maller (Vol. Eds.), *On Thinking: Vol. 2. Towards a Theory of Thinking,* pp. 35–48. Berlin: Springer-Verlag.

Gentner, D., & Goldin-Meadow, S. (Eds.). (2003). *Language in mind.* Cambridge, MA: MIT Press.

Geshwind, N. (1964). Development of the brain and the evolution of language. *Monograph Series in Language and Linguistics, 17*, 155–169.

Gibson, J. J. (1979). *The ecological approach to visual perception.* Boston, MA: Houghton Mifflin.

Gick, M. L., & Holyoak, K. J. (1980). Analogical problem solving. *Cognitive Psychology, 12*, 306–355.

Gick, M. L., & Holyoak, K. J. (1983). Schema induction and analogical transfer. *Cognitive Psychology, 15*, 1–38.

Gierhan, S. M. E. (2013). Connections for auditory language in the human brain. *Brain & Language, 127*, 205–221.

Gigerenzer, G. (2004). Dread risk, September 11, and fatal traffic accidents. *Psychological Science, 15*, 286–287.

Gigerenzer, G. (2011). Personal reflections on theory and psychology. *Theory and Psychology, 20,* 733–743.

Gigerenzer, G., & Hoffrage, U. (1995). How to improve Bayesian reasoning without instruction: Frequency formats. *Psychological Review, 98,* 506–528.

Gigerenzer, G., & Todd, P. M. (1999). *Simple heuristics that make us smart.* Oxford, UK: Oxford University Press.

Gilboa, A., Winocur, G., Grady, C. L., Hevenor, S. J., & Moscovitch, M. (2004). Remembering our past: Functional neuroanatomy of recollection of recent and very remote personal events. *Cerebral Cortex, 14,* 1214–1225.

Glanzer, M., & Cunitz, A. R. (1966). Two storage mechanisms in free recall. *Journal of Verbal Learning and Verbal Behavior, 5,* 351–360.

Glass, A. L., & Holyoak, K. J. (1975). Alternative conceptions of semantic memory. *Cognition, 3,* 313–339.

Gleason, J. B., & Ratner, N. B. (1998). Language acquisition. In J. B. Gleason & N. B. Ratner (Eds.), *Psycholinguistics* (2nd ed., pp. 347–407). Fort Worth, TX: Harcourt.

Gleick, J. (1992). *Genius: The life and science of Richard Feynman.* New York: Pantheon.

Glickstein, M., & Whitteridge, D. (1987). Tatsuki Inouye and the mapping of the visual fields in the human cerebral cortex. *Trends in Neuroscience, 10,* 350–353.

Gobet, F., Land, P. C. R., Croker, S., Cheng, P. C.-H., Jones, G., Oliver, I., et al. (2001). Chunking mechanisms in human learning. *Trends in Cognitive Science, 5,* 236–243.

Gobbini, M. I., & Haxby, J. V. (2007). Neural systems for recognition of familiar faces. *Neuropsychologia, 45,* 32–41.

Godden, D. R., & Baddeley, A. D. (1975). Context-dependent memory in two natural environments: On land and underwater. *British Journal of Psychology, 66,* 325–331.

Goldenberg, G., Podreka, I., Steiner, M., Willmes, K., Suess, E., & Deecke, L. (1989). Regional cerebral blood flow patterns in visual imagery. *Neuropsychologia, 27,* 641–664.

Goldinger, S. D., Papesh, M. H., Barnhart, A. S., Hansen, W. A., & Hout, M. C. (2016). The poverty of embodied cognition. *Psychonomic Bulletin & Review, 23,* 959–978.

Goldin-Meadow, S. (1982). The resilience of recursion: A study of a communication system developed without a conventional language model. In E. Wanner & L. R. Gleitman (Eds.), *Language acquisition: The state of the art* (pp. 51–77). Cambridge, UK: Cambridge University Press.

Goldman, S. R., Graesser, A. C., & Van den Broek, P. (Eds.). (1999). *Narrative comprehension, causality, and coherence.* Mahwah, NJ: Erlbaum.

Goldman-Rakic, P. S. (1990). Cellular and circuit basis of working memory in prefrontal cortex of nonhuman primates. *Progress in Brain Research, 85,* 325–336.

Goldman-Rakic, P. S. (1992, September). Working memory and the mind. *Scientific American,* pp. 111–117.

Goldreich, D., & Tong, J. (2013). Prediction, postdiction, and perceptual length contraction: A Bayesian low-speed prior captures the cutaneous rabbit and related illusions. *Frontiers in Psychology, 4,* Article 221. 1–26.

Goldstein, A. G., Chance, J. E., & Schneller, G. R. (1989). Frequency of eyewitness identification in criminal cases: A survey of prosecutors. *Bulletin of the Psychonomic Society, 27,* 71–74.

Goldstone, R. L., Kersten, A., & Carvalho, P. F. (2012). Concepts and categorization. In I. B. Weiner (Ed.), *Handbook of psychology* (2nd ed., Vol. 4, pp. 607–630). Hoboken, NJ: Wiley.

Goodale, M. (2010). Action and vision. In E. B. Goldstein (Ed.), *Sage encyclopedia of perception.* Thousand Oaks, CA: Sage. Vol 1, pp. 6–11.

Graesser, A. C., & Wiemer-Hastings, K. (1999). Situation models and concepts in story comprehension. In S. R. Goldman, A. C. Graesser, & P. Van den Broek (Eds.), *Narrative comprehension, causality, and coherence* (pp. 77–92). Mahwah, NJ: Erlbaum.

Graesser, A. C., Singer, M., & Trabasso, T. (1994). Constructing inferences during narrative text comprehension. *Psychological Review, 101,* 371–395.

Graf, P., Mandler, G., & Haden, P. E. (1982). Simulating amnesic symptoms in normal subjects. *Science, 218,* 1243–1244.

Graf, P., Shimamura, A. P., & Squire, L. R. (1985). Priming across modalities and priming across category levels: Extending the domain of preserved function in amnesia. *Journal of Experimental Psychology: Learning, Memory, and Cognition, 11,* 386–396.

Grant, H., Bredahl, L. S., Clay, J., Ferrie, J., Goves, J. E., Mcdorman, T. A., et al. (1998). Context-dependent memory for meaningful material: Information for students. *Applied Cognitive Psychology, 12,* 617–623.

Greenberg, D. L., & Rubin, D. C. (2003). The neuropsychology of autobiographical memory. *Cortex, 39,* 687–728.

Gregory, E., McCloskey, M., & Landau, B. (2014). Profound loss of general knowledge in retrograde amnesia: evidence from an amnesic artist. *Frontiers in Human Neuroscience, 8,* Article 287.

Gregory, E., McCloskey, M., Ovans, Z., & Landau, B. (2016). Declarative memory and skill-related knowledge: Evidence from a case study of amnesia and implications for theories of memory. *Cognitive Neuropsychology,* http://dx.doi.org/10.1080/0264329 4.2016.1172478.

Greicius, M. D., Krasnow, B., Reiss, A. L., & Menon, V. (2003). Functional connectivity in the resting brain: A network analysis of the default mode hypothesis. *Proceedings of the National Academy of Sciences, 100,* 253–258.

Griggs, R. A., & Cox, J. R. (1982). The elusive thematic-materials effect in Wason's abstract selection task. *British Journal of Psychology, 73*, 407–420.

Grill-Spector, K., Knouf, N., & Kanwisher, N. (2004). The fusiform face area subserves face perception, not generic within-category identification. *Nature Neuroscience, 7*, 555–562.

Grimes, J. A. (1996). On the failure to detect changes in scenes across saccades. In K. Akins (Ed.) *Perception (Vancouver Studies in Cognitive Science)* (pp. 89–110). New York: Oxford University Press.

Gross, C. G. (2002). The genealogy of the "grandmother cell." *The Neuroscientist, 8*, 512–518.

Gross, C. G., Bender, D. B., & Rocha-Miranda, C. E. (1969). Visual receptive fields of neurons in inferotemporal cortex of the monkey. *Science, 166*, 1303–1306.

Gross, C. G., Rocha-Miranda, C. E., & Bender, D. B. (1972). Visual properties of neurons in inferotemporal cortex of the macaque. *Journal of Neurophysiology, 5*, 96–111.

Guariglia, C., Padovani, A., Pantano, P., & Pizzamiglio, L. (1993). Unilateral neglect restricted to visual imagery. *Nature, 364*, 235–237.

Guilford, J. (1956). The structure of intellect. *Psychological Bulletin, 53*, 267–293.

Gurung, R. A. R., Weidert, J., & Jeske, A. (2010). Focusing on how students study. *Journal of the Scholarship of Teaching and Learning, 10*, 28–35.

Haigney, D., & Westerman, S. J. (2001). Mobile (cellular) phone use and driving: A critical review of research methodology. *Ergonomics, 11*, 132–143.

Hamann, S. B., Ely, T. D., Grafton, S. T., & Kilts, C. D. (1999). Amygdala activity related to enhanced memory for pleasant and aversive stimuli. *Nature Neuroscience, 2*, 289–293.

Hamilton, D. L. (1981). Illusory correlation as a basis for stereotyping.

In D. L. Hamilton (Ed.), *Cognitive processes in stereotyping and intergroup behavior*. Hillsdale, NJ: Erlbaum.

Harmelech, T., & Malach, R. (2013). Neurocognitive biases and the patterns of spontaneous correlations in the human cortex. *Trends I Cognitive Sciences, 17*, 606–615.

Harrison, S. A., & Tong, F. (2009). Decoding reveals the contents of visual working memory in early visual areas. *Nature, 458*, 632–635.

Hartline, H. K. (1940). The receptive fields of the optic nerve fibers. *American Journal of Physiology, 130*, 690–699.

Hassabis, D., Kumaran, D., Vann, S. D., & Maguire, E. A. (2007). Patients with hippocampal amnesia cannot imagine new experiences. *Proceedings of the National Academy of Sciences, 104*, 1726–1731.

Hauk, O., Johnsrude, I., & Pulvermuller, F. (2004). Somatotopic representation of action words in human motor and premotor cortex. *Neuron, 41*, 301–307.

Haviland, S. E., & Clark, H. H. (1974). What's new? Acquiring new information as a process in comprehension. *Journal of Verbal Learning and Verbal Behavior, 13*, 512–521.

Haxby, J. V., Hoffman, E. A., & Gobbini, M. I. (2000). The distributed human neural system for face perception. *Trends in Cognitive Science, 46*, 223–233.

Hayes, J. R. (1978). *Cognitive psychology*. Homewood, IL: Dorsey Press.

Hayhoe, M., & Ballard, C. (2005). Eye movements in natural behavior. *Trends in Cognitive Sciences, 9*, 188–194.

Hebb, D. O. (1948). *Organization of behavior*. New York: Wiley.

Hecaen, H., & Angelergues, R. (1962). Agnosia for faces (prosopagnosia). *Archives of Neurology, 7*, 92–100.

Heffner, C. C. & Slevc, R. (2015). Prosodic structure as a parallel to musical structure. *Frontiers in Psychology, 6*, Article 1962.

Hegarty, M. (2010). Visual imagery. In E. B. Goldstein (Ed.). *Sage Encyclopedia of Perception* (pp. 1081–1085). Thousand Oaks, CA: Sage Publishers.

Helmholtz, H. von. (1866/1911). *Treatise on physiological optics* (J. P. Southall, Ed. & Trans.; 3rd ed., Vols. 2 & 3). Rochester, NY: Optical Society of America. (Original work published 1866)

Helson, H. (1933). The fundamental propositions of Gestalt psychology. *Psychological Review, 40*, 13–32.

Henkel, L. A. (2004). Erroneous memories arising from repeated attempts to remember. *Journal of Memory and Language, 50*, 26–46.

Herz, R. S., & Schooler, J. W. (2002). A naturalistic study of autobiographical memories evoked by olfactory and visual cues: Testing the Proustian hypothesis. *American Journal of Psychology, 115*, 21–32.

Hickock, G. (2009). Eight problems for the mirror neuron theory of action understanding in monkeys and humans. *Journal of Cognitive Neuroscience, 21*, 1229–1243.

Hillis, A. E., Rapp, B., Romani, C., & Caramazza, A. (1990). Selective impairment of semantics in lexical processing. *Cognitive Neuropsychology, 7*, 191–243.

Hinton, G. E., & Shallice, T. (1991). Lesioning an attractor network: Investigations of acquired dyslexia. *Psychological Review, 98*, 74–95.

Hoffman, E. J., Phelps, M. E., Mullani, N. A., Higgins, C. S., & Ter-Pogossian, M. M. (1976). Design and performance characteristics of a whole-body positron transaxial tomography. *Journal of Nuclear Medicine, 17*, 493–502.

Hoffman, H. G., Doctor, J. N., Patterson, D. R., Carrougher, G. J., & Furness, T. A., III. (2000). Virtual reality as an adjunctive pain control during burn wound care in adolescent patients. *Pain, 85*, 305–309.

Hoffman, H. G., Patterson, D. R., Seibel, E., Soltani, M., Jewett-Leahy, L., & Sharar, S. R. (2008). Virtual reality pain control during burn wound debridement in the hydrotank. *Clinical Journal of Pain, 24,* 299–304.

Hoffman, P., & Lambon Ralph, M. A. (2013). Shapes, scenes and sounds: Quantifying the full multi-sensory basis of conceptual knowledge. *Neuropsychologia, 51,* 14–25.

Hofmann, W., Schmeichel, B. J., & Baddeley, A. D. (2012). Executive functions and self-regulation. *Trends in Cognitive Sciences, 16,* 174–180.

Holmes, G., & Lister, W. T. (1916). Disturbances of vision from cerebral lesions, with special reference to the cortical representation of the macula. *Brain, 39,* 34–73.

Holyoak, K. J., & Thagard, P. (1995). Analogical mapping by constraint satisfaction. *Cognitive Science, 13,* 295–355.

Horikawa, T., & Kamitani, Y. (2017). Generic decoding of seen and imagined objects using hierarchical visual features. *Nature Communications* 8:15037/.doi: 10.1038/ncomms15037

Horowitz, J. (2017). In Italian schools, reading, writing and recognizing fake news. *New York Times,* October 18, 2017.

Horton, W. S., & Brennan, S. E. (2016). The role of metarepresentation in the production and resolution of referring expressions. *Frontiers in Psychology, 7,* Article 1111.

Howe, M. L. (2013). Memory development: implications for adults recalling childhood experiences in the courtroom. *Nature Reviews Neuroscience, 14,* 869–876.

Hubel, D. H. (1982). Exploration of the primary visual cortex, 1955–1978. *Nature, 299,* 515–524.

Hubel, D. H., & Wiesel, T. N. (1959). Receptive fields of single neurons in the cat's striate cortex. *Journal of Physiology, 148,* 574–591.

Hubel, D. H., & Wiesel, T. N. (1961). Integrative action in the cat's lateral geniculate body. *Journal of Physiology, 155,* 385–398.

Hubel, D. H., & Wiesel, T. N. (1965). Receptive fields and functional architecture in two non-striate visual areas (18 and 19) of the cat. *Journal of Neurophysiology, 28,* 229–289.

Hupbach, A., Gomez, R., Hardt, O., & Nadel, L. (2007). Reconsolidation of episodic memories: A subtle reminder triggers integration of new information. *Learning and Memory, 14,* 47–53.

Huth, A. G., deHeer, W. A., Griffiths, T. L., Theunissen, F. E., & Gallant, J. L. (2016). Natural speech reveals the semantic maps that tile human cerebral cortex. *Nature, 532,* 453–460.

Huth, A. G., Nishimoto, S., Vo, A. T., & Gallant, J. L. (2012). A continuous semantic space describes the representation of thousands of object and action categories across the human brain. *Neuron, 76,* 1210–1224.

Hyman, I. E., Jr., Husband, T. H., & Billings, J. F. (1995). False memories of childhood experiences. *Applied Cognitive Psychology, 9,* 181–197.

Iacoboni, M., Molnar-Szakacs, I., Gallese, V., Buccino, G., Mazziotta, J. C., & Rizzolatti, G. (2005). Grasping the intentions of others with one's own mirror neuron system. *PLoS Biology, 3(3),* e79.

Innocence Project (2012). *250 Exonerated: Too many wrongfully convicted.* Benjamin N. Cardozo School of Law, Yeshiva University.

Intons-Peterson, M. J. (1983). Imagery paradigms: How vulnerable are they to experimenters' expectations? *Journal of Experimental Psychology: Human Perception and Performance, 9,* 394–412.

Intons-Peterson, M. J. (1993). Imagery's role in creativity and discovery. In B. Roskos-Ewoldson, M. J. Intons-Peterson & R. E. Anderson (Eds.), *Imagery, creativity, and discovery: A cognitive perspective* (pp. 1–37). New York: Elsevier.

Isaacs, E. A., & Clark, H. H. (1987). References in conversation between experts and novices. *Journal of Experimental Psychology: General, 116,* 26–37.

Ishai, A. (2008). Let's face it: It's a cortical network. *Neuroimage, 40,* 415–419.

Ishai, A., Pessoa, L., Bikle, P. C., & Ungerleider, L. G. (2004). Repetition suppression of faces is modulated by emotion. *Proceedings of the National Academy of Sciences, 101(26),* 9827–9832.

Ishai, A., Ungerleider, L. G., Martin, A. & Haxby, J. V. (2000). The representation of objects in the human occipital and temporal cortex. *Journal of Cognitive Neuroscience, 12, Supplement 2,* 35–51.

Itti, L., & Koch, C. (2000). A saliency-based search mechanism for overt and covert shifts of visual attention. *Vision Research, 40,* 1489–1506.

Izuma, K., & Adolphs, R. (2011). The brain's rose-colored glasses. *Nature Neuroscience, 14,* 1355–1356.

Jack, F., & Hayne, H. (2007). Eliciting adults' earliest memories: Does it matter how we ask the question? *Memory, 15(6),* 647–663.

Jacoby, L. L., Kelley, C. M., Brown, J., & Jaseckko, J. (1989). Becoming famous overnight: Limits on the ability to avoid unconscious inferences of the past. *Journal of Personality and Social Psychology, 56,* 326–338.

Jalbert, A., Neath, I., Bireta, T. J., & Surprenant, A. M. (2011). When does length cause the word length effect? *Journal of Experimental Psychology: Learning, Memory, and Cognition, 37,* 338–353.

James, W. (1890). *Principles of psychology.* New York: Holt.

Janata, P., Tomic, S. T., & Rakowski, S. K. (2007). Characterisation of music-evoked autobiographical memories. *Memory, 15(8),* 845–860.

Jansson, D. G., & Smith, S. M. (1991). Design fixation. *Design Studies, 12,* 3–11.

Jefferies, E. (2013). The neural basis of semantic cognition: Converging evidence from neuropsychology, neuroimaging and TMS. *Cortex, 49*, 611–645.

Jenkins, J. J., & Russell, W. A. (1952). Associative clustering during recall. *Journal of Abnormal and Social Psychology, 47*, 818–821

Jobs, S. (2005). Stanford University commencement address.

Johnson, E. J., & Goldstein, D. (2003). Do defaults save lives? *Science, 302*, 1338–1339.

Johnson, E. J., Hershey, J., Meszaros, J., & Kunreuther, H. (1993). Framing, probability distortions, and insurance decisions. *Journal of Risk and Uncertainty, 7*, 35–51.

Johnson, K. E., & Mervis, C. B. (1997). Effects of varying levels of expertise on the basic level of categorization. *Journal of Experimental Psychology: General, 126*, 248–277.

Johnson, M. K. (2006). Memory and reality. *American Psychologist, 61*, 760–771.

Johnson, M. K., Foley, M. A., Suengas, A. G., & Raye, C. L. (1988). Phenomenal characteristics of memories for perceived and imagined autobiographical events. *Journal of Experimental Psychology: General, 117*, 371–376.

Johnson, M. K., Hashtroudi, S., & Lindsay, D. S. (1993). Source monitoring. *Psychological Bulletin, 114*, 3–28.

Johnson, M. R., & Johnson, M. K. (2014). Decoding individual natural scene representations during perception and imagery. *Frontiers in Human Neuroscience, 8*, Article 59. 1–14.

Johnson, S., & Coxon, M. (2016). Sound can enhance the analgesic effect of virtual reality. R. Soc. open sci. 3: 150567. http://dx.doi.org/10.1098/rsos.150567

Johnson-Laird, P. N. (1995). Inference and mental models. In S. E. Newstead & J. St. B. T. Evans (Eds.), *Perspectives on thinking and reasoning: Essays in honour of Peter Wason*. Hove, UK: Erlbaum.

Johnson-Laird, P. N. (1999a). Deductive reasoning. *Annual Review of Psychology, 50*, 109–135.

Johnson-Laird, P. N. (1999b). Formal rules versus mental models in reasoning. In R. Sternberg (Ed.), *The nature of cognition* (pp. 587–624). Cambridge, MA: MIT Press.

Jonides, J., Lewis, R. L., Nee, D. E., Lustig, C. A., Berman, M. G., & Moore, K. S. (2008). The mind and brain of short-term memory. *Annual Review of Psychology, 59*, 193–224.

Joordens, S. (2011). *Memory and the human lifespan*. Chantilly, VA: The Teaching Company.

Kabat-Zinn, J. (2003). Mindfulness-based interventions in context: Past, present, and future. *Clinical Psychology: Science and Practice, 10*, 144–156.

Kahneman, D. (2003). A perspective on judgment and choice. *American Psychologist, 58*, 697–720.

Kahneman, D. (2011). *Thinking fast and slow*. New York: Farrar, Straus and Giroux.

Kaldy, Z., & Sigala, N. (2017). Editorial: The cognitive neuroscience of working memory. *Frontiers in Systems Neuroscience, 11*, Article 1.

Kandel, E. R. (2001). A molecular biology of memory storage: A dialogue between genes and synapses. *Science, 294*, 1030–1038.

Kandel, E. R. (2006). *In search of memory*. New York: Norton.

Kanwisher, N. (2003). The ventral visual object pathway in humans: Evidence from fMRI. In L. M. Chalupa & J. S. Werner (Eds.), *The visual neurosciences* (pp. 1179–1190). Cambridge, MA: MIT Press.

Kanwisher, N., McDermott, J., & Chun, M. M. (1997). The fusiform face area: A module in human extrastriate cortex specialized for face perception. *Journal of Neuroscience, 17*, 4302–4311.

Kaplan, C. A., & Simon, H. A. (1990). In search of insight. *Cognitive Psychology, 22*, 374–419.

Karpicke, J. D., & Roediger, H. L. (2008). The critical importance of retrieval for learning. *Science, 319*, 966–968.

Karpicke, J. D., Butler, A. C., & Roediger, H. L. (2009). Metacognitive strategies in student learning: Do students practise retrieval when they study on their own? *Memory, 17*, 471–479.

Kassin, S. M., Drizin, S. A., Grisso, T., Gudjonsson, G. H., Leo, R. A., & Redich, A. D. (2010). Police-induced confessions: Risk factors and recommendations. *Law and Human Behavior, 34*, 3–38.

Kassin, S. M., & Kiechel, K. L. (1996). The social psychology of false confessions: Compliance, internalization, and confabulation. *Psychological Science, 7(3)*, 125–128.

Kassin, S. M. (2012). Why confessions trump innocence. *American Psychologist, 67(6)*, 431.

Kassin, S. M. (2015). The social psychology of false confessions. *Social Issues and Policy Review, 9(1)*, 25–51.

Katzner, S., Busse, L., & Treue, S. (2009). Attention to the color of a moving stimulus modulates motion-signal processing in macaque area MT: Evidence for a unified attentional system. *Frontiers in Systems Neuroscience, 3*, 1–8.

Kaufman, J. C. (2009). *Creativity 101*. New York: Springer Publishing Company.

Kaufman, S. B., & Gregoire, C. (2015). *Wired to create: Unraveling the mysteries of the creative mind*. New York: Perigee.

Kay, R. H., & Lauricella, S. (2011). Exploring the benefits and challenges of using laptop computers in higher education classrooms: A formative analysis. *Canadian Journal of Learning and Technology, 37(1)*, 1–18.

Keren, G., & Schul, Y. (2009). Two is not always better than one: A critical evaluation of two-system theories. *Perspectives on Psychological Science, 4*, 533–550.

Keri, S., Janka, Z., Benedek, G., Aszalos, P., Szatmary, B., Szirtes, G., et al. (2002). Categories, prototypes and memory systems in Alzheimer's disease. *Trends in Cognitive Sciences, 6*, 132–136.

Kermer, D. A., Driver-Linn, E., Wilson, T. D., & Gilbert, D. T. (2006). Loss aversion is an affective forecasting error. *Psychological Science, 17*, 649–653.

Kersten, D., Mamassian, P., & Yuille, A. (2004). Object perception as Bayesian inference. *Annual Review of Psychology, 55*, 271–304.

Kida, S., Josselyn, S. A., Peña de Oritz, S., Kogan, J. H., Chevere, I., Masushige, S., et al. (2002). CREB required for the stability of new and reactivated fear memories. *Nature Neuroscience, 5*, 348–355.

Kiefer, M., & Pulvermüller, F. (2012). Conceptual representation in mind and brain: Theoretical developments, current evidence and future directions. *Cortex, 48*, 805–825.

Killingsworth, M. A., & Gilbert, D. T. (2010). A wandering mind is an unhappy mind. *Science, 330*, 932.

Killingsworth, M.A. (2011). Want to be happier? Stay in the moment. TED Talk. https://ed.ted.com/lessons /want-to-be-happier-stay-in-the -moment-matt-killingsworth.

Kilner, J. M. (2011). More than one pathway to action understanding. *Trends in Cognitive Sciences, 15*, 352–357.

Kindt, M., Soeter, M., & Vervliet, B. (2009). Beyond extinction: Erasing human fear responses and preventing the return of fear. *Nature Neuroscience, 12*, 256–258.

Kleffner, D. A., & Ramachandran, V. S. (1992). On the perception of shape from shading. *Perception and Psychophysics, 52*, 18–36.

Klein, S. B., Loftus, J., & Kihlstrom, J. (2002). Memory and temporal experience: The effects of episodic memory loss on an amnesic patient's ability to remember the past and imagine the future. *Social Cognition, 20*, 353–379.

Klein, S. B., Robertson, T. E., & Delton, A. W. (2010). Facing the future:

Memory as an evolved system for planning future acts. *Memory & Cognition, 38(1)*, 13–22.

Klein, S. B., Robertson, T. E., & Delton, A. W. (2011). The future-orientation of memory: Planning as a key component mediating the high levels of recall found with survival processing. *Memory, 19*, 121–139.

Kneller, W., Memon, A., & Stevenage, S. (2001). Simultaneous and sequential lineups: Decision processes of accurate and inaccurate eye witnesses. *Applied Cognitive Psychology, 15*, 659–671.

Knoch, D., Pascual-Leone, A., Meyer, K., Treyer, V., & Fehr, E. (2006). Diminishing reciprocal fairness by disrupting the right prefrontal cortex. *Science, 314(5800)*, 829–832.

Knutson, B., Rick, S., Wimmer, G. E., Prelec, D., & Loewenstein, G. (2007). Neural predictors of purchases. *Neuron, 53(1)*, 147–156.

Koelsch, S. (2011). Toward a neural basis of music perception—a review and updated model. *Frontiers in Psychology, 2*, Article 110.

Koelsch, S. (2005). Neural substrates of processing syntax and semantics in music. *Current Opinion in Neurobiology, 15*, 207–212.

Koelsch, S., Gunter, T., Friederici, A. D., & Schroger, E. (2000). Brain indices of music processing: "Nonmusicians" are musical. *Journal of Cognitive Neuroscience, 12*, 520–541.

Koffka, K. (1935). *Principles of Gestalt psychology.* New York: Harcourt Brace.

Kohler, W. (1929). *Gestalt psychology.* New York: Liveright.

Konnikova. M. (2013). *Mastermind: How to think like Sherlock Holmes.* New York: Penguin Books.

Koppel J., & Bernsten, D. (2014). Does everything happen when you are young? Introducing the youth bias. *Quarterly Journal of Experimental Psychology, 67(3)*, 417–423.

Körding, K. P., & Wolpert, D. M. (2006). Bayesian decision theory in sensorimotor control. *Trends in Cognitive Sciences, 10*, 319–326.

Kornell, N., & Son, L. K. (2009). Learners' choices and beliefs about self-testing. *Memory, 17*, 493–501.

Kosslyn, S. M. (1973). Scanning visual images: Some structural implications. *Perception & Psychophysics, 14*, 90–94.

Kosslyn, S. M. (1978). Measuring the visual angle of the mind's eye. *Cognitive Psychology, 10*, 356–389.

Kosslyn, S. M. (1980). *Image and mind.* Cambridge, MA: Harvard University Press.

Kosslyn, S. M. (1994). *Image and brain: The resolution of the imagery debate.* Cambridge, MA: MIT Press

Kosslyn, S. M., Ball, T., & Reiser, B. J. (1978). Visual images preserve metric spatial information: Evidence from studies of image scanning. *Journal of Experimental Psychology: Human Perception and Performance, 4*, 47–60.

Kosslyn, S. M., Pascual-Leone, A., Felician, O., Camposano, S., Keenan, J. P., Thompson, W. L., et al. (1999). The role of area 17 in visual imagery: Convergent evidence form PET and rTMS. *Science, 284*, 167–170.

Kosslyn, S. M., & Thompson, W. L. (2000). Shared mechanisms in visual imagery and visual perception: Insights from cognitive neuroscience. In M. Gazzanaga (Ed.), *The cognitive neurosciences* (2nd ed., pp. 975–985). Cambridge, MA: MIT Press.

Kosslyn, S. M., Thompson, W. L., & Ganis, G. (2006). *The case for mental imagery.* Oxford, UK: Oxford University Press.

Kosslyn, S. M., Thompson, W. L., Kim, I., J., & Alpert, N. M. (1995). Topographical representations of mental images in primary visual cortex. *Nature, 378*, 496–498.

Kotabe, H. P., & Hofmann, W. (2015). On integrating the components of self-control. *Perspectives on Psychological Science, 10(5)*, 618–638.

Kotovsky, K., Hayes, J. R., and Simon, H. A. (1985). Why are some problems hard? Evidence from Tower of Hanoi. *Cognitive Psychology, 17*, 248–294.

Kounios, J., & Beeman, M. (2014). The cognitive neuroscience of insight. *Annual Review of Psychology, 65*, 71–93.

Kounios, J., Fleck, J. I., Green, D. L., Payne, L., Stevenson, J. L., Bowden, E. M., & Jong-Beeman, M. (2008). The origins of insight in resting-state brain activity. *Neuropsychologia, 46*, 281–291.

Kounios, J., Frymiare, J. L., Bowden, E. M., Fleck, J. I., Subramaniam, K., Parrish, T. B., & Jong-Beeman, M. (2006). The prepared mind: Neural activity prior to problem presentation predicts subsequent solution by sudden insight. *Psychological Science, 17*, 882–890.

Kozhevnikov, M., Kosslyn, S., & Shephard, J. (2005). Spatial versus object visualizers: A new characterization of visual cognitive style. *Memory & Cognition, 33*, 710–726.

Kozhevnikov, M., Motes, M.A., & Hegarty, M. (2007). Spatial visualization in physics problem solving. *Cognitive Science, 31*, 549–579.

Kreiman, G., Koch, C., & Fried, I. (2000). Imagery neurons in the human brain. *Nature, 408*, 357–361.

Kruglanski, A. W., & Gigerenzer, G. (2011). Intuitive and deliberative judgments are based on common principles. *Psychological Review, 118*, 97–109.

Krumhansl, C. L. (1985). Perceiving tonal structure in music. *American Scientist, 73*, 371–378.

Kuffler, S. W. (1953). Discharge patterns and functional organization of mammalian retina. *Journal of Neurophysiology, 16*, 37–68.

Kuhn, T. (1962). *The structure of scientific revolutions*. Chicago, IL: University of Chicago Press.

Kuhn, T. (1970). *The structure of scientific revolution* (2nd ed.). Chicago, IL: University of Chicago Press.

Kuperberg, G. R. (2013). The proactive comprehender: What event-related potentials tell us about the dynamics of reading comprehension. In B. Miller, L. Cutting, & P. McCardle (Eds.), *Unraveling the behavioral, neurobiological, and genetic components of reading comprehension*. Baltimore: Paul Brookes.

Kuperberg, G. R., & Jaeger, T. F. (2015). What do we mean by prediction in language comprehension? *Language, cognition and neuroscience.* 10.1080/23273798.2015.110299.

Kuznekoff, J. H., & Titsworth, S. (2013). The impact of mobile phone usage on student learning. *Communication Education, 62*, 233–252.

LaBar, K. S., & Cabeza, R. (2006). Cognitive neuroscience of emotional memory. *Nature Reviews Neuroscience, 7*, 54–64.

LaBar, K. S., & Phelps, E. A. (1998). Arousal-mediated memory consolidation: Role of the medial temporal lobe in humans. *Psychological Science, 9*, 490–493.

Lakoff, G., & Turner, M. (1989). *More than cool reason: The power of poetic metaphor*. Chicago: Chicago University Press.

Lamble, D., Kauranen, T., Laakso, M., & Summala, H. (1999). Cognitive load and detection thresholds in car following situations: Safety implications for using mobile (cellular) telephones while driving. *Accident Analysis and Prevention, 31*, 617–623.

Lambon Ralph, M. A., Howard, D., Nightingale, G., & Ellis, A. W. (1998). Are living and non-living category-specific deficits causally linked to impaired perceptual or associative knowledge? Evidence from a category-specific double dissociation. *Neurocase, 4*, 311–338.

Lambon Ralph, M. A. Jefferies, E., Patterson, K., & Rogers, T. T. (2017) The neural and computational bases of semantic cognition. *Nature Reviews Neuroscience,* online.

Lambon Ralph, M. A., Lowe, C., & Rogers, T. T. (2007). Neural basis of category-specific deficits for living things: Evidence from semantic dementia, HSVE, and a neural network model. *Brain, 130*, 1127–1137.

Lanagan-Leitzel, L. K., Skow, E., & Moore, C. M. (2015). Great expectations: perceptual challenges of visual surveillance in lifeguarding. *Applied Cognitive Psychology, 29*, 425–435.

Land, M. F., & Hayhoe, M. (2001). In what ways do eye movements contribute to everyday activities? *Vision Research, 41*, 3559–3565.

Langer, E. (2014). Personal communication, November 7, 2014, cited Kaufman, S. B., & Gregoire, C. (2015). *Wired to create: Unraveling the mysteries of the creative mind*. New York: Perigee.

Lanska, D. J. (2009). Historical perspective: Neurological advances from studies of war injuries and illnesses. *Annals of Neurology, 66*, 444–459.

Larkin, J. H., McDermott, J., Simon, D. P., & Simon, H. A. (1980). Expert and novice performance in solving physics problems. *Science, 208*, 1335–1342.

Larsson, M., & Willander, J. (2009). Autobiographical odor memory. *International Symposium on Olfaction and Taste. Annals New York Academy of Sciences, 1170*, 318–323.

Lavie, N. (2010). Attention, distraction, and cognitive control under load. *Current Directions in Psychological Science, 19*, 143–148.

Lavie, N., & Driver, J. (1996). On the spatial extent of attention in object-based visual selection. *Perception & Psychophysics, 58*, 1238–1251.

Lea, G. (1975). Chronometric analysis of the method of loci. *Journal of Experimental Psychology: Human Perception and Performance, 2*, 95–104.

Le Bihan, D., Turner, R., Zeffiro, T. A., Cuenod, A., Jezzard, P., & Bonnerdot, V. (1993). Activation of human primary visual cortex during visual recall: A magnetic resonance imaging study. *Proceedings of the National Academy of Sciences, USA, 90*, 11802–11805.

Lee, D. (2006). Neural basis of quasi-rational decision making. *Current Opinion in Neurobiology, 16,* 191–198.

Lee, D., & Seo, H. (2016). Neural basis of strategic decision making. *Trends in neurosciences, 39(1),* 40–48.

Lee, S.-H., & Baker, C. I. (2016). Multi-voxel decoding and the topography of maintained information during visual working memory. *Frontiers in Systems Neuroscience, 10, Article 2.*

Lee, S-H., Kravitz, D. J., & Baker, C. I. (2012). Disentangling visual imagery and perception of real-world objects. *Neuroimage, 59,* 4064–4073.

LePort, A. K. R., Mattfeld, A. T., Dickinson-Anson, H., Fallon, J. H., Stark, C. E. L., Kruggel, F., et al. (2012). Behavioral and neuroanatomical investigation of Highly Superior Autobiographical Memory (HSAM). *Neurobiology of Learning and Memory, 98,* 78–92.

Lerner, N., Baldwin, C, Higgins, J. S., Lee, J., & Schooler, J. (2015). Mind wandering while driving: What does it mean and what do we do about it? *Proceedings of the Human Factors and Ergonomics Society, 59th Annual Meeting.* 1686–1690.

Leshikar, E. D., Dulas, M. R., & Duarte, A. (2015). Self-referencing enhances recollection in both young and older adults. *Aging, Neuropsychology, and Cognition, 22(4),* 388–412.

Lesgold, A. M. (1988). Problem solving. In R. J. Sternberg & E. E. Smith (Eds.), *The psychology of human thoughts.* New York: Cambridge University Press.

Levelt, W. J. M. (2001). Spoken word production: A theory of lexical access. *Proceedings of the National Academy of Sciences, 98,* 13464–13471.

Levine, B., Turner, G. R., Tisserand, D., Hevenor, S. J., Graham, S. J., & McIntosh, A. R. (2004). The functional neuroanatomy of episodic and semantic autobiographical remembering: A prospective functional fMRI study. *Journal of Cognitive Neuroscience, 16,* 1633–1646.

Levinson, S. C. (2016). Turn-taking in human communication—origins and implications for language processing. *Trends in Cognitive Sciences, 20,* 6–14.

Levy, I., & Glimcher, P. W. (2013). Neuroeconomics. In H. Pashler (Ed.), *Encyclopedia of the mind* (vol. 14, pp. 565–569). Thousand Oaks, CA: SAGE Publications.

Lewis, M. (2016). *The Undoing Project: A Friendship that changed the world.* Penguin UK.

Lichtenstein, S., Slovic, P., Fischoff, B., Layman, M., & Combs, B. (1978). Judged frequency of lethal events. *Journal of Experimental Psychology: Human Learning and Memory, 4,* 551–578.

Lindsay, D. S. (1990). Misleading suggestions can impair eyewitnesses' ability to remember event details. *Journal of Experimental Psychology: Learning, Memory, and Cognition, 16,* 1077–1083.

Lindsay, D. S., & Hyman, I. E. (2017). Commentary on Brewin and Andrews. *Applied Cognitive Psychology, 31,* 37–39.

Lindsay, R. C. L., & Wells, G. L. (1980). What price justice? Exploring the relationship of lineup fairness to identification accuracy. *Law and Human Behavior, 4,* 303–313.

Lippmann, W. (1920). *Liberty and the news.* New York: Harcourt, Brace & Howe. Dover edition reprint (2010).

Lister-Landman, K. M., Domoff, S. E., & Dubow, E. F. (2015). The role of compulsive texting in adolescents' academic functioning. *Psychology of Popular Media Culture. http://dx.doi .org/10.1037/ppm0000100.* 1–15.

Loewenstein, R. J. (1991). Psychogenic amnesia and psychogenic fugue: A comprehensive review. In A. Tasman & S. M. Goldfinger, *American Psychiatric Press Review of Psychiatry* (Vol. 10, pp. 189–221). Washington, DC: American Psychiatric Press.

Loftus, E. F. (1979). *Eyewitness testimony.* Cambridge, MA: Harvard University Press.

Loftus, E. F. (1993a). Made in memory: Distortions in recollection after misleading information. In D. L. Medin (Ed.), *The psychology of learning and motivation: Advances in theory and research* (pp. 187–215). New York: Academic Press.

Loftus, E. F. (1993b). The reality of repressed memories. *American Psychologist, 38,* 518–537.

Loftus, E. F. (1998). Imaginary memories. In M. A. Conway, S. E. Gathercole, & C. Cornoldi (Eds.), *Theories of memory II* (pp. 135–145). Hove, UK: Psychology Press.

Loftus, E. F., & Palmer, J. C. (1974). Reconstruction of an automobile destruction: An example of the interaction between language and memory. *Journal of Verbal Learning and Verbal Behavior, 13,* 585–589.

Loftus, E. F., Miller, D. G., & Burns, H. J. (1978). Semantic integration of verbal information into visual memory. *Journal of Experimental Psychology: Human Learning and Memory, 4,* 19–31.

Lomber, S. G., & Malhotra, S. (2008). Double dissociation of "what" and "where" processing in auditory cortex. *Nature Neuroscience, 11,* 609–616.

Lorayne, H., & Lucas, J. (1996). *The memory book.* New York: Ballantine Books.

Lord, C. G., Ross, L., & Lepper, M. (1979). Biased assimilation and attitude polarization: The effects of prior theories on subsequently considered evidence. *Journal of Personality and Social Psychology, 46,* 1254–1266.

Lovatt, P., Avons, S. E., & Masterson, J. (2000). The word-length effect and disyllabic words. *The Quarterly Journal of Experimental Psychology, 53A,* 1–22.

Lovatt, P., Avons, S. E., & Masterson, J. (2002). Output decay in immediate serial recall: Speech time revisited. *Journal of Memory and Language, 46,* 227–243.

Lovett, M. C. (2002). Problem solving. In D. L. Medin (Ed.), *Stevens' Handbook of Experimental Psychology* (3rd ed., pp. 317–362). New York: Wiley.

Lowenstein, G., Rick, S., & Cohen, D. (2008). Neuroeconomics. *Annual Review of Psychology, 59*, 647–672.

Lubart, T. I., & Mouchiroud, C. (2003). Creativity: A source of difficulty in problem solving. In J. E. Davidson and R. J. Sternberg (Eds.), *The psychology of problem solving* (pp. 127–148). New York: Cambridge University Press.

Lucas, P. A. (1999). Context effects in lexical access: A meta-analysis. *Memory & Cognition, 27*, 385–398.

Luchins, A. S. (1942). Mechanization in problem solving—the effect of Einstellung. *Psychological Monographs, 54*(6), 195.

Luck, S. J., & Vogel, E. K. (1997). The capacity of visual working memory for features and conjunctions. *Nature, 390*, 279–281.

Luminet, O., & Curci, A. (Eds.). (2009). *Flashbulb memories: New issues and new perspectives.* Philadelphia: Psychology Press.

Lundquist, M., Rose, J., Herman, P., Brincat, S. L., Buschman, T. J., & Miller, E. K. (2016). Gamma and beta bursts underlie working memory. *Neuron, 90*, 152–164.

Luria, A. R. (1968). *The mind of a mnemonist* (L. Solotaroff, Trans.). New York: Basic Books.

Luus, C. A. E., & Wells, G. L. (1994). The malleability of eyewitness confidence: Co-witness and perseverance effects. *Journal of Applied Psychology, 79*, 714–724

MacKay, D. G. (1973). Aspects of the theory of comprehension, memory and attention. *Quarterly Journal of Experimental Psychology, 25*, 22–40.

Macmillan, M. (2002). *An odd kind of fame: Stories of Phineas Gage.* Boston, MA: MIT Press.

Maess, B., Koelsch, S., Gunter, T. C., & Friederici, A. D. (2001). Musical syntax is processed in Broca's area: an MEG study. *Nature Neuroscience, 4*, 540–545.

Maguire, E. (2014). Memory consolidation in humans: new evidence and opportunities. *Experimental Physiology, 99 (3)*, 471–486.

Mahon, B. Z., & Caramazza, A. (2011). What drives the organization of object knowledge in the brain? *Trends in Cognitive Sciences, 15*, 97–103.

Mahon, B. Z., Milleville, S. C., Negri, G. A. L., Rumiati, R. I., Caramazza, A., & Martin, A. (2007). Action-related properties shape object representations in the ventral stream. *Neuron, 55*, 507–520.

Maier, N. R. F. (1931). Reasoning in humans: II. The solution of a problem and its appearance in consciousness. *Journal of Comparative Psychology, 12*, 181–194.

Malcolm, G. L., & Shomstein, S. (2015). Object-based attention in real-world scenes. *Journal of Experimental Psychology: General, 144*, 257–263.

Malik, J. (1987). Interpreting line drawings of curved objects. *International Journal of Computer Vision, 1*, 73–103.

Malpass, R. S., & Devine, P. G. (1981). Eyewitness identification: Lineup instructions and absence of the offender. *Journal of Applied Psychology, 66*, 482–489.

Malt, B. C. (1989). An on-line investigation of prototype and exemplar strategies in classification. *Journal of Experimental Psychology: Learning, Memory and Cognition, 4*, 539–555.

Maner, J. K., & Schmidt, N. B. (2006). The role of risk avoidance in anxiety. *Behavior Theory, 37*, 181–189.

Manktelow, K. I. (1999). *Reasoning and thinking.* Hove, UK: Psychology Press.

Manktelow, K. I. (2012). *Thinking and reasoning.* New York: Psychology Press.

Mantyla, T. (1986). Optimizing cue effectiveness: Recall of 500 and 600 incidentally learned words. *Journal of Experimental Psychology: Learning Memory, and Cognition, 12*, 66–71.

Marino, A. C., & Scholl, B. (2005). The role of closure in defining the "objects" of object-based attention. *Perception & Psychophysics, 67*, 1140–1149.

Marsh, R., Cook, G., & Hicks, J. (2006). Gender and orientation stereotypes bias source-monitoring attributions. *Memory, 14*, 148–160.

Mast, F. W., & Kosslyn, S. (2002). Visual mental images can be ambiguous: insights from individual differences in spatial transformation abilities. *Cognition, 86*, 57–70.

Mattar, M. G., Cole, M. W., Thompson-Schill, S. L., & Bassett, D. S. (2015). A functional cartography of cognitive systems. *PLOS Computational Biology, 11(12)*:e1004533. doi: 10.1371/journal.pcbi.1004533. doi:10.1016/j.neuroimage.2015.11.059, 2015

Maurer, L., Zitting, K-M., Elliott, K., Czeisler, C. A., Ronda, J. M., & Duffy, F. F. (2015). A new face of sleep: The impact of point-learning sleep on recognition memory for face-name associations. *Neurobiology of Learning and Memory, 126*, 31–38.

Mayseless, N., Eran, A., & Shamay-Tsoory, S. G. (2015). Generating original ideas: The neural underpinning of originality. *Neuroimage, 116*, 232–239.

Mazza, S., Gerbier, E., Gustin, M.-P., Kasikci, Z., Koenig, O., Toppino, T. C., & Magnin, M. (2016). Relearn faster and retain longer: Along with practice, sleep makes perfect. *Psychological Science, 27*, 1321–1330.

McCarthy, J., Minsky, M. L., & Shannon, C. E. (1955). A proposal for the Dartmouth summer research project on artificial intelligence. Downloaded from http://www.formal.stanford .edu/jmc/history/dartmouth /dartmouth.html

McClelland, J. L., & Rogers, T. T. (2003). The parallel distributed processing approach to semantic cognition. *Nature Reviews Neuroscience, 4*, 310–322.

McClelland, J. L., & Rumelhart, D. E. (1986). *Parallel distributed processing: Explorations in the microstructure of cognition.* Cambridge, MA: MIT Press.

McClelland, J. L., McNaughton, B. L., & O'Reilly, R. C. (1995). Why there are complementary learning systems in the hippocampus and neocortex: Insights from the successes and failures of connectionist models of learning and memory. *Psychological Review, 102,* 419–457.

McDaniel, M. A., Anderson, J. L., Derbish, M. H., & Morrisette, N. (2007). Testing the testing effect in the classroom. *European Journal of Cognitive Psychology, 19,* 494–513.

McDermott, K. B., & Chan, J. C. K. (2006). Effects of repetition on memory for pragmatic inferences. *Memory & Cognition, 34,* 1273–1284.

McDermott, K. B., Wooldridge, C. L., Rice, H. J., Berg, J., J., & Szpunar, K. K. (2016). Visual perspective in remembering and episodic future thought. *Quarterly Journal of Experimental Psychology, 69,* 243–253.

McGaugh, J. L. (1983). Hormonal influences on memory. *Annual Review of Psychology, 34,* 297–323.

McKenzie, C. R. M. (2004). Hypothesis testing and evaluation. In D. J. Koehler & N. Harvey (Eds.), *Blackwell handbook of judgment & decision making* (pp. 200–219). Malden, MA: Blackwell.

McMenamin, B. W., Langeslag, S. J. E., Sirbu, M., Padmala, S., & Pessoa, L. (2014). Network organization unfolds over time during periods of anxious anticipation. *Journal of Neuroscience, 34,* 11261–11273.

McMillan, R. L., Kaufman, S. B., & Singer, J. L. (2013). Ode to positive constructive daydreaming. *Frontiers in Psychology, 4,* Article 626.

McNeil, D. G. (2013). Car mechanic dreams up tool to ease births. *New York Times,* November 13, 2013.

McNeil, J. E., & Warrington, E. K. (1993). Prosopagnosia: A face-specific disorder. *Quarterly Journal of Experimental Psychology, 46A,* 1–10.

Melzack, R., & Wall, P. D. (1965). Pain mechanisms: A new theory. *Science, 150,* 971–979.

Memon, A., Meissner, C. A., & Fraser, J. (2010). The cognitive interview: A meta-analytic review and study space analysis of the past 25 years. *Psychology, Public Policy, and Law, 16,* 340–372.

Mervis, C. B., Catlin, J., & Rosch, E. (1976). Relationships among goodness-of-example, category norms and word frequency. *Bulletin of the Psychonomic Society, 7,* 268–284.

Metcalfe, J., & Wiebe, D. (1987). Intuition in insight and noninsight problem solving. *Memory and Cognition, 15,* 238–246.

Metusalem, R., Kutas, M., Urbach, T. P., Hare, M., McRae, K., & Elman, J. (2012). Generalized event knowledge activation during online sentence comprehension. *Journal of Memory and Language, 66,* 545–567.

Meyer, D. E., & Schvaneveldt, R. W. (1971). Facilitation in recognizing pairs of words: Evidence of a dependence between retrieval operations. *Journal of Experimental Psychology, 90,* 227–234.

Miller, G. A. (1956). The magical number seven, plus or minus two: Some limits on our capacity for processing information. *Psychological Review, 63,* 81–97.

Miller, G. A. (1965). Some preliminaries to psycholinguistics. *American Psychologist, 20,* 15–20.

Miller, G. A. (2003). The cognitive revolution: A historical perspective. *Trends in Cognitive Sciences, 7,* 141–144.

Milner, A. D., & Goodale, M. A. (1995). *The visual brain in action.* New York: Oxford University Press.

Minda, J. P., & Smith, J. D. (2001). Prototypes in category learning: The effect of category size, category structure, and stimulus complexity. *Journal of Experimental Psychology: Learning, Memory, and Cognition, 27,* 775–799.

Mishkin, M., Ungerleider, L. G., & Macko, K. A. (1983). Object vision and spatial vision: Two central pathways. *Trends in Neuroscience, 6,* 414–417.

Misiak, H., & Sexton, V. (1966). *History of psychology: An overview.* New York: Grune & Stratton.

Mitchell, K. J., & Johnson, M. K. (2000). Source monitoring. In E. Tulving & F. I. M. Craik (Eds.), *The Oxford handbook of memory* (pp. 179–195). New York: Oxford University Press.

Molenbergs, P., Hayward, L., Mattingley, J. B., & Cunnington, R. (2012). Activation patterns during action observation are modulated by context in mirror system areas. *NeuroImage, 59,* 608–615.

Mooneyham, B. W., & Schooler, J. E. (2013). The costs and benefits of mind-wandering: A review. *Canadian Journal of Experimental Psychology, 67,* 11–18.

Morley, N. J., Evans, J. St. B. T., & Handley, S. J. (2004). Belief bias and figural bias in syllogistic reasoning. *Quarterly Journal of Experimental Psychology A, 57,* 666–692.

Morris, C. D., Bransford, J. D., & Franks, J. J. (1977). Levels of processing versus transfer appropriate processing. *Journal of Verbal Learning and Verbal Behavior, 16,* 519–533.

Moscovitch, M., Winocur, G., & Behrmann, M. (1997). What is special about face recognition? Nineteen experiments on a person with visual object agnosia and dyslexia but normal face recognition. *Journal of Cognitive Neuroscience, 9,* 555–604.

Mueller, P. A., & Oppenheimer, D. M. (2014). The pen is mightier than the keyboard: Advantages of longhand over laptop note taking. *Psychological Science, 25,* 1159–1168.

Mukamel, R., Ekstrom, A. D., Kaplan, J., Iacoboni, M., & Fried, I. (2010). Single-neuron responses in humans during execution and observation of actions. *Current Biology, 20,* 750–756.

Mullen, B., Johnson, C., & Salas, E. (1991). Productivity loss in brainstorming groups: A meta-analytic integration. *Basic and Applied Social Psychology, 12,* 3–23.

Müller, G. E., & Pilzecker, A. (1900). Experimentelle Beitrage zur Lehr vom Gedachtniss *Zeitschrift fur Psychologie, 1,* 1–300.

Mumford, M. D., Medeiros, K. E., & Partlow, P. J. (2012). Creative thinking: Processes, strategies, and knowledge. *Journal of Creative Behavior, 46,* 30–47.

Murdoch, B. B., Jr. (1962). The serial position effect in free recall. *Journal of Experimental Psychology, 64,* 482–488.

Murphy, G. L. (2016). Is there an exemplar theory of concepts? *Psychonomic Bulletin & Review, 23,* 1035–1042.

Murphy, G., L., Hampton, J. A., & Milovanovic, G. S. (2012). Semantic memory redux: An experimental test of hierarchical category representation. *Journal of Memory and Language, 67,* 521–539

Murphy, K. J., Racicot, C. I., & Goodale, M. A. (1996). The use of visuomotor cues as a strategy for making perceptual judgments in a patient with visual form agnosia. *Neuropsychology, 10,* 396–401.

Murray, D. J. (1968). Articulating and acoustic confusability in short-term memory. *Journal of Experimental Psychology, 78,* 679–684.

Murray, J. D., Bernacchia, A., Roy, N. A., Constantinidis, C., Romo, R., & Wang, X-J. (2017). Stable population coding for working memory coexists with heterogeneous neural dynamics in prefrontal cortex. *Proceedings of the National Academy of Sciences, 114(2),* 394–399.

Naci, L., Cusack, R., Anello, M., & Owen, A. M. (2014). A common neural code for similar conscious experiences in different individuals. *Proceedings of the National Academy of Sciences, 111,* 14277–14282.

Naci, L., Sinai, L., & Owen, A. M. (2015). Detecting and interpreting conscious experiences in behaviorally non-responsive patients. *NeuroImage.* doi:10.1016/j.neuroimage.2015.11.059, 2015

Nadel, L., & Moscovitch, M. (1997). Memory consolidation, retrograde amnesia and the hippocampal complex. *Current Opinion in Neurobiology, 7,* 217–227.

Nader, K., & Einarsson, E. O. (2010). Memory reconsolidation: An update. *Annals of the New York Academy of Sciences, 1191,* 27–41.

Nader, K., Schafe, G. E., & Le Doux, J. E. (2000a). Fear memories require protein synthesis in the amygdala for reconsolidation after retrieval. *Nature, 406,* 722–726.

Nader, K., Schafe, G. E., & Le Doux, J. E. (2000b). The labile nature of consolidation theory. *Nature, 1,* 216–219.

Nairne, J. S. (2010). Adaptive memory: Evolutionary constraints on remembering. *Psychology of Learning and Motivation, 53,* 1–32.

Naselaris, T., Olman, C. A., Stansburh, D. E., Uurbil, K., & Gallant, J. (2015). A voxel-wise encoding model for early visual areas decodes mental images of remembered scenes. *Neuroimage, 105,* 215–228.

Nash, R. A., & Wade, K. A. (2009). Innocent but proven guilty: Eliciting internalized false confessions using doctored-video evidence. *Applied Cognitive Psychology, 23,* 624–637.

Nash, R. A., Wade, K. A., Garry, M., Loftus, E. F., & Ost, J. (2017). Misrepresentations and flawed logic about the prevalence of false memories. *Applied Cognitive Psychology, 31,* 31–33.

National Academy of Sciences (2014). *Identifying the culprit: assessing eyewitness identification.* Washington, DC: National Academy of Sciences Press.

Neisser, U. (1967). *Cognitive psychology.* New York: Appleton-Century-Crofts.

Neisser, U. (1988). New vistas in the study of memory. In U. Neisser & E. Winograd (Eds.), *Remembering reconsidered: Ecological and traditional approaches to the study of memory* (pp. 1–10). Cambridge, UK: Cambridge University Press.

Neisser, U., & Becklen, R. (1975). Selective looking: Attending to visually specified events. *Cognitive Psychology, 7,* 480–494.

Neisser, U., & Harsch, N. (1992). Phantom flashbulbs: False recollections of hearing the news about *Challenger.* In E. Winograd & U. Neisser (Eds.), *Affect and accuracy in recall: Studies of "flashbulb" memories* (pp. 9–31). New York: Cambridge University Press.

Neisser, U., Winograd, E., Bergman, E. T., Schreiber, C. A., Palmer, S. E., & Weldon, M. S. (1996). Remembering the earthquake: Direct experience vs. hearing the news. *Memory, 4,* 337–357.

Nesterak, E. (2014). Coerced to confess: The psychology of false confessions. Thepsychreport.com, October 14, 2014, in Conversations, Society.

Nichols, E. A., Kao, Y.-C., Verfaellie, M., & Gabrieli, J. D. E. (2006). Working memory and long-term memory for faces: Evidence from fMRI and global amnesia for involvement of the medial temporal lobes. *Hippocampus, 16,* 604–616.

Newell, A., & Simon, H. A. (1972). *Human problem solving.* Englewood Cliffs, NJ: Prentice-Hall.

Nietzsche, F. (1889). *Twilight of the idols.* See *Twilight of the Idols and the Anti-Christ.* (2003). Translated by R. J. Hollingsworth. New York: Penguin Books.

Noton, D., & Stark, L. W. (1971). Scanpaths in eye movements during pattern perception. *Science, 171,* 308–311.

Nyberg, L., McIntosh, A. R., Cabeaa, R., Habib, R., Houle, S., & Tulving, E. (1996). General and specific brain regions involved in encoding and retrieval of events: What, where and when. *Proceedings of the National*

Academy of Sciences, USA, 93, 11280–11285.

Nyhan, B., & Reifler, J. (2010). When corrections fail: The persistence of political misperceptions. *Political Behavior, 32*(2), 303–330.

Ogawa, S., Lee, T. M., Kay, A. R., & Tank, D. W. (1990). Brain magnetic resonance imaging with contrast dependent on blood oxygenation. *Proceedings of the National Academy of Sciences, 87,* 9868–9872.

Oliva, A., & Torralba, A. (2007). The role of context in object recognition. *Trends in Cognitive Sciences, 11,* 521–527.

Olshausen, B. A., & Field, D. J. (2004). Sparse coding of sensory inputs. *Current Opinion in Neurobiology, 14,* 481–487.

Olson, A. C., & Humphreys, G. W. (1997). Connectionist models of neuropsychological disorders. *Trends in Cognitive Sciences, 1,* 222–228.

Oppezzo, M., & Schwartz, D. L. (2014). Give your ideas some legs: The positive effect of walking on creative thinking. *Journal of Experimental Psychology: Learning, Memory and Cognition, 40,* 1142–1152.

Orban, G. A., Vandenbussche, E., & Vogels, R. (1984). Human orientation discrimination tested with long stimuli. *Vision Research, 24,* 121–128.

Osborn, A. F. (1953). *Applied imagination.* New York: Scribner.

Osman, M. (2004). An evaluation of dual-process theories of reasoning. *Psychonomic Bulletin and Review, 108,* 291–310.

Ost, J., Vrij, A., Costall, A., & Bull, R. (2002). Crashing memories and reality monitoring: Distinguishing between perceptions, imaginations and "false memories." *Applied Cognitive Psychology, 16,* 125–134.

Osterhout, L., McLaughlin, J., & Bersick, M. (1997). Event-related brain potentials and human language. *Trends in Cognitive Sciences, 1,* 203–209.

Paczynski, M., & Kuperberg, G. R. (2012). Multiple influences of semantic memory on sentence processing: Distinct effects of semantic relatedness on violations of real-world event/state knowledge and animacy selection restrictions. *Journal of Memory and Language, 67,* 426–448.

Paivio, A. (1963). Learning of adjective-noun paired associates as a function of adjective-noun word order and noun abstractness. *Canadian Journal of Psychology, 17,* 370–379.

Paivio, A. (1965). Abstractness, imagery, and meaningfulness in paired-associate learning. *Journal of Verbal Learning and Verbal Behavior, 4,* 32–38.

Paivio, A. (2006). *Mind and its evolution: A dual coding theoretical approach.* Hillsdale, NJ: Erlbaum.

Palmer, S. E. (1975). The effects of contextual scenes on the identification of objects. *Memory and Cognition, 3,* 519–526.

Palmer, S. E. (1992). Common region: A new principle of perceptual grouping. *Cognitive Psychology, 24,* 436–447.

Palmer, S. E., & Rock, I. (1994). Rethinking perceptual organization: The role of uniform connectedness. *Psychonomic Bulletin and Review, 1,* 29–55.

Palombo, D. J., Alain, C., Soderlund, H., Khuu, W., & Levine, B. (2015). Severely deficient autobiographical memory (SDAM) in healthy adults: A new mnemonic syndrome. *Neuropsychologia, 72,* 105–118.

Parker, E. S., Cahill, L., & McGaugh, J. L. (2006). A case of unusual autobiographical remembering. *Neurocase, 12,* 35–49.

Parkhurst, D., Law, K., & Niebur, E. (2002). Modeling the role of salience in the allocation of overt visual attention. *Vision Research, 42,* 107–123.

Parkin, A. J. (1996). *Explorations in cognitive neuropsychology.* Oxford, England: Blackwell.

Patel, A. D. (2013). Sharing and nonsharing of brain resources for language and music. M. A. Arbib (Ed), *Language, Music and the Brain.* 329–361. Cambridge, MA: MIT Press.

Patel, A. D., Gibson, E., Ratner, J., Besson, M., & Holcomb, P. J. (1998). Processing syntactic relations in language and music: An event-related potential study. *Journal of Cognitive Neuroscience, 10,* 717–733.

Patel, A. D., Iversen, J. R., Wassenaar, M., & Hagoort, P. (2008). Musical syntactic processing in agrammatic Broca's aphasia. *Aphasiology, 22,* 776–779.

Patterson, K., Nestor, P. J., & Rogers, T. T. (2007). Where do you know what you know? The representation of semantic knowledge in the human brain. *Nature Reviews Neuroscience, 8,* 976–987.

Paulus, M. P., & Yu, A. J. (2012). Emotion and decision-making: Affect-driven belief systems in anxiety and depression. *Trends in Cognitive Sciences, 16,* 476–483.

Pavlov, I. (1927). *Conditioned reflexes.* New York: Oxford University Press.

Payne, J. D., Chambers, A. M., & Kensinger, E. A. (2012). Sleep promotes lasting changes in selective memory for emotional scenes. *Frontiers in Integrative Neuroscience, 6,* 1–11.

Payne, J. D., Stickgold, R., Swanberg, K., & Kensinger, E. A. (2008). Sleep preferentially enhances memory for emotional components of scenes. *Psychological Science, 19,* 781–788.

Pearce, J. M. S. (2009). Marie-Jean-Pierre Flourens (1794–1867) and cortical localization. *European Neurology, 61,* 311–314.

Pearson, J., & Kosslyn, S. M. (2015). The heterogeneity of mental representation: Ending the imagery debate. *Proceedings of the National Academy of Sciences, 112,* 10089–10092.

Pearson, J., Clifford, C. W. G., & Tong, F. (2008). The functional impact of mental imagery on conscious perception. *Current Biology, 18,* 982–986.

Peretz, I., & Hyde, K. (2003). What is specific to music processing? Insights from congenital amusia. *Trends in Cognitive Sciences, 7,* 362–367.

Peretz, I., & Zatorre, R. (2005). Brain organization for music processing. *Annual Review of Psychology, 56,* 89–114.

Peretz, I., Vuvan, D., Lagrois, M.-E., & Armony, J. L. (2015). Neural overlap in processing music and speech. *Philosophical Transactions of the Royal Society, B370,* 20140090.

Perfect, T. J., & Askew, C. (1994). Print adverts: Not remembered but memorable. *Applied Cognitive Psychology, 8,* 693–703.

Perky, C.W. (1910). An experimental study of imagination. *American Journal of Psychology, 21,* 422–442

Perrett, D. I., Rolls, E. T., & Caan, W. (1982). Visual neurons responsive to faces in the monkey temporal cortex. *Experimental Brain Research, 7,* 329–342.

Pessoa, L. (2014). Understanding brain networks and brain organization. *Physics of Life Reviews, 11,* 400–435.

Peters, E., Vastfjall, D., Garling, T., & Slovic, P. (2006). Affect and decision making: A "hot" topic. *Journal of Behavioral Decision Making, 19,* 79–85.

Petersen, S. E. (1992). The cognitive functions of underlining as a study technique. *Reading Research and Instruction, 31,* 49–56.

Petersen, S. E., & Posner, M. I. (2012). The attention system of the human brain: 20 years after. *Annual Review of Neuroscience, 35,* 73–89.

Petersen, L. R., & Peterson, M. J. (1959). Short-term retention of individual verbal items. *Journal of Experimental Psychology, 58,* 193–198.

Petrican, R., Gopie, N., Leach, L., Chow, T. W., Richards, B., & Moscovitch, M. (2010). Recollection and familiarity for public events in neurologically intact older adults and two brain-damaged patients. *Neuropsychologia, 48,* 945–960.

Phelps, E. A., & Sharot, T. (2008). How (and why) emotion enhances the subjective sense of recollection. *Current Directions in Psychological Science, 17,* 147–152.

Philippi, C. L., Tranel, D., Duff, M., and Rudrauf, D. (2015). Damage to the default mode network disrupts autobiographical memory retrieval. *SCAN, 10,* 318–326.

Pillemer, D. B. (1998). *Momentous events, vivid memories.* Cambridge, MA: Harvard University Press.

Pillemer, D. B., Picariello, M. L., Law, A. B., & Reichman, J. S. (1996). Memories of college: The importance of specific educational episodes. In D. C. Rubin (Ed.), *Remembering our past: Studies in autobiographical memory* (pp. 318–337). Cambridge, UK: Cambridge University Press.

Plaisier, M. A., & Smeets, J. B. J. (2015). Object size can influence perceived weight independent of visual estimates of the volume of material. *Scientific Reports.* doi: 10.10.1038/srep17719

Plaut, D. C. (1996). Relearning after damage in connectionist networks: Toward a theory of rehabilitation. *Brain and Language, 52,* 25–82.

Pobric, G., Jefferies, E., & Lambon Ralph, M. A. (2010). Category-specific versus category-general semantic impairment induced by transcranial magnetic stimulation. *Current Biology, 20,* 964–968.

Poldrack, R. A., Laumann, T. O., et al. (2015). Long-term neural and physiological phenotyping of a single human. *Nature Communications,* DOI: 10.1038/ncomms9885.

Pollack, I., & Pickett, J. M. (1964). Intelligibility of excerpts from fluent speech: Auditory vs. structural context. *Journal of Verbal Learning and Verbal Behavior, 3,* 79–84.

Porter, S., & Birt, A. R. (2001). Is traumatic memory *special*? A comparison of traumatic memory characteristics with memory for other emotional life experiences. *Applied Cognitive Psychology, 15,* S101–S117.

Posner, M. I., Nissen, M. J., & Ogden, W. C. (1978). Attended and unattended processing modes: The role of set for spatial location. In H. L. Pick & I. J. Saltzman (Eds.), *Modes of perceiving and processing information* (pp. 137–157). Hillsdale, NJ: Erlbaum.

Post, T., van den Assem, M. J., Baltussen, G., & Thaler, R. H. (2008). Deal or no deal? Decision making under risk in a large-payoff game show. *American Economic Review, 98,* 38–71.

Proust, M. (1922/1960). *Remembrance of Things Past: Swann's way.* (C.K. Scott Moncrieff, Trans). London: Chatto & Windus.

Ptak, R. (2012).The Frontoparietal Attention Network of the Human Brain: Action, Saliency, and a Priority Map of the Environment. *The Neuroscientist, 18,* 502–515.

Pulvermüller, F. (2013). How neurons make meaning: Brain mechanisms for embodied and abstract-symbolic semantics. *Trends in Cognitive Sciences, 17,* 458–470.

Putnam, A. L., Sukngkhasettee, V. W., & Roediger, H. L. (2016). Optimizing learning in college: Tips from cognitive psychology. *Perspectives on Psychological Science, 11,* 652–660.

Pylyshyn, Z. W. (1973). What the mind's eye tells the mind's brain: A critique of mental imagery. *Psychological Bulletin, 80,* 1–24.

Pylyshyn, Z. W. (2001). Is the imagery debate over? If so, what was it about? In E. Dupoux (Ed.), *Language, brain, and cognitive development* (pp. 59–83). Cambridge, MA: MIT Press.

Pylyshyn, Z. W. (2003). Return of the mental image: Are there really pictures in the brain? *Trends in Cognitive Sciences, 7,* 113–118.

Quillian, M. R. (1967). Word concepts: A theory and simulation of some basic semantic capabilities. *Behavioral Science, 12,* 410–430.

Quillian, M. R. (1969). The Teachable Language Comprehender: A simulation program and theory of language. *Communications of the ACM, 12,* 459–476.

Quinlivan, D. S., Wells, G. L., & Neuschatz, J. S. (2010). Is manipulative intent necessary to mitigate the eyewitness post-identification feedback effect? *Law and Human Behavior, 34,* 186–197.

Quiroga, R. Q., Reddy, L., Koch, C., & Fried, I. (2007). Decoding visual inputs from multiple neurons in the human temporal lobe. *Journal of Neurophysiology, 98,* 1997–2007.

Quiroga, R. Q., Reddy, L., Kreiman, G., Koch, C., & Fried, I. (2008). Sparse but not "grandmother-cell" coding in the medial temporal lobe. *Trends in Cognitive Sciences, 12,* 87–91.

Raichle, M. E. (2011). The restless brain. *Brain Connectivity, 1,* 3–12.

Raichle, M. E., MacLeod, A. M., Snyder, A. Z., Powers, W. J., Gusnard, D. A., & Shulman, G. L. (2001). A default mode of brain function. *Proceedings of the National Academy of Sciences, 98,* 676–682.

Ranganath, C., & Blumenfeld, R. S. (2005). Doubts about double dissociations between short- and long-term memory. *Trends in Cognitive Sciences, 9,* 374–380.

Ranganath, C., & D'Esposito, M. (2001). Medial temporal lobe activity associated with active maintenance of novel information. *Neuron, 31,* 865–873.

Raphael, B. (1976). *The thinking computer.* New York: Freeman.

Rathbone, C. J., Moulin, C. J. A., & Conway, M. A. (2008). Self-centered memories: The reminiscence bump and the self. *Memory & Cognition, 36,* 1403–1414.

Ratiu, P., Talos, I.F., Haker, S., Lieberman, D., Everett, P. (2004) The tale of Phineas Gage, digitally remastered. *Journal of Neurotrauma, 21,* 637–643.

Rauchs, G., Feyers, D., Landeau, B., Bastin, C., Luxen, A., Maquet, P., et al. (2011).

Sleep contributes to the strengthening of some memories over others, depending on hippocampal activity at learning. *Journal of Neuroscience, 31,* 2563–2568.

Raveh, D., & Lavie, N. (2015). Load-induced inattentional deafness. *Attention, Perception, & Psychophysics 77,* 483–492.

Rayner, K., & Duffy, S. A. (1986). Lexical complexity and fixation times in reading: Effects of word frequency, verb complexity, and lexical ambiguity. *Memory and Cognition, 14,* 191–201.

Rayner, K., & Frazier, L. (1989). Selection mechanisms in reading lexically ambiguous words. *Journal of Experimental Psychology: Learning, Memory and Cognition, 15,* 779–790.

Reali, F., & Christiansen, M. (2007). Processing of relative clauses is made easier by frequency of occurrence. *Journal of Memory and Language, 53,* 1–23.

Reber, A. S. (1995). *Penguin dictionary of psychology* (2nd ed.). New York: Penguin Books.

Redelmeier, D. A., & Shafir, E. (1995). Medical decision making in situations that offer multiple alternatives. *Medical Decision Making, 273,* 302–305.

Reder, L. M., & Anderson, J. R. (1982). Effects of spacing and embellishment for the main points of a text. *Memory and Cognition, 10,* 97–102.

Reid, C. A., Green, J. D., Wildschut, T., & Sedikides, C. (2015). Scent-evoked nostalgia. *Memory, 23(2),* 157–166.

Reitman, J. (1976). Skilled perception in Go: Deducing memory structures from inter-response times. *Cognitive Psychology, 8,* 336–356.

Renoult, L., Davidson, P. S. R., Palombo, D. J., Moscovitch, M., & Levine, B. (2012). Personal semantics: at the crossroads of semantic and episodic memory. *Trends in Cognitive Sciences, 16,* 550–558.

Rensink, R. A. (2002). Change detection. *Annual Review of Psychology, 53,* 245–277.

Rensink, R. A., O'Regan, J. K., & Clark, J. J. (1997). To see or not to see: The need for attention to perceive changes in scenes. *Psychological Science, 8,* 368–373.

Richardson, A. (1994). *Individual differences in imaging: Their measurement, origins, and consequences.* Amityville, NY: Baywood.

Riley, M. R., & Constantinidis, C. (2016). Role of prefrontal persistent activity in working memory. *Frontiers in Systems Neuroscience, 9, Article 181.*

Rips, L. J. (1995). Deduction and cognition. In E. Smith & D. N. Osherson (Eds.), *An invitation to cognitive science* (Vol. 2, pp. 297–343). Cambridge, MA: MIT Press.

Rips, L. J., Shoben, E. J., & Smith, E. E. (1973). Semantic distance and the verification of semantic relations. *Journal of Verbal Learning and Verbal Behavior, 12,* 1–20.

Rips, L. J. (2002). Reasoning. In D. L. Medin (Ed.), *Stevens' handbook of experimental psychology* (3rd ed., pp. 363–411). New York: Wiley.

Ritchey, M., Dolcos, F., & Cabeza, R. (2008). Role of amygdala connectivity in the persistence of emotional memories over time: An event-related fMRI investigation. *Cerebral Cortex, 18,* 2494–2504.

Rizzolatti, G., & Sinigaglia, C. (2016). The mirror mechanism: A basic principle of brain function. *Nature Reviews Neuroscience, 17,* 757–765.

Rizzolatti, G., Forgassi, L., & Gallese, V. (2006, November). Mirrors in the mind. *Scientific American,* pp. 54–63.

Robbins, J. (2000, July 4). Virtual reality finds a real place. *New York Times.*

Robertson, L., Treisman, A., Freidman-Hill, S., & Grabowecky, M. (1997). The interaction of spatial and object pathways: Evidence from Balint's syndrome. *Journal of Cognitive Neuroscience, 9,* 295–317.

Rocha-Miranda, C. (2011). Personal communication.

Rock, I. (1983). *The logic of perception.* Cambridge, MA: MIT Press.

Roediger, H. L. (1990). Implicit memory: Retention without remembering. *American Psychologist, 45,* 1043–1056.

Roediger, H. L., Guynn, M. J., & Jones, T. C. (1994). Implicit memory: A tutorial review. In G. d'Ydewalle, P. Eallen, & P. Bertelson (Eds.), *International perspectives on cognitive science* (Vol. 2, pp. 67–94). Hillsdale, NJ: Erlbaum.

Roediger, H. L., & McDermott, K. B. (1995). Creating false memories: Remembering words not presented in lists. *Journal of Experimental Psychology: Learning, Memory, and Cognition, 21,* 803–814.

Rogers, T. B., Kuiper, N. A., & Kirker, W. S. (1977). Self-reference and the encoding of personal information. *Journal of Personality and Social Psychology, 35,* 677–688.

Rogers, T. T., & Cox, C. (2015). The neural basis of conceptual knowledge: Revisiting a Golden-Age hypothesis in the era of cognitive neuroscience. In D. R. Addis, M. Barense, & A. Duarte (Eds.), *Wiley handbook on the cognitive neuroscience of memory.* New York: Wiley.

Rogers, T. T., & McClelland, J. L. (2004). *Semantic cognition: A parallel distributed processing approach.* Cambridge, MA: MIT Press

Rogin, M. P. (1987). *Ronald Reagan, the movie and other episodes in political demonology.* Berkeley, CA: University of California Press.

Rolls, E. T. (1981). Responses of amygdaloid neurons in the primate. In Y. Ben-Ari (Ed.), *The amygdaloid complex* (pp. 383–393). Amsterdam: Elsevier.

Rolls, E. T., & Tovee, M. J. (1995). Sparsness of the neuronal representation of stimuli in the primate temporal visual cortex. *Journal of Neurophysiology, 73,* 713–726.

Roozendaal, B., & McGaugh, J. L. (2011). Memory modulation. *Behavioral Neuroscience, 125,* 797–824.

Rosch, E. H. (1973). On the internal structure of perceptual and semantic categories. In T. E. Moore (Ed.), *Cognitive development and the acquisition of language* (pp. 111–144). New York: Academic Press.

Rosch, E. H. (1975a). Cognitive representations of semantic categories. *Journal of Experimental Psychology: General, 104,* 192–233.

Rosch, E. H. (1975b). The nature of mental codes for color categories. *Journal of Experimental Psychology: Human Perception and Performance, 1,* 303–322.

Rosch, E. H., & Mervis, C. B. (1975). Family resemblances: Studies in the internal structures of categories. *Cognitive Psychology, 7,* 573–605.

Rosch, E. H., Mervis, C. B., Gray, W. D., Johnson, D. M., & Boyes-Braem, P. (1976). Basic objects in natural categories. *Cognitive Psychology, 8,* 382–439.

Rose, N. S., Olsen, R. K., Craik, F. I. M., & Rosenbaum, R. S. (2012). Working memory and amnesia: The role of stimulus novelty. *Neuropsychologia, 50,* 11–18.

Rosen, L. D., Carrier, L. M., & Cheever, N. A. (2013). Facebook and texting made me do it: Media-induced task-switching while studying. *Computers in Human Behavior, 29,* 948–958.

Rosenbaum, R. S., Köhler, S., Schacter, D. L., Moscovitch, M., Westmacott, R., Black, S. E., et al. (2005). The case of K.C.: Contributions of a memory-impaired person to memory theory. *Neuropsychologia, 43,* 989–1021.

Ross, D. F., Ceci, S. J., Dunning, D., & Toglia, M. P. (1994). Unconscious transference and mistaken identity: When a witness misidentifies a familiar but innocent person. *Journal of Applied Psychology, 79,* 918–930.

Ross, E. D. (2010). Cerebral localization of function and the neurology of language: Fact versus fiction or is it something else? *The Neuroscientist, 16,* 222–243.

Rossato-Bennet, M., director (2014). *Alive Inside: A Story of Music and Memory.*

Rubin, D. C., Rahhal, T. A., & Poon, L. W. (1998). Things learned in early adulthood are remembered best. *Memory & Cognition, 26,* 3–19.

Rumelhart, D. E., & McClelland, J. L. (1986). *Parallel distributed processing: Explorations in the microstructure of cognition.* Cambridge, MA: MIT Press.

Rundus, D. (1971). Analysis of rehearsal processes in free recall. *Journal of Experimental Psychology, 89,* 63–77.

Sachs, J. (1967). Recognition memory for syntactic and semantic aspects of a connected discourse. *Perception & Psychophysics, 2,* 437–442.

Saffran, J. R., Aslin, R. N., & Newport, E. L. (1996). Statistical learning by 8-month old infants. *Science, 274,* 1926–1928.

Saffran, J., Hauser, M., Seibel, R., Kapfhamer, J., Tsao, F., & Cushman, F. (2008). Grammatical pattern learning by human infants and cotton-top tamarin monkeys. *Cognition, 107,* 479–500.

Saletin, J. M., Goldstein, A. N., & Walker, M. P. (2011). The role of sleep in directed forgetting and remembering of human memories. *Cerebral Cortex, 21,* 2534–2541.

Sanfey, A. G., Lowenstein, G., McClure, S. M., & Cohen, J. D. (2006). Neuroeconomics: Cross-currents in research on decision-making. *Trends in Cognitive Sciences, 10,* 106–116.

Sanfey, A. G., Rilling, J. K., Aronson, J. A., Nystrom, L. E., & Cohen, J. D. (2003). The neural basis of economic decision making in the Ultimatum Game. *Science, 300,* 1755–1758.

Schacter, D. L. (1987). Implicit memory: History and current status. *Journal of Experimental Psychology: Learning, Memory and Cognition, 13,* 501–518.

Schacter, D. L. (2001). *The seven sins of memory.* New York: Houghton Mifflin.

Schacter, D. L. (2012). Adaptive constructive processes and the future of memory. *American Psychologist, 67,* 603–613.

Schacter, D. L., & Addis, D. R. (2007). The cognitive neuroscience of constructive memory: Remembering the past and imagining the future. *Philosophical Transactions of the Royal Society of London B, 362,* 773–786.

Schacter, D. L., & Addis, D. R. (2009). On the nature of medial temporal lobe contributions to the constructive simulation of future events. *Philosophical Transactions of the Royal Society of London B, 364,* 1245–1253.

Scheck, B., Neufeld, P., & Dwyer, J. (2000). *Actual innocence.* New York: Random House.

Schenkein, J. (1980). A taxonomy for repeating action sequences in natural conversation. In B. Butterworth (Ed.), *Language production* (Vol. 1, pp. 21–47). San Diego, CA: Academic Press.

Schiller, D., Monfils, M.-H., Raio, C. M., Johnson, D. C., LeDoux, J. E., & Phelps, E. A. (2010). Preventing the return of fear in humans using reconsolidation update mechanisms. *Nature, 463,* 49–54.

Schmeichel, B. J., Volokhov, R. N., & Demaree, H. A. (2008). Working memory capacity and the self-regulation of emotional expression and experience. *Journal of Personality and Social Psychology, 95,* 1526–1540.

Schmolck, H., Buffalo, E. A., & Squire, L. R. (2000). Memory distortions develop over time: Recollections of the O. J. Simpson trial verdict after 15 and 32 months. *Psychological Science, 11,* 39–45.

Schneider, W., & Chein, J. (2003). Controlled and automatic processing: Behavioral and biological mechanisms. *Cognitive Science, 27,* 525–559.

Schrauf, R. W., & Rubin, D. C. (1998). Bilingual autobiographical memory in older adult immigrants: A test of cognitive explanations of the reminiscence bump and the linguistic encoding of memories. *Journal of Memory and Language, 39,* 437–457.

Schweickert, R., & Boruff, B. (1986). Short-term memory capacity: Magic number or magic spell? *Journal of Experimental Psychology: Learning, Memory, and Cognition, 12,* 419–425.

Scorbia, A., Wade, K. A., Lindsay, D.S., Azad, T., Strange, D., Ost, J., & Hyma, I. E. (2017). A mega-analysis of memory reports from eight peer-reviewed false memory implantation studies. *Memory, 25(2),* 146–163.

Scoville, W. B., & Milner, B. (1957). Loss of recent memory after bilateral hippocampal lesions. *Journal of Neurology, Neurosurgery, and Psychiatry, 20,* 11–21.

Sederberg, P. B., Gershman, S. J., Polyn, S. M., & Norman, K. A. (2011). Human memory reconsolidation can be explained using the temporal context model. *Psychonomic Bulletin & Review, 18,* 455–468.

Segal, S. J., & Fusella, V. (1970). Influence of imaged pictures and sounds on detection of visual and auditory signals. *Journal of Experimental Psychology, 83,* 458–464.

Seidenberg, M. S., & Zevin, J. D. (2006). Connectionist models in developmental cognitive neuroscience: Critical periods and the paradox of success. In Y. Munakata & M. Johnson (Eds.), *Processes of change in brain and cognitive development: Attention and performance XXI.* Oxford, UK: Oxford University Press.

Seiler, S. J. (2015). Hand on the wheel, mind on the mobile: an analysis of social factors contributing to texting while driving. *Cyberpsychology, Behavior, & Social Networking, 18,* 72–78.

Seung, S. (2012). *Connectome: How the brain's wiring makes us who we are.* New York: Houghton Mifflin Harcourt Publishing.

Shallice, T., & Warrington, E. K. (1970). Independent functioning of verbal memory stores: A neuro-psychological study. *Quarterly Journal of Experimental Psychology, 22,* 261–273.

Shannon, B. J., Dosenbach, R. A., Su, Y., Vlassenko, A. G., Larson-Prior, L. J., Nolan, T. S., Snyder, A. Z., & Raichle, M. E. (2013). Morning-evening variation in human brain metabolism and memory circuits. *Journal of Neurophysiology, 109,* 1444–1456.

Sharot, T., Korn, C. W., & Dolan, R. J. (2011). How unrealistic optimism is maintained in the face of reality. *Nature Neuroscience, 14,* 1475–1479.

Shaw, J., & Porter, S. (2015). Constructing rich false memories of committing crime. *Psychological Science, 26,* 291–301.

Shek, D. T. L., Yu, L., & Sun, Rachel, C. F. (2016). Internet addiction. In D. W. Pfaff and N. D. Volkow (Eds.). *Neuroscience in the 21st Century.* New York: Springer. pp. 3737–3750.

Sheldon, S., Amaral, R., & Levine, B. (2017). Individual differences in visual imagery determine how event information is remembered. *Memory, 25,* 360–369.

Shen, O., Rabinowitz, R., Geist, R. R., & Shafir, E. (2010). Effect of background case characteristics on decisions in the delivery room. *Medical Decision Making, 30,* 518–522.

Shepard, R. N., & Metzler, J. (1971). Mental rotation of three-dimensional objects. *Science, 171,* 701–703.

Shinoda, H., Hayhoe, M. M., & Shrivastava, A. (2001). What controls attention in natural environments? *Vision Research, 41,* 3535–3545.

Shulman, G. L., Fiez, J. A., Corbetta, M., Buckner, R. L., Miezin, F. M., Raichle, M. E., & Petersen, S. E. (1997). Common blood flow changes across visual tasks: II. Decreases in Cerebral Cortex. *Journal of Cognitive Neuroscience, 9,* 648–663.

Simons, D. J., & Chabris, C. F. (2011). What people believe about how memory works: A representative survey of the U.S. population. *PLoS ONE, 6*(8), e22757.

Simonsohn, U. (2007). Clouds make nerds look good. *Journal of Behavioral Decision Making, 20,* 143–152.

Simonsohn, U. (2009). Weather to go to college. *Economic Journal, 20,* 1–11.

Simonson, I., & Tversky, A. (1992). Choice in context: Tradeoff contrast and extremeness aversion. *Journal of marketing research, 29*(3), 281–295.

Simonton, D. K. (1984). Creative productivity and age: A mathematical model based on a two-step cognitive process. *Developmental Review, 4,* 77–111.

Simonton, D. K. (2012). Taking the U. S. Patent office criteria seriously: A quantitative three-criterion creativity definition and its implications. *Creativity Research Journal, 24,* 97–106.

Simonyan, K., Aytar, Y., Vedaldi, A., & Zisserman, A. (2012). Presentation at Image Large Scale Visual Recognition Competition (ILSVRC2012).

Singer, J. L. (1975). Navigating the stream of consciousness. Research in daydreaming and related inner experience. American *Psychologist, 30,* 727–738.

Singer, M., Andrusiak, P., Reisdorf, P., & Black, N. L. (1992). Individual differences in bridging inference processes. *Memory and Cognition, 20,* 539–548.

Sinha, P. (2002). Recognizing complex patterns. *Nature Neuroscience 5,* 1093–1097.

Skinner, B. F. (1938). *The behavior of organisms.* New York: Appleton Century.

Skinner, B. F. (1957). *Verbal behavior.* New York: Appleton-Century Crofts.

Slameka, N. J., & Graf, P. (1978). The generation effect: Delineation of a phenomenon. *Journal of Experimental Psychology: Human Learning and Memory, 4,* 592–604.

Slevc, L. R., Faroqi-Shah, Y., Saxena, S., & Okada, B. M. (2016). Preserved processing of musical structure in a person with agrammatic aphasia. *Neurocase, 22,* 505–511.

Slovic, P., Monahan, J., & MacGregor, D. G. (2000). Violence risk assessment and risk communication: The effects of using actual cases, providing instructions, and employing probability versus frequency formats. *Law and Human Behavior, 24,* 271–296.

Smallwood, J. (2011). Mind-wandering while reading: Attentional decoupling, mindless reading and the cascade model of inattention. *Language and Linguistics Compass, 5,* 63–77.

Smallwood, J., & Schooler, J. W. (2006). The restless mind. *Psychological Bulletin, 132,* 946–958.

Smallwood, J., & Schooler, J. W. (2015). The science of mind wandering: Empirically navigating the stream of consciousness. *Annual Reviews of Psychology, 66,* 487–518.

Smith, C. N., Frascino, J. C., Kripke, D. L., McHugh, P. R., Tresiman, G. J., & Squire, L. R. (2010). Losing memories overnight: A unique form of human amnesia. *Neuropsychologia, 48,* 2833–2840.

Smith, E. E. (1989). Concepts and induction. In M. L. Posner (Ed.), *Foundations of cognitive science* (pp. 501–526). Cambridge, MA: MIT Press.

Smith, E. E., Rips, L. J., & Shoben, E. J. (1974). Semantic memory and psychological semantics. In G. H. Bower (Ed.), *The psychology of learning and motivation* (Vol. 8, pp. 1–45). New York: Academic Press.

Smith, J. D., & Minda, J. P. (2000). Thirty categorization results in search of a model. *Journal of Experimental Psychology: Learning, Memory, and Cognition, 26,* 3–27.

Smith, S. M., Kerne, A., Koh, E., & Shah, J. (2009). The development and evaluation of tools for creativity. In A. B. Markman and K. L. Wood (Eds.), *Tools for innovation* (pp. 128–152). Oxford, UK: Oxford University Press.

Smith, S. M., & Rothkopf, E. Z. (1984). Contextual enhancement and distribution of practice in the classroom. *Cognition and Instruction, 1,* 341–358.

Smith, S. M., Ward, T. B., & Schumacher, J. S. (1993). Constraining effects of examples in a creative generation task. *Memory & Cognition, 21,* 837–845.

Smith, Z. (2010). Rules for writers. *Guardian.* The guardian.com /books/2010/feb/22/Sadie-smith -rules-for-writers.

Soderstrom, N. C., & McCabe, D. P. (2011). Are survival processing memory advantages based on ancestral priorities? *Psychonomic Bulletin & Review, 18,* 564–569.

Solomon, K. O., Medin, D. L., & Lynch, E. (1999). Concepts do more than categorize. *Trends in Cognitive Science, 3,* 99–105.

Spence, C., & Read, L. (2003). Speech shadowing while driving: On the difficulty of splitting attention between eye and ear. *Psychological Science, 14,* 251–256.

Sperling, G. (1960). The information available in brief visual presentations. *Psychological Monographs, 74*(11, Whole No. 498), 1–29.

Sporns, O. (2015). Cerebral cartography and connectomics. *Philosophical Transactions of the Royal Society B, 370:* 20140173.

Sporns, O., Tuoni, G., & Kotter, R. (2005). The human connectome: A structural description of the human brain. *PloS Computational Biology, 1(4),* e42.

Squire, L. R., & Zola-Morgan, S. (1998). Episodic memory, semantic memory, and amnesia. *Hippocampus, 8,* 205–211.

Stanfield, R. A., & Zwaan, R. A. (2001). The effect of implied orientation derived from verbal content on picture recognition. *Psychological Science, 12,* 153–156.

Stanny, C. J., & Johnson, T. C. (2000). Effects of stress induced by a simulated shooting on recall by police and citizen witnesses. *American Journal of Psychology, 113*, 359–386.

Stanovich, K. E. (1999). *What is rational? Studies of individual differences in reasoning.* Mahwah, NJ: Lawrence Erlbaum Associates Inc.

Stanovich, K. E. (2011). *Rationality and the reflective mind.* New York: Oxford University Press.

Stanovich, K. E., & West, R. F. (2000). Individual differences in reasoning: Implications for the rationality debate? *Behavioral and Brain Sciences, 23*, 645–726.

Stanovich, K. E., West, R. F., & Toplak, M. E. (2013). Myside bias, rational thinking, and intelligence. *Current Directions in Psychological Science, 22*, 259–264.

Stellmann, P., & Brennan, S. E. (1993). Flexible perspective-setting in conversation. In *Abstracts of the Psychonomic Society, 34the Annual Meeting* (p. 20), Washington, D.C.

Stevens, K. (2002, May 7). Out of the kitchen, and other getaways. *New York Times.*

Stokes, M. G. (2015). "Activity-silent" working memory in prefrontal cortex: A dynamic coding framework. *Trends in Cognitive Sciences, 19(7)*, 394–405.

Strayer, D. L., Cooper, J. M., Turrill, J., Coleman, J., Medeiros-Ward, N., & Biondi, F. (2013). *Measuring driver distraction in the automobile.* Washington, DC: AAA Foundation for Traffic Safety.

Strayer, D. L., & Johnston, W. A. (2001). Driven to distraction: Dual-task studies of simulated driving and conversing on a cellular telephone. *Psychological Science, 12*, 462–466.

Stroop, J. R. (1935). Studies of interference in serial verbal reactions. *Journal of Experimental Psychology, 18*, 643–662.

Suddendorf, T., Addis, D. R., & Corballis, M. C. (2009). Mental time travel and the shaping of the human mind.

Philosophical Transactions of the Royal Society of London B, 364, 1317–1324.

Sui, J., & Humphreys, G. W (2015). The integrative self: How self-reference integrates perception and memory. *Trends in Cognitive Sciences, 19*, 719–728.

Suri, G., Sheppes, G., Schwartz, C., & Gross, J. J. (2013). Patient inertia and the status quo bias: When an inferior option is preferred. *Psychological Science, 24*, 1763–1769.

Swinney, D. A. (1979). Lexical access during sentence comprehension: (Re) consideration of context effects. *Journal of Verbal Learning and Verbal Behavior, 18*, 645–659.

Taber, C. S., & Lodge, M. (2006). Motivated skepticism in the evaluation of political beliefs. *American Journal of Political Science, 50*, 755–769.

Talarico, J. M. (2009). Freshman flashbulbs: Memories of unique and first-time events in starting college. *Memory,17*, 256–265.

Talarico, J. M., & Rubin, D. C. (2003). Confidence, not consistency, characterizes flashbulb memories. *Psychological Science, 14*, 455–461.

Talarico, J. M., & Rubin, D. C. (2009). Flashbulb memories result from ordinary memory processes and extraordinary event characteristics. In O. Luminet & A. Curci (Eds.), *Flashbulb memories: New issues and new perspectives.* Philadelphia, PA: Psychology Press.

Tambini, A., Rimmele, U., Phelps, E. A., & Davahi, L. (2017). Emotional brain states carry over and enhance future memory function. *Nature Neuroscience, 20(2)*, 271–278.

Tanaka, J. W., & Taylor, M. (1991). Object categories and expertise: Is the basic level in the eye of the beholder? *Cognitive Psychology, 23*, 457–482.

Tarkan, L. (2003, April 29). Brain surgery, without knife or blood, gains favor. *New York Times,* p. F5.

Tenenbaum, J.B., Kemp, C., Griffiths, T. L., & Goodman, N. D. (2011). How to grow a mind: Statistics, structure, and abstraction. *Science, 331*, 1279–1285.

Tanenhaus, M. K., & Trueswell, J. C. (1995). Sentence comprehension. J. L. Miller & P. Eimas (Eds.), *Speech, language, and communication* (2nd ed., Vol. 11, pp. 217–262). San Diego, CA: Academic Press.

Tanenhaus, M. K., Leiman, J. M., & Seidenberg, M. S. (1979). Evidence for multiple stages in the processing of ambiguous words in syntactic contexts. *Journal of Verbal Learning and Verbal Behavior, 18*, 427–440.

Tanenhaus, M. K., Spivey-Knowlton, M. J., Beerhard, K. M., & Sedivy, J. C. (1995). Integration of visual and linguistic information in spoken language comprehension. *Science, 268*, 1632–1634.

Tatler, B. W., Hayhoe, M. M., Land, M. F., & Ballard, D. H. (2011). Eye guidance in natural vision: Reinterpreting salience. *Journal of Vision, 11(5)*, 1–23.

Ter-Pogossian, M. M., Phelps, M. E., Hoffman, E. J., & Mullani, N. A. (1975). A positron-emission tomograph for nuclear imaging (PET). *Radiology, 114*, 89–98.

Time Special Edition (2017) Innocent: The fight against wrongful convictions. *New York: Time Magazine.*

Tindall, D. R. & Bohlander R. W. (2012). The use and abuse of cell phones and text messaging in the classroom: A survey of college students. *College Teaching, 60*, 1–9.

Toffolo, M. B. J., Smeets, M. A. M., & van den Hout, M. A. (2012). Proust revisited: Odours as triggers of aversive memories. *Cognition and Emotion, 26(1)*, 83–92.

Toga, A. W. (1992). Editorial. *Neuroimage, 1*, 1.

Tolman, E. C. (1938). The determinants of behavior at a choice point. *Psychological Review, 45*, 1–41.

Tolman, E. C. (1948). Cognitive maps in rats and men. *Psychological Review, 55*, 189–208.

Tooley, V., Bringham, J. C., Maass, A., & Bothwell, R. K. (1987). Facial recognition: Weapon effect and attentional focus. *Journal of Applied Social Psychology, 17*, 845–859.

Traxler, M. J. (2012). *Introduction to psycholinguistics*. Malden, MA: Wiley-Blackwell.

Traxler, M. R., Morris, R., & Seely, R. (2002). Processing subject and object relative clause: Evidence from eye movements. *Journal of Memory and Language, 47*, 69–90.

Treadeau, K. (1997). *Mega memory*. New York: William Morrow.

Treisman, A. M. (1964). Selective attention in man. *British Medical Bulletin, 20*, 12–16.

Treisman, A. M. (1986). Features and objects in visual processing. *Scientific American. 225*, 114–125.

Treisman, A. (1988). Features and objects: The fourteenth Bartlett memorial lecture. *Quarterly Journal of Experimental Psychology, 40A*, 207–237.

Treisman, A. (1999). Solutions to the binding problem: Progress through controversy and convergence. *Neuron, 24*, 105–110.

Treisman, A. M. (2005, February 4). *Attention and binding*. Presentation to the Cognitive Science Group, University of Arizona.

XTreisman, A. M., & Schmidt, H. (1982). Illusory conjunctions in the perception of objects. *Cognitive Psychology, 14*, 107–141.

Tsao, D. Y., Freiwald, W. A., Tootell, R. B., & Livingstone, M. S. (2006). A cortical region consisting entirely of face-selective cells. *Science, 311*, 670–674.

Tulving, E. (1972). Episodic and semantic memory. In E. Tulving & W. Donaldson (Eds.), *Organization of memory* (pp. 381–403). New York: Academic Press.

Tulving, E. (1985). How many memory systems are there? *American Psychologist, 40*, 385–398.

Tulving, E., & Markowitsch, H. J. (1998). Episodic and declarative memory: Role of the hippocampus. *Hippocampus, 8*, 198–204.

Tulving, E., & Pearlstone, Z. (1966). Availability versus accessibility of information in memory for words. *Journal of Verbal Learning and Verbal Behavior, 5*, 381–391.

Turatto, M., Vescovi, M., & Valsecchi, M. (2007). Attention makes moving objects be perceived to move faster. *Vision Research, 47*, 166–178.

Tversky, A., & Kahneman, D. (1973). Availability: A heuristic for judging frequency and probability. *Cognitive Psychology, 5*, 207–232.

Tversky, A., & Kahneman, D. (1974). Judgment under uncertainty: Heuristics and biases. *Science, 185*, 1124–1131.

Tversky, A., & Kahneman, D. (1981). The framing of decisions and the psychology of choice. *Science, 211*, 453–458.

Tversky, A., & Kahneman, D. (1983). Extensional versus intuitive reasoning: The conjunction fallacy in probability judgment. *Psychological Review, 90*, 293–315.

Tversky, A., & Kahneman, D. (1991). Loss aversion in riskless choice. *Quarterly Journal of Economics, 106*, 1039–1061.

Tyler, L. K., & Moss, H. E. (2001). Towards a distributed account of conceptual knowledge. *Trends in Cognitive Sciences, 5*, 244–253.

Ungerleider, L. G., & Mishkin, M. (1982). Two cortical visual systems. In D. J. Ingle, M. A. Goodale, & R. J. Mansfield (Eds.), *Analysis of visual behavior* (pp. 549–580). Cambridge, MA: MIT Press.

Valtonen, J., Gregory, E., Landau, B., & McCloskey, M. (2014). New learning of music after bilateral medial temporal lobe damage: Evidence from an amnesic patient. *Frontiers in Human Neuroscience, 8*, Article 694.

Van den Broek, P. (1994). Comprehension and memory of narrative texts. In M. A. Gernsbacher (Ed.), *Handbook of psycholinguistics* (pp. 539–588). San Diego, CA: Academic Press.

Van den Heuvel, M.P., & Pol, H. E. H. (2010). Exploring the brain network: A review on resting-state fMRI functional connectivity. *European Neuropsychopharmacology, 20*, 519–534.

van Dongen, E. V., Thielen, J.-W., Takashima, A., Barth, M., & Fernandez, G. (2012). Sleep supports selective retention of associative memories based on relevance for future utilization. *PLoS ONE, 7, e43426.*

Van Essen, D. C. (2004). Organization of visual areas in Macaque and human cerebral cortex. In L. Chalupa and J. Werner (Eds.), *The visual neurosciences.* Cambridge, MA: MIT Press.

van't Wout, M., Kahn, R. S., Sanfey, A. G., & Aleman, A. (2005). Repetitive transcranial magnetic stimulation over the right dorsolateral prefrontal cortex affects strategic decision-making. *Neuroreport, 16*(16), 1849–1852.

Vedaldi, A., Ling, H., & Soatto, S. (2010). Knowing a good feature when you see it: Ground truth and methodology to evaluate local features for recognition. In R. Cipolla, S. Battiato, & G. M. Farinella (Eds.) *Computer vision* (pp. 27–49). Berlin: Springer-Verlag.

Venema, V. (2013). Odon childbirth device: Car mechanic uncorks a revolution. *BBC News Magazine*, December 3, 2013.

Violanti, J. M. (1998). Cellular phones and fatal traffic collisions. *Accident Analysis and Prevention, 28*, 265–270.

Viskontas, I. V., Carr, V. A., Engel, S. A., & Knowlton, B. J. (2009). The neural correlates of recollection: Hippocampal activation declines as episodic memory fades. *Hippocampus, 19,* 265–272.

Vogel, E. K., McCollough, A. W., & Machizawa, M. G. (2005). Neural measures reveal individual differences in controlling access to working memory. *Nature, 438,* 500–503.

Voss, J. F., Greene, T. R., Post, T., & Penner, B. C. (1983). Problem-solving skill in the social sciences. In G. Bower (Ed.), *The psychology of learning and motivation.* New York: Academic Press.

Vossel, S., Geng, J. J. & Fink, G. R. (2014). Dorsal and ventral attention systems: Distinct neural circuits but collaborative roles. *The Neuroscientist, 20,* 150–159.

Vuust, P. Ostergaard, L., Pallesen, K. J., Bailey, C., & Roepstorff, A. (2009). Predictive coding of music—Brain responses to rhythmic incongruity. *Cortex, 45,* 80–92.

Wade, K. A., Garry, M., Read, J. D., & Lindsay, S. D. (2002). A picture is worth a thousand lies: Using false photographs to create false childhood memories. *Psychonomic Bulletin & Review, 9,* 597–603.

Wagenaar, W. A. (1986). My memory: A study of autobiographical memory over six years. *Cognitive Psychology, 18,* 225–252.

Waldrop, M. M. (1988). A landmark in speech recognition. *Science, 240,* 1615.

Ward, T. B., Smith, S. M., & Vaid, J. (Eds.). (1997). *Creative thought: An investigation of conceptual structures and processes.* Washington, DC: American Psychological Association.

Warrington, E. K., & McCarthy, R. A. (1987). Categories of knowledge. *Brain, 110,* 1273–1296.

Warrington, E. K., & Shallice, T. (1984). Category specific semantic impairments. *Brain, 107,* 829–854.

Wason, P. C. (1960). On the failure to eliminate hypotheses in a conceptual task. *Quarterly Journal of Experimental Psychology, 12,* 129–140.

Wason, P. C. (1966). Reasoning. In B. Foss (Ed.), *New horizons in psychology* (pp. 135–151). Harmondsworth, UK: Penguin Books.

Watson, J. B. (1913). Psychology as the behaviorist views it. *Psychological Review, 20,* 158–177.

Watson, J. B. (1928). *The ways of behaviorism.* New York: Harper and Brothers.

Watson, J. B., & Rayner, R. (1920). Conditioned emotional reactions. *Journal of Experimental Psychology, 3,* 1–14.

Wearing, D. (2005). *Forever today.* London: Doubleday.

Weisberg, R. W. (2015). Toward and integrated theory of insight in problem solving. *Thinking & Reasoning, 21,* 5–39.

Weisberg, R. W. (2009). On "out-of-the-box" thinking in creativity. In A. B. Markman and K. L. Wood (Eds.) *Tools for innovation* (pp. 23–47). Oxford, UK: Oxford University Press.

Weisberg, R. W., & Alba, J. W. (1981). Gestalt theory, insight, and past experience: Reply to Dominowski. *Journal of Experimental Psychology: General, 110,* 193–198.

Weisenberg, M. (1977). Pain and pain control. *Psychological Bulletin, 84,* 1008–1044.

Weisenberg, M. (1999). Cognitive aspects of pain. In P. D. Wall & R. Melzak (Eds.), *Textbook of pain* (4th ed., pp. 345–358). New York: Churchill Livingstone.

Wells, G. L., & Bradfield, A. L. (1998). "Good, you identified the suspect": Feedback to eyewitnesses distorts their reports of the witnessing experience. *Journal of Applied Psychology, 83,* 360–376.

Wells, G. L., Steblay, N. K., & Dysart, J. E. (2015). Double-blind photo lineups using actual eyewitnesses: An experimental test of a sequential versus simultaneous lineup procedure. *Law and Human Behavior, 39,* 1–14.

Wells, G. L., & Quinlivan, D. S. (2009). Suggestive eyewitness identification procedures and the Supreme Court's reliability test in light of eyewitness science: 30 years later. *Law and Human Behavior, 33,* 1–24.

Wernicke, C. (1874) Der aphasische Symptomenkomplex. Breslau: Cohn.

Wertheimer, M. (1912). Experimentelle Studien über das Sehen von Beuegung. *Zeitchrift für Psychologie, 61,* 161–265.

Westmacott, R., & Moscovitch, M. (2003). The contribution of autobiographical significance to semantic memory. *Memory and Cognition, 31,* 761–774.

Westmacott, R., Black, S. E., Freedman, M., & Moscovitch, M. (2003). The contribution of autobiographical significance to semantic memory: evidence from Alzheimer's disease, semantic dementia, and amnesia. *Neuropsychologia, 42,* 25–48.

Wheeler, M. E., Stuss, D. T., & Tulving, E. (1997). Toward a theory of episodic memory: The frontal lobes and autonoetic consciousness. *Psychological Bulletin, 121,* 331–354.

Wickelgren, W. A. (1965). Acoustic similarity and retroactive interference in short-term memory. *Journal of Verbal Learning and Verbal Behavior, 4,* 53–61.

Wickens, D. D., Dalezman, R. E., & Eggemeier, F. T. (1976). Multiple encoding of word attributes in memory. *Memory & Cognition, 4,* 307–310.

Wiech, K., Ploner, M., & Tracey, I. (2008). Neurocognitive aspects of pain perception. *Trends in Cognitive Sciences, 12,* 306–313.

Wiederhold, B. K. (2016). Why do people still text while driving? *Cyberpsychology, Behavior, and Social Networking, 19,* 473–474.

Wiernicke, C. (1874). Der aphasische Symptomenkomplex. Breslau: Cohn.

Wilding, J., & Valentine, E. R. (1997). *Superior memory.* Hove, UK: Psychology Press.

Wilhelm, I., Diekelmann, S., Molzow, I., Ayoub, A., Molle, M., & Born, J. (2011). Sleep selectively enhances memory expected to be of future relevance. *Journal of Neuroscience, 31,* 1563–1569.

Wilson, T. D., & Gilbert, D. T. (2003). Affective forecasting. In L. Berkowitz (Ed.), *Advances in experimental social psychology* (Vol. 35, pp. 345–411). San Diego, CA: Academic Press.

Wineburg, S., McGrew, S., Breakstone, J., & Ortega, T. (2016). Evaluating Information: The Cornerstone of Civic Online Reasoning. Retrieved from https://purl.stanford.edu /fv751yt5934.

Wiseman, S., & Neisser, U. (1974). Perceptual organization as a determinant of visual recognition memory. *American Journal of Psychology, 87,* 675–681.

Wissman, K. T., Rawson, K. A., & Pyc, M. A. (2012). How and when do students use flashcards? *Memory, 20,* 568–579.

Wittgenstein, L. (1953). *Philosophical investigations* (G. E. M. Amnscombe, Trans.). Oxford, UK: Blackwell.

Wixted, J. T., Mickes, L., Clark, S. E., Gronlund, S. D., & Roediger, H. L. III (2015). Initial eyewitness confidence reliably predicts eyewitness identification accuracy. *American Psychologist, 70,* 515–526.

Wolfe, J. M. (2012). The binding problem lives on: comment on Di Lollo. Trends in *Cognitive Sciences, 16,* 307–308.

Wozniak, S., & Smith, G. (2007). *iWoz: Computer geek to cult icon.* New York: Norton.

Xu, J., Vik, A., Groote, I. R., Lagopoulos, J., Holen, A., Ellingsen, O., Haberg, A. K., & Davanger, S. (2014). Nondirective meditation activates default mode network and areas associated with memory retrieval and emotional processing. *Frontiers in Human Neuroscience, 8,* Article 86.

Yeh, F.-C., Vettel, J. M., Singh, A., Poczos, B., Grafton, S. T., Erickson, K. I., et al. (2016). Quantifying differences and similarities in whole-brain white matter architecture using local connectome fingerprints. *PLoS Computational Biology.* doi:10.1371/journal. pcbi.1005203

Yuille, A., & Kersten, D. (2006). Vision as Bayesian inference: Analysis by synthesis. *Trends in Cognitive Sciences, 10,* 301–308.

Yule, G. (1997). *Referential communication tasks.* New York: Routledge.

Zabelina, D. L., & Andrews-Hanna, J. R. (2016). Dynamic network interactions supporting internally-oriented cognition. *Current Opinion in Neurobiology, 40,* 86–93.

Zhang, W., & Luck, S. J. (2009). Sudden death and gradual decay in visual working memory. *Psychological Science, 20,* 423–428.

Zwaan, R. A. (1999). Situation models: The mental leap into imagined worlds. *Current Directions in Psychological Science, 8,* 15–18.

Zwaan, R. A., Stanfield, R. A., & Yaxley, R. H. (2002). Language comprehenders mentally represent the shapes of objects. *Psychological Science, 13,* 168–171.

Name Index

N

Nadel, L., 211
Nader, K., 208, 216–217, 220
Nairne, J. S., 197
Naselaris, T., 308
Nash, R. A., 247–248, 254
Neisser, U., 16, 18, 116, 200, 233–234
Newell, A., 15, 362–364, 366
Newton, I., 13, 384
Nichols, E. A., 171
Nietzsche, F., 387
Norman, D. A., 98
Noton, D., 104
Nyberg, L., 173
Nyhan, B., 402

O

Odón, J., 377–379, 388
Ogawa, S., 18
Oliva, A., 67
Olshausen, B. A., 38
Olson, A. C., 285
Oppenheimer, D., 201–202
Oppezzo, M., 387
Orban, G. A., 74
Osborn, A. F., 379
Osman, M., 423
Ost, J., 234

P

Paczynski, M., 341
Paivio, A., 299–300
Palmer, S., 19
Palmer, S. E., 73, 76, 244
Palombo, D. J., 172
Parker, E. S., 243
Parkhurst, D., 103–104
Pasteur, L., 386
Patel, A. D., 348–350
Patterson, K., 291
Pauling, L., 378
Pavlov, I., 10–11
Payne, J. D., 215
Pearce, J. M. S., 38
Pearce, G., 186
Pearlstone, Z., 203
Pearson, J., 304, 312
Peretz, I., 350
Perfect, T. J., 184
Perky, C. W., 304
Perrett, D. I., 35
Peters, E., 417

Petersen, S. E., 123
Peterson, L. R., 138
Peterson, M. J., 138
Peterson, S., 201
Petrican, R., 176
Phelps, E. A., 231–232
Philippi, C. L., 178
Picasso, P., 386
Pickett, J. M., 326
Pillemer, D. B., 228, 231
Pilzecker, A., 208
Pinker, S., 114
Plaisier, M. A., 87
Pobric, G., 292
Poincaré, H., 384
Pol, H. E. H., 49–50
Poldrack, R. A., 49
Porter, S., 186, 254
Posner, M. I., 105–106, 123
Post, T., 416
Proust, M., 256
Ptak, R., 103
Pulvermüller, F., 264, 293
Putnam, A. L., 202
Pylyshyn, Z. W., 301–303, 312

Q

Quillian, M. R., 276–279
Quinlivan, D. S., 249, 252
Quiroga, R. Q., 37

R

Racicot, C. I., 84
Raichle, M., 48, 50–51
Ramachandran, V. S., 74
Ranganath, C., 171
Raphael, B., 363
Ratiu, P., 150
Ratner, N. B., 324
Rauchs, G., 215
Raveh, D., 116
Rayner, K., 325, 329
Rayner, R., 10
Read, L., 112
Reali, F., 336
Reber, A. S., 413
Redelmeier, D. A., 417
Reder, L. M., 200
Reid, C. A., 256
Reifler, J., 402
Reisberg, D., 312
Reitman, J., 375

Renoult, L., 174
Rensink, R. A., 117
Richardson, A., 299
Riley, M. R., 154
Rips, L. J., 279, 408
Ritchey, M., 232
Rizzolatti, G., 85–87
Robertson, L. C., 121
Rocha-Miranda, C. E., 35
Rock, I., 73
Roediger, H. L., 184, 197, 242
Rogers, T. B., 194
Rogers, T. T., 264, 281, 283–284, 288
Rogin, M. P., 237
Rolls, E. T., 35
Romona, G., 248
Roozendaal, B., 231
Rosch, E. H., 268–269, 271, 274–275
Rose, N. S., 171
Rosen, L. D., 113
Rosenbaum, R. S., 171–172
Ross, D. F., 250–251
Ross, E. D., 44–45
Rossato-Bennett, M., 256
Rothkopf, E. Z., 200
Rubin, D. C., 227, 229–230, 235
Rumelhart, D. E., 280
Rundus, D., 165
Russell, W. A., 195

S

Sachs, J., 167, 169
Saffran, J., 68
Saffran, J. R., 326
Saletin, J. M., 215
Sandler, A., 187
Sanfey, A. G., 420–422
Schacter, D. L., 177–178, 185
Scheck, B., 249
Scherer, K. R., 347
Schiller, D., 220
Schmeichel, B. J., 155
Schmidt, H., 120–121
Schmidt, N. B., 416
Schmolck, H., 234
Schneider, W., 110–111
Scholl, B., 106–107
Schooler, J. E., 51, 114, 256
Schooler, L. J., 243
Schrauf, R. W., 229
Schul, Y., 423
Schunn, C. D., 373

Subject Index

ISBN-13: 978-1337616287
ISBN-10: 1337616281

9 781337 616287